The Old Rose Advisor, Volume II

No. 3 in The Old Rose Researcher Series

The Old Rose Advisor, Volume II

Updated, Enlarged, and Revised Second Edition

Brent C. Dickerson

Authors Choice Press
San Jose New York Lincoln Shanghai

The Old Rose Advisor, Volume II
Updated, Enlarged, and Revised Second Edition

Authors Choice Press
an imprint of iUniverse.com, Inc.

For information address:
iUniverse.com, Inc.
5220 S 16th, Ste. 200
Lincoln, NE 68512
www.iuniverse.com

ISBN: 0-595-17299-7

Printed in the United States of America

Contents

Preface to Volume II

"Happy is the Man that has no other Acquaintance with Booksellers, than what is Contracted by Reading the News in their Shops, and perhaps now and then Buying a Book of them; but he, that is so unfortunate, as to have Business with them about Translating, Printing, or Publishing any Thing to the World, has a Miserable Time of it, and ought to be endued with the Patience of *Job*. Some days after I had parted with this Copy, my Bookseller asked me when I would go about the Preface; the Preface! Said I, what do you mean? Mean! Says he, I mean the Preface, the Preface to the Reader. I told him, that what he had bought was all I had to say to the Reader, as for my Part; and if he had any Thing to add for himself, he was at Liberty to do as he thought fit. I leave it to any Impartial Judge, if this was not Fair between Man and Man. Yet the Bookseller, far from being satisfied with so Reasonable an Answer, seemed to be very angry, and strenuously insisted on a Preface, telling me over and over, that he never heard of an Author that denied a Preface before, that it was a Folly to dispute it, that he could not Sell the Book without, and that in short a Preface he must have. Having no Mind to be huff'd, and bubbled out of my Labour into the Bargain, I grew angry in my Turn, and told him plainly, he should have none of me; the Book was his own, if he would not Sell it, he might stop Ovens with it if he pleased; at last, seeing me thus resolute, and knowing, that there was no Act of Parliament that obliged People to make Prefaces in spite of their Teeth, he put on a more obliging Countenance, and came to Persuasions, which having more influence on me than his rougher Language, I began to be more tractable, we went to the Tavern, where talking of Prefaces, I grew very good Humour'd, and that Prefacing might not be wanting, instead of One, I promised him

Two. The next Day considering what a Ridiculous Promise I had made, and yet willing to be as good as my Word, I thought on this Expedient of letting you know what had happened between us, and as a Wheel within a Wheel, prefixing it to this Preface.

"Is it possible, says the Ingenious Critick, that a Man of any Brains should be such a Coxcomb, as to put down such Balderdash, and play the Buffoon without Wit or Sense, in the very Beginning of a Book; thus People judge, when they are ignorant of a Man's Aim. I have a mortal Antipathy against Prefaces, this I had a Fancy to acquaint my Reader with, which being supposed, I'll justify to any Critick's Face, that I have said nothing but what is very much to the Purpose; that is, to my Purpose, because I conceive, that the best Way a Man can show the Reluctancy of his Mind to an Undertaking, is by being Impertinent in the Execution; but why, says another, should you hate Prefaces? The Reason is plain, because I am Honest, and I never saw any (those of Saints excepted) but what were full of Hypocrisie and Dissimulation. Does ever People tell you in their Prefaces, that they write for Profit, or for Glory? And yet it is most certain, that they do it either for the one or the other; but instead of that, with abundance of Impudence, they'll protest that they have no other Aim than the Reader's Good, which commonly is an Abominable Lie. One would make you believe that he is more Learned and Knowing than in his own Conscience he knows himself to be; another points at some of the best Things in the Book, and confesses they are Faults, whilst in Profound Silence he passes by those Things which he knows to be really such. I was once with an Author, that was about the same Business as I am now; he had occasion for Three or Four *Latin* Words, but not being very well acquainted with one of them, he ran to his Dictionary to see what Gender it was of; I don't blame him for taking the Benefit of another Man's Labour; but don't you think he would have been Hang'd before he'd have put this in his Preface; therefore believe me, good Reader, no Man of Integrity can love a Sort of Writing, in which hitherto People have not thought fit to speak the real Sentiments of their Hearts; if I had been let alone, this would have been the first; and I'll tell ye how: Since these Dialogues have been made, I found a great many Faults in the Contrivance, the Language, and a great many other Things, which I design'd to have made a Catalogue of, and showed you in the Front, with the same Candour as the Printer has owned this in the Rear. But, says the Earthly-minded Bookseller, what d'you mean? Have you a Mind to Damn the Book? What Mortal that sees so many Mistakes before, and so many Errata behind, will be such a Fool as to give Money for the Middle, that contains 'em? So you see, gentle Reader, my Hands are tied. The next I design'd, was to take away whatever might create Misunderstandings between you and me; for tho' I would have been very glad to show you my Faults, yet I am as unwilling that you should take those Things to be Faults, which in Reality are not. But now I have talked away my Time, to do it as I should do." [Mdv]

Chapter Eight

Noisettes and Climbers

"The Noisettes originated during John Champneys' time in Charleston, South Carolina. From *R. moschata* pollinated by the pink *R. bengalensis* [*presumed to intend 'Parsons' Pink China'*], he obtained a variety which he named 'Champneys' Pink Cluster'. The date of this development is not certain, and could be any time between 1802 and 1805. Philippe Noisette, who lived in Charleston and who was related to Champneys, sowed the seeds of this rose, which gave a remontant variety with flesh-white flowers [*'Blush Noisette'*]. Much contented, he took it to his brother Louis, who was a Parisian Horticulturist. These [*cuttings?*] would propagate the new race." [JR25/152] "It was raised by a gentleman on Long Island [*New York state*]; a plant was brought from there by Monsieur Landonne [*or Lendormi; see below*], an intimate acquaintance of the raiser, to Rouen, where it was cultivated in large quantities. Pailland, a gardener at Rouen [*was growing it already*], when Noisette of Paris received a plant from his brother in America…[*Noisette*] grew it under an iron cage in one of his houses for protection, while it was being commonly sold in Rouen at a moderate price! Prévost, the well-known nurseryman at Rouen, can attest to these facts." [HstI:46-47] "A note from John D. Legare, Esq., of Charleston, S.C.,…informs us that the account…of its having been originated on Long Island…is entirely a fabrication. Its true history, he says, is that it was raised from seed by Mr. Philip Noisette, of Charleston. Mr. L. informs us that he was for many years acquainted with Mr. Noisette, who owned a small farm on Charleston neck. From his own lips Mr. Legare heard the account of the origin of this rose more than once…Mr. Noisette frequently spoke of the attempts of the nurserymen in Europe to rob him of the honor of originating the first of this beautiful class of Roses…Mr. Noisette mentioned to Mr. Legare the sorts of roses between which the original Noisette was a hybrid—but the latter does not recollect which were the varieties. 'Certain it is, however,' says Mr. Legare, 'no one in the neighborhood of Charleston but knows as to its originating here and by the hands of Mr. Philip Noisette.'" [HstI:145] "These [*the Noisettes*] are from the seeds of the rose found by John Champney[s] and sown by Philippe Noisette, florist, also of Charleston, which [*seeds*] gave rise to that [*rose*] which bears the name of a distinguished family of horticulturists, a rose which the American nurseryman sent to his brother Louis in 1814, who possessed at that time at 51 rue du faubourg St.-Jacques, Paris, an immense horticultural establishment well known throughout the world. Independently of this parcel sent to his brother, Philippe Noisette, two years later, sent two specimens of his rose to Monsieur Jacques Durand, a Rouen businessman, who took delivery in March of 1816, and put them under the care of Monsieur Prévost fils, able horticulturist on the rue de Champ-des-Oiseaux of that city. In 1829, one could see at the home of the fancier Monsieur Lendormi, *also* of Rouen, one of those two plants sent by the Philippe Noisette establishment thirteen years before." [JR6/13] "*Noisette Rose. Rosa Noisettiana, Bosc.*—Taken from America by

Philippe Noisette, my brother, in 1814." [No] "One sees that Louis Noisette is very cautious in his *Manual* about speaking of the origin of the Rose which bears his name...Without the Noisette Rose, who today would know Noisette?" [JR34/81]

For a number of reasons, there has always been much confusion in the story of these two Noisettes, 'Champneys' Pink Cluster' and 'Blush Noisette'. What are these reasons? To begin with, the year in which Champneys crossed the Musk Rose with 'Parsons' Pink China'—producing, as it happens, what was not only the first Noisette, but also the first cross in the Occident between a China Rose and any other kind of rose—is lost in the mists of time: "any time between 1802 and 1805" is what we must content ourselves with. Further, the first Noisette to appear among the horticultural circles of *Europe* was not Champneys' rose but rather its offspring, Philippe Noisette's 'Blush Noisette', which was evidently developed by 1814; Europeans consequently became accustomed to referring to 'Blush Noisette' as "the first Noisette." Confusion compounds when we come to consider the date of introduction of 'Blush Noisette'. When was it introduced? We see claims for 1814, 1816, 1817...Rosarians have focused on France; but if we accept the "Long Island story" given above—though disputed by "John D. Legare, Esq."—we must look to the West. What appears to be the crux of Legare's complaint is that, to his own certain knowledge, 'Blush Noisette' was not raised on Long Island, but rather at Charleston, South Carolina. If we consider the case, and suppose that there was simply a misunderstanding at the point of sale on Long Island, when Monsieur Landonne/Lendormi purchased the plant(s), the Frenchman understanding "raised" to mean "bred," whereas the Long Island nurseryman—possibly William Prince, of Flushing, on Long Island—simply meant by "raised" that cuttings were rooted and brought to maturity there, there is nothing intentionally deceptive in this nor unreasonable nor objectionable in the rest of the tale; indeed, in its details and likelihoods, it shows every ability to conform to what others wrote. I discuss this in greater detail elsewhere (see my entry on 'Blush Noisette');

but the series of events seems to be this: In 1814, Philippe Noisette's seedling 'Blush Noisette' had reached a state of maturity such that he decided to start distributing it and profiting from it; he sent cuttings to his brother Louis in Paris, and it appears that he sent cuttings to a nurseryman on Long Island. The cuttings sent to Paris in 1814 seem not to have succeeded; those sent to Long Island appear to have rooted, where, in perhaps 1816, a traveling Rouennais businessman bought one or more, and took it to Rouen, where it grew and was distributed (and seemingly another Rouen native, Jacques Durand, also received cuttings directly from Philippe Noisette in that same year), while in 1817 another shipment to Louis Noisette finally began to meet with some success such that, in 1818, the Parisian crop began to bloom and be distributed there, the first mentions of the rose there being made in 1819 and 1820 under the names 'Rosier de Philippe Noisette' and simply 'Noisette Rose'. But, despite what was happening in France all this time, it appears that—at least on Long Island, New York state—the rose had already been introduced in its original homeland, the U.S.A.

"The first Noisette rose, as all good rosarians know, was produced in Charleston, S.C., by a horticulturalist heretofore known as John Champney. It is pleasant to have the interesting contact with his memory provided by the following letter from Julia R. Tunno, of Atlanta, Ga.: 'I would be glad if you will correct the name of my great-great-grandfather which was Champneys, and not Champney. His daughter, Sarah Champneys, was the last of the name, and when she married my great grandfather William Tunno, the name of Champneys ended. John Champneys was a rice planter, but a great lover of flowers, especially roses, and he had a wonderful flower-garden. In an old family Bible is this record, "John Champneys, son of John and Sarah Champneys (whose maiden name was Saunders), born December 28th, 1743, in Charleston, S.C., and baptized by Rev. Mr. Gay at Ashley River"; and on another page is this, "John Champneys died Wednesday, July 26th, 1820." ' " [ARA29/214]

Between the time of 'Champneys' Pink Cluster' and 'Blush Noisette', however, one Fraser—also of Charleston—had produced around 1810 a new rose, 'Fraser's Pink Musk', usually classified with the Musks, but which appears to have been a product of the same parentage as Champneys' rose. At length, in France, the Noisettes began to proliferate. Vibert offered his own, 'Azélie', so soon as 1820; and others were hard at work. "More than 25 varieties of Noisettes are comprised in that quantity [*of selections in Vibert's 1824 collection*]...which are mostly full-flowered...[*They are*] destined to exercise a great influence on the cultivation—and the pleasure—of this beautiful family...The deportment, the foliage, the form of the flowers and of the petals in these roses present more variety than is to be found in the Chinas...Nature has given the Noisettes a liberality without precedent; scarcely born, already they have happily supplies us with all the colors from the most delicate to the darkest. The whites, the flesh, the pink, the rosy-pink, and the crimson have already shown up, the first three particularly, in a number of varieties; the white, so rare in the Chinas, leaves little to be desired. As for the perfume, lacking up till now in these, it has yielded to these essays, and I believe that I am able to assure you that we now possess one or two fragrant sorts." [V2] "Ten years after the introduction into France of the Noisette, the horticulturists had raised a hundred and two varieties!" [PlB] "As the Champney [*sic*] rose produces seeds far more abundantly than the 'Blush Noisette', it has doubtless been the parent of much the greatest number." [WRP] "Since that time [*i.e., the time of the original introduction of the Noisette into France*], Monsieur Robert, director of the Toulon botanical garden, has raised an identical rose from a Musk Rose seed." [JF] "What do I receive from Monsieur Robert, director of the marine garden at Toulon, but a rose pretty nearly just like the [*original*] Noisette [*probably intending 'Blush Noisette' rather than 'Champneys' Pink Cluster'*] in all ways, except that the flowers, instead of being white with a light touch of pink on the outer petals, are entirely the latter color. Hm! This new rose of Monsieur Robert's came from a seed which he himself gathered from the

Musk Rose in a garden in Hyères in Provence. Thus, it is evident that the Noisette Rose and that of Monsieur Robert can't be considered as otherwise than as having come from the Musk Rose." [L-D] "At Coubert, a small town in Brie, Monsieur Cochet the elder [*i.e., Pierre Cochet père*], in 1862 or 1863, obtained from seeds of an ordinary *R. semperflorens* [*which name usually intends the race of 'Slater's Crimson China' rather than that of 'Parsons' Pink China'*], usually called the Bengal Rose, which had been naturally pollinated by a Moschata hybrid—'Princesse de Nassau'—which was close by, a seedling which was quite identical with *R. Noisettiana*, save that the flowers were single, and more carminy than the Type." [JR6/12]

"There was a time when the Noisettes, complex hybrids though they were, preserved their characteristics to some degree, and were easy to recognize in the garden. But not for long. When the Tea roses were, naturally or artificially, crossed with the Noisettes or their hybrids, it suddenly brought into being a whole new series of Roses which the rosarians were at their wits' ends to classify." [JR34/96]

Those wishing to survey all the roses in this book which can be used as climbers should also check among the Bourbons, Hybrid Bourbons, Hybrid Chinas, and Hybrid Noisettes, many of which are "climberish," and among the Teas, most of which will "climb" under the right conditions. Many Hybrid Perpetuals and Hybrid Teas of extra-vigorous growth may also serve as pillar-type climbers. "With so many climbing roses to choose from…monotony should not exist. It can only be blamed upon a lack of knowledge that different kinds of roses can be obtained and to a certain sheep-like tendency in many humans to follow where their neighbors lead." [GAS]

Adele Frey (Walter, 1911)
Hybrid Tea
"Deep pink, large, very full, light scent, tall." [Sn]

[Adrienne Christophle] (Guillot fils, 1868) syn., 'Adrienne Christophe'
Noisette
"The flowers attain a diameter of up to 4 inches [ca. 1 dm]...borne on a flower-stem which frequently is feeble and bends under the weight of the blossom, as do the branches which bear the clusters of flowers. The growth is of moderate vigor, fairly floriferous; the drooping branches are not unpleasant in effect. The only fault I can find with this rose...is that sometimes its petals are clustered in three or four entirely separate groups, giving the impression of a blossom which has been broken apart." [JR9/54-55] "Thorns hooked and remote; leaves of five leaflets, sometimes seven, but the uppermost pair always very small, often abortive and represented by a simple foliole; petiole prickly; flowers in a cluster of 10-12, usually nodding under their weight...coppery apricot yellow, shaded peach pink, sometimes deep yellow...planted in the north, it blooms little or not at all." [JR10/10] "Growth vigorous; branches slender and nodding, with reddish-green bark, and long, sharp, brown thorns. Foliage smooth, pale green; leaves composed of 3-5 oval-acuminate, finely dentate, red-bordered leaflets; leafstalk slender, of the same color as the branches and armed with some small thorns. Flowers about three inches across [ca. 7.5 cm], nearly full, slightly globular, cupped, solitary on the little branchlets, clustered on vigorous branches; color, coppery pink-yellow, apricot, shaded pink; petals large, central petals smaller; stem slender, nodding under the weight of the blossom. Calyx rounded. Because of the variety of its colors, this rose is very beautiful. Hardy, and proof against winter's cold." [JF] "Distinct and beautiful." [JC] A parent of 'Erzherzogin Franz Ferdinand' (T).

Aimée Vibert (Vibert, 1828)
Noisette
From an early Noisette × *R. sempervirens* 'Plena'.
"Flowers pure white, medium size, full, freely borne in umbel-like clusters. Buds tinted with red. Foliage shining, deep green. Branches springing up

from the base, hence this rose is particularly suitable for planting on graves." [Hn] "Cup., pure white, in clusters, beautiful." [CC] "White, blushing." [JR2/60] "Pure white, produced in large clusters, of medium size, full; form compact; growth vigorous...foliage of a dark green and shining." [P1] "Flowers mid-sized, full, well-formed, erect when opening, nodding in maturity, milk-white, musk-scent very marked, in clusters of many flowers on big canes, giving a charming appearance of a well-made bouquet, and bearing simultaneously both the milky flowers and the many attractive buds which are often shaded carmine—all in all, a very pretty sight." [JR5/24] "Branches covered with very rich and brilliant foliage; and when it blooms it produces veritable garlands of snowy white to very charming effect." [JR18/136] "Very free-flowering." [H] "Of beautiful form; the foliage is a dark lustrous green; growth vigorous." [EL] "A very delicate grower." [HstXI:225] "Very vigorous." [J] "Not among the most vigorous in growth of the Noisettes." [FP] "Good for pillars." [F-M] "Perfect in form, a profuse bloomer...exquisite." [Bu] "Branches of moderate size, more or less long depending upon the vigor of the particular specimen; bark green, smooth, nearly thornless; thorns sparse, small, short, and somewhat reflexed. Leaves a handsome green, divided into 5 or 7 leaflets, with 3 of those subtending the inflorescence; the leaflets are oval-elongate, pointed, and finely toothed; leafstalk green, weak, often curled, having a number of small light green prickles beneath. Flower, about two inches across [ca. 5 cm], very full, rounded, blooming in clusters of 3-20 and sometimes more, depending upon the vigor of the branch; color, pure white; outer petals concave; those of the center, small and rumpled; bud washed carmine; flower stem slender, green, a little reddish where the sun hits. Calyx medium-sized, rounded; sepals leaf-like. Lightly fragrant, this variety is notable for its vigor." [JF] "One of the introductions of Monsieur Vibert, who raised it at his breeding-grounds at Longjumeau, near Paris, in 1828. Though 18 years separate us from the day this Rose bloomed for the first time, and despite the more than four thousand introductions which have been paraded before our eyes since

1828, of which nearly 500 have been Noisettes, not one of these conquerors has been able to dethrone 'Aimée Vibert'. As the Rose of the King [*unexplained*], it is popular in the markets, well-liked by both proud lady and trullion; its white splashes appear in both royal garden and doorstep plot. Some people believe that this rose was a sport of *R. semperflorens* perpetuated by grafting.—This is of little importance. Let us admire the flower without caring whether it be seedling or sport. In either case, all we would have to show for our trouble would be to be able to say '...which was sown...' or '...which was grafted...'. 'Aimée Vibert' is the sort of Noisette that has short branches, all or nearly all flower-bearing, in the way of the Chinas...The flower...is composed of numerous small petals which unite in a veritable rosette. In all regards, this is a charming rose." [PlB] "This very exquisite variety was grown from seed of a rose that blooms only once in the season (Sempervirens Pleno) by J.P. Vibert, of Lonjeameaux [*sic*], near Paris. When I visited him, in 1839, whilst discoursing upon roses, he directed my attention with great enthusiasm to this plant, and said, 'Celle si est si belle, que Je lui ai donné le nom de ma fille chérie—Aimée Vibert' [*sic; 'This one is so pretty that I gave it the name of my dear daughter—Aimée Vibert'*]. This enthusiasm can be easily understood by those who, like myself, have been so fortunate as to see the two Aimée Viberts—the rose and the young girl—both in their full bloom, and both as lovely as their sweet name." [Bu] "Aimée Vibert" was also the name of Vibert's mother.

Aimée Vibert, Climbing (Curtis, 1841)
Noisette
Sport of 'Aimée Vibert' (N).
"White." [LS] "It's an excellent rose for fences, giving canes of 4-5 meters [ca. 13-16 feet], and is pretty robust. I prune it back to 15 to 20 eyes, and I get wonderful bloom." [JR10/10] "Heavy everblooming groundcover with fine foliage and horizontal growth." [Th2]

Aimée Vibert Jaune
Listed as 'Mme. Brunner'.

Albert La Blotais (Pernet père, 1887)
Hybrid Tea
From 'Gloire de Dijon' (N) × 'Général Jacqueminot' (HP).
"Bush vigorous; flower very large, nearly full, globular, stem upright and strong, very good hold; beautiful bright red, sometimes darker, passing to crimson...Reblooms freely; of the first merit." [JR11/163] "Red, large, very full, tall." [Sn] Not a sport of the Moreau-Robert HP 'Albert La Blotais'!

Alister Stella Gray (A.H. Gray/G. Paul, 1894)
Noisette
"Pale yellow with orange center, changing to white as flowers expand; small, and produced in fine clusters. A continuous bloomer." [P1] "Yolk-yellow...flower 3 inches across [ca. 7.5 cm]." [T2] "Pale yellow." [J] "Buff." [J] "Deep yellow with lighter edges; flowers in clusters." [Th] "Pale and rather dull yellow." [F-M2] "Self yellow clusters summer and autumn." [E] "Buff-yellow buds...flowers that fade to ivory-white...15 [ft; ca. 4.5 m]." [HRG] "Flowers beautifully formed." [Hk] "Shapely...Rich tea scent...long flowering season...15 × 10 [ft; ca. 4.5×3 m]." [B] "Free-flowering miniature." [H] "Growth: 10-12 [ft; ca. 3-3.5 m]. Repeats bloom well." [Lg] "Very vigorous. The buds are quite pretty and seem made to be painted." [JR23/42] "Short zigzag shoots, horizontally poised glossy leaves, few thorns." [T2] "Good in South." [ARA18/119] "A slow starter." [Hk] "Of vigorous growth and upright rather branching habit; it throws up good strong branches to about 8-ft. high [ca. 2.25 m], which arch if left untrained, and have smooth green bark bronzing in autumn to a nice russet tint on the sunny side...The flowering period is long...The flowers are about a couple of inches across [ca. 5 cm], semi-double, sometimes full, and are carried in fair trusses or rather sprays. They possess a fragrance that is not strong, but quite distinct

[*suggesting*] the musk rose...The buds are pretty and lasting and of a deep buff yellow and the expanded flowers are pale yellow with a centre of light orange yellow...it often takes some time to 'get started'...The strong point of this Rose is its early autumn flowering...Its weak points are that though a pretty little Rose, in neither colour nor shape is it very striking, and the early flowers are poor." [NRS/11] "Throughout the whole Summer and Autumn it was a solid mass of blossom, every little new brown shoot from the ground upward being tipped with flower buds." [K1] "The best of all Roses for stumps." [Wr]

American Beauty, Climbing (Hoopes, Bro. & Thomas, 1909)
HP Climber or Wichuraiana
From an unnamed seedling (which resulted from crossing *R. wichuraiana* and the Tea 'Marion Dingee') × 'American Beauty' (HP).
"Carmine to rich imperial pink—blues in heat, fades quickly; fine buds; large, double flowers...Gives one large burst of bloom only. Vigorous, foliage usually lost early." [Th2] "Cerise flowers blue with age. Very large, cupped...Vigorous to 12 to 15 feet [ca. 3.5-4.5 m]. Best grown in semishade to slow up fading...sweet and heady damask fragrance." [W] "Rich rosy crimson...remarkable amount of spring bloom...practically no summer or fall bloom. Loses foliage early." [ARA17/26] "Flower red nuanced vermilion as in its mother, and similarly perfumed as well. Grows very strongly, and annually gives scions of 9 to 12 feet [ca. 2.75-3.5 m], durable as an oak; flower large; blooms profusely and early, over four weeks, then less abundantly up to Fall. A good variety for pillars and columns." [JR38/88-89] "Very useful and very glorious in spring." [ET] "The '[Climbing] American Beauty' reposed in luxury less than a foot above the body of a finally useful cat that had been run over on the highway." [ARA25/23]

[**Anna Olivier, Climbing**] (Breeder/Introducer unknown, date uncertain)
Tea

Presumably a sport of 'Anna Olivier' (T).
"Golden pink, large, full, medium scent, medium height." [Sn, speculating it came from England] Alas, it is now evidently extinct.

Anne-Marie Côte (Guillot fils, 1875)
Noisette
"Blush, medium size, full, tall." [Sn] "Well-formed...pure white, very often nuanced lilac pink." [S] "Appeared in 1871 among Monsieur Guillot fils' seedlings, and entered into commerce by him in 1875. Growth vigorous with upright canes armed with long and straight thorns; beautiful dark green foliage, leafstalk green or purplish; blossom medium-sized, full, globular, pure white, sometimes tinted pink; blooms in clusters. Grows poorly in pots, and can't be forced. Freezes at 12°. Prune to 4-6 eyes." [JR10/19]

Annie Vibert (Vibert?, -1871)
Noisette
"Double, medium-sized and pink on opening, then white... fragrant...vigorous...4 metres or more [ca. 12 ft or so]...glossy green foliage and long arching young growths." [G] Listed as a "standard blooming" rose in HstXXV:262. We know of no one in Vibert's family named "Annie."

Apeles Mestres (Dot, 1926)
Hybrid Perpetual
From 'Frau Karl Druschki' (HP) × 'Souvenir de Claudius Pernet' (Pernetiana).
"Sunflower-yellow, full, globular flowers which are very lasting and fragrant. Vigorous growth, with abundant May, and June bloom." [C-Ps31] "Remarkable for gigantic, very double, bright yellow flowers, which, alas, are only sparingly produced. The plant is a mean grower but well worth coddling." [GAS]

Apotheker Georg Höfer, Climbing (Vogel, 1841)
Hybrid Tea
Sport of 'Apotheker Georg Höfer' (HT).
"Red, very large, full, very fragrant, tall." [Sn]

[**Archiduchesse Charlotte**] (Earing/Kern Rose Nurs., 1975)
China
Sport of 'Archiduc Charles' (Ch).
Rose-pink climbing China.

Ards Rambler (A. Dickson, 1908)
Hybrid Tea
"Orange-red, large, full, very fragrant, tall." [Sn]

Ards Rover (A. Dickson, 1898)
Hybrid Perpetual
"Crimson, shaded maroon; a good pillar rose, and moderate climber." [P1] "Flowers globular, deep crimson." [W/Hn] "Good-sized flowers with stiff petals." [F-M2] "Medium size; good form...spring only...very fragrant." [ARA17/26] "Shapely...strong scent...occasionally recurrent...15×10 [ft; ca. 4.5×3 m]." [B] "Fine growth." [ARA18/119] "Handsome foliage...best as a Pillar Rose." [F-M2] "[*Excellent in Norway*]." [ARA20/46] "For a low wall, say 4-ft. to 6-ft. high [ca. 1.25-1.75 m], is a gem, flowering very profusely quite early in the season." [NRS/17] "For a rose planted for a grand effect during its bloom, considering the color, size, and its vigorous growth, it easily surpasses those varieties for which one searches either because of their renown, or because of the magniloquent descriptions with which catalogs try to woo amateurs...The word 'Rover' means 'Rambler'...the Ards Peninsula, where the introducer resides. It is very vigorous, climbing, quite floriferous, giving large blossoms, full, well-formed, crimson shaded maroon-brown. The

graceful bud is supported by a long and rigid stem." [JR28/43] "Carries its foliage late into the autumn...flowers freely and well in early summer, the blooms being fairly large, nicely shaped in the bud, and of a fine crimson colour, which looks well in the garden. The autumn flowering is sparse and, particularly in wet weather, the colour is not so bright as in summer, but in favourable weather they look well. The sparseness of the autumn flowers, and a slight tendency at that time of year to mildew, are its worst defects as a Pillar Rose; its good qualities are its ready and rapid growth, the ease with which it adapts itself to life on a Pillar, and its bright handsome colour and fragrance." [NRS/14]

Autumnalis (Noisette?, 1812?)
Noisette
"White flushed pink and red...in many flowered corymbs...8×6 [ft; ca. 2.25 × 1.75 m]." [B] Jäger calls it an English Hybrid Musk of unknown date. Phillips & Rix equate it with 'Princesse de Nassau', Laffay's 1827 Musk or Noisette. Problematical and probably spurious.

[**Baronne Charles de Gargan**] (Soupert & Notting, 1893)
Tea
From 'Mme. Barthélemy Levet' (T) × 'Socrate' (T).
"Climbing, flower large, full, beautiful form, outer petals light daffodil yellow, inner ones shining Naples yellow. Fragrant." [JR17/147] "A climber of good growth, very fine retained foliage, and double, sulphur-yellow bloom of medium size." [ARA28/101]

Beauté de l'Europe (Gonod, 1881) trans., "Europe Beauty"
Noisette
Seedling of 'Gloire de Dijon' (N).
"Flowers, which are globular and full, of dark yellow to salmon-colour. Has vigorous growth, free-flowering and pretty." [B&V] "Very vigorous, of good bearing, heavy wood and nearly thornless reddish canes. The

foliage is comprised of 5-7 rounded, dark green, serrated leaflets. The flower stem is strong, and the large flowers very full and well formed, of the Centifolia shape. Color, dark yellow, with a reverse of coppery yellow. This variety...is very floriferous, and the most notable yellow to date of this sort." [JR5/136] "Small growth; attractive blooms scattered throughout season; requires winter protection." [ARA18/119]

Beauté de Lyon
Listed as 'Beauté Inconstante'.

Beauté Inconstante (Pernet-Ducher, 1892) syn., 'Beauté de Lyon'; trans., "Inconstant Beauty"
Noisette
"Metallic red shaded yellow; vigorous. Distinct and charming in colour, but variable in this respect, as its name implies." [J] "Even more brilliant orange-scarlet tones than any hybrid China . . .free and hardy, as well as solid in petal, coppery red, shaded with carmine and yellow...variable...of irregular shape. Distinct and beautiful. Very fragrant." [P1] "A red-orange rose. Oh! such a colour...sometimes...Rather a weak grower, but one bloom will repay the growth." [HmC] "Carmine shaded to yellow, very variable in colour, large, full and of good form, in every respect an acquisition; has a more free habit, but in many ways reminds one of 'L'Idéal'." [B&V] "Very vigorous, making a rather tall bush; thorns protrusive and somewhat numerous; foliage bronze-green; flower large, full or semi-double, nasturtium red with yellow-tinted carmine reflections...sometimes bears paler colored blossoms." [JR16/166] "Extremely climbing branches...probably from the Noisette 'Earl of Eldon'." [JR21/99] "Very pretty buttonhole variety." [H]

Beauty of Glazenwood
Listed as 'Fortune's Double Yellow'.

Belle Blanca (Breeder unknown, date uncertain)
Hybrid Gigantea
Presumably a sport of 'Belle Portugaise' (HGig).
"Large climbing shrub, large semi-double white flowers." [HRG87]

[**Belle d'Orléans**] (Conard & Jones, 1902)
Noisette?
"A new constant blooming Cluster Rose, flowering continuously through the whole season; pure white flowers in grape form clusters, sometimes tinted rose; semi-climbing habit, best for low trellises and beds, from which roses can be picked from June to December." [C&Js02]

Belle de Bordeaux
Listed as 'Gloire de Bordeaux'.

Belle Lyonnaise (Levet, 1870) trans., "Lyon Beauty"
Noisette
Seedling of 'Gloire de Dijon' (N).
"Deep lemon." [H] "Well-shaped, fragrant, yellow." [ARA29/98] "Dark canary passing to salmon shades." [JR8/26] "Deep canary-yellow, changing to white, slightly tinted with salmon, large, full, and of fine form." [P1] "Large or very large, very full, cup-shaped, canary-yellow. Very vigorous...A beautiful sweet-scented rose." [Hn] "Large yellow blooms, which are not very freely produced." [OM] "One is always sure of some of its huge, solid blossoms till November." [K1] "Very vigorous grower." [FRB] "One of the most remarkable and best...The occupation of a part of France by the German army in 1870-1871 restricted the distribution of this beautiful rose to its source...This rose, of the highest merit,...is a very vigorous plant...[I]ts flower is large, full, and well-formed...with a very satisfying fragrance...very floriferous." [JR1/1/14] "Very handsome

foliage, ample." [JR3/142] "Leaves...strongly toothed...very floriferous and vigorous, but only for the first two or three years." [JR10/36]

Belle of Portugal
Listed as 'Belle Portugaise'.

Belle Portugaise (Cayeux, ca. 1905) syn., 'Belle of Portugal'; trans., "Portuguese Beauty"
Hybrid Gigantea
From *R. gigantea* × 'Souvenir de Mme. Léonie Viennot' (N).
"Flesh-pink, spring only, but very profuse." [W] "Loosely double flower...composed of silky quilled petals, rolled at the edges, creamy salmon with deeper reverse." [T2] "Vigorous...beautiful pointed buds." [HRG] "Profuse foliage...10×10 [ft; ca. 6×3 m]." [B] "He [*Dr. Franchesci Fenzi*] imported 'Belle of Portugal' from the Lisbon Botanical Garden...From Dr. [*Fenzi's*] garden in Santa Barbara [*California*], 'Belle of Portugal' gradually found it way over California and into other Southern states." [ARA32/92]

Belle Siebrecht, Climbing
Listed as 'Mrs. W.J. Grant, Climbing'.

Belle Vichysoise (Lévêque, 1895) "Vichy Beauty"
Noisette
"A climbing perpetual variety with pale pink flowers, produced in clusters." [P1] "Extra vigorous, handsome slightly glaucous foliage, blooms in clusters of 20-30 of medium or small size, pinkish white or light pink, the two colors appearing simultaneously in the same panicle. Very pretty; superb." [JR19/164] "A vigorous bush or pillar 8 ft or more high [ca. 2.25m +] with recurrent clusters of 30 to 50 white or pinkish flowers." [GAS] "Taking the cure at Vichy, Monsieur Lévêque noticed the pretty flowers of a rose climbing on the orangery wall...Struck by its astonishing vigor as well as by the abundant bloom of the variety, resembling nothing

he had [*heretofore*] seen in cultivation, this rosarian took a cutting to his friend Monsieur Eugène Verdier...The plant...is of extraordinary growth, producing very long branches covered with quite numerous clusters of a pretty blush white, sometimes deeper in color...For two years, we have scrutinized this Noisette in full bloom, and, compared with the variety 'Cornélie', from Moreau-Robert [*actually, Robert & Moreau*], 1858, there seems to be no difference." [JR27/88]

Billard et Barré (Pernet-Ducher, 1898)
Noisette
From 'Mlle. Alice Furon' (HT) × 'Mme. la Duchesse d'Auerstädt' (N).
"Climbing Tea with double, sweet-scented, golden yellow flowers." [GAS] "Dependable grower...bright yellow." [ARA28/99] "Semi-climbing, canes strong and erect; large leaves of a lustrous somber green; bud superb when half open; flower large, nearly full, globular." [JR22/163]

Black Boy (A. Clark, 1919)
Hybrid Tea
From 'Étoile de France' (HP) × 'Bardou Job' (B).
"Dark red satin petals shaded with black velvety." [ARA32/120] "Semi-double." [Th2] "Deep crimson, shaded with blackish maroon, overlaying scarlet...good mildew-proof foliage and fine climbing habit...opens quickly, retains its rich color." [TS] "Without a peer...in formation of flower, richness of color, and freedom of bloom." [PP28] "Excellent growth the first season, giving a few superb, dark red flowers, which blackened agreeably instead of fading." [ARA27/129] "Lustrous, mildew-free leaves." [ARA23/119] "Highly resistant to mildew and an intermittent bloomer until midsummer but sparingly thereafter." [ARA35/171] "15 feet tall [ca. 4.5 m] in a season." [ARA31/186] "Dark crimson blooms of medium size. A vigorous climber which comes into bloom early. It makes a fine splash of color." [ARA30/153]

Blairii No. 1 (Blair, 1845)
Hybrid China
From 'Parks' Yellow Tea-Scented China' (T) × 'Tuscany' (Gallica).
"Brilliant roseate, splendid, very fragrant." [WRP] "Flowers bright rose, sometimes tinged with lake, large and semi-double; form, cupped. Raised at Stamford Hill, near London, a few years since, by Mr. Blair...habit, branching; growth, vigorous." [P] "Very double." [JR9/162] "Large, blowsy, scented...soft blush pink...good climber...8×6 [ft; ca. 2.25×1.75 m]." [B]

Blairii No. 2 (Blair, 1845)
Hybrid China
From 'Parks' Yellow Tea-Scented China' (T) × 'Tuscany' (Gallica).
"Blush, rose center." [HpBpIV/318] "Delicate flesh." [H] "Large, flattish blooms of pale pink. Fragrant. Very double and free flowering." [B] "Flower rosy blush, very large and double. Habit, branching; growth, vigorous; foliage, fine. One of the largest of Roses, and one of the freest growers, often attaining to ten or twelve feet [ca. 3-3.5 m] in one season." [P] "There is no rose tree more generally useful. If its luxuriant shoots are only reduced one fourth of their length in pruning (the weakly wood being altogether excised), it produces its blushing beauties in abundance, amid foliage large and glossy." [R1/159] "Much esteemed in England as a Pillar rose. We do not value it highly for this climate [*that of New York*]." [EL] "A very distinct and unique variety, so impatient of the knife, that, if pruned at all severely, it will scarcely put forth a flower: it is perhaps better as a pillar rose than grown in any other mode, as it shoots ten or twelve feet [ca. 3-3.5 m] in one season, and its pendulous clusters of flowers, which are produced from these long shoots unshortened, have a beautiful effect on a pillar." [R8] "A rare charm." [J]

[**Blairii No. 3**] (Blair, 1845)
Hybrid China

From 'Parks' Yellow Tea-Scented China' (T) × 'Tuscany' (Gallica).
"Pink." [LS]

Blanc Pur (Mauget, 1827) trans., "Pure White"
Noisette
"White, exterior greenish shades, large-flowered, double; growth very strong, to…13.2 ft [ca. 4 m]." [Kr] "Extremely vigorous and has large lush leaves, big thorns and enormous pure white full flowers which are fragrant." [G]

Blush
Listed as 'Fraser's Pink Musk'. See also 'Blush Noisette'.

Blush Noisette (P. Noisette, 1814) syn., 'Belle Noisette', 'Carnée', 'Commun', 'Noisettiana', 'Rose Noisette', 'Rosier de Philippe Noisette', 'Vulgaris'
Noisette
Seedling of 'Champneys' Pink Cluster' (N).
"White, washed with pink." [RG] "Flesh-white; flower small; very vigorous; climbing." [Cx] "More double than its parent, and of much more dwarf and compact growth; the flowers in very large dense panicles." [WRP] "This rose originated in the United States, and bears the name of Monsieur Noisette because it was sent to him by the brother of that celebrated grower, who dedicated it to him, and who first found it in southern America. Its stem grows from eight to ten feet high. The Noisette rose is notable for the profusion of its buds, which are colored pink before opening—it comes close to the Multiflora rose by the abundance of its flowers—and by its Musk Rose stature. It could be considered a sort of China rose. This rose is nearly thornless. Its leaves for the most part are of seven obtuse, crenelate leaflets. Its flowers, of the size of those of the Musk Rose, are white lightly nuanced with pink, double, and arranged in strong panicles. It is delicate and requires a temperate house…; however, let us not

despair of acclimating it to the open air by the simple means of wrapping it in straw, if grafted. It is propagated by grafting very low, shield-grafting the new shoots, cuttings in a frame, and graft." [LeR] "Superb *shrub* 2.4-3 meters high [ca. 7-9 m]; *canes* glabrous; *prickles* fairly strong, slightly hooked, reddish on the flowering branches, brown on the adult stems. *Leaflets* 5-7, acute ovate, rarely obtuse, simply and finely crenulate, glabrous, green above, paler beneath; petioles villose, with many small recurved prickles sometimes extending up to the midrib of the odd leaflet; stipules acute, denticulate, gland-edged. *Flowers* lateral and terminal, (1-) 3-6, often grouped in panicles of up to 130, opening successively, the first out being larger than those of the Musk Rose, the others about the same size, very sweetly scented; peduncles, elongate; pedicels, and ovoid *receptacles*, shortly and densely lanate; *sepals* 2 entire, 3 pinnate, acute, lanate within, gland-edged; *petals* 7-8-eriate, white flushed pink, a little yellowish towards the base, irregularly notched; *styles* free; *stigmas* a little reddish. This was produced by Philippe Noisette, one of the most skilful North American nurserymen, and propagated in France by his brother Louis Noisette. Our specimen came from his choice collection where it bloomed in 1818. We consider it a hybrid of *R. moschata* and *R. chinensis*, the foliage, flower disposition, and season of which it shares. However, the former is distinguished by its coherent styles and smaller, pure white flowers; the latter by its reflexed sepals, long tortuous stamens bent inwards over the styles, and continuous flowering. Seed raising may show us if it will breed true and constitute a new species. It blooms abundantly from July up to frost, and a young specimen was frost-hardy in 1820, although we took the precaution of covering it with leaves. When acclimated, it will be an ornament to our gardens, above all for the perfume, which is as good as that of the *Centifolia*, though different." [T&R] "It must be said that this rose has much more in common with its mother the Musk Rose than with the China rose. The bouquets of flowers, both numerous and pretty, with which it is covered during eight months of the year develop like those of the Musk Rose; its ovaries are of the same form, and its styles are collected into a column like theirs. Contrarily, in the China rose, the styles are free for their whole length." [BJ24] "The villose peduncles bear a great number of small double flowers, flesh- white upon opening, exhaling a very agreeable scent." [BJ30]

"Sent from America by Philippe Noisette, my brother, in 1814. Shrub of four to six feet, with branches of a brownish green; thorns strong, sparse, hooked; leaves fairly close-set, of a bright green; ordinarily of seven oval-acute leaflets, glabrous, finely and sharply dentate, glossy above, pale beneath, with villose, prickly petioles; flowers medium-sized, numerous, double, flesh-colored; petals entire; exhaling an agreeable scent." [No] "One sees that Louis Noisette is very cautious in his *Manual* about speaking of the origin of the Rose which bears his name." [JR34/81] "[R]aised from seed in America by Monsieur Philippe Noisette, and sent by him to his brother, Monsieur Louis Noisette, the well-known nurseryman at Paris, in the year 1817." [R4] "*Bush*, of great vigor. *Canes*, flexuose, very smooth. *Thorns*, large and strong. *Leaflets*, close-set, oval, acute, or avoid acuminate, and of an agreeable green. *Ovary*, ovoid-fusiform. *Flower*, medium-sized, regular, very multiplex, flesh. *Styles*, 20 to 40, glabrous. This beautiful rose, the Type of the species, originated in southern America. Monsieur Philippe Noisette, horticulturist at Charleston, after having raised it and propagated it, sent it to France in 1816. At least, that's the year—in March—that I received and looked after two own-root specimens which he sent to the late Monsieur Jacques Durand, then a businessman at Rouen. One of these two specimens is still at Monsieur Lendormi's, a fancier, at Rouen." [Pf] "It was raised by a gentleman on Long Island [*New York state*]; a plant was brought from there by Monsieur Landonne, an intimate acquaintance of the raiser, to Rouen, where it was cultivated in large quantities. Pailland, a gardener at Rouen [*was growing it already*], when Noisette of Paris received a plant from his brother in America…[*Noisette*] grew it under an iron cage in one of his houses for protection, while it was being commonly sold in Rouen at a moderate price! Prévost, the well-known nurseryman at Rouen, can attest to these facts." While this story seems at first glance to be at odds with what we know from other sources usually considered more reliable, it still appears upon deeper consideration to have some possible kernel of truth, hazily, at third- or fourth-hand. The Prince firm was early involved with Noisettes; the Prince firm was located in Flushing, New York—on Long Island. Meantime, "Monsieur Landonne" seems rather to be the Monsieur Lendormi just mentioned by Prévost. If the story has any truth, then—and we believe it does—it would seem to indicate that Lendormi purchased stock of 'Blush Noisette', perhaps from the Prince Co., and brought it to Rouen supposing it to have been originated by the Princes rather than simply raised from cuttings by them, all this taking place either before Louis Noisette had received propagation material of the plant from his brother, or at least before Louis Noisette had had success with propagation material sent by his brother. It is credible that Philippe Noisette would have begun distributing his rose domestically in America at once; and meantime we note that, whatever careful phraseology Louis Noisette might resort to, we see no evidence of the plant being in Paris before it blooms—seemingly for the first time—for Louis Noisette in 1818, and LeRouge mentions it in 1819. Rivers' "1817" perhaps accurately indicates the first *successful* sending of the plant by Philippe N. to Louis N.

What is the correct name of this rose? The name 'Carnée' has been proposed as the proper name for the rose which Philippe Noisette raised and sent around. People have concentrated upon what they suppose it was being called in France; they are wrong, it would seem, on two counts. As we have seen, it appears that the variety was introduced in the U.S. Would the U.S. sellers give a U.S.-born rose a French name? Unlikely. Prince, whose father's firm may well have been the one supplying the rooted cuttings taken to Rouen, calls it 'Blush Noisette' in his own book published thirty years later. In 1826, in his own book, Louis Noisette strictly speaking doesn't call it anything at all; he just lists it under the category of Noisette Rose, describes its color not as "*carnée*" but rather as its synonym "*chair*"—and there you have it. LeRouge just calls it the Noisette Rose in 1819. Vibert calls it 'Belle Noisette' in 1820. Thory in 1820 calls it "the rose of Ph. Noisette," which is also the name ("*Rosier de Philippe Noisette*") used by Thory and Redouté in *Les Roses.* So far along as 1828, Desportes, who revels in synonymy, fails to record 'Carnée' as a synonym; and it is only finally in the next year that Prévost fils finally gives it. What is the name, then? If we accept the U.S. introduction, we can perhaps trust in tradition and William R. Prince's referring to it as 'Blush Noisette'. If we cannot accept that and consequently look to France as the site of original introduction, LeRouge's unpublished 1819 'Noisette Rose' beckons, as does, more substantially, Thory's published 1820 'Rosier de Philippe Noisette' and Vibert's published 1820 'Belle Noisette'. Our choice is made clear by the title of this entry.

Bougainville (Cochet père/Vibert, 1824)
Noisette
"Lilac-pink." [TCN] "Bright pink." [RG] "Small, purple." [God] "Flowers medium-sized, full, well-formed, petals undulate, of a delicate pink tending towards lilac." [BJ30] "Here is the description which Monsieur Prévost fils, of Rouen, gives this rose…'Canes very thorny. Leaflets slender, wavy; ovary obconical or oblong, and glabrous. Buds red. Flower medium-sized, full, pink, paler and more lilac at the edge.'…This variety prefers open ground…It is dedicated to Admiral Bougainville, owner of the château of Suisnes." [JR10/59] "Vigorous; canes with magnificent lustrous dark green foliage; flower medium-sized, well formed, cupped; color, peachy lilac-red." [S] In some marginalia found in the Cochet copy of Prévost fils' *Catalogue*, we find the following, referring first to the now-extinct 'Philemon': "Found from seed at Suisnes by Pierre Cochet-Aulriot [*sic*] and sold with Bougainville [*for*] 20 francs to Monsieur Vibert."

Bouquet d'Or (Ducher, 1872) trans., "Bouquet of Gold"

Noisette
Seedling of 'Gloire de Dijon' (N).
"Dark coppery yellow, a beautiful variety; a good climber." [FRB] "A handsome bright yellow with touches of orange, a semi-climber." [JR10/46] "Dark yellow. An improved 'Gloire de Dijon'." [H] "Buff and orange...very vigorous." [J] "A lot of pink." [Hk] "Very double, yellow with coppery salmon center. Good repeat bloom...15-20 [ft; ca. 4.5-6.6 m]." [Lg] "Coppery-salmon with yellow centre. Slightly scented. Vigorous...10×6 [ft; ca. 3×1.75 m]." [B] "Large, finely formed, lemon-yellow, fragrant...shaded rose." [ARA29/98] "Buff yellow.—Vigorous pillar." [JP] "Pale yellow, centres coppery, large and full, and of good form; growth vigorous. One of the best." [P1] "Somewhat similar to 'Gloire de Dijon'; the blooms, which are of fairly good shape in the bud, are creamy yellow with deeper centre." [OM] "Exquisite when half open." [Hn] "Very vigorous; flower large, full, fragrant, cupped." [S] "Vigorous branches, green on one side, brownish on the other; foliage of 5-7 leaflets, shiny, thick, reddish in youth." [JR10/59-60] "Superior to 'Gloire de Dijon'...in form...color and freedom from mildew...[*but*] not so prolific." [Capt28] "A capital rose." [HRH]

Bouquet Tout Fait (Laffay, 1834) trans., "Perfect Bouquet"
Noisette
"Creamy white, produced in large handsome clusters, of medium size, very double; form, expanded. Growth, vigorous. Very sweet." [P] "Middle-sized, full; of a nankin-tinted white, bearing numerous flowers." [Go] "Very fragrant." [S] "A pillar noisette...a most vigorous grower, forming immense corymbs; this may be taken for the original Noisette at first sight, but it is more fragrant, and its flowers buff towards their center." [WRP] "Repeats blooms well...5-10 [ft; ca. 1.5-3 m]." [Lg]

[**Bridesmaid, Climbing**] (Dingee & Conard, 1897)
Tea

Sport of 'Bridesmaid' (T).
"Pink." [CA06] " 'Bridesmaid' is well known as one of the grandest Ever-blooming Roses we have, and is more extensively grown for cut-flowers than any other variety except 'American Beauty'. The 'Climbing Bridesmaid' is exactly like the other, except that the plant is a strong vigorous climber, sometimes growing 8 to 10 feet [ca. 2.6-3.3 m] in a season, and producing a constant succession of the most lovely roses imaginable. The color is clear rose-pink, with crimson shading, and both buds and flowers are exquisitely beautiful and deliciously sweet—not entirely hardy, but will usually stand the winter with moderate protection." [C&Js02]

Camélia Rose (Prévost?, ca. 1830?) trans., "Pink Camellia"
"Flowers bright rosy pink, double; form, cupped." [P] "Growth vigorous with very flexuose canes, pretty climbing, dark green leaves, thick on the plant; flower medium-sized, full, well formed, bright pink shaded lilac." [S]

Capitaine Soupa, Climbing (Vogel, 1983)
Hybrid Tea
Sport of 'Capitaine Soupa' (HT).
"Rose-red, large, full, tall." [Sn]

Captain Christy, Climbing (Ducher Children and Successors, 1881)
Hybrid Tea
Sport of 'Captain Christy' (HT).
"Blush and pink." [J] "Large, full double blooms of soft pink with darker center, vigorous...to 8 [ft; ca. 2.25 m]." [HRG] "Globular flowers are generously produced and fragrant...12×10 [ft; ca. 3.5×3 m]." [B] "Delicate flesh colour, deeper in the centre, large." [P1] "Seldom gives fall blooms." [Th2] "Same as 'Captain Christy', except more floriferous, and of a climbing habit." [JR5/186] "Poor grower; shy bloomer." [ARA18/121] "Even more delightful [*than the bush form*], because more

vigorous and abundant in blossoms...With me it certainly does better than its dwarf original; and nothing could exceed the perfection of its blossoms outside a south window on a day in early June; while as I write these words on almost the last day of October, a great six-inch flower [ca. 1.5 dm] as well as many half-open buds look in at that same window on the Chrysanthemums that fill the vases within. In a neighbour's sheltered garden a much older plant than mine climbs over a wide wooden arch, and when in full bloom it is worth a journey to behold its huge blossoms, borne so freely on long stalks, and set off by the singularly fine foliage." [K1]

Captain Hayward, Climbing (W. Paul, 1906)
Hybrid Perpetual
Sport of 'Captain Hayward' (HP).
"Healthy disposition...Pinkish-crimson flowers large and cupped until fully open...84 [ft; ca. 2.6×1.3 m]." [B1]

Carnée
Listed as 'Blush Noisette'. See also 'Fraser's Pink Musk'.

Caroline Marniesse (Roeser, 1848)
Noisette
"An old cluster-flowering Noisette, nearly hardy in the North, with small, globular flowers of pale flesh-pink, almost white. Blooms continuously, and should be a good rose in the South." [GAS] "Creamy white, small and full; seven leaflets, nearly hardy." [EL] "This rose, by its stature, foliage, and the placement of its white, clustered flowers, bears a great resemblance to the Sempervirens rose 'Félicité et Perpetué' [*sic*], but is not a climber. It blooms continuously up to frost; its blossoms are medium-sized, very full, globular, and of a light flesh white. It is hardy, and in growth is like 'Aimée Vibert'." [R-H48]

[**Caroline Schmitt**] (Schmitt/Schwartz, 1881) syn., 'Mme. Caroline Schmitt'
Noisette
"Blooms in large clusters; flowers full and regular; color coppery rose, passing to buff and white; very pretty and fragrant." [CA90] "Vigorous bush with branching, climbing canes; foliage somber green; flowers medium-sized or large, full, well-formed, salmon yellow fading to yellowish white. This variety is freely remontant; its manner of blooming is the same as that of the Noisette 'Narcisse', but with much larger flowers." [JR5/148]

Catalunya (Nonin, 1917)
Bourbon
Sport of 'Gruss an Teplitz' (B).
"Bright maroon." [Ÿ] "Brilliant red flowers more or less continuously." [GAS] Catalunya, alias Catalonia, the region of north-east Spain where Barcelona is located.

Cécile Brunner, Climbing
Listed as 'Mlle. Cécile Brunner, Climbing'.

Céline Forestier (Trouillard, 1842) syn., 'Liésis', 'Lusiadas'
Noisette
Affiliated with 'Lamarque' (N).
"Pale yellow, deepening toward the centre." [EL] "A pretty canary-yellow." [BJ] "Large very full delicate flowers of white shading to lemon-yellow, blushing delicate pink…to 6 [ft; ca. 1.75 m]." [HRG] "Fairly free flowering; old-gold." [ARA17/26] "Medium-sized, full, well-formed, light yellow." [JR1/2/8] "Free bloomer, fair autumnal…prettily coloured buds add much to the beauty of the truss." [F-M2] "Pale primrose to white…abundant, healthy, light green foliage. Well scented…64 [ft; ca. 2×1.25 m]." [B] "Vigorous, large-flowered, blossoms full, well-formed, of a handsome

and magnificent golden yellow." [JR4/153] "Not, I think, a very quick grower...though, perhaps, it is never showy, I find the nicely shaped and pointed flowers of sulphur-yellow with a deeper centre very homely and attractive. When a situation suits it and it is doing well, it flowers fairly freely and continuously." [NRS/14] "Large and full; form cupped." [P1] "Medium-sized, flat." [JR3/29] "A pleasant scent." [JR18/136] "Spicy fragrance." [G] "Flowers freely in clusters." [Hn] "Of good growth, but not sufficiently lengthy to make a climber." [F-M2] "An old variety, but an excellent climber." [FRB] "Good growth; wood and foliage very distinct, latter nearly evergreen and glazed, a proof against mildew." [B&V] "Vigorous, somewhat climbing, with divergent branches with green bark, brown flat thorns, sparse and small and towards the extremities of the branches...flower about 2.5 inches across [ca. 6.25 cm], fragrant, flat, cupped, either in a cluster or solitary; pale yellow, darker at the center, often washed pink, outer petals pointed red...It bears the name of a close friend of Monsieur Trouillard" [JR10/93]

Champneys' Pink Cluster (Champneys, ca. 1802) syn., 'Chamnagagna', 'Chamnagaa', 'Champagagna', 'Champneyana', 'Champuciana', 'Changnagana'

Noisette

From *R. moschata* × 'Parsons' Pink China' (Ch).

"Rosy white." [Sx] "A very pale pink hybrid, less double and as small as [*'Blush Noisette'*], but very pretty." [J-A] "Small blush pink double blooms in clusters." [HRG] "Semi-double, flesh." [TCN] "Very pale pink and heavily clustering." [ARA36/17] "Light pink, a rampant grower, profuse bloomer, quite hardy...it is universally cultivated." [Bu] "Although not full double, is still quite a favorite for its rapid growth, its appropriateness for pillars and other climbing positions, and for the profusion of its flowers which are in very large panicles much more diffuse than [*those of 'Blush Noisette'*]...produces seed far more abundantly than the 'Blush Noisette'." [WRP] "Has much in common with the Type of the Noisette Rose [*referring to 'Blush Noisette'*]; but its leaves are larger; it was first grown and published at the Luxembourg." [BJ30] "Five to seven oval acute leaflets, crenelate, green above, pale beneath." [MaCo] "[*In comparison to 'Blush Noisette'*], this rose differs from the preceding by the following characteristics: *Epidermis*, purplish. *Leaflets* and *stipules* narrower or longer. *Corolla* larger, with higher color, more single, slightly fragrant." [Pf] Vibert groups it, in 1826, with the group of "Noisettes, encompassing those of which the main canes, much longer [*than those of his other grouping of Noisettes, comprising the more China-like Noisettes*], are not totally floriferous, at least without having recourse to technique." [V3] "A rose long well known and very widely diffused. It was raised from seed by the late John Champney[s], Esq., of Charleston, S.C., an eminent and most liberal votary of Flora, from the seed of the White Musk Rose, or *Rosa Moschata*, fertilized by the old Blush China, and as he had been for a long period in constant correspondence with the late William Prince, he most kindly presented him with two tubs, each containing six plants, grown from cuttings of the original plant. From these an immense number were propagated and sent to England and France." [WRP]

Château de Clos-Vougeot, Climbing (Morse, 1920)
Hybrid Tea
Sport of 'Château de Clos-Vougeot' (HT).
"Deep velvety red…highly scented. Glossy foliage but of sprawly habit…15×8 [ft; ca. 4.5×2.25 m]." [B] "Superb, everblooming, blackish red rose, turning darker with age…Fine growth (8 feet [ca. 2.25 m])…holds foliage better than dwarf." [PP28] "Foliage is lost early." [Th2] "Bud very large; flower very large, full, open form, very double, borne singly and together on long stems; very lasting; strong fragrance…Foliage abundant, medium size, leathery, rich green; disease resistant. Very vigorous and free blooming, producing its blooms from June to September. Very hardy." [ARA20/126] "Though a shy bloomer, is

well worth growing." [ARA18/79] "Growth usually poor...distinct. Valuable." [Capt28]

Cherubim (A. Clark, 1923)
Noisette
Seedling of 'Mlle. Claire Jacquier' (N).
"Small, pointed, yellow-and-salmon-pink buds; semidouble flowers in huge, clear-pink clusters, May into June. This looks like the Sweetheart Rose, '[Mlle.] Cécile Brunner'...The foliage is small, wrinkled, glossy, and rich green; the canes almost thornless. Very vigorous where it is hardy." [W] "Clusters of exquisitely formed little pale yellow flowers, flushed with salmon-pink. Charming, and somewhat like 'Phyllis Bide'." [GAS]

[**Cheshunt Hybrid**] (G. Paul, 1872)
Hybrid Tea
From 'Mme. de Tartas' (T)? × 'Prince Camille de Rohan' (HP).
"Cherry-carmine, large, full, open flower, very hardy, free, and distinct." [JC] "Maroon-crimson, changing to slatey red, large and full; a useful climbing Rose, its principal defect being the dull hue of the expanded flowers." [P1] "Cherry-carmine, shaded violet. A good early and very free-flowering variety." [H] "Dark brown leaves, and reddish brown stems reveal the Tea ancestor, while the color of the flower and growth of the plant proclaim its descent from Bourbons or HPs." [JR8/157-158] "Shows the Tea blood in its veins in its foliage more than in any other way; what fragrance it has is more like that of 'Alfred Colomb' or 'Prince Camille [de Rohan]' than like a Tea; it seldom shows a flower after the first of August." [EL] "A tall, straight, gawky plant, fit to be tied to a clothes post. It was the first red Hybrid Tea, but was virtually sterile." [Hk] "The first Rose to be known and recognized as a Hybrid Tea. Very vigorous in growth, hardy and free flowering, it will do well for a pillar or paling. An early bloomer and good autumnal, with large flowers, but the shape is open and the colour wanting in brightness." [F-M2] "A glorious rose." [HRH]

China Doll, Climbing (Weeks, 1977)
Polyantha
Sport of 'China Doll' (Pol).
Light pink; semi-double; in clusters.

Chromatella (Coquereau/Vibert, 1843) syn., 'Cloth of Gold'
Noisette
Seedling of 'Lamarque' (N).
"Sulphur-yellow, deeper center; large." [ARA17/26] "Large; double, deep golden yellow, fragrant." [ARA29/98] "Flowers creamy white, their centre yellow, varies as to colour and fulness, usually very large and very double; form, globular. Growth, vigorous. A beautiful Rose, and sweet, but a shy bloomer...when thoroughly established it will flower." [P] "Quartered centers and stiff petals...Continuous bloom...8-12 [ft; ca. 2.25-3.5 m]...outstanding." [Lg] "Has charms of colour which...make it very desirable. It is described as...'large double yellow, of as bright a shade as our old yellow rose [*R. hemisphærica*]; colour as yet unique in the group of Noisettes.' The English advertise it under the name of 'Cloth of Gold Noisette, with very large flowers and fine bold stiff petals, withstanding the effects of the sun, retaining its colour, a perfect yellow, equal to the Yellow Harrison Rose'...It is very rare, and sells at twenty-five francs in France." [Bu] "Its flowers were like large golden bells...each flower was pendulous so that their bright yellow centres were most conspicuous...no yellow rose has approached in beauty this grand and remarkable variety." [R8] "A magnificent yellow rose, but opens with difficulty, and late." [S] "Large, unique, splendid." [CC] "Well formed, of a weakish color." [JR10/44-45] "A noble rose, of exquisite odor, and strong growth." [HstXI:225] "I have never seen a strong plant." [Hk] "Buds bruise...easily...Special prey to mildew." [J] "A grand rose, but difficult to grow well." [EL] "The original plant still [*in 1857*] exists in Angers at Coquereau's." [VH57/77]

"This new rose...upon which so many praises have been lavished...will, I fear, prove a downright disappointment. I have had six plants in my possession for eighteen months, and have never seen but two flowers." [HstI:145] "Is, when in perfection, the most beautiful of all the yellow roses; but it is shy of bloom, and difficult of culture." [FP] "The wood requires roasting on a south wall to bring it to sufficient maturity to enable it to produce a full crop of blossoms." [NRS/17] "Flowers are borne February to May. Dormant in hot season, rampant in autumn—September to Christmas, if not frost." [ARA40/36-37] "This plant, with two others, budded...on seedling Noisette stocks, had last autumn made shoots from eight to ten feet high [ca. 2.25-3 m]...These plants, in November and October, produced from ten to fifteen flowers each—the color, at this season, nearly equal to ['Harison's Yellow'], or one shade deeper than what they are." [HstII:35] "Vigorous, very climbing, giving magnificent and numerous flowers of a straw yellow." [JR10/140] "I have just seen several specimens...in full bloom. The flowers were very full, of a rather deep creamy yellow, yellowest in the center, and of a handsome cup shape. When compared with its twin sister, the 'Solfaterre' [*sic*]...the 'Cloth of Gold' was seen to be much superior in size and shape...It quite answers the description of it as given by Rivers himself...Near Natchez, I have seen it really blooming well, but never at the North." [HstI:196]
"Outer petals pale yellow, with golden centre—globular—large and magnificent—sometimes a shy bloomer, of the most luxuriant growth...There can be but little doubt that this is the finest of yellow autumnal Roses...'In the month of July, 1842, I [*Rivers*] was at Angers, and looking over the gardens of Monsieur Vibert, when his foreman brought me a bouquet of yellow Roses, some in bud and some about half expanded. I had never in my life seen anything so beautiful, and I warmly expressed my admiration...it had been raised from the seed of Noisette 'Lamarque' by an amateur, living in the neighbourhood'...Most beautiful foliage...blossoms, distinctly Tea scented, are of the most beautiful globular-shape, petals of great substance, with centres of the richest golden yellow. In spring the flowers are

more frequently produced singly of a great size, but in the autumn it assumes its Noisette habit, blooming in clusters." [C] "Foliage large and spreading...of a dark green tint...flowers large, three inches in diameter [ca. 7.5 cm], (I have often seen them four [ca. I dm],) very double, petals firm, particularly the two outer rows, which are of a round form, guarding the interior ones well; these are smaller, more pointed, a little reflexed at the apex, becoming more irregular in their arrangement towards the centre of the flower, lasting long; not so fugacious as Noisette 'Solfaterre' [*sic*]...blooms freely in early summer, and late autumn; frequently transient flowers between these periods." [HstII:36] "The finest of climbing roses in the 'Cloth of Gold'. The finest of yellow roses in the 'Cloth of Gold'. The finest of Noisettes is the 'Cloth of Gold'. And yet how few know it except as a dwarf, grown in a pot or border, and bearing there a scanty supply of its noble blossoms. Nevertheless, it yields to none in the power of flowering, producing, if well managed, enormous quantities of golden balls...To bloom it in perfection, it should never be pruned; and we add, that the plant must have some age to insure a profuse bloom." [HstXII:94] "It is indeed the queen of roses. In the bud, and until it is half expanded, it is impossible to conceive of an object more exquisite...Nor indeed is it less perfect when fully blown." [HstII:47] "Queen Victoria carried the 'Cloth of Gold' rose when, with Albert, her consort, she opened in Crystal Palace in 1847." [ARA40/36] "Still, for its purpose, without equal as a mild-climate climber." [ARA31/30]

Cinderella (Page, 1859)
Noisette
"Salmon." [l'H59/137] "Carmine pink." [JR4/60] Not to be confused with Walsh's Wichuraiana of 1909.

Claire Carnot
Listed as 'Mme. Claire Carnot'.

Claire Jacquier
Listed as 'Mlle. Claire Jacquier'.

Claudia Augusta (Damaizin, 1856)
Noisette
"Vigorous; canes dark green; leaves brilliant dark green; flower large, full; color, white with a cream center." [S]

Cloth of Gold
Listed as 'Chromatella'.

Clotilde Soupert, Climbing (Dingee & Conard, 1902)
Polyantha
Sport of 'Clotilde Soupert' (Pol).
"One of the very finest varieties, unequalled for quick and abundant bloom and healthy, vigorous growth. The flowers are 2.5 to 3 inches across, and perfectly double; rich creamy white, sometimes tinted with blush. Not subject to insects or disease, and is altogether one of the most beautiful and satisfactory hardy ever-blooming climbing roses for porch or trellis yet produced." [C&Js10] "Poor growth; blooms not of good form." [ARA18/122]

Colcestria (B.R. Cant, 1916)
Hybrid Tea
"Satin pink." [Cw] "Fair growth and bloom. A pillar rose." [ARA18/118] "Strong Pillar in habit of growth, with good stout foliage of a light green shade, and retained well in winter. The blooms are large and full; satin-rose in the centre, shading off to silvery-pink in the outer petals, which are beautifully reflexed. It possesses a most delightful perfume...Very free flowering when established." [NRS/17]

Columbia, Climbing (Lens, 1929)
Hybrid Tea
Sport of 'Columbia' (HT).
"Pink changing to brighter pink." [Ÿ] "Best in cool dampness. One of the best of the pink Hybrid Tea climbers, with the fault of discoloration in heat, but fine growth and foliage, long stems and lovely perfume; not a prolific bloomer, yet always furnishes a few fine blooms for cutting." [Capt28]

Commun
Listed as 'Blush Noisette'.

Comte de Torres (A. Schwartz, 1905)
Hybrid Tea
From 'Kaiserin Auguste Viktoria' (HT) × 'Mme. Bérard' (N).
"Light salmon Hybrid Tea with pink center." [GAS] "Growth very vigorous; foliage somber green; flower large, full, well formed, opening well; outer petals salmony white, those of the center coppery salmon yellow lightly tinted pink; climbing." [JR29/150]

Comtesse de Galard-Béarn (Bernaix, 1893)
Noisette
"Long bud, the flower is pretty large, flesh-white, and it seems to be very floriferous." [JR17/84] "Very vigorous and very floriferous, with climbing canes having thick, beautiful, bright green foliage. Blossom of large size, beautifully double, with large and numerous petals which spread out and recurve; light canary yellow which fades upon expansion to chrome, brightened with incarnadine towards the center. Remarkable due to the delicate tint of its large blossoms, the beautiful form of its buds, its vigor, and its abundant bloom." [JR17/164]

Comtesse Georges de Roquette-Buisson (Nabonnand, 1885)
Noisette
"Very vigorous, climbing, big-wooded; flower medium-sized, perfect, very full, globular, imbricated, erect; color, a novel bright yellow." [JR8/166]

Condesa da Foz
Listed as 'Rêve d'Or'.

Cooper's Burmese Rose (Cooper?, 1927)
Hybrid Gigantea?
Possibly *R. lævigata* × *R. gigantea.*
"Fantastic, creamy-white rose...large, glossy foliage...large, single, scented flowers of immense attraction. Very vigorous...35 × 20 [ft; ca. 11.25×6 m]." [B] "Very strong climber...8 to 10 metres [ca. 30 ft or so]...single white flowers up to 50 mm [ca. 2 inches]." [G]

Cornélie (Robert & Moreau, 1858)
"5-6 cm [ca. 2-2¼ inches], full, bright pink, passing to light lilac, strong corymbs of from 12-25 flowers." [R&M62] See also 'Belle Vichysoise'.

Cracker, Climbing (A. Clark, 1927)
Hybrid Gigantea
"Red with white, large, single, very fragrant, tall." [Sn]

Cramoisi Supérieur, Climbing
Though seen listed under the above name, such a rose would be either of the following two varieties: 'Mme. Couturier-Mention' or 'James Sprunt', *qqv.*

Crépuscule (Dubreuil, 1904) trans., "Twilight"
Noisette

"Copper, yellow and pink shades." [OM] "Double, shapely...orange and apricot. Light green, plentiful foliage...8×5 [ft; ca. 2.25×1.5 m]." [B] "In color and simple beauty its coppery fawn flower of exquisite grace, borne all season long, and its handsome foliage, are without a superior in my garden." [ARA34/44] "Of good vigor, bushy, elongated bud of perfect form and of pretty chamois yellow, the exterior petals striped nasturtium red. Flower, medium-sized, full, salmon-chamois, in clusters of 3-5, fragrant." [JR28/157] "Copper orange fading to apricot...Continuous bloom...5-8 [ft; ca. 1.5-2.25 m]...outstanding." [Lg] "Eager bloomer...to 12 [ft; ca. 3.5 m]." [HRG] "A climbing Noisette resembling 'Ma Capucine'." [JR31/73]

Crimson Conquest (Chaplin Bros., 1931)
Hybrid Tea
Sport of 'Red Letter Day' (HT).
"Medium-sized, semi-double, rich crimson...healthy plant with dark green, glossy foliage...15×8 [ft; ca. 4.5×2.25 m]." [B1]

Cupid (B.R. Cant, 1915)
Hybrid Tea
"Blush-colour." [OM] "Superbly formed...Large, single, peachy...tawny gold anthers. Sparse bloom...12×2 [ft; ca. 3.5×3.5 m]." [B] "Small growth; single blooms; attractive color, fading quickly." [ARA18/120] "A pillar Rose of strong growth...of good habit and abundant foliage. The flowers are single, four to five inches across [ca. 1-1.25 dm], sometimes larger, and the colour in the half-developed stage is a glowing flesh, with a touch of peach, softening to delicate flesh and opal when fully expanded. In the Autumn it produced pretty rose-coloured seed pods." [NRS/15] Cupid, ubiquitous and troublesome factor in the human drama.

Dainty Bess, Climbing (VanBarneveld, 1935)
Hybrid Tea

Sport of 'Dainty Bess' (HT).
Single pink. "Pointed buds…3.5-4 inch [ca. 7.75 cm-1 dm] flowers with wine-colored stamens…Heavy resistant foliage…vigorous…8 to 10 feet [ca. 2.25-3 m]." [W] "An ideal Climber with flowers larger than the bush form…a few flowers all season." [ARA39/182-183] "Perfect foliage." [ARA38/181] "Grew well…should be in every garden." [ARA37/213]

Dame Edith Helen, Climbing (Howard & Smith, 1930)
Hybrid Tea
Sport of 'Dame Edith Helen' (HT).
"Dark pink, very large, very full, very fragrant, tall." [Sn]

Dawn (G. Paul, 1898)
Hybrid Tea
From 'Mme. Caroline Testout' (HT) × 'Mrs. Paul' (HP).
"Semi-double, rosy pink Hybrid Tea." [GAS] "Light pink, large, lightly full, tall." [Sn] "Silvery pink, shaded rose. —Very vigorous. —Bush, pillar." [Cat12/22] "Quite easy to grow…If tied in too closely it may often refuse to break from the bottom, and then becomes woefully leggy, and when this state of affairs becomes established nothing seems to avail but digging it up and starting afresh with a new plant…Its beautiful shiny pink flowers come freely in summer and fairly continuously, though more sparingly, later…Very little pruning is required, and that should be directed to the encouragement of young growths. Consequently, thinning will be freely practised. It is somewhat, though not very, liable to mildew, but suffers badly from black spot if that is anywhere near…Only semi-double, or nearly single." [NRS14/70]

Député Debussy (Buatois, 1902)
Hybrid Tea
"Flesh white, yellow nub." [Ÿ]

Deschamps (Deschamps, 1877)
Noisette
"Cerise red fading to pink." [JR32/173] "Bright carmine, of medium size, but produced in great profusion. Grand in Autumn, and almost evergreen." [P1] "Cerise...cupped...very vigorous." [Cx] "An old rose that is free flowering, though the blooms are small and not very shapely. The colour is light crimson. [OM] "One of the best autumnal climbers that we have. The cerise-pink flowers are very pretty." [JR22/74] 'Longworth Rambler' is an 1880 climber from Liabaud which might—or might not—be synonymous. It is very doubtful that a long-established, reputable *rosiériste* such as Liabaud would intentionally mislead his patrons (nor have we seen any accusations to that effect).

Desprez
Listed as 'Desprez à Fleur Jaune'.

Desprez à Fleur Jaune (Desprez/Sisley, 1830) syn., 'Desprez', 'Jaune Desprez'; trans., "Yellow-Flowered Desprez"
Noisette
"Rosy yellow." [Sx] "Coppery yellow and pink." [TCN] "Red, buff, and sulphur." [WD] "Double, flat, strongly fragrant; very light yellow with apricot tints, fading to white. Repeats...15-20 [ft; ca. 4.5-6 m]." [Lg] "Buff or Fawn, deliciously fragrant, blooms freely in autumn...beautiful foliage." [H] "Double flowers fairly large, give the impression of soaking up the sun's warmth and paying it back with a sleepy scent...said to be shaded peach and apricot...rather white when I visited it." [Hk] "Pale yellow overshot with pink blush...to 20 [ft; ca. 6.3 m]." [HRG] "Rose, blended with coppery yellow, highly scented." [EL] "Cup., bright fawn color, large, very fragrant." [CC] "Sulphur-color tinged with red, very large and fragrant." [FP] "Large, full, very well formed, cupped; copper yellow mixed with sulphur yellow." [S] "Bud, bright pink.—Flower, semi-double and cupped, or full and more or less flat.—Color, pink; reverse

washed salmon yellow." [JR23/151] "Reddish, buff-coloured flowers. It is a vigorous grower, retaining its foliage during the greater part of the winter." [OM] "Red, buff, flesh, and sulphur, very large and full; form cupped; growth vigorous; the flowers forming in clusters; the foliage large and fine; very sweet. A most desirable kind for a wall." [P1] "Grown against a west wall here, it covered a space some 20×20 ft [ca. 6.6×6.6 m] in three years, throwing laterals five feet [ca. 1.5] and more every summer; and from the ends of these in late autumn the great heads of bloom hang down, filling the whole air with fragrance; in one cluster alone I have counted seventy-two blossoms, soft sulphur, salmon, and red." [K2] "Flowers of a ravishing beauty. Though the form may be irregular, the general effect is most agreeable to the eye." [JR22/74] "Apricot scented." [R33/101] "Flower stem stiff, short, somewhat slender. Calyx oblong; sepals leaf-like; scent agreeable." [JF] "A well-known and much esteemed rose, of rapid growth and quite hardy...its fragrance is also very remarkable. This was originated by Monsieur Desprez about eighteen years since, and is still, and will be for some time to come, a very popular rose...Its rosy copper-colored flowers are very singular, and so powerfully fragrant that one plant will perfume a large garden in the cool weather of autumn." [WRP] "It has been cultivated about Philadelphia these ten years past...[W]hen well established, [*produces a*] profusion of flowers...in large clusters. The colour is a rosy-buff inclining to orange, and perfectly double. It should always be planted where it will be under the eye, as its colour does not make it a remarkable object from a distance." [Bu] "At one time highly esteemed, and even now its fawn-coloured and very fragrant flowers are often, in autumn, very beautiful." [R8] "Rapidity of its growth and the magnificence of its foliage." [P2] "The lovely and fragrant old Noisette...has in these few years spread over a space 18 by 20 feet [ca. 5.5×6.6 m] and more, with its light green, graceful foliage and great clusters of sweet-scented flowers...sometimes ten or twelve feet long [ca. 3-4 m] in a year." [K1]

"Monsieur Pirolle described this rose in the August and September 1831 numbers of the *Annals of the Society of Practical Agriculture*...The bearing and vigor of the plant resemble those of a Bourbon...Noisette Desprez is a vigorous bush, well supported, and its thorns are purplish and sparse; its foliage is large, outspread, leathery, of a nice shiny green, with five oval-acuminate leaflets bordered with numerous blunt teeth. The leafstalk has prickles beneath, and often the base of the terminal leaflet's vein has a prickle as well when the leaves are large. Flowers terminal, 3-5 on each cane, borne on stems which are fairly long and flexible enough that they don't interfere with each other; the peduncles are purplish and slightly pubescent, as are the ovaries and calyces, which stay green. The ovaries are oval-oblong, and the sepals somewhat lacinated. The blossom is full, large to 4 inches [ca. 1 dm], with large exterior petals which are concave and saucer-shaped like those of the Centifolia; inner petals muddled; color, nankeen yellow or fawn washed pink towards the edge. The scent is elegant; many people say that it resembles that of a ripe banana. No one can confuse this rose with any other." [R-H33] "*Shrub*, very vigorous. *Thorns*, purplish, scattered. *Leaves*, coriaceous, glossy, large, of a dark green. *Flowers*, usually in a cluster of three; three inches wide [ca. 7.5 cm]; yellow in the centre, pale at the circumference.' [Go] "Large branches, which are very long and flexile; bark, yellowish-green, somewhat reddish where exposed to the sun; thorns not numerous, short, hooked, of the same green as that of the bark, but tinged red; leaves, handsome green, paler beneath, pointed and finely toothed; leafstalks green, slender, armed beneath with five or six little prickles which are hooked and sharp; flower, about 2.5 inches across [ca. 7 cm], full, expanded, in clusters at the ends of the branches; color, flesh-colored saffron yellow, going to light pinkish yellow, outer petals concave, obovate, and rounded, while those of the center are narrower." [S]

"Grown from seed around 1828 by Monsieur Desprez...who sold it for the exorbitant sum of 3,000 francs to Monsieur Sisley-Vandael with the proviso that he would not give it to anyone else for several years...This rose is not one to be victimized by changing fashions; it will stand always in the forefront of the Noisettes." [R-H34] "Such was [*Monsieur*] Desprez that, after being so often inclined while on this Earth to admire one of these most perfect works of creation [*referring to rose blossoms*], this fancier/enthusiast had brought to him, on his death-bed, one of these beloved roses, the one which bears his name, to take one last look before sinking into the peace of death." [JF]

Devoniensis, Climbing (Pavitt/Curtis, 1858) syn., 'Magnolia Rose'
Tea
Sport of 'Devoniensis' (T).
"Very pale creamy white...centres sometimes buff, sometimes yellowish; very large and full; form cupped." [P1] "Pink-tinged white, recurrent." [W] "Blush centre. Fragrant." [H] "Large, full, handsome white with some sulphur-yellow." [Sx] "Very large flowers of cream/white with an occasional blush of pink...10×6 [ft; ca. 3×1.75 m]." [B] "Often come divided...deficient in size." [F-M2] "Richly perfumed." [ARA29/98] "The strongest, most untidy, and irregular grower of all Tea Roses. Growing is its strong point." [F-M2] "The early, strong, sappy wood should be pinched or stopped when about a foot in length [ca. 3 dm], in order to cause it to break into several shoots...which almost invariably flower at each point the first season." [R1/278] "Vigorous; branches very climbing, of a dark green, not very thorny; foliage brilliant green, regularly toothed; flower large, quite full; the inner petals are curled and artistically arranged, giving the appearance of a smaller rose placed within a larger; color, white, yellower towards the center of the petal, flesh towards the base." [S] "When established, very vigorous, and bearing its small cream-coloured flowers freely." [OM]

Distinction, Climbing (Lens, 1935)
Polyantha
Sport of 'Distinction' (Pol).

"Pink, medium size, semi-double, tall." [Sn]

Doris Downes (A. Clark, 1932)
Hybrid Gigantea
Pink, semi-double.

Dr. Domingos Pereira (De Magalhaes, 1925)
Tea
"Big, fragrant flowers of lilac-pink and yellow. A vigorous Tea reported to be very floriferous." [GAS]

[**Dr. Kane**] (Pentland, 1856)
Noisette
"Vigorous; flowers large, sulphur yellow, held in much esteem in the [*American*] South." [JR4/60]

Dr. Lande (Berger/Chauvry, 1901)
Tea
"Very vigorous, semi-climbing; foliage deep bronze green, buds medium, very long; flower large, semi-double; color, deep salmon pink in Spring, coppery brick red nuanced salmon on a ground of golden bronze in Fall. Petals recurved and ruffled; fragrant and very floriferous. Dedicated to Monsieur Dr. Lande, mayor of Bordeaux." [JR25/163]

Dr. Rouges (Widow Schwartz, 1893)
Tea
"China pink." [LS] "Deep coppery red, with orange shading. Very free-flowering." [H] "The most intensely brilliant shade of orange-red that I know...The rich claret-red shoots in January are almost as brilliant as any flower could be." [J] "Red, with yellowish centres...[*flowers*] of good effect on the plant." [P1] "Vigorous, foliage beautiful green with purplish leafstalks. Flower irregular in form, like that of a cactus Dahlia; petals

rolled into a horn, China red on a dawn-gold ground." [JR17/165] "Needs coolness and dryness for best results. Another distinct color, much like wine; good growth; lots of bloom; some liability to mildew; and little perfume or cutting value." [ARA28/95] "A fine Tea...Good as a shrub." [GAS]

Dr. W. Van Fleet (Van Fleet/Henderson, 1910)
Hybrid Tea or Wichuraiana
From an unnamed seedling (resulting from crossing *R. wichuraiana* with the Tea 'Safrano') × 'Souvenir du Président Carnot' (HT).
"Soft flesh, shading to delicate peach-pink." [ARA21/93] "Pale pink fading to blush...to 20 [ft; ca. 6.6 m]." [HRG] "Vigorous, robust, covered with handsome shiny bronze foliage. The flowers are cupped, about four inches across [ca. 1 dm]; petals are wavy, flesh-pink at the base, more of a delicate pink towards the edges. The flowers are full, on strong stems, and are very fragrant." [JR33/135] "Beautiful flowers of good form; blooms well in spring, an occasional bloom thereafter." [ARA18/120] "Bloom free last three weeks of June." [ARA18/130] "A grand show if there is enough cold weather to render dormant in winter." [ET] "Foliage very good." [ARA17/27] A much longer entry on 'Dr. W. Van Fleet' will be found in our other book *The Old Rose Adventurer*.

Duarte de Oliveira (Brassac, 1879)
Noisette
From 'Ophirie' (N) × 'Rêve d'Or' (N).
"Salmon-rose, coppery at base, medium size, full." [EL] "Dedicated to our brother the editor of the *Portuguese Horticultural Review*...Very vigorous, flower of medium size, full, well-formed, coppery salmon-pink; climbing." [JR2/167] "Monsieur Brassac...delivers into commerce this year a new rose [*'Duarte de Oliveira'*] which he had intended to release *last* year, a rose whose entry into the world of flowers was delayed due to an error in propagation." [JR3/167]

Duchesse d'Auerstädt
Listed as 'Mme. la Duchesse d'Auerstädt'.

Duchesse de Grammont (Laffay?, -1838)
Noisette
"*Flowers*, small, full; flesh-coloured." [Go] "To about 2 metres [ca. 6 ft]...fragrant small double pink flowers which appear in clusters." [G] Not to be confused with Cels' 1825 pink Damask of the same name, nor with Laffay's pinkish-lilac Tea of 1825, 'Duc de Grammont'.

E. Veyrat Hermanos (Bernaix, 1894) syn., 'Pillar of Gold'
Tea
"The flower is ravishing with a beautiful color of sulphur enhanced by apricot pink and washed with a light tint of carmine, marvelous when the blossom is half open. The plant is very vigorous, but should not be pruned much." [JR23/42] "Another lovely rose, though not generally very free [*with*] its flowers, which are of apricot-yellow and rose." [OM] "Flower very large, full, cupped, very fragrant; very vigorous." [Cx] "Very sweet, distinct, and good, but rather a shy bloomer." [P1] "Best in heated zones...Good strong growth; foliage only fair; blooms well but balls in damp; some blooms very fine. Well worth growing even with its fault. Color varies from light yellow to apricot red, and bronze." [Capt28] "Branches strong and big, foliage thick and bright, flowers large, nicely double, very fragrant, bud of pretty form, flower bi-colored, with petals of apricot yellow and delicate carmine-pink with amaranth pink reflections. The contrast produced by these two noteworthy shades, its great vigor, its intense and pleasant scent, all make it an elite variety of great merit." [JR18/163]

Earl of Eldon (Eldon/Coppin/G. Paul, 1872)
Noisette

"Coppery gold." [Ÿ] "Copper-orange." [LS] "Bud yellow. Flower semi-full or full, large, flat; color, chamois yellow, orange yellow." [JR23/154] "Orange buff, a loose semi-double flower, very attractive, and highly fragrant; a good climbing rose." [JC] "Flesh and copper-coloured, handsome large regular flowers, and sweet scented. Well worth growing; a large successfully cultivated plant is a splendid feature in any collection." [B&V] "Growth vigorous." [S]

Edmée Cocteau
Listed as 'Mme. Edmée Cocteau'.

Effective (Hobbies, 1913)
Hybrid Tea
From an unnamed seedling (of the HT 'General MacArthur') × 'Paul's Carmine Pillar' (HCh).
"Brilliant scarlet red." [Ÿ] "Continuous bloom. We hope to have found [*in this*] the best autumnal climber...pretty color [*of 'General MacArthur'*] and [*from 'Paul's Carmine Pillar'*] its early blooming and climbing habit. The long buds are much prized." [JR37/26]

Elie Beauvilain (Beauvilain, 1887)
Noisette
From 'Gloire de Dijon' (N) × 'Ophirie' (N).
"Two-toned pink and yellow, recurrent, very showy." [W] "Very floriferous. Very vigorous. Flowers large, full, copper-pink." [Lc] "Climbing, vigorous, growing shoots nine or ten feet in length [ca. 2.75-3 m]; foliage very large and of a nice brilliant green; very numerous and strong thorns; flower large, full, imbricated; prettily colored silvery blush, copper-veined with a ground of red, the reverse of the petals pink; all in all, a quite novel coloration for this sort; very floriferous, quite remontant." [JR11/163-164]

Emilia Plantier
Listed in the chapter on Bourbons.

Emilie Dupuy
Listed as 'Mme. Emilie Dupuy'.

Emmanuella de Mouchy (P. Nabonnand, 1922)
Hybrid Gigantea
R. gigantea × 'Lady Waterlow' (HT).
"A vigorous Gigantea hybrid with medium-sized, globular flowers of pale flesh-pink." [GAS]

Empress of China (Jackson/Elizabeth Nursery Co., 1896)
China
"Bright red." [Ÿ] "Resembles a beautiful Tea Rose; blooms the first year and all through the season. The color is soft dark red passing to light pink or apple blossom; the flowers are medium size and quite fragrant, and borne on long stems, nice for cutting. It is a rapid grower, of slender twining habit, bearing few thorns and valuable for having over porches and arches. It is entirely hardy—needs no protection, and will thrive in any locality." [C&Js99] "Widely distributed everblooming Bengal or China rose of little value, with reddish pink, semi-double flowers." [GAS]

Étendard de Jeanne d'Arc (Garçon/Margottin fils, 1882) syn., 'Jeanne d'Arc'; trans., "Jeanne d'Arc's Banner"
Noisette
Seedling of 'Gloire de Dijon' (N).
"Creamy white changing to pure white; very large and full, opening well…very free." [P1] "Opens quickly, free, fragrant." [Hn] "Very good scent." [JR5/106] "An inferior 'Lamarque'." [EL] "Reminds one a little of 'Souvenir de la Malmaison'." [JR9/146] "This new Tea rose…is a very vigorous variety, but is nevertheless not so vigorous as its parent 'Gloire de

Dijon'; its flowers are very large, very full, and open well; they are of good form, having much in common with 'Gloire de Dijon'." [JR7/153] "Repeats...8-12 [ft; ca. 2.25-3.5 m]." [Lg] "To 15 [ft; ca. 4.5 m]." [HRG]

Étoile de Holland, Climbing (Leenders, 1931)
Hybrid Tea
Sport of 'Étoile de Hollande' (HT).
"Bright red, double...very large, cupped...Color is quite sun-resistant. Recurrent...soft foliage...to 8 feet [ca. 2.25 m]...Beautiful buds...Marvelous old-rose fragrance." [W] "Highly scented...rich velvety crimson...12×10 [ft; ca. 4×3.3 m]." [B] "During the spring blooming period the flowers completely cover the plant, with some recurrence on old wood." [ARA36/178] "One of the finest red climbers...Large blooms all season." [ARA37/213]

Étoile de Portugal (Cayeux/Chénault & fils, 1909)
Hybrid Gigantea
From *R. gigantea* × 'Reine Marie Henriette' (HT).
"Most notable as being the first Gigantea hybrid. The ample foliage is light green. The large, well-formed blossoms, with regular petals, are a nice salmon shrimp pink, yellow at the nub; the bud is of perfect form and long duration. The color is superb and a novelty among Climbers." [JR33/152] "Vigorous...to...12 [ft; ca. 3.5 m]. Large, loose, double rose-red blooms." [HRG] "Of astonishing vigor, as with 'Reine Marie Henriette', a very great quantity of flowers of a handsome silvery carmine-pink, shaded yellow at the base. The fragrant blossom is large, full, and becomes slightly lighter when fully open. Monsieur Cayeux doesn't yet know if it will be remontant; such is to be hoped." [JR29/120] "Once-blooming only." [GAS] "The first of these [*Gigantea*] hybrids bloomed here after two years...Luxuriantly vigorous, the plant would seem to have borrowed [*from 'Reine Marie Henriette'*] its great floriferousness. The buds are elongated, often in twos or threes, of a pretty silvery carmine-pink,

shaded yellow at the base. The flower is large, full, and fragrant, and fades lighter after opening." [JR29/77-78] Evidently developed around 1905.

[**Eugene Jardine**] (Conard & Jones, 1898)
Noisette?
"A hardy, everblooming climber, fully tested and highly recommended for its rapid, vigorous growth, and constant and abundant bloom. The flowers are pure white, large, full and fragrant, and borne in solid wreaths and clusters all over the vine; entirely hardy and sure to please." [C&Js98]

Eva Teschendorff, Climbing (Opdebeek, 1926)
Polyantha
Sport of 'Eva Teschendorff' (Pol).
"Creamy white, small, full, light scent, moderately tall." [Sn]

Fellemberg (Fellemberg, 1834) syn., 'Fellenberg'
Noisette
"Light carmine, double, cupped, beautiful." [LF] "Bright red." [V4] "Light purple." [TCN] "Rosy crimson, very free bloomer." [FP] "Maroon." [R-H35] "Bright crimson, strong, very free." [H] "Bright pink to crimson...attractive cascading habit if grown free...7×4 [ft; ca. 2×1.25 m]." [B] "Has no equal for brilliancy of colour, during the autumnal months; in the early part of the season, it is of a pale red, but in the fall its colour approaches a scarlet, with large flowers produced in clusters of thirty to fifty. It is perfectly hardy...the foliage, when young, has also a peculiar red colour." [Bu] "Pretty crimson." [R8] "Delightfully fragrant." [NRS/13] "Medium size, double, cupped; bright crimson. Slightly fragrant...continuous...6-10 [ft; ca. 1.75 m]." [HRG] "Of medium size, double, form cupped; growth vigorous. An abundant bloomer...dark foliage, showy, but rather loose...fine late in the year." [P1] "Medium size, carmine-pink, well-filled, vigorous growth; flowers free till late autumn." [Hn] "Flowering from the end of June to the end of November...bright

crimson, flowers double and small, joints short as the crimson china [*which usually means 'Slater's Crimson China', but could also mean 'Cramoisi Supérieur'*]." [HsV:46] "The pretty little 'Fellemberg', poorest in quality of any, but flowering the most profusely, in colour and habit indicates a near relationship to the semperflorens type [*'Slater's Crimson China'*]." "Believed by some authorities to be a cross of China with Multiflora." [ARA38/13] "Good in damp climates...does not last well." [Capt28] "Good growth. Very fine foliage. Blooms over long period...Specially recommended in the Southern Zones." [Th2] "This rose, when grown luxuriantly, is a most charming plant." [R9] "Beautiful." [CC]

Flesh-Coloured
Listed as 'Fraser's Pink Musk'. See also 'Blush Noisette'.

Florence Haswell Veitch (W. Paul, 1911)
Hybrid Tea
From 'Mme. Émile Metz' (HT) × 'La Tulipe' (T).
"Blossom bright scarlet, shaded black, large, moderately full, perfect form, stiff petals. Bush very vigorous, nearly climbing. Wonderful scent, continuous bloom; excellent as a large bush, or for clothing walls of medium height." [JR35/101] "One of the best rich crimsons." [NRS20/69] "Rich blackish crimson colour. It is not a fast grower, but with a little patience one is rewarded with a fine plant that yields its blossoms until quite late in the year." [NRS22/162] "Many of the qualities of 'Sarah Bernhardt', but it is a far better shaped flower, and seems to me most promising." [NRS14/63-64]

Flying Colours (A. Clark, 1922)
Hybrid Gigantea
"Striking, bright purplish red, single flowers about five inches across [ca. 1.25 dm]." [GAS] "Very large, single, lasting; light red; slight fragrance. Foliage disease-resistant. Very vigorous climber; abundant bloomer in

spring only." [ARA24/175] "Large, single, rich cerise-pink...If grown on a sheltered wall or trellis facing the morning sun, it comes into bloom three weeks before the flush, simply covering itself with bloom and making a glorious sight. It is spring-blooming only, but well worth having." [ARA30/153] "Lustrous, mildew-free leaves." [ARA23/119] Not to be confused with 'Flying Colors', a Miniature.

Fortune's Double Yellow (Fortune, 1845) syn., 'Beauty of Glazenwood', 'Gold of Ophir', 'Wang-Jang-Ve'
Hybrid Gigantea?
"Bronzed yellow." [EL] "Of a bright fawn-color, with a tinge of copper." [FP] "Rich salmon and pink." [K1] "A dull buff, with a tinge of purple; flowers small, semi-double, and loose...at its best, it falls far below expectation." [HstVIII:380] "The flecked flowers, semi-double, washed carmine-pink, of changing color...the buds are superb and much liked...It is a plant of the first merit." [JR18/135] "Very vigorous; flower of medium size, fairly full; color, yellow shaded rosy-red. Do not prune." [S] "Large golden blooms washed with pink and apricot, sometimes splashed with red...early...to 15 [ft; ca. 4.5 m]." [HRG] "Semi-double, shapely...loosely formed clusters. Glossy foliage...8×5 [ft; ca. 2.25×1.5 m]." [B] "In a cold spring the flowers are vivid; in a warm spring they pale." [ARA40/37] "One of the roses which thrive best in Madeira, bearing its burden of yellow and pink-tipped blossoms in the spring." [DuC] "A source of pride and delight to its happy possessor...vivid recollections of its exquisite effect tumbling over a high grey stone wall by the dusty roadside from Genoa to Pegli...And each year from the ground to the roof it is showered over with scores of lovely blossoms...it is without exception the most cruelly prickly, thorny Rose I know—every dainty twig, every shiny leaf being armed with ferocious fish-hooks. The flowers are borne singly on the well-ripened branchlets of last year's growth." [K1] "Must be treated [*in pruning, etc.*] similar to the Banksian [*i.e., summer pruning only*]...it is a rapid grower, and quite hardy, excellent for covering a wall

or trellis, or grown as a pillar rose." [WHoIII] "Small grower." [ARA18/120] "40, 50 and even 60 feet high [ca. 1.25-2 dkm]." [ARA19/133] "The best example I have seen is in Nabonnand's garden at Golfe Juan; an old plant which grows in a Pergola covered with other creepers, so much shaded that neither its stem nor roots can feel the sun's influence, has forced its head through this ceiling of other growths, and extending its arms on every side produces a mass of flowers innumerable and beautiful. It requires shading in burning weather, or the striking tints of the flowers are soon reduced to a yellowish white." [B&V] "Discovered in the garden of a rich mandarin at Ningpo. It completely covered an old wall in the garden, and was in full bloom at the time of my visit; masses of glowing yellowish and salmon colored flowers hung down in the greatest profusion...It is called by the Chinese the 'Wang-jang-ve' or 'Yellow Rose'. They vary, however, a good deal in color; a circumstance which, in my opinion, adds not a little to the beauty and character of the plant." [Mr. Fortune, being quoted secondhand in WHoIII]

François Crousse (P. Guillot, 1900)
Tea
"Cherry crimson, shaded dark." [RR] "Large, globular, crimson flowers, both double and fragrant." [GAS] "Vigorous and hardy, climbing, flower large, full, well-formed, cupped, fragrant, bright crimson red, sometimes fiery red." [JR24/146] "One of the best crimson pillar roses, rather late flowering, hardy and perpetual." [F-M] "Small growth; fair foliage; color attractive, tending to fade quickly; an occasional bloom during season; needs winter protection." [ARA18/120] "A real acquisition." [P1]

Fraser's Pink Musk (Fraser, ca. 1810) syn., 'Blush', 'Carné', 'Flesh-Coloured', 'Frazerii'
Noisette
"Small, semi-double, cupped, pale red." [JR5/133] "Not a pure Musk Rose, but a hybrid of the Noisette class, which was raised at Charleston,

S.C., about the same time as the Champney[s] and [Blush] Noisette Roses, and was carried thence to England by Mr. John Fraser; it is of a blush color, and quite fragrant; its flowers are semi-double, in large clusters, but it has now been cast aside." [WRP] "Rose with oval seed-buds and many-flowered panicles: footstalks prickly: leaflets oblong, pointed, finely sawed, and smooth: stem climbing: spines of the branches scattered and straight. This Rose, we believe, was first raised from seed in America, sent to France, and from thence to England. It is evidently a hybrid of the old Autumnal Rose, beginning in the summer season to unfold its delicate pink blossoms with an abundant succession till the month of November. [*Andrews'*] figure is from a large plant trained against an old barn in the Hammersmith Nursery, in 1824." [A] "It is true we have the 'Pink Musk Cluster', 'Red Musk Cluster', 'Frazerii', and some others, but...they are worthless." [Bu] One wonders if this rose was actually raised by Mr. John Fraser, or only "carried thence to England" by him. Coming as it did from Charleston, and considering the time it appeared, it is conceivable that it could be some sibling of 'Champneys' Pink Cluster', raised by Champneys; but this is only pure speculation. At any rate, it is the second Noisette.

Frau Geheimrat Dr. Staub (Lambert, 1908)
Hybrid Tea
From 'Mrs. W.J. Grant' (HT) × 'Duke of Edinburgh' (HP).
"Deep red, large, full, very fragrant, tall." [Sn] A "geheimrat" is a privy councillor.

Frau Karl Druschki, Climbing (Lawrenson, 1906)
Hybrid Perpetual
Sport of 'Frau Karl Druschki' (HP).
White. "A little inferior, however, to its mother; the flowers are smaller, and the buds pinker." [JR30/69] "It grows as vigorously as the Tea and Hybrid Tea climbers." [ET] "It frequently reverts to the type...[*it has an*]

inveterate desire to grow from the top and leave the base bare...the long straggling shoots are difficult to control in autumn...it is worth a good deal of care, for a well grown pillar of 'Frau Karl Druschki' is most decorative, its glistening white flowers showing up from distant parts of the garden, while it blooms more or less all summer and autumn, and Mr. Courtney Page adds, 'I think I might add winter too'." [NRS/14]

Frazerii
Listed as 'Fraser's Pink Musk'.

Fun Jwan Lo (China, -1811) syn. 'Indica Major', 'Odorata 22449'
Tea
"[*Discovered*] in a garden at Pautung Fu, Chihli Province...It produces small, double white flowers with pale pink centers; its canes are slender, smooth and of very rapid growth." [ARA23/92] "Plant has branches which are thin and climbing; the foliage is very shiny, lasting well on the plant; styles, free; flower, of medium size, very double, flesh-colored with tints of pink." [S] "With slender, scandent branches, more or less climbing, is the most appropriate subject for warm climates with prolonged summers, arid terrain, desert-like conditions, stony, or quite damp." [JR21/141] "[*Nowhere*] does it bear the slightest resemblance to the Tea roses which comprise the true species *R. odorata*." [ARA32/45]

Fürst Bismarck (Drögemüller/Schultheis, 1887) trans., "Prince Bismarck"
Noisette
Seedling of 'Gloire de Dijon' (N).
"Growth, foliage, and bearing like those of [*'Gloire de Dijon'*]; color, brilliant golden yellow, darker than 'Belle Lyonnaise'. This rose has all the

good qualities of its mother, adding to them the advantage of being more floriferous; hardy; good for forcing." [JR11/93]

Fürstin Bismarck (Drögemüller/Schultheis, 1887) trans., "Princess Bismarck"
Hybrid Tea
From 'Gloire de Dijon' (B) × 'Comtesse d'Oxford' (HP).
"Cherry." [LS] "Large, very full, imbricated, and well-held; color changes from China pink to cerise pink, but is very pretty despite the changes; reblooms freely. Growth very vigorous...foliage large, bright green." [JR11/92]

Gainesborough (Good & Reese, 1903) syn., 'Climbing Viscountess Folkestone'
Hybrid Tea
Sport of 'Viscountess Folkestone' (HT).
"Pinkish white, very large, full, medium scent, tall." [Sn] "A lovely Hybrid Tea with well-shaped, delicate shell-pink flowers flushed rose. Relatively hardy, but a shy summer bloomer." [GAS] Thomas Gainesborough, English painter; lived 1727-1788.

Gaston Chandon (Schwartz, 1884)
Noisette
Seedling of 'Gloire de Dijon' (N).
"Very vigorous...flower large or of medium size, full, well-formed, cherry-pink, shaded delicate pink, on a ground of coppery yellow." [JR8/133]

Général Lamarque
Listed as 'Lamarque'.

General MacArthur, Climbing (H. Dickson, 1923)
Hybrid Tea

Sport of 'General MacArthur' (HT).
"Large, loosely formed, scented, deep rosy-red...Very free flowering and vigorous...15×10 [ft; ca. 4.5×3 m]." [B] "About 5 feet high [ca. 1.5 m] the first year." [ARA25/183] "Best near coast. Wonderful as a decorative rose; continuous bloomer, and fine in every way, though fails somewhat in cutting value." [Capt28] "The best tender climber of its color." [PP28]

General-Superior Arnold Janssen, Climbing (Böhm, 1931)
Hybrid Tea
Sport of 'General-Superior Arnold Janssen' (HT).
"Deep rose-red, large, full, moderate scent, tall." [Sn]

George Dickson, Climbing (Woodward, 1949)
Hybrid Perpetual
Sport of 'George Dickson' (HP).
Red.

Georges de Cadondal
Listed as 'Monsieur Georges de Cadoudal'.

Geschwind's Gorgeous (Geschwind, 1916)
Hybrid Tea
"Light red, medium size, not very full, light scent, tall." [Sn]

Gigantea Blanc (Colett, 1889) *R. gigantea*
Gigantea
"The principal attraction of *R. gigantea* is the exceptional size of the blossoms, which attain six inches across [ca. 1.5 dm], and have been compared to those of the Clematis. Their color is an undecided one, fading from pale primrose yellow to ivory white. The bud is long, pointed...The leaves have from five to seven large oval leaflets...The branches are lengthily climbing." [JR29/30] "Imported from Upper Burmah at an altitude of

4,000 to 5,000 feet, and also found in Manypore 2,000 feet higher. It is said never to have produced blooms in Europe till we had the good fortune to flower it in this garden last month. A splendid plant, making growths of forty feet or more, with rambling branches armed with irregular prickles of moderate size, often in pairs at base of leaves, which are about three inches long and glabrous. The flowers are solitary, about six inches in diameter [ca. 1.5 dm], which size will not unlikely be increased when the plant is older and stronger, of a golden white with yellow centre, containing an unusual quantity of pollen. Petals large, broad, imbricated, disk large, styles much exserted, free, villous, stamens long. The most desirable and by far the finest single rose I have ever seen. It does not seem to be very hardy, and is subject to mildew. The bud is long, larger, but very closely resembles that of 'Mme. Marie Lavallée' [*sic*; 'Mme. Marie Lavalley'] and of pure gold colour. This rose when in flower should obviously be shaded, as the sun soon extracts the gold from the blooms, leaving behind a substitute of dirty white. At a short distance, the flowers bear a close resemblance to a Clematis." [B&V]

Gloire de Bordeaux (Lartay, 1861) syn., 'Belle de Bordeaux'; trans., "Bordeaux' Glory"
Noisette
Seedling of 'Gloire de Dijon' (N).
"Large, bright pink flowers silvered with white." [GAS] "Rose color, tinged with fawn." [EL] "Silvery-rose, the back of the petals rosy, very large and full." [FP, about 'Gloire de Bordeaux'] "Pink, large and full, habit and growth of 'Gloire de Dijon'." [FP, about 'Belle de Bordeaux'] "Vigorous habit of the Bourbon 'Sir Joseph Paxton', to which it bears some resemblance; its large, coarse rose-coloured flowers are however very fragrant, and the variety is well calculated for training to walls." [R8]

Gloire de Dijon (Jacotot, 1853) trans., "Dijon's Glory"
Noisette

From 'Desprez à Fleur Jaune' (N) × 'Souvenir de la Malmaison' (B), though the 'Desprez à Fleur Jaune' contribution is not fully established. "After two weeks in the steerage of an army transport, and two weeks of quarantine in a bitterly cold French camp, the last Sunday of December, 1917, found us in the railroad station of Dijon, with five hours between trains. As soon as our eyes lighted upon the sign 'Dijon', one of my friends and I made up our minds to visit the home of the rose which I had grown and admired for so many years, but when we started out I was dismayed to find that I had forgotten the originator's name. It did not occur to us, however, that we would have any trouble finding such a famous place, until we had, in our very bad French, asked the way of several shopkeepers. They were quite polite—'Yes, there were nurseries in Dijon; which one did we want to see? Roses? Yes, they all grew roses!' After getting these answers in four or five places, we gave it up and began to search blindly. Luck was with us, for after walking about an hour, we turned a corner, and beheld, painted in large letters on the brick wall of the house opposite, '*Jacotot, Horticulteur*'. Like a flash, the name I had been trying to remember came back to me, and we crossed the street, entered the little gate, and walked toward the house. The brick walk leading from the gate to the house divided the little enclosure in half. On the right was a formal rose-garden, 60 or 80 feet wide [ca. 2-2.5 dkm], and perhaps a hundred long [ca. 3 dkm], with little rectangular beds, having standard (tree) roses marking their corners, and with occasional arches or posts for climbers, these two types of roses standing out boldly while the dwarfer roses were mostly hidden with snow. On the left were three greenhouses, about 18 by 50 each [ft; ca. 5.5×1.5 dkm], and between them and beyond them, roses and other plants in nursery rows. Entering the little office, we announced that we were American soldiers, interested in roses, and that we would like to see the original vine of 'Gloire de Dijon', which we knew well in America. A woman, who told us that she was Jacotot's daughter, greeted us, and took us outside and showed us an old climbing rose, which, however, hardly seemed old enough to be the original vine, unless it had been pruned back so severely as to leave to trace of old wood. Then she took us into the greenhouses, which were indeed a pitiable sight. They were of the steep-roof type, with small glass, houses such as are now but seldom seen in this country [*U.S.A.*]. The framework, and even the doors and benches[,] were of steel. Owing to fuel restrictions, there was no heat, and the houses were covered with straw mats, so that they were as dark as a cellar, getting light from the ends only...We came away marveling that from this little place could have come a rose so fine that, after more than sixty years' trial in nearly every civilized country in the world, it is still so grown and loved that it has made a place for itself which but few other roses have ever attained." [ARA20/20-22]

"Cream and salmon yellow; climber or bush." [WD] "Buff and orange." [J] "Amber-flushed, pale pink." [W] "In color a combination of rose, salmon and yellow; flowers very large, very full, good globular form, the outer petals inclined to fade. A very useful rose." [EL] "Soft pink, suffused yellow; fragrant." [ARA29/98] "Yellow shaded with salmon, very large and full; a superb variety for wall or pillar." [P1] "Buff, very vigorous and hardy climber; still one of the best." [FRB] "Magnificent...cream-coloured blooms, tinted with fawn and blush." [Ed] "Almost an exact resemblance of the Bourbon Rose 'Souvenir de la Malmaison', and, like that fine Rose, it requires dry warm weather to open its flowers in perfection. Its perfume is Tea-like and powerful, and in color it is quite unique, being tinted with fawn, salmon, and rose, and difficult to describe." [HstX:85] "Certainly the colour, an ochraceous yellow, the size, as large as 'Jaune Desprez', and the Tea scent, made it a great acquisition." [HstX:398] "In Southern California, the blossoms range in color from being predominantly buff-yellow in the Winter to being predominantly light pink in the Summer, always with hints of burnt orange, gold, and rose." [BCD] "Luscious shades of pink, buff, apricot and peach...to 15 [ft; ca. 4.5 m]." [HRG] "Little beauty of colour or form...except perhaps quite in the bud...and even these are comparatively fat and squat." [F-M2] "Beautiful, old fashioned flowers, delicious Tea fragrance...never out of bloom until the frost stops it." [ARA29/50] "Will supply more good roses in a season than any other variety, for it is first in spring and last in winter to produce its abundant flowers, exquisite in colour, form, and fragrance." [R1/159] "It has one defect—a crumpled appearance of the central petals, which gives them a somewhat withered look, even when just open." [FP] "Gives more flowers than any Hybrid Tea sport, being a continuous bloomer; growth is good." [ARA18/120] "Large, very full, the cupped buds becoming flatter with age. Salmon-yellow with fiery copper-red towards center. Growth very vigorous; should not be pruned severely. The flowering period is extended by bending down the shoots...Flowers from June till November. Very fragrant." [Hn]

"We [*at Jacotot's*] have grown it since 1850; we wanted, before releasing it to commerce, to assure ourselves of its true merit...Since 1852, we have been propagating it *en masse*; we now have a very great quantity in heads of one, two, and three years, on wonderful Briar stock in all sizes; we have noted with pleasure that it bears with ease the cold of the worst Winters. Exhibited at Dijon in June, 1852, the Société d'Horticulture de la Côte-d'Or awarded it First Prize; it was at this meeting that the jury gave it the name 'Gloire de Dijon'." [VH53/39] "A new variety, exhibited in 1853, in Paris, raised at Dijon...is a great acquisition; its flowers are as large and as durable as those of the Bourbon 'Souvenir de la Malmaison', which they much resemble in shape; but their colour, nearly as deep as the buds of 'Safrano', is most striking; its foliage is as thick and large, and its habit as robust, as those of the above well-known Bourbon Rose, and as it opens freely in our climate it is highly popular...near Aberdeen it has bloomed beautifully." [R8] "It is a hybrid of Tea and Bourbon, with a large, full flower which resembles in form and delicate flesh tint Malmaison, from which it differs in the icy saffron-salmon tint which brightens at the base of the corolla." [l'H53/242] "We saw this beautiful rose at the Paris exposition in June, 1853, where it received a gold medal. The flowers exhibited were of a beautiful clear yellow with a light salmon tint. In a picture which Monsieur Jacotot sent his correspondents, the color was slightly exaggerated; instead of light salmon reflections, the artist added pink tints which were not quite to be found in the blossom." [l'H54/55] "Admirable...This variety appeared in [*Jacotot's*] acreage of Teas, and, by its elegant bearing, its handsome foliage, its remontant qualities, its perfect form, its beautiful coloration, and its delicious scent, it has not been surpassed to this day...Very vigorous; its branches are upright, reddish when young, aging to ashy-green; the stem is smooth and furnished with reddish prickles which are hooked and of differing sizes; the leaves are of five to seven leaflets, an attractive brilliant green on top, and, on the bottom, reddish when young, aging to a glaucous green. The general foliation is vigorous and quite characteristic; it is easy to recognize among the group's varieties. The foliage of 'Souvenir de la Malmaison' would be quite the same were it larger and more rounded; it is nearly of the same character. The flowers develop at the ends of the branches, supported by a large and firm stem, and nearly always supported by two or three large, expanding buds—inevitably opening, however, with the greatest of ease. The flower, of good form and full, attains a breadth of about 4.5 to 5 inches [ca. 1-1.25 dm]; the shape resembles that of Malmaison; the petals are large at the outer edge of the blossom, reflexing a little, and diminishing in size towards the center, which itself is formed of rolled petals, and is 'quartered'. The color of the rose is a yellow strongly suffused with salmon." [JR1/10/5-6] "The foliage is very large, thick, and lustrous; thorns comparatively few." [EL]

"Very vigorous, and the canes, generally big and limber, develop leafy branchlets at the nodes which terminate in blossoms; bark, light green, reddish where the sun hits, with homogeneously reddish thorns which are large, hooked, sharp, and thick. Foliage shiny, light green, divided into 3-5 leaflets which are oval-rounded, slightly acuminate, and dentate; leafstalk strongly nodding, slightly reddish, with several little prickles beneath. Flowers about 3.5 inches across [ca. 8.75 cm], very full, globular, sometimes solitary, or in clusters of 2 or 3 on the branchlets, but always in bouquets of 5-10 or more on the vigorous canes. Color, salmon yellow; petals large and concave, those of the center smaller and inter-folded; flower stem pretty long, nodding under the weight of the blossom. Calyx rounded pear-shape; sepals unfurl onto the calyx at expansion...[O]ne of the most beautiful varieties of its section." [JF] "Equal to any demands that can be made upon a wall, pole, or pillar Rose. This splendid variety is first-rate for all purposes...further a most prolific parent." [WD] "[*For*] climates without extremes of damp or heat. Fine strong climber, with prolific bloom...mildews badly at times, and requires equable conditions for best results." [Capt28] "Not liable to mildew." [F-M2] "Liable, oddly, to both mildew and rust, though more as a host than as a victim." [BCD] "[*Excellent in Norway.*]" [ARA20/46] "The best and hardiest of all the Teas." [HRH]

An unintroduced gold-leafed sport is recorded: "All the leaves are golden, with veins and blotches of green...the flower is perfectly similar to 'Gloire de Dijon'." [JR3/172]

"I decided to investigate the 'Gloire de Dijon' pedigree when in Dijon, France, in July, 1925. From the originator Jacotot's grand-daughter I heard that while no written record was in existence it was the oral tradition in the family that 'Souvenir de la Malmaison' was the pollen parent and a vigorous unnamed climbing yellow Tea the seed bearer." [K] "At a recent sitting of the Central Horticultural Society of France, Monsieur Andry, in alluding to the death of the late Monsieur Lucy, remarked that the latter was the first to recognize the peculiar merits of the 'Gloire de Dijon' Rose, after it had been obtained from seed by Monsieur Jacotot, who scarcely noticed it amongst many others. Monsieur Lucy advised him to propagate and send it out, which was done." [R7/378] "Monsieur de Lucy, former president of the Dijon society, now in Marseilles." [l'H57/61] "The famous old 'Gloire de Dijon' at Toulon, France, is described as being seventy-five feet in height [ca. 2.25 dkm], producing fifty thousand roses at a tie." [Dr] "On the occasion of this meeting of rose-men at Dijon, a special fête was organized in honor of the Rose, and,

naturally, 'Gloire de Dijon', that variety so well known and esteemed, took the place of honor." [JR32/101]
"On June 27 [*1922*], I stopped off at Dijon to visit again the home of the famed rose 'Gloire de Dijon', which was originated...in a little garden near the center of the city. The nursery is now kept up by the grandson, but roses are no longer the chief specialty. The original plant, which grew for many yeas in the corner of the property, is now dead." [ARA23/129] "This, to me, is the rose par excellence." [ARA24/184] "Stands unrivalled and alone." [P2] "If ever, for some heinous crime, I were miserably sentenced, for the rest of my life, to possess but a single Rose-tree, I should desire to be supplied, on leaving the dock, with a strong plant of 'Gloire de Dijon'." [H]

Glory of California (A. Clark, 1935)
Hybrid Gigantea
"Light pink, large, full, moderate fragrance, tall." [Sn] Possibly by Franceschi-Fenzi?

Glory of Waltham (Vigneron/W. Paul, 1865)
Hybrid Perpetual
Seedling of 'Souvenir de Leveson-Gower' (HP).
"Purplish-carmine." [Ÿ] "Rich crimson, very large and full...larger, brighter, darker, and of better form, than the parent; a superb rose, of hardy, vigorous growth." [FP] "Very floriferous; color, crimson nuanced carmine." [S] "Very large, very double, and very sweet; growth vigorous. One of the best Climbing or Pillar roses." [P1]

Gribaldo Nicola (Soupert & Notting, 1890)
Noisette
From 'Bouquet d'Or' (N) × 'La Sylphide' (T).
"Very vigorous growth; climbing; foliage large and glossy; flower very large, fairly full, form of 'Souvenir de la Malmaison'; color, silvery white

on a ground of blush pink; center tinted nankeen yellow, reverse of petals isabelle pink. Fragrant...blooms little on new growth, but the two year old canes are covered with flowers." [JR14/147]

Gruss an Aachen, Climbing (Kordes, 1937)
Hybrid Tea
Sport of 'Gruss an Aachen' (HT).
"Ivory-white...enriched with apricot pink ...rich fragrance." [T2] "Very vigorous." [ARA38/239]

Gruss an Friedburg (Rogmans/Metz, 1902) trans., "Greetings to Friedburg"
Noisette
Sport of 'Duarte de Oliveira' (N).
"Vigorous, flowers medium or large, full, pale yellow with a golden center. The bloom lasts from July to frost." [JR26/114]

Gruss an Teplitz, Climbing (Storrs & Harrison Co., 1911)
Bourbon
Sport of 'Gruss an Teplitz' (B).
Red. "Blooms with great freedom in June but seldom thereafter. Its delightful fragrance and brilliant color make this a most popular climber." [C-Ps27] "For interior districts without dampness. Fine growth; little bloom on some plants unless root-pruned; foliage mildews; no cutting value but fine perfume." [ARA28/95]

Hadley, Climbing (Heizmann, 1927)
Hybrid Tea
Sport of 'Hadley' (HT).
"Large, double, very fragrant blooms of deep, dark crimson, vigorous climber up to 10 [ft; ca. 3.3 m]." [HRG] "Too thin for great heat. The best red climber for cutting, and certainly the best dark red; fine grower

and better foliage than the dwarf, with long stems and fine perfume...a splendid bloomer, and better all around than 'Climbing Château de Clos-Vougeot', which varies in growth and loses foliage." [Capt28] "I wish that someone would suggest a red climbing rose that would take the place of our splendid old 'Hadley'. It blooms in the spring with long stems and there is always a rose to be had, if it is given half a chance; but oh, the mildew!" [CaRoIII/6/6]

Henry Irving (Conard & Jones, 1907)
Hybrid Perpetual
From a cross of an unnamed HP with an unnamed Multiflora.
"Light orange red, medium size, not very full, tall." [Sn] "New, fine large full flowers; deep rich crimson, an early and abundant bloomer, fragrant and good every way." [C&Js03] Henry Irving, English actor; lived 1838-1905.

Hermosa, Climbing
Listed as 'Setina'.

Indiana (E.G. Hill, 1907)
Hybrid Tea
From 'Rosalind Orr English' (HT) × 'Frau Karl Druschki' (HP).
"The bloom is pretty abundant; the blossoms, medium to large, are a beautiful light silvery pink, with light violet reflections. We have seen it used to great advantage in many rosaries." [JR33/125]

Indica Major
Listed as 'Fun Jwan Lo'.

Irène Bonnet (P. Nabonnand, 1920)
Hybrid Tea
"Salmon pink, medium size, full, medium scent, tall." [Sn]

Irish Beauty (A. Dickson, 1900)
Hybrid Tea
"Produces blossoms 7-8 cm across [ca. 3 inches], resembling those of *R. lævigata* [*that is, they are single and white*]." [JR26/86]

Irish Fireflame, Climbing (A. Dickson, 1916)
Hybrid Tea
Sport of 'Irish Fireflame' (HT).
"Large, single...quiet orange-yellow and peach. Healthy and vigorous...10×6 [ft; ca. 3.3×1.75 m]." [B] "A grand introduction...not a tall climber, but bushy, and must be left to grow quite freely." [ARA18/47] "Foliage good." [Capt28]

[**Isabella Gray**] (Gray/Buist, 1857)
Noisette
Seedling of 'Chromatella' (N).
"Of a most beautiful bright yellow...its buds are, however, so hard that they open very rarely. It should be planted against a wall with a warm aspect." [R8] "Vigorous; flower very large, full, of very good form; color, golden yellow. Very sensitive to dampness." [S] "Reputedly the parent of 'Maréchal Niel'. It has large, full, globular blooms of deep colouring." [OM] "Monsieur Andrea Gray, long-time chief gardener to Monsieur Buist...settled in Charleston, South Carolina. On his property, he flowered and obtained seed from...'Chromatella'...and grew from this seed two specimens; one he dedicated to his elder daughter Isabelle, and the other to his wife Jane Hardy. The first of these two bloomed well in America, but without the felicities of 'Chromatella'...'Isabella [Gray]' was sent to England by Monsieur Buist, who gave us these details; he had not, however, seen a blossom up to that time [*1857*]." [JR13/107-108] Introduced into France by Portemer.

Isis (Robert, 1853)
Noisette
"Flowers medium-sized, full, well-formed, pure white, in corymbs of 8 to 10." [l'H54/12] "Growth vigorous; branches short, clothed with sturdy thorns which are hooked and flat; leaves bright dark green; flower large, full, very well formed, in a cluster; color, virginal white." [S] Isis, Egyptian goddess of fertility; manure itself, however, seems not to have been apportioned a goddess yet.

Jacques Amyot
See the listing in the chapter on Damask Perpetuals.

James Sprunt (Sprunt, 1858)
China
Sport of 'Cramoisi Supérieur' (Ch).
"Carmine-red, just the same as its parent, but fuller and larger. Couldn't be better for exhibitions in *le Midi* [*in France*]." [JR16/36] "Deep cherry red flowers, rich and velvety, medium size, full, very double and sweet. A strong quick grower and good bloomer." [C&Js05] "Medium-sized, double, bright red flowers. Not notably valuable." [GAS] "Advise against its use. So bad it is mentioned only to be avoided." [Capt28] Rev. James M. Sprunt, D.D., a Presbyterian clergyman of Kenansville, North Carolina, divided some strong plants of 'Agrippina' [*supposedly 'Cramoisi Supérieur'*]. Afterwards he observed a *single* shoot from one of these plants growing vigorously without flowers or branches; it grew over *fifteen* feet [ca. 5 m] before it showed any flower buds, the rest of the plant retaining its normal characteristics. This shoot branched out very freely the following year, and cuttings taken from it invariably retained the same climbing habit. The flowers...are somewhat larger and fuller than 'Agrippina', but are, of course, not produced till the plant has made considerable growth. It is a valuable greenhouse climber." [EL]

Jaune Desprez
Listed as 'Desprez à Fleur Jaune'.

Jeanne Corbœuf (Corbœuf-Marsault, 1901)
Hybrid Tea
From 'Mme. la Duchesse d'Auerstädt' (N) × 'Mme. Jules Grolez' (HT).
"Growth very vigorous, climbing, floriferous, flower very large, very full, cupped, long bud; color, satiny pink with carmine reflections on a yellow ground, fragrant." [JR26/2]

Jeanne d'Arc
Listed as 'Étendard de Jeanne d'Arc'.

Jonkheer J.L. Mock, Climbing (Timmermans, 1923)
Hybrid Tea
Sport of 'Jonkheer J.L. Mock' (HT).
"Whitish pink, large, full, very fragrant, tall." [Sn] "Best for interior with some altitude giving dry heat. A fine grower with good stem and fragrance, but balls easily in damp and mildews." [Capt28]

Jules Margottin, Climbing (Cranston, 1874)
Hybrid Perpetual
Sport of 'Jules Margottin' (HP).
"Light purplish crimson." [Ÿ] "Flower large, full, very well formed; color, brilliant carmine. Magnificent exhibition rose." [S] "Vigorous...Flowers are the same as in the old sort, except being a little smaller, and for this reason it is finer in the bud state. The best of all the climbing sports; highly commended as a useful pillar rose." [EL] "Free and vigorous habit; not in a robust form, but branching as freely as an evergreen climbing rose; a great acquisition as a free growing perpetual climbing rose." [JC]

Kaiser Wilhelm der Siegreiche (Drögemüller/Schultheis, 1887) trans., "The Victorious Kaiser Wilhelm"
Noisette
From 'Mme. Bérard' (N) × 'Perle des Jardins' (T).
"Flower large, very full, opens well, of good form and well held; exterior of petals yellowish-white, interior brilliant deep yellow with carmine-pink reflections; very fragrant. Vigorous, good bright green foliage. More floriferous and hardy than 'Mme. Bérard." [JR11/92]

Kaiserin Auguste Viktoria, Climbing (A Dickson, 1897) syn., 'Mrs. Robert Peary'
Hybrid Tea
Sport of 'Kaiserin Auguste Viktoria' (HT).
"Primrose." [Th] "Very large, double; cream-white. Excellent repeat bloom...8-10 [ft; ca. 2.25-3 m] one of the best." [Lg] "Only gives scattering blooms throughout the season." [ARA17/26] "Constantly in bloom from the earliest to the latest of the season. Elegant climbing habit. Rich, luxuriant, clean, healthy foliage. The climbing white rose for everybody." [Dr] "The buds are very beautiful, of good form, and creamy-yellow." [OM] "[*For*] everywhere. Better than the dwarf; good to very good grower; nice foliage; not a very free bloomer, but yields some exceptionally fine cut flowers, and gives them through a long season; distinct in color." [Capt28] "A person needn't hesitate to compare its vigor...to that of specimens of 'Gloire de Dijon'." [JR25/36] "[*Of white climbers in Houston, Texas,*] we favor 'Climbing Kaiserin Auguste Viktoria' most." [ET] "Reliable in every way." [Th2] Also attributed to the Americans De Voecht and De Wilde, 1897—perhaps a separate sporting—whence comes the name 'Mrs. Robert Peary'.

Kaiserin Friedrich (Drögemüller/Schultheis, 1889) trans., "Empress Friedrich"
Noisette

From 'Gloire de Dijon' (N) × 'Perle des Jardins' (T). "This rose resembles 'Marie Van Houtte' in color, and 'Gloire de Dijon' in form." [JR13/20] "A good autumn-flowering Tea, with large, very fragrant, pale pink flowers tinged with yellow." [GAS] "Flowers shaded with red when dying off; good and hardy." [P1] "Dedicated to the late Empress of Germany...very vigorous and floriferous. The blossoms, most often solitary, are large, and despite their size always open well...As for the coloration, it varies quite a bit. At expansion, the rose is an overall brilliant intense yellow; then the petals develop carmine pink." [JR25/120] "Growth vigorous, foliage shiny, young growths reddish; thorns thinner and sharper than those of 'Gloire de Dijon'. Flowers large, solitary, well held on the long branches, very full, and opening well. Held perfectly, and also perfect is the bright yellow blossom. The petals are large, carmine-red, lighter in the interior, and, on the reverse, shading gradually to white. Very fragrant." [JR13/20]

Kitty Kininmonth (A. Clark, 1922)
Hybrid Gigantea
"Bud large, globular; flower very large, semi-double, cupped, very lasting; pink—almost fadeless—with many golden stamens; slight fragrance. Very vigorous climber; moderate bloomer in spring." [ARA24/176] "[*For*] everywhere. A wonderful decorative rose with a specially clear, brisk color; flower very large; growth fine; foliage fair and will hold." [Capt28] "To 12 feet [ca. 3.5 m]. Dark wrinkled foliage, few thorns. Heavy June bloom...sparingly repeated. Slight fragrance." [W] "Will repeat...if dead blooms are removed." [Lg] "It does especially well in Southern California, with mildew-proof foliage and very large, semi-double, rose-pink flowers...to 15 feet or more [ca. 4.5 m +]...very nearly the same vivid carmine-pink...as the old favorite 'Zéphirine Drouhin'." [ARA31/186] "It is my idea of a perfect rose; the heavy waxy petals of brilliant pink form a shapely flower that lasts for three days outdoors in our [*Georgian*] hot southern sunshine." [ARA32/120]

König Friedrich II von Dänemark, Climbing (Vogel, 1940)
Hybrid Perpetual
Sport of 'König Friedrich II von Dänemark' (HP).
"Deep red, medium size, full, light scent, tall." [Sn]

L'Abondance (Moreau-Robert, 1887) trans., "Abundance"
Noisette
"Flesh-pink, double flowers on well spaced clusters, moderate climber to 8 [ft; ca. 2.25 m]." [HRG] "Flower medium-sized, full, pure white lightly tinted pink while opening." [LR] "10×6 [ft; ca. 3.3×1.75 m]." [B] "Extremely vigorous, semi-climbing; foliage handsome shiny green; flower of medium size, of pretty form, pure white, lightly blushing upon opening, blooming abundantly and in clusters of 50-100 flowers; the plant is a sight to see." [JR11/150]

L'Arioste (Moreau-Robert, 1859)
Noisette
"Delicate pink." [Ÿ] Lodovico Ariosto, Italian poet; lived 1474-1533.

[**L'Idéal**] (Nabonnand, 1887) syn., 'L'Idéale'; trans., "The Ideal"
Noisette
"Lovely old Noisette, with big, coppery pink and golden yellow flowers. Extremely tender." [GAS] "Extremely vigorous climbing bush; flower large, semi-full, pretty form; color, yellow and metallic red, shaded, washed indefinably with sparkling golden tints. Thoroughly distinct from all other shadings found till now. This delectable variety is without a doubt the *ne plus ultra*, being, of all colorations, the most beautiful and striking. It's ideal! Very fragrant, very floriferous, extraordinary." [JR11/165] "That's the trouble with ''L'Idéale'—wonderful as to color, but to be faulted for a too-single blossom which is only beautiful in the bud." [JR19/66] "In 'L'Idéal' we find together both a ravishing color and

an exquisite perfume; but it is far from being as vigorous as is believed." [JR22/75] Parent of 'Vicomtesse Pierre de Fou'.

La Biche (Toullier, 1832) trans., "The Doe"
Noisette
"White with a pink heart." [R-H35] "Flesh-white, large and full." [FP] "Pale rose and white." [HoBoIV/319] "Cup., deep blush, extra large [*and marked as being* 'particularly fragrant']." [CC] "Yellowish flesh." [LS] "White...centres flesh-colour, very large and very double; form cupped; growth vigorous. A fine Pillar Rose." [P1] "Globular." [LF] "Still a good rose when first open, of a pale flesh colour, though almost instantly changing to pure white, rather large and double...of free growth." [Bu] "Inclining to fawn color at the center...a very fragrant, beautiful, and distinct variety." [WRP] "Large, flat; pure striking white. Continuous...6-8 [ft; ca. 1.75-2.25 m]...unexpected beauty." [Lg] "Very dainty." [OM] "Stem purple; bushy, very vigorous; alternate leaves, petiole sharp, usually seven bright green leaflets, serrated, prickles beneath on the mid-vein; thorns big, pointed, pretty numerous. Blossoms well formed, full, flesh-white, wafting the characteristic tea scent, well-held; borne on a moderately long stem accompanied by a purplish bract. This very remontant, beautiful rose blooms from the end of May until heavy frost...It is not very delicate, and does well in all areas and exposures. It's just the thing for arbors and beds because of its rapid growth making canes from six to seven feet long [ca. 1-1.3 m]; and, above all, because of the persistence of its leaves, which hold for a long time." [An32/26] "Vigorous; branches large or of medium size, elongated and fairly 'climbing'; bark is smooth, olive-green, armed with brown, longish thorns which are very sharp and clinging; leaves are smooth, divided into 5 or 7 leaflets which are rounded and somewhat pointed, and with very small teeth; the stalks are weak and thin, with 2 or 3 small, sharp, and pointed prickles; the flower is 2.5 to 3 inches in diameter [ca. to 7.5 cm], pretty full, cupped, somewhat muddled, rarely solitary, usually in fairly full clusters, depending upon the

strength of the branch; color, flesh-white, lightly yellowish at the center; outer petals are concave, with smaller ones towards the center; flower stems bend under the weight of the blossom; calyx green, smooth, ovoid; a very pretty variety, thoroughly remontant; best for fences; hardy." [S] "It was a defender of his country turned gardener—retired Lieutenant-Colonel Toullier, who rests on his laurels in the cozy community of Reuil, near Paris—who captured the beautiful Noisette 'La Biche'...Branches of a brownish or purplish green, long thorns which are very thick and pointed, light red in youth and brown in age, sometimes recurved, looking like the beak of a parakeet. Foliage of seven leaflets which are curled, glabrous, rounded, very slightly dentate and feebly petiolate; leafstalk bristling with small hairs, short, remote, stiff, and bearing two or three small thin prickles beneath. Stipules long and narrow, glabrous, finely ciliate with glandular hairs; flowers large, to about 3 inches [ca. 7.5 cm], handsome flesh white on a yellowish ground by way of contrast. The rose's scent is like that of the Teas...What charm and what grace in those long and vigorous canes, which fountain majestically to the ground!" [PlB] "This variety is absolutely unknown in our region...Nevertheless, it is one of the most noteworthy." [JR20/60]

La France, Climbing (Henderson, 1893)
Bourbon
Sport of 'La France' (B)
"Rich peach pink, delicious perfume, same beautiful buds as 'La France', but a vigorous climber and abundant bloomer, and quite hardy." [C&Js98] "Flowers equal to the old variety, but growth very vigorous." [P1] "It seems that the roses are enormous and abundant." [JR17/81] "Not of much use." [F-M2] "Individual charms." [ET] "Often a tendency to revert to the dwarf type...It is quite likely not to flower much for the first two or three years; Mr. Frank Cant notices it is most important to secure free root action, and Mr. Easlea lays stress on the fact that it must become well established before it will flower well. When this is attained,

however, it often flowers better, if not more profusely, than do the dwarf plants, the flowers expanding more readily; and it is stated that on heavy soils some have discarded the dwarf plants in its favour. It is slightly subject to mildew and readily infected by black spot...There are few more fragrant Roses than 'La France'." [NRS/14] "An elegant standby in any garden." [ARA40/37]

La France de 89 (Moreau-Robert, 1889) trans., "France of [17]89," also with a pun on the variety's parent 'La France'.
Hybrid Tea
From 'Reine Marie Henriette' (HT) × 'La France' (B).
"Large, dark red flowers occasionally marked with white." [GAS] "A bright large showy red Rose, sometimes pretty good." [F-M3] "Dedicated to the memory of the Revolution of 1789. It is still one of the most beautiful roses known, its blossoms in our climate [*that of Tunisia*] attaining the size of Peonies. Color superb and variable, bright red, scarlet, and sometimes deep pink; the long bud opens very well, and is borne on a short but erect and strong stem. Very fragrant...Its Fall bloom is not so good as that of 'La France', but it is nevertheless of the first merit, considering its vigor and bloom." [JR34/14] "Very large, fragrant, and deep rose-red flower of great beauty, which makes prodigious shoots in autumn, and flowers be degrees, beginning at the top in December and continuing to do so down the long shoots throughout the season. It is of the very largest size, fragrant, and double, but I think it is capricious in some gardens." [J] "Extra-vigorous, always growing, wood strong and robust, with slightly recurved thorns; beautiful light green foliage...bud very long, big as an egg and always opening well; flower enormous, well formed, sparkling bright red, sometimes lined white, in effect quite a Peony, extra-floriferous...needs several years to develop its growth." [JR13/99]

La Sylphide
Listed as a Tea.

Lady Clonbrock (Smith of Daisy Hill, -1903)
Noisette
"Light pink, medium size, full, tall." [Sn] "A vigorous-growing Noisette, which produces immense trusses of pale rose-coloured flowers in summer and late autumn." [sDH/03] "Found in an old Irish garden." [sDH/29] Information kindly supplied by Dr. E. Charles Nelson, formerly of Dublin, Ireland.

Lady Hillingdon, Climbing (Hicks, 1917)
Tea
Sport of 'Lady Hillingdon' (T).
"Outstanding...shapely, apricot-yellow...healthy plum-coloured shoots and gray-green leaves. Scented...12×6 [ft; ca. 3.5×1.75 m]." [B] "Rampant growth to 20 [ft; ca. 6.3 m]. Excellent repeat bloom...excellent low-maintenance hedge, if watered." [Lg] "A wonderful plant for sunny walls." [T2] "[*Liked in Texas.*]." [ET] "Takes time to become established." [GAS]

Lady Sylvia, Climbing (Stevens/Low, 1933)
Hybrid Tea
Sport of 'Lady Sylvia' (HT).
Pink, cream, and apricot. "Superb...rich pink...fine perfume. Outstanding as a climber . . .10×10 [ft; ca. 3.3×3.3 m]." [B] "Its 'Ophelia'-like flowers are of a little darker color and of the finest quality, produced throughout the entire season." [ARA36/178]

Lady Waterlow (Nabonnand, 1902)
Hybrid Tea
From 'La France de 89' (HT) × "Mme. Marie Lavalley' (N).
"Light salmon pink, saffron nub; flower large, semi-double; very vigorous." [Cx] "Soft pink salmon with deeper edges...healthy and

robust...12×6 [ft; ca. 3.5×1.75 m]." [B] "Salmon-rose, golden centres." [P1] "Very beautiful semi-double...clear salmon-pink petals edged with crimson; and when gathered in large bunches its effect is most striking." [K1] "Should become more popular not only for its intrinsic beauty, but it flowers freely in late autumn...There is an alluring charm in the large half-double flowers with petals of softest pink and white." [NRS/12] "Lovely light green foliage, which is not only distinct...but...immune from disease [excepting black spot]...carries twice, and often three times in the year[,] quantities of most lovely pale salmon pink flowers, nearly single, with large petals held well up above the foliage. The bright cherry-coloured buds are very pleasing." [NRS/13] "Bud well formed; very large and handsome foliage; plant very vigorous, very floriferous." [JR26/149] "The hardihood of the growth is superlative, the foliage wonderful. I have had leaves 5 inches long by 4 inches wide [ca. 1.25×1 dm]...It is exempt from disease, both mildew and rust; it is one of the first to leaf out, and one of the last to shed in the fall; it climbs quite as high as 'Mme. Alfred Carrière', while remaining clothed to the ground...The best climber I know." [JR36/106] "Extremely climbing, with strong, thorny wood...Three-year-olds have attained 18 feet in height [ca. 5.25 m]...Pruned specimens make very pretty shrubs." [JR36/123] "A very charming rose." [OM]

Lafollette (Busby, 1910)
Hybrid Gigantea
"Salmon-pink." [ARA35/98] "Beautiful...loose, long-pointed shape." [T2]

Lamarque (Maréchal, 1830) syn., 'Général Lamarque', 'Thé Maréchal'
Noisette
From 'Blush Noisette' (N) × 'Parks' Yellow Tea-Scented China' (T).
"Outer petals soft white; inner, pale straw." [H] "Sulphur yellow." [HoBoIV/319] "White, with sulphur centre, sometimes pure white, very

large, full, somewhat fragrant, generally seven leaflets. A superb climbing rose, quite too much neglected." [EL] "Cup., large straw col'd, lemon centre, sup'rb." [CC] "White…centres deep straw colour, very large and full; form cupped; growth vigorous. A splendid kind for a wall with a sunny aspect, producing its elegant flowers in large clusters. Raised by Monsieur Maréchal, a shoemaker, from his window-garden at Angers." [P1] We learn from *Les Amis des Roses* no 215 (p. 4) that Monsieur Maréchal was gardener at la Croix Montaillé. "Magnificent, large, perfectly double, yellowish-white, pendulous flowers, which it produces in clusters of three to ten in each. In good dry rich soils it will grow twenty feet in a season [ca. 3.6 m]." [Bu] "A continuous bloomer with white, violet-scented flowers." [ARA31/30] "Lemon-centred and lemon-scented." [J] "Blend of Musk and Tea [*perfumes*]." [NRS/17] "Approaching to the Tea-scented rose in the size and fragrance of its flowers. It is of most vigorous growth but not quite as hardy as 'Jaune Desprez'…Its large pale sulphur-colored or nearly white flowers are pendant from their weight, and have a fine effect…In a rich warm soil, it will grow fifteen to twenty feet [ca. 3.6 m] in a season, and produce from May to December a profusion of its drooping clusters, comprised of five to ten flowers each. In the Southern States it attains a magnificent development, extending its branches in some cases for fifty feet in length [ca. 1.6 dkm] and above twenty feet in height [ca. 3.6 m]." [WRP] "Continuous." [Capt28] "Bud is high-centred, delicate. Lovely healthy gray-green foliage…8-12 [ft; ca. 2.25-3.5 m]. Good repeat bloom." [Lg] "To 15 [ft; ca. 4.5 m]." [HRG] "10×6 [ft; ca. 3.3×1.75 m]." [B] "Tremendous grower." [W] "Flower…widely cupped." [S] "Unfortunately little known today…its cupped flowers are very pretty and of long duration." [JR18/135]

"Around 1830, Monsieur Maréchal, cobbler—so it is said—at Angers, raised this variety from seedlings grown in a pot in his window. It had, at that time, the name 'Thé Maréchal' because of its tea-like features." [PlB] "Here is the description given by Monsieur Maréchal himself, who wasn't a professional, but rather a very distinguished amateur: 'Shrub very vigorous, branches flexile and big, with light green bark, sometimes smooth, with numerous reddish prickles which are somewhat flattened and hooked, enlarged at the base, and very sharp. The foliage is smooth, shiny, and a nice green, with 5-7 leaflets which are oval-lanceolate, pointed, and finely toothed; the leafstalk is slender, slightly reddish green, armed with five or six little prickles of the same color, unequal, hooked, and very sharp. The flower is three or so inches in diameter [ca. 7.5 cm], very full, flat, blooming in clusters of 3-6 roses at the ends of the branches. Color, a yellowish white; outer petals large, those of the center a little smaller and muddled with the stamens. Flower stalk big enough, somewhat glandular and nodding, calyx nearly globular, light green, sepals long, narrow, and downy. Slight tea-scent'." [JR20/43] "It has always been a great favorite with me, and when in its full beauty I think it almost the most beautiful of white roses...It has the reputation of being rather tender, which I very much doubt, my plant having been in the same place for certainly over fifty years, during which it must have passed through many a severe winter with little injury. Its numerous trusses of pure white sweet-scented roses are most beautiful, especially in dry seasons." [GG] "A superior old white rose...it retains the clustering tendency...and produces an immense quantity of flowers during the season. It is a noble rose." [EL]

[**Le Vésuve, Climbing**] (P. Guillot, 1904)
China
Sport of 'Le Vésuve' (Ch).
"Blood red, sometimes red with a white center; flower large, full; very floriferous; very vigorous." [Cx] "Climbing, bushy, robust...flower large, full, color variable, bearing on the same bush blossoms of dark red, bright red, delicate pink, and red-edged pink." [JR28/154]

Lemon Queen (Hobbies, 1912)
Hybrid Tea
From 'Frau Karl Druschki' (HP) × 'Mme. Ravary' (HT).

"Large, very fragrant, pale lemon-yellow flowers tinted deeper. A pillar roes." [GAS] "As for the form of the blossom, one can't do much better than to say it is the same as that of Druschki, but much prettier, with a yellow tint to each petal—very pretty. It is excellent for decoration, and is a semi-climber with nearly continuous bloom." [JR37/26]

[**Les Fiançailles de la Princesse Stéphanie et de l'Archiduc Rodolphe**] (Levet, 1880) syn., 'Princesse Stéphanie', 'Stéphanie et Rodolphe', etc., etc.; trans., "The Engagement of Princess Stéphanie and Archduke Rodolphe"
Noisette
Seedling of 'Gloire de Dijon' (N).
"Climbing; foliage dark green; thorns long and hooked; flower medium-sized; color, orange salmon yellow." [JR4/167] "Vigorous; strong growth; the flowers are borne several to a cluster at the tip of the cane, which is long and tendentially nodding; flower quite full, petals all the same length, making it neither cupped nor globular; the later it is in the year, the smaller the blossom." [S]

Liberty, Climbing (H.B. May, 1908)
Hybrid Tea
Sport of 'Liberty' (HT).
"Dark red." [Ÿ] "Velvety crimson; good bloomer." [Th2]

Liésis
Listed as 'Céline Forestier'.

Lilliput (G. Paul, 1897)
Polyantha
"Red, small, full, tall." [Sn] Lilliput, the land of the diminutive and pusillanimous in Swift's *Gulliver's Travels*.

Lily Metschersky (Nabonnand, 1877)
Noisette
"Blossom medium-sized, very full, well formed, very remontant, violet red, the only one of its color among the Noisettes; wood dark, climbing, very thorny, and very vigorous." [JR1/12/14] The name has suffered many orthographic vicissitudes.

Longworth Rambler
See 'Deschamps'.

Lorraine Lee, Climbing (McKay, 1932)
Hybrid Gigantea
Sport of 'Lorraine Lee' (HGig).
"Golden apricot-pink, recurrent, fragrant." [W] "Very vigorous." [G]

[**Louis-Philippe, Climbing**] (Breeder/Introducer unknown, date uncertain)
China
Sport of 'Louis-Philippe' (Ch)?
"Deep-red, recurrent." [W]

Lucy Thomas (P. Nabonnand, 1924)
Hybrid Perpetual
From 'Ulrich Brunner fils' (HP) × 'Georg Arends' (HP).
"Pink, large, semi-double, tall." [Sn]

Lusiadas
Listed as 'Céline Forestier'.

Madeleine Lemoine (Franceschi-Fenzi, date uncertain)
Noisette or Hybrid Gigantea
From *R. moschata* × *R. gigantea*.

Griffiths relays that the blossoms are cream-white, slightly semi-double, large, and fragrant.

Magnolia Rose, Climbing
Listed as 'Devoniensis, Climbing'.

Maman Cochet, Climbing (Upton, 1909)
Tea
Sport of 'Maman Cochet' (T).
Shades of pink and cream. "Less fine in cool dampness. Wonderful in every way except strength of stem…tendency to ball in dampness." [Capt28] "Recurrent." [W] "Vigorous…to 12 [ft; ca. 3.5 m]." [HRG] "Individual charms." [EL]

Manettii (Manetti/Crivelli/Rivers, 1835)
Noisette
"Violet-rose, small size, single, not productive…dark, brownish wood, and always seven leaflets, sometimes nine." [EL] "Vig. Shrub with red shoots and pink fl. 2-inch diam." [MR8] "I am rejoiced to have it; for its charming foliage and bunches of delicate pink blossoms make it well worth growing for its own sake." [K1] "A variety of great vigor, coming I believe from *R. fraxinifolia*, and which was developed in 1820 by Messer Manetti, director of the gardens at Monza in Lombardy. It is pretty hardy, and takes easily to budding; but it is being abandoned as a stock because of certain faults. These faults are, firstly, overly continuous growth which hinders the harvesting of the plants; also, it forms numerous suckers, which exhaust the plant." [JF] "The Rosa Manetti is a rose I [*Rivers*] received some thirty years since, from Como, from Signor Crivelli, who recommended it as the very best of all roses for a stock. It was raised from seed by Signor Manetti, of the Botanic Garden at Monza." [R8] "Bred in 1832 from the seed of a Bourbon—I cannot say which." [JR7/79] "Considered as a hybrid of *R. semperflorens* [*i.e., the 'Slater's Crimson*

China' race] and *R. moschata*." [JR25/138] "It was the late Monsieur Granger who was the first to recommend 'Manettii' as a stock on which to graft." [JR27/64] "It was found so vigorous, so easy to propagate from cuttings, and the bark ran so readily, that it soon became a general favorite...There was one class of Roses, however, which it did not suit—Teas; its growth was too strong, and overpowered the more delicate growth of the [*Tea*] Rose, and consequently for these the Briar still held its own." [DO]

Maréchal Niel (Pradel, 1864)
Noisette
Seedling of 'Isabella Gray' (N).
"Deep yellow, very large, very full, globular form, delightfully fragrant, the finest of all yellow roses...of delicate constitution...requires very careful treatment to produce satisfactory results." [EL] "Deep golden yellow, the yellow of all the yellows, its only fault for exhibition being that it flowers rather too early, and is not sufficiently perpetual...It must be very slightly pruned, and not allowed to flower too freely, as this probably exhausts the plant and hastens on canker, which seems inevitable to this variety." [FRB] "A vigorous growing rose, more free blooming than 'Chromatella'. Its color is yellow, deepening at the center to a rich golden yellow. It is, perhaps, the largest and most beautiful yellow rose known, and very fragrant." [SBP] "Strongly Tea-scented...magnificent foliage...very liable to mildew...blooms...lose colour when exposed to the sun...fine in petal, centre, shape, colour, fragrance, and size: of fair lasting qualities if kept dry and fairly cool." [F-M2] "Large, full, fine form." [ARA17/26] "Perfectly shaped buds and flowers of soft deep yellow, with richer fragrance than any other rose." [ARA29/98] "Blend of Musk and Tea [*perfumes*]." [NRS/17] "Raspberry-scented." [JR33/101] "Very tender, and mildews and balls easily." [Capt28] "Truly yellow and a real climber [*in Brazil*]." [PS] "Rich-green foliage...12-15 feet [ca. 3.5-4.5 m]." [W] "The most aristocratic [*foliage*] of any climbing rose—like smooth kid in texture;

with its tender, reddish tips." [ARA29/101] "Shoots well clothed with large shining leaves." [FP] "A most rampant growing kind." [P1] "A rapid climber, which requires time before it blooms. Patience is of primary importance to get this into order." [WD]

"The circular which announced its release to commerce in 1864 gives the following description: 'Vigorous plant, with large, long branches producing slender branchlets. Bark smooth, of a glabrous green, or perhaps a little yellowish, numerous hooked, very dark and sharp thorns. Foliage plain green, glossy, wavy, divided into 5 or 6 pointed oval leaflets; the leafstalk, which is pretty long, bears three or four hooked and very sharp prickles beneath. The superb flower is 3-4 inches in diameter [ca. 7.5cm-1 dm], full, globular, borne singly on the branches, but usually in a cluster on the stronger limbs. Its color is a beautiful golden yellow which is quite dark indeed; petals, large. The flower-stalk is slender and somewhat too weak for the blossom, which consequently nods. Calyx flared'." [JR20/43] "By its vigor and bloom, the Rose 'Maréchal Niel' surpasses 'Chromatella', 'Solfatare', 'Isabella Gray', etc., other varieties with yellow flowers. Its wood is deep olive green nuanced brownish red where the sun strikes; it is armed with dark red thorns which are laterally flattened, and hooked like the beak of a parakeet. The ample leaves are composed of 3-5 leaflets of a beautiful glossy green above, pale green beneath, finely dentate—the lateral leaves, slightly petiolate, are obovate, pointed, or shortly acuminate; the terminal leaflet is larger, longly petiolate, and acuminate; the rachis is glandular-hirsute above, and armed beneath with very fine hooked prickles; it is slightly winged at the base due to its stipules which, where free, are subulate, and at a right angle to the petiole. The blossoms are very beautiful, full, globular at first, then opening out, large to 12-14 cm [ca. 4½-6 inches], beautiful deep yellow, and very fragrant. This beautiful Tea comes from the South [*of France*], raised a few years ago by a horticulturist in *le Midi*; it is not known to commerce." [l'H64/327] "Branches large, elongate, and limber, producing equally both slender and strong branchlets...Calyx rounded." [JF] "The *Canada Farmer* mentions the fact that this new and splendid rose has been exposed to a temperature of eighteen degrees below zero [*Fahrenheit*] without injury...We have some doubts of the general hardiness of this variety." [HstXXIV:91] "As a variety, 'Maréchal Niel' seems to be suffering from old age." [ARA37/152] "When budding it is advisable to use only buds from those shoots that are seen to produce flowers freely." [Hn]

"Monsieur Pradel responded that the rose came from a sowing made by himself, and was one which he had grafted on many stocks; that the previous year he had planted one of these stocks in the garden of Monsieur Château to replace a 'Chromatella' which he had lost...It was [*continues correspondent G.T.*] in 1858 that Monsieur Géraud Pradel the younger sowed a certain quantity of seed gathered from his collections, there being among others the seed of 'Chromatella'. He had the satisfaction of seeing born one plant which attracted his attention. It repaid his attentions. The following year, a yellow rose appeared; it was grafted by him on the Briar; it became magnificent. Instead of taking advantage of this great find,...Monsieur Pradel became jealous about it. He hid it mysteriously. In 1860, the wife of one of his clients having lost a very pretty 'Chromatella' which had grown on one of her garden walls,...she said to him, 'Never will you be able to replace it!'; 'Yes, madame,' responded Pradel, 'I will replace it for you with another even prettier which you will hold dear, because *my* yellow rose is a veritable marvel.' He gave it to her. The Rose was well looked after, and grew wonderfully. Some time later, Monsieur R—, a great fancier, went to pay a visit to the woman, and saw the rose..." [JR19/85-87] "This magnificent rose, always held in esteem and sought out, has given rise to a little horticultural fraud at its place of origin, 'Isabella Gray' being supplied in place of what everyone wanted to have, 'Maréchal Niel', commerce not being able to supply enough. This did not last long." [JR1/3/12] "The marks of resemblance to 'Isabella Gray', particularly the birthmark of indented petals, are unmistakable." [Dr]

"Outside of commerce commonly and justly called the Queen of Roses, one is not able to confuse it with 'Lamarque' or 'Isabella Gray'; neither the one nor the other has the pleasurable perfume of 'Maréchal Niel'...Though every year we see newcomers, it must be said that not one of them is the equal of 'Maréchal Niel' in form or the freshness of its color." [S] "The 'Maréchal Niel' Rose...is, like the 'Général Jacqueminot', most extensively forced under glass for its buds; probably three acres of glass surface are used for it in the vicinity of New York City, but it is now [*1889*] superseded by some of the yellow 'Teas' which, though not quite equal to it in quality, flower continuously." [pH] "It used to abound in the southern states, but nowadays it is rarely met with, although its fame abides." [GAS] "By the unreversed judgment of over forty years, 'Maréchal Niel' is the most remarkable rose of the nineteenth century. It is a proud triumph of nature that exceeds all expectation and defies criticism." [Dr] "Named after a French general, Minister of War of Napoleon III." [K]

Margo Koster, Climbing (Golie, 1962)
Polyantha
Sport of 'Margo Koster' (Pol).
Coral-orange, and different from the dwarf only in its climbing growth. I have seen some very nice weeping standards made from it.

Marguerite Carels (P. Nabonnand, 1922)
Hybrid Tea
From 'Frau Karl Druschki' (HP) × 'General MacArthur' (HT).
"Pink, large, full, tall." [Sn]

Marguerite Desrayaux (P. & C. Nabonnand, 1906)
Noisette
From 'Mme. Alfred Carrière' (N) × 'Mme. Marie Lavalley' (N).
"Pink, large, semi-double, tall." [Sn]

Marie Accary (Guillot fils, 1872)

Noisette
"White tinted pink and yellow." [JR8/26] "Creamy-blush, changing to nearly white, somewhat similar to 'Acidalie', flowers small, full, and compact." [JC] "Very vigorous and climbing; flower medium-sized, full, well-formed; white lightly tinted salmon pink at the center. For forcing." [S]

[**Marie Bülow**] (Welter, 1903)
Noisette
From 'Maréchal Niel' (N) × 'Luciole' (T).
"This is a very promising climber of the 'Maréchal Niel' type. It has long pointed buds that open into large full flowers. Color, china rose, changing to carmine and pure yellow." [C&Js08]

[**Marie Guillot, Climbing**] (Dingee & Conard, 1898)
Tea
Sport of 'Marie Guillot' (T).
"Yellowish white." [LS] "—Among White Roses, this splendid variety stands at the head, the flowers are extra large, full and fragrant, the petals are thick and durable, lasting a long time when cut; color pure snowy white; it is a most constant and abundant bloomer, covered with beautiful buds and flowers the whole season; one of the best for garden planting, always in bloom and always satisfactory." [C&Js04]

Marie-Jeanne
Listed in the Polyantha chapter.

Marie Robert (S. Cochet, 1893)
Noisette
Seedling of 'Isabella Gray' (N).
"Bright rose marbled with salmon and apricot, outer petals paler; a free and continuous bloomer." [P1] "Of the color of 'Blairii No. 2'." [JR22/74] "Good Noisette with large, dark pink flowers flushed salmon

and apricot." [GAS] "Extremely vigorous, climbing, extremely abundant bloom. Flower large, full, center bright pink marbled light apricot salmon, outermost petals paler. A child of 'Isabella Gray', from which it takes its growth and beautiful, distinctive foliage. An excellent climber, blooming from Spring to Fall." [JR17/163-164] "Dedicated to Mlle. Marie Robert, the well-known innkeeper at Antony (Seine)." [JR17/180] Not to be confused with the Damask Perpetual of the same name.

Marie-Thérèse Dubourg (Godard, 1888)
Noisette
"Deep coppery golden yellow." [P1]

[**Marie Van Houtte, Climbing**] (Hjort, ca. 1940)
Tea
Sport of 'Marie Van Houtte' (T).
"Creamy, pink-tinged yellow, recurrent." [W] "It was a sport discovered here [*at the Thomasville Nurseries, Georgia*] in 1936. It appeared in our catalogs in the early 40's for several years and there is no further reference to it. We have no stock now." [Hj]

[**Mélanie Soupert**] (Nabonnand, 1881)
Noisette
Seedling of 'Gloire de Dijon' (N).
"Very vigorous bush, the same as 'Gloire de Dijon'...flower large, very full, pure white." [JR5/148]

Merveille
Listed as 'Tausendschön'.

Meteor (Geschwind, 1887)
Noisette

"Crimson, shaded." [LS] "A beautiful brilliant red color nuanced fiery red, very vigorous." [JR34/17] "Requires a warm, sunshiny location to get the best buds out." [BSA] "Fair growth; bloom not of best form; requires winter protection." [ARA18/121] "One of the finest yet introduced, makes exquisite buds and large, beautifully shaped flowers of the true '[Général] Jacqueminot' color. A vigorous grower and most constant and profuse bloomer, produces immense numbers of magnificent roses all through the season." [C&Js98]

Mikado (Kiese, 1913)
Hybrid Tea
"Red, large, not very full, tall." [Sn] Not to be confused with either the Rugosa nor the modern HT, both of the same name. *The Mikado, or, The Town of Titipu*, the comic opera by Gilbert and Sullivan.

Milkmaid (A. Clark/Brundrett, 1925)
Noisette
From 'Crépuscule' (N) × ?.
"A strong-growing Noisette with large sprays of rather small white or creamy yellow, single flowers. Recommended as a fragrant spring-blooming climber for the South." [GAS]

Miniature, Climbing (Lambert, 1908)
Polyantha
Sport of 'Miniature' (Pol).
"Whitish pink, very small, very full, medium scent, tall." [Sn]

Miss G. Mesman (Mesman, 1910) syn., 'Climbing Baby Rambler'
Polyantha
Sport of 'Mme. Norbert Levavasseur' (Pol).
"Clusters of purplish red flowers throughout the season." [GAS] "Foliage very plentiful, black-spots badly in midsummer, slightly in late summer,

leaves held on; bloom moderate early and late, profuse in July, almost continuous into November." [ARA18/130] "Rather low, bushy growth; fair bloomer—occasionally some fall bloom; needs winter protection." [ARA18/121]

Miss Marion Manifold (Adamson/Brundrett, 1913)
Hybrid Tea
"A vigorous climbing rose with full, large, well-formed flowers of rich, velvety crimson, and a free and continuous bloomer, opening well in all weathers. It has a slight Bourbon scent. In this country [*Australia*] it sends out strong, vigorous canes each year up to, and sometimes exceeding, nine feet [ca. 3 m], and when covered with bloom is a glorious sight. One of our growers recently counted 150 blooms on his bush, and experts here consider it the finest climbing rose in the world." [ARA28/112]

[**Mlle. Adèle Jougant**] (Lédéchaux/V. & C. Verdier, 1862)
Tea
Seedling of 'Mlle. de Sombreuil' (T).
"Clear yellow, medium size." [FP] "Leaves beautiful light green; flower medium-sized, nearly full, light yellow." [l'H62/277] "Very vigorous; branches climbing; leaves small, much serrated, yellowish green; flower medium-sized, nearly full; sulphur yellow." [S]

Mlle. Cécile Brunner, Climbing (Hosp, 1894; and Kerschaw, 1905)
Polyantha
Sport(s) of 'Mlle. Cécile Brunner' (Pol).
"[*For*] everywhere. A good, large-growing decorative pink with perfect, well-held foliage and a most prolific bloomer. Flower…fades in sun. Plant stands shade or sun." [Capt28] "Flowers…are sparsely distributed…25×20 [ft; ca. 7.5×6 m]." [B] "Always blooming, with large foliage which doesn't drop until December." [JR36/188] "In clusters…Sparse, soft, light foliage." [W] "Black-spots somewhat; bloom abundant in May

and June, free in July, moderate later, almost continuous." [ARA18/129] "Graceful vine, with uncommonly beautiful foliage." [Dr]

Mlle. Claire Jacquier (Bernaix, 1887) syn., 'Claire Jacquier'
Noisette
"Buff-yellow." [J] "Deep orange…and thornless." [BSA] "Finishes pale." [Hk] "Medium size, double, yellow fading to white…blooms once yearly…10-12 [ft; ca. 3-3.5 m]." [Lg] "Flowers nankeen-yellow, small, but produced in very large clusters; exceedingly pretty and distinct, and remarkably, and remarkably vigorous." [P1] "Well foliated…shapely…pleasing perfume…Recurrent. 25×10 [ft; ca. 7.5×3.3 m]." [B] "Flowers very numerous, at the ends of the branches, in clusters; small (an inch or so in diameter [ca. 2.5 cm +]), of perfect form, erect, very double; petals self-colored, nankeen-yellow, not fading more than a little upon opening…climbing, of great vigor, in one season growing to 15 feet [ca. 4.5 m]…large leaves, glossy green on top, purplish beneath." [JR11/151] "20 [ft; ca. 6.6 m]." [HRG] The Lyonnais nurseryman Claude Jacquier is mentioned in *Les Amis des Roses* no. 245.

Mlle. de Sombreuil
Listed in the chapter on Teas.

Mlle. Geneviève Godard (Godard/E. Verdier, 1889)
Tea
"Growth vigorous, flowers large, very full; color, handsome carmine red." [JR13/181]

[**Mlle. Jeanne Ferron**] (Widow Schwartz, 1887)
Polyantha
"Climbing bush; foliage large, bronzy, then becoming green on both sides; canes floriferous, tipped with three or four obtuse flower-buds, peduncles upright, fairly firm and medium in length; flower very large for the sort,

opens well, with many petals which are well rounded and slightly wavy, giving when completely open a plump flower of a pretty satiny pink at the center, fading along the edges to a very tender flesh. The plant reblooms freely from Spring to Fall on big bloomy bushes to very pretty effect." [JR11/87]

Mlle. Madeleine Delaroche (Corbœuf, 1890)
Noisette
Seedling of 'Mlle. Mathilde Lenaerts' (N).
"Climbing, flower large, very full, well formed, flesh pink, very floriferous, superb plant." [JR14/178]

Mlle. Marie Gaze (Godard, 1892)
Noisette
"Yellow." [Ÿ]

Mlle. Mathilde Lenaerts (Levet, 1879)
Noisette
Seedling of 'Gloire de Dijon' (N).
"Large, double, bright pink flowers silvered white." [GAS] "Rose colour." [EL] "Very vigorous, climbing, leaves large, composed of seven leaflets which are a beautiful intense pink, distinctly bordered white, making a most charming appearance, a new coloration in the 'Gloire de Dijon' clan." [JR3/165] "[*One of the*] hybrids of Tea and Bourbon." [JR24/44] Daughter of B. Lenaerts, president of the Antwerp Circle of Rosarians.

Mme. Abel Chatenay, Climbing (Page/Easlea, 1917)
Hybrid Tea
Sport of 'Mme. Abel Chatenay' (HT).
Pink shades. "*The* climbing rose for autumn…most beautiful flowers." [RATS] "Larger flowers than the dwarf." [Th2] "[*For*] everywhere. Very find grower…well-held foliage; flower medium-size; lasts well; slight perfume;

continuous bloomer in occasional bursts." [Capt28] "Semi-vigorous…10×6 [ft; ca. 3.3×1.75 m]." [B]

Mme. Alfred Carrière (Schwartz, 1879)
Noisette
"White, yellowish base. Large, fragrant, very perpetual." [H] "Pure white, very free; a good pillar rose." [Th] "Pearly-white, with long stems…good foliage…one of the most constant." [BSA] 'Pinky-white to white clusters…globular flowers. Vigorous…12×10 [ft; ca. 4×3.3 m]." [B] "White, not free blooming, undesirable." [EL] "Free-blooming." [F-M] "Its white blossoms, which some liken to the porcelain roses manufactured abroad, are borne singly on the stalk, and last long in water, while it is never out of flower from June to November." [K2] "One of the earliest climbing roses to open its blossoms, which are produced profusely." [NRS/17] "Large pale leaves of the tea-rose character, and large loose flowers of a low-toned warm white." [E] "Very big grower; good foliage; double, flat flowers with blush at center." [Capt28] "One of the most beautiful climbing roses we possess…flesh white shaded with salmon; large and full. Sweet-scented, growth extra vigorous." [P1] "Ample foliage of a handsome brilliant green." [JR3/165] "Foliage mildews in shade or extreme damp, but [*the variety*] is indispensable in Southern Zones." [Th2] "Fine upright growths, branching the second season…quite free from mildew. So continuously does this beautiful Rose flower that its flowering period may almost be said to be the whole season…The flowers are large, almost full, and carried singly of in small loose clusters. They are very sweetly scented…the wood of the previous year must be retained." [NRS/11] "Most artistic flower. It suffers from mildew occasionally, but not badly. [NRS/13] "It requires thinning out freely every year…The foliage is of a lightish green and very good, lasting long on the plant…it is liable to make a dense growth which hides the flowers." [NRS/14] "Very vigorous…20 feet [ca. 6.6 m]." [W] "[*Excellent in Norway.*]." [ARA20/46]

"Dedicated to the wife of a great lover of roses from our province Dauphiné." [JR10/57]

Mme. Auguste Choutet (Godard, 1901)
Hybrid Tea
From 'William Allen Richardson' (N) × 'Kaiserin Auguste Viktoria' (HT). "Yellow nuanced dawn gold." [LS] "Golden yellow, semi-climbing." [JR32/140] "Large, semi-double, dark orange-yellow, fragrant flowers." [GAS] "Grows 6 feet [ca. 2 m] the first year. Foliage dark green, without disease; flower very large, double, deep saffron-yellow, lasting well. Somewhat shy but so beautiful it is most valuable…much superior in lasting quality to 'Climbing Lady Hillingdon'." [ARA28/103] "This is a most charming, continuous-flowering, yellow pillar Rose which appears to be so little known that I venture to direct special attention to it. I was myself not impressed with it in the first two or three seasons of its life with me; but now that it is established it is charming. It forms a compact, evergreen pillar clothed from the base; it has small glossy leaves, apparently mildew and vermin proof, and is covered with perfectly formed but smallish flowers, the colour of 'Mme. Pierre Cochet', not so vivid as 'William Allen Richardson', and which does not fade. It is a perfect companion for 'Lady Waterlow', and with that and 'Johanna Sebus' makes a lovely trio." [NRS13/148] "None other than that old favorite 'Crépuscule'." [NRS18/148]

Mme. Auguste Perrin
Listed in the chapter on Bourbons.

Mme. Bérard (Levet, 1870)
Noisette
From 'Mme. Falcot' (T) × 'Gloire de Dijon' (N).
"Bright buff or fawn colour with a slight salmon tint, flowers very large, full, and well formed; a very distinct and superb rose…vigorous." [JC]

"Large, semi-double, salmon-yellow flowers edged with pink; fragrant." [GAS] "Without perfume." [JR3/62] "Very similar to [*'Gloire de Dijon'*]; the flowers are somewhat less full, of a fresher shade, and are better in the bud state." [EL] "From 'Gloire de Dijon', its flowers are better formed, its colors darker (light pink with salmon), and it has a darker yellow heart. It is more vigorous than Gloire, but not so floriferous. This variety is good for breeding." [JR10/47] "Foliage a very handsome dark green, blooms profusely; flower medium-sized to large; very prettily colored coppery yellow at the center; outer petals a beautiful salmon pink. Coppery yellow in the shade." [S] "One of the best in shape and colour, very pretty at times, but not as hardy or free-flowering as [*'Gloire de Dijon'*]." [F-M2]

[**Mme. Brunner**] (Brunner/Froebel, 1890) syn., 'Aimée Vibert Jaune'
Noisette
Sport of 'Aimée Vibert' (N).
"Pale yellow." [LS] "A rampant, rambling shrub of evergreen, everblooming habit, very like Yellow Banksia, but of deeper color." [ARA31/28] There was also an 'Aimée Vibert à Fleur Jaune' by Perny/Cochet, 1904: "A seedling from the rose 'Aimée Vibert', in which the flowers are salmon yellow and not white...All the characteristics are those of 'Aimée Vibert', except for the differing color." [JR28/185]

Mme. Butterfly, Climbing (Smith, 1926)
Hybrid Tea
Sport of 'Mme. Butterfly' (HT).
Pale pink. "[*As compared with 'Mme. Butterfly' bush form:*] Flower longer, outer petals cleaner, more fragrant, and altogether superior...vigorous...to 7 feet [ca. 2.3 m]." [ARA26/181] "10×10 [ft; ca. 3.3×3.3 m]." [B]

Mme. Caroline Küster
Listed in the chapter on Teas.

Mme. Caroline Testout, Climbing (Chauvry, 1901)
Hybrid Tea
Sport of 'Mme. Caroline Testout' (HT).
"Satin pink with a deeper...Huge blooms...strongly scented...strong stems...15×8 [ft; ca. 4.5×2.25 m]." [B] "Good blooms when you get them; not one of the best growers; susceptible to mildew." [ARA18/122] "Good grower, fair foliage, good bloomer but balls in dampness. Best in Pacific Northwest." [Capt28] "[*Favorite in Houston, Texas*]." [ET] "*Splendid in Norway*]." [ARA20/46] "A gorgeous show in early June but seldom another bloom the rest of the season." [K] "Vigorous growth characterises this Rose, and an upright but branching habit...more or less constantly in flower...Its strong points are its vigor, reliability, and bold big blossoms, and continuity of flowering. Its weakness that it is apt to become bare at the base unless carefully treated, and from its stiff growth bending the shoots down to prevent this is often difficult." [NRS/11] "Branches climbing, excellent variety for pyramids." [JR25/163]

Mme. Chabanne (Liabaud, 1896)
Tea
"Very vigorous and very floriferous, metallic foliage, flower medium or large, full, opening into a cup, center petals numerous, canary yellow, outermost petals cream white." [JR20/147]

[**Mme. Chauvry**] (Bonnaire, 1886)
Noisette
From 'Mme. Bérard' (N) × 'William Allen Richardson' (N).
"Nankeen shaded with rose, reverse of petals coppery, distinct and handsome; one of the best." [P1] "Very large, full, fragrant flowers of deep nankeen-yellow, shaded with copper and pink." [GAS] "Very vigorous, with long, climbing, branches, very floriferous and remontant. Foliage very handsome, large, glossy dark green above, glaucous and often reddish

beneath. Flower very large measuring about 4.5 inches across [ca. 1.25 dm], good form, numerous concave petals, imbricated, nankeen yellow upon opening, nuanced China pink on the backs of the petals, and coppery yellow towards the tips." [JR10/137] "Dedicated to Mme. Chauvry, wife of a well-known rosarian of the Bordelais region." [JR10/184]

[**Mme. Claire Carnot**] (Guillot fils, 1873) syn., 'Claire Carnot'
Noisette
Seedling of 'Ophirie' (N).
"Yellow, bordered with white and carmine rose; medium size; full and well formed; growth vigorous." [CA88] "Bush very vigorous and climbing; flower medium-sized, full; beautiful bright coppery yellow, sparkling, edged white and carmine pink; flower cupped, fragrant, opening easily, in clusters. Resembles 'Céline Forestier', but is more fragrant." [S]

Mme. Couturier-Mention (Couturier/Moser, 1885) syn., 'Climbing Cramoisi Supérieur'
China
Seedling of 'Cramoisi Supérieur' (Ch).
"Shining crimson; flower medium-sized, cupped, semi-double; floriferous; vigorous." [Cx] "Full, crimson red. Continuous flowering." [LR] "Dark scarlet. Fine foliage and continuous bloom; not a tall grower; train on a fence or pillar; does well in shade." [Th2] "Rather large, double, purplish red flowers, borne more or less continuously." [GAS] "A fine climber, though it is not very free flowering until well established." [OM] "Fair everywhere...only slight perfume." [Capt28] "12×10 [ft; ca. 3.6×3.3 m]." [B] "Will climb to fully twenty feet high [ca. 6.6 m], and cover itself with its rich crimson flowers." [J] "We have the pleasure of making known to fanciers of pretty roses that the China roses have been enriched by a new variety which will certainly not be considered the least attractive of that race. This new offering was raised from seed by Monsieur Couturier-Mention...Contrary to the type, known to be naturally weak in all its

parts, this variety is vigorous, and is able to attain—after a few years—seven feet or so [ca. 2.3 m] on a pillar, nearly always covered with flowers. The flowers, borne on long stems, nod, and are cupped and regularly formed, with large, concave petals, rather large for the sort, bright crimson-maroon, and showing that distinctive mark of this race, a certain number of central petals marked longitudinally down the middle with a white, readily apparent, stripe. Its foliage, of a green rather darker than lighter, has leaflets deeply toothed, and more oval than those of 'Bengale cerise' and 'Bengale sanguin'. The thorns are not a problem, being rather sparse. Its raiser, Monsieur Couturier-Mention, considers it the hardiest of the Chinas, assuring us that it weathers the frosts of central France without much trouble. Last September, the young plants we saw were quite as full of blossoms as their brother 'Cramoisi Supérieur'." [JR9/167] "Bears a great resemblance to 'James Sprunt'." [JR22/21]

Mme. Creux (Godard, 1890)
Tea
"Fine rose colour to salmon, reverse of petals having a tint of bronze." [B&V] "Like a higher-colored, better-shaped 'Gloire de Dijon'; better (disease-resistant) foliage and fragrance, too; a very fine climber, vigorous once established." [BCD] "First class certificate." [JR16/20]

Mme. Driout (Bolut & Thiriat, 1902)
Hybrid Tea
Sport of 'Reine Marie Henriette' (HT).
"Pink striped cerise." [LS] "The flower is a delicate shaded satin-pink, plumed and striped bright carmine, making a most agreeable contrast. The striping is constant, and pretty regular on all the flowers, though at times a very large and distinct splotch might be formed, or perhaps one big stripe." [JR28/27] "Admirably plumed, flamed, striped bright carmine on pale pink…Its vigor and floriferousness are not inferior to those of 'Reine Marie Henriette'. The striping varies with the flower: sometimes

the red predominates...other times, the pink, at which times the blossom gains in freshness, I think." [JR27/153] "Deep red. This rose resembles the shape of 'Gloire de Dijon'...10×8 [ft; ca. 3.3×2.25 m]." [B] "This novelty was noted by Messrs. Bolut and Thiriat when on a visit to the gardens at St.-Dizier at the home of Monsieur Driout, mayor of that community. The striping is sharper in Spring, and less pronounced in Fall. The characteristics of the variety are exactly the same as those of the mother, except that it is of a little less vigor." [JR26/113]

Mme. E. Souffrain (Chauvry, 1897)
Noisette
From 'Rêve d'Or' (N) × 'Duarte de Oliveira' (N).
"Large, richly fragrant, golden yellow flowers tinged with salmon and marked pink." [GAS] "Smooth reddish canes, thornless; very climbing; foliage glossy green; buds large, ovoid; flower large, very full, imbricated; ground color golden yellow, shading to salmon yellow at the center, touched white at the edge of the petals; lined and bordered pink and very light violet; very fragrant." [JR21/149]

Mme. Edmée Cocteau (Margottin fils, 1903) syn., 'Edmée Cocteau'
Hybrid Tea
Seedling of 'Captain Christy' (HT).
"Climbing, very vigorous; foliage resistant, dark; flower enormous, beautiful delicate pink; long stem." [JR28/27]

Mme. Emilie Dupuy (Levet, 1870)
Noisette
From 'Mme. Falcot' (T) × 'Gloire de Dijon' (N).
"Large, full, globular flowers of creamy yellow, suffused salmon." [GAS] "Pale fawn, buds long and handsome, flowers large, full, and tolerably well formed." [JC] "Climbing, blossom well formed, large and full, coppery yellow." [JR6/136] "Magnificent exhibition rose." [S]

[**Mme. Eugène Verdier**] (Levet, 1882)
Noisette
From 'Gloire de Dijon' (N) × 'Mme. Barthélemy Levet' (T).
"A very pretty rose, with large shell-shaped petals of a pleasant pink." [JR4/97] "Rich golden yellow. Requires a warm wall." [H] "Climbing, with heavy wood and occasional thorns; its foliage is a beautiful dark green…Its blossoms vary in color depending upon the season: sometimes canary yellow, one may also encounter deep yellow in the center with the reverse of the petals straw yellow, and, later in the season, when flowers are abundant, one can find the most beautiful deep chamois color imaginable." [JR14/39] "Canes strong, very handsome shiny green foliage; flower large and well formed, surpassing all the other 'Gloire de Dijon' brood in this respect, thorns straight and light…very fragrant." [JR6/149] "Vigorous with strong canes, which are upright and short, and light green; numerous thorns of varying size, slightly hooked, pink; leaves comprised of 2-5 oval-elongate leaflets with large petals which are well held; color, the most beautiful satiny bright pink, much nuanced and shaded silver; a splendid, vigorous variety, very remontant." [JR2/187]

Mme. Foureau (Viaud-Bruant, 1913)
Noisette
Seedling of 'Rêve d'Or' (N).
"Yellowish salmon, medium size, full, medium height." [Sn] "Extremely vigorous, with beautiful foliage, and strong-growing canes; flower well-formed, light salmon pink with pale Indian yellow; very good and hardy variety." [JR37/26]

Mme. Gaston Annouilh (Chauvry, 1899)
Noisette
"Climbing, with slender, bronze green canes, nearly thornless; foliage purplish passing to ashy delicate green; buds medium long, canary yellow;

flower semi-double, fairly large, white tinted canary with greenish reflections; very floriferous and fragrant." [JR24/2]

Mme. Hector Leuilliot (Pernet-Ducher, 1903)
Hybrid Tea
"Golden yellow Hybrid Tea tinged pink." [GAS] "Tinted with carmine in the center; large; full; gives scattering blooms throughout the entire season; most attractive color." [ARA17/27] "Growth semi-climbing, beautiful bright bronzy green foliage; flower large, globular, quite full, superbly colored golden yellow on a red ground. This magnificent variety has a hardiness equal to that of the HPs, and may be grown as either a climber or a bush, as with 'William Allen Richardson'." [JR27/131] "Hard to establish in southern climates but worth extra effort. Produces in its second year distinct and lovely double blooms of orange-yellow, sometimes splashed with crimson; good cutting value; exquisite perfume." [ARA28/103] "Practically no disbudding...Tops winter kill badly. Splendid in South without cutting back." [Th]

Mme. Jules Bouché, Climbing (California Roses, 1938)
Hybrid Tea
Sport of 'Mme. Jules Bouché' (HT).
White, flesh center.

Mme. Jules Franke (Nabonnand, 1887)
Noisette
"Extremely vigorous, climbing; flower medium-sized, very full, imbricated, a paragon in form; pure white, finally yellowish. Floriferous." [JR11/165]

Mme. Jules Gravereaux (Soupert & Notting, 1900)
Hybrid Tea
From 'Rêve d'Or' (N) × 'Viscountess Folkestone' (HT).

"Buff-white, shaded peach…free and good." [P1] "Flesh, shaded yellow." [NRs/10] "Pink undertones…slight scent. Good foliage…12×8 [ft; ca. 4×2.6 m]." [B] "Very vigorous and climbing, magnificent foliage; bud, very long and pointed; flower extremely large, very full; color, chamois yellow, with a peach-pink canter and dawn-gold reflections. Of the best, very floriferous and fragrant." [JR24/148] "This variety has big, well-formed blooms of buff-white with rose and yellow shading, and is often grown for exhibition. It is disappointing as a garden rose." [OM] "Flowers of great size and beautiful form. Mildews badly…does not develop well in dampness." [Capt28] "Exquisite buds." [ARA18/79] "Very double blooms…vigorous to 12 [ft; ca. 4 m]." [HRG] "Tall, compact, vigorous, hardy; foliage plentiful, blackspots slightly; bloom free, continuous." [ARA18/126] "It resembles, in the form of the plant as well as in its abundant autumnal flowering, 'Gloire de Dijon'." [JR32/34] "Gravereaux (Jules).—Former administrator of 'Bon Marché', died in 1916 at the age of 71. Great rose fancier. He created in 1899 a magnificent rosarium at his estate at l'Haÿ (Seine)." [R-HC]

Mme. Julie Lassen (Nabonnand, 1881)
Noisette
"Very vigorous, wood short and stout, flower large, very full, perfectly cupped…deep pink." [JR5/148]

Mme. la Duchesse d'Auerstädt (Bernaix, 1887) syn., 'Duchesse d'Auerstädt'
Noisette
Seedling of 'Rêve d'Or' (N).
"Golden yellow; flower very large, very full, imbricated, cupped, fragrant; vigorous." [Cx] "Deep buff, very double…to 10 [ft; ca. 3.3 m]." [HRG] "Bright yellow, shaded with nankeen at the centre. Very vigorous." [P1]

"More intense colouring [*than has 'Gloire de Dijon'*]. Good foliage...10×6 [ft; ca. 3.3×2 m]." [B] "A lovely rose, but shy flowering. It is of good growth on a warm wall, but the shapely flowers...are usually sparsely produced." [OM] "Remarkably vigorous growth. Blooms constantly in Southern Zones...does not open well in dampness." [Th2] "The bush grows somewhat larger than medium size; great big leaves, thick, leathery, shiny, in stiff stalks; flowers large, of perfect form, most often solitary at the end of the branch, very double and opening well; large concave petals, thick, firm, imbricated in the outer rows." [JR11/151] "Wonderful...equal to 'Maréchal Niel' and a better grower." [ARA25/113] "Excellent in every way." [J]

Mme. la Général Paul de Benoist (Berland/Chauvry, 1901)
Noisette
Seedling of 'Mme. Chauvry' (N).
"Climbing, buds very large, rounded, nuanced light violet, opening well; flower very large and full, salmon on a dawn-gold ground, petal edges reflexed creamy white; fragrant." [JR25/163]

Mme. Léon Constantin (Bonnaire, 1907)
Tea
"Free-flowering Tea, producing large, fragrant, full flowers of rosy white." [GAS] "Very vigorous with strong branches...ornamented with handsome foliage. Beautiful long bud, flower extra-large, very full, always opens well, beautiful satiny pink with a light salmon interior. Very distinct and floriferous. Climbing." [JR31/135]

Mme. Louis Blanchet (Godard, 1894)
Noisette
"Lilac pink, marbled." [Ÿ]

Mme. Louis Henry (Widow Ducher, 1879)
Noisette
"Pale yellow, fragrant; in the way of 'Solfaterre' [*sic*]. [EL] "Very vigorous, with branches climbing, thorns somewhat numerous, short and reddish, handsome light green foliage composed of seven leaflets, flower medium or large, full, very well formed; color white, slightly yellowish in the center, reblooms freely." [JR3/164]

Mme. Louis Ricard, Climbing (Boutigny, 1904)
Hybrid Perpetual
Sport of 'Mme. Louis Ricard' (HP).
"Flower large, bright pink, beautiful form, blooming in a cluster, very vigorous." [JR28/89]

[**Mme. Marie Berton**] (Levet, 1875)
Noisette
Seedling of 'Gloire de Dijon' (N).
"Flower very large, full; color, straw yellow fading to cream." [S] "Particularly good in autumn." [GAS]

[**Mme. Marie Lavalley**] (Nabonnand, 1881)
Noisette
"Growth extra vigorous, big-wooded, few thorns; flower very large, nearly single, well formed, bright pink, shaded, lined white in an indefinite reflection; very floriferous; a superb effect, from the ample supply of flowers." [S] "Not a long-lived sort. The flowers from young plants being greatly superior to those of say four years or more. The petals are delicate and easily injured by wind or sun; answers very well under glass." [B&V]

Mme. Martignier (Dubreuil, 1903)
Noisette
"Vigorous Tea with medium-sized, bright red flowers tinged purple and flushed with gold." [GAS] "Climbing, extremely floriferous, with medium-sized blossoms, leaves bronzy, glossy green. Buds ovoid-elongate, 3-4 at the ends of the canes. Flower cupped...brilliantly colored intense cochineal nuanced mauve-aniline with amaranth reflections when fully open. Petals neatly and abruptly acuminate-mucronate with a fawn-yellow nub; very fragrant." [JR27/163]

Mme. Pierre Cochet (S. Cochet, 1891)
Noisette
Seedling of 'Rêve d'Or' (N).
"Yellow, striped." [Ÿ] "First-rate Noisette with beautiful, fragrant, chrome-yellow flowers, tinged pink and apricot." [GAS] "Climbing, strong canes, nearly thornless, leaves and wood greenish brown. Flowers medium-sized, full, basically golden yellow fading to yellowish white, reverse dark coppery yellow. Long buds. This variety...is 'William Allen Richardson' perfected." [JR15/164]

Mme. Rose Romarin (Nabonnand, 1888)
Tea
From 'Papillon' (T) × 'Chromatella' (N).
"Extremely vigorous, climbing; wood red; leaves thick, of a handsome glossy green resembling those of 'Chromatella' very much; bud long and of perfect form; flower large, semi-double, very erect; color, bright red, shaded, center coppery...very floriferous. Extraordinary in all respects." [JR12/148] "[*For*] everywhere. Not a solid red, but with sufficiently dark marking to be so classed, although much of the center is lighter; very prolific, fine foliage, some fragrance, and although of only fair form, lasts; valuable for cutting." [ARA28/95] "Small growth; winterkilled." [ARA18/122]

[**Mme. Schultz**] (Beluze, 1856)
Affiliated with 'Lamarque' (N).
"Primrose, shaded with carmine, very sweet." [FP] "Medium-sized, yellow or yellowish." [JDR56/53] "Canary yellow." [S] "Another new yellow rose…it is the most vigorous grower of all, but appears to be very chary in giving its flowers." [R8] "Centre pale yellow, outer petals straw, flowers full, of moderate size and good substance; a fine rose of vigorous habit." [JC]

Mme. Segond-Weber, Climbing (Reymond, 1929)
Hybrid Tea
Sport of 'Mme. Segond-Weber' (HT).
"Salmon pink, very large, full, medium scent, tall." [Sn] "[*For*] everywhere. A new introduction which gives very large blooms with fine stems for cutting. Seems most promising; strongly recommended." [Capt28]

Mme. Therese Roswell
Listed in the chapter on Teas.

Mme. Trifle (Levet, 1869)
Noisette
Seedling of 'Gloire de Dijon' (N).
"Pale fawn changing to cream, shape of the flower and habit like 'Gloire de Dijon', flowers somewhat paler, a good rose; habit vigorous." [JC] "Without perfume." [JR3/62] "Inferior to [*'Gloire de Dijon'*] in value." [EL] "Stands out because of its large and handsome foliage, and because of its large, very full, cupped flowers which are nearly upright; deep yellow; sometimes the center of the blossom is salmon yellow with coppery reflections. Like 'Gloire de Dijon', it blooms freely up till frost." [S]

Mock's Rosa Druschki (Mock, ca. 1935) trans., "Mock's Pink Druschki"
Hybrid Perpetual

We alas have no information on this climbing Hybrid Perpetual—presumably it is a cross between 'Frau Karl Druschki' (HP) and some worthy red or pink rose—but we record the name here to spur on others to research.

Monsieur Désir (Pernet père, 1888)
Noisette
Seedling of 'Gloire de Dijon' (N).
"Growth vigorous, climbing, foliage reddish green; flower very large, pretty full, perfect form, well held, of a handsome crimson red often much darkened with violet." [JR12/165] "Fine in dry heat. Very fine in spring; only fault, foliage mildews in dampness; good cutting value; fine fragrance; good lasting." [ARA28/95] "Good form and habit. One of the best dark colored climbers." [P1]

Monsieur Georges de Cadoudal (Schwartz, 1904) syn., 'Georges de Cadondal'
Tea
"Vigorous, foliage purplish green; flower large, very full, globular; color bright pink nuanced carmine on a coppery ground. Fragrant." [JR28/154]

Monsieur Paul Lédé, Climbing (Low, 1913) syn., 'Paul Lédé'
Hybrid Tea
Sport of 'Monsieur Paul Lédé' (HT).
"Honey-amber with pink glow and delicious fruity scent; the buds are particularly beautiful." [BCD] "Carmine pink and dawn yellow." [JR38/109] "Yellow and apricot. Graceful in vigor and color, 'Climbing Paul Lédé' is a precious enrichment in yellow climbers." [JR38/72] "[*For*] everywhere. Not pure yellow, but otherwise very fine, with splendid growth, good foliage, and cutting value. A prolific and constant bloomer." [Capt28] "Large shapely pink flowers with apricot overtones, sweetly fra-

grant and very free flowering, 12 [ft; ca. 4 m]." [HRG] "A sight to remember…12×8 [ft; ca. 4×2.6 m]." [B]

Monsieur Rosier (Nabonnand, 1887)
Noisette
Seedling of 'Mlle. Mathilde Lenaerts' (N).
"Vigorous; flower large, full, well formed, cupped; color, bright pink on a ground of translucent yellowish white…very floriferous." [JR11/165]

Montecito (Franceschi-Fenzi, 1930)
Hybrid Gigantea
From *R. gigantea* × *R. brunonii.*
Presumably white or cream-white single. "Grown to some extent in California." [GAS] Montecito, an elite precinct of Santa Barbara, California. Also, of the same provenance, **Montarioso** (syn., 'Montariosa'), concerning which we have no reports.

[**Mosella, Climbing**] (Conard & Jones, 1909)
Polyantha
Sport of 'Mosella' (Pol).
"The flower is precisely like the golden yellow, cream colored blossoms of the Bush Rose by the same name; a healthy vigorous climber that continues producing its lovely clusters almost without interruption from Spring till frost." [C&Js10]

Mrs. Aaron Ward, Climbing (A. Dickson, 1922)
Hybrid Tea
Sport of 'Mrs. Aaron Ward' (HT).
"Yellow, very large, full, medium scent, tall." [Sn]

[**Mrs. B.R. Cant, Climbing**] (Hjort, 1960)
Tea

Sport of 'Mrs. B.R. Cant' (T).
Rose-red to silvery-pink. "A very vigorous climber, reaching...ten to twelve feet [ca. 3.3-4 m]...the same good foliage and bloom of the bush 'Mrs. B.R. Cant'...a good spring bloom and intermittent bloom the rest of the ...season...We doubt that it is still growing anywhere now." [Hj]

Mrs. Henry Morse, Climbing (Chaplin Bros., 1929)
Hybrid Tea
Sport of 'Mrs. Henry Morse' (HT).
"Yellowish pink, very large, full, medium scent, tall." [Sn]

Mrs. Herbert Stevens, Climbing (Pernet-Ducher, 1922)
Hybrid Tea
Sport of 'Mrs. Herbert Stevens' (HT).
"Lovely white...stamina. Fragrant and vigorous...12×16 [ft; ca. 4×5.3 m]." [B] "Semi-double and delightfully fragrant...a rampant grower." [GAS] "[*For*] everywhere. Fine grower; good foliage; a rose for cutting and far ahead of 'Niphetos' and 'Devoniensis'. Blooms through a long season. Prefer this to 'Climbing Frau Karl Druschki'." [Capt28]

Mrs. Robert Peary
Listed as 'Kaiserin Auguste Viktoria, Climbing'.

Mrs. Rosalie Wrinch (W. & J. Brown, 1915)
Hybrid Perpetual
From 'Frau Karl Druschki' (HP) × 'Hugh Dickson' (HP).
"A fine climbing single H.T....The flowers are a delightful shade of pink, and withstand all weathers." [NRS18/140] "A vigorous Hybrid Tea with stout stems and very large, single pink flowers. Fine pillar." [GAS] "Has...become very popular, and deservedly so. There is a brilliancy and charm about its rose-coloured flowers, and they are excellent for decorative purposes." [NRS18/148]

Mrs. W.H. Cutbush, Climbing (Paling, 1911)
Polyantha
Sport of 'Mrs. W.H. Cutbush' (Pol).
"Flowers and leaves of this newcomer are similar to those of its mother...Its deportment is strong and upright...blooms without interruption; the blossoms are erect rather than nodding. Having grown to four feet [ca. 1.25 m], it begins to bloom at the base; it will grow that same year to perhaps six feet [ca. 2 m]. In Fall, the rose is covered with pale pink blossoms, and is ornamented with pretty light green foliage resistant to all diseases." [JR35/118]

Mrs. W.J. Grant, Climbing (E.G. Hill, 1899) syn., 'Climbing Belle Siebrecht'
Hybrid Tea
Sport of 'Mrs. W.J. Grant' (HT).
"Light pink, large, full, medium scent, tall." [Sn] "Fair to good growth; not a good bloomer." [ARA18/121]

Multiflore de Vaumarcus (Menet, 1875) trans., "Multifloral [Rose] from Vaumarcus"
Noisette
"Soft pink, very double, medium large, in large trusses, continuous bloom; growth bushy, medium, foliage healthy." [Kr]

Nancy Hayward (A. Clark, 1937)
Hybrid Gigantea
From 'Jessy Clark' (HGig) × ?
Cherry red, single. No doubt a "once-bloomer," like most Hybrid Giganteas.

Nardy (Nabonnand, 1888)
Noisette

Seedling of 'Gloire de Dijon' (N).
"Very large, fragrant, globular flowers of coppery yellow." [GAS] "Growth extremely vigorous, climbing; heavy-wooded; foliage bronzy green; bud like that of 'Gloire de Dijon', but larger; flower very large, very full, globular, stout; color, coppery salmon yellow; very floriferous. More vigorous than 'Gloire de Dijon'." [JR12/148] "The foliage...is very ornamental." [JR22/9] "Nardy (Sébastien).—Landscape gardener from Hyères, where he died in 1909 at the age of 79. Following a trip to America, he introduced, around 1876, the peach 'Amsde' into cultivation." [R-HC]

Neervelt (Verschuren, 1910)
Hybrid Tea
From 'Gloire de Dijon' (N) × 'Princesse de Béarn' (HP).
"Fiery red." [Jg] "Red, large, full, tall." [Sn]

New Dawn (Somerset/Dreer, 1930)
Hybrid Tea
Sport of 'Dr. W. Van Fleet' (HT).
Light pink. "Outstanding...Shapely and perfumed...10×8 [ft; ca. 3.3×2.25 m]." [B] "Bloomed continuously all summer...smaller [*flowers*] than 'Dr. W. Van Fleet' but otherwise similar...Vigor is equal to 'Dr. W. Van Fleet'...bloomed continuously until late in November." [ARA32/199] "Never disappointed anyone!...[T]remendous display...slightly fragrant." [W] "Of no value in Texas." [ARA34/204]

Niphetos, Climbing (Keynes, Williams & Co., 1889) syn., 'Paul Krüger'
Tea
Sport of 'Niphetos' (T).
"Pure white, a good climber." [FRB] "The flowers are long and shapely and pure white, but the stalks are weak." [OM] "Lovely, creamy bud...Highly scented...10×6 [ft; ca. 3.3×2 m]." [B] "[*As compared to the bush form*], the flowers are larger, whiter, and considerably more fragrant."

[JR17/35] "Does not ball, but discolored by rain. Medium foliage. Better as a climber than a dwarf...The flowering is continuous." [Th2] "Another example of a luxuriant climber, exceeding the parent rose in the substance of the flowers." [Dr] "Constant supply of fine pure white flowers...much appreciated in hot climates." [F-M2] "A bit stingy with its flowers." [Hk] "Very vigorous." [DO] "Sometimes a little difficulty in getting it to commence 'running'." [F-M2] "Habit thoroughly climbing." [P1]

Noëlla Nabonnand (Nabonnand, 1900)
Tea
From 'Reine Marie Henriette' (HT) × 'Bardou Job' (B).
"Velvety crimson red, white nub." [Cx] "Velvety crimson and carmine." [RR] "A gorgeous semi-double velvety crimson Rose with extra large petals...extra vigorous in growth." [P1] "Flower very large, even enormous, semi-double; color, velvety crimson-red; very large petals; elongated bud, well-formed, well-held; very large and handsome foliage; growth very vigorous, very floriferous. Fragrant. More vigorous than 'Reine Marie Henriette'." [JR25/4] "Sweet scented and of good shape and size...crimson having a bluish tinge." [F-M] "Fair growth...color good, tending to blue somewhat." [ARA18/121] "A most magnificent rose, still classed as a Tea, though it seems more closely allied to the Hybrid Teas. It grows vigorously, and bears very long, fragrant buds of the most vivid velvety-crimson shade; they soon become full-blown, but in the bud are splendid. It flowers freely." [OM] "Rich old-rose fragrance. Canes to 10 [ft; ca. 3.3 m]." [HRG] "Foliage well retained." [Th2] "Foliage perfectly healthy; heavy spring bloom; light subsequently." [BCD] "A really good winter-blooming deep red Rose." [J]

Noisette de l'Inde (Noisette, 1814)
Noisette
"Blush white." [Ÿ] We give the received attribution for this rose; but—unless it is a synonym of 'Blush Noisette'—this variety is spurious.

Noisette Moschata (Schwartz, 1873)
Noisette
"Blush white." [LS]

Noisettiana
Listed as 'Blush Noisette'.

Nymphe (Türke, 1910)
Noisette? Lambertiana?
From 'Mignonette' (Pol) × 'Maréchal Niel' (N).
"White, center yellow, medium size, full, medium scent, tall." [Sn]

Odorata 22449
Listed as 'Fun Jwan Lo'.

Old Blush, Climbing (Breeder/Introducer unknown, date uncertain)
China
Presumably sport of 'Parsons' Pink China' (Ch).
"Medium size, double, loose spray; bright to medium pink. Repeats…builds up to 15-20 [ft; ca. 5-6.6 m]." [Lg]

Ophelia, Climbing (A. Dickson, 1920)
Hybrid Tea
Sport of 'Ophelia' (HT).
"Large, double, flat, fragrant; soft salmon pink. Repeats…8-10 [ft; ca. 2.25-3 m]." [Lg] "Very valuable. In great heat, this rose opens flat. If possible, should be given partial shade in Southern Zones." [Th2] "Vigorous, healthy plant. Outstanding…12×8 [ft; ca. 4×2.6 m]." [B] "Will become exceedingly popular…superior flowers to the dwarf variety." [NRS22/159]

[**Ophirie**] (Goubault, 1841)
Noisette
"Reddish copper, the outer petals rosy and fawn, of medium size, very double; form cupped; growth vigorous; distinct and sweet; foliage handsome." [P1] "Nasturtium-yellow, suffused with coppery-red, medium-size, double; a very distinct sort, but very shy." [EL] "Queerly coloured and queerly shaped, as they are nearly always quartered, flowers abundantly in clusters. Except as a curiosity, hardly worth growing." [B&V] "In colour quite unique; a rose without rose-colour, for it is of a bright fawn and salmon colour, with scarcely a tint of rose: its habit is robust and vigorous: like many others of this class, it will form an excellent pillar rose, requiring, however, protection in winter." [R9]

Orange Triumph, Climbing (Koopmann, 1948)
Polyantha
Sport of 'Orange Triumph' (Pol).
"Salmon orange red, small, semi-double, light scent, tall." [Sn]

Oscar Chauvry (Chauvry, 1900)
Noisette
Seedling of 'Elise Heymann' (T).
"Canes flexuose and very climbing; bud pretty large, full, beautiful deep China pink with metallic reflections on a golden yellow ground; central petals touched and lined white, purple reverse. Reblooms fairly freely; fragrant." [JR24/165]

Pale Pink China, Climbing (Breeder/Introducer unknown, date uncertain)
China
Sport of 'Pale Pink China' (Ch).
"Light pink, medium size, semi-double, tall." [Sn]

Papa Gontier, Climbing (Hosp, 1898)
Tea
Sport of 'Papa Gontier' (T).
"Intense pink, shaded yellow towards the center; reverse of petals purplish-red." [JR32/173] "The buds are long and shapely, of rose-red colour, but they are thin and soon become full-blown." [OM] "Very fine foliage; does not mildew in shade." [Th2] The same sport also occurred for Vigneron/Chevrier in 1904 and for Chase & Co. in 1905.

Papillon (Nabonnand, 1878) trans., "Butterfly"
Tea
"Pink and white, with coppery shading. Fine pillar rose." [H] "Coppery salmon-rose, of medium size, semi-double; very free in blooming." [P1] "Quite a curious rose in the form of its flower and the disposition of its petals." [JR14/132] "Very vigorous, climbing, flowers of medium size, and semi-double. Color is the coppery-pink of dawn, the underside of the petals being bright pink; bloom is profuse, and the blossoms look, in their form and arrangement, like a flock of butterflies perched on the bush. This variety of such originality is one of the best of the climbing sort." [JR3/9] "Foliage deep green and coppery." [B1] "Rather tender." [OM] "4×3 [ft; ca. 1.25×1 m]." [B] "[*One of the*] Hybrids of Tea and Noisette." [JR24/44] "This Rose is quite easy to grow on an 8-ft. or 9-ft. Pillar [ca. 2.25-2.75 m]. I incline to think I should call it the best Tea Rose we possess for this purpose. It so readily clothes itself right up from the base and allows…much latitude in pruning…The first plant I had of this variety absolutely refused to grow more than about three feet [ca. 1 m], and it still remains about that height, though I have had it undisturbed for some ten years…On getting a strong plant, however, I found it would readily make a 15-ft. Pillar [ca. 5 m]…It is extremely free flowering all the season through, and the flowers, which are borne in large trusses, are very fresh and decorative, particularly if picked young…They are wanting in form it

is true, but I think this is the only bad quality my friends have been able to find in this Rose as a Pillar." [NRS/14]

Paul Krüger
Listed as 'Niphetos, Climbing'.

Paul Lédé, Climbing
Listed as 'Monsieur Paul Lédé, Climbing'.

Paul's Lemon Pillar (G. Paul, 1915)
Hybrid Tea
From 'Frau Karl Druschki' (HP) × 'Maréchal Niel' (N).
"Exquisite large pale yellow double blooms with Tea fragrance…10 [ft; ca. 3.3 m]." [HRG] "Probably this is the most beautiful white of any class." [GAS] "Massive blooms, off-white suffused with lemon…Scented…vigorous…very thick branches and large leaves…15×10 [ft; ca. 5×3.3 m]." [B] "Wonderful blooms—large and of fine form; fair growth; rather shy bloomer." [ARA18/120] "Best in Pacific Northwest. Balls in dampness; mildews." [Capt28]

Paul's Single White Perpetual (G. Paul, 1883)
Hybrid Perpetual
"Hybrid Perpetual with large, single white flowers, sometimes freely produced in autumn." [GAS] "Growth vigorous; flower medium-sized, single; remontant; color, pure white." [S] "There can be no question that this is an easy Rose to grow. Mr. Dickson calls it of extraordinary vigour and hardiness, requiring abundant room, the most vigorous Rose he knows…long, rather straggling growth…It flowers well and freely summer and autumn, and its pure white flowers are very pleasing. Moreover, it opens freely in any weather, and in a wet year is particularly useful. It has good rather light green foliage which is practically free from mildew, but sometimes touched by black spot, and the plant makes long lax laterals,

which flower late into the autumn, and altogether the growth is clean and satisfactory. There is generally a good deal of thinning to be done at pruning time, and laterals that have flowered may be closely cut back. Almost its only fault is that it is rather too vigorous, a fault at least on the right side." [NRS14/75] Phillips & Rix report *R. moschata* ancestry.

Pavillon de Prégny (Guillot père, 1863)
Noisette
"Purplish pink, medium size, full, medium scent, moderate height." [Sn] "Growth vigorous, floriferous; flower medium-sized, full; color, wine pink, reverse of petals white." [S]

Pennant (A. Clark, 1941)
Hybrid Gigantea
Pink; non-remontant. No further information!

Perle des Jardins, Climbing (J. Henderson, 1889)
Tea
Sport of 'Perle des Jardins' (T).
"Golden-yellow, recurrent, fragrant." [W] "Intense yellow fading to very light yellow." [JR32/139] "Pure yellow…a fine addition to the climbing kinds." [P1] "Intense straw yellow; flower very large, very full, cupped; very floriferous; very vigorous." [Cx] "Richly fragrant." [ARA29/98] "The buds of this rose…are very pretty though small." [OM] "Better than the dwarf. Easier to grow than 'Maréchal Niel', and of much the same color. Balls in ocean climates early and late." [Th2]

[**Perle d'Or, Climbing**] (Breeder/Introducer unknown, date uncertain)
syn., 'Climbing Yellow Cécile Brunner'
Polyantha
Presumably sport of 'Perle d'Or' (Pol).

"Deep yellow, opening lemon-yellow, outer edges yellow-cream. Foliage slightly different from the pink climber [*i.e., 'Climbing Mlle. Cécile Brunner'*]...Does not flower as continuously as the pink, and is not as strong a grower." [Th2] "Great clusters of small double flowers even more abundantly than in bush form." [SHj]

Philomèle (Vibert, 1844)
Noisette
"Flesh." [Ÿ] Philomel is a poetic name for the Nightingale.

Phyllis Bide (Bide, 1923)
Polyantha
From 'Perle d'Or' (Pol) × 'Gloire de Dijon' (N).
"Golden yellow shaded pinkish carmine." [Cw] "Pink, salmon and gold. Slight scent. Medium growth...10×6 [ft; ca. 3.3×2 m]." [B] "Small, double blooms of pale gold, shaded pink, borne in clusters, vigorous to 6 [ft; ca. 2 m]." [HRG] "Long, loose clusters in June...old blooms stay too long, turning green...to 6 feet [ca. 2 m]." [W] "Very pretty perpetual-flowering Polyantha variety of fairly vigorous habit, the plants growing to a height of about 6 feet [ca. 2 m]. The blooms, which are produced in loose sprays, are almost double, the color pale gold, tipped with pale pink. The foliage is handsome." [ARA24/166] "Not very high-climbing, with clusters of few flowers, neither large nor small, mostly yellow in the bud, but pink in age...some scented bloom...pretty buds have a delicious color." [ARA30/172]

Pink Pet, Climbing (Breeder/Introducer unknown, date uncertain)
Polyantha
Presumably sport of 'Pink Pet' (Pol).
"Mid-sized, double bright pink blooms in clusters...to 10 [ft; ca. 3.3 m]." [HRG]

Pink Rover (W. Paul, 1890)
Hybrid Tea
"Very pale pink, deeper in the centre, buds long, clean, and handsome...growth semi-climbing." [P1] "Very fragrant." [GAS] "Appeared in a row of HTs; but, considering its principal characteristics, it seems more of a Bourbon, looking a lot like 'Souvenir de la Malmaison', only darker pink and somewhat more vigorous...[B]eautiful green, persistent foliage, an abundance of flowers from Spring to very late Fall, pale pink in Summer, darker at the end of the season...flowers fragrant, nearly always solitary, strong stem." [JR31/42]

Pinkie, Climbing (Dering, 1952)
Polyantha
Sport of 'Pinkie' (Pol).
"Large clusters of semidouble, 1.75 to 2.5 inch [ca. 2.75-6.25 cm], rose-colored, cupped flowers in...constant profusion...Soft, glossy foliage. Vigorous to 8 to 9 feet [ca. 2.25-3 m]...slightly fragrant." [W] "Not a typically huge-growing climbing Polyantha...3-5 [ft; ca. 1-1.5 m]. Repeats bloom well." [Lg]

Pompon de Paris, Climbing (Breeder/Introducer unknown, date uncertain)
Miniature China
"Blush." [Ÿ] "Pink, small, full, moderately tall." [Sn] "Vigorous...small, greyish-green foliage and twiggy growth. Flowers small and button-like, produced profusely in small clusters." [B1]

Pride of Reigate, Climbing (Vogel, 1941)
Hybrid Perpetual
Sport of 'Pride of Reigate' (HP).
"Red, striped white, large, full, moderate scent, tall." [Sn]

Princes van Oranje (Sliedrecht & Co., 1933) trans., "Princess of Orange"
Polyantha
Sport of 'Gloria Mundi' (Pol).
"Huge clusters of blazing red and orange flowers produced more or less continuously throughout the season." [GAS] "6 feet [ca. 2 m] and is literally covered with masses of blazing red flowers in trusses." [ARA33/179] "Very strong growth…the color burns less than that of the dwarf form." [ARA34/208]

Princess May (W. Paul, 1893)
Noisette
Seedling of 'Gloire de Dijon' (N).
"From 'Gloire de Dijon', this new variety is however somewhat less vigorous than its mother, and in color differs much from its siblings. The blossoms are an opaque pink which is very light and sweet, large, full, and globular. It forces well, and under those conditions produces very pretty foliage." [JR17/85-86]

Pumila Alba (Hardy/Margottin, 1847) trans., "Small White"
Noisette
"Flower very small, full, pure white." [JR4/21] "Form, cupped. A free bloomer of small growth." [P] "Origin and raiser unknown. Salmon-rose, seeming to have 'Safrano' blood, very free." [EL] "I have also seen—at Monsieur Margottin's—an interesting dwarf rose; it is 'Pumila Alba' (Hardy), a type of Noisette. Small bushy plant with dark green foliage and medium-sized pure white flowers; should be used in borders, where it is very decorative." [An47/210] Vibert also had a dwarf Noisette 'Pumila' about 1824, evidently unreleased but shared around; it is not inconceivable that this 1847 rose could be the same variety, saved by Hardy for study (Hardy was indeed very much around and in the thick of things in the mid-1820s).

Purity (Hoopes, Bro. & Thomas, 1917)
Hybrid Tea
From an unnamed seedling (resulting from crossing *R. wichuraiana* × the Tea 'Marion Dingee') × 'Mme. Caroline Testout' (HT).
"Big, cup-shaped, pure white flowers borne with remarkable freedom. Plant is excessively thorny and extremely vigorous." [GAS] "Semi-double." [ARA18/91] "One blooming season. Vigorous growth, varying sometimes…Foliage good and well held. Very fine when well grown." [Th2] "Rather low, bushy growth; good foliage; blooms attractive." [ARA18/121] "Foliage black-spots in midsummer; bloom sparse in June." [ARA18/131] "A sturdy trellis or pillar Rose." [McF]

Purple East (G. Paul, 1901)
Noisette? Lambertiana?
From 'Turner's Crimson Rambler' (Multiflora) × 'Beauté Inconstante' (N).
"Deep carmine purple." [Ÿ] "Huge clusters of rather large, semi-double, brilliant purple flowers. It is a strange and rather violent color, bound to attract attention. An outstanding characteristic is its earliness." [GAS]

Queen of Hearts (A. Clark, 1919)
Hybrid Tea
From 'Gustav Grünerwald' (HT) × 'Rosy Morn' (HP).
"Orange pink, large, semi-double, very fragrant, tall." [Sn] "An easy-growing tall climber of Hybrid Tea appearance, although its everblooming qualities are slight in this country [*U.S.A.*]. Flowers are large, semi-double, bright reddish pink, sometimes tending toward crimson." [GAS]

[**Queen of Queens, Climbing**] (W. Paul, 1892)
Hybrid Perpetual
Sport of 'Queen of Queens' (HP).

"Of strong climbing habit producing pink flowers of extra size and fine form." [CA96]

Radiance, Climbing (Griffing, 1926)
Hybrid Tea
Sport of 'Radiance' (HT).
"Salmon pink with yellow, large, full, very fragrant, tall." [Sn]

Rathswell
Listed as 'Mme. Therese Roswell' in the chapter on Teas.

Reine Maria Pia (Schwartz, 1880)
Noisette
Seedling of 'Gloire de Dijon' (N).
"Deep rose-colored flowers stained red in the center." [GAS] "Very vigorous, flower large, full, deep pink with a crimson center…A very beautiful variety." [JR4/165]

Reine Marie Henriette (Levet, 1878) trans., "Queen Marie Henriette"
Hybrid Tea
From 'Mme. Bérard' (N) × 'Général Jacqueminot' (HP).
"Rosy-red." [J] "Fulgent crimson, large and full; magnificent and effective." [P1] "Cherry-carmine, another hybrid tea; an excellent climber." [FRB] "Brilliant red clusters…the foliage is sparse and shabby in color." [BSA] "Vigorous, very floriferous, nice foliage, flower cupped, of good form, cherry-red." [JR3/142] "Cherry-red, a pure shade, large, double, somewhat fragrant; a beautiful, but rather unproductive sort." [EL] "Free-flowering and vigorous…12×8 [ft; ca. 4×2.6 m]." [B] "Blooms prolifically in the spring…good form and petalage…fragrant; it occasionally gives blooms in summer and autumn." [ARA17/27] "The most constant of autumnals." [F-M2] "A new rose, and on being entered into commerce it was put out as being a red 'Gloire de Dijon'. I can hardly see why it should

be thus compared with that old favorite. The shoots are different, being more wiry; the buds are more pointed; and, once open, the blossoms are poorly held and have no perfume; it isn't as floriferous, though it certainly grows vigorously enough." [JR6/110] "Large, three-parts full, globular to cup-shaped, of a distinct fiery cherry-red...should not be severely pruned...very fragrant." [Hn] "Scent of plums in marmalade." [JR33/101] "Peculiar sweet vinous odour." [Dr] "It has shapely buds, of fair size and red colouring...I always expected (and rarely was disappointed) to gather the first blossoms late in May and the last in November or December...This variety has a fault, but it is only that of most red roses, which on fading take on a depressing purplish tint. This, however, soon ensures their being cut off, so the evil is not a very great one." [OM] "Vigorous with heavy wood, green, strong, and slightly thorny, foliage dark green." [JR2/153] "Mildews; foliage lost early." [Th2] "[*Excellent in Norway*]." [ARA20/46] "Dedicated to Queen Marie-Henriette of Belgium." [JR34/15]

Reine Olga de Wurtemberg (Nabonnand, 1881)
Noisette
"Crimson, almost a summer-flowering climbing Rose, as it yields so few blooms in the autumn. There is no red climber to equal it in colour." [J] "Flower very large, well-formed, semi-double, sparkling red—as brilliant a color as it is possible to see. Luxuriant growth." [JR5/147] "Fragrant flowers of reddish scarlet." [GAS] "Bright light crimson. A fine climber, with magnificent foliage." [H] "Though so good in England is here [*on the French Riviera*] so fleeting and ugly in colour that I regret to see it." [J] "Vivid cherry red, which exposure to the sun converts to a false crimson...semi-double, but very graceful and perfect in shape before it is too full blown. A climber, and most free-flowering. A wall covered with this rose in full bloom before the sun has sucked the flowers, is a truly beautiful sight." [B&V] "Vigorous, almost evergreen, foliage handsome." [P1] "[*For the*] interior South. Reported fine in Texas. I have discarded it on

Southern California seacoast." [Capt28] "Nice growth and foliage; large attractive blooms; needs winter protection." [ARA18/121]

Rêve d'Or (Ducher, 1869) syn., 'Condesa da Foz'; trans., "Golden Dream"
Noisette
Seedling of 'Mme. Schultz' (N).
"Buff-yellow...free-flowering." [H] "Deep rich yellow; fragrant." [ARA29/98] "Buff yellow flowers partly lighter, and going over paler." [Hk] "Sometimes, a hint of pink...10×6 [ft; ca. 3.3×2 m]." [B] "Deep yellow, sometimes coppery yellow, large and full; growth vigorous. A good wall Rose. One of the best." [P1] "Large, double, fragrant; buff-yellow with pinkish center. Repeats bloom well...10 to 15 [ft; ca. 3.3-5 m]. A healthy plant, lovely foliage and blooms; graceful. One of the best Noisettes. Easy." [Lg] "Lovely, tea-rose shaped blooms...to 12 [ft; ca. 4 m]." [HRG] "Usually gives semi-double flowers of a salmon-yellow, sometimes golden yellow." [JR10/47] "Flower large, full, chamois yellow. Very fragrant." [LR] "Seldom bears a cluster of more than three flowers...One of the most useful and hardy of the race, a rampant grower, with buff-yellow blossoms borne in immense numbers both in summer and autumn, while its rich red shoots and reddish-green foliage make it a beautiful object before and after it blooms. It strongly resents any pruning beyond shortening its vigorous summer shoots." [K2] "One of the best climbers and nearly evergreen." [FRB] "Its foliage is one of its chief attractions, clothing the plant to its base, coming very early and continuing late...I, and most of my friends, have found it free from mildew...During its flowering periods the blossoms are very freely produced and cover the plant well...The flowers have a Tea scent, their colour generally resembles 'Mme. Falcot' and the rose has, in fact, been called a climbing 'Mme. Falcot', but when more closely examined the opened flowers will be found to have two colours, a buff yellow and a coppery yellow tint. They are borne in clusters and are fairly shapely, but not good enough for exhibi-

tion...requires some time to get established before it is at its best." [NRS/11] "A charming Rose, with its copper-tinted foliage, which associates well with the yellow apricot-tinted blooms, which are produced in huge clusters." [NRS/17] "The most prolific climber of medium size...very vigorous growth; resistant, restrained foliage...better than '[Mme. la] Duchesse d'Auerstädt'." [Capt28] "Foliage well retained." [Th2] "[*Especially good in Florida*]." [ARA24/85]

"The original of this beautiful rose...exists still...and each year, in June, it is covered with flowers to the great admiration of visitors. This variety...is one of the most vigorous of climbing roses. As compared to others, it grows with astonishing rapidity. Its branches are slender and its foliage large and shiny dark green, and is composed of 5 or perhaps 7 leaflets. The beautiful flowers are large, full, well-formed, and of a nice dark yellow, light at the edges, coppery towards the center. At the first bloom, the blossoms come in clusters of 8-10; afterwards, they come one at a time." [JR6/185] "Though in point of perfection and size the flowers are not to be compared with many other roses, it is to my mind one of the most delightful of all climbers; for even when out of bloom its handsome foliage and reddish shoots are highly decorative." [K1]

Richmond, Climbing (A. Dickson, 1912)
Hybrid Tea
Sport of 'Richmond' (HT).
"Bright red." [Ÿ] "Pure red scarlet...of fair form only and blooming less freely in the autumn and summer." [Th] "A grand colour, rather stiff perhaps in growth...The flowers seem to have more substance than the dwarf form." [NRS22/160] "Many basal shoots attained a length of from 6-ft. to 10-ft. [ca. 2-3.3 m]. These I carefully trained in, merely 'tipping' the ends...The result was largely a thicket of flowerless laterals and only about a half-dozen blooms." [NRS22/173] "Best near coast. The best of the lighter reds, and a very prolific bloomer. Has fair cutting value; superior to

'Liberty'." [Capt28] "Very vigorous...the best addition to the climbers for many years." [JR36/92]

Rosabelle (Bruant, 1900)
Tea
From 'Fortune's Double Yellow' (HGig) × 'Mme. de Tartas' (T).
"Pale rose reflexed with salmon." [P1] "Brownish pink." [LS] "Great vigor...climbing, canes purplish, ample and superb foliage, which is glossy, bronze, and purplish when young. Blooms in clusters, large or very large, of elegant form; petal edges crinkled, reflexed; light pink with salmon reflections, contrasting China pink on the back; very pretty long bud; elegant and pronounced scent. In this variety, the influence of the pollen parent, the Tea rose, comes to the fore...reblooms in Fall." [JR23/167] "Producing in one season canes more than six feet long [ca. 2 m], covered beginning to end with pretty clusters of flowers." [JR27/99-100]

Rose Noisette
Listed as 'Blush Noisette'.

Rosemary, Climbing (Dingee & Conard, 1920)
Hybrid Tea
Sport of 'Rosemary' (HT).
"Light pink, very large, full, tall." [Sn]

Rosier de Philippe Noisette
Listed as 'Blush Noisette'.

Rouletii, Climbing (Breeder/Introducer unknown, date uncertain)
Miniature China
Presumably sport of 'Rouletii' (Min Ch).
Pink miniature climber. No further information!

Sarah Bernhardt (Dubreuil, 1906)
Hybrid Tea
"Rosy scarlet flowers shaded velvety red, semi-double and fragrant." [GAS] "Deep red, large, semi-double, moderate scent, tall." [Sn] "Growth very hardy, very vigorous and floriferous, with upright semi-climbing canes. Blossom full, very large, with large incarnadine petals, bright scarlet crimson red nuanced velvety purple. The blossom is very fragrant with a scent of violets, and does not burn in the sun." [JR30/150] "Non-remontant." [JR33/185] "Has a fine crimson colour and good perfume, and gets up to the top of an 8-ft. [ca. 2.3 m] bamboo without difficulty. The flowers are perhaps a little thin and sometimes apt to be rather ragged, but it is a Rose that has been rather overlooked, and seems to me quite useful for our purpose [*of making Pillars*]." [NRS14/63] Sarah Bernhardt, French actress; lived 1844-1923.

Scorcher (A. Clark, 1922)
Hybrid Tea
Seedling of 'Mme. Abel Chatenay' (HT).
"Early. Scarlet. Four-inch [ca. 1 dm], semi-double, ruffled flowers of crimson-scarlet. The September bloom of 'Scorcher' in our test-garden was very striking last fall. It is fragrant, too." [C-Ps34] "Stunning Australian variety of most vigorous growth, with very large, ruffled, semi-double flowers of blazing rosy-scarlet, a different 'Paul's Scarlet Climber' and even brighter. It is evidently a throw-back to the Bourbon type, as its parent was a Hybrid Tea. Occasional blooms are produced in midsummer and autumn. One of the finest modern climbers." [GAS]

Sénateur Amic (P. Nabonnand, 1924)
Hybrid Gigantea
From *R. gigantea* × 'General MacArthur' (HT).
"Bud large...Nilson red; flower large...cupped, brilliant cochineal-carmine with cochineal reflex. Foliage rich green, many thorns. Very vigorous;

makes 32-foot shoots [ca. 1 dkm] in a season." [ARA25/188] "A striking, single-flowered Gigantea, with beautiful warm red, single flowers. Enormously vigorous." [GAS] "Light green foliage with seven leaflets. Flower rather large, cupped, almost single, borne gracefully, very large petals, coloring superb." [ARA26/174] "Bright carmine…superb perfume. Healthy and vigorous…10×8 [ft; ca. 3.3×2.3 m]." [B]

Setina (Henderson, 1879) syn., 'Climbing Hermosa'
Bourbon
Sport of 'Hermosa' (B).
"A beautiful new introduction from the U.S., bearing many well-formed blossoms of a beautiful silvery-rose." [JR3/114] "Sometimes bright pink." [JR3/166] "Very fragrant." [CA93] "A deeper shade of pink than the bush 'Hermosa', and the roses are larger." [Dr] "Flower medium-sized, full, globular; very vigorous." [Cx] "A strong grower and a free bloomer." [CA96] Introduced in France by Schwartz.

[**Smith's Yellow China**]
Listed in the chapter on Teas.

Snowbird, Climbing (Weeks, 1949)
Hybrid Tea
Sport of 'Snowbird' (HT).
"Exquisite buds, large, very double, high-centered white flowers, tinged lemon-yellow. Leathery foliage and very vigorous. Blooms dependably all season…Heavy tea fragrance." [W]

Solfatare (Boyau/Vibert, 1843) syn., 'Solfaterre'
Noisette
Seedling of 'Lamarque' (N).
"Cup., sulphur, large, double, splendid." [CC] "Creamy white…centres bright sulphur, very large and full; form cupped; growth vigorous. A fine

Rose, with handsome foliage and very sweet." [P1] "The most useful yellow [*as compared to 'Maréchal Niel' and 'Chromatella'*];...hardier, of better habit, and more certain to flower...and the blooms are but little inferior." [EL] "The flowers are not so globular as [*those of 'Chromatella'*], but rather flat like those of 'Jaune Desprez', very large, of a deeper saffron yellow than [*'Chromatella'*], and retaining its color more permanently. It is a splendid rose, universally esteemed...vigorous." [WRP] "Bright lemon. When half opened, the buds are superb...its growth is very luxuriant." [SBP] "Bright straw, with a deeper sulphur centre...though not so fine in either color or form as the 'Cloth of Gold' [*i.e., 'Chromatella'*], is truly a superb variety, ever repays high cultivation by constantly producing fine clusters of sulphur flowers at the points of every shoot...Care should be taken to stop all *very strong* young shoots when about eighteen inches long [ca. 4.5 dm], to induce a more branching growth and greater number of flowers." [C] "Sent to me, by its grower, two years ago [*making 1842*], as a 'superb Yellow Tea Rose, not equalled,' and when it first bloomed it fully maintained its Tea character, but as soon as I grew it on its own roots, it directly assumed the habit of our favorite 'Lamarque'...an agreeable fragrance...When fully established it flowers freely, and grows rapidly...An eastern or northern aspect, where it will have a portion of sun, will suit it best, and fully preserve its beautiful colour." [Bu] "Fugacious." [HstII:36] "Foliage very good." [Th2] "Apt to cast its leaves." [P2] "10×8 [ft; ca. 3.3×2.6 m]." [B] "[*Liked in Texas*]." [ET] "An excellent climbing rose, and valuable as a stock on which to bud Teas." [EL] As for the name:

*A **Solfatare**'s a sulphur spring;*
*A **Solfaterre**'s not anything.*

Sombreuil
Listed as 'Mlle. de Sombreuil' in the chapter on Teas.

Souvenir d'Emile Zola (Begault-Pigné, 1907) trans., "In Memory of Emile Zola"

Hybrid Tea
Seedling of 'La France de 89' (HT).
"Bright pink in bud, delicate silvery pink upon opening, very large, full, very fragrant, distinctive fragrance; vigor and bearing of 'La France de 89'." [JR31/166]

Souvenir de Claudius Denoyel (Chambard, 1920) trans., "In Memory of Claudius Denoyel"
Hybrid Tea
From 'Château de Clos-Vougeot' (HT) × 'Commandeur Jules Gravereaux' (HP).
"A magnificent, perfectly formed flower of glistening crimson with shadings of vermilion. It will grow 7 to 8 feet high and is the most desirable Red *Pillar Rose* we know. The fall blooms are exceptionally fine." [C-Ps28] "Large, double, cupped, intensely fragrant; bright crimson red. Pillar type climber; repeats…well with good fertilizing and water." [Lg] "Good in all districts. A peculiar color, verging on dark brown; very large grower with particularly fine foliage. Opens a trifle flat, but with clothed center and good stems and perfume. A continuous but not prolific bloomer." [Capt28] "One of the best red climbers. It has the happy faculty of blooming all the way up the stalk. It is very fragrant and is of good color." [CaRoI/5/7] "Does not blue nor pale, it is of a vigorous habit and is very sweet scented." [CaRoII/1/8] "Shapely, double, cupped…rich red to scarlet. Fragrant. Vigorous, angular growth…12×8 [ft; ca. 4×2.6 m]." [B]

Souvenir de la Malmaison, Climbing (Bennett, 1893)
Bourbon
Sport of 'Souvenir de la Malmaison' (B).
"Blush white; flower very large, very full, flat, fragrant; floriferous; very vigorous." [Cx] "Well formed, flesh-white." [JR26/56] "Among the very choicest…Huge, double, pale-pink…cupped and quartered…a great spring mass…to 20 feet [ca. 6.6 m]…fine fragrance." [W] "Does not

repeat bloom well when established...10-12 [ft; ca. 3.3-4 m]." [Lg] "Has no superior. It is luxuriant, profuse, strong and vigorous, and the large, double roses are light pink low down on the vines, but higher up, appear white, with charming effect." [Dr] "Foliage sparse and poor; growth fair." [ARA18/122]

Souvenir de Lucie (Widow Schwartz, 1893) trans., "In Memory of Lucie"
Noisette
From 'Fellemberg' (N) × 'Ernestine de Barante' (HP).
"Very vigorous, climbing, leaves glaucous green washed purple. Flower medium-sized, well formed, in a cluster; color varies from ruby red to pale carmine pink; center blush white; reverse whitish. The mid-vein of the petal is often white." [JR17/165]

Souvenir de Mère Fontaine
Listed in the chapter on Hybrid Bourbons, Hybrid Chinas, and Hybrid Noisettes.

Souvenir de Mme. Joseph Métral (Bernaix, 1887) trans., "In Memory of Mme. Joseph Métral"
Hybrid Tea
From 'Mme. Bérard' (N) × 'Eugène Fürst' (HP).
"Bright cerise, illumined with crimson and vermilion; very large, full, and of splendid shape and substance." [GAS] "Climbing canes; of the 'Gloire de Dijon' class; vigorous and hardy; leaves very large with oval leaflets, rather long, of a brilliant and handsome green; flower very large, very double, with many petals, regularly imbricated...This variety, by its abundance and the brightness of its flowers, enriches the climbing Teas with its distinct and novel characteristics." [JR11/150-151]

Souvenir de Mme. Ladvocat (Veysset, 1899) trans., "In Memory of Mme. Ladvocat"
Noisette
Sport of 'Duarte de Oliveira' (N).
"Salmon pink on a light copper ground, medium size, full, fragrant. Vigorous growth, foliage striped." [JR23/178]

Souvenir de Mme. Léonie Viennot (Bernaix fils, 1898) trans., "In Memory of Mme. Léonie Viennot"
Noisette
From 'Gloire de Dijon' (N) × ?
"Jonquil yellow, shading to China rose. Distinct." [H] "Light rose-pink with yellow shading." [Capt28] "Fully double, sometimes quartered blooms of deep primrose yellow with coppery tints, fragrant and free flowering…10 [ft; ca. 3.3 m]." [HRG] "Tremendous amount of bloom…little fall bloom…Foliage only fair." [Capt28] "Climbing, sumptuous foliage, purple-green in the shoots, shiny and somber when older. Flower-stalk hirsute, stiff, holding the blossom erect. Flower very large, of exquisite form, very double, and lasts well. Handsomely colored jonquil yellow shading to amber yellow at the nub, aging subtly to China pink tinted cochineal of a very fresh tone, with azalea red; and, on the reverse, a silvery grayish-white with reddish tinge. Center petals numerous, chamois at the heart, illumined with pink." [JR21/149] "Vigorous…10×8 [ft; ca. 3.3×2.6 m]." [B] "One of the main booths [*at the 1890 exhibition at Dijon*]—the best, perhaps—was that of Messrs. Viennot & fils, Dijon rose-men…This magnificent booth…gained for Messrs. Viennot the Exhibition's grand prize." [JR15/4-5]

Souvenir of Wootton, Climbing
Listed as 'Wootton, Climbing'.

Spray Cécile Brunner
Eventually "climbs," but listed in the Polyantha chapter.

Summer Snow, Climbing (Couteau/Jackson & Perkins, 1936)
Polyantha
Seedling of 'Tausendschön' (Mult).
"White." [Ÿ]

Sunday Best (A. Clark, 1924)
Hybrid Perpetual
From 'Frau Karl Druschki' (HP) × an unnamed seedling.
"Its gorgeous, single red flowers have conspicuous white centers and are borne very freely early in the season. Autumn blooms scarce." [GAS] "Long, pointed bud; 3-inch [ca. 7.5 cm], semi-double, ruffled flowers, vivid crimson to carmine with a white eye, richer coloring in partial shade. Starts to bloom early and goes right on even past a first light frost. Wrinkled foliage, not too attractive...It appears to me...it should branch more, great long canes springing from the base are garlanded the entire length with bloom. Grows to 8 to 10 feet [ca. 2.6-3.3 m]." [W]

Tea Rambler (G. Paul, 1903)
Tea or Multiflora
From 'Turner's Crimson Rambler' (Mult) × "a climbing Tea."
"Beautiful...deep coppery pink in the bud, changing to soft pink in the older flowers." [F-M] "Clusters of mid-sized double flowers...salmon-pink, fragrant, one profuse bloom, vig. To 12 [ft; ca. 4 m]." [HRG] "Very vigorous upright stems...The foliage is particularly good and persistent; the leaves are moderately dark green in colour, surrounded with a faint red edge, with a fine glossy surface, while the young undeveloped leaves at the end of the shoots are delicate and fern-like. It is particularly free from mildew...only one flowering period...large clusters...tea-scented. The

individual blossoms are rather large for a rambling rose, a little fuller than semi-double, and somewhat loosely put together. The colour of the buds is cherry-carmine, that of the open flowers coppery pink, fading to 'La France' pink…more form than most ramblers." [NRS/11] "Among the novelties of Fall, 1902, it was also mentioned that Messrs. Paul & sons…announced one of their origination, The Tea Rambler, which made quite a stir…The bush is very vigorous, developing numerous and large leaves, and bearing quantities of petite blossoms of 'La France' coloration." [JR26/161] "Growth not of best; profuse bloomer; most attractive." [ARA18/121] "The leaves are unusually handsome, and persist on the stems until midwinter." [OM] "12×8 [ft; ca. 4×2.6 m]." [B] "Unsuitable for northern gardens." [NRS/14]

Thé Maréchal
Listed as 'Lamarque'.

Triomphe de Bollwiller
Listed as 'Fun Jwan Lo'.

Triomphe des Noisettes (Pernet père, 1887) trans., "Noisette Triumph"
Noisette
From 'Général Jacqueminot' (HP) × 'Ophirie' (N).
"Bright rose colour; large, full and vigorous. Gives an abundance of sweet-scented flowers. A good thing." [B&V] "Vigorous, climbing; foliage very dark; thorns protrusive and numerous; flower very large, nearly full; blooming in clusters; beautiful intense pink; very fragrant; quite remontant…a variety of the first order." [JR11/163]

Vicomtesse d'Avesnes (Roeser, 1848)
Noisette
"Light salmon-rose, large, full, and distinct." [FP] "A very neat rose-coloured rose, blooming most abundantly." [R8] "Growth vigorous;

flower medium sized, full; color, delicate pink." [S] "Very vigorous plant; flowers medium-sized, full, well-formed, lilac pink. Very good variety, good for bedding, arbors, etc., pretty freely remontant, as vigorous grafted as own-root." [l'H53/155]

Vicomtesse Pierre de Fou (Sauvageot, 1921)
Noisette
From 'L'Idéal' (N) × 'Joseph Hill' (HT).
"Deep pink to magenta-red, with a tip of yellow. Foliage large, dark green." [ARA24/173] "Large, quartered bloom...to 15 [ft; ca. 5 m]." [HRG] "Bud medium size, ovoid; flower large, very double and lasting; red passing to deep pink...short stem; strong fragrance. Foliage...glossy dark green, disease-resistant. Few thorns. Climbing, bushy habit; profuse bloomer; all season; very hardy." [ARA22/151] "Luxuriant, glossy foliage of coppery, dark green...fragrant...flowers...are coppery-pink...15×10 [ft; ca. 5×3.3 m]." [B] "The finest climber in the garden. An immense grower, it produces a constant succession of large double blooms of a wonderfully brilliant shrimp pink with gold shadings. By disbudding, excellent flowers for cutting may be secured. It made twenty-foot canes [ca. 6.6 m] the second year from budding, and has handsome, glossy, disease-resistant foliage." [CaRoI/6/6]

Viscountess Folkestone, Climbing
Listed as 'Gainesborough'.

Vulgaris
Listed as 'Blush Noisette'.

Waltham Climber I (W. Paul, 1885)
Noisette
Seedling of 'Gloire de Dijon' (N).

"Bright rosy-crimson, shaped like a Camellia when expanded; growth extra vigorous." [P1] "[*Waltham Climbers I, II, and III*] are seedlings of 'Gloire de Dijon', possessing all the best qualities of that variety, but of better form, and of brighter color than other Gloire seedlings...They bloom abundantly in autumn, and have very pretty foliage. The flowers last a long time, and are bright until the end...The color of the three new-comers is crimson red, but different for each...'I' is the brightest, 'III' the darkest, and 'II' the most climbing." [JR10/19]

Waltham Climber II (W. Paul, 1885)
Noisette
Seedling of 'Gloire de Dijon' (N).
"Bright pink." [Ÿ] "Large, flame-red flowers tinged with crimson." [GAS] See also under 'Waltham Climber I'.

[**Waltham Climber III**] (W. Paul, 1885)
Noisette
Seedling of 'Gloire de Dijon' (N).
"Vigorous...with large, bright rosy-crimson flowers." [GAS] See also under 'Waltham Climber I'.

[**Weisser Maréchal Niel**] (Deegan, 1896) syn. and trans., 'White Maréchal Niel'
Noisette
Sport 'Maréchal Niel' (N).
"Identical in every way with 'Maréchal Niel' except in color, which is pure creamy-white; splendid large roses, full and deep and deliciously tea-scented." [C&Js02] "This rose is a veritable treasure for hothouse culture or indeed under glass, what is more leaving nothing to be desired as an outdoor plant...It is a seedling of our old favorite 'Maréchal Niel' [*An editorial note adds:* 'It is a sport. As for the rest, it is more often yellow than

white.']...It is equally good in warm-house or cool. Its flowers are splendid." [JR23/42]

Wenzel Geschwind, Climbing (Vogel, 1940)
Hybrid Tea
Sport of 'Wenzel Geschwind' (HT).
"Deep purple, large, full, medium scent, tall." [Sn]

White Maman Cochet, Climbing (Knight, 1907 and/or Needle & Co., 1911)
Tea
Sport of 'White Maman Cochet' (T).
"Very large, double; white streaked pink. Repeats...8-12 [ft; ca. 2.25-3.5 m]." [Lg] "Best in reasonable heat. The best light-colored climber—a light yellow 'Maman Cochet'." [Capt28] "Small grower; blooms attractive, but shy." [ARA18/119] "Vigorous canes to 12 [ft; ca. 4 m]." [HRG]

White Pet, Climbing (Corbœuf-Marsault, 1894)
Polyantha (or, construably, Sempervirens)
Sport of 'Little White Pet' (Pol).
"This is a superb new variety that will please and delight everyone who wishes a pure white constant blooming Climbing Rose. It is a true ever bloomer, and bears great clusters of snowy white blossoms continually all through the season. The flowers are deliciously fragrant. It blooms the first year, and is a most rapid and graceful climber, surpassing nearly all others, in quick growth, early and constant bloom, and the astonishing number of flowers produced." [C&Js98] "This variety will be able, it would seem, to rival 'Turner's Crimson Rambler' [*the Multiflora cultivar, discussed in* The Old Rose Adventurer]; it 'creeps' the same way, and is also vigorous. It is not remontant, but gives flowers just like those of 'White Pet'." [JR18/162]

William Allen Richardson (Ducher, 1878)
Noisette
Sport of 'Rêve d'Or' (N).
"Colour of a cut apricot." [E] "A real orange...quite small." [F-M] "Very deep orange yellow, sometimes pale straw, with beautiful foliage; one of the best noisette varieties for button-holes." [FRB] "Medium size, fairly well filled, fiery orange-yellow, usually white at the edges. Very strong-growing and free-flowering, continuing into the autumn. Exquisite when half-expanded, but flatter and rather irregular with age." [Hn] "It stands alone as regards depth of yellow." [DO] "Buff to apricot. Free-flowering and vigorous...12×8 [ft; ca. 4×2.6 m]." [B] "Deep orange, with white edges. A most distinct and valuable climbing Rose. Early in the season the flowers often come almost white." [J] "Striking...fragrant." [ARA29/98] "Easy to grow, particularly where there is some shelter...sadly wanting in form of flower." [NRS/14] "Very showy and distinct; growth vigorous." [P1] "Long branches, climbing, of a dark green, well branched; the blossoms are borne in clusters at the ends of the branches, and are of a nice shade of orange and saffron yellow." [S] "Not, it is true, a model rose, as the blossoms are too small, but these flowers are nevertheless charming and of use in bouquets." [JR7/178] "At first of quite modest appearance, parsimonious with its flowers...with age...the bloom becomes more generous, the rebloom is greater, and the color gains intensity...It was dedicated to a rich American fancier...'Vigorous as a bush or climber, with branches both flexible and divergent, wood a lightly browned green, furnished with short, recurved thorns, somewhat numerous; the leaves are composed of 5-7 leaflets of a handsome though somber brilliant green; flowers in clusters on the large branches, singly on the branchlets, varying from pretty orange-yellow tinted with saffron to a very fresh nankeen-yellow'." [JR10/40] "Suffers somewhat from mildew, but this is easily kept in check on this plant." [NRS/13] "It is a Rose of singularly dirty habits, attracting every vile form of blight and caterpillar." [K1] "The writer, Mr. W.R. Belknap, roundly states himself to be William Allen Richardson's

nephew. He continues:—'William Allen Richardson was born in New Orleans, La., on Feb. 20, 1819. When he was but two years old his father moved to Lexington, Ky., where he resided until his death, in October, 1892...[M]uch interested in the cultivation and propagation of Roses. He imported a good many, and in this way became acquainted by correspondence with Madame Ducher." [NRS/10] "Indefinable individuality." [Hk] "Popular all over the world." [H]

Wootton, Climbing (Butler/Craig, ca. 1897) syn., 'Souvenir of Wootton, Climbing"
Hybrid Tea
Sport of 'Souvenir of Wootton' (HT).
"Bright magenta red." [CA97] "Flower rosy crimson, full, cup-shaped, fair to good form; strong, enduring fragrance. The medium to large flowers come singly and in small clusters and last three to four days. Fine foliage. Very vigorous grower. Averages 300 to 500 blooms per season; most in spring, a few in summer and autumn. Suitable for arches and pillars. Very hardy." [ARA21/93] "I have a plant in my garden which has stood the test of fifteen winters and a very changeable climate without loss of any kind. It is situated in an open spot subject to all the elements except a direct northern wind. It is a strong, vigorous climber, on an arch eight feet high [ca. 2.6 m] with a span of four feet [ca. 1.3 m], growing way beyond this distance if allowed. The strong canes are produced annually from the base right through the season, these branching at different distances from the bottom. The canes bountifully produce fragrant, large, fine looking buds, opening into double, cup-shaped flowers of fair to good form, coming singly and in clusters of two to eight, on stems, some short but most from long to extra long, making them fine for cutting as well as garden decoration. In the spring of 1917 and 1918 the plant showed by actual count over 500 buds and flowers. There is a heavy crop in spring always, and almost as many flowers in the fall (but at this time variable), with a scattering of blooms through the summer. The

color ranges from deep pink to a rosy crimson, deeper in cool weather and the fall, the lighter flowers being produced in the shade of the foliage, which is large, luxuriant, healthy and lasting, remaining on the plant till heavy frosts appear." [ARA19/126] "Entirely new [*in 1898*] and believed one of the best and most beautiful ever-blooming climbing roses yet produced. Pure, rich velvety red, fully equal to Jacqueminot in color; delightfully sweet, and a most constant and profuse bloomer, every shoot producing a bud; extra large fully double flowers, frequently over 6 inches across [ca. 1.5 dm]. A vigorous grower and quite hardy; a real treasure; for partially sheltered places." [C&Js98] "One of the best of the climbing Hybrid Tea sports." [Th]

Yellow Cécile Brunner, Climbing
Listed as 'Perle d'Or, Climbing'.

Zéphirine Drouhin
Listed in the chapter on Bourbons.

Chapter Nine

Early Polyanthas

"In February 1869, I [*Guillot fils*] sowed a great quantity of seed which I had harvested from the variety 'Polyantha', a Multiflora variety originating in Japan which was very much a climber, and non-remontant, having a quite small single white blossom much like that of a bramble or strawberry, and blooming in panicles. Among the many seedlings, there were many which, in their wood and foliage, resembled multifloras and Noisettes. Quite a few bore flowers of moderate quality, singles, semi-doubles, and full blossoms, with petals as large as the roses of our gardens, and with a variety of colors: yellow, white, bright pink, etc. I didn't have so many as two which resembled their mother! Among the seedlings which didn't bloom until the second or third year there was found one which had blossoms with two rows of petals, an inch to an inch and a half across [to ca. 3.75 cm], not remontant as the others were, but which gave me wonderful seeds which I sowed in February, 1872. Out of this came my dear little 'Pâquerette', which I put into commerce in November, 1875." [JR2/137-138] One sees a certain amount of speculation that China cultivars supposedly in the proximity of Guillot's *R. multiflora* 'Polyantha' played a paternal role in the generation of these first Polyanthas. The nature and range of variation evident in the "many seedlings" mentioned in Guillot's account would certainly lend an air of plausibility to this speculation—*but* seedlings of a similar nature and range of variation were also produced independently by other specimens of *R. multiflora* 'Polyantha', most notably that owned by Guillot's fellow Lyonnais breeder Rambaux (see our Appendix Four). It thus seems probable that the similar *R. chinensis* characteristics manifested in these two separate crops of seedlings from different specimens—seedlings which in the aggregate seem to be of the nature of an F2 generation rather than an F1—were due to *R. chinensis*-like genes inherent in *R. multiflora* 'Polyantha', in which flowers having a yellowish tint and a tea-like perfume further hint at a hybrid Oriental background.

We learn from *Les Amis des Roses* (no. 243) that the Polyanthas did not really surpass 'Hermosa' and the various Chinas as most-favored bedding roses until Ernest Levavasseur had released 'Mme. Norbert Levavasseur', 'Maman Levavasseur', 'Triomphe Orléanais', and 'Orléans-Rose', which, with their progeny, also in large part replaced the older Polyanthas.

"The growth on most varieties is quite compact, but the foliage varies greatly, some kinds being extremely susceptible to mildew. The flowers usually come in sprays, trusses, or corymbs, each individual blossom being of small to very small size. With a few exceptions, the class may be divided into two distinct types, one of which is either semi-double or double, with short, flat buds that open into shallow, cupped flowers, generally coming in large clusters. The other division produces a perfect miniature rose, beautifully formed, with a long, spiral bud and a lovely half-open flower, which is very attractive even when fully matured, this type being usually produced in small sprays, but occasionally singly. Neither of these types balls, but the flat forms often discolor very badly." [Th2] "The little Polyanthas rise to the occasion. The little tree-like bushes are well-clothed with delicate foliage, and the way they bloom is to send up stiff, straight stems with panicles of tiny roses by dozens, each tall stem holding up its ready-made bouquet. The fascination of the true Polyantha roses is very much that each perfectly formed double rose is not beyond the circumference of a silver dime, and the little buds seem like something Nature might have made for fun." [Dr]

Polyanthas generally only require the removal of crossed, dead, or dying branches, resenting the heavy-handed approach with the shears. Occasionally unusually vigorous canes shoot up which destroy the symmetry of the bush. These should be pruned back just beneath the inflorescence *after* they have bloomed, as it is senseless to sacrifice the immense clusters to which such shoots give rise simply to maintain a strict—and unnatural—neatness. Further information on the parent of this class, *R. multiflora* 'Polyantha', will be found in Appendix Four, as well as in *The Old Rose Adventurer*. This group has persevered into modern times; we list all extant or important varieties introduced prior to 1920, and glance very quickly at many of the more modern ones.

Abondant (Turbat, 1914) trans., "Abundant"
"Pink, medium-sized, full, dwarf." [Sn]

Alberich (De Ruiter, 1954) syn., 'Happy'
Red. As with the others in the "7 Dwarfs" series ('Bashful'/'Giesebrecht', 'Doc'/'Degenhard', 'Dopey'/'Eberwein', 'Grumpy'/'Burkhard', 'Sleepy'/'Balduin', and 'Sneezy'/'Bertram', and perhaps 'Snow White'/'Sneprinsess'), we give preference to the European name of the European introduction.

[**Amélie-Suzanne Morin**] (Soupert & Notting, 1898)
From 'Clotilde Soupert' (Pol) × 'Léonie Osterrieth' (T).
"Vigorous and compact bush, beautiful foliage, flower of medium size, admirably imbricated; color, pure white with a yellow glow; blooms in large erect corymbs. Very remarkable variety due to its great floriferousness...A magnificent pendant to 'Clotilde Soupert'. Very fragrant." [JR22/147]

Ännchen Müller (Schmidt, 1906)
From 'Turner's Crimson Rambler' (Multiflora) × 'Georges Pernet' (Pol).
"Dark pink." [Ÿ] "The blossoms are a fascinating shade of deep rose with petals curled and twisted, producing a fluffy effect. Its hardiness, vigorous habit of growth, with healthy, rich green foliage, all commend it to the careful buyer. 'A magnificent bedding variety, and very persistent in holding its flowers.'" [C&Js10] "Rigid branches to a meter [yard] in height, growth much like that of 'Mme. Norbert Levavasseur'. Very abundant bloom, particularly in June when it gives pretty and effective red blossoms." [JR30/182-183]

Anne Marie de Montravel (Widow Rambaux & Dubreuil, 1879) syn., 'Anna Maria de Montravel'
From 'Polyantha Alba Plena Sarmentosa' (Multiflora) × 'Mme. de Tartas' (T).
"Pure white, small, full and imbricated; produced in clusters and in extraordinary quantities. One of the best." [P1] "Dwarf, to about 12 or 15 inches [ca. 3-4 dm], well-branched, and the greater number of the branches bear flower clusters, distinctive in that the flower stems carry the blossoms well above the foliage, bearing a great quantity of blooms. I have counted 65 on the same stem, which seems quite extraordinary to me. The blossoms are pure white, and last well. They are about an inch and a quarter [ca. 3 cm] in diameter, very full, and of the 'expanded' form—a worthy

relative of the pretty 'Pâquerette'." [JR3/153] "Gives a particular scent of rose and lily-of-the-valley." [JR3/166] "Foliage very plentiful, holds well, black-spots slightly; bloom profuse last two and a half weeks in June, few in July." [ARA18/129] "The flowers are very large, but quite irregular in form, sometimes open, but when only half open much more beautiful." [JR7/15] "Flowers flat, very well formed, large to 2 inches [ca. 5 cm], pure white, large petals, imbricated, spread out, sometimes showing a few stamens. Very remontant and ornamental." [JR9/7] "Best of the white Pompons." [J] "Lovely '[Mlle.] Cécile Brunner' form. Very small growth. Not as continuous as rest of class." [Th2] "Slightly sprawly plant but fairly dense...globular flowers...in profusion...2×3 [ft; ca. 6.6×10 dm]." [B]

Apfelblüte (Wirtz & Eicke, 1907) trans., "Appleblossom"
Seedling of 'Mme. Norbert Levavasseur' (Pol).
"Light pink, small, full, medium scent, dwarf." [Sn]

[**Archiduchesse Elisabeth-Marie**] (Soupert & Notting, 1898)
From 'Mignonette' (Pol) × 'Luciole' (T).
"Vigorous bush, beautiful foliage, flower medium-sized, full, imbricated, blooming in corymbs, bud of a beautiful chrome yellow, the flower of a pure silky yellow, the center bright Naples yellow, passing to pure white. Very fragrant and floriferous. Very good variety for beds and pot-culture. Novel coloration among the Polyantha roses." [JR22/20]

Baby Alberic (Chaplin Bros., 1932)
"Bud yellow; flower double, creamy white. Vigorous; perpetual bloomer." [ARA33/171]

Baby Doll
Listed as 'Tip-Top'.

Baby Faurax (Lille, 1924)
"Violet-purple with slate tones…to 2 [ft; ca. 6.6 dm]." [HRG] "Bud small; flower small, double, sweet fragrance, violet-blue, borne in large clusters. Growth dwarf (12 to 15 inches [ca. 3-3.75 dm])." [ARA27/222] "Dark amethyst…small, very double, and fragrant…The plant…stumpy and rather ugly…an interesting curiosity." [Hk]

Baby Herriot
Listed as 'Étoile Luisante'.

Baby Tausendschön
Listed as 'Echo'.

Baptiste Lafaye (Puyravaud, 1909)
"Flower pale currant red, lined white, fading to pink, well formed, like a daisy, large for the sort, full, abundant bloom, in a cluster; very vigorous bush for the center of the bed with 'Mme. Norbert Levavasseur', good for pot culture, very vigorous on its own roots, foliage dark green, thorns large and not very numerous. Dedicated to a horticulturist from Coutras (Gironde)." [JR33/152]

Balduin (De Ruiter, 1955) syn., 'Sleepy'
From an unnamed seedling (resulting from crossing the Polyantha 'Orange Triumph' with the Pernetiana HT 'Golden Rapture') × "a Polyantha seedling."
Pink. Not to be confused with the Hybrid Tea of the same name.

Bashful
Listed as 'Giesebrecht'.

[**Bellina Guillot**] (Widow Schwartz, 1889)
"Vigorous bush, flowers numerous in a corymb, well-filled, medium in size, of a greenish white; the buds are entirely covered by yellowish green sepals which are long and lacinate; freely remontant." [JR13/163]

Bertram (De Ruiter, 1955) syn., 'Sneezy'
Deep pink.

Betsy van Nes (Van Ryn/Münch & Haufe, 1914)
Sport of 'Mrs. W.H. Cutbush' (Pol).
"Pure bright red; flowers unusually large and double for this class. Does not fade or mildew." [C&Js15] "Small, semi-double, in clusters, short stems. Foliage fair, sparse. Growth weak; hardy. Light red which fades badly." [ARA23/156]

Bloomfield Abundance (Capt. Thomas, 1920)
From 'Sylvia' (Wichuraiana) × 'Dorothy Page-Roberts' (HT).
"A dwarf Wichuraiana, 'Sylvia', crossed with the Hybrid Tea 'Dorothy Page-Roberts', gave 'Bloomfield Abundance'...the stem, the flower-form, and the number of blooms of the stem were those of 'Sylvia'; the color, fragrance, and blooming continuity were the same as those of 'Dorothy Page-Roberts'." [ARA31/34] "Flowers double, salmon-pink, produced singly and in sprays. Foliage glossy, dark green, not susceptible to mildew. Grows 3 to 6 feet high [ca. 1-2 m], bushy. Similar to '[Mlle.] Cécile Brunner', with flowers larger and more full in bud, and darker in color." [ARA24/94] "A failure [*in Massachusetts*], producing very few flowers and giving no second crop." [ARA22/43] "Blooms constantly from June to heavy frost." [ARA20/36] "Lacks substance." [ARA25/105] "Vigorous." [B] "A low hedge rose, or, if not cut back, a five to six foot [ca. 1.6-2 m] pillar rose...blooms in sprays...it is double and lasting...foliage nearly perfect, dark green varnished. A dainty little rose." [Th]

Border King (De Ruiter, 1952)
Red.

Bordure (Barbier, 1911) trans., "Edging"
Seedling of 'Universal Favorite' (Wichuraiana).
"Completely dwarf, not about 3 dm high [ca. 1 foot], with stocky growth. Covered all season long with cascades of blossoms to the point of obscuring the foliage. Flowers 3-5 cm across –ca. 1-2 inches], double, well formed, pure carmine. Bud bright carmine. The color doesn't fade in the sun, and in the clusters of 25-50 flowers, a person can't make out any difference between old blossoms and those newly opened. Magnificent plant for borders and pot culture. Dwarfer than 'Mme. Norbert Levavasseur'." [JR36/10] "Low-growing, moderate; foliage very plentiful till late summer, when it black-spots, causing it to become sparse; bloom abundant till September then moderate, continuous." [ARA18/128]

Bouquet Blanc (Corrard/Vigneron, 1914) trans., "White Bouquet"
"Dwarf bush, pretty vigorous, early blooming. Blossom medium-sized, full, very fragrant; color, pure white with some sulphur towards the middle. Good for pot culture." [JR38/72]

Bouquet de Neige (Vilin, 1899) trans., "Bouquet of Snow"
"Growth dwarf, very hardy, handsome foliage, flower very bright white, medium size for the sort, pretty double, very pretty form; blooms abundantly in clusters of 20-30 blossoms on each stem. Very pretty." [JR24/2]

Burkhard (De Ruiter, 1956) syn., 'Grumpy'
Pink.

Caid (Delforge, 1971)
From 'Orangeade' (Floribunda) × a seedling.
Orange.

Cameo (De Ruiter, 1932)
Sport of 'Orléans-Rose' (Pol).
"Bud ovoid, salmon-pink; flower small, semi-double, cupped, very lasting; slightly fragrant...turning to shell-pink, in cluster...15 to 18 inches high [ca. 3.75-4.25 dm]; profuse bloomer." [ARA32/220-221] "A peculiar mixture of salmon, coral, and orange." [ARA35/134] "Its much softer color makes it easier to handle in the garden than either 'Paul Crampel' or 'Golden Salmon'." [ARA35/174] "[*One gardener*] likes the way it drops its dead petals." [ARA36/176] "Very worth-while." [ARA37/210]

Casque d'Or (Delbard, 1979) trans., "Cask of Gold"
From a seedling (resulting from crossing the Floribunda 'Zambra' with the Floribunda 'Jean de la Lune') × a seedling (resulting from crossing the HT 'Michèle Meilland' with the HT 'Tahiti').
Gold.

Cécile Brunner
Listed as 'Mlle. Cécile Brunner'.

Charles Métroz (Widow Schwartz, 1900)
"Delicate pink bordered light pink." [Ÿ] "Foliage bright green, as if varnished; flower small, well formed, China pink tinted salmon pink and carmine." [JR24/164]

Chatillon Rose (Nonin, 1923)
From 'Orléans-Rose' (Pol) × an unnamed seedling.
"A light cerise-pink with white center, semi-double and very lasting." [ARA25/102] "Silvery crimson, shading to white...grows in large bunches. Very attractive." [ARA25/121] "The prettiest truly pink of its class, providing, without stopping, enormous thyrses of flowers, semi-double, large, and of long duration." [ARA26/175] "Large clusters of sparkling pink...tinged with bronze." [ARA29/97] "Bud small, long-pointed; flower

medium-size, semi-double…very lasting…slight fragrance. Foliage disease-resistant. Very vigorous, bushy, 1 to 2 feet high [ca. 3-6 dm]; profuse and continuous bloomer." [ARA24/172] "Never out of bloom all summer, never had black-spot." [ARA31/118] "Fades brown in great heat; ten to twelve petals; comes in corymbs, about a hundred blooms in a corymb; does not shatter easily…Stems strong. Vigorous grower; continuous bloomer. A remarkable novelty." [Th2]

China Doll (Lammerts, 1946)
From 'Mrs. Dudley Fulton' (Pol) × 'Tom Thumb' (Min).
"Light pink, yellow base, small…1.2-2 inches [3-5 cm], double, some scent, many in clusters together, abundant; growth strong, dwarf…14 inches [ca. 3.5 dm], branched; foliage coarse." [Kr] A '**Weeping China Doll**', evidently a sport of 'China Doll', of unknown provenance, is also to be found.

Cineraria (Lambert, 1909)
"Light red, white in the center, small, single, dwarf." [Sn] Not to be confused with Leenders' semidouble Polyantha of 1934 of the same name.

[**Clara Pfitzer**] (Soupert & Notting, 1888)
From 'Mignonette' (Pol) × 'Marquise de Vivens' (T).
"Bright carmine, fairly big. Rounded bush, grows tall." [Ck] "Dwarf bush; flower small, imbricated; color, light carmine iced and marbled on a silvery white ground. Excellent variety, very floriferous and *fragrant.*" [JR12/55]

Clotilde Soupert (Soupert & Notting, 1889) syn., 'Mme. Hardy du Thé', 'Mme. Melon du Thé'
From 'Mignonette' (Pol) × 'Mme. Damaizin' (T).
"Vigorous, upright, about 1.5 feet high [ca. 4.5 dm], handsome mid-green foliage, healthy. Flower large, very full, magnificently imbricated…exterior

of petals, pearly white; center, lake-pink tinted soft Paris red...bears on the same plant both pink and white blossoms...very floriferous and fragrant." [JR12/147] "The flower is held upright, slightly inclined when fully open...blooms pretty continuously." [JR13/41] "Fairly good in autumn." [Hn] "Too lazy to...open her buds properly...dropsical yet constricted blossoms that blighted instead of bloomed." [ARA2-/16] "Flowers large for its class, but of perfect shape; outer petals white, centres rosy; full and imbricated. Liable to vary, but at all times a most beautiful kind." [P1] "Too unsightly after blooming." [ARA25/105] "Continuous bloom. Shiny light green foliage." [Lg] "The flower changes color beautifully depending upon its exposure to the air, going from a darker pink to pure white...In dampness, the flowers open with difficulty if at all, and in rainy areas it is certainly better to cultivate it under glass." [JR23/38] "The petals are lovely little shells, closely compacted together, forming an indescribably beautiful rose." [Dr]

Colibri (Lille, 1898)
"Buds coppery yellow; flowers medium, full, well formed, white tinted coppery yellow fading to pure white. Growth vigorous; blooms in clusters, producing a most charming effect by the contrast of the yellow buds and white blossoms." [JR22/166]

[**Comtesse Antoinette d'Oultremont**] (Soupert & Notting, 1899)
From 'Mignonette' (Pol) × 'Luciole' (T).
"Vigorous and compact bush, beautiful foliage, bud magnificent in form; flower medium-sized, imbricated, blooming in erect corymbs; color, pure white, silky yellow center. Very floriferous with a strong Stocks scent. Magnificent variety for forcing and bedding." [JR23/170]

Coral Cluster (Murrell, 1920)
Sport of 'Orléans-Rose' (Pol).

"An entrancing soft coral." [ARA25/103] "Pale coral-pink, rather a new color, and comes in fairly large trusses; fades in great heat. More susceptible to black-spot than most...Vigorous grower." [Th2] "It resembles [*'Orléans-Rose'*] in every way except color." [ARA21/153] "Semi-double...slight fragrance...bushy...2×2 [ft; ca. 6×6 dm]." [B]

Coronet (W. Paul, 1912)
"Yellow tinted pink...very beautiful. Very floriferous, quite distinct." [JR36/103] Not to be confused with the Dingee-Conard HT of 1897 of the same name, which was silvery carnation pink.

Corrie Koster (W. Paul, 1923)
Sport of the pale salmon Polyantha 'Juliana-Roos' (den Ouden, 1921), which was itself a sport of 'Orléans-Rose' (Pol).
"Coral red and salmon yellow." [Ÿ]

Cyclope (Dubreuil, 1909) trans., "Cyclops"
Seedling of 'Mme. Norbert Levavasseur' (Pol).
"Dwarf, blooming in clusters of ten to twenty flowers, which are small, and of a bizarre coloration: velvety carmine purple, lined white, with pale yellow stamens forming an eye in the center of the blossom, giving it the look of a garden primrose. Very hardy and remontant; does not lose its leaves." [JR33/169]

Degenhard (De Ruiter, 1954) syn., 'Doc'
From 'Robin Hood' (Hybrid Musk) × "a Polyantha seedling."
Pink.

Denise Cassegrain (Grandes Roseraies, 1922)
"White." [Ÿ]

Diamant (Robichon, 1908) trans., "Diamond"
Seedling of 'Marie Pavic' (Pol).
"Bush vigorous, foliage small, flowers fringed and ruffled like a carnation, clusters of 6-12, large for the sort, very full; petals lustrous sulphur white, water-green reflections; bud conical; almond scent." [JR32/152-153]

Dick Koster (Koster, 1929)
Sport of 'Anneke Koster' (Pol), the lineage at length tracing back to 'Tausendschön' (Multiflora).
"Orange-red, dwarf, and compact, suitable for low hedges and for forcing in pots." [ARA37/196] "Flower large, bright salmon-rose to orange, in cluster. Vigorous; free-flowering all season." [ARA37/268]

Doc
Listed as 'Degenhard'.

Dopey
Listed as 'Eberwein'.

Dr. Raimont
Listed as 'Dr. Reymont'.

[**Dr. Reymont**] (Alégatière, 1888) syn., 'Dr. Raimont'
From 'Général Jacqueminot' (HP) × a Polyantha.
"Extra-reblooming bush, canes bronzy green, thorns numerous, foliage of 3-5 dark green leaflets; blossom of medium size, full, always opening well, color crimson red at first, passing then to violety pink, darker at the center." [JR12/165]

Dr. Ricaud (Corbœuf-Marsault, 1907)
Seedling of 'Little White Pet' (Pol).

"Salmony flesh on a ground of copper." [Ÿ] "Vigorous, bushy, 12-15 inches in height [ca. 3-4 dm]. Blooms profusely from May to October…blooms in clusters, large blossoms for the class, well formed, fragrant. Color, light pink on a light sulphur ground, center nuanced coppery, fading after opening." [JR31/38]

Eberwein (De Ruiter,1954) syn., 'Dopey'
From 'Robin Hood' (Hybrid Musk) × "a Polyantha seedling."
Crimson.

Éblouissante (Turbat, 1918) trans., "Dazzling"
From 'Bengale Rose' (presumably 'Parsons' Pink China') × 'Cramoisi Supérieur' (Ch).
"The best red dwarf perpetual Polyantha. Flowers of good size, in bouquets of ten to twenty, in color similar to 'Cramoisi Supérieur' and 'Fabvier', with the advantage that they are produced on a true dwarf perpetual Polyantha. They last a long time without fading or turning violet, and when fully open take a cactus form. Wood and foliage purplish green. Erect grower…shapely bud." [ARA19/101] "Quilled flowers of gleaming dark crimson." [ARA29/97] "Brilliant deep velvety red—holds color well; small clusters. Bushy growth. Very good foliage." [Th2] A China in ancestry, a Polyantha in use.

Echo (Ludorf/Lambert, 1914) syn., 'Baby Tausendschön'
Sport of 'Tausendschön' (Multiflora).
"Dwarf, or nearly so—about two feet high [ca. 6 dm]—vigorous, hardy, erect thornless branches, handsome foliage. Blooms in bouquets which are quite large and fairly flat—perhaps a foot in diameter [ca. 3 dm]—on firm and upright stems. The blossoms are fairly large, full, pink and white mottled, much like 'Tausendschön'. Blooms June to November…the flower lasts eight days in water." [JR38/75] "Fairly wide blooms with the outer petals curving up to make a bowl-shaped flower." [Hk] "A free bloomer,

remaining in flower throughout the season." [ARA18/133] "Foliage mildews. Continuous bloomer. Vigorous grower for this class. Discolors badly in California." [Th2]

Eileen Loow (Levavasseur, 1910)
From 'Mme. Norbert Levavasseur' (Pol) × 'Orléans-Rose' (Pol).
"Vigorous bush, foliage glossy green, as abundant as that of 'Orléans-Rose'; color, China pink, grading to cream at the base of the petals." [JR34/167]

Elise Kreis
Listed as 'Frau Elise Kreis'.

Ellen Poulsen (Poulsen, 1911)
From 'Mme. Norbert Levavasseur' (Pol) × 'Dorothy Perkins' (Wichuraiana).
"Dark brilliant pink." [ARA16/20] "Large, full; sweet-scented; vigorous, bushy habit, most floriferous; very fine." [C&Js16] "Medium height, moderate [*growth*]; foliage very plentiful till midsummer, then sufficient, black-spots somewhat; bloom moderate, continuous." [ARA18/128] "Sweet-scented." [Bk] "Doesn't grow more than perhaps two feet high [ca. 6 dm]; it blooms all Summer, giving large bouquets of quite full blossoms...of a pretty carnation pink with light yellow at the base of the petal. The growth is vigorous; the leaves are dark green and shiny, resembling those of the Wichuraianas." [JR36/40] "Mildew and black-spot resistant...always so fresh and clean." [ARA24/94]

Erna Teschendorff (Teschendorff, 1911)
Sport of 'Mme. Norbert Levavasseur' (Pol).
"Deep red flowers in clusters. Medium growth." [Th2] "Low-growing, vigorous; foliage very abundant till late summer, mildews most of season, black-spots in late summer; bloom free, continuous." [ARA18/128]

"Born three years ago as a sport of 'Mme. Norbert Levavasseur', has been watched all this time with much attention; and I am able to state that it has all the growth, bloom, and hardiness of its mother. The umbel of flowers is much the same as that of Levavasseur; the blossoms, too, are much the same size, but they are fuller and the incurved petals, which are an intense, deep carmine red, closely resemble those of 'Gruss an Teplitz'. The great benefit of this variety is that the flowers last a very long time, and without fading. Cut stems have lasted, still fresh, for more than eight days, without showing even the least change in color." [JR34/140]

Étoile de Mai (Gamon, 1892) trans., "May Star"
"Blooms in fine yellow buds, clusters quite full and double, orange passing to pale canary yellow when open." [C&Js02] "Dwarf, vigorous, blooming abundantly, producing a seductive effect as the pretty buds expand, starting as they do nankeen yellow, and finishing up yellowish white. The blossoms always open well, are small, but very fragrant." [JR26/88-89] "Flowers large for this class." [JR17/166] "Sulphury white, flower small, full, very fragrant, very floriferous, vigorous." [Cx] "Unusually profuse." [Dr]

Étoile Luisante (Turbat, 1918) syn., 'Baby Herriot'; trans., "Shining Star"
"Long, pointed, vermilion-red buds; flowers in long, pyramidal corymbs of forty to fifty, scarlet-red and bright shrimp-rose, with coppery red reflexes; golden yellow aiglets. Wood and leaves clear green. Dwarf; vigorous grower." [ARA19/101] "Orange-red bud, opening coral and carmine, base golden yellow, much on the order of 'Mme. Édouard Herriot'. '[Mlle] Cécile Brunner' form. Doing well in California and well worthy of trial." [Th2]

[**Eugénie Lamesch**] (Lambert, 1899)
From 'Aglaia' (Lambertiana) × 'William Allen Richardson' (N).

"An exquisite Rose, orange-yellow, passing to clear yellow, heavily shaded with rose." [C&Js21] "Dwarf bushy plant, very vigorous and hardy; foliage bright green, medium sized; thorns rare but strong. The medium-sized flowers appear in a bunch of 5-30 in large but closely-packed corymbs; the dormant buds open very easily...Color, pure bright ochre yellow passing to light yellow shaded pink. Beautiful, very regular form, cupped. Bud coppery yellow/red; quite full. Very fine perfume, smelling like a Pippin." [JR23/171]

Eva Teschendorff (Grünewald/Teschendorff, 1923)
Sport of 'Echo' (Pol).
"The best [*white Polyantha*] we have today...a greenish white color. The blooms are not spoiled by rain...the plant is healthy and blooms freely." [ARA25/137] "Bud small, long-pointed; flower medium-size, double, very lasting, slight fragrance, greenish white (like 'Kaiserin Auguste Viktoria'), borne in clusters on long, strong stems. Foliage small, abundant, light green, glossy, disease-resistant. Thornless. Very vigorous, bushy habit (15 to 20 inches [ca. 4-5 dm]; abundant; intermittent bloomer in June and July and September and October. Tips freeze." [ARA25/190]

Evaline (Prosser, 1920)
From 'Orléans-Rose' (Pol) × 'Rayon d'Or' (Pernetiana).
"Light pink, edged bright pink, small, full, petals rolled; in clusters, fragrance 6 [*on a scale of 10*], constant, growth 6 [*on a scale of 10*], bushy." [Jg]

Evelyn Thornton (Bees, 1919)
From 'Léonie Lamesch' (Pol) × 'Mrs. W.H. Cutbush' (Pol).
"Bud medium size; flower medium size, full, double, open form, borne in clusters on medium-length stems; very lasting; fragrant. Color shell-pink, deepening to salmon and lemon with orange shading. Foliage abundant, large, leathery, glossy, dark, bronzy green; disease-resistant. Vigorous grower of bushy habit; blooms profusely all season." [ARA20/127] "A free

growing little Polyantha Rose, of dwarf and bushy habit. The blooms are of a soft pink colour, with a golden glow at the base of the petals, the golden stamens making the blooms very attractive. Perpetual flowering." [NRS20/150]

Excellens (Levavasseur, 1913) syn., 'Excelsior'
"Bush vigorous, hardy, blooming in clusters; the wood is nearly thornless. Color, Nilson pink washed white, petals' edges cochineal carmine; considered altogether, making a blossom which appears delicate pink washed white when fully open." [JR37/119]

Excelsior
Listed as 'Excellens'.

Fairy Changeling (Harkness, 1979)
From 'The Fairy' (Pol) × 'Yesterday' (Floribunda).
Pink.

Fairy Damsel (Harkness, 1981)
From 'The Fairy' (Pol) × 'Yesterday' (Floribunda).
"Dense, spreading, well-foliaged shoots...deep red, semi-double flowers...2×5 [ft; ca. 6×15 dm]." [B]

Fairy Maid (Harkness, 1979)
From 'The Fairy' (Pol) × 'Yesterday' (Floribunda).
Pink.

Fairy Prince (Harkness, 1979)
From 'The Fairy' (Pol) × 'Yesterday' (Floribunda).
Red.

Fairy Ring (Harkness, ca. 1980)
From 'The Fairy' (Pol) × 'Yesterday' (Floribunda).
Rose-pink.

Fairyland (Harkness, 1979)
From 'The Fairy' (Pol) × 'Yesterday' (Floribunda).
Pink. "2×5 [ft,] 60 cm × 1.5 m." [B]

Fireglow (Wezelenburg, 1929)
Sport of 'Orange King' (Pol).
"Bud small, ovoid; flower medium size, single, open, very lasting, slightly fragrant, brilliant vermilion-red, shaded orange, borne in cluster on short stem. Foliage sufficient, medium size, rich green, glossy. Growth moderate (15 inches [ca. 3.75 dm]), dwarf, compact; abundant bloomer all season. Very hardy." [ARA31/239]

Flamboyant (Turbat, 1931)
"Flower large, double, bright scarlet, passing to crimson-carmine which does not blue, in cluster of 10 to 20. Foliage glossy, serrated. Dwarf." [ARA]

Flocon de Neige (Lille, 1897) trans., "Snowflake"
"Flowers small, full, very well formed, pure white. Bush dwarf, bearing clusters of flowers, and very floriferous." [JR22/166] Not to be confused with the Knapper/Blanc Polyantha 'Snowflake' of 1900.

[**Flora**] (Widow Schwartz, 1888)
"Bush with foliage of a light green; flowers full, large for the sort, arranged in large corymbs, opening very easily, color cream white passing to pure white, fragrant. Vigorous plant, remontant, good for borders." [JR12/163]

Floribunda (Dubreuil, 1885)
"Flowers pale rose color, medium size, very double and fragrant, and borne in large clusters; constant bloomer." [CA90] "Growth bushy with vigorous shoots topped by large clusters of 30-50 blossoms; buds ovoid; flowers very double, expanding well; petals striped with very fresh pink and lilac. This variety has the stature and bloom of the charming variety 'Anne Marie de Montravel', from which it differs only in the shading of the blossoms." [JR9/167]

Frau Alexander Weiss (Lambert, 1909)
From 'Petite Léonie' (Pol) × *R. fœtida* 'Bicolor'.
"Yellowish pink, small, full, dwarf." [Sn]

Frau Anna Pasquay (Walter, 1909)
From 'Trier' (Lambertiana) × 'Mme. Norbert Levavasseur' (Pol).
"Deep pink, small, full, dwarf." [Sn]

Frau Cecilie Walter (Lambert, 1904)
From 'Aglaia' (Lambertiana) × 'Kleiner Alfred' (Pol).
"Light yellow, small, full, very fragrant, dwarf." [Sn]

Frau Elise Kreis (Widow Kreis, 1913)
Seedling or sport of 'Ännchen Müller' (Pol).
"The form of the blossom is the same [*as that of 'Ännchen Müller'*], but the color is bright carmine, which it holds throughout bloom. 'Frau Elise Kreis' grows 4-5 dm high [ca. 20 inches], is elegantly branched, and blooms without interruption from June till Fall. The blossoms are about 5 cm across [ca. 2 inches], and grow in large clusters. Due to its great floriferousness, this introduction may be used along or in a group." [JR38/30]

Frau Oberhofgärtner Schultze (Lambert, 1909)
From 'Euphrosine' (Lambertiana) × 'Mrs. W.J. Grant' (HT).

"Deep pink, small, full, dwarf." [Sn]

Frau Rudolf Schmidt (Schmidt, 1919)
Sport of 'Jessie' (Pol).
"Dark red, small, not very full, dwarf." [Sn]

Gabrielle Privat (Barthélemy-Privat, 1931)
"Brilliant carmine-pink." [ARA33/174]

George Elger (Turbat, 1912)
"A dainty yellow." [ARA24/94] "Deepest and most lasting yellow of the class; lovely '[Mlle.] Cécile Brunner' form. Very continuous bloomer. Medium growth." [Th2] "[*Listed as giving between 100 and 200 blossoms annually*]." [ARA20/84] "Singly and in small sprays, double, fine form, small, Tea fragrance...fine foliage, plentiful." [ARA23/162] "Very floriferous, growth erect, wood smooth, reddish green, foliage dark green, glossy above, reddish brown beneath, blooms in large clusters, coppery golden yellow changing to light yellow at expansion, buds golden yellow. The yellowest reblooming Polyantha. Could be called a dwarf 'W[illiam] A[llen] Richardson'." [JR36/183]

Georges Pernet (Pernet-Ducher, 1887)
Seedling of 'Mignonette' (Pol).
"Flowers bright rosy pink, medium size with petals beautifully rayed and reflexed; very fragrant and beautiful." [C&Js98] "Growth very dwarf, making a compact bush, good for border work or pots, blooming constantly and abundantly; blossom large for the class, graceful in form, very bright pink nuanced yellow, fading to peach pink nuanced white." [JR11/164]

Giesebrecht (De Ruiter, 1955) syn., 'Bashful'
"Single, red with a white eye." [Hk]

Gloire d'Orléans (Levavasseur, 1912) trans., "Orléans Glory"
"Vigorous bush, with strong, erect canes. Foliage dark green; blooms in terminal panicles which are numerous; color, very dark red. It is, when all is said and done, 'Mme. Norbert Levavasseur', but with a much redder blossom having the great advantage of not bluing." [JR36/153]

[**Gloire de Charpennes**] (Lille, 1897) trans., "Charpennes Glory"
"Blossoms small, full, well-formed, varying from purplish pink to bluish purple-red. Growth dwarf, blooming in tight clusters, very floriferous, the plant looking like a ball of bloom." [JR22/166]

[**Gloire des Polyantha**] (Guillot & fils, 1887) trans., "Polyantha Glory"
Seedling of 'Mignonette' (Pol).
"Growth dwarf; flower small, from 2-3 cm in diameter [ca. 1 inch], full, very well formed, petals imbricated; color, bright pink on a white ground; the middle of each petal is often striped deep pink or red; bloom very abundant, in a panicle of 60-80 blossoms, forming a striking bouquet." [JR11/149] "Lovely little roses, somewhat cup-shaped, color salmon rose flamed with carmine, blooms in clusters." [C&Js02]

Gloire du Midi (De Ruiter, 1932) trans., "Glory of *le Midi*"
Sport of 'Gloria Mundi' (Pol).
Orange-red. "Like 'Gloria Mundi', but keeps color outside." [ARA33/178]

Gloria Mundi (Sliedrecht/De Ruiter, 1929) trans., "World's Glory"
Sport of 'Superb' (Pol).
"Neat, full, well-formed flowers of the most brilliant scarlet-orange color imaginable, said to be unfading." [ARA29/227] "Flower large for the class, fully double, very lasting...orange-scarlet, borne in clusters. Foliage abundant, medium size, light green, glossy. Growth vigorous, upright,

bushy; free, intermittent bloomer for ten weeks, from July to September." [ARA30/228] "Has a more double flower than 'Golden Salmon', and a faster color." [ARA32/128] "It is good but nothing to rave about...the color is harsh and ugly at its best and it turns just as blue as any of them." [ARA32/185] "It is oak-hardy." [C-Pf33] "2×2 [ft; ca. 6×6 dm]." [B]

Golden Fairy (Bennett, 1889)
"Flower bright fawn-yellow with lighter edges. Growth moderate." [GeH] "This Polyantha which was bred by the late Bennett certainly couldn't be compared with 'Gloire des Polyantha' as a decorative plant; but the form is so perfect and the blossoms so full that it deserves to be much more often grown than it is at present. It's quite an exaggeration to say that this rose is golden: The open flower is pure white with a light touch of cream tone at the nub of the petals. Sometimes, however, you can find several blossoms lightly tinted pale apricot. The bushy plant is more vigorous than the major part of varieties in this category." [JR22/145] Previously thought extinct, it has recently been found living in a Finnish collection.

Golden Salmon (Cutbush/De Ruiter, 1926)
Sport of 'Superb' (Pol).
"Vivid orange." [RATS] "Shows up." [ARA29/50] "Healthy plant about 15 inches high [ca. 3.75 dm], with a fair amount of bloom of striking color, which becomes rather tiresome...Blooms more persistently than any other Polyantha...Fascinating when it opens, the blooms soon turn a peculiar slaty blue-purple which is exceedingly painful to look at." [ARA30/182] "Strong growth and prolific bloom." [ARA32/186] "Large clusters of small, semi-double, rich bright salmon...2×2 [ft; ca. 6×6 dm]." [B]

Golden Salmon Superior (De Ruiter, 1929)
Sport of 'Golden Salmon' (Pol).
"Color almost like 'Golden Salmon', perhaps a little more yellow-salmon, and stands weather conditions better and does not fade." [ARA32/221]

"Bud small, globular; flower small, cupped, semi-double, very lasting, golden salmon that does not fade or burn, in cluster on long stem. Foliage wrinkled, light green. Vigorous (30 inches [ca. 7.5 dm]), upright; profuse bloomer (1000 blooms in a season)." [ARA33/178]

Greta Kluis (Kluis & Koning, 1916)
Sport of either 'Echo' (Pol) or 'Louise Walter' (Pol).
"Deep crimson-pink. Very free." [ARA25/121] "Medium-sized, globular blooms of deep pink, passing to carmine-red. A continuous, even bloomer." [C-Ps28]

Grete Schreiber (Altmüller, 1916)
"Pink, medium size, full, dwarf." [Sn]

Grumpy
Listed as 'Burkhard'.

Gustel Mayer (Lambert, 1909)
From 'Turner's Crimson Rambler' (Multiflora) × an unnamed seedling (which resulted from crossing the Noisette 'Mme. Pierre Cochet' with the Bourbon 'Dunkelrote Hermosa').
"Light red, middle yellow, small, full, dwarf." [Sn]

Happy
Listed as 'Alberich'.

Hermine Madèlé (Soupert & Notting, 1888)
From 'Mignonette' (Pol) × 'Marquise de Vivens' (T).
"Dwarf, flower small, full, very well formed; color, creamy white with yellowish reflections. Center darker." [JR12/55]

Herzblättchen (Geschwind, 1889) trans., "Darling"
"Pink, small, full, medium height." [Sn]

Ideal (Spek, 1920)
Sport of 'Miss Edith Cavell' (Pol).
"Small, brilliant red blooms in compact clusters." [ARA29/97] "Very dark garnet, in large clusters; grows quite dwarf; vigorous." [ARA25/121]"The darkest of all." [ARA29/50] "The flowers are semi-double, come in great heads of thirty or more, and the color is retained remarkably well until they drop. A neat and compact grower. Has everything a Polyantha of this type needs, except fragrance." [C-Ps25] "Bud globular; flower medium size, double, full open, globular…very lasting…slight fragrance. Growth moderate; bushy; blooms abundantly all season. Hardy." [ARA21/165]

Indéfectible (Turbat, 1919) trans., "Indestructible"
Sport of a seedling of 'Ännchen Müller' (Pol).
"Buds medium size, long-pointed; flowers medium size, cupped, semi-double, borne in clusters of 15 to 20 on long stems; very lasting; slight fragrance. Color bright, clear red. Foliage abundant, medium size, bronzy green; disease resistant. A very vigorous grower of bushy habit, reaching a height of two to three feet [to ca. 1 m], and blooming continuously the whole season." [ARA20/131]

Ivan Misson (Soupert & Notting, 1912)
From 'Jeanny Soupert' (Pol) × 'Katharina Zeimet' (Pol).
"Pink, then white." [Ÿ]

Jacques Proust (Robichon, 1904)
"Stocky bush, with dark green foliage; flower large for the sort; color, velvety grenadine red tinted amaranth when fully open. Very floriferous and fragrant." [JR28/155]

Jean Mermoz (Chenault, 1937)
From *R. wichuraiana* × "a Hybrid Tea."
Pink.

Jeanne d'Arc (Levavasseur, 1909)
Seedling of 'Mme. Norbert Levavasseur' (Pol).
"A seedling of 'Mme. Norbert Levavasseur', from which it takes its abundance, having however smaller leaves and magnificent pure milk-white blossoms." [JR33/169] Not to be confused with the Noisette 'Étendard de Jeanne d'Arc'.

Jeanne Drivon (Schwartz, 1883)
"A lovely rose; perfect, full form; very double and sweet; color, pure white, faintly tinged with crimson." [CA90] "Growth dwarf, very remontant, foliage glossy; blooms in terminal clusters, amply furnished with numerous buds; flowers very double, looking like those of the camellia-flowered balsam, rather large for the sort, white bordered and shaded pink, reverse of petals white. Unique coloration. Distinct from other Polyanthas in commerce." [JR7/121]

Jeanny Soupert (Soupert & Notting, 1912)
From 'Mme. Norbert Levavasseur' (Pol) × 'Petite Léonie' (Pol).
"Very delicate light flesh pink. Flower small, very regular in form, produced in large, tight bouquets. It blooms constantly. For bedding and borders, it is just the thing. It is a wonderful child of Levavasseur, from which it takes all the other's well-known qualities." [JR37/19]

Jessie (Merryweather, 1909)
Sport of 'Phyllis' (Pol).
"Brilliant red shaded pink." [Ÿ] "A fine Rose for massing as it flowers profusely. The color is glowing crimson, which does not fade until the blooms are ready to fall. If you have anywhere in your garden that needs a touch of

bright red all summer you should try this excellent, continuous-flowering variety." [C&Js23] "Very small, cerise red, and single. Of feeble growth, it nevertheless grows more vigorously than 'Maman Levavasseur' [*Pol, Levavasseur, 1908, "bright pink of the 'Dorothy Perkins' shade" [C&Js08].*]." [JR24/140]

Joséphine Morel (Alégatière, 1891)
"Bush to 35-40 cm [ca. 15 inches], same deportment as 'Miniature', and blooming continuously; flowers small, very full, bright intense pink." [JR15/148] "Pink, small, full, dwarf." [Sn]

Katharina Zeimet (Lambert, 1901)
Two parentages are given: (1), 'Étoile de Mai' (Pol) × 'Marie Pavic' (Pol); or (2), 'Euphrosine' (Lambertiana) × 'Marie Pavic' (Pol).
"Very small, double, fragrant, pure white...large clusters. Free, continuous bloom. Compact...102 [ft; ca. 3-6 dm]. Shiny, healthy foliage...perhaps the best white Polyantha." [Lg] "Bright green glossy foliage." [HRG] "Stocky plant, twiggy growth...2×2 [ft; ca. 6×6 dm]." [B] "Fine for massing." [P1] "Moderate vigor." [Cx] "Low-growing, vigorous; foliage very plentiful till late summer, then plentiful, black-spots somewhat; bloom free, continuous." [ARA18/128] "One of the most remarkable among white varieties. It is more floriferous than 'Marie Pavie' [*sic*], its parent." [JR28/128] "Fades to brown in heat; double, flat flowers, in clusters...shows black open center in California...reported better in East...Strong growth." [Th2] "A record-breaker for bloom and hardiness." [MLS] "A little plant of great refinement." [Hk]

Kersbergen (Oosthoek/Kersbergen, 1927)
Sport of 'Miss Edith Cavell' (Pol).
Red.

Kleiner Alfred (Lambert, 1903) trans., "Alfred Minor"
From 'Anne Marie de Montravel' (Pol) × 'Shirley Hibberd' (T).
"Red-yellow with nasturtium red." [Ÿ] "Colors grade from orange yellow to pale yellow...buds prettily tinted grenadine." [JR28/128]

[**Kleiner Liebling**] (Kiese/J.C. Schmidt, 1895) trans., "Little Darling"
From 'Polyantha Grandiflora' (Multiflora) × 'Fellemberg' (N).
"An entirely new and very handsome variety; blooms in beautiful clusters, frequently 100 roses in a bunch; the flowers are medium size, somewhat cupped form; lovely carmine rose; very constant and free bloomer." [C&Js98]

La Marne (Barbier, 1915)
From 'Mme. Norbert Levavasseur' (Pol) × 'Comtesse du Caÿla' (Ch).
"Semi-double flowers, bright salmon-rose at the edges, rosy blush inside...glossy and mildew-proof foliage." [ARA24/94] "Apple-blossom-pink clusters." [ARA29/97] "Clusters of double flowers of rich pink with creamy centers...to 4 [ft; ca. 1.25 m]." [HRG] "The growth is uniform and the bluish-green foliage very distinctive...Its foliage is retained until well into the winter." [C-Ps27] "Very handsome." [ARA31/118] La Marne, the French river.

La Proserpine (Ketten Bros., 1897)
From 'Georges Schwartz' (Pol) × 'Duchesse Marie Salviati' (T).
"Peach, yellow center." [Ÿ] "Peach-colored Multiflora tinted yellow." [GAS] "Blossom reach red, center tinted orange chrome yellow, edge fading to blush white, medium-sized, fairly full, fragrant, long stem. Vigorous, heavy continuous bloom. Valuable for cutting." [JR21/135] Proserpine, alias Persephone, unwilling co-regent of Hades who returns seasonally to visit us.

La Rosée (Turbat, 1920) trans., "Dew"
"Sulphur-white fading to pure white." [Ÿ]

Lady Reading (Van Kleef? Van Herk?, 1921)
Sport of 'Ellen Poulsen' (Pol).
"Bright red, semi-double flowers in clusters; holds color well. Very attractive. Black spots. Fine. [*Rhode Island, U.S.A.*]/...of good growth...not an attractive color...[*Massachusetts*]/...one of the finest Polyanthas [*Ontario, Canada*]/...washed-out, pale pink [*Iowa*]/...muddy color...profuse...for forcing." [PP28]

Le Loiret (Turbat, 1920)
"Flowers very brilliant pink, passing to tender salmon-rose, borne in clusters of 10 to 15 on very long stems. Foliage disease-resistant. Vigorous; bushy." [ARA21/161] "Flower brilliant rose with fire-red shading, changing to soft salmon-rose. Growth vigorous, branching; foliage deep glossy green." [GeH] Loiret, *département* of France in which is situate Turbat's city of Orléans.

Leonie Lamesch (Lambert, 1899)
From 'Aglaia' (Lambertiana) × 'Kleiner Alfred' (Pol).
"A quaint but novel variety, producing flowers of a coppery red colour with terra-cotta edges...rather imperfect in shape, but...valuable...vigorous." [P1] "The blooms are medium size and very durable and ten distinctly colored flowers are frequently shown on the bush at one time, varying from cochineal red in the bud to glowing coppery red tinged with orange when the flower opens." [C&Js10] "Shrub bushy, vigorous, and hardy; upright branches, height about two feet [ca. 6 dm]; wood brownish, with red prickles, which are very large and not very numerous. Foliage medium-sized, dark green, new foliage reddish-brown...The flowers often come singly, and often 25 to the cluster; they are small or medium-sized, well-formed, globular, and quite full; the color is distinct and unique in its

group…deep copper-red, darker beneath, and the edges are shaded, bordered, and striped copper-red…the semi-open bud is deep blood-red. Strong perfume." [JR23/171] "Medium height, moderate [*vigor*], foliage plentiful, healthy; bloom moderate, continuous." [ARA18/128] "Perfect foliage. Large grower." [Th2] "A most charming little rose." [Wr]

Lillan (De Vink, 1958)
From 'Ellen Poulsen' (Pol) × 'Tom Thumb' (Min).
Deep red.

Lindbergh (Croibier, 1927)
Sport of 'Orléans-Rose' (Pol).
"Very brilliant geranium-red—does not burn in sun and retains color until petals fall. Foliage mildew-resistant; growth vigorous, upright; very free-flowering." [ARA28/239] Charles A. Lindbergh, aviator; lived 1902-1974.

Little Dorrit (Reeves, 1920)
Sport of 'Coral Cluster' (Pol).
"Bud and flower large, semi-double, full, open, very lasting, slightly fragrant, coral-salmon, borne in large cluster on long stem. Foliage abundant, medium size, glossy. Growth vigorous, bushy, dwarf; profuse, continuous bloomer. Very hardy." [ARA31/232] *Little Dorrit*, the 1856-1857 novel by Charles Dickens; or, more probably, its eponymous character.

Little Dot (Bennett, 1889)
"Pale pink, very pretty but apt to be too small." [JR17/9]

[**Little Gem**] (Conard & Jones, 1898)
"Loaded with perfectly double little roses all season; pure white and very sweet." [C&Js98]

Little White Pet (Henderson, 1879) syn., 'White Pet'
Sport of 'Félicité-Perpétue' (Sempervirens).
"White, small, and double; a pretty miniature Rose, and exceedingly free in flowering." [P1] "Double, flat, fragrant; white sometimes tinged pink on the edges...2 [ft; ca. 6 dm]...outstanding...healthy." [Lg] "Huge trusses of pure white pompon-like blooms throughout the Summer...3×2 [ft; ca. 10×6 dm]." [B] "Vigorous." [J] "Much to be admired for its charm...graceful." [JR4/111] "A beautiful rose to own." [Hk] This variety's parent, a climber, was known in some areas as 'White Pet', hence 'Little White Pet' for its dwarf sport.

Loreley (Kiese, 1913)
From 'Tausendschön' (Multiflora) × ? .
"From a cross involving 'Tausendschön'; it gained from its mother a very fresh pink color. The flowers grow in big clusters, and have the great advantage of lasting a very long time. The flowers are quite full, which however doesn't keep the buds from opening easily. Blooming lasts far into the Fall, up to frost. The foliage is glossy and similar to that of 'Mme. Norbert Levavasseur'. In coloring, it can't be beaten by any other Polyantha. Its small stature—3-4 dm [ca. 12-16 inches]—recommends it for bedding." [JR38/40] Loreley, alias Lorelei, the Siren of the Rhine river, in this case luring us to purchase rather than to destruction.

Louise Walter (Walter, 1909)
From 'Tausendschön' (Multiflora) × 'Rösel Dach' (Pol).
"Pink, changing to rosy carmine. Resembles considerably the standard 'Tausendschön'." [Th2] "Medium size, in clusters, double, fair form, delicate fragrance, medium stems. Good foliage, sufficient. Medium dwarf growth; hardy. Blush pink to white." [ARA23/165-166] "Very like new Rose 'Echo'!" [C&Js16]

Lullaby (Shepherd, 1953)
From an unnamed seedling (arising from a cross of *R. soulieana* with the pink Polyantha 'Mrs. Joseph Heiss') × 'Mlle. Cécile Brunner' (Pol).
White, center blush.

[**Ma Fillette**] (Soupert & Notting, 1897) trans., "My Little Girl"
From 'Mignonette' (Pol) × 'Luciole' (T).
"Compact bush, corymbiferous; outer petals large, peach pink on a yellow ground; center petals more compact and colored glossy lake carmine red with dawn reflections. Novel colorations among the Polyanthas. Very fragrant and floriferous. Excellent variety for beds and forcing in pots." [JR21/146]

Ma Pâquerette
Listed as 'Pâquerette'.

[**Ma Petite Andrée**] (Chauvry, 1898) syn., 'Red Soupert'; trans., "My Little Andrée"
Seedling of 'Étoile de Mai' (Pol).
"Flower pretty large, a beautiful deep carmine red (of the '[Mlle.] Blanche Rebatel' sort, but darker); more vigorous, very floriferous." [JR22/165] "Vigorous growth and dwarf bushy habit, mostly covered with bright crimson buds, fully double flowers, the whole season. It is a very useful rose and quite hardy." [C&Js06] "Dedicated to the grand-daughter of the breeder." [JR22/165] In one of the sad moments of rosedom, we note that Chauvry's beloved little Andrée had perished by 1900, when he introduced in her memory the Tea 'Souvenir de ma Petite Andrée'. Rest in peace, my wee one; we remember you.

Madeleine Orosdy (Gravereaux, 1912)
"Fresh pink." [Ÿ]

Magenta (Barbier, 1916)
"Flowers semi-double, cup-shaped, of medium size, in long spikes of twenty to forty; violet-red, the middle of the petal magenta-violet—a new shade in the dwarf Polyanthas—sometimes turns reddish violet. Dwarf grower; very floriferous." [ARA19/100]

Maman Turbat (Turbat, 1911) trans., "Mama Turbat"
From 'Mme. Norbert Levavasseur' (Pol) × 'Katharina Zeimet' (Pol).
"Very vigorous, very hardy; growth erect; wood very smooth and thornless; persistent glossy green foliage. Strong panicles of 30-40 blossoms, very long-lasting, delicate China pink nuanced light peachblossom pink and dawn gold as well as delicate flesh white." [JR36/10]

Maréchal Foch (Levavasseur, 1918) trans., "Marshal Foch"
Sport of 'Orléans-Rose' (Pol).
"Cerise red." [Ÿ] "Bud medium size; flower medium size, open form, semi-double, borne in clusters on medium length stems; very lasting; strong fragrance. Color deep red." [ARA20/131] Also attributed to a cross between 'Orléans-Rose' (Pol) and 'Jessie' (Pol). Marshal Ferdinand Foch, French general in World War I; lived 1851-1929.

Margo Koster (Koster, 1931)
Sport of 'Dick Koster' (Pol).
"Flower large, orange-red, in cluster. Fine forcer." [ARA37/269]"Varies from intense orange salmon (in cool weather) to light pinkish salmon (in warm weather). No scent. Twiggy. May lose leaves during the Summer, but compensates for this by blooming straight through Winter, just when one needs some cheerful-looking flowers. Mildews; no rust. My thirty-year-old plants, unpruned for fifteen years, never exceeded the dimensions they attained their first season—2.5×2.5 feet (ca. 7.5×7.5 dm)." [BCD]

Margo's Sister (Ratcliffe, 1954)
Sport of 'Margo Koster' (Pol).
Light pink.

Marguerite Rose (Robichon, 1904) trans., "Pink Marguerite [Daisy]"
"Growth vigorous, compact, stout-wooded, foliage light green, blossom full, well formed, imbricated at the edges, color Hermosa pink [*referring to the Bourbon by that name*], larger than this last, blooms in well-held clusters." [JR28/155]

Marie Brissonet (Turbat, 1913)
"Plant dwarf, with delicate green foliage which disappears completely under the abundant bloom. Large pyramidal clusters, with 75-100 medium-sized blossoms, delicate flesh pink in color, with petal tips light carmine. This variety, of such abundance, will be very useful for bedding and borders." [JR37/137]

Marie-Jeanne (Turbat, 1913)
"Very vigorous, with handsome shiny green foliage; wood without thorns; enormous clusters of 40-60 blossoms, large for the type, of long duration and pure white, sometimes shaded very light salmon as it opens. Quite remontant, all in all producing a very decorative effect by its white masses of flowers at first bloom." [*Listed as climbing, a quality not cited in more recent descriptions.*] [JR37/137] "Pale blush-cream in clusters. Almost thornless...2×2 [ft; ca. 6×6 dm]." [B]

Marie Pavic (Alégatière, 1888) syn., 'Marie Pavie', 'Marie Pavié', 'Marie Parvie'
"Rosy white." [P1] "Flower medium sized, full, flesh-white, center tinted pink." [LR] "Thornless, extra floriferous, handsome green foliage of 5-7 leaflets; flower large for a Polyantha; principally blush-white to the center, the same as 'Souvenir de la Malmaison', and much more floriferous."

[JR12/165] "Fragrant...very vigorous." [Cx] "Medium height, vigorous; foliage very plentiful, black-spots slightly; bloom free, continuous." [ARA18/129] "Holds its foliage among the best." [ARA20/58] "Very lasting...Foliage large, abundant, rich green, soft, disease-resistant. Vigorous grower, reaching 15 to 20 inches [ca. 3.75-5 dm], very bushy. Blooms profusely in June and at intervals the remainder of the season." [Th2] "A good scent." [Hk] "Large cluster. Continuous...1-3 [ft; ca. 3-10 dm]." [Lg] "Upright...4×3 [ft; ca. 1.3×1 m]." [B] The question of the spelling of the rose's name remains to be settled; both surnames "Pavic" and "Pavie" are to be found.

Martha (Lambert, 1905)
From 'Thalia' (Lambertiana) × 'Mme. Laurette Messimy' (Ch).
"Copper red, flowers in large corymbs." [K2] "A 'Bengale Multiflora' rose...blooms in profusion over a great part of the season, developing corymbs of small, full blossoms." [JR29/179] "Shrub dwarf, bushy, very floriferous, flower small, coppery pink." [JR30/25] Not to be confused with the 1912 Bourbon of the same name.

Martha Keller (Walter, 1912)
"Yellowish white, medium size, very full, medium height." [Sn]

Mary Bruni (Gratama, 1914)
"Pink, small, full, dwarf." [Sn]

Marytje Cazant (Van Nes, 1927)
Sport of 'Jessie' (Pol).
"Buds salmon-pink on white ground, globular, lasting." [ARA29/227] "A charming flesh-colored Polyantha." [ARA33/155]

Mauve (Turbat, 1915)
"Mauve pink." [Ÿ]

Melle Fischer (Pfitzer, 1914)
"Pink, small, full dwarf." [Sn]

Merveille des Polyanthas (Mermet, 1909) trans., "Polyantha Wonder"
"Very vigorous, flowers pure white passing to lilac pink upon opening; very fragrant and floriferous; foliage light green." [JR32/153]

Merveille des Rouges (Dubreuil, 1911) trans., "Red Wonder"
"Very bright red." [Ÿ] "Dwarf, much branched, continuous bloom. Branches strong and robust, bearing clusters of 7-15 little blossoms of a color as bright as that of 'Général Jacqueminot'. Thick foliage, 5-7 beautiful somber green leaflets; buds turbinate, with crested sepals. Blooms in elegant clusters, small, cupped, intense velvety crimson with a small white halo at the center which only adds to the sparkle. The plant is extra floriferous, does not lose its leaves, and surpasses in abundance and color all Polyanthas previously developed." [JR35/167]

Mevrouw Nathalie Nypels (Leenders, 1919)
From 'Orléans-Rose' (Pol) × an unnamed seedling (arising from crossing the China 'Comtesse du Caÿla' with *R. fœtida* 'Bicolor').
"Bud large; flower large, open form, double, borne in clusters; very lasting; strong fragrance. Color, hydrangea-pink. Foliage abundant, small, leathery bronze-green. A vigorous grower of bushy habit and a profuse bloomer." [ARA20/135] "Reddish orange, changing to hydrangea pink—a striking color." [ARA25/102]

Mignon (Mille-Toussaint, 1904)
From 'Mme. Laurette Messimy' (Ch) × 'Marie Pavic' (Pol).
"Flesh yellow fading to white." [Ÿ]

Mignonette (Guillot fils, 1881)

Seedling of a seedling of *R. multiflora* 'Polyantha'; the immediate parent is probably the 'Polyantha Alba Plena Sarmentosa' one sees to have been much used in breeding in Lyon, though unreleased.

"Dwarf, of the Lawrenciana sort, very vigorous, with small flowers in the shape of full tulips, well formed, ruffled. The color is flesh-pink, brighter at the center." [JR3/9] "Vigorous, quite remontant, with very small flowers of about an inch [ca. 2.5 cm], well formed and held well, colored pale pink fading to white, in clusters of 30-40 making a single stem into a pretty bouquet." [JR5/147] "Very beautiful, full regular flowers about the size of a twenty-five cent piece, perfectly double, deliciously perfumed; bright rosy pink; immense bloomer." [C&Js98] "Very dwarf, bushy, floriferous. Stature of China roses. Branches compact, short, with dark reddish-brown bark, twiggy, bearing strong hooked prickles of a reddish color. Leaves glabrous, of 5-7 leaflets, narrowly oval, slender, smooth, dark green on top, reddish below. The young foliage is reddish-brown edged, and finely serrated. The inflorescence is a short panicle, like that of the Chinas. The flowers are full, pink, sometimes flesh, bordered or blotched with rose." [JR9/6-7] "Weak in growth." [Hn] "Foliage very plentiful till late summer, then sufficient, some black-spot...mildew...bloom free, continuous." [ARA18/129] "One of the best." [P1]

"In February, 1869, I sowed a great quantity of seed which I had harvested from the variety 'Polyantha', a multiflora variety originating in Japan which was very much a climber, and non-remontant, having a quite small single white blossom much like that of a bramble or strawberry, and blooming in panicles. Among the many seedlings, there were many which resembled Multifloras and Noisettes in their wood and foliage. Quite a few bore flowers of moderate quality, single, semi-doubles, and full blossoms, with petals as large as the roses of our gardens, with a variety of colors: yellow, white, bright pink, etc. I didn't have so many as two which resembled their mother! Among the seedlings which didn't bloom until the second or third year, there was found one which had blossoms with two rows of petals, an inch to an inch and a half across, not remontant as the others were, but which gave me wonderful seeds which I sowed in February 1872. Out of this came my dear little 'Pâquerette', which I put into commerce in November, 1875. From these seedlings, I further got many varieties equally dwarf and very remontant, one giving yellowish-white double flowers, more petite than those of 'Pâquerette' and keeping the form and character of the climbing 'Polyantha', as well as another similarly remontant dwarf, of the same sort as 'Pâquerette', but with soft pink flowers which were full and well-formed though small [*this, presumably, is 'Mignonette'*]; I am going to propagate a quantity sufficient to deliver them into commerce in November 1880" [JR2/137-138]

Milrose (Delbard-Chabert, 1965)
From 'Orléans-Rose' (Pol) × a seedling (resulting from crossing the Floribunda 'Français' with the Floribunda 'Lafayette').
Light pink.

Mimi Pinson (Barbier, 1919)
"Flower clear crimson, passing to purplish rose and then to 'Paul Neyron' pink." [ARA21/161] "Rose-red, medium size, full, dwarf." [Sn]

Miniature (Alégatière, 1884)
"Pink, then yellowish white." [Ÿ] "Bushy, vigorous, extra remontant; to a foot in height [ca. 3 dm], stout, with thick foliage…The buds are in a cluster and are of a deep pink tint; they always open well. The flowers are very fragrant, small, hardly larger than a double violet, very full, well formed, blush white fading to white." [JR8/178] "This is the smallest of all roses, but perfect full regular flowers, borne in wreaths and clusters, cover the plant with a mass of fairy roses; rosy blush, delightfully perfumed and very pretty. 10 cts." [C&Js98] "Dwarf and bushy plant, average growth to 40 to 50 cm [ca. 16-20 inches]. Flowers numerous, full,

white, in a short, compact panicle. Bloom uninterrupted from May to November." [JR30/54-55]

[**Minutifolia Alba**] (Bennett, 1888)
"White." [LS]

Miss Edith Cavell (Meiderwyk/Spek, 1917)
Sport of 'Orléans-Rose' (Pol).
"Brilliant dark red." [Cw] "Color brilliant scarlet, overlaid with deep, velvety crimson or maroon. The blooms come in great open clusters all season. The most attractive red Polyantha Rose in existence." [C&Js22] "Very floriferous." [Lc] "Little flowers...close in the large trusses." [Hk] "Semi-double, scarlet-crimson flowers amid dark green foliage...3×2 [ft; ca. 10×6 dm]." [B] "Foliage disease-resistant." [ARA21/165] Not to be confused with the single white HT 'Edith Cavell' of 1918, nor with the red Polyantha 'Miss Edith Cavell' from De Ruiter in 1932.

[**Miss Kate Schultheis**] (Soupert & Notting, 1887)
From 'Mignonette' (Pol) × 'Mme. Damaizin' (T).
"White and salmon." [LS]

Mlle. Alice Rousseau (Vilin, 1903)
"Bush vigorous, canes Van Dyck red, foliage emerald green, bud golden pink, which opens into the form of a small cactus Dahlia, taking on the tints of an Italian fresco of pretty vivid color; at full expansion, the blossom becomes a delicate flesh pink. Very pretty variety." [JR28/27]

[**Mlle. Bertha Ludi**] (Pernet-Ducher, 1891)
"Vigorous bush forming a compact plant growing 30-40 cm in height [ca. 12-16 inches], erect habit, foliage abundant, flower large, 8-10 cm in size [to ca. 4 inches], full, beautiful form, color pure white passing to flesh pink when fully open, continuous bloom...I especially recommend this

variety for pot culture and for forcing; it should be noted that good-forcing white roses are not very common." [JR15/166]

Mlle. Blanche Rebatel (Bernaix, 1888) syn., 'Blanche Rebatel'
"Stocky, vigorous, small growth, extraordinarily floriferous. Inflorescence nearly a thyrse before expansion, then a large corymb of 40-50 buds. Often all the small, charming blossoms open at once. Color uniformly bright carmine red nuanced pink on the reverse, with a white nub. A new coloration." [JR12/164] "Purplish crimson, shaded rose; a somewhat dull colour, but prettily shaped." [P1]

[**Mlle. Camille de Rochetaillée**] (Bernaix, 1889)
"Dwarf bush, compact, producing large corymbs at the tips of the canes. Flowers very numerous, very fragrant, pure white when opening, the sun bringing out the nuances, stripes, and spots of carmine; very double, convex form, many petals, recurved back and imbricated Camellia-style. Very beautiful." [JR13/163]

Mlle. Cécile Brunner (Widow Ducher, 1880)
From 'Polyantha Alba Plena Sarmentosa' (Mult) × 'Mme. de Tartas' (T). "Dwarf, very vigorous and suitable for bedding…blooms in clusters; pretty, bright pink on a yellowish ground, outside petals light pink; very fragrant." [JR4/167] "Spreading branches, diverging, looking like a Tea rose, thornless, or here and there a thorn or two; bark smooth, glossy, of a rusty green; leaves of 3-5 fairly oval leaflets…flowers numerous, small, very full, delicately scented; an exquisite miniature." [EL] "Perfect pink buds, diffused with yellow." [ARA29/97] "I have never found it set seed." [Hk] "Low-growing, weak; foliage barely sufficient, black-spots slightly; bloom moderate, but continuous." [ARA18/128] "Practically free from mildew…graceful habit." [NRS/12] "Blooms of HT shape. Continuous…3×2 [ft; ca. 10×6 dm]." [B] "Vigorous to 4 [ft; ca. 1.3 m]." [HRG] "Dedicated to the charming daughter of the late Ulrich Brunner,

rose-grower at Lausanne." [JR30/53] 'Mlle. Cécile Brunner' has not lost any of her charms over the years. Recently, I was strolling meditatively down an aisle of modern roses at a local nursery when I heard a housewife in the neighboring aisle call out to her husband, "Oh, *look*!" as if she had found the dearest jewel in all the world. I peeked through some intervening canes of 'Peace' to find that she was gazing at an unfurling bud of 'Mlle. Cécile Brunner', holding its own easily against the heavy artillery of more recent times.

Mlle. Fernande Dupuy (Vigneron, 1899)
"Dwarf, compact, and vigorous, bearing clusters of flowers; blossom small and full, zinnia-formed, beautifully colored currant pink, sometimes a little darker. Good for pot and border work." [JR23/149] "Penetrating scent." [JR25/11]

Mlle. Joséphine Burland (Bernaix, 1886)
"Much branched, moderate vigor, continuously covered with flowers throughout the whole season. Flower large for the class, very double, petals longly acuminate, upright in the center, inclining in the middle, and reflexing in the outer rows. Pure white upon opening, taking on nuances of carmine pink. Distinguished from others in this class by having solitary blossoms." [JR10/172]

Mlle. Marcelle Gaugin (Corbœuf-Marsault, 1910)
"Light salmon pink, small, full, dwarf." [Sn]

Mlle. Marthe Cahuzac (Ketten Bros., 1901)
From 'Mignonette' (Pol) × 'Safrano' (T).
"Flower yellowish white, center silky yellow passing to whitish pink, medium sized, full, flat, bud long and pointed, opening well. Bush dwarf, vigorous, hardy, blooming in clusters." [JR25/146]

Mlle. Suzanne Bidard (Vigneron, 1913)
From 'Georges Pernet' (Pol) × 'Perle d'Or' (Pol).
"Bush vigorous, compact; flowers medium-sized, full, in clusters; very pretty coloration, light coppery salmon, petal bases lighter yet, stamens golden yellow; buds very long, salmon, superb. Very beautiful variety which will be much sought out for pot culture." [JR38/71]

Mme. Alégatière (Alégatière, 1888)
From 'Polyantha Alba Plena Sarmentosa' (Multiflora) × 'Jules Margottin' (HP).
"Bright rose." [CA96] "Bright pink.—Blossom large, fragrant; floriferous; vigorous." [Cx] "Always in bloom, branches upright, numerous thorns of a fawn-green; foliage small, of 3-5 leaflets; blossom of moderate size, beautiful bright pink, full, and staying in good form for a long time." [JR12/165]

Mme. Arthur Robichon (Robichon, 1912)
From 'Mme. Norbert Levavasseur' (Pol) × 'Mrs. W.H. Cutbush' (Pol).
"Color, beautiful and very fresh purplish pink, previously unknown among Polyanthas; blooms in very compact panicles; wood smooth, few thorns, foliage reddish green; plant dwarf." [JR36/153]

Mme. E.A Nolte (Bernaix, 1892)
"Nankeen yellow, passing to white." [H] "Buds chamois-yellow, changing to rosy white as they expand; very free. A lovely variety." [P1] "Dwarf, very floriferous. Corymbs profuse, buds very unique in form and color, stocky, flattened, wider than high when opening; chamois yellow paling with age to blush white. Flowers of perfect form, making, with their differing nuances, a delightful contrast between flower and bud." [JR16/165]

Mme. Hardy du Thé
Listed as 'Clotilde Soupert'.

Mme. Jules Gouchault (Turbat, 1912)
From 'Maman Turbat' (Pol) × 'George Elger' (Pol).
"In large and in small sprays, double, good form, medium size, medium stems. Good foliage, sufficient. Growth strong; hardy. Vermilion-pink shaded orange, passing to brilliant pink." [ARA23/169] "Light green wood and foliage; blooms in large erect panicles of 25-50 blossoms, well held, long lasting. Bud bright vermilion red nuanced orange vermilion, fading to bright pink, then to light pink when open." [JR37/137]

Mme. Jules Thibaud (Breeder/Introducer unknown, date uncertain)
Presumed to be a sport of 'Mlle. Cécile Brunner' (Pol).
"A deeper peachy-pink [*than 'Mlle. Cécile Brunner'*]. Young foliage is deep bronze...rolled centre with a button eye." [G]

Mme. Melon du Thé
Listed as 'Clotilde Soupert' (Pol).

Mme. Norbert Levavasseur (Levavasseur, 1903)
From 'Turner's Crimson Rambler' (Multiflora) × 'Gloire des Polyantha' (Pol).
"This Rose is in many ways one of the most remarkable that has been introduced in many years. It is a cross between '[Turner's] Crimson Rambler' and 'Glory of Polyanthas' [*sic*], retaining the color of the former with the exceeding free flowering of dwarf growing habit of the latter. The plants are very vigorous and grow to 18 or 24 inches [ca. 4.5-6 dm]. The foliage is dark, glossy green and remarkably free from insects and fungus. The flowers are borne in clusters of 20, 30 or more to the cluster." [C&Js06] "Growth vigorous, dwarf, very handsome foliage, glossy green; flower large for the sort, very double, magnificent very bright carmine red, extremely floriferous and remontant. Resembles in its floribundity '[Turner's] Crimson Rambler', whence it sprang." [JR27/131]

Mme. Taft (Levavasseur, 1909)
From 'Turner's Crimson Rambler' (Multiflora) × 'Mme. Norbert Levavasseur' (Pol).
"Red." [Ÿ] "Color is rosy crimson. Habit is similar to 'Baby Red Rambler'. Splendid for massing or for borders." [C&Js11] "Lighter than ['Mme. Norbert Levavasseur']. The foliage is identical to that of Levavasseur, as is the blossom. Blooms continuously in large panicles all Summer." [JR33/169]

[**Mosella**] (Lambert & Reiter, 1895)
From 'Mignonette' (Pol) × a seedling (which resulted from crossing the two Teas 'Mme. Falcot' and 'Shirley Hibberd').
"Large flowers of a pretty cream white. This variety is, according to my experience, pretty hardy." [JR23/42] "Makes a neat handsome bush, loaded with flowers all the time...medium size, finely formed flowers borne in large clusters and quite fragrant; color, pretty buff or peachy-yellow; fine for bedding and house culture." [C&Js98] Mosella, alias the river Moselle, river shared by France and Germany.

Mrs. R.M. Finch (Finch, 1923)
Seedling of 'Orléans-Rose' (Pol).
"Flowers of bright rose-pink come in branching fragrant clusters." [C-Pf33] "Medium...double, cupped, cluster; rosy pink, fading lighter. Repeats...2-3 [ft; ca. 6-10 dm]." [Lg]

Mrs. W.H. Cutbush (Levavasseur, 1907)
Sport or seedling of 'Mme. Norbert Levavasseur' (Pol).
"Very light pink." [JR32/161] "More vigorous than 'Mme. Norbert Levavasseur', from which it however takes its stature and mode of flowering...A pretty, delicate pink, sometimes washed slightly with a light salmon...blooms throughout the Winter under glass, and furthermore is very hardy." [JR33/12] "Flower large, full; moderate vigor; for borders."

[Cx] "Coral pink...Clean, healthy growth." [Dr] "The foliage is rather small but sufficiently dense, light green in colour, as also are the stems of the current year's growth. The habit of the plant is dwarf, bushy and compact, very suitable for bedding purposes...almost continuously in flower until November. The flowers are small and slightly cup-shaped; they are produced in large compact trusses and are bright clear pink in colour. These trusses are carried on strong stems well above the foliage and the flowers stand wet weather very well for a Rose of this class...little affected by mildew...Its weakness lies in its want of perfume and the absence of any pronounced form in the flowers." [NRS/12] "Medium height, vigorous; foliage very plentiful till late summer, then sparse, black-spots badly; bloom abundant till late summer, then moderate, continuous." [ARA18/129] "This rose was sold in 1904 to Messrs. Cutbush and Son of London, who bought 10,000 slips and propagated it the following year." [JR33/25]

Mrs. William G. Koning (Kluis & Koning, 1917)
Sport of 'Louise Walter' (Pol).
"White, medium size, full, moderate scent, dwarf." [Sn]

Multiflora Nana Perpétuelle
Listed as 'Multiflore Nain Remontant'.

Multiflore Nain Remontant (Lille, 1893) syn., 'Multiflora Nana Perpétuelle'
"This variety is so floriferous that I have seen bloom on seedlings having no more foliage than their cotyledons...In their fourth year, they make little spreading bushes varying from 3-4 dm [ca. 12-16 inches]. The foliage is of two sorts: small, oval-rounded, or shortly lanceolate on the regular branches, sometimes more lengthily lanceolate on the young canes. The stipules, which are pretty large, are elegantly lacinated. In the inflorescence, which is in the form of a thyrse or irregular cyme, the multiplex flo-

ral axes give rise to caducous bracts. The peduncle, which is obscurely segmented, bristles with glandular hairs, and grades into a fusiform calyx. The sepals do not extend beyond the conical bud, and the outer lobes have one or two pairs of lanceolate auricles. The blossom is usually white, small, full or semi-double, sometimes nearly single. The styles adhere into a column, and the stigmata are capitate. The hips are red and turbinate. The calyx-lobes [*sepals*] are deciduous. In this sort, the dwarfness is only relative; the bushes which provide the seed [*of this strain*] have grown, in the fourth year, over 8 dm tall [ca. 30 inches]." [JR24/4] "Floriferous…makes a very pretty border and a superb potted plant." [JR18/105]

Muttertag (Grootendorst, 1949) trans., "Mother's Day"
Sport of 'Dick Koster' (Pol).
Deep red.

Neiges d'Été (Gailloux, 1984) trans., "Snows of Summer"
Sport of unnamed seedling (arising from a selfing of the Miniature 'Baby Masquerade').
White.

Nypels Perfection (Leenders, 1930)
Sport of 'Mevrouw Nathalie Nypels' (Pol).
"Bud ovoid; flower large, semi-double, open, lasting, hydrangea pink, shaded rose-neyron-red, borne in a cluster on medium-strength stem. Foliage sufficient, medium size, rich green. Growth vigorous, bushy; profuse bloomer." [ARA31/240]

Orange Koster (Introducer unknown, date uncertain)
Presumably a sport from 'Margo Koster' (Pol) or 'Dick Koster' (Pol) or the like.
Orange.

Orange Morsdag (Grootendorst, 1956) trans., "Orange Mother's Day"
Sport of 'Muttertag' (Pol).
Orange.

Orange Triumph (Kordes, 1937)
From 'Eva' (Hybrid Musk) × 'Solarium' (Wichuraiana).
"Bud small, ovoid; flower small, semi-double, cupped, very lasting, slightly fragrant, salmon-red, with orange shadings, in cluster. Foliage abundant, glossy. Very vigorous (2 feet [ca. 6 dm]), compact, bushy; profuse, continuous bloomer." [ARA37/270] "Orange only under special conditions; usually is coral…is really a triumph…1.5-foot [ca. 4.5 dm] plants with enormous clusters of deep salmon-pink bloom. It is a good Polyantha, but apparently wrongly named." [ARA39/215] "No fragrance…free from mildew, constant in bloom, and holds its color well in heat." [ARA40/215]

Orléans-Rose (Levavasseur, 1909)
From 'Mme. Norbert Levavasseur' (Pol) × an unnamed seedling.
"Very floriferous…has the advantage of innumerable buds on one upright stem on which the flower-stems have small, rigid brown bristles…geranium red, tinted Neyron pink, whitish at the center, with carmine petals, very decorative, keeping its color until completely open. Very vigorous, attaining perhaps 2.5 to 3 feet [ca. 7.5-10 dm]; foliage a handsome shiny light green, quite hardy, and healthy." [JR33/169] "Foliage dark." [JR34/24] "Flower medium-sized, full." [Cx] "Small, bright red blooms with white center." [ARA29/97] "Nearer pink…to call it rose-red is generous enough." [Hk] "Medium height, vigorous; foliage very plentiful till late summer, then sparse, black-spots some…bloom profuse in June, grading to moderate in October and November, continuous." [ARA18/129] "Said to be the best Polyantha Rose ever raised." [C&Js12]

Pacific Triumph (Heers, 1949)
Sport of 'Orange Triumph' (Pol).

Papa Hémeray (Hémeray-Aubert, 1912)
From 'Hiawatha' (Multiflora) × 'Parsons' Pink China' (Ch).
"Scarlet-crimson." [NRS/15] "Single red with white centre, produced in clusters. Vigorous...4×3 [ft; ca. 1.25×1 m]." [B] "Foliage dark green." [B1] "Single flowers of a very intense vermilion red around the edges, with a white center. This dwarf continuously reblooming variety is only a copy of the climber 'Hiawatha' with a very abundant flowering; it blooms in clusters which are very full, and has the same blossoms as 'Hiawatha'. This rose, which is very vigorous, blooms very well until frost...Its brilliant color is not 'washed out' by rain, nor does it 'blue' in the sun." [JR36/184] "It is a China hybrid...One is able to say that it is, at one and the same time, a China and a dwarf 'Hiawatha'; but it is remontant and always blooms up to the Autumn frosts...Very vigorous, could be used for bedding where, because of the nature of its blossoms, it would produce a grand sight." [JR37/145] "Its nature is much closer to its Multiflora parent than to its China parent, as its growth, bloom, and leaves are those of a Polyantha, not of a China. The more shade the plant gets, the pinker the blossoms are; but, red or pink, they are always a gladsome sight. The little glossy orange-red hips are distinctive and attractive in their own right, having a slender elongated oval shape which would not seem to be derived from any of its ancestors even unto the second generation back. Seems to resent pruning. Blooms all year in Southern California." [BCD]

Pâquerette (Guillot fils, 1875) syn., 'Ma Pâquerette'; trans., "Daisy"
Seedling of a seedling of *R. multiflora* 'Polyantha'.
"Pure white, about one inch [ca. 2.5 cm] in diameter, full, prettily formed, recalling blossoms of the double flowering cherry; there are five to seven leaflets, the growth is slender." [EL] "'Pâquerette'...attains a height of one foot to fifteen inches [ca. 3-3.8 dm]." [JR2/138]

"Moderately vigorous; a variety of many merits, well-branched, blooms abundantly and constantly; the plant is dwarf and bushy; has branches of shiny green bark, fairly thornless; leaves of three to five smooth leaflets, which are glossy." [S] "Has the general aspect of a Noisette'." [JR9/6] "Continuous...excellent." [Lg] For the history of this, the first Polyantha, see the chapter headnote.

Paris (De Ruiter, 1929)
"Flower bright red, unfading. Vigorous." [ARA32/221] "Crimson...with some tendency to fade and blue." [ARA35/196]

Paul Crampel (Kersbergen, 1930) syn., 'Paul Grampel'
"Flower deep orange-scarlet (does not burn), in large cluster; brighter than 'Gloria Mundi'—not as double, but larger." [ARA32/221] "Moderately vigorous...with clean foliage...orange-scarlet flowers which scarcely fade or blue." [ARA35/196] "Its orange color is not as hard as that of some others." [ARA34/205] "A vigorous erect plant with light green foliage...2×2 [ft; ca. 6×6 dm]." [B] "Still-glorious." [ARA35/143]

Paul Grampel
Listed as 'Paul Crampel'.

Perle (Kiese, 1913) trans., "Pearl"
"Considering stature, this introduction bears much resemblance to 'Katharina Zeimet'. The light pink color is very delicate, but the blossoms aren't fragile. Each inflorescence is composed of forty blossoms, and indeed forms a perfect bouquet." [JR38/40]

Perle Angevine (Délépine, 1920) trans., "Angers Pearl"
From 'Jeanne d'Arc' (Pol) × 'Mrs. W.H. Cutbush' (Pol).
"Blush pink, small, full, open, long-lasting, in clusters, floriferous, constant, few thorns, growth 5 [*on a scale of 10*], upright." [Jg] "Bud small;

flower small, open, double, lasting, pale rose, borne in cluster on strong stem. Foliage sufficient, medium size, rich green, disease-resistant. Few thorns. Moderate grower, upright, bushy; blooms profusely from June to October." [ARA22/150]

Perle d'Or (Widow Rambaux & Dubreuil, 1883) trans., "Pearl of Gold"
From 'Polyantha Alba Plena Sarmentosa' (Mult) × either 'Mme. Falcot' (T) or 'Mme. Charles' (T).
"Apricot, pink and cream tones…to 3 [ft; ca. 1 m]." [HRG] "A golden copper." [ARA24/94] "Clusters of buff-yellow…with pink shadings…shapely…rich green foliage…43 [ft; ca. 1.3×1 m]." [B] "Double, small, fragrant; light golden yellow, center pinkish. Continuous." [Lg] "Fragrant…vigorous." [Cx] "[*As compared to other early Polyanthas,*] more blossoms, better shaped and larger, plant dwarfer, with handsome foliage of a bright green. The flowers are in a tight cluster of 20-30, buds long-oval, stems strong and upright, flowers large for the type, well formed, expanding well, of nankeen-yellow with an orange center and elongated elliptical petals which are imbricated and recurved. Surpasses all others of this sort by reason of its bearing and coloration." [JR7/169] "Developed by P. Rambaux in 1875 and released to commerce in 1883 by F. Dubreuil." [JR24/5] "Plant healthy, dense, and vigorous. Blossoms slightly larger than those of 'Mlle. Cécile Brunner', foliage slightly larger, plant slightly more compact; ever-delightful, a good poster-boy for the Polyanthas in its shapeliness, varying hues, and air of frank generosity." [BCD]

Perle des Rouges (Dubreuil, 1896) trans., "Pearl of the Reds"
"Deep velvety crimson, produced in clusters, and blooming abundantly and late in the season." [P1] "Dwarf, very floriferous, blooms in clusters, blooming until frost, as sparkling as those of 'Cramoisi Supérieur', shallowly cupped, numerous petals, thick, regularly imbricated, stiff, looking

like a pompon when opening, superb velvety crimson red with bright cerise reflections." [JR21/3] "The best of the red Pompons." [J]

Perle Orléanaise (Duveau, 1912) trans., "Orléans-ish Pearl"
From 'Mme. Norbert Levavasseur' (Pol) × 'Frau Cecilie Walter' (Pol).
"Bush vigorous, canes strong, erect, red-tinted; foliage brilliant dark green, glossy, tinted purple-red, very hardy, healthy; thorns rare. Flowers in terminal panicles, quite erect, profuse, medium-sized, rosette-form, quite double, of a pretty coloration: bright salmon pink nuanced saffron, particularly at the base of the petals, making a most charming effect with the bronzy-green foliage; bloom continuous." [JR37/9]

[**Petit Constant**] (Soupert & Notting, 1899) trans., no doubt referring to a little boy named "Constant," but also punning on the blossoms' being petite and appearing constantly.
From 'Mignonette' (Pol) × 'Luciole' (T).
"Vigorous bush; pretty reddish foliage; graceful bud; blooming in very large corymbs of good hold; flower small, full; color, dark nasturtium red and carmine with reflections of dawn and orange yellow. A variety all its own, unique in its genre. Very fragrant and floriferous." [JR23/170]

Petite Françoise (Gravereaux, 1915) trans., "Little Françoise"
"Delicate pink." [Ÿ]

Petite Léonie (Soupert & Notting, 1892) trans., "Little Léonie"
From 'Mignonette' (Pol) × 'Duke of Connaught' (HT).
"Dwarf, bushy, flower small, full, imbricated, outer petals porcelain white tinted light pink, the center shining carmine lake." [JR16/139]

Petite Marcelle (Dubreuil, 1910) trans., "Little Marcelle"
"Bush of small dimensions, much branched, always in bloom, clothed in beautiful dark green leaves. Inflorescence a cluster of 5 to 10 small flowers,

the buds when opening looking much like those of 'Rose du Roi' in miniature, making a very pretty rosette. Flowers very double, snow white, opening well, numerous muddled petals, imbricated like those of a big daisy." [JR34/168]

[**Phyllis**] (Merryweather, 1908)
"Beautiful cerise pink. Flowers are borne in great clusters on a little bush from a foot to eighteen inches high [ca. 3-4.5 dm] and very symmetrical in shape. As a bedding variety it is splendid." [C&Js11]

[**Picotte**] (Geschwind, 1890) trans., "Picotee"
"Striped." [Jg]

[**Pink Cécile Brunner**] (Western Rose Co., 1918)
Presumably a sport from 'Mlle. Cécile Brunner' (Pol).
"Rose-pink, darker than '[Mlle.] Cécile Brunner', with darker colored foliage, and not quite as large a grower. Continuous. Tested only in California." [Th2] *Cf.* 'Rita Sammons' (Pol).

Pink Pet (Lilley, 1928)
"Flower double, bright pink, borne in large clusters. Growth upright; early bloomer." [ARA29/222] "Small stocky plant…deep green foliage, plant 2 [ft; ca. 6 dm]." [HRG] "Small, double, flat; bright soft pink. Continuous…1-3 [ft; ca. 3-10 dm]. Healthy, shiny green foliage…outstanding." [Lg]

Pink Posy (Cocker, 1983)
From 'Trier' (Lambertiana) × 'New Penny' (Min).
Pink.

Pink Soupert (Dingee & Conard, 1896)
From 'Clotilde Soupert' (Pol) × 'Lucullus' (Ch).

"Perfectly full and double, very sweet, blooms all the time; fine rose pink, sometimes striped with white." [C&Jf97] "A seedling from 'Clotilde Soupert', with rosette-shaped flowers varying from pale pink to red." [VA97] "Very low-growing, weak; foliage barely sufficient, black-spots very slightly in midsummer, mildews in late summer; bloom hardly more than sparse, continuous." [ARA18/129]

Pinkie (Swim, 1947)
Sport of 'China Doll' (Pol).
"Small, double; deep rose pink. Profuse...1 [ft; ca. 3 dm]...excellent border plant." [Lg] Keen fans of Eighteenth-Century British painting may wish to plant 'Pinkie' in association with the Centifolia 'Blue Boy'.

Prevue (James, 1978)
From a seedling (which resulted from crossing the Multiflora 'Tausendschön' with a seedling resulting from crossing 'Perle d'Or' and "old China" [presumably 'Parsons' Pink China']) × 'Safrano' (T). Seems like a lot of trouble to go to to come up with a little white Polyantha! White.

Primula (Soupert & Notting, 1900)
From 'Mignonette' (Pol) × an unnamed seedling.
"Carmine pink with a white eye." [Ÿ] "Vigorous and stocky; graceful bud; flower small, fullish; color, bright China pink, center snow white. Distinctive coloration, like that of *Primula chinensis.*" [JR24/148]

Princess Ena (H.B. May, 1906)
Sport of 'Mme. Norbert Levavasseur' (Pol).
"Pink." [Ÿ] "Pretty little flowers which are very effective, quite another 'Mrs. W.H. Cutbush' of the 'Gloire des Polyantha' type, only slightly paler." [JR31/74]

[**Princesse Elisabeth Lancellotti**] (Soupert & Notting, 1892)
"Bush and foliage like 'Clotilde Soupert'; flower large, full, flat form, blooming in corymbs, color light yellow-white, center canary yellow, very floriferous and fragrant." [JR16/139]

[**Princesse Henriette de Flandres**] (Soupert & Notting, 1888)
From 'Mignonette' (Pol) × 'Marquise de Vivens' (T).
"Vigorous bush; flower small, full, beautiful form; color, salmony yellow, nankeen yellow center, on a ground of flesh-pink. *Scent of violets.*" [JR12/55]

Princesse Joséphine de Flandres (Soupert & Notting, 1888)
From 'Mignonette' (Pol) × 'Marquise de Vivens' (T).
"Dwarf, flower small, full; color, blush pink on a ground of salmon; very fragrant." [JR12/55]

Princesse Marie Adélaïde de Luxembourg (Soupert & Notting, 1895)
Seedling of 'Mignonette' (Pol).
"Bushy, blooming in corymbs; flower small, very full, magnificently imbricated; color, ovary white nuanced flesh pink, center bright pink. Very attractive fragrance." [JR19/148] "Neat compact grower…flowers medium size with over-lapping petals, very double; color rosy flesh with carmine centre; very sweet." [C&Js98]

[**Princesse Wilhelmina des Pays-Bas**] (Soupert & Notting, 1885)
From 'Mignonette' (Pol) × 'Mme. Daimaizin' (T).
"Compact bush; flower small, well filled, imbricated, color sparkling white, sometimes green in the center; has the look of a double Stocks; the flowers remain fresh and beautiful for 8 to 10 days. This rose…is remontant." [JR9/149]

Radium (Grandes Roseraies/Houry, 1913)
"Dwarf, very vigorous and hardy bush, with erect canes, well-held, foliage persistent. Blooms in profuse panicles of 15-20 buds opening successively; color, very delicate pink, pearly gold at the center, a very pretty look for beds and the open border." [JR38/25]

Red Soupert
Listed as 'Ma Petite Andrée'.

Red Triumph (Morse, 1956)
Sport of 'Orange Triumph' (Pol).
Very dark red.

Renoncule (Barbier, 1913) trans., 'Ranunculus'
"Dwarf; foliage cheerful green, glossy. Continuous bloom, abundant, clusters of 15-50 blossoms. Flowers of medium size, double, in the form of a Ranunculus, very prettily colored bright salmon pink, very fresh, quite different from other varieties." [JR37/167]

Rita Sammons (Clarke, 1925)
Sport of 'Mlle. Cécile Brunner' (Pol).
"One shade deeper pink than that of 'Mlle. Cécile Brunner', and fading less than that variety. Stature and blooming the same; but the entire plant is ruddier, very attractively so—canes, leaves, and indeed hips all handsomely and richly darker in color than those of 'Mlle. Cécile Brunner'. The plant sets more hips, and indeed these become quite an attractive feature of the plant in the Fall and Winter. Compact, healthy, and—once established—vigorous. An outstanding rose with a distinctive character in the garden." [BCD] *Cf.* 'Pink Cécile Brunner'.

Rödhätte (Poulsen, 1911) trans., "Red-Hat" (alias "Little Red Riding-Hood")

From 'Mme. Norbert Levavasseur' (Pol) × either 'Liberty' (HT) or 'Richmond' (HT).
"Flower clear cherry-red, fairly large, semi-double. Growth vigorous and free-flowering." [GeH] "Cherry-red; semi-double, large, continuous bloomer. Foliage mildews in damp conditions. Rather small growth." [Th2]

[**Rösel Dach**] (Walter, 1906)
"Cherry-red, edge lighter, very full." [Jg]

Rottkäppchen (Geschwind, 1887) trans., "Little Red Cap" (alias "Little Red Riding-Hood")
"Bright red." [JR17/9] "Red, large, full, dwarf." [Sn]

[**Schneeball**] (Türke, ca. 1890) trans., "Snowball"
From 'Mignonette' (Pol) × 'Maréchal Niel' (N).
"White." [Jg]

[**Schneekopf**] (Lambert, 1903) trans., "Snow-Head"
From 'Mignonette' (Pol) × 'Souvenir de Mme. Sablayrolles' (T).
"Shell pink." [CA07] "Yellow, turning white." [CA10] "Has the same vigorous habit of growth as 'Clotilde Soupert'—a bush thick with branches and usually quite full of bloom; the blossoms open perfectly, showing beautiful cup-shaped petals, waxy white and sometimes tinged flesh pink." [C&Js08]

Schneewitchen (Lambert, 1901)
From 'Aglaia' (Lambertiana) × an unnamed seedling (resulting from crossing the Polyantha 'Pâquerette' with the Tea 'Souvenir de Mme. Levet').
"Yellowish white, small, moderately full, moderate scent, dwarf." [Sn] "Bushes candelabra shaped and each branch bearing from 15 to 50 lit-

tle flowers, creamy-white passing to snow-white." [C&Js07] Floriferous." [Ck]

Schöne von Holstein (Tantau, 1919) trans., "Holstein Beauty"
Seedling of 'Orléans-Rose' (Pol).
"Pink, medium size, full, dwarf." [Sn] "Flower full, pure 'Hermosa'-pink, better than 'Mrs. W.H. Cutbush'. A free bloomer." [ARA21/164]

Siegesperle (Kiese, 1915) trans., "Victory-Pearl"
Seedling of 'Tausendschön' (Multiflora).
"Yellowish white, small, not very full, dwarf." [Sn] "Flower semi-double, white, light red along the edge. The bush grows 40-50 cm high [ca. 16-20 inches], heavy and continuous bloom." [Ck]

Sisi Ketten (Ketten Bros., 1900)
From 'Mignonette' (Pol) × 'Safrano' (T).
"Blossom peach pink veined carmine on a ground of yellowish white, large for the sort, full, starry, opening well. Growth dwarf, vigorous, erect, very floriferous...Dedicated to a daughter of the breeders. Excellent for borders and pots." [JR24/147]

Sleepy
Listed as 'Balduin'.

Sneezy
Listed as 'Bertram'.

Sneprinsesse (Grootendorst, 1946) syn., 'Snow White'; trans., "Snow Princess"
Sport of 'Dick Koster' (Pol).
White.

[**Snowball**] (Walsh, 1901)
"A most charming little rose, everyone wants it, blooms in large clusters, completely covering the plant—pure snow white and delightfully perfumed." [C&Js02] Also attributed to Henderson, 1899. Not to be confused with 'Schneeball'.

Snow White
Listed as 'Sneprinsesse'.

[**Souvenir de Mlle. Élise Châtelard**] (Bernaix, 1890) trans., "In Memory of Mlle. Élise Châtelard"
"Dwarf bush, much branched at the base, forming a compact bush which is rounded and regular as the canes develop in a fairly uniform manner. Foliage relatively small, very brilliant, deep green above, paler beneath, flowers numerous, from 3-4 cm in diameter [to ca. 1½ inches], of beautiful form, beautiful very fresh carmine red color. The outer petals are mucronate, the center ones are creped, giving the flower a very fetching crimpled look." [JR14/163-164]

Sparkler (De Ruiter, 1929)
Sport of 'Golden Salmon' (Pol).
"Sparkling brilliant red." [ARA32/222] "Bud small, globular; flower small, cupped, semi-double, very lasting, red, burning in the sun, in cluster on long stem. Foliage light green. Growth moderate (1.5 feet [ca. 4.5 dm]), upright; profuse bloomer (1000 blooms in season)." [ARA22/179]

Spray Cécile Brunner (Howard Rose Co., 1941)
Sport of 'Mlle. Cécile Brunner' (Pol).
"Small, double, very fragrant; light to medium pink. Excellent repeat…when established…10-15 [ft; ca. 3.3-5 m]…shorter, and repeats bloom much better than 'Climbing [Mlle.] Cécile Brunner'." [Lg] Said to be much confused in commerce with 'Bloomfield Abundance'.

Stadtrat Meyn (Tantau, 1919)
Seedling of 'Orléans-Rose' (Pol).
"Light orange-red, medium size, full, dwarf." [Sn] "Large, full flowers in very large clusters; luminous brick-red. Vigorous." [ARA21/164]

Summer Dawn (Proctor, 1950)
Sport of 'Margo Koster' (Pol).
Dawn pink to light rose.

Sunshine (Robichon, 1927)
"Charming…best yellow of the race…While the plants are only moderate in vigor, and the pale orange flowers fade almost white in hot weather, the light scarlet buds are most attractive and it is decidedly worth having if you like Polyanthas." [ARA34/213] "Fades too quickly but is really worth keeping because of the yellow shades of the newly opened buds." [ARA35/204]

Susanna (Weigand, 1914)
2nd generation seedling of 'Tausendschön' (Multiflora).
"The plant maintains a bearing which is both very dwarf and compact, without shooting out the long stems produced by the liked of 'Mme. Norbert Levavasseur'. The coloration is that of 'Tausendschön'. The blossoms are small, quite full, with petals slightly folded back like those of 'Ännchen Müller'; they are produced in large clusters which cover the whole plant and last a very long time. The flower clusters strike one as those expected of a climber rather than of a dwarf Polyantha, and are indeed much like those of 'Tausendschön'. The good keeping qualities of the cut flowers have impressed those who have seen it for themselves." [JR38/75]

The Allies (Heers, 1930)
"Bud small, globular; flower small, double, full, open, lasting, slightly fragrant, white suffused pale pink, in cluster. Foliage small, glossy. Growth dwarf (16 inches [ca. 4 dm]), bushy; free bloomer in May, June, and November." [ARA33/178]

The Fairy (Bentall, 1932)
Two parentages have been reported: (1), from 'Paul Crampel' (Pol) × 'Lady Gay' (Wichuraiana); (2), sport of 'Lady Godiva' (Wichuraiana).
"Flower salmon-pink, in cluster. Beautiful foliage." [ARA33/173] "Ideal for massed, groundcover planting. Clusters of bead-like buds open to globular, pink flowers…flowering almost continuously…Good foliage…2×4 [ft; ca. 6×13 dm]." [B]

Tip-Top (Lambert, 1909) syn., 'Baby Doll'
From 'Trier' (Lambertiana) × a seedling of *R. fœtida* 'Bicolor'.
"Coppery, orange towards the center, edges pink and white; flower very large, full, very floriferous, moderate vigor; good for bedding." [Cx] "Low-growing…foliage plentiful until midsummer, then barely sufficient, black-spots very little…mildews some…bloom moderate, continuous." [ARA18/129] "Its blooms are rather large, the petals beautifully crimped and white, with a broad margin of clear pink…not as floriferous as many others…growth relatively weak…eighteen inches [ca. 4.5 dm]. The foliage is also small, which helps to give the plant an undernourished appearance." [ARA20/59] "The open flowers look like balls of pink and white pop-corn." [ARA29/50] "Lovely little blossoms of rose and copper." [ARA29/97] "Lovely bud, opening with high but loose center, petals often reflexed, lasting. Continuous bloomer. Vigorous. Small to medium growth. Fine foliage. A distinct and desirable rose." [Th2]

Topaz (Tantau/Conard-Pyle, 1937)
From 'Johanna Tantau' (Pol) × an unnamed seedling (arising from crossing the HT 'Professor Gnau' with the Pernetiana 'Julien Potin').
"Small blooms like tiny H.T. blooms, light golden yellow on petite twiggy plant, 12 inches [ca. 3 dm]." [HRG]

Triomphe Orléanais (Peauger, 1912) trans., "Orléans-ish Triumph"
"Growth vigorous, foliage a handsome glossy green, with erect branches. Flowers large for the sort , in clusters, a pretty and intense cherry-red, lasting well and long without bluing, and weather-resistant...Superior to and distinct from the beautiful variety 'Mme. Norbert Levavasseur'. In color, this newcomer resembles 'Jessie' and 'Eva Teschendorff'; but it is more vigorous, more disease-resistant, and the flower clusters are larger." [JR36/184] "The best red-colored, as well as the most vigorous growing, Polyantha. Flower-clusters very large; holds its color well over a long period." [ARA18/134] "Of the clearest and brightest red, borne in abundance." [ARA20/59] "Tall, vigorous; foliage very plentiful till late summer, then barely sparse, black-spot increasing from midsummer, mildew in late summer; bloom profuse till late summer, then decreasing to moderate in October and November, continuous." [ARA18/129]

Vatertag (Tantau, 1959) trans., "Father's Day"
Sport of 'Muttertag' (Pol).
Coral-orange.

Verdun (Barbier, 1918)
"Purplish carmine-red." [Cw] "Flowers are borne in pyramidal trusses of twenty-five to fifty, and are rather large, well-formed, globular, of a splendid carmine-purple, brighter than '[Turner's] Crimson Rambler'. Do not fade or turn violet. Dwarf, branching shrub; exceedingly floriferous."

[ARA19/101] A **Verdun Superior**, of which we have no further reports and which is of unknown provenance, is also to be found.

Waverly Triumph (Poulter, 1951)
Sport of 'Orange Triumph' (Pol).
Pink, yellow at the nub. Writing a book seems to us a very waverly triumph indeed, all things considered.

White Cécile Brunner (Fauque & fils/Vigneron, 1909)
Sport of 'Mlle. Cécile Brunner' (Pol).
"Cream-yellow to white, light yellow or fawn center, bleaches when fully open to white cream. Foliage lighter in color than '[Mlle.] Cécile Brunner'. Continuous bloomer. The smallest grower of the '[Mlle.] Cécile Brunner' type." [Th2] "Maintains all of the good qualities of '[Mlle.] Cécile Brunner'...flowers of pure white, sulphur yellow, and chamois may be found on the same plant." [JR33/152] "Not a white." [ARA25/105]

White Koster (Introducer unknown, date uncertain)
Presumably a sport from 'Margo Koster' (Pol) or 'Dick Koster' (Pol) or the like.
White.

White Pet
Listed as 'Little White Pet'.

Yvonne Rabier (Turbat, 1910)
From an *R. wichuraiana* cultivar × a Polyantha cultivar.
"Double, flat; pure white, center tinted soft yellow. Continuous...compact, vigorous...1-2 [ft; ca. 3-6 dm]." [Lg] "Very free and perpetual flowering." [NRS/13] "Clusters of small double white flowers...hints of lemon in the base...Glossy rich green foliage...2×2 [ft; ca. 6×6 dm]." [B] "Very hardy, foliage ample and abundant, brilliant green, persistent, very

decorative. Its numerous, sturdy scapes bear great clusters of good-sized flowers, pure white with a very light touch of sulphur. The buds are white with a light tinge of green, open easily, and are well poised." [JR34/167] "Medium height, vigorous; foliage very plentiful, black-spots slightly...bloom abundant and moderate by turns, but continuous." [ARA18/129] "Discolors badly in heat...Very strong grower." [Th2]

Chapter Ten

Early Hybrid Teas

"The Hybrid Tea Rose (*Rosa Indica odorata hybrida*) is a group produced from crossing Teas with Hybrid Perpetuals." [pH] The cultivar which was often advanced as the "first Hybrid Tea," 'La France', is of course not this at all, having been introduced and recognized as a Bourbon hybrid, while other, earlier, roses which were indeed the product of crossing Teas with Hybrid Perpetuals, such as 'Victor Verdier', were put into the *Hybrid Perpetual* class: "These, like the Hybrid China roses, are usually classed with the Hybrid Perpetuals; indeed, there is practically very little difference between them…[*they*] possess the delicacy of color and fragrance of the Teas, and the vigor of those Hybrid Perpetuals owing their parentage to the Damask Rose." [TW] "They have all the qualities of the tea-rose but their color is not so rich." [G&B] "In hardiness it excels the Teas as a class, and in blooming it is more constant than the Hybrid Perpetuals, but, *per contra*, it is seldom as hardy as the best of the Hybrid Perpetuals and flowers less continuously than the Teas...In the North it is much smaller than the Hybrid Perpetual, and in the Southwest and South it is rivaled or excelled by the Tea in vigor. The foliage is more resistant to mildew than most Hybrid Perpetuals, yet generally inferior to the Tea in this respect. Loss of foliage varies also between the easily-lost leaves of the Hybrid Perpetual to the long-lived Tea foliage...Altogether, the Hybrid Teas combine everything and anything!" [Th2]

What, then, was the first Hybrid Tea? We begin to see, dimly, some candidates emerging in 1849, with Vibert's 'Élise Masson', Odier's 'Gigantesque', and Portemer's 'Léonore d'Este', and in 1852 Robert's 'Adèle Bougère', all of which are included below in the listings. In Lyon, Lacharme, perhaps at least partially as a byproduct of his quest to produce a white Hybrid Perpetual, took to crossing Teas with Hybrid Perpetuals, and had already made important contributions to the HTs by the time Henry Bennett in England began to systematically develop the class. As Bennett tells us, "For quite a long time, I had been a rose propagator, and, over forty years, had gotten to know many introductions. In 1865, I began to make roses the object of my study, and indeed found that during all this time no one had made great progress; I thought at that point that one should be able to get good results from intelligent cross breeding. I had had a great deal of experience in breeding domestic animals, and the wonderful results I had obtained encouraged me to continue my experimentation on flowers. In 1870, I visited the nurseries of the various rosarians at Lyon, but nowhere saw any progress being made in breeding roses by scientific methods. Jean Sisley lamented continually that he had brought artificial pollination to the attention of his comrades in vain. Looking closer, I saw that raising seedlings in France was comparable to raising livestock on the Mexican prairies—everything was left to itself; a person would simply choose the best of what nature had to offer. This made me certain that before me lay an open, unexplored field. I made my first attempts, and found that there were many difficulties to surmount before I would be able to gather the first seeds from the crosses; it was necessary to know which of the different types differed from one another in their individual characteristics. Tea roses were often crossed with the remontants, and vice-versa; I have found that Moss Roses, and Chinas, etc., are equally easy to cross. For my main tries, I ordinarily use 'Alba Rosea' [*poss. 'Mme. Bravy'*] and 'President' [*'Adam'*] as the seed-bearer, crossing them with 'Louis Van Houtte', 'Victor Verdier', and so forth. My purpose was to raise remontant roses of pure white and of yellow, as well as purplish-red Tea roses of a color both intense and dark. In token of my progress, I offer the first six Hybrid Teas to be released to commerce." [JR10/23] The six would be: 'Beauty of Stapleford', 'Duchess of Connaught', 'Duchess of Westminster', 'Duke of Connaught', 'Jean Sisley', and 'Michael Saunders'. These are bush HTs; it should meantime be borne in mind that the climbing 'Cheshunt Hybrid' from George Paul in 1872, found in our chapter on Noisettes and Climbers, was "the first Rose to be known and recognized as a Hybrid Tea." [F-M2]

"In the year 1879, when Bennett came out in Stapleford for the first time with the so-called Hybrid Tea Roses, most of his fellow countrymen shook their heads in disbelief about his undertaking, particularly since he was no gardener, denying him any success at it because his roses produced no firm stems, and what was more were good only for greenhouse culture! I am still amused by the recollection of William Paul showing me Bennett's first six Hybrid Teas in his greenhouse at Waltham, and saying, 'These are good for nothing but the greenhouse.'—What successes he has had with his seedlings since then!" [RZ86/5-6]

Our focus in this chapter is on the early Hybrid Teas, in particular to 1900, including as well a generous sprinkling of other, slightly later, ones often of interest to lovers of old roses. The next phase in the story of Hybrid Teas, and the inception of the closely-related—but oh what a difference!—Pernetianas will be found in the companion to this book, *The*

Old Rose Adventurer, the chapters there focusing on the exciting period 1900-1920 when these groups, at first in parallel, began to converge to produce at length the modern Hybrid Tea. Perhaps because "Hybrid Tea" is not so exotic a name as "Bourbon" or "Hybrid Perpetual," the original Hybrid Teas are very much neglected today, a most unfortunate situation. "So what shall remain of that whole riot of fine, gloriously colored and gracefully shaped Hybrid Teas? They will disappear like the old Hybrid Perpetuals." [ARA37/197]

Abbé André Reitter (Welter, 1901)
"Delicate flesh." [LS] "Light pink, large, full, light fragrance, medium height." [Sn]

Abbé Millot (Bénard/Corbœuf-Marsault, 1899)
"Silvery pink." [LS] "Large, full, medium height." [Sn]

Adam Rackles (Rommel, 1905)
Sport of 'Mme. Caroline Testout' (HT).
"Pink on a white ground." [LS] "Light pink, very large, full, light fragrance, moderately tall." [Sn]

[**Adèle Bougère**] (Robert, 1852)
"Bush not very vigorous; branches bend under the weight of the rose; thorns reddish green, leaves smooth, not very dentate; flower from 6-7 cm in diameter [ca. 3½ inches], full, well held; color, velvety purple-black." [S] The bending branches and lack of vigor typified the early HTs.

Admiral Dewey (Taylor, 1899)
Sport of 'Mme. Caroline Testout' (HT).
"A splendid new Constant-Blooming Rose; flowers large and beautifully formed, quite full and double, with broad, shell-shaped petals, delightfully

tea-scented; color, rich creamy rose, delicately shaded with fine golden-yellow and peach blossom tints. A clean, healthy grower and abundant bloomer, very handsome." [C&Js02] "A light-coloured sport of ['Mme. Caroline Testout'] from America." [F-M2] "Color a beautiful light blush pink, clear and distinct; free bloomer and very fragrant." [CA01] But there was also evidently another, and mysterious, 'Admiral Dewey': "Velvety cinnabar." [LS] "Red, large, full, medium height." [Sn]

Amateur André Fourcaud (Puyravaud, 1903)
Seedling of 'Mme. Caroline Testout' (HT).
"Light pink, reverse darker." [Ÿ] "Flower handsome pink, reverse of petals very bright pink, very large, high-centered, bud very long, semi-double, fragrant, borne on a firm stem, very well branched, very floriferous, very beautiful." [JR27/149]

Andenken an Moritz von Frölich (Hinner, 1905) trans., "In Memory of Moritz von Frölich"
From 'Mme. Caroline Testout' (HT) × ? 'Princesse de Béarn' (HP).
"Dark red, large, full, light scent, tall." [Sn]

Antoine Rivoire (Pernet-Ducher, 1895)
From 'Dr. Grill' (T) × 'Lady Mary Fitzwilliam' (HT).
"In the soft shell pink or cream-tinted pinks, the beautiful old 'Antoine Rivoire', a clean-foliaged plant, is the sturdiest and best." [ARA40/42] "A charming rose of rose-pink colouring, shaded with yellow. The flowers are rather flat, and borne moderately freely. Its growth is fairly vigorous and erect, displaying the blossoms perfectly." [OM] "Cream, touched with salmon rose." [E] "Cream with orange centre. Camellia-like flower; very free." [H] "Fresh pink and white." [J] "Rosy flesh shaded and bordered carmine, base of petals yellow…large, full, and imbricated. A splendid Rose for all purposes." [P1] "Pale creamy buff." [Hk] "It grows with vigor, giving very pretty flowers which are large, well-formed, flesh-pink and

even salmon-pink, the edges of the petals shaded carmine." [JR21/98] "Frequently five inches in diameter [ca. 1.25 dm]. Full and double." [Dr] "Flesh to cream-yellow-peach center, sometimes with lilac shading; perfume mild...growth high and strong but lacking in bushiness." [ARA17/22-23] "Lacks perfume." [ARA25/99] "Holds center in heat; slight fragrance. Best in spring, not only in bloom, but in strength of stem. Owing to loss of foliage, cannot be recommended for [*the warmest zones*], but being almost immune from mildew is splendid in damp climates. Form seldom beautiful enough for exhibition." [Th2] "Early, and good in autumn.—(Prune medium)." [JP] "Vigorous free bloomer." [HRG] "The flowers, cupped, are the prettiest color one could desire: flesh pink with a yellow center...It has a quantity of good qualities not possessed by other varieties—the very delicate tone of the blossoms, and their pretty form, their upright bearing, its dark foliage, and the longevity of the flowers. This last is not a worthless quality because, even while lasting so long as eight days, the flower doesn't change at all." [JR23/42] "Bud not of the best; opens flat but attractive and pleasing...Foliage, leathery, and of great substance; seldom affected by mildew, but sometimes lost by [*black-*] spot...Its worst fault is that in most seasons there is very little August bloom." [Th] "While not rampant, this Rose is vigorous in growth and of a rather branching habit; it is capable of making a good shaped plant, but does not always do so when grown as a dwarf...The foliage is fine, large, and leathery, of a dark green color with a bronzy tint, while the upper surface of the leaves is rather shiny. It is not subject to mildew, but rather liable to black spot. It flowers freely both early (mid-June) and late, the early blooms being the largest. The flowers are carried on erect stems and are of good shape and fairly full, pale cream in colour with a deeper centre, sometimes almost approaching very light orange at the base of the petals, which are of good substance, stout, and clean-cut, large for the size of the flower, deep and shell-shaped...Though best in fair weather, they will stand a fair amount of wet. They are fragrant, but not very sweet-scented." [NRS/10] "Branches slightly divergent; handsome foliage of a light green." [JR19/148] "Dark green foliage…3×3 [ft; ca 1×1 m]." [B] "Good blooms [*in Madeira*]." [DuC] "Blooms abundantly, nearly continuously in Tunisia…very vigorous, hardy…dedicated to a well-known horticulturist of Lyon." [JR34/170] Monsieur Antoine Rivoire was a president of the Lyon Horticulturists' Association.

Antonine Verdier (Jamain, 1872)
"Flower large, full, light carmine." [S] Parent of the early HTs 'Camoëns', 'Mlle. Brigitte Viollet', and 'Mme. Étienne Levet'.

Archiduchesse Marie-Dorothée Amélie
Listed as 'Erzherzogin Marie Dorothea'.

Argentine Cramon
Listed as 'Mlle. Argentine Cramon'.

Astra (Geschwind/Ketten Bros., 1890)
"Light pink, large, full, tall." [Sn] "Flower flesh pink, petals sometimes edged lighter, large, full, cupped, solitary. Moderate vigor, very floriferous. 'Astra' is probably 'Astrée', goddess of Justice." [JR14/146]

Attraction (Dubreuil, 1886)
"Of good vigor, very floriferous and extra-remontant, with somber green foliage, matte above, glaucescent beneath. Inflorescence an erect corymb of 3-5 upright blossoms with strong stems. Buds ovoid. Petals numerous, concave, mucronate, imbricated in the outer rows, light carmine, nuanced China pink, with a paler edging, yellowish nub; in appearance and scent intermediate between Centifolias and Teas." [JR10/149]

Augustine Guinoisseau
Listed as 'Mlle. Augustine Guinoisseau'.

Augustine Halem (Guillot & fils, 1891)
"Carmine rose shaded with purple; medium size and good form; free flowering and sweet." [P1] "Bright pink deepening to deep rose colour." [Dr] "Copper overlaid with pink, with deeper reverse...3×3 [ft; ca. 1×1 m]." [B] "Vigorous, robust, very floriferous, flower large, globular, full, very well formed, well-held; color, carmine-purplish-pink; fragrant; a very pretty variety." [JR15/148] "Of good habit and sweet." [CA95]

Augustus Hartmann (B.R. Cant, 1914)
"Light red, large, full, medium scent." [Sn]

[**Aurora**] (W. Paul, 1898)
"Pretty vigorous bush with beautiful dark green foliage, and abundant bloom; flower large, full, petals ragged; very fragrant and long lasting; color, salmon towards the center, paler at the petal edges. The very long buds and beautiful form make it easy to use for making bouquets." [JR22/58]

Australia Felix (A. Clark, 1919) trans., "Felicitous Australia"
From 'Jersey Beauty' (Wichuraiana) × 'La France' (B).
"Pink, medium size, moderately full, moderate fragrance, medium height." [Sn]

Australie (Kerslake, 1907)
"Dark pink, large, full, tall." [Sn]

Aviateur Michel Mahieu (Soupert & Notting, 1912) trans., "Aviator Michel Mahieu"
From 'Mme. Mélanie Soupert' (HT) × 'Lady Ashtown' (HT).
"Coral red with a bright center. Flower large, perfect form, held upright above the ample and rich foliage. Petals thick. Splendid rose for

bedding...Blooms without interruption until the first frosts. Very fragrant. Of the greatest value for all purposes." [JR37/10]

Avoca (A. Dickson, 1907)
"Crimson scarlet, buds very long and pointed, flowers large and sweetly perfumed, foliage large and very dark green." [C&Js09] "A beautiful shaped flower, of medium size, only useful for the late shows, as it is produced on the ends of long shoots which take time to grow...Not very free flowering. Fragrant." [H] "Very vigorous, semi-climbing; flower scarlet-red." [JR35/14] "Another crimson Rose I grow as a pillar is 'Avoca'. Grown in this way it is far more free flowering than as a cutback, and has given me some fine flowers...It is somewhat difficult to keep furnished at the base as a pillar, and...it is hardly sufficiently decorative in the garden, and is perhaps best grown pegged down." [NRS14/64]

Balduin (Lambert, 1898) syn., 'Helen Gould'
From 'Charles Darwin' (HP) × 'Marie Van Houtte' (T).
"Pure carmine; flower large, very full, globular, Camellia form; very floriferous; vigorous." [Cx] "Bright watermelon-red. Extensively used throughout the South." [Th2] "This newcomer of 1898 is a ravishing variety for planting in any bed one wishes to have constantly in bloom. It is one of the best introductions of P. Lambert of Trèves who has carefully tested this rose over several years before releasing it to commerce...This new rose should be placed, considering its quality, in the first rank with such varieties as 'La France' or 'K[aiserin] A[uguste] Viktoria'. The flower is large, very full, and of a crimson pink; the buds are long and usually in threes or fives at the ends of the vigorous branches; this variety is very remontant, and the flower buds keep developing without interruption until late in the season; the foliage of a nice shiny green is very ornamental...perfectly hardy...[*In Trèves there was a*] charming bed around the statue of the celebrated archbishop Balduin, to whom this rose was dedicated." [JR23/34-35] Not to be confused with the Polyantha 'Balduin'.

Baronne G. de Noirmont (S. Cochet, 1891)
"Vigorous, with upright branches; strong and reddish thorns which are remote; wood and leaves light green. Buds rounded; flowers large and full, having the form of the rose 'La France', globular, large petals, flesh pink with some salmon fading to blush white. The flowers open well, the stem is strong, the poise is good, and the bush is very floriferous." [JR15/163]

Béatrix, Comtesse de Buisseret (Soupert & Notting, 1899)
From an unnamed seedling × 'Mme. Caroline Testout' (HT).
"In the way of '[Mme.] Caroline Testout';...lovely silver rose passing to rosy carmine red." [C&Js02] "Bush vigorous with magnificent foliage; bud of extraordinary beauty; flower very large, full, of beautiful form and well-held; outer petals large and thick, those of the middle smaller and pointed. Color, silvery pink with carmine pink. Very floriferous and fragrant. Excellent for forcing and cutting." [JR23/170]

Beauty of Stapleford (Bennett, 1879)
From 'Mme. Bravy' (T) × 'Comtesse d'Oxford' (HP).
"Foliage like that of 'Alba Rosea' [*supp. syn. of 'Mme. Bravy'*], but more rounded; flowers large; petals large and well placed. Beautiful form; color, pale pink, darker towards the center. Beautiful exhibition rose." [JR3/114] "No particular merit, having flowers of pale rose colour, with darker centre." [B&V]

[**Becker's Ideal**] (Becker, 1903)
Sport of 'La France' (B).
"This new obtention differs from [*'La France'*] by way of its unique configuration, which is that of a perfect cup with the petals incurving rather than spreading out." [JR27/17] The placement of the sports of 'La France' is problematical—Bourbons like the parent, or Hybrid Teas as originally introduced? We opt for the latter, and salve our nagging conscience by noting the former.

Bedford Belle (Laxton, 1884)
From 'Gloire de Dijon' (N) × 'Souvenir du Comte de Cavour' (HP). "Light red." [Ÿ] "Flower large, very full, cupped, always opens easily; reddish white; of the 'La France' tribe; sometimes redder towards the outside. This variety, one of the most vigorous Hybrid Teas known so far, blooms from May until October…Very beautiful exhibition rose." [S] "Very vigorous…Flower very double, well formed, opens well, marbled pink, somewhat resembles 'La France'. Abundant bloom early to late. The bluish-green foliage is very distinct." [JR8/179]

Belle Siebrecht
Listed as 'Mrs. W.J. Grant' (HT).

Beryl
Listed in the chapter on Teas.

Bessie Brown (A. Dickson, 1900)
"Creamy white; immense flowers of perfect shape and great substance; free blooming and vigorous. The flowers are impatient of wet, and they also droop." [P1] "Fine form, full, large to extra large, fine fragrance, medium long stems. Good foliage, sufficient. Growth strong; hardy. Soft ivory-white, very lightly blushed in cool weather." [ARA23/156] "Lovely peachy pink, delicately shaded with rose and fawn." [C&Js02] "For exhibition, it is quite one of the best…The growth and foliage are strong, stout, and stiff; the blooms come exceedingly well, being rarely divided, and if there is any malformation it is usually of a slight nature. They are very large, sweet-scented, of perfect pointed semi-globular shape, and the fine petals open just as they should do, neither too stiffly nor too easily. The colour is a good true creamy white unstained; but it does not display the beauty of the flowers well upon the plant, for the stalk, though stout, is pliable, and the heavy blooms hang their heads…I have not found it affected by mildew; and though rain will harm it as it will all white Roses,

its pendant position protects the centre. It is not so good in autumn, and I fear it will be rather an exhibitor's Rose." [F-M2]

Betty (A. Dickson, 1905)
"A coppery rose overspread with golden yellow. Its flowers are extremely large, flowers all season and is deliciously perfumed." [C&Js08] "A superb novelty with marvelous coloration...its coppery salmon color is difficult to describe." [JR29/153] "Strong and upright growth; beautiful color; good bloomer, attractive bud." [ARA18/110] "Opens well in wet; rather thin." [NRS14/159]

Bona Weillschott (Soupert & Notting, 1889)
From 'Goubault' (T) × 'Marie Baumann (HP).
"Growth vigorous, flower large, full, centifolia-form; color, vermilion pink, center orange red; fragrant." [JR13/147]

British Queen (McGredy, 1912)
"The most beautiful white rose existing, surpassing, in perfection of form, all other white roses. The floriferousness is notable; it blooms from June to Winter. The blossom type is between 'Maman Cochet' and 'Frau Karl Druschki' with a Tea rose form. The petals are large, and well arranged; we often note in the bud a light pink tint which disappears when the flower opens, and is transformed into immaculate white." [JR36/171] "Small growth; shy bloomer." [ARA18/115]

[**Camoëns**] (Schwartz, 1881)
Seedling of 'Antonine Verdier' (HT).
"Extra large, full flowers; color China rose, suffused with pale yellow, passing to white, flushed with carmine; fragrant and fine." [CA90] "Red on a yellow ground." [LS] "The flowers, in a thick cluster, are of normal size, long, beautifully colored China pink striped white; the long pedicel is very bristly; the slightly glossy leaves are somewhat bronze; the wood is of moderate

strength, with strong, widely-spaced thorns." [JR5/117] "Moderate growth, very floriferous, very fragrant." [S] "Plant regular in form and very upright." [JR20/58] "One of Schwartz's best. Found in 1877, it didn't make its horticultural debut until November 1, 1881...Canes delicate green with some purple...the blossoms are about 9 cm [ca. 4 inches] across, well held, with central petals both short and long of a bright China pink which is very often striped white; not much scent; bud long, pointed. Blooms abundantly, and in clusters...Dedicated by the breeder to the author of *The Lusiad*, who died in 1579...Prune to 5 or 6 eyes." [JR10/76] Luiz Vaz de Camoëns (or Camões), Portuguese poet; lived 1524-1580.

Captain Christy (Lacharme, 1873)
From 'Victor Verdier' (HP) × 'Safrano' (T).
"Light salmon, petals edged in white, a new and fine distinct habited kind." [HstXXVIII:350] "Fine, fragrant soft pink." [ARA29/96] "Delicate flesh, deeper in center...flowers well in Autumn." [H] "Tea-scented, a most charming and delicate white, very large and fine." [HRH] "Peach-blow, deepening to rose-colour." [Dr] "Medium-size, sometimes large, full; the foliage when young somewhat resembles Mahonia leaves. Ill-shaped flowers are not uncommon, but it is a most lovely sort when in perfection." [EL] "Open." [F-M2] "[*Occasional ideal flowers with minimum care*]." [L] "Very large and very full, short-jointed, erect, delicate pink, with deeper centre; cup-shaped, becomes flatter" [Hn] "Has never given me seeds." [JR26/101] "Robust...handsome foliage, beautifully colored in Spring, coming well up under the flowers." [F-M2] "Ample foliage of a handsome lustrous green on top, paler beneath...As for the flower, it is the simple expression of grace and freshness—it is large, full, cupped, well-formed, well held, and, in color, tender flesh-white with tints of pink. Unfortunately, it has little scent, and has difficulty opening in unfavorable weather. The bud is very pretty." [JR10/77] "Plant is rather dwarf but sturdy. It is a dependable autumn bloomer." [ARA34/77] "[*Very satisfactory in Brazil*]." [PS] "In the breeding of 1869, [*Lacharme*] created a new

rose of the first order which he dedicated to Capt. Christy of London, one of the great amateur rosarians of England...The buds are much sought-after by florists." [JR2/25] "Talking of judging at the Lyons Exhibition, he [*George Paul*] tells me he well remembers suggesting Captain Christy's name being attached to Lacharme's new Rose of the year." [NRS20/27] "The flowers produced in the South of France are certainly more delicate and beautiful than those we are accustomed to in England...Foliage when young somewhat resembles Mahonia leaves." [B&V] "I can find no fault as to colour, shape, foliage, or anything else, save that I cannot have enough of his glorious blossoms set in the midst of their strong, handsome leaves, as if each one intended to be placed in a glass alone." [K1]

Captain Christy à Fleurs Panachées (Letellier, 1896)
Sport of 'Captain Christy' (HT).
"Striped white and pink." [Ÿ]

[**Cardinal**] (Cook, 1904)
From 'Liberty' (HT) × an unnamed seedling.
"Cardinal-red; medium size, full, but opens flat and blues in heat. Stems strong. Foliage lasts." [Th2] "Excels in perfume and blooming qualities." [ARA18/110] "Growth strong." [ARA23/157] "Form fair; fragrance good and enduring. Foliage susceptible to mildew and spot. Growth bushy but not tall; average stem. Averages 48 blooms per season. Prune to 5 eyes. Hardy." [ARA21/90]

Carmen Sylva (Heydecker/Dubreuil, 1891)
From 'Baronne Adolphe de Rothschild' (HP) × 'Mme. Barthélemy Levet' (T).
"Cream and carmine." [LS] "Seems to have sprung from 'Captain Christy'. The deportment and form of the rose are those of 'Captain Christy'. The only difference is in the yellowish color of the blossom. This variety is extremely floriferous." [JR23/39]

Caroline Testout
Listed as 'Mme. Caroline Testout'.

Cecil (B.R. Cant, 1926)
"Rich, deep golden yellow...in clusters, but each flower has a ten-inch stem [ca. 2.25 dm]." [ARA34/81] "The growth and vitality of the plant is all that can be asked of any rose...Free-flowering...[*but*] at Breeze Hill it is one of the stingiest bloomers we know." [ARA32/178] "A very attractive yellow single rose, freely borne on a rather reluctant plant until the end of June and very sparingly afterward...It is most attractive." [ARA31/186] "Succession of large, single buttercups." [ARA28/150] "Pretty golden stamens." [ARA28/150]

[**Charles J. Graham**] (A. Dickson, 1906)
"Thoroughly remarkable HT; its enormous flowers...are a superb orange crimson." [JR29/153] "Vigorous, flower large, full, sparkling crimson orange." [JR22/190]

[**Charlotte Gillemot**] (P. Guillot, 1894)
Descendant of 'Lady Mary Fitzwilliam' (HT).
"Vigorous bush, very floriferous, foliage shiny, stems and canes upright, strong; long, thick peduncles; buds in the form of an elongated egg, relatively large, pure white. Flower very regular, with petals reversed..., imbricated in an unbelievable perfection resembling that of the Camellias 'Alba Plena' and 'Alba Fimbriata'..." [JR18/147]

Château de Clos-Vougeot (Pernet-Ducher, 1908)
"Velvety maroon red nuanced and shaded dark maroon." [Riv] "Keeps its brilliant coloration despite the temperature." [JR32/85] "The darkest red, black as night, to be stroked with the eyes, velvety and voluptuous...spindly, sprawling growth." [Hk] "Growth above average; wonderful color; good fragrance; fair bloomer." [ARA18/110] "Good

vigor, branching; foliage somber green; thorns occasional and slightly protrusive; flower large, globular, full, richly colored crimson scarlet nuanced fiery red passing to blackish velvety purple." [JR32/25] "Delicious perfume." [JR32/124]

Chloris (Geschwind/Ketten Bros., 1890)
"Scarlet, large, very double, 1 m [ca. 3 feet]." [EU] "Blossom light purple crimson, very large, full, very fragrant. Bush of medium vigor and very floriferous. One of the biggest Hybrid Tea roses. Chloris, spouse of Zephyrus." [JR14/146-147]

Christobel (Croibier, 1937)
From 'Frau Karl Druschki' (HP) × 'Mme. Butterfly' (HT).
"Yellowish orange salmon, very large, full, tall." [Sn]

[**Clara Barton**] (Van Fleet/Conard & Jones, 1898)
From 'Climbing Clotilde Soupert' (Pol) × 'American Beauty' (HP).
"The color is a rare and exquisite shade of delicate amber pink, entirely different from any other rose with which we are acquainted. The flowers are quite large, three to three and one-half inches in diameter [ca. 7.5-8 cm], and double to the center; they are delightfully fragrant, and each one is set in a lovely rosette of leaves, completely encircling the flower and making it an elegant bouquet in itself. It is a most constant and abundant bloomer, continuously loaded with flowers during the whole growing season, and if taken indoors before cold weather, will bloom all winter as well. We think the plant will prove hardy with usual protection as far north as New York, unless in very exposed situations...It is an exquisite Rose in every way." [C&Js99] "After years of careful study and hybridizing the most beautiful varieties, we at last succeeded in obtaining this *grand new constant-blooming rose*, which has attracted so much attention, and proved of such remarkable beauty and value that we requested permission

of Miss Clara Barton, President of the world's Red Cross Society, to give it her name." [C&Js98]

[**Clara Watson**] (Prince, 1894)
"Silvery flesh with deep pink center." [CA17] "Bright salmon, center tinted rosy peach, free, fine form and habit." [HuD/04] "Fair growth and foliage; pretty color." [ARA18/118] "It has pretty pink flowers which last a long time, and when it is still a bud, it is particularly pretty...It seems superior to 'Souvenir du Président Carnot'." [JR24/129] "The flowers are very graceful, resembling 'Bridesmaid' in form, and are produced in remarkable profusion. The buds are very beautiful and are supported on long stems, making it desirable for cutting. The color is salmon pink, very difficult to describe." [C&Js07] "A very pretty hybrid tea, of a slightly fawn pink which everybody likes." [JR23/42]

Columbia (E.G. Hill, 1917)
From 'Ophelia' (HT) × 'Mrs. George Shawyer' (HT).
"Hydrangea pink." [Cw] "Light pink, with full petalage; opens somewhat flat in heat; deliciously fragrant. Good but not strong grower...Of exceptional value in cool conditions; must be given careful protection. Good in early and late seasons in Southern California. Scorches in heat." [Th2] "Perfume is its best point, although its keeping quality and form make it valuable as a cut-flower...The color does not spot in partial shade. It blooms freely." [ARA31/99] "Beautiful foliage and fine, healthy growth." [ARA18/96]

Commandant Letourneux (Bahaud/Ketten Bros., 1903)
Sport of 'Joséphine Marot' (HT).
"Bright, soft pink." [Ÿ]

[**Comte Henri Rignon**] (Pernet-Ducher, 1888)
From 'Baronne Adolphe de Rothschild' (HP) × 'Ma Capucine' (T).

"For many years, I [*Pernet-Ducher*] have doggedly pursued creating a hybrid tea which was not only yellow but which also had all the good qualities for which one might hope. In 1882, I fertilized some blossoms of the HP 'Baronne Adolphe de Rothschild' with pollen from 'Mme. Falcot', from which I got several seeds, among which was the one which gave me, the following year, 'Mlle. Germaine Caillot'...Since then, I have crossed Teas with Rothschild on a grand scale, and have gotten very curious and diverse results. From one of the crosses came, in 1885, the Hybrid Tea 'Comte Henri Rignon'." [JR12/136] "Dwarf, very hardy, strong growth, bloom abundant and constant; beautifully colored coppery yellow with a salmon pink center nuanced dawn gold, fading to salmon flesh white." [JR12/166] "Large, to very large, full, cupped, but flattish afterwards, delicate creamy-yellow, with a salmon-colored rose-red centre, unique. A magnificent rose, but owing to its short-jointed growth and very prickly stems, is not very suitable for cutting." [Hn] Joseph Pernet, known initially as Pernet fils, born in Lyon in November of 1859, died in November of 1928; took the name "Pernet-*Ducher*" upon his marriage to Marie Ducher, daughter of the rose-breeders, in 1882; their two sons Claudius and Georges were killed within days of each other early in the First World War. Monsieur Pernet-Ducher's "dogged pursuit" was the initial step in his contribution to the creation of the *modern* Hybrid Tea. Not finding his ideal yellow Hybrid Tea by crossing Teas with Hybrid Perpetuals—results not yellow enough—he turned to crossing *R. fœtida* with Hybrid Perpetuals, an ancestry which is latent in this present rose, as 'Ma Capucine' is the product of crossing a Tea with *R. fœtida*. We do not know how many of the crosses took; but that with the old HP 'Antoine Ducher' resulted in the Pernetiana class, also called "Lutea Hybrids," which, subsequently crossed and recrossed with the "true" or "old" Hybrid Teas, produced the initial members of our present race of Hybrid Teas, which thus are in effect Hybrid Hybrid Teas.

Comtesse Icy Hardegg (Soupert & Notting, 1907)
From 'Mrs. W.J. Grant' (HT) × 'Liberty' (HT).
"Shining pure carmine, always constant...The blossoms are larger and fuller than are those of 'Belle Siebrecht' [*i.e., 'Mrs. W.J. Grant'*], with larger petals of better consistency; the perfect bud is longer than that of its mother." [JR31/137]

[**Coronet**] (Dingee & Conard, 1897)
From 'Paul Neyron' (HP) × 'Bon Silène' (T).
"The flowers are very large, full and round; the color is clear pink, petals beautifully edged with reddish violet; they have a delicious tea fragrance, and are produced in great profusion." [C&Js99] "Like a continuous-blooming 'Paul Neyron'. The blossom is as large as tat of 'Paul Neyron', but the bloom is much more abundant. The perfume is as delicious as that of the Damask, and the flower as beautiful as that of a Peony. The breeders kept it under study for four years, and have scrutinized its various characteristics...The plant begins to bloom early, and all season produces long, large, beautiful, and quite full flowers. The bud is deep carmine and the expanded blossom is carnation pink with a silvery tone. The bush has the form and 'cut' of that of 'Paul Neyron', and takes the same culture as 'Bon Silène'. Very pretty plant." [JR21/68]

[**Countess of Caledon**] (A. Dickson, 1897)
"Large, full, and well formed, very free and good." [HuD/04] "Of good growth and foliage, rather of the H.P. character, and a fine Rose, hardly as well appreciated, I think, as it deserves. The stems are stiff and the flowers show themselves well; they are sweet-scented, of good semi-globular shape and a fine rich pink colour. The variety is a good example of the H.P. side of this class; but its thorough reliability for autumnal blooms shows the Tea cross. Good, as a half-standard, for exhibition, cutting, or garden decoration." [F-M2]

Dainty Bess (Archer, 1925)
From 'Ophelia' (HT) × 'K. of K.' (HT).
"Very lovely and attractive, single, sweet-scented blooms in clusters on strong, upright stems...a delightful shade of salmon-pink, the daintiness of which is greatly increased by prominent red stamens and somewhat frilled petals...Its growth is robust and its foliage free of mildew. Considered the finest single rose introduced for some years." [ARA26/178] "Flower 3.5 to 4 inches across [ca. 7.5-8.5 cm], single, broad petaled, fimbriated petals, rose color, borne several together." [ARA26/181] "Very little autumn bloom...the notched petals form a flower more nearly square than round...exceedingly lovely." [ARA30/174] "Has won friends everywhere. All reports are favorable...it is more or less stingy, giving very few flowers throughout the summer and in autumn." [ARA31/187] "There seems to be no halting the flow of enthusiastic adjectives concerning this rose...We still stick to our opinion, expressed last year, that, in spite of her beauty, Bess is a stingy and ungrateful girl." [ARA32/180] "The most delicately beautiful single rose, in both form and color...two tones of either light rose or rose-pink...from three to four inches in diameter [ca. 7.5cm-1 dm]...in clusters." [ARA34/81] "Very free bloom...3-4 [ft; ca. 1-1.3 m." [Lg] "Exquisitely beautiful." [ARA40/43]

Dame Edith Helen (A. Dickson, 1926)
From 'Mrs. John Laing' (HP) × ?
"A large, finely shaped, clear pink bloom, with plenty of substance, freely produced on long, stiff stems; sweetly scented. Vigorous; foliage free of mildew; good for garden purposes." [ARA26/181] "Beautiful, but not vigorous...shy after the first blooming...plants grow little, and seem to get smaller every year...leaves fall of early...very beautiful, fragrant blooms...Throughout the South, it seems to do well." [ARA30/175] "Did wonderfully the first year but has done nothing since." [ARA31/97] "Its

long-pointed buds develop into perfect, double pink flowers which do not fade and whose fragrance is also pleasing." [ARA] "Very lazy bloomer." [Kr]

Danmark (Zeiner-Lassen & Dithmer, 1890)
Sport of 'La France' (B); or from 'La France' × either 'Safrano' (T) or 'Isabella Sprunt' (T).
"Pink, large, full, very fragrant, medium height." [Sn] "Not so good [*as 'La France'*] in growth and very apt to ball." [F-M2] "Large, cupped, silvery rose-red, like 'La France, but darker outside. Flowers erect, and not so drooping as in 'La France'. Free, vigorous, bushy." [Hn] "Very like 'La France', but stouter in growth and stiffer in petal." [HuD/04]

Dean Hole (A. Dickson, 1904)
Sport of 'Mme. Caroline Testout' (HT).
"Silvery carmine tinted salmon; flower very large, full, high-centered; very floriferous, very vigorous." [Cx] "Pretty form; petals thick and strong." [JR31/177] "Occasionally comes split…impatient of too much wet…very free-flowering." [F-M] "Blooms of excellent form, long and pointed, though the colour is rather unattractive—silvery rose and salmon." [OM] "Subject, but not badly, to mildew…Good grower." [F-M] "Fair growth; color not of best; mildews." [ARA18/115] "Low, weak grower; foliage sufficient; bloom sparse, well scattered through season." [ARA18/124] "Often not a clear color. In autumn, usually muddy." [Th] "The variety 'Dean Hole' is one of the best of today's roses, and indeed one of the best roses of any time. The growth is very vigorous, branching, and very floriferous. The bud is long and pointed, and of pretty shape; the flower is very large, very full, with a high center. The color is superb and very fresh, and is silvery carmine with salmon-tinted reflections." [JR37/30] "Pale silvery rose, with deep shading, sometimes muddy; nice shape; substance varies; above average size and cuts well; fragrant. Very nice growth and stem. Foliage mildews badly." [Th2] "Plenty of buds, some of which failed to open on account of the wet. It requires shading to get the best out of this

Rose." [NRS14/159] "It was a singular coincidence that the last letter the Dean wrote on Roses had as its subject matter this Rose that had been named after him. He saw a flower of it, but never saw the plant growing." [F-M]

Directeur Constant Bernard (Soupert & Notting, 1886) trans., "Director Constant Bernard"
From 'Abel Grand' (HP) × 'Mlle. Adèle Jougant' (T).
"Vigorous, floriferous, flower large, very full, well imbricated; color, very delicate magenta pink on a silvery ground; edge of outer petals often light violet; very fragrant." [JR10/148]

[**Distinction**] (Bennett, 1882)
Two parentages have been published: (1) 'Mme. de St.-Joseph' (T) × 'Eugène Verdier' (HP); or, (2) 'Mabel Morrison' (HP) × 'Devoniensis' (T). "Growth very vigorous; flower not very full but well formed; color tinted with peach, difficult to describe; opens easily; magnificent exhibition rose; cupped; Centifolia scent." [S] "Flowers of shaded peach. No particular merit." [B&V]

Double White Killarney (Budlong, 1913) syn., 'Killarney Double White'
Sport of 'Killarney White' (HT).
"[*Liked in Houston, Texas*]...beautiful in the bud in early spring, but...not a good summer boarder," [ET] "The only good, first-class white rose that we have available today, commercially." [ARA21/138] Much used as a florist's rose in the Teens.

Dr. Cazeneuve (Dubreuil, 1899)
"Extra large flowers of beautiful form and texture, color rich dark velvety crimson, somewhat resembling 'Jean Liabaud'; almost black, and one of the finest dark hybrid tea roses yet produced. Very beautiful." [C&Js02]

"Bush with dark brilliant foliage; branches with true vigor, blooming all year. Blossom of the color and form of that of 'Géant des Batailles'; bud purple, so deep when opening that it seems black. The open rose bears comparison to the splendid HPs 'Jean Liabaud', 'Louis Van Houtte', and 'Charles Lefebvre', as far as color goes, by the intensity and depth of its velvety crimson. This will be one of the best deep-colored HTs." [JR23/167-168]

[**Dr. Pasteur**] (Moreau-Robert, 1887)
"A strong, vigorous-growing variety, with very dark, rich foliage; flowers finely formed, globular, but becoming reflexed when over half open; color, a very pleasing soft rosy crimson with satiny shading." [CA93] "Vigorous bush; magnificent dark green foliage; flower large, full, opening well, bud very long, form globular, beautiful intense carminy pink nuanced currant red, extremely floriferous." [JR11/150]

Dr. Schnitzler
Listed as 'Emin Pascha'.

Duchess of Albany (W. Paul, 1888) syn. 'Red La France'
Sport of 'La France' (B).
"Fine deep pink, in the way of 'La France', but darker in colour; quite first-rate; growth vigorous." [P1] "Clear red, broad petals of silky texture." [Dr] "Vigorous; flower very large, full, globular, a nice rose color, very fragrant…maintains all the characteristics of 'La France, from which it differs only by its rosy color." [JR30/17] "Dark pink." [LS] "Low moderate growth, hardy; foliage sufficient to plentiful, healthy; bloom moderate, continuous." [ARA18/125] "Bright pinkish-red…shapely…well proportioned bush with good foliage…3×2 [ft; ca. 1 m × 6 dm]." [B] Not to be confused with Lévêque's Tea of 1903, 'Duchesse d'Albe', which was red with yellow tints.

Duchess of Connaught (Bennett, 1879)
From 'Adam' (T) × 'Duchesse de Vallombrosa' (HP).
"Large, cupped, silvery-pink; free-flowering; fragrant, similar to 'La France'." [Hn] "At first glance, might readily be mistaken for 'La France', having much the same shade of color, but the flowers are somewhat smaller and of rounder form; it is the only variety which resembles 'La France' in perfume." [EL] "Foliage and flowers very distinct, well-formed, delicate silvery-pink, center salmon, very fragrant, a charming rose." [JR3/114] "Foliage larger and better [*than that of 'La France'*]...petals recurving to a less extent." [EL]

Duchess of Westminster (Bennett, 1879)
From 'Adam' (T) × 'Marquise de Castellane' (HP).
"Flowers quite large without seeming 'gross'; well formed; bright cerise." [JR3/114] "Growth and foliage above average; color and form good; variably hardy; shy in blooming." [ARA18/110]

Duke of Connaught (Bennett, 1879)
From 'Adam' (T) × 'Louis Van Houtte' (HP).
"Rosy-crimson, large, full, well formed, good in bud, almost without fragrance; the buds do not always open. A fine rose when well grown, but it will never be useful for ordinary cultivators." [EL] "Beautiful foliage, flowers very large, of very beautiful form, dark velvety crimson bordered brilliant red." [JR3/114] "A free autumnal bloomer; rather small; very hardy." [H] "Buds large and of good form...dwarf in growth." [S] "Its foliage is that of the Tea; it has an elongated bud as in that class...bloom is...continuous." [JR3/171] "Almost without fragrant." [CA88]

Edmée et Roger (Ketten Bros., 1902)
From 'Safrano' (T) × 'Mme. Caroline Testout' (HT).

"Flesh white, center salmon flesh pink, darker ground, large or very large, long bud, opens well, stem long and firm. Vigorous, floriferous...Dedicated to Dr. Dumas of Faverny and his wife." [JR26/163]

[**Élise Masson**] (Vibert, 1849)
"Perpetually-blooming hybrid. Flowers full, 9 cm across [ca. 3¾ inches], deep pink; very beautiful." "8-9 cm, carminy-pink, in a rosette, flat." [R&M62] "Very vigorous growth, forming a strong bush; flower medium-sized, full, in the form of a cup; color, deep intense pink." [S]

Ellen Wilmott (Archer, 1936)
From 'Dainty Bess' (HT) × 'Lady Hillingdon' (T).
"Fair growth with beautiful single flowers of cerise, with red calyx." [ARA40/197] "Flower large, lasting, creamy lemon, flushed rosy pink with pink at edges of petals, on long stem. Foliage leathery, dark green. Vigorous, upright; abundant, continuous bloomer all season." [ARA37/264] "Golden anthers framed by wavy petals of cream and pink. Upright growth. Foliage and stems tinted purple...3×3 [ft; ca. 1×1 m]." [B] "Glossy foliage...superb." [G] Not to be confused with Bernaix's 1898 similarly colored double HT of the same name.

Emin Pascha (Drögemüller, 1894) syn., 'Dr. Schnitzler'
From 'Gloire de Dijon' (N) × 'Louis Van Houtte' (HP).
"Deep pink, large, full, tall." [Sn] "A very bold and handsome rose borne well up on strong stiff stems, the flowers are extra large and massive, with broad thick petals—very double full and sweet and a profuse bloomer. Color, deep carmine, rose shaded crimson." [C&Js98]

Erinnerung an Schloss Scharfenstein (Geschwind, 1892) trans., "Remembrance of Scharfenstein Castle"
"Purplish red, large, full, very fragrant, medium height." [Sn]

Erzherzogin Marie Dorothea (Balogh, 1892) syn., 'Archiduchesse Marie-Dorothée Amélie'
From 'Mme. Falcot' (T) × 'Général Jacqueminot' (HP).
"Yellowish rose-red, large, very full, very fragrant, tall." [Sn] "Very vigorous. Its blossoms are a yellowish pink which is most agreeable to the eye. They are only barely full; but the plant is so floriferous that this alone makes it valuable." [JR23/39]

Étoile de Hollande (Verschuren, 1919) trans., "Dutch Star"
From 'General MacArthur' (HT) × 'Hadley' (HT).
"Large, semi-double flowers of a very beautiful scarlet-red." [ARA21/148] "Medium-sized, ovoid buds and medium to small, cupped, deep bright red, double flowers of good lasting quality and strong fragrance, borne singly or several together on long, strong stems. Soft, disease-resistant foliage. Moderate, upright growth." [ARA27/132] "The rose of roses to me; a great, big, loose fellow of velvety crimson." [ARA29/48] "Large; rich, deep red, gleaming with color." [ARA29/96] "Buds opened too quickly." [Hk]

Exquisite (W. Paul, 1899)
"Very bright crimson shaded magenta, large, full, globular; the buds are large and long; the expanded blossom is very open and quite regular; this variety blooms continuously and profusely...its fragrance is that of 'La France'...very vigorous." [JR23/81]

Ferdinand Batel (Pernet-Ducher, 1896)
"Variable from rosy flesh on a yellow ground to nankeen orange; remarkable for the contrasts of its colour. [P1] "Fair size." [HuD/04] "Vigorous, well-branched; foliage somber green; flower fairly full, oval; bi-colored, varying from very delicate flesh to a ground of orange nankeen yellow...blooms abundantly." [JR20/164]

Ferdinand Jamin (Pernet-Ducher, 1896)
"Growth very vigorous; canes branching; foliage bronzy green; flower large, full, globular; color, carmine pink nuanced salmon. The coloration of this variety much resembles that of 'Mme. Abel Chatenay', except the flowers are larger and fuller, and will be much appreciated for cutting purposes." [JR20/164] "Fine form, long pointed bud; good." [HuD/04] Not to be confused with the Hybrid Perpetuals 'Ferdinand Jamin' and 'Mme. Ferdinand Jamin', *qqv*.

Frances Ashton (DuPuy/Stocking, 1937)
From 'Lady Battersea' (HT) × 'Hawlmark Crimson' (HT).
"Bud large, long-pointed; flower large, single, lasting, slightly fragrant, carmine, no variations, wine-colored stamens, on long stems. Foliage leathery. Vigorous, upright; profuse bloomer." [ARA38/232] "Good growth and good foliage and…the flowers beautiful." [ARA40/199] "Continuous…3-4 [ft; ca. 1-1.3 m]…outstanding." [Lg] "One of the best of the singles…no serious faults after two years of observation." [ARA39/193]

Frau J. Reiter (Welter, 1904)
From 'Mlle. Augustine Guinoisseau' (HT) × an unnamed seedling (which resulted from crossing the HTs 'Viscountess Folkestone' and 'Kaiserin Auguste Viktoria').
"Pure white, or slightly coppery." [Ÿ] "Flower very large, very full, cupped, very delicate flesh pink, or pure white." [JR31/178]

Gardenia (Soupert & Notting, 1898)
From 'Comtesse Dusy' (T) × 'Mlle. Hélène Cambier' (HT).
"Vigorous, handsome foliage, long pure white bud sometimes tinted virginal blush; flower large, full, imbricated like a camellia; color, gardenia

white...Very floriferous and fragrant." [JR22/148] Not to be confused with the Wichuraiana of the same name and era.

General MacArthur (E.G. Hill, 1905)
Possibly descended from 'Gruss an Teplitz' (B).
"Vivid scarlet, almost vermilion. Dazzling, with the effect of scarlet geraniums." [Dr] "Flower large, full, flat, fragrant." [JR30/25] "Bright crimson; perfume good...of all-round worth." [ARA17/24] "Tending to blue; fragrance strong and enduring; buds attractive...about 35 flowers in season." [ARA21/90] "Lacks substance." [ARA25/105] "One of the very best of the Hybrid Teas. It is of strong growth, and bears bright red flowers, which, if somewhat thin, are very freely produced. A splendid rose for the garden." [OM] "Always good, but too pinkish a red...fragrance, form, fine foliage...free-flowering." [RATS] "Color tends to blue...small in hot weather...almost immune from mildew; slightly susceptible to [*black-*] spot." [Th] "Cherry red...thin, open quickly, and possess no great charm in form...Healthy, it grew well, and flowered freely." [Hk] "Scarlet-crimson; tall, bushy." [ARA17/31] "Low, spreading, compact, weak; foliage plentiful, healthy; bloom moderate, intermittent." [ARA18/125] "Very vigorous, floriferous and remontant...develops solitary blossoms on stems up to eighteen inches long [ca. 4.5 dm]! The flowers are a dark crimson of a very brilliant shade, and are deliciously fragrant." [JR28/80] "[*Does*] only passably well [*in Houston, Texas, as compared to 'Red Radiance'*]." [ET] "Growth above average." [ARA18/110] "Very vigorous." [M] "It was a failure on my light soil till I took it down to the wettest and heaviest part of my garden, where it received a half shade...[*Its*] foliage...is noteworthy. It has a blackish tinge in the green, joined with a bluish black shade, which pervades the whole plant...The carriage of the flowers is excellent...the open flowers rather soon lose their shape...Very free flowering and continuous and not to suffer from mildew." [NRS/13] "Blend of Musk and Damask [*perfumes*]." [NRS/17] "Perfectly magnificent in flower." [Fa]

General-Superior Arnold Janssen (Leenders, 1912)
From 'Farbenkönigin' (HT) × 'Général MacArthur' (HT).
"Fiery red." [Ÿ] "Excellent in color and lasting qualities; nice growth; fairly good bloomer." [ARA18/110] "Particularly intense deep carmine…large, full, and very fragrant flowers. The perfectly formed buds are very distinctive. The plant is vigorous, compact, and continuous." [JR36/74]

George Dickson
Listed in the chapter on Hybrid Perpetuals.

Gertrude (A. Dickson, 1903)
Sport of 'Countess of Caledon' (HT).
"Flesh pink." [Ÿ] "A blush sport of 'Countess of Caledon' which it resembles in all save color." [HuD/04]

[**Gigantesque**] (Odier, 1849) trans., "Gigantic"
"Vigorous growth; flower large, full, very well formed; color, deep pink." [S] From James Odier of Bellevue, near Paris; most likely the Bourbon 'Louise Odier' introduced by Margottin in 1851 was named after his wife or daughter.

Gladys Harkness (A. Dickson, 1901)
"Deep salmon pink, silvery pink reflections; cupped." [JR30/16] "Very large, good constitution and fragrant. A fine Rose." [P1] "Inclining to the H.P. side of the class, this variety is sturdy and hardy in growth and foliage, and the pink blooms, though not of the most refined shape, are large, with fine petals, sweet-scented, and good in the autumn." [F-M] "Growth very erect and vigorous; large and beautifully formed buds and flowers, resembling the famous 'American Beauty' in size and fullness; color, bright rich salmon pink; very fragrant and first-class in every way." [C&Js02]

Golden Ophelia (B.R. Cant, 1918)
From 'Ophelia' (HT) × 'Mrs. Aaron Ward' (HT).
"A seedling from 'Ophelia', possessing many of its characteristics. Flower of fair size, very compact, opening in perfect symmetrical form, golden yellow in center, and paling to almost white at outer petals." [ARA19/102] "Odor slight; fine shape, rather small but exquisite; lasts well when cut. Bush slim but strong." [ARA26/94] "Shorter bud than 'Ophelia', but holding center better; smaller and less pointed; slight fragrance; petals have less substance than its parent, but lasts. Nice grower, with very fine and retained foliage; stems not so stout as 'Ophelia'. Does well in Pacific South-West and very well in winter in Southern zones. Much to be preferred to most yellows for general garden cultivation and ordinary cut-flowers." [Th2] "Shapely flowers of delicate texture with good fragrance. More yellow than golden...3×2 [ft; ca. 1 m × 6 dm]." [B] "Popular [*in Houston, Texas*]." [ET]

Grace Darling (Bennett, 1884)
"It is necessary that the kingdom of flowers fairly teem with quite amiable creatures since we inevitably turn to it when we want to symbolize joy, happiness, friendship, gratitude, and other such warm, heart-felt sentiments. When we feel the need of catharsis by some gesture, we charge Flowers with the responsibility of being our intermediators, our interpreters. Thus it can be believed, then, that no one would ever have dreamed of dedicating a Rose to the daughter of an English lighthouse keeper, to Grace Darling, if, one stormy night, she had not, alone, saved the crew of a ship-wrecked vessel. That heroic act was sung by the English poets, but the poems were quickly forgotten...In seeing the beautiful [*Hybrid*] Tea rose 'Grace Darling, we remember her act of courage and dedication...The blossom is large, very full, and of a beautiful coloration: basically a cream white, strongly tinted peach pink; the flower opens well, and is sufficiently fragrant. The bush is vigorous, and blooms abundantly on each branch; it begins to flower early, and blooms late as well."

[JR15/43-44] "The blossoms are large, very full, and open well in greenhouse or garden. The color is new." [JR8/54] "Very pretty sometimes when half open...Colour rather confused...Of good growth." [F-M2] "Cupped." [Hn] "Moderate vigor." [Cx] "3×3 [ft; ca. 1×1 m]." [B] "One of the newest and best." [JR11/50] Grace Horsley Darling, lived 1815-1842; rescued, with her father, nine survivors of the ship *Forfarshire* in 1838 during a storm sweeping over the Farne Island off Bamburgh in Northumberland, England. It was thought that the fame and celebrity proceeding from this feat contributed to her early death.

Grand-Duc Adolphe de Luxembourg (Soupert & Notting, 1891)
From 'Triomphe de la Terre des Roses' (HP) × 'Mme. Loeben de Sels' (HP).
"Vigorous, floriferous, giving well-formed buds...The flower is very large, nearly full, with large petals, light brick pink within, bright geranium lake without." [JR23/154]

[**Grossherzog Ernst Ludwig von Hesse**] (Müller/Lambert, 1898) syn., 'Red Maréchal Niel'; trans., "Grand Duke Ernst Ludwig of Hesse"
From 'Pierre Notting' (HP) × 'Maréchal Niel' (N); Jäger replaces 'Pierre Notting' with 'Général Jacqueminot' (HP).
"Bright pink." [LS] "Bright rosy red." [CA11] "Flower very large, well formed, quite full, flower and bud like those of 'Maréchal Niel', and held similarly [*i.e., nodding*]. Color, carmine red, very fragrant; very floriferous on last season's canes; foliage ample, glossy. Very vigorous bush, nearly climbing." [JR22/20] "Though climbing, is not as vigorous as 'Maréchal Niel'...It is, what is more, not very abundant, and doesn't rebloom...*Further*, we have noted that this rose is very susceptible to mildew...It's a fraud that this newcomer is described in rose catalogs as 'Red Maréchal Niel'!...[W]e have found on the flowers we have seen *not one trace* of what might *properly* be called Red...[T]hey are simply a more

or less bright pink which one could compare to the coloration of the common pink China [*i.e., 'Parsons' Pink China'*], or 'Hermosa'." [JR25/84]

[**Grossherzogin Viktoria Melitta von Hessen**] (Lambert, 1897) syn., 'Grand Duchess Victoria Melita'; trans., "Grand Duchess Viktoria Melitta of Hesse"
From 'Safrano' (T) × 'Mme. Caroline Testout' (HT).
"Very vigorous plant, one of the most floriferous, freely remontant. The wood is reddish brown and the leaves are large. The flower is very large, quite full, of a nearly closed form, usually solitary on the stem, and drying there without shedding its petals. The buds are long and open easily; the color is cream with a yellow center, resembling 'K[aiserin] A[uguste] Viktoria' somewhat, though being more vigorous. The plant is busy and takes to all sorts of fantastical pruning. The perfume is sweet but penetrating. Dedicated to her highness the Grand Duchess of Hesse." [JR21/50-51]

Gruss an Aachen (Geduldig, 1909) trans., "Greetings to Aachen"
From 'Frau Karl Druschki' (HP) × 'Franz Deegen' (HT).
"Large, very double blooms of warm pink with peach tones, low growing, 2 [ft; ca. 6 dm]." [HRG] "Superb...very tidy habit. Flesh-pink changing to cream...shapely...Slightly fragrant. Good, glossy foliage...2×2 [ft; ca. 6×6 dm]." [B] "Low growing...flowers open flat...creamy pink, richly fragrant and recurrent." [G] "Color fades quickly in hot weather, becoming almost white; perfume mild...growth fair." [ARA17/22] "Buds gold and red." [ARA29/97] "Of good vigor; the branches are strong, rigid, fairly erect. Continuous-flowering...The bud is long and of attractive form; color, orange red strongly tinted yellow. The color of the rose is quite difficult to describe...truly very beautiful. One gathers that the blossom will attain perhaps six inches across [ca. 1.5 dm]—but I have never seen it that large." [JR36/124] "Tall, vigorous; foliage very plentiful till late summer, then plentiful, black-spots...mildews...bloom moderate,

continuous, size and quality compensate for lack of quantity." [ARA18/128] Aachen, alias Aix-la-Chapelle, was Charlemagne's capital city. Those partial to 'Gruss an Aachen' may wish to collect its sports as well: 'Climbing Gruss an Aachen', 'Gruss an Aachen Superior', 'Jean Muraour', 'Minna', 'Rosa Gruss an Aachen'.

Gruss an Aachen Superior (Leenders, 1942)
Presumably a "superior" sport of 'Gruss an Aachen' (HT).
"Blush white, large, full, moderate height." [Sn]

Gruss an Pallien
Listed in the chapter on Hybrid Perpetuals.

Gruss an Teplitz
Listed in the chapter on Bourbons.

Gustav Grünerwald (Lambert, 1903)
Two distinct parentages have been published: (1), 'Safrano' (T) × 'Mme. Caroline Testout' (HT); (2) 'Grossherzogin Viktoria Melitta von Hessen' (HT) × *R. fœtida* 'Bicolor'.
"Carmine pink with a radiant center of yellow; flower large, full, fragrant; floriferous; very vigorous." [Cx] "Flowers…cupped, with a high centre…buds yellowish red, long and pointed." [W/Hn] "A beautiful flower…of a very distinct shade of bright carmine pink with pale orange shading at the base of the petal which lights up the flower well. It has a delicious perfume, being one of the best of the pink Roses in this respect. The flowers are not badly affected by either sun or rain, but in hot weather, especially in mid season, they are apt to get loose and lose their shape…The autumnal blooming is generally good and free." [NRS/12] "Free vigorous growth of an upright yet branching habit, and good though rather sparse dark green bold leathery foliage but little liable to mildew. It flowers fairly continuously and freely from early July till late

autumn. The flowers are carried erect singly and on good stems, though full flowers will droop at times. The petals are strong and of good substance, bright carmine pink in colour, rather paler in hot weather...sweetly fragrant." [NRS/10] "Good autumnal." [JP] "A good early variety...must be disbudded freely." [F-M] "Not the most floriferous, despite being very vigorous." [JR32/33] "Pretty vigorous, floriferous, having buds which are elongated, pointed, and good for vases. The flowers are large, cupped, of a pretty and fresh pink, the interior of the petals being saffron yellow. Were it not for this last color, it would very much resemble the charming 'Mme. Caroline Testout', with which it shares many other characteristics, notably form, wood, and thorns." [JR29/92] "Moderate height, compact, vigorous, hardy; foliage plentiful, black-spots slightly; bloom almost free, continuous." [ARA18/125] "3×3 [ft; ca. 1×1 m]." [B] "Good...not one of the best." [ARA18/111] "Everyone should grow this variety if only for the sake of the bright rose-pink colour of the flowers. There are many pink roses, but this is distinct from them all. It grows well and flowers freely." [OM]

Gustave Regis (Pernet-Ducher, 1890)
Possibly a seedling of 'Mlle. Blanche Durrschmidt' (T).
"Pale yellow." [Ÿ] "Large, semi-double, canary yellow with saffron-yellow centre; erect growing, free flowering." [Hn] "Distinct and beautiful in bud." [H] "A very vigorous Hybrid Tea pillar with semi-double, nankeen-yellow flowers." [GAS] "Tall growth; very good bloomer. Useful mainly as a decorative rose." [ARA18/111] "Another strong growing garden Rose which should not be closely pruned. The blooms are quite thin, and fall abroad as soon as expanded, though even then the clean petals give the idea of a Rose of good quality. It is in the very early bud state that this Rose is at its best, for the shape is long and pointed, and the three colours, red, yellow, and white, are present together in a more charming combination than I am aware of in any other Rose." [F-M2] "The best and most vigorous of the yellow garden Roses." [J]

Hadley (Pierson/Montgomery Co., 1914)
From an unnamed seedling (which resulted from crossing the HT 'Liberty' with the HT 'Richmond') × 'General MacArthur' (HT).
"A rich crimson-red flower with velvety texture, lovely form, and perfume. Moderate in growth and bloom. Splendid color which blues very little. Flowers small in summer, superb in fall." [ARA26/110] "Velvety crimson to darkest black-purple—blues in extreme heat more than 'Hoosier Beauty'; double and attractive in form; fine fragrance. Foliage good. Stem usually long and strong. Weak grower in Central zone; satisfactory in cool, moist climates of Pacific North-West and Pacific South-West. Reported by Miss Creighton, of western Florida, as continuous." [Th2] "In the summer-time and all the time, 'Hadley' yields wonderfully fine blooms for cutting." [ARA29/106] "Free and constant flowerer." [Au] "The pre-disposition to blind wood…is the weak spot in 'Hadley'." [ARA16/116] "Produces so few flowers that it is hardly worth growing [*in the florist trade*]." [ARA22/140] "With its wonderful color and quality, is considered ideal by the buyer [*of cut flowers*], but not by the grower." [ARA23/108] "Has been almost entirely discarded [*by commercial growers of cut flowers*]." [ARA26/158] "'Hadley' certainly is not [*easy to grow*]." [ARA25/170] "The plant grows well, but is of a rather straggling habit, and the carriage of the flowers is not good." [NRS21/51] "Of our dark red roses 'Hadley' is the favorite." [ARA21/142] "Superior to the reds I previously had." [ARA25/98] "Color distinct; growth and blooming fair; foliage quite good; best in the spring." [ARA18/111] "A grand rose." [ARA25/144] "In 1916 there was a flower show at Philadelphia…Basing my opinion on the opinion of those with whom I talked after the show, it seems that 'Hadley' is 'some rose.' Those who saw this finest of the crimson roses at Philadelphia have something to remember…Growers have decided that 'Hadley' is worth all the extra care which a good variety needs. It has come into its own. 'Montgomery's mistake' was the nickname tacked onto 'Hadley' by those who thought they knew more about roses than the originator of 'Hadley'." [ARA17/110] "Alexander W. Montgomery, Jr., of Hadley, Mass." [ARA16/44]

Helen Gould
Listed as 'Balduin'.

Henri Brichard (Bonnaire, 1890)
"Bush of great vigor, with upright canes; beautiful large leaves, bronzy somber green; flower large, very full, on a very strong stem; color, pure white outside; within, very bright carmine red shaded salmon pin; abundant, continuous bloom; distinct among HTs." [JR14/146] "A splendid grower, producing quantities of buds which are large and quite double; nearly white, shading into a bright rosy carmine center." [CA96]

His Majesty (McGredy, 1909)
"Large growth without being climbing; the quite upright blossoms are large, of good substance...beautiful deep crimson shaded blackish vermilion. One might call it the Red Frau Karl Druschki due to its resemblance to that variety in form and growth...Wafts the most elegant fragrance." [JR33/10]

Hofgärtendirektor Graebener (Lambert/Ketten Bros., 1899)
From 'Mme. Caroline Testout' (HT) × 'Antoinette Durieu' (T).
"Graebener, director of the court gardens...Blossom pinkish yellow or coppery orange yellow, medium sized, full, opens well. Vigorous, erect, abundant bloom." [JR23/171]

[**Honourable George Bancroft**] (Bennett, 1880)
From 'Mme. de St.-Joseph' (T) × 'Lord Macaulay' (HP).
"Red, shaded with violet crimson; large, full flowers, and good pointed buds." [CA88] "Large flower the same form as that of 'Lord Macaulay'; color, beautiful crimson pink shaded purple; very beautiful; semi-globular; very fragrant; medium growth; very good rose to force." [S] "[*Flowers*] fade very quickly...if grown so that the original color is retained, will generally give satisfaction, though many more malformed

blooms are produced than we expect to see in a variety put down as desirable." [EL]

Innocence (Chaplin Bros., 1921)
"A lovely, large...single-flowering white rose that opens well. The delicate wave of the petals, coupled with the golden stamens, makes it a very attractive variety...The perfume is not pronounced." [ARA23/145] "Pure white, five-inch [ca. 1.25 dm] beauty with yellow stamens...both in clusters and singly on long, thick, thorny stems." [ARA34/81] "Very lovely...of twelve petals, with unusual stamens." [ARA40/43] "Tapering buds, and fine, large, white, single blooms of great beauty...Very vigorous. Free from mildew; some black-spot...lovely...Bore 57 blooms [*Rhode Island*]...Odorless [*Indiana*]...No special merit [*California*]." [PP28]

Irish Brightness (A. Dickson, 1904)
"Light orange red, medium size, single, moderate height." [Sn]

Irish Elegance (A. Dickson, 1905)
Supposedly *R.* ×*hibernica* × "a Hybrid Tea."
"Single flowers of a bronze and orange color, from which the roses turn completely to a shade of apricot at maturity." [JR29/153] "A medley of apricot, pink and orange-red." [Hk] "A variegated rose with a lot of pink in the combination; it is beautiful but nothing to get excited about." [ARA34/81] "Buds are orange-scarlet. Vigorous...4×3 [ft; ca. 1.25×1 m]." [B] "A delightful fragrance of cloves." [ARA24/95] "A wonderfully free bloomer." [ARA20/149] "Fades in heat...opens quickly. Very good foliage. Very fine growth in Pacific Horst-West." [Th2] "The foliage is specially beautiful and harmonises well with the flowers, particularly in autumn, when it turns a ruddy green. The early foliage is also most beautiful, of a rich red tint. The habit is good and branching...free flowering and fairly continuous...The colour of the single flower is unique, the buds are a fine orange scarlet, and the petals of the open flower coppery fawn with a pink

shade running through it. It has a sweet but not very strong fragrance, and good lasting flowers for a single Rose...Its charm lies not merely in the flowers, lovely as they are, but in their delightful harmony with the foliage and in the good and healthy habit of the plants...Decidedly liable to mildew." [NRS/12] "A very beautiful rose." [K2]

Irish Fireflame (A. Dickson, 1913)
Supposedly *R.* ×*hibernica* × "a Hybrid Tea."
"The sumptuous color of 'Irish Fireflame' immediately conveys the notion of a flame; its color is dark Madeira orange, veneered with maroon which changes to crimson orange; when the buds are developing, they are a pure delicate orange which changes, when the blossoms expand, to a rich, satiny old gold, deliciously veined and mottled as if a beam of sunlight had tinted the crimson and the lemon yellow shading the crimson, which makes, considering the large size of the flowers (which reach 5.25 inches [ca. 1.25 dm]), the prettiest contrast and the most delicious coloration. The buds have a special feature: the oval receptacles are chocolate-color, and the base, hidden from the sun, is apple-green; the foliage is oval. Strongly and deliciously perfumed with a Persian-Tea scent. The vigorous branches are never without flowers." [JR37/105-106] "Orange yellow and red." [OM] "Fiery crimson at the base, shading to orange-salmon...in the bud state they are very attractive." [ARA16/117] "Deep madder-orange...blossoms all season." [ARA25/121] "A reddish bronze yellow...brilliant and very pleasing in the sunshine. A feature is the contrast in the varying shades of colour in the bud, half open and fully expanded flower; it is very striking and, combined with the deep bronze-green foliage, the whole makes a very fine decorative garden plant." [NRS/13] "Perfumed. Foliage good. Stem weak; growth good in Southern zones; does well in shade in Pacific South-West, but flower and stem wilt in heat." [Th2] "Dependable." [Capt28]

Irish Glory (A. Dickson, 1900)
"Light pink, large, single, moderate scent, tall." [Sn]

Irish Modesty (A. Dickson, 1900)
"Light orange pink, large, single, tall." [Sn]

Isobel (McGredy, 1916)
"Flame, copper, and gold...my favorite among the singles of these blended shades." [ARA24/95] "Although single, the enormous petals, with their mingled shades of carmine, red, and orange, make a plant of 'Isobel', in bloom, a beautiful sight, and the manner in which the petals fold up after sundown is also delightful." [ARA29/48] "A large flower on a large bush...light rose-pink, with apricot shadings." [ARA34/80-81] "Said to be good." [ARA18/47] "Of remarkable color. Fair growth." [ARA18/118] "Growth rather small, not bushy. Wonderful decorative rose where well grown." [Th2] "Huge, warm, pink, five petaled, fragrant flowers...an enchanting rose by any standards." [DP]

Jean Lorthois (Widow Ducher, 1879)
Seedling of 'Gloire de Dijon' (N).
"Splendid large flowers, very full and double, and exceedingly sweet; color, bright glossy pink, deepening at center to intense carmine; reverse of petals silver rose." [CA90] "Growth very vigorous with short, upright canes; thorns occasional, upright, and brown; beautiful dark green foliage composed of 5 leaflets; flower large, full, very well formed; color, China pink, darker at the center, passing to lilac; reverse of petals whitish; very beautiful plant." [JR3/164]

Jean Muraour (Vogel,1935)
Sport of 'Gruss an Aachen' (HT).
"White, large, full, medium height." [Sn]

Jean Sisley (Bennett, 1879)
From 'Adam' (T) × 'Emilie Hausbourg' (HP, Lévêque, 1868, lilac-rose; parentage unknown).
"Large flowers, very full, beautifully formed petals, lilac-pink around the perimeter, bright pink in the center; flowering perfect and of long duration." [JR3/114] "Moderate vigor, floriferousness; no scent. Opens with difficulty." [S] "[*Has a tendency to*] fade very quickly...difficult to open...rather a muddy shade...very subject to mildew. The color is bad, and the buds rarely open well; it is entirely worthless." [EL] "22 [ft; ca. 6×6 dm]." [B]

[**Johannes Wesselhöft**] (Welter & Hinner/Ketten Bros, 1899)
From an unnamed seedling (resulting from crossing the HTs 'Kaiserin Auguste Viktoria' and 'William Francis Bennett') × 'Comtesse de Frigneuse' (T).
"Flower sulphur yellow passing to light yellow, large, full, very fragrant; long bud; long stem. Bush vigorous, branching...Dedicated to a rosarian from Langensalza." [JR23/171] "A strong growing, free blooming Hybrid Tea Rose, valuable for garden planting, as it is quite hardy and a great bloomer; soft pale sulphur yellow, passing to ivory-white; bears beautiful buds and fine handsome flowers in great profusion." [C&Js09]

Jonkheer J.L. Mock (Leenders, 1909)
From an unnamed seedling (which resulted from crossing the HTs 'Mme. Caroline Testout' and 'Mme. Abel Chatenay') × 'Farbenkönigin' (HT).
"Mixture of ochre and light red." [Ÿ] "Large to extra large, full, fine form, tea fragrance, medium to long stem. Foliage good, sufficient. Growth vigorous, hardy. Inside of petals silvery pink, outside bright cherry-rose—very thick and leathery." [ARA23/164] "Distinct; notable for color, size, stem, and lasting qualities; tall growth, lacking in bushiness; fairly good bloomer." [ARA18/111] "In growth resembles 'Mme. Caroline Testout' to some degree. Its blossoms are borne on upright and rigid stems, and are

held well above the foliage; they are large, full, very fragrant, pink and light red with dawn-gold reflections, resembling 'Farbenkönigin' (HT) a little. The long bud opens well, and the form of the blossom much resembles that of 'La France'. Dedicated to Monsieur J.L. Mock, president of the Dutch rosarian's society." [JR33/102]

Joséphine Marot (Bonnaire, 1894)
"Very vigorous bush with erect canes; somber green foliage; flower large, full, beautiful muslin white; bud lightly washed pink." [JR18/131]

Jules Girodit (Buatois, 1899)
"Light orange pink, large, full, medium height." [Sn]

Jules Toussaint (Bonnaire, 1899)
"Brownish red, base of petals citron yellow, and reverse of petals slightly silvery; growth vigorous." [P1] "Very vigorous, foliage…somber glossy green. Flower very large, quite full, always opening well…notable variety." [JR23/168]

Julius Finger (Lacharme, 1879)
From 'Victor Verdier' (HP) × 'Mlle. de Sombreuil' (T).
"Salmon pink, in the style of 'Captain Christy'; a promising sort." [EL] "'Captain Christy' perfected." [S] "Very vigorous, flower stem long, flowers large, full, form and poise the most perfect; color, pure white, center pink, towards the end of bloom, the pink predominates." [JR3/164] "[*Julius Finger*] died December 19, 1894, at Millstatt, Austria. Despite his high duties with the Imperial Court, he was much occupied with roses." [JR19/18]

K. of K. (A. Dickson, 1917) syn., 'Kitchener of Khartoum'
"Bright crimson…half double, with large petals. Seems to be extremely floriferous." [ARA20/123] "Each petal resembling a piece of fine scarlet

velvet." [ARA29/49] "A Rose of vigorous free-branching habit, with dark green foliage. The blooms, which are freely produced and sweetly scented, are carried on fairly stiff stems. The colour is a brilliant scarlet crimson, which does not burn. [NRS/17] "Beautiful but somewhat weak-necked." [ARA26/21] "3×3 [ft; ca. 1×1 m]." [B] "Does well in California…Continuous bloomer." [Th2] "Quite took our fancy." [ARA18/47]

Kaiserin Auguste Viktoria (Lambert & Reiter, 1891) syn., 'Grande Duchesse Olga', 'K.A. Viktoria', 'Reine Augusta Victoria'
Two parentages have been published: (1) 'Perle des Jardins' (T) × 'Belle Lyonnaise' (N); (2) 'Coquette de Lyon' (T) × 'Lady Mary Fitzwilliam' (HT).
"Pure white with an orange-yellow center; flower large, very full, globular; very floriferous; vigorous." [Cx] "Cream…one of the best…Vigorous." [J] "A dainty, creamy-white rose of moderately vigorous growth. The flowers are of perfect form." [OM] "Primrose. Very beautiful glossy leathery foliage…unique in color and must be included in any large collection." [Th] "Splendid large buds and full flowers like camellias." [BSA] "Pure white with yellow centre, outer petals reflexed; a very free and effective decorative Rose; also fine for exhibition; growth vigorous." [P1] "This variety was obtained by crossing 'Perle des Jardins' and 'Belle Lyonnaise'; it has preserved a slight resemblance to this latter." [JR22/56] "Vigorous, with strong and upright branches; thorns sparse but big; foliage large, brownish red, shiny when young, brilliant dark green with age; flower, large or very large, very full, well-held…imbricated, opening easily, and of long duration. Exterior petals, pure white; those of the interior, Naples yellow; center of the flower, orange yellow…very fragrant. The blossoms are usually solitary, rarely two or three on the long stalks, which are erect and strong. Bloom is very abundant up to frost…resists cold well." [JR15/5] "Semi-globular…stands hot weather well…Fair growth and foliage, requiring 'liberal treatment'." [F-M2] "Bushy, tall, moderately

compact...foliage plentiful, black-spots; bloom free most of the time, almost continuous." [ARA18/125] "Does not discolor under rain, wind, or heat." [Th2] "Another superb rose, particularly as a bud or half-open...White, or often with some orange, globular...dedicated to [*the German*] Empress...Blooms in Fall and Winter; very nice under the north African skies." [JR34/170] "Most planted [*of white roses in Houston, Texas*]." [ET] "3 [ft; ca. 1 m]." [HRG] "Its majestic bearing, its graceful form, its fine coloration—all these place it in the first range of beautiful roses." [JR30/18] "No white rose has yet surpassed old 'Kaiserin Auguste Viktoria', at least in shape." [ARA35/92] "A true aristocrat in rosedom." [ARA29/102]

[**Kaiserin Goldifolia**] (Conard & Jones, 1909)
Sport of 'Kaiserin Auguste Viktoria' (HT).
"The flower of this variety is identical with 'Kaiserin Auguste Viktoria' but the distinction between the two Roses is the bright, golden yellow foliage of 'Kaiserin Goldifolia'. It is a decided novelty, beautifully attractive in leaf and flower." [C&Js09]

Kathleen (A. Dickson, 1895)
"Coral pink." [Ÿ] Single. Not to be confused with the 1908 Multiflora nor with the 1922 Hybrid Musk, both of the same name.

Kathleen Mills (Le Grice, 1934)
"Bud large, long-pointed, carmine; flower large, semi-double, open, intense briar fragrance, pale pink, washed silvery sheen, reverse deep pink, on a long stem. Foliage leathery. Vigorous (3 feet [ca. 1 m]), upright, open; profuse, continuous bloomer all season." [ARA37/264] "Iridescent pink petals and stamens shining like particles of gold...truly beautiful. Of all the roses I know it is the most prolific...the display is continuous...not a lusty plant." [DP] "3-5 [ft; ca. 1-1.5 m]...striking, unique." [Lg]

Killarney (A. Dickson, 1899)
From 'Mrs. W.J. Grant' (HT) × 'Charles J. Graham' (HT).
"Flesh colour shaded with white and suffused with pale pink. A showy flower with large petals and fine long buds; growth vigorous. A splendid Rose." [P1] "Large, good to fine form, semi-double, quite fragrant, medium to long stem. Sufficient foliage, slight [*black-*] spot and mildew. Growth poor; hardy. Clear bright pink." [ARA23/164] "Several marked faults. Growth and blooming qualities good; color beautiful; attractive in bud form but not in open flower; foliage mildews." [ARA18/111] "A fairly good grower, flowering freely in summer and autumn. The blooms are very large, of quite first-class pointed shape, and the colour a lovely shade of pale pink. The petals are long and stout, but there are not enough of them, the centre being badly filled." [F-M2]

Killarney Brilliant (A. Dickson, 1914)
Sport of 'Killarney' (HT).
"Large to very large, double, good to fine form, very fragrant, medium to long stem. Fine foliage, sufficient. Growth strong; hardy. Clear rosy crimson." [ARA23/164] "Fair, having the faults of parent, but not so good growers or bloomers." [ARA18/111]

Killarney Double White
Listed as 'Double White Killarney'.

Killarney Queen (Budlong/Pierson, 1912)
Sport of 'Killarney' (HT).
"Bright pink...vigorous...30 to 4o blooms per season." [ARA21/91] "The best of the Killarneys for outdoor planting. Flowers larger, color deeper and more lasting than 'Pink Killarney'; growth more vigorous." [ARA18/133] "Extremely heavy foliage...lesser production in bloom." [ARA18/99] "Tall, compact, free-growing, hardy; foliage sufficient, black-spots; bloom

free, almost continuous." [ARA18/125] "For decoration or hedges in Interior South districts with dry conditions." [Th2]

Kitchener of Khartoum
Listed as 'K. of K.'.

Kootenay (A. Dickson, 1917) syn., 'Mary Greer'
"Almost white, faint blush, tinged yellow; large; odor slight to good. Bush tall and strong." [ARA26/94] "Yellowish white with pink, large, full, medium scent, medium height." [Sn] "Of vigorous growth and branching habit; the blooms are freely produced on long rigid stalks. They are large and full and of perfect form, of primrose yellow colour, and strongly perfumed. The Rose is described as an improved 'Kaiserin Auguste Viktoria'." [NRS16/141] "Obtained some triumphs in America." [NRS21/57] Kootenay, regional name applied to several geographic features (lake, river, etc.) in Canada.

[**L'Innocence**] (Pernet-Ducher, 1897) trans., "Innocence"
From an unnamed seedling × 'Mme. Caroline Testout' (HT).
"Very vigorous well-branched bush, thorns small and occasional, foliage bronze green; flower large, full, globular; color, sparkling white. The blossoms are nicely double without being full, and [*thus*] are light [*enough to be*] well-held on their erect stems." [JR21/146] "Most lovely buds and flowers of beautiful form and delightful fragrance." [C&Js01]

La Favorite (Widow Schwartz, 1899) trans., "The Favorite"
From 'Mme. Caroline Testout' (HT) × 'Reine Emma des Pays-Bas' (T).
"Blush white washed cream.—Flower fairly large, full, cupped; floriferous; vigorous." [Cx] "Pink, large, full, medium height." [Sn]

La France
Listed in the chapter on Bourbons.

La Tosca (Widow Schwartz, 1900)
From 'Joséphine Marot' (HT) × 'Luciole' (T).
"Soft pink tinted with rosy white and yellow, large and full; very free flowering." [P1] "Medium to medium-large, double, good to fine form, very fragrant, medium to long stems. Fine foliage, sufficient, slight [*black-*] spot. Growth very vigorous, tall, bushy; hardy. Silvery pink with deeper center." [ARA23/165] "Vigorous, growth well disposed, branches tinted purple, terminating in a solitary blossom which is large, well formed, borne on a strong stem, beautiful delicate pink nuanced blush white, nubs yellowish." [JR24/163] "Splendid for garden decoration. Noteworthy in growth, blooming, and hardiness; color good; bud fair in shape, but opens loose." [ARA18/112]

Lady Alice Stanley (McGredy, 1909)
"Deep coral-rose on outside...inside pale flesh; perfume mild to fair...growth fair." [ARA17/23] "Silvery pink; moderate [*height*], spare [*in leafage*]." [ARA17/23] "The arrangement of petals, gently curved back just a trifle, even in the center, so gracefully overlapping and supporting one another, like the studied folds of a lovely frock, all so uniform, so well-proportioned, so regular, so strongly placed on its stem, and the whole so well guarded by its outer rows of petals—this it is which gives us the essence of ladyhood, the two tones of softer and deeper rose, together with a bountiful fragrance, that give it its lovableness." [ARA30/36] "Good form." [OM] "Bloom lasts well; fair grower; moderately good bloomer." [ARA18/111] "Growth is vigorous and the flowers large and of good shape and distinct colour." [F-M] "Good foliage. Medium grower. Averages 34 blooms per season." [ARA21/92] "Open flower very attractive...very little affected by mildew, but susceptible to [*black-*] spot...growth fair." [Th] "Height and compactness medium, vigorous,

hardy; foliage plentiful, black-spots slightly; bloom free, almost continuous." [ARA18/125] "[*Very satisfactory in Brazil*]." [PS]

Lady Ashtown (A. Dickson, 1904)
Seedling of 'Mrs. W.J. Grant' (HT).
"Flower very large, full, well held, pale pink shaded yellow with silvery reflections." [JR31/178] "Medium large, fine form, double, faint fragrance, medium stem. Fine foliage, sufficient. Growth medium strong; hardy. Light rose with silvery reflex, bases light yellow." [ARA23/165] "Distinct and attractive in color and form; good growth and foliage; blooming qualities fairly good." [ARA18/111]

[**Lady Clanmorris**] (A. Dickson, 1900)
"Distinct and different from all others; flowers very large and graceful, petals large and of excellent substance, color rich creamy-white with pale rose centre, edge of petals beautifully bordered with deep rose; altogether a rose of unusual excellence." [C&Js02]

[**Lady Henry Grosvenor**] (Bennett/W. Paul, 1892)
"Pale pink." [LS] "Flowers flesh color; large, full, and globular; an exceedingly free and effective variety; also a fine young forcing rose." [CA96]

Lady Mary Fitzwilliam (Bennett, 1882)
From 'Devoniensis' (T) × 'Victor Verdier' (HP).
"Robust, well-branched, enormous flowers, globular, very full, pale delicate flesh, of the 'Captain Christy' sort; excellent for exhibition." [JR6/69] "Blooms in abundance on short branches, giving blossoms of 3 inches [ca. 7.5 cm] at the height of bloom." [JR7/136] "Flowers which would be difficult to surpass in beauty." [JR8/156] "Of moderate vigor, giving enormous globular blossoms which are full and of a light flesh-white. The large bud is well-formed, and has the advantage of lasting a long time before opening…lightly fragrant." [JR14/84] "Of a delicate rosy flesh-colour,

very large globular well-formed flowers with long and fine petals, dwarf growth, hardy and robust, but its growth seems to be checked by the habit of producing too many of these large and exhausting flowers." [B&V] "One of the best...dwarf, but robust and very floriferous." [JR7/83]

Lady Sylvia (Stevens, 1926)
Sport of 'Ophelia' (HT).
"A clear fresh pink, as pleasing a pink Hybrid Tea, I think, as there has ever been." [Hk] "Lovely, shapely buds opening to full flowers of flesh-pink with deeper undertones...bushy and fairly vigorous. Superb scent...3×2 [ft; ca. 1 m × 6 dm]." [B]

[**Léonore d'Este**] (Portemer, 1849)
"Vigorous growth, large plump very full flowers; flesh colored, with whitish edges." [M-V49/233] "Very vigorous growth; canes irregular and of differing sizes; not much covered with thorns; leaves nearly round, deeply dentate, of a blackish green; flower medium-sized, flat; color, bright yellow nuanced chamois." [S] Such coloration would likely proceed from a Tea parent such as 'Safrano'.

Liberty (A. Dickson, 1900)
From 'Mrs. W.J. Grant' (HT) × 'Charles J. Graham' (HT).
"Rich velvety crimson, fine stiff petals...Growth fairly vigorous." [P1] "Very floriferous, producing deliciously perfumed blossoms like those of 'American Beauty'; they are perhaps paler in Summer; but in the Fall their tint is much the same deep crimson as that of 'Gruss an Teplitz'." [JR24/21] "Fairly mediocre by the end of September. Its color has a lilac tint." [JR28/10-11] "It seems to be a fairly good grower, with well-formed flowers not large enough for exhibition, but of a colour—bright crimson—which is much wanted in this section [*HTs*]." [F-M2] "The *ne plus ultra* of red roses...very floriferous, remontant, and irreproachably held;

the growth is vigorous, stocky, and furnished with handsome glossy foliage." [JR25/20]

Lina Schmidt-Michel (Lambert, 1905)
From 'Mme. Abel Chatenay' (HT) × 'Kleiner Alfred' (Pol).
"A newcomer dedicated to the artist whose watercolors…have appeared these last several years in the *Journal des Roses*. It is a vigorous rose…it grows six to ten feet in height [ca. 1.75-3.3 m], and blooms profusely in season. Its flowers are semi-double, bright pink nuanced carmine, staying fresh and open a long time." [JR29/179] The Floribunda-formula parentage is perhaps worth noting.

Lulu (Easlea, 1919)
"Orange-salmon and pink." [ARA25/102] "Pretty buds; opens too quick; too thin; fades quickly. Foliage crinkly; no [*black-*] spot." [ARA26/117] "Foliage mildews. Growth good." [Th2] "Bud very long-pointed; flower orange, salmon, and pink. Vigorous grower of bushy habit…abundance of bloom all season." [ARA] "This is said to hold the record for the longest bud yet produced." [ARA20/120] "A tall, eight petaled, very slender orange bud which was eye-catching…a charmer." [DP]

Ma Tulipe (Bonnaire, 1899)
"Extremely vigorous, though without being climbing; blossom semi-full, with large, very firm petals, beautiful dark crimson red. This variety, noteworthy because of its long buds which resemble tulips, will serve well for cutting." [JR23/168]

Madeleine Gaillard (Bernaix fils, 1908)

Magnafrano (Van Fleet/Conard & Jones, 1900)
From 'Magna Charta' (HP) × 'Safrano' (T).

"It combines the hardiness and vigor of the 'Magna Charta' with the free-blooming habit and delightful fragrance of the Tea Roses. The flowers are extra large, frequently four to five inches across [ca. 1-1.25 dm]; very regular, full and double, and deliciously sweet. The color is deep, bright, shining rose, very rich and handsome. The bush is a strong, upright grower and a constant and most abundant bloomer." [C&Js02] "Low-growing, compact, reasonably hardy; foliage plentiful, healthy; bloom moderate, intermittent." [ARA18/126]

Mamie (A. Dickson, 1902) syn., 'Mrs. Conway Jones'
"Rosy carmine, with yellow base. Beautiful shape; growth vigorous." [P1] "Vigorous, well-spaced branches, very floriferous. It blooms early and continuously. The blossoms are fragrant, beautifully colored carmine pink with a splotch of yellow very evident at the base of the petals, which are large, smooth, and very sturdy. The blossom lasts a long time." [JR25/100] "A well-formed flower of good pointed shape, but rather undecided in colour. [F-M2] "Of strong healthy growth with good foliage. The buds are large and open slowly into very full flowers having fine petals and globular shape with high centre. A fine Rose for exhibition." [F-M]

Marchioness of Salisbury
Listed as 'Marquise de Salisbury'.

Marie Girard (Buatois, 1898)
"Vigorous and bushy; leaves large, beautiful dark green; flowers very large, with large petals, cupped; full; color, flesh white nuanced yellowish salmon; fragrant. Strong stem, good for cutting." [JR22/164]

Marie Zahn (Müller/Lambert, 1897)
From an unnamed seedling (resulting from crossing the Bourbon 'Reine des Île-Bourbons' with the Noisette 'Maréchal Niel') × an

unnamed seedling (resulting from crossing the HP 'Pierre Notting' with the Tea 'Safrano').
"Light pink, yellow at the center, large, full, medium height." [Sn] "Hybrid of Tea and Bourbon…The bush is of vigorous growth, with thick foliage, light green in color. The flower is large, full, cupped; the buds are long and pointed. The color is silvery pink shaded carmine on a yellowish ground; very floriferous and hardy." [JR21/68]

Marjorie (A. Dickson, 1895)
"White with a pink center. Magnificent." [JR19/67] "White, suffused with salmon-pink; of medium size and exquisite form; growth robust." [P1] "Very free-flowering." [H] "Growth and blooming fair; flower not distinctive." [ARA18/117]

Marquise de Salisbury (Pernet père, 1890) syn., 'Marchioness of Salisbury'
"Bright velvety pink." [Ÿ] "Bright crimson. A semi-double bedding Rose." [H] "Brilliant velvety red, almost full, buds long…growth vigorous." [P1] "Handsome very velvety intense red; flower medium-sized, fairly full, imbricated; very floriferous; vigorous." [Cx] "Glowing crimson flowers and deep green leaves." [Ro] "Brilliant crimson, sometimes sparkling scarlet; very abundant bloom, semi-double, a good garden rose." [JR22/106] "Vigorous, branches upright and strong, thorns prominent and numerous, foliage very thick and conspicuous, of a handsome somber green bordered reddish, flowers of moderate size or large, fairly full, of a handsome and very velvety bright red; bud, elongated and in the form of a **T**; bloom, continuous and abundant; this wonderful variety will be much sought out for bedding…of the highest merit." [JR14/164] "Moderately bushy; flower large, pretty full, very floriferous." [JR30/32] "A good bright rose for bedding. I am persuaded that the best results with this variety are secured by cutting the branches very short." [JR28/10] "Gorgeous and

thorny." [K2] "Dark red to maroon. Fragrant and free-flowering...3×3 [ft; ca. 1×1 m]." [B]

Marquise Litta de Breteuil (Pernet-Ducher, 1893)
"A splendid carmine-rose colour, and very large blooms. It grows on a strong upright stalk, and is proud of its beauty. Every one asks its name, as a matter of course, on entering the rosary. Mine grows in the shade, and is apt to lose its leaves in the autumn." [HmC] "Elegantly formed large full flowers with broad thick petals of good substance, delightfully sweet-scented." [C&Js05] "Growth very vigorous, handsome foliage, flower very large, to five inches [ca. 1.25 dm], very full, cupped, carmine pink, center vermilion red." [JR17/165] "This very soon became a well-known and popular variety, as being practically the only dark-red Show Rose among the H.T.s. It is of stout stiff thorny growth, with foliage and general appearance of a H.P. character; and the flowers are very distinct, there being something characteristic in the arrangement of the inner petals which is often very regular and pleasing. They are large, very bright and fairly lasting. Free-flowering, and a good autumnal even in hot climates, it is a Rose to be much recommended as a short Standard for any purposes or situation." [F-M2]

Mary Greer
Listed as 'Kootenay'.

Mavourneen (A. Dickson, 1895)
Sport from 'Killarney' (HT).
"Silvery flesh. Unrivalled." [JR19/67] "Pale pink. A strong grower." [P1]

[**Michael Saunders**] (Bennett, 1879)
From 'Adam' (T) × 'Victor Verdier' (HP).
"A superb rose; flowers extra large, finely formed, very double and full; petals of good substance and beautifully reflexed; color deep rich crim-

son; very brilliant." [CA93] "It is large, of good form, of a curious pink color, with a very distinct Tea fragrance." [JR3/171] "Quite full...Growth moderate." [S]

Mildred Grant (A. Dickson, 1901)
From 'Niphetos' (T) × 'Mme. Mélanie Willermoz' (T).
"Blush white, large, full, medium height." [Sn] "The flowers...grow up to 12-15 cm across [ca. 6 inches]...The roses are a silvery white tinted crimson pink towards the center, and deliciously perfumed. It is very floriferous...This variety is dedicated to a charming Miss, the daughter of one of the principal English rosarians." [JR27/20] "The blossoms are quite large, have a high center, and keep a long time. The petals, which are very long, are very well formed, and, what is more, are enormous. The bush is vigorous, with the branches well placed and separate, each crowned by a flower, which is borne on an absolutely upright and very strong stem. The wood and foliage are very attractive, the latter being light green." [JR25/100] "Small growth; attractive blooms." [ARA18/113] "It appears to be the largest Rose of good pointed shape yet issued...Very fine indeed in form, petal and substance, but unfortunately undecided and whitish in colour." [F-M2]

Minna (Kordes, 1930)
Sport of 'Gruss an Aachen' (HT).
"Pink, medium size, very full, light scent, dwarf." [Sn] "Bloom not so full [*as that of 'Gruss an Aachen'*]. Bud medium size, ovoid, deeper in color than the flower; flower large, double, full, high-centered, very lasting, slightly fragrant, fine rosy pink, borne in cluster on medium-length, strong stem. Foliage sufficient, medium size, rich green, leathery, disease-resistant. Growth moderate, bushy, dwarf; profuse, intermittent bloomer all season. Tips freeze." [ARA31/243]

[**Mlle. Alice Furon**] (Pernet-Ducher, 1895)
From 'Lady Mary Fitzwilliam' (HT) × 'Mme. Chédane-Guinoisseau' (T). "Vigorous, with strong and upright branches, foliage ample, somber green; flower large, globular, full, yellowish white, resembling 'Gloire Lyonnaise'. Very floriferous, and has the deportment of 'Lady Mary Fitzwilliam', being however more vigorous." [JR19/149] A parent of the climber 'Billard et Barré'.

Mlle. Argentine Cramon (Chambard, 1915) syn., 'Argentine Cramon'
"A very double white Rose carried on rigid stems." [NRS18/155] "White, very large, full, medium height." [Sn] "Fair growth; color clear and attractive." [ARA18/118]

Mlle. Augustine Guinoisseau (Guinoisseau fils, 1889) syn., 'Augustine Guinoisseau', 'White La France'
Sport of 'La France' (B).
"A nearly white sport, tinted blush...As a bedding Rose, '[Mlle.] Augustine Guinoisseau' is one of the very best; it is thinner than 'La France', and therefore better for this purpose, and if possible even freer in flower. Having les substance, it seldom balls...it has all the delightful 'La France' perfume." [NRS/10] "Rosy white...produced in great profusion...Deliciously fragrant and vigorous." [P1] "Flowers large, full, beautiful light pink, erect; growth moderately vigorous. Branches slender, buds small." [Hn] "White with some flesh; flower large, full, imbricated; floriferous, vigorous." [Cx] "As good a white garden rose as a heart can desire." [K2] "Not white—a poor thing." [ARA25/105] "Nearly white, very free and late in flowering." [E] "Especially fine in the autumn." [Ro] "A fair degree of perfection [*in cool seasons*]." [L] "Good in heat." [Th2] "Oh, no! The rose is rather disheveled, wilts quickly, the petals don't hold well, the blossom is skimpy, the hardiness precarious." [JR37/170] "A branch-sport of 'La France', known to advantage for its abundant bloom and vigor, the only difference being in its color, lightly-fleshed white...Cultivated for

over eight years, it has always been of good behavior. Thoroughly of the first order." [JR13/166] "Flowers very inferior in size, color, and shape [*to those of 'La France'*]." [F-M2] "We know all of La France's advantages—abundant bloom, vigor, the shape of the bud, the fragrance, etc.—there is nothing lacking in these. And her child 'Mlle. Augustine Guinoisseau' is no different—except in color." [JR21/56] "Somewhat less vigorous than [*'La France'*]. It blooms remarkably freely, and the recurving petals give it a quaintly attractive appearance. A rose for the beginner." [OM] "Most of my friends agree in describing the foliage as good; it is, I think, slightly lighter in colour than that of its parent...The stems are smooth and a nice light green colour...delightfully fragrant, the scent being that described as sweet or honeyed in character...this scent resembles that of no other Rose excepting 'La France'...Perhaps not mildew proof, it is very little affected by this, or indeed, any other fungus pests...Free-flowering and continuous." [NRS/12] "Medium height, compact, winterkills somewhat; foliage plentiful, black-spots somewhat; bloom free, continuous." [ARA18/128] "Very strong in growth, and highly scented; perhaps a little stiff and artificial looking, but a fine variety." [Wr]

Mlle. Brigitte Viollet (Levet, 1878)
Seedling of 'Antonine Verdier' (HT).
"Silvery-rose, slightly tinged with violet; not highly scented, but quite a pleasing sort." [EL] "Vigorous, flower large, full, well-formed, blooms in clusters; color, bright pink with some violet, petals edged salmon; a plant of the first order." [JR2/165-166]

[**Mlle. Germaine Caillot**] (Pernet-Ducher, 1887)
From 'Baronne Adolphe de Rothschild' (HP) × 'Mme. Falcot' (T).
"The bush is vigorous, with strong and upright canes; foliage, beautiful dark green; thorns, remote, nearly straight; flower stalk strong; long bud; flower very large, quite full, very well formed; color, salmon flesh pink, brighter at the center, creamy white at the edge of the petals; the open

flower has recurving petals. The plant blooms abundantly, and the blossoms are solitary." [JR11/99] "Vigorous, dwarf...flower very large (12 to 14 cm across [ca. 5 inches])." [JR11/164] See also 'Comte Henri Rignon' (HT).

Mlle. Hélène Cambier (Pernet-Ducher, 1895)
"Very pretty and desirable, makes a neat handsome bush, bears abundantly, large, very double Roses. Color, lovely canary yellow, with deep peachy red centre, becoming lighter as the flowers open. Very sweet and handsome." [C&Js99] "Very vigorous, bushy, erect, beautiful bronzy green foliage; flower medium-sized or large, very full, color varying from salmon flesh-pink to coppery pink, often having a beautiful dawn gold tint which fades at full expansion of the blossom. Very abundant bloom." [JR19/149]

[**Mme. A. Schwaller**] (Bernaix, 1886)
"The flowers are large and globular and of excellent substance. Color fine, soft coral pink, delicately edged with violet rose and richly perfumed. A strong healthy grower and constant bloomer, fine in every way." [C&Js02] "Thick, bushy plant with non-climbing canes; flower large, full, very well formed; color uniformly incarnate pink to be base of the petals, and fading towards the tip. Plant extremely floriferous." [JR10/172]

Mme. Abel Chatenay (Pernet-Ducher, 1894)
From 'Dr. Grill' (T) × 'Victor Verdier' (HP).
"Carmine pink shaded vermilion, tinted pale salmon; flower large, very full, cupped; vigorous." [Cx] "Salmon pink, very free." [H] "Carmine-rose-buff mixture...distinctive." [Hk] "Light pink deepening towards the centre." [T2] "Carmine rose, shaded with salmon. Very popular in England." [Th] "One of the best roses of recent introduction, not so much as a show bloom as for its excellent decorative qualities and attractive colour...rosy carmine shaded with vermilion rose and tinged with

salmon; base of petals deeper. Flowers of exquisite shape, not large, but full and fragrant; growth vigorous." [P1] "The prettiest decorative Rose in the world." [NRS/12] "One of the prettiest Hybrid Teas. The growth is vigorous, hardy, with branching canes armed with strong, sparse thorns. The foliage is a pretty bronze green; bloom is continuous. The bud is very elegant, opening in a spiral. The blossom is large and full; the petals recurve on themselves in the most graceful fashion, giving the variety a particular distinction and an unequaled elegance. The magnificent color is carmine pink shaded pale vermilion pink and touched with salmon; the tone is very intense and warm around the petals' nub." [JR37/93] "Utterly distinct in color and form with a sharp, penetrating fragrance, carmine shading on salmon with wonderful reflexing. The flower is medium sized and the growth rather straggling." [RP] "Good blooms [*in Madeira*]." [DuC] "Tall, moderately compact, fairly hardy; foliage sufficient, black-spots slightly; bloom free, almost continuous." [ARA18/126] "Subject to mildew and the blooms decrease in size as the season advances, but its long season, great productiveness, beautifully formed buds, and fine color make it desirable." [ARA25/99] "Both in bud and when fully open an exquisite Rose of lovely shape and colour, it grows freely and flowers freely, and is quite hardy." [NRS/14]

"This beautiful Rose has free, vigorous, if somewhat erratic growth and a branching habit rather apt when closely pruned to push up single strong flower shoots in panicles, and if not closely pruned to become 'leggy.' The foliage is strong and good, but scattered, not disposed well on the plant, and not enough of it…rather liable to mildew…It flowers very freely and continuously from the third week of June till late autumn. The flowers, carried on long erect stems, come as long-pointed buds opening to beautifully shaped flowers of moderate size. The petals are of good substance, the centre and outside of a deep salmon pink, the inner side much lighter towards the edges, giving the effect of blended shades of colour in sunshine or rain; they last long in water (four days) and on the plant, and their fragrance, though not strong, is very sweet…One of the very best all-round Roses."

[NRS/10] "Certainly a short-lived Rose...decidedly liable to mildew, and I have found it suffer from black-spot." [NRS/12] "Very vigorous." [M] "Poor grower." [NRS/14] "One of the most beautiful." [E]"Opens easily...Dedicated to the wife of the secretary-general of the Société Nationale d'Horticulture." [JR34/171] "3×3 [ft; ca. 1×1 m]." [B] "Fair; good in color and growth, but superseded by better roses of the same type." [ARA18/116] "A general perfection all round which I should imagine that it would be very long before any Rose could rival—much less out-do." [Fa]

[**Mme. Adolphe Loiseau**] (Buatois, 1897)
From 'Merveille de Lyon' (HP) × 'Kaiserin Auguste Viktoria' (HT). "Elegantly formed and deliciously sweet; color, fine rosy flesh, passing to rich creamy white, delicately tinged with blush." [C&Js99] "Vigorous bush with smooth thornless wood; foliage glossy yellowish green; flower very full, sometimes as large as that of 'Paul Neyron'." [JR21/148]

Mme. Alfred Sabatier (Bernaix fils, 1904)
"Sturdy handsome dark green foliage, plant of good vigor. Bud of pretty form, blossom fairly large, with thick petals, wavy, gracefully intermingled at the center and delicately pleated towards the outside, bright satiny peach red, fading when open." [JR28/155]

[**Mme. André Duron**] (Bonnaire, 1887)
"Clear red." [CA97] "Growth very vigorous, with strong, upright canes; beautiful foliage; flower very large, sometimes attaining the size of 'Paul Neyron'; beautiful fresh light red; continuous bloom; very good for cutting." [JR11/149]

Mme. Angèle Favre (Perny, 1888)
"Pink and salmon." [Ÿ]

Mme. Angélique Veysset (Veysset, 1890) syn., 'Striped La France'
Sport of 'La France' (B).
"Pink, striped and plumed bright red; more floriferous than 'La France'." [JR14/149] "Distinctly striped with pearl-white and satin rose; a most pleasing combination." [C&Js99] "A magnificent new rose, identical in every respect with its parent 'La France', except it is much stronger in growth, and the flowers are beautifully striped and shaded with a delicate white. The coloring is exquisite. It forces freely, and produces magnificent large buds and flowers." [CA96]

Mme. Augustine Hamont (Vigneron, 1897)
"Clear satin-rose, very large and sweet; vigorous." [P1] "Blossom very large, full, globular, satiny flesh pink, lighter at the petal edges. The growth is vigorous, with handsome light green foliage; very strong stem." [JR21/147]

[**Mme. Bessemer**] (Conard & Jones, 1898)
"A beautiful new rose, producing flowers of elegant form and substance. Color, beautiful peachy-pink, delicately shaded and clouded. Large, very full, sweet and handsome." [C&Js98]

Mme. Blondel (Veysset, 1899)
Seedling of 'La France de 89' (HT).
"Blossom bright pink; petals very thick, with a silvery edge; very large, full; opens well; fragrant. Growth, very vigorous; floriferous." [JR23/178]

Mme. Butterfly (E.G. Hill, 1918)
Sport of 'Ophelia' (HT).
"Soft flesh, shaded rose; beautiful spiral bud; attractive open flower of good size; lasts quite well; very fragrant. Stem very good. Foliage good...Should be planted in partial shade in hot climates. In California coast areas does not discolor as quickly as its parent, and must be given the

preference." [Th2] "Rather more salmon to apricot [*than 'Ophelia'*]." [RP] "Very feminine...shades of pale pink to blush with lemon centre. Very fragrant." [B] "A glorified 'Ophelia'. Much larger in flower...more vigorous...and more prolific." [ARA20/xiii] "Similar to 'Ophelia' in all characteristics, except that the color is greatly intensified." [ARA19/159] "Very free-flowering." [ARA29/48] "A hot weather rose." [ARA24/95] "Many admirers [*in Houston, Texas*]." [ET] We note early references to "*Madam* Butterfly,' under which pronunciation, we find, both the rose and the opera by Puccini are usually cited.

Mme. C. Chambard (Chambard, 1911)
From 'Frau Karl Druschki' (HP) × 'Prince de Bulgarie' (HT).
"Very vigorous with erect canes; beautiful light green resistant foliage; solitary, long bud, borne on a long rigid stem, silvery flesh pink with some salmon; flowers very large, opening well, flesh pink, salmon nuanced dawn gold, nub deep yellow, fragrant and floriferous...It takes from Druschki its great vigor, and from 'Prince de Bulgarie' its beautiful foliage and floriferousness." 'JR35/156]

Mme. Caroline Testout (Pernet-Ducher, 1890)
From 'Mme. de Tartas' (T) × 'Lady Mary Fitzwilliam' (HT).
"Satin rose with brighter center...color, most beautiful; fragrance, very distinct...slightly susceptible to mildew and [*black-*] spot...sometimes tends to have a weak neck...a universal favorite." [Th] "Very large, deep pink...showing the eye...sweet scented also, like a wild Rose." [HRH] "Bright pink...well-formed." [Hk] "A light salmon-pink. This magnificent variety makes a fine bush, has the longest flowering season of all the roses, except 'Frau Karl Druschki', and is suitable for both the garden and exhibition." [JP] "Very large, well-filled, cupped, centifolia form, beautiful rosy-red like 'La France', but the petals are stronger and less tinted with silvery white. A magnificent rose of recent years, with vigorous growth." [Hn] "Opens quickly." [Th2] "The bud is of a pretty form, quite elongated; the

blossom, which opens easily, bears something of a resemblance to a variety which one would have though inimitable—'La France'—in its satiny flesh-pink color, though a little brighter at the center; it wafts a fragrance which is very agreeable, though a little less strong than that of 'La France'." [JR16/99] "Good decided self-pink...very free bloomer...Fair foliage and thorny growth." [F-M2] "Splendid...strong leafy stems...pink colouring is clear and pretty." [E] "Notable in color and fragrance; good bloomer; not of the best in form or growth." [RA18/112] "Growth good." [ARA17/23] "One of the most beautiful introductions of recent years. In many respects it resembles 'La France', but differs in form, and the growth is more vigorous. Petals large and shell-shaped. Abundant bloomer." [P1] "The flowers for the most part are too coarse and loose for close inspection." [NRS/12] "Carnation-scented." [JR33/101] "A good hot weather rose." [L]
"Of free, vigorous growth and branching habit, armed with many and strong thorns. The foliage is thick, large, and green, and free from mildew till August...stems, which are erect with young flowers...apt to bend over with a full bloom. [*The blossoms are*] rather round in shape, large, full, and of great substance, bright, full, pink in colour, but rather lighter in hot weather...They fade rather quickly on the plant when open, but this is of less importance, as they open slowly so that the plants generally seem to have plenty of bloom. It stands rain well, and is perhaps at its best in dull weather or where it will get shade part of the day, but it is apt somewhat to 'ball' in bad weather...It is fairly fragrant, and the perfume is clean and pleasing...Its special characteristic is its regular branching habit and freedom of flowering...One of the most reliable...it fails to inspire me with that personal affection which is quite inexplicable, and yet often arises is respect of some far less satisfactory Rose." [NRS/10] "Tall, rather upright, hardy; foliage sufficient, black-spots somewhat; bloom moderate, continuous." [ARA18/126] "It has no serious fault other perhaps than that of being very spiny." [JR23/39] "Can hardly be beaten in all-round good qualities." [ARA20/46] "Indeed a treasure." [K1] "A generation old and still in the front rank." [McF] "The rose-advance of the past dozen years

has, in a sense, outmoded Testout." [ARA36/23] "Dedicated to a lady of Grenoble, a flower fancier." [JR34/14]

Mme. Charles Boutmy (Vigneron, 1892)
"Very vigorous, very beautiful light green foliage, flower very large, full, cupped, perfect form, well held, beautifully colored flesh pink, becoming, when fully open, beautiful light pink." [JR16/153]

Mme. Charles Détraux (Vigneron, 1895)
"Velvety red." [Ÿ] "Very vigorous, beautiful glaucous green foliage, flower very large, quite full, globular, bright red with some carmine. Very fragrant...extremely floriferous." [JR19/147]

Mme. Cunisset-Carnot (Buatois, 1900)
"Vigorous, medium-sized blossom, bud very long, solitary; color, salmony carnation pink." [JR23/169]

Mme. Dailleux (Buatois, 1900)
From 'Victor Verdier' (HP) × 'Dr. Grill' (T).
"Salmon pink, outer petals somewhat imbricated; center brighter pink on a coppery yellow ground; large, full, central petals muddled and for the most part folded at an angle for the greater part of their length; very fragrant; conical bud opens well. Very vigorous growth." [JR24/163]

[**Mme. de Loeben-Sels**] (Soupert & Notting, 1879)
"Flower large, very full. Flat form like that of 'Souvenir de la Malmaison'. Color, silvery white nuanced salmon/dawn-gold, reverse of petals flesh lake; very abundant bloom." [JR3/168] Not to be confused with the Hybrid Perpetual 'Mme. Loeben de Sels'.

Mme. Elisa de Vilmorin Lévêque, 1864)
"Carmine-rose." [JR8/27] "Flower large, full; color, scarlet red with tints of brown." [S] "Blood red." [LS] "Very large, handsome dark vermilion red, shaded brown." [BJ] "Like an amaranth peony." [l'H67/54] "Vigorous; branches short, furnished with stickers that are both short and hooked; leaves, dark green, often touched with yellow; flower, of medium size, full; color, crimson." [S] "Double, deep carmine, fragrant with upright growth…3×3 [ft; ca. 1×1 m]." [B] Also called a Hybrid Perpetual. "Vilmorin (Mme. Elisa).—wife of Louis Lévêque de Vilmorin, née Bailly, associated with Maison Vilmorin [*French seedsmen*] from 1860 to 1866. A woman of great culture and intelligence. Produced a notable book *Les Fraisiers*." [R-HC]

Mme. Emilie Lafon (Morainville, 1905)
Seedling of 'La France de 89' (HT).
"Light red, large, full, medium height." [Sn]

Mme. Ernest Piard (Bonnaire, 1887)
"Bright silvery pink." [Ÿ] "Handsome bright red, with a kind of silver polish." [B&V] "Extra-vigorous, with upright, very firm branches; foliage large, to eight inches [ca. 2 dm], a handsome blackish dark green; flower very large, cupped, beautiful bright red with a silvery edging. Reblooms freely." [JR11/149]

Mme. Étienne Levet (Levet, 1878)
From 'Antonine Verdier' (HT) × a Tea.
"Vigorous; flower large, full, well formed; color, beautiful cerise red with superb coppery yellow nubs. This beautiful plant is one of the most remontant." [JR2/166]

[**Mme. Eugénie Boullet**] (Pernet-Ducher, 1897)
"Magnificent flowers and buds; extra large; fine cup form, well filled and delightfully fragrant; color, fine buff pink, shading to yellow and rich carmine. Very handsome." [C&Js99] "Vigorous bush with upright reddish canes, rare thorns, beautiful bright bronze green foliage; bud of elegant form, superb half open; flower large, cupped, nearly full; color, China pink nuanced yellow and bright carmine. Very beautiful variety." [JR21/146]

Mme. Georges Bénard (Bénard/Corbœuf-Marsault, 1899)
Seedling of 'Grace Darling' (HT).
"Pink, yellow center, large, full, medium height." [Sn]

Mme. Gustave Metz (Lamesch, 1905)
From 'Mme. Caroline Testout' (HT) × 'Viscountess Folkestone' (HT).
"Vigorous, large and handsome bright foliage. Flower very large, large petals, magnificent form, quite full, nearly always solitary...Color, creamy white, going to pink. The bloom is very abundant, and lasts until the Fall." [JR29/22]

Mme. Jean Favre (Godard, 1900)
From 'La France de 89' (HT) × 'Xavier Olibo' (HP).
"Compact, foliage light green, bud long, deep carmine, flower large, well formed; when fully open, light carmine with bluish reflections." [JR25/6] "White, pink reverse." [Ÿ]

Mme. Joseph Bonnaire (Bonnaire, 1891)
From 'Adam' (T) × 'Paul Neyron' (HP).
"Bright China rose, reverse of petals silvery, extra large; in the way of 'Paul Neyron', but paler...a very handsome and showy Rose." [P1] "Supported by a strong stem, its enormous bud, beautifully colored bright China pink with the reverse of the petals silvery, will most certainly be a delicacy much

prized by florists. It is a 'Paul Neyron' of much more delicate color, but of equal vigor." [JR19/146] "Vigorous, with upright branches...Flower very large, very full, opening very well, growing to seven inches across [ca. 1.75 dm]...Handsome foliage, thorns rare. Very remontant, blooming until frost." [JR15/164] "Monsieur Joseph Bonnaire, dead at the age of 68. Born at St.-Chef (Isère) in 1842, Bonnaire went while still quite young to Lyon, where he worked at the establishments of Damaizin and Ducher, going then to Paris...[*At length, he returned to Lyon*] where he ultimately set up shop in 1878." [JR34/136]

Mme. Joseph Combet (Bonnaire, 1893)
"A continuation of the type of which 'Gloire Lyonnaise' was the inception. Its flowers are very large and full, and the petals well arranged; the colour is creamy white. A beautiful Rose, but does not always open well; growth almost climbing, with bold and massive foliage." [P1] "Beautifully cup-shaped." [Hn] "Extremely vigorous, branches upright, handsome somber green foliage, nearly thornless, flower large, very full, perfectly imbricated, always opens well, beautiful creamy white shaded pink, interior dawn-gold, very fragrant, very remontant, blooming until frost." [JR17/147]

[**Mme. Joseph Desbois**] (Guillot & fils, 1886)
From 'Baronne Adolphe de Rothschild' (HP) × 'Mme. Falcot' (T).
"Very vigorous bush; flower very big, measuring 14-16 cm across [ca. 6 inches], quite full, very well formed; color, flesh white with a very delicate salmon pink center." [JR10/147]

Mme. Jules Bouché (Croibier, 1910)
"Vigorous, branches slender and strong, bud very long, flower large, full, well formed, petals of great substance, folding back at expansion. Color, salmon-white, center nuanced virginal pink, stem very strong. Good for all purposes." [JR24/169] "Best light-colored rose; useful both for cutting

and decorative purposes; growth and blooming qualities splendid; color clear, beautiful." [ARA18/112]

Mme. Jules Finger (P. Guillot, 1893)
"Creamy white changing to almost pure white, fine globular form, full; growth moderate." [P1] "Vigorous bush; flower very large, quite full, very well formed, globular and of good hold; color, beautiful creamy white nuanced salmon pink at the center passing to pure white; very floriferous, nicely perfumed." [JR17/131] "Extra large, handsome buds and flowers…delicately tinted with rose and salmon." [C&Jf97] "Free bloomer. A distinct and novel variety, in all respects very desirable." [B&V]

Mme. Jules Grolez (P. Guillot, 1896)
From 'Triomphe de l'Exposition' (HP) × 'Mme. Falcot' (T).
"Bright silvery rose.—Vigorous.—Garden, standard, bedding.—A good and distinct garden rose. Fragrant." [Cat12/40] "Very floriferous; numerous branches; flower large, full, very well formed, beautiful frosty China pink, very bright." [JR20/147] "It is a colour which does not harmonise with some other Roses, especially with those of pink, or pink and copper shades." [NRS12/73] "Growth and color not of best; good bloomer, but superseded by better roses of same type." [ARA18/116] "Disbud." Th] "Moderate height, bushy, hardy; foliage very plentiful, healthy; bloom free first half of season, moderate last half, continuous." [ARA18/126] "Growth rather dwarf, but fairly vigorous habit, bushy, making a good shaped plant. Foliage distinct, dark bronze when young and effective, but decidedly liable to mildew. Flowers from the end of June to October, good early and late. The flowers are freely produced, and carried erect on short, moderately thick stems. The petals are of a very silky texture, and a clear deep rosy pink. The flowers last well in water (four days) and stand wet well, if there be not too much of it, but they become paler in damp weather…It flowers well on light soil and, I am told, also on the clay." [NRS/10/33] "Bright China rose, not always clear—blues in heat; nice

bud; center held quite well; fair size only; lasting; fragrant. Foliage practically perfect, and holds. Bushy but not tall growth in Central and Northern Zones; stem long with fair strength. Shows distinct Tea characteristics, especially in its retention of foliage, while its hardiness makes it useful where late frosts are encountered. Fair for cutting and requires little attention…very fine and continuous." [Th2] "Messrs. Grolez Bros., of Ronchin, [*were among the exhibitors at the 1881 general meeting of the members of the Société Regionale du Nord de la France in Lille, where*] in their 600 roses exhibited, there was not even one which could be regarded as anything but first-choice." [JR5/150]

Mme. Jules Grévy (Schwartz, 1881)
From 'Triomphe de l'Exposition' (HP) × 'Mme. Falcot' (T).
"Salmon-pink." [EL] "Dark red shaded grenadine." [Ÿ] "Growth very vigorous…foliage purple at first, like Tea foliage; flower medium-sized or large, full, salmon-white within, bright carmine-pink without. Not very floriferous, and subject to mildew." [S] "Large, full, very fragrant and, in form, campanulate; its novel color is salmon white inside and salmon pink outside. The pedicel is short, with numerous fine prickles; the wood is strong; the foliage is bright and purplish." [JR5/117]

[**Mme. Julie Weidmann**] (Soupert & Notting, 1881)
Seedling of 'Antonine Verdier' (HT).
"Flower very large, full; petals large; color, silvery salmony pink, center carmine and ochre, reverse of petals satiny violet; very floriferous;…medium-sized bush, coming from 'Antonine Verdier', which it resembles, except when the petals fall the flower is paler." [S]

Mme. Lacharme (Lacharme/Schwartz, 1872)
From 'Jules Margottin' (HP) × 'Mlle. de Sombreuil' (T).
"White, the centre the palest blush colour, beautifully clear and wax-like, a large circular cupped shaped flower, and highly scented; requires fine dry

weather to open." [JC] "Vigorous; flower large, full, Centifolia form, opens with difficulty, white lightly blushing, fades to white." [S] "Shy in the autumn. Of bushy growth, and quite hardy." [EL] "Of fair growth and foliage, with characteristic habit. The shoots themselves require to be severely thinned, and then they must be looked over from top to bottom several times during the growing season, as it is such a free bloomer that every wood bud will break and try to form a flower bud before the top one has begun to swell. Very liable to mildew, and absolutely spoilt by any rain even at quite an early stage. Even a heavy dew will sometimes soil the blooms. These are of a pure white, and for years this was the best HP of its colour [*we call it an HT*], a row of it in full bloom looking most charming just as the desk of a July evening comes on...The shape is good and lasting, globular with the centre well filled, but the size is not up to the average. It will come again well in the autumn, if it should be particularly dry and fine." [F-M3] "The most beautiful white hybrid known till now." [l'H72/261]

Mme. Léon Pain (P. Guillot, 1904)
From 'Mme. Caroline Testout' (HT) × 'Souvenir de Catherine Guillot' (Ch).
"Flesh, center vermilion." [LS] "Vigorous, robust, numerous somewhat branching canes, occasional thorns, handsome purplish foliage; flower very large, quite full, very well formed, fragrant, silvery flesh white, center brightened by orange yellow, petals' reverse salmon tinted vermilion and chamois yellow; very beautiful." [JR28/154] "A good rose. Color most attractive; satisfactory in form, growth, and blooming qualities." [ARA18/112]

Mme. Marie Croibier (Croibier, 1901)
Seedling of 'Mme. Caroline Testout' (HT).
"Very vigorous, foliage deep maroon green, thorns upright and numerous, flower full, very large, deep China pink, long bud, strong stem, very

floriferous. This superb rose comes from 'Mme. Caroline Testout', from which it takes it vigor, and the main characteristics of its growth; its bud is longer, making the blossom more graceful; its color doesn't blue, and keep until the petals fall." [JR25/147]

Mme. Maurice de Luze (Pernet-Ducher, 1907)
From 'Mme. Abel Chatenay' (HT) × 'Eugène Fürst' (HP).
"Of good vigor, with upright canes, cheerful green foliage, superb buds borne on long and strong stems; flower very large, with large petals, in the form of a full cup. Color, Nilsson pink, center cochineal carmine, reverse of petals lighter." [JR31/103]

Mme. Méha Sabatier (Pernet-Ducher, 1916)
From an unnamed seedling × 'Château de Clos-Vougeot' (HT).
"Deep crimson." [Ÿ] "Red, large, full, medium height." [Sn]

Mme. Moser (Vigneron, 1889)
"Growth very vigorous, with strong and upright canes, handsome dark green foliage, numerous brown thorns, large and beautiful buds, strong flower-stems; flower very large, full, globular, beautifully colored silvery white and lilac-pink in the interior, well held. Quite remontant; very fragrant…dedicated to the wife of Monsieur Moser, a well-known horticulturist of Versailles." [JR13/165]

Mme. P. Euler (P. Guillot, 1907)
From 'Antoine Rivoire' (HT) × 'Killarney' (HT).
"Vermilion silvery pink; extra-fine for cut-flowers." [C&Js12] "Vigorous, flower very large, supported on a long, strong stem, very full, long duration, very beautifully colored…fragrant." [JR31/139]

Mme. Paul Lacoutière (Buatois, 1897)
From 'Ma Capucine' (T) × 'Baronne Adolphe de Rothschild' (HP).

"Bud very long; flower large, semi-full, coppery saffron yellow, center golden yellow, petal edges slightly touched carmine; very fragrant; growth vigorous with upright canes; foliage bright dark green. The blossoms are sometimes solitary and sometimes in clusters of three to six." [JR21/148] The *R. fœtida* heritage of 'Ma Capucine' makes 'Mme. Paul Lacoutière' very close to being able to be considered as the first commercial Pernetiana.

Mme. Pernet-Ducher (Pernet-Ducher, 1891)
From an unnamed Tea × 'Victor Verdier' (HP).
"Vigorous, making a compact, erect bush; flower medium-sized or large, nearly full, bud conical, nicely colored canary yellow, outer petals washed carmine, fading to creamy white by the time the petals fall...The plant has handsome foliage, blooms continually and abundantly, and, what is more, is very hardy." [JR15/166]

Mme. Ravary (Pernet-Ducher, 1899)
"The blossoms...are large, cupped, and beautiful orange-yellow; its fairly long bud is golden yellow. The growth is excellent and the blooming abundant." [JR34/69-70] "A kind of light chamois pink." [Hk] "Good vigor, well-branched, strong thorns, handsome brownish green foliage, bud conical, beautiful golden yellow; flower very large, globular, nearly full, orange yellow." [JR23/149] "Color very pretty; good growth, foliage, and bloom; bud attractive." [ARA18/112]

Mme. Segond-Weber (Soupert & Notting, 1907)
From 'Antoine Rivoire' (HT) × 'Souvenir de Victor Hugo' (T).
"Pure salmon pink, very delicate, new among HTs, bright center. The enormous blossom, with its large and strong petals, lasts a very long time; it is cupped, quite regular, and faultless in form...blooms without interruption from Spring to November." [JR31/136-137] "Beautiful color; almost perfect form; growth fair; blooming qualities very good; lasts well;

splendid cut-flower." [ARA18/112] "Very large, fragrant, long stem. Fine foliage, sufficient. Growth poor; fairly hardy." [ARA23/167]

Mme. Tony Baboud (Godard, 1895)
"Very vigorous without being a climber, somewhat branching, thorns strong and somewhat numerous, foliage beautiful light green, flower large, semi-double, pretty fawn nankeen yellow fading to canary, deliciously perfumed; bud always solitary, borne on a long and strong stem." [JR19/163] "Baboud, of Thoissey, the nursery-maker of l'Ain." [JR22/160]

[**Mme. Veuve Ménier**] (Widow Schwartz, 1891)
Seedling of 'Camoëns' (HT).
"Pale light rose." [CA97] "Vigorous bush; canes tinted purple; foliage glaucous green; flower large, very full, perfect form, ruffled; color, pale pink on a blush white ground nuanced dawn gold and a very delicate carmine; petals' nubs yellowish. From 'Camoëns', and showing all the characteristics of that precious variety." [JR15/149]

Mme. Viger (Jupeau, 1901)
From 'Heinrich Schultheis' (HP) × 'G. Nabonnand' (T).
"Vigorous, upright branches, wood glaucous green, thorns rare, handsome foliage, very long and graceful buds, well held; borne on a long, strong stem, goes well with the foliage, nearly always solitary; flower very large, imbricated form, opens well; the most beautiful delicate pink, edges and reverse silvery pink touched carmine; nearly white in Fall...Extra floriferous, always blooming." [JR24/146]

Mme. Wagram, Comtesse de Turenne (Bernaix, 1895)
"Bright satin-rose in opening, changing to carnation; extra large bud and flower. A very fine Rose; growth vigorous." [P1] "Rosy red with yellow base...Full blooms...healthy bush...4×3 [ft; ca. 1.3×1 m]." [B] "Buds very large, ovoid; flower very large, of admirable form (like 'Merveille de

Lyon'), surpassing 4.5 inches in diameter [ca. 1.1 dm]. Beautiful color, satiny pink and flesh-pink upon opening, with a sulphur nub to the petal, fading to intense incarnadine with deep rose reflections when the flower is open. One of the biggest Tea roses, having the form of a hybrid." [JR18/163] [*We take it to indeed be a hybrid.*] "One of the most vigorous Tea roses. The beautiful coloration of sulphur yellow tinted pink makes this flower one of the best introductions of these last few years." [JR23/42] "Rather shy; might be better in a dry summer." [NRS/14] "Sometimes muddy. Fine rose in heat." [Th2] "Very vigorous, covered with superb foliage, and blooming abundantly from June until frost." [JR23/71-72]

Monsieur Bunel (Pernet-Ducher, 1899)
"Rosy peach, shaded with yellow and edged with bright rose; very full and compact; somewhat flat, but a fine Rose; growth vigorous." [P1] "Erect branches, beautiful cheerful green foliage, flower very large, quite full, imbricated, peachblossom pink, ground yellow, petals edged bright pink." [JR23/149]

Monsieur Charles de Lapisse (Laroulandie, 1909)
Sport of 'Mme. Caroline Testout' (HT).
"Vigorous, well-branched, pretty buds, virginal pink upon opening; flower very large, full, pearly white, sometimes blush white fading to creamy white, very pretty coloration." [JR23/153]

Monsieur Fraissenon (Gamon, 1911)
Seedling of 'Lady Ashtown' (HT).
"Vigorous, long bud, flower large, full, deep frosty pink." [JR35/167]

[**Monsieur Paul Lédé**] (Pernet-Ducher, 1902)
"Very vigorous, bushy; beautiful dark green foliage; flower very large, full, cupped, superbly colored carmine pink nuanced and shaded yellow; very

fragrant; continuous bloom." [JR26/131] Not to be confused with its own climbing sport 'Climbing Monsieur Paul Lédé', often called simply and confusingly 'Paul Lédé'.

Mrs. Charles J. Bell (Mrs. C.J. Bell/Pierson, 1917)
Sport of 'Red Radiance' (HT).
"Color light or shell-pink on a salmon-shaded background. Superior in growth to 'Radiance', being equally vigorous but more robust in habit." [ARA17/140] "Of an unusual color…Very fine." [ARA24/90] "Described…as a constant and steady bloomer." [Th2]

Mrs. Conway Jones
Listed as 'Mamie'.

Mrs. Cynthia Forde (A. Dickson, 1910)
"The flowers, large, numerous, and always opening well, are borne upright on very rigid stems; they have a unique form; the center juts out, and the petals fall back gracefully around it. The perfectly formed blossom is of a splendid color…delicate carmine red nuanced pink; it has a chrome yellow zone at the base of each petal. The branches are particularly strong and robust; the plant is much branched; the foliage is lime-green; each branch is crowned with a bud…a very strong, delicious Tea scent." [JR36/91-92]

Mrs. Henry Morse (McGredy, 1919)
From 'Mme. Abel Chatenay' (HT) × 'Lady Pirrie' (HT).
"Brilliant pink shaded vermilion red." [Riv] "Bright rose, darker shadings; beautiful spiral bud, holding high center when open; good size; lasting; very free; thirty petals; fragrant. Tall but somewhat spindly growth, with good stem. Foliage mildews…would seem to mildew in moist heat rather than damp coolness, but would do better still in dry climates. A rose well worth test, particularly adapted to Central Zone conditions with altitude."

[Th2] "We have never raised or sent out a Rose with a feeling of greater pride than we do in offering this wonderful novelty to the Rose-loving world." [NRS19/163]

Mrs. Herbert Stevens (McGredy, 1910)
From 'Frau Karl Druschki' (HP) × 'Niphetos' (T)—but see also below. "Nearly pure white, with a fawn and peach base to the petal. Habit free and vigorous for a Tea [*mainly because it is a Hybrid Tea!—BCD*], of excellent bedding type. The flowers are remarkable for their 'pointed' character, with good length of petal and excellent shape." [NRS/10] "White, slim, prone to weather damage." [Hk] "Grows strongly, has perfectly formed flowers, white tinged with a faint pink." [OM] "Growth and color good; foliage inclined to mildew; fairly good bloomer." [ARA18/113] "The best bloomer in whites in my garden." [ARA24/96] "Beautiful buds of rather thin petalage, and balls slightly, although frequently of exhibition value." [Th2] "Tall, compact, hardy; foliage very plentiful, black-spots and mildews somewhat; bloom free, continuous." [ARA18/127] "Very branching growth…To myself and some of my friends the foliage appears rather small and scanty, but others have referred to it as good dark foliage. It is always in flower throughout the season, and the blossoms are a nearly pure white (some notice and fawn and peach shading which I have not observed), and are a very beautiful shape, usually rather thin, and particularly elegant…One of the most beautiful decorative Roses we have had for a long time…rather bad in respect to mildew." [NRS/13] "I prefer this to any other white, for its shapely buds, its delicately toned color, and its healthy foliage. Not a rampant grower, but a very constant bloomer." [ARA29/52] "I asked him [*McGredy*] if it was not from 'Niphetos'. He said, No! but it had some of that blood in it, but only indirectly. It was the result of no less than 6 different crossings with his own seedlings." [NRS22/26]

Mrs. Oakley Fisher (B.R. Cant, 1921)
"A single tinted salmon-copper." [ARA23/125] "A uniform egg-yellow. It seems to be a good keeper, and the blooms appear in masses." [ARA23/140] "A very large, single-flowering rose, somewhat after the style of 'Irish Fireflame'...dark red stems...of good form, [*the blossoms are*] not apt to crinkle with age...pale golden buff, with deeper-colored stamens." [ARA22/145] "Orange and yellow without...harshness...Highly scented...3×3 [ft; ca. 1×1 m]." [B] "In constant flower...deliciously fragrant." [T3]

Mrs. Robert Garrett (J. Cook, 1898)
Several parentages have been published: (1), from 'Mlle. de Sombreuil' (T) × 'Mme. Caroline Testout' (HT); (2), from 'Mlle. de Sombreuil' (T) × an unnamed seedling (resulting from a cross of the Tea 'Mme. la Comtesse de Caserta' with the HP 'Mme. Eugène Verdier'); or (3), from 'Mme. la Comtesse de Caserta' (T) × 'Mme. Eugène Verdier' (HP).
"Shell pink with deeper center." [CA10] "Pink, medium size, full, medium scent, medium height." [Sn] "Both flowers and buds are of grand size and perfect full form. The flowers are of remarkable depth and sweetness. The petals are broad and of excellent substance. The color is exquisite shell pink, passing to soft glowing rose, delicately tinged with creamy yellow...The bush is a strong, vigorous grower, with handsome foliage and quite hardy. It is a constant and abundant bloomer, and can not be recommended too highly." [C&Js99] "A variety of really vigorous growth, appearing to be thoroughly hardy and healthy. The flowers are large and rather inclined to hang their heads, the colour being somewhat similar to '[Mme.] Caroline Testout'. I was somewhat disappointed on finding that the flowers came rather 'balled' in the season, but I have had one or two very long buds of fine pointed shape late in the autumn. This looks rather as if it would prefer not being closely pruned, which I think is likely. Being very free flowering and a good autumnal, it seems to be a variety of considerable promise for all purposes." [F-M2]

[**Mrs. W.C. Whitney**] (May, 1894)
From 'Mme. Ferdinand Jamin' (HP) × 'Souvenir d'un Ami' (T).
"Clear, deep pink color, and very fragrant; flowers large, combing with long buds A very free bloomer." [CA96]

Mrs. W.J. Grant (A. Dickson, 1895) syn., 'Belle Siebrecht'
From 'Lady Mary Fitzwilliam' (HT) × 'La France' (B).
"Brilliant intense pink with large petals." [JR22/107] "Large camellia-like flowers, bright pink. Beautiful long buds." [Hn] "The plant is unfortunately not strong in growth, and is best as a maiden…it is excessively free-flowering until quite late in the autumn, and the blooms at their best are very large, of a bright deep pink colour, very fragrant, and may be taken, I think, as a type of the finest and best pointed form with pointed petals known among Roses. The flowers generally come good, if the plant can be grown strongly enough, for it requires 'liberal treatment': and a good specimen is indeed something for a Rosarian to feast his eyes upon. The weak growth is an unfortunate drawback." [F-M2]

Mrs. Wakefield Christie-Miller (McGredy, 1909)
"Soft pearly blush, shaded salmon; outside of petal clear vermilion rose; loosely built with petals of good size." [Th] "Silvery pink shaded salmon; exterior light vermilion pink; flower very large, full, peony-shaped; very floriferous; very vigorous." [Cx] "Blush, shaded salmon. The flowers open out like a big tree Pæony, and are most decorative. They are produced on erect, strong growths." [OM] "The deeper colour being on the outside of the petal and the lighter shade inside, respectively clear vermilion rose and soft blush shaded salmon—a very striking combination. Habit, very vigorous, branching and with good foliage. Flowers of an enormous size, as large as any of the Hybrid Teas, quite full, and retaining their colour well in the hottest sun. A remarkable decorative Rose." [NRS/10] "28 to 57 blooms per season." [ARA21/92] "Growth, fairly good; lacks in blooming; color and form not of best." [ARA18/117] "Tall, bushy, vigorous,

hardy; foliage very plentiful, black-spots very much, bloom abundant, continuous." [ARA18/127] "Does exceedingly well here [*Denver, Colorado*], especially in hot weather." [ARA24/95]

Old Gold (McGredy, 1913)
"Orange red, very beautiful in the bud." [OM] "Reddish orange, semi-double.—Moderately vigorous." [JP] "Strong growth…a deep coppery old gold." [NRS/13] "Best in the bud. While it is orange at first, the color fades to light buff as the flower opens." [ARA34/81] "Great beauty of colour, which the raisers call reddish rouge, with rich coppery red and apricot shadings…a very beautiful and a striking decorative plant…spreading and not too tall. It has very dark coppery foliage, which appeared quite mildew proof…very free-flowering. It is sweetly scented and lasts well when cut." [NRS/13] "Does not last; especially fragrant…Foliage good." [Th2] "Without a doubt the most beautiful decorative existing, its color never having been equaled by another rose; the color is orange-red tinted apricot-red. It is a gem for vases, as the roses last a very long time in the best condition. The foliage is a somber coppery green, making a delicious contrast. The blossom is pleasantly perfumed; this variety is continuously in bloom and grows vigorously; the roses are always borne singly at the ends of the long stems." [JR37/89]

Ophelia (W. Paul, 1912)
Seedling of 'Antoine Rivoire' (HT).
"Salmon color, with pink reflections, perfect form, well-held—upright at the end of a long stem. Excellent for forcing and the garden." [JR36/103] "Delicate touches of blush pink, a suggestion of yellow art the petal's foot…clean, trim shape of the petals around a simple and upright heart…Its growth is free." [Hk] "Salmon-flesh shaded rose…with a flush of pale apricot whilst in the opening stage…honey scent." [RP] "Shapely buds…rich flesh pink with deeper shadings. Slight lemon tints in the center…Good foliage and highly fragrant…3×2 [ft; ca. 1 m × 6 dm]." [B]

"One unfurling bud on the desk fills one with awe and happiness. It is one of the most dependable bloomer and seldom has blackspot. In the early morning these creamy, pink-toned flowers with their high, deeper pink centers are lovely." [ARA31/99] "Fragrance quite marked for light-colored rose." [ARA18/114] "Brighter in autumn." [ARA26/95] "Growth good; fine foliage, stem good; perfect form, lasts well; color beautiful." [ARA16/20] "30 blooms a season." [ARA21/92] "Fragrance, fair, very delicate; shape, very good in bud and open flower." [Th] "Foliage mildews slightly and may be lost by black-spot...In extreme heat, 'Ophelia' blasts in the bud." [Th2] "Blooms perfectly in our cool [*Norwegian*] summers." [ARA20/47] "Many admirers [*in Houston, Texas*]." [ET] "I cannot but feel that 'Antoine Rivoire' must have been very close to the place in the nursery from which that pod [*containing the seed originating 'Ophelia'*] was gathered." [ARA31/146]

Papa Lambert (Lambert, 1898)
From an unnamed seedling (resulting from crossing the HT 'White Lady' with the HP 'Marie Baumann') × 'Oskar Cordel' (HT).
"Large, full, beautifully cupped form. Vivid pink, darker inside. Growth erect, straight, flowers solitary with a strong centifolia fragrance." [Hn] "Very floriferous, remontant, and extremely fragrant. The vigorous branches are erect and amply covered with attractive glossy leaves; the solitary buds come at the ends of the very long stems. They are more or less oval, and delicate pink, being slightly darker without; the half-opened blossom is regularly formed and quite full; its petals are large and slightly recurved...This rose is very hardy...As for appearance, we unhesitatingly compare it to 'Baronne Adolphe de Rothschild', being however darker and, above all, deliciously perfumed." [JR22/180]

Paul Meunier (Buatois, 1902)
"Very vigorous with heavy, upright wood, and handsome bronzy green foliage. Flower large, full, long bud. Color, straw yellow, strongly tinted

salmon." [JR26/178] "Strong stem, held on heavy wood, upright and strong...hardy and floriferous." [JR29/184]

[**Pearl**] (Bennett, 1879) trans., 'Perle'
From 'Adam' (T) × 'Comtesse de Serenye' (HP).
"Flesh pink, well formed, large." [JR3/114] "Soft rosy pink, or pale flesh-color, shaded carmine, passing to white; medium size, very full, perfect form; delightfully scented; a constant and very free bloomer." [CA90]

Pharisäer (Hinner, 1901) trans., "Pharisee"
Seedling of 'Mrs. W.J. Grant' (HT).
"Pinkish yellow." [LS] "Large, full, whitish-pink with salmon-pink; fairly long-stalked, free-flowering." [Hn] "Buds long on stiff stems, of splendid texture, flower very large, rose colour shading to silver, with centre of salmon; very free." [P1] "The most perfect Rose in the garden; the blooms open in any weather; a good size, and when disbudded are very large." [NRS/14] "Opens somewhat loose but holds its center...Only fair foliage, but holds in long seasons. Fine, tall, fairly bushy growth...continuous bloomer." [Th2] "Perfume mild...growth well above the average." [ARA17/22] "Low-growing, compact, hardy; foliage sufficient, black-spots somewhat; blooms free, continuous." [ARA18/ 127] "A very pretty variety; its outstanding features are the vigor of its canes, and the abundance of its bloom." [JR32/33] "The flowers are carried erect and well above the foliage, and are sweet scented. Its strong points are the beautiful shape of its flowers and elongated buds, its good constitution and its autumnal blooming and erect habit. Its weak ones are not many, but it is too tall for an ideal bedder, and the substance of petal is rather thin." [NRS/12] "Vigorous and rather tall (4-ft. [ca. 1.3 m]) with a branching but erect habit. The young foliage is a beautiful red, getting greener with age, and it is not subject to mildew...It flowers very freely and continuously from the end of June till October...the flower, though nicely pointed, is not very full. The colour is somewhat difficult to describe.

'Rosy white, shaded pale salmon...the centre is somewhat deeper...The buds are long and specially beautiful...It is a very beautiful garden Rose...though a fair-sized (often large) Rose, it never looks heavy...It has moderate fragrance. This is not perhaps everybody's Rose, but it is one of my chief favorites...The shade of colouring of the flowers is very delicate and they harmonise well with the foliage." [NRS/10] "Bronzy foliage...3×3 [ft; ca. 1×1 m]." [B]

Pierre Guillot (Guillot fils, 1879)
From 'Mme. Falcot' (T) × an unnamed HP.
"Vigorous, flower large to very large, full, well formed, and well held; color, bright sparkling red, petals bordered white, very floriferous, extra pretty." [JR3/164] "Very sweet." [B&V] "Moderately vigorous...canes upright, purplish green; leaves dark green; 5-7 leaflets; very good for forcing." [S]

Pierre Wattinne (Soupert & Notting, 1901)
From 'Papa Gontier' (T) × an unnamed seedling.
"Vigorous, handsome foliage; long bud; flower large, full, of a beautiful form; color, glossy cherry pink nuanced salmon yellow. Floriferous and fragrant." [JR25/162]

Pink Radiance
Listed as 'Radiance'.

Prince de Bulgarie (Pernet-Ducher, 1901)
"Very vigorous; leaves large, bright green; bud long, very graceful; flower very large, quite full, in the form of an elongated cup; outer petals large; coloration superb, difficult to describe; silvery flesh pink, very delicately nuanced or shaded salmon and dawn-gold...[F]orm resembles that of 'Souvenir du Président Carnot'. Like it, Bulgarie holds its blossom on a strong and quite erect stem." [JR25/131]

Radiance (J. Cook/Henderson, 1908) syn., 'Pink Radiance'
From 'Enchanter' (HT) × 'Cardinal' (HT).
"Light silver flesh to salmon pink…tends to blue slightly…shape, only fair…growth, very strong…splendid constitution…the best pink rose in cultivation today [*1920*]." [Th] "Carmine-rose; tall, bushy." [ARA17/31] "Brilliant rosy-carmine displaying beautiful opaline pink tints in the open flower." [C&Js11] "Blooms medium to large…Lasts well…slightly subject to mildew and [*black-*] spot…average of 51 blooms per season." [ARA21/91] "A hot weather rose." [ARA24/95] "We can depend on it for blossoms at all times. While the form is not always good, nevertheless it is never so poor that it doesn't add to a bouquet…strong, disease-resisting plant." [ARA31/99] "Foliage very abundant, blackspots slightly; bloom free, continuous all season." [ARA18/127] "A beauty both novel and remarkable. Its foliage is luxuriant; the plant, bushy, with voluptuous foliage, freely bearing buds emerging above the plant, everblooming…The blossoms have large rounded petals and long stems, are upright, and are of a brilliant carmine-lake, resembling a pretty 'Mme. Abel Chatenay'; the coppery shadings and gradations of red and yellow contrast strongly. These remarkable characteristics are accompanied by a sweet fragrance and lengthy bloom…beautiful and productive in Fall, and, so far, healthy." [JR34/76] "Valuable because of its all-round worth and wonderful constitution. Particularly notable for fragrance, strong growth, and very good blooming qualities." [ARA18/114]

Red La France
Listed as 'Duchess of Albany'.

Red Maréchal Niel
Listed as 'Grossherzog Ernst Ludwig von Hesse'.

Red Radiance (Gude, 1915)
Sport from 'Radiance' (HT).

"Dark, rich red...quite fragrant; fine form; lasting about five days...Growth vigorous...average [*in one season*] 45 blooms." [ARA21/91] "Red; tall, bushy." [ARA17/32] "Lighter in heat." [Th2] "Moderate height, compact, hardy; foliage very abundant, black-spots very slightly; bloom free, continuous." [ARA18/127] Pierson Co. introduced its own different, and supposedly inferior, 'Red Radiance' in 1916.

Reine Carola de Saxe (Gamon, 1902) trans., "Queen Carola of Saxony"
"Vigorous, flower large, full, very well formed, flower solitary, beautiful delicate silvery pink on a deep salmony pink ground, fragrant...Dedicated to the memory of the great care exercised by Her Majesty on behalf of an ill, restless gentleman of Lyon [*doubtless Gamon himself*] at the town of Strehlen in Saxony, 1870-1871 [*during, one should note, the Franco-Prussian War*]." [JR26/147]

Reine Marguerite d'Italie (Soupert & Notting, 1904) trans., "Queen Marguerite of Italy"
From 'Baron Nathaniel de Rothschild' (HP) × 'Mme. la Princesse de Bessaraba de Brancovan' (T).
"Vigorous, handsome dark green foliage; the bud is magnificently formed, and held proudly above the foliage. Flower very large, very full, of great beauty, and excellently held. Color, shining carmine red, the center brightened with vermilion red...literally covered with blossoms and buds throughout the season. Centifolia fragrance." [JR28/153]

Richmond (E.G. Hill, 1905)
From 'Lady Battersea' (HT) × 'Liberty' (HT). 'Général Jacqueminot' (HP) is mentioned in place of 'Liberty' in NRS/10.
"Pure red scarlet. At times varies greatly. Fragrant." [Th] "Scarlet crimson; flower large, full, fragrant; blooms continuously; very vigorous." [Cx] "Very small in heat and its form is flat; fragrant." [Th2] "Too single (many better reds)." [ARA25/105] "Continuous bloom...gorgeous in the spring

and fall, although they fade and blue in the sun, and the midsummer blooms are not very attractive." [ARA29/70] "Brilliant color; fairly good growth; blooming qualities good on Multiflora; not dependable; varies greatly; seldom grown well." [ARA18/118] "The roses are generally solitary and...develop on long, firm, and erect stems. The foliage...is a dark green...the color of this variety, which is delicately perfumed, is a bright scarlet crimson." [JR28/182] "Another florist's rose, like 'Mme. Abel Chatenay'." [JR37/171] "Long slim buds...colour burned in hot sun." [Hk] "Moderately high, compact, and hardy; foliage abundant, black-spots some; bloom moderate, continuous spring and fall, almost continuous in midsummer." [ARA18/127] "Delightful...more continuously produced with me than those of any other Rose in my garden...a most grateful and refreshing perfume." [NRS/12] "This Rose makes but moderate growth with stems rather twiggy and thin, in habit rather a poor bush, not very hardy. The foliage is nice when young and only of fair substance, but clean and little affected by mildew. The flowers are carried splendidly erect and well above the foliage in a way that is quite remarkable considering their thin stems. The flowers are produced most freely...the bud and half opened flowers are very beautiful, and the summer flowers come an almost perfect shape...bright crimson without any trace of purple...It flowers so much that it seems almost to flower itself to death, and the plants are apt to dwindle away...I was inclined to think it a weakly edition of 'Liberty'." [NRS/10]

Rosa Gruss an Aachen (Spek, 1930) trans., "Pink Gruss an Aachen"
A pink sport, presumably, of 'Gruss an Aachen' (HT).
"Yellowish pink, large, full, moderate height." [Sn]

Rosette de la Légion d'Honneur (Bonnaire, 1895) trans., "Rosette of the Legion of Honor"
"Carnation red, veined yellow.—Semi-climber.—Garden, pillar.—A pretty and distinct variety. A good buttonhole rose. Fragrant." [Cat12/53]

"Extra vigorous, semi-climbing, continuous blooming, canes numerous, growing to 1.5 m [ca. 4.5 feet]; leaves glossy, thick; buds small, well formed, ovoid, red nuanced cerise at the tip, and colored vermilion-grenadine; petals salmon-carmine, with a yellow line in the center. The bud looks singularly like the medal of an officer of the Legion of Honor." [JR19/147]

Rosomane Gravereaux (Soupert & Notting, 1899) trans., "Rose-Enthusiast Gravereaux"
"Growth bushy, of great vigor, magnificent foliage; enormous long bud of the 'Souvenir du Président Carnot' sort; blossom very large, very full, borne on a long, strong stem; beautiful form, perfectly held, petals large and thick; color, silvery white, exterior tinted very lightly with a very delicate flesh pink...Very fragrant and floriferous." [JR23/170] "Blooms well." [JR25/11]

Ruhm der Gartenwelt (Jacobs/Lambert, 1905) trans., "Glory of the Garden-World"
From 'American Beauty' (HP) × 'Francis Dubreuil' (T).
"Brilliant fiery red." [Ÿ] "Very vigorous, blooms profusely, giving globular blossoms, a non-bluing blood red." [JR28/166]

Sachsengruss (Neubert/Hoyer & Klemm, 1913) trans., "Saxon Greeting"
From 'Frau Karl Druschki' (HP) × 'Mme. Jules Gravereaux' (HT).
"Delicate flesh on a white ground. Center blush with China pink reflections. Form and placement of the blossoms just like 'Frau Karl Druschki'." [JR37/10]

Shandon (A. Dickson, 1899)
"Growth vigorous, flower large, full, deep carmine. Fragrant and beautiful." [JR25/11] "Center light red." [JR32/140] "Very fragrant, medium height." [Sn]

Sheila (A. Dickson, 1895)
"Bright pink." [Ÿ]

Snowbird (Hatton, 1936)
From 'Chastity' (Cl. HT) × 'Louise Cretté' (HP).
"Large, very double, fragrant; white with creamy center. Profuse, continuous bloom...2-3 [ft; ca. 6 dm-1 m]." [Lg] "Production is incessant on a practically disease-proof plant...exquisite white flowers." [ARA37/250] "Bud long-pointed; flower double, high centered, very sweetly fragrant, white, creamy white center. Foliage abundant, leathery. Vigorous (2.5-3 ft. [ca. 7.5-9 dm]), compact, bushy; profuse, continuous bloomer." [ARA36/225] "Apparently a lasting addition to our very few worth-while and dependable white roses. Plants are vigorous, with intensely fragrant white flowers with a cream center." [ARA36/212] "I have grown 'Snowbird' for about thirty years; and, having had the opportunity to scrutinize it under all conditions afforded by my Southern California climate, have little but praise for it. Chubby yet graceful urn-shaped buds, ivory sometimes spattered with rose-red, open into large, flat, very fragrant blossoms with the 'old' look to them, reminding me of a 'Souvenir de la Malmaison' in which the pink tints are changed to yellow—rather like 'Kronprinzessin Viktoria von Preussen'. 'Snowbird' is frequently mistaken for a Tea. It does indeed look very Tea-like, and has certain Tea characteristics: the blossoms will ball in extreme dampness; the dark green foliage is Tea-like in appearance, and is held in a characteristically stiff Tea manner; in shady conditions, the bush form does not grow tall and spindly as do most HTs—it climbs, as Teas frequently will; lastly, the fragrance is, to a great degree, that associated with the Teas. Unlike most Teas, however, 'Snowbird' will host a certain amount of mildew and rust, both of which are fortunately easily controlled on this variety. The plant itself is as handsome and bushy a *rosier* as can be desired, producing blossoms in great spurts throughout the year." [BCD] "The most satisfactory

of all white roses...dainty blossoms on a shapely plant...an indispensable white rose." [ARA39/230]

[**Souvenir d'Auguste Métral**] (P. Guillot, 1895) trans., "In Memory of Auguste Métral"
"Pure deep red, large full flowers of good form and substance, delightfully fragrant." [C&Js98] "Vigorous bush, very floriferous, canes numerous and thick, bud crimson red. Flower large, full, very well formed, varying from purple red to crimson red; fragrant; very beautiful." [JR19/147]

[**Souvenir de Mme. Ernest Cauvin**] (Pernet-Ducher, 1898) trans., "In Memory of Mme. Ernest Cauvin"
"Bush of good vigor with not very thorny upright canes; foliage shiny; flower large, very full, well formed, imbricated; color, delicate flesh, petals bordered a brighter pink, center light yellow, very often beautiful orange yellow. Very beautiful variety with abundant bloom. From an unreleased variety." [JR22/163]

[**Souvenir de Mme. Eugène Verdier**] (Pernet-Ducher, 1894) trans., "In Memory of Mme. Eugène Verdier"
From 'Lady Mary Fitzwilliam' (HT) × 'Mme. Chédane-Guinoisseau' (T). "Very vigorous with upright canes branching somewhat; foliage finely serrated, and handsome green; the blossom is borne on a strong stem and is large, very full, oval, with the petals gracefully recurving beneath; beautiful coloration, electric white on a ground of saffron yellow, sometimes shaded darker yellow." [JR19/25]

Souvenir de Monsieur Frédéric Vercellone (A. Schwartz, 1906) trans., "In Memory of Monsieur Frédéric Vercellone"
From 'Antoine Rivoire' (HT) × 'André Schwartz' (T).

"Vigorous, flower large, full, very well formed, good poise, opens well, fragrant; carmine pink, lightly coppery, nuanced blush white tinted bright carmine." [JR30/136]

Souvenir du Président Carnot (Pernet-Ducher, 1894) trans., "In Memory of President Carnot"
Seedling of 'Lady Mary Fitzwilliam' (HT).
"Light pink, very delicate at the center; flesh white around the edges; flower very large, full, imbricated; bud elongated; floriferous; vigorous." [Cx] "White, vigorous…very free-flowering." [J] "Flesh shaded white. With us, flesh to shell pink center…Fragrance, mild; shape, very good in bud and open flower…foliage, very good…tall, but not uniform." [Th] "Rosy flesh shaded with white, fine long buds on stiff and long stems, quite first-rate; growth vigorous." [P1] "Clear, bright rose colour on ivory-white ground. Large, full buds of 'Niphetos' shape…Experts of the world concede this to be one of the finest roses in existence. Exquisitely lovely." [Dr] "It is a strong, healthy grower and profuse bloomer, and so wonderfully beautiful that it has already [*1897*] taken more medals and certificates of merit than any other rose. It is elegantly formed, very large, full and double, and deliciously sweet. Color, lovely sea-shell pink, delicately tinted with golden fawn on rich creamy white." [C&Jf97] "Large, well-filled, white, with a delicate fleshy-pink centre. Free-flowering, strong-growing, erect, with sturdy stems. Beautiful tulip-like form when expanding, becoming flatter with age." [Hn] "Clear and attractive color, good form and foliage; growth tall…blooming qualities fair." [ARA18/114] "Very low-growing, slender, winterkills some; foliage sufficient, black-spots in midsummer; bloom free, intermittent during warm months." [ARA18/128] "Very vigorous with lightly bronzed branches; very floriferous; bud as long as that of 'Niphetos', admirably poised on a firm and long stem; flower very large, full, with large petals throughout…A magnificent variety, very floriferous and perfectly hardy, and will be much sought out for its prettily-shaped blossoms." [JR18/149] "This

pretty rose, dedicated to the unfortunate president of the Republic who fell under the dagger of the miserable Caserio, was raised in 1890." [JR19/132]

Souvenir of Wootton (J. Cook/Strauss & Co., 1888)
From 'Bon Silène' (T) × 'Louis Van Houtte' (HP).
"Pure rich, velvety red, delightfully sweet and constant bloomer; extra large fully double flowers. A vigorous grower and quite hardy." [C&Js06] "Cup-shaped, double flowers of a rosy crimson; very fragrant. Fine healthy foliage. Strong grower. Gives 34 blooms per season. Hardy." [ARA21/91] "Its coloration is a very beautiful display of crimson carmine, being meanwhile very fragrant and of strong growth. Whenever it appears, it attracts attention, but its manner of bloom makes in inappropriate for the frame, where it produces many blossoms wanting in form and color. For this reason, it isn't very popular; it is, nevertheless, a quite notable introduction." [JR16/37] "Medium height, compact, winterkills some; foliage sufficient, some black-spot in July; bloom abundant in July, free rest of season." [ARA18/128] "Take for example 'Souvenir of Wootton', which does very well in pots, blooming well enough, as long as it is not placed on the north side." [JR26/118] "Said to be the first Hybrid Tea rose raised in the United States." [ARA22/187]

Striped La France
Listed as 'Mme. Angélique Veysset'.

Sunny South (A. Clark, 1918)
From 'Gustav Grünerwald' (HT) × 'Betty Berkeley' (T).
"The color is pink, flushed with carmine on a yellow base—a most distinct and charming combination. It possesses a strong constitution and good habit, growing naturally five to six feet high, sometimes very much taller, and flowering practically throughout the year." [ARA28/112] "An Australian introduction of highest value for decorative purposes and as a

cut-flower. Very bushy up to 10 feet [ca. 3 m]. Flowers continuously and freely; soft pink with yellow shadings. Foliage remarkably resistant to disease. Almost in a class by itself for hedge or massing." [Capt28] "Not a strong climber, but makes a fine pillar or is good trained fan-wise on a lattice wall. The blooms are large, fairly double, and of a lovely deep shell pink shading to white in the center. It is a very constant bloomer." [CaRoI/6/6]

The Dandy (G. Paul, 1905)
Seedling of 'Bardou Job' (B).
"Fiery maroon crimson." [Ÿ] "Flower small, sparkling blackish crimson." [JR30/25]

The Meteor (Evans, 1887)
"Rich velvety crimson, exceedingly bright and striking; buds and flowers are large, and elegantly formed, and borne on nice long stems. It is a vigorous, strong grower, and free bloomer." [CA93] "Dark red, medium size, not very full, medium scent, dwarf." [Sn] "'[The] Meteor' and 'Liberty', having such beautiful coloration, grow too feebly, and the length of the stem makes for poor lasting qualities." [JR26/118] "One of the best for all purposes." [C&Jf97]

[**The Puritan**] (Bennett, 1886)
From 'Mabel Morrison' (HP) × 'Devoniensis' (T).
"In size and shape resembles 'Mabel Morrison'; flowers large, pure white, sweet; fine foliage." [CA90] "[*It*] caused a veritable sensation when exhibited at South Kensington, [*the exhibited flowers*] coming from America. It is indeed a precious rose for forcing, evidently being able to bear any rise in temperature. Its white flowers are tinged light yellow at the base, are lush, and retain for a long time their freshness." [JR12/107]

Triomphe de Pernet père (Pernet père, 1890) trans., "Triumph of Pernet père"
From 'Monsieur Désir' (N) × 'Général Jacqueminot' (HP).
"Vigorous, good growth, growing upright and strongly; wood and foliage very dark; flowers large, nearly full, beautiful bright red, very well held; bud very long, in the form of a **T**, opening very well, continuously and abundantly blooming…as vigorous as 'Souvenir de la Malmaison', and reblooms freely." [JR14/164] "A magnificent rose…The flowers are extra large, full and double and deliciously tea scented. Color brilliant carmine lake, with rich crimson shading, exquisitely beautiful. The plant is a neat compact grower, quite hardy and a free bloomer." [C&Js02] "Jean Pernet, who died last March 31st [*1896*] at Charpennes, near Lyon, at the age of 64…Born October 15, 1832, at Passin…of a family of modest gardeners, Jean Pernet early devoted himself to horticulture, and worked at Lyon at the establishment of Guillot père from 1853 to 1855, when he left for Paris, staying first with Portemer père at Gentilly, then with Victor Verdier père at Paris, returning to Lyon in 1856 to complete his horticultural education at the establishment of J.-B. Guillot fils…We hear the happy news that the business of the late Jean Pernet will not fall into the hands of strangers, but will be united with that of his son, Monsieur J. Pernet-Ducher." [JR20/65-66]

Vesuvius (McGredy, 1923)
"Six petals…soft dark crimson flowers of good form." [ARA34/81] "Long buds, opening to beautiful single blooms of a deep velvety crimson; slightly fragrant. Moderate growth and both mildews and black-spots [*Rhode Island*]. A poor harsh shade. Strong grower but unattractive in habit and form [*California*]. A five-petal rose that is a winner. Growth, vigorous and upright…I am very partial to it [*California*]. Pretty, single, dark red flower, shaped like California poppies, but…very shy-blooming." [ARA28/193]

Violette Bouyer
Listed in the chapter on Hybrid Perpetuals.

Violiniste Émile Lévêque (Pernet-Ducher, 1897) trans., "Violinist Émile Lévêque"
"Growth vigorous and bushy; foliage purplish green; long buds; blossom medium or large, full, and very well formed; color, bright flesh pink nuanced yellow with orange reflections within. Very floriferous." [JR21/146]

[**Viscountess Falmouth**] (Bennett, 1879)
From 'Adam' (T) × 'Soupert & Notting' (Mossy Remontant)
"A very extraordinary plant, the color of the blossom is very distinct, being pale pink with the reverse of the petals darker, very fragrant." [JR3/171] "Wood nearly as thorny as that of Moss Roses, though the bud isn't [*isn't mossy, that is*]. Blossom very large, well formed; color, delicate pink, with a darker reverse; globular; scent like that of the Moss." [S]

Viscountess Folkestone (Bennett, 1886)
"Creamy pink, centre salmon-pink, large and sweet. Very distinct and attractive. One of the best for garden decoration and massing; growth vigorous." [P1] "Very large, full, delicate pink, centre deep salmon-pink. Strong-growing, free-flowering." [Hn] "Beautiful...creamy white, shaded flesh...The most charming white, or nearly white, garden rose." [J] "As free-flowering a rose as I know, even till late into the Autumn...flowers very distinct, sweetly scented, and of quiet but taking colour, but they open quickly." [F-M2] "A good hot weather rose." [L] "Great petalage; bloom heavy, stem usually drooping. An old favorite. Very fragrant. Foliage, fair." [Th] "Of exquisite shape." [DO] "Strong but not long growth...much like the Chinas." [F-M2] "Good growth and color; fragrant; large flowers, generally too heavy for stems; good bloomer." [ARA18/114] "Low-growing, moderately compact, not entirely hardy; foliage plentiful, black-spots somewhat; bloom moderate, occasional."

[ARA18/128] "An old favorite, still worth growing. The blooms are large, though not of good form, and the colour is cream-pink. It grows vigorously...liable to mildew." [OM] "Growth fairly vigorous but not tall, habit rather spreading and bushy, foliage a fair size and good, but I fear (though all do not agree) rather subject to mildew. The flowers are borne on somewhat thin stems generally drooping, but sometimes erect, and are produced freely and continuously...always seems to be in flower, and it is at its best in early autumn...large heavy-shaped blooms with petals of good substance, the colour creamy white, shaded salmon flesh. The flowers...open quickly, becoming loose and shapeless. They will stand some bad weather, and are quite fragrant...'Viscountess Folkestone' is a highly artistic Rose...I should be very sorry to be without it." [NRS/10] "A lovely flower." [E]

W.E. Lippiatt (A. Dickson, 1907)
"Probably the best dark HT in cultivation—the colour is deep crimson shaded maroon. Rather late flowering, but particularly good un autumn...a good grower, free from mildew, fragrant, and the flowers are of good size and shape." [F-M] "The flowers are large, full, symmetrically formed canter." [C&Js09] "Tall, bushy, hardy; foliage very plentiful, black-spots somewhat; bloom moderate and intermittent first half of season." [ARA18/128] "Very deep, velvety crimson with sweet scent. Shapely with mid green foliage...3×3 [ft; ca. 1×1 m]." [B] W.E. Lippiatt, rosarian; introduced, *inter alia*, the China 'Primrose Queen', *q.v.*

Westfield Star (Morse, 1920)
Sport of 'Ophelia' (HT).
"Dwarf; stems short; disease-resistant; very little bloom. Buds good shape but blooms open flat, lemon-yellow which soon fades to creamy white [*Ontario, Canada*]. Yellowish buds, opening to nearly perfect glistening white blooms of delightful fragrance, the same lovely shape as 'Ophelia'. Foliage large, free from disease; blooms singly on strong stems...the best white rose we have [*Rhode Island*]." [ARA28/194-195]

White La France
Listed as 'Mlle. Augustine Guinoisseau'.

White Wings (Krebs, 1947)
From 'Dainty Bess' (HT) × an unnamed seedling.
Single. "Papery white with pronounced, chocolate anthers. Foliage is leathery and dark green…4×3 [ft; ca. 1.3×1 m]." [B]

[**William Francis Bennett**] (Bennett/Evans, 1886)
From 'Adam' (T) × 'Xavier Olibo' (HP).
"Velvety crimson." [LS] "Large, loosely filled, glossy carmine-red, becoming violet with age; flowers continuously. Highly prized as a good forcing rose, but not much favored as a standard, as it is not full enough." [Hn] "A fine Tea Rose, in profusion [*of*] bloom unsurpassed by any of the monthly roses. It produces extra fine buds of the most brilliant crimson, with a delicious fragrance." [CA88] "The buds of 'William Francis Bennett' resemble those of the well-known 'Niphetos', up to but excluding the color—we think that we are seeing a rich fiery carmine-red 'Niphetos' before our eyes—that is 'William Francis Bennett'." [RZ86/6] "Moderate, bushy growth, with very dark leaves; long buds; color, carmine red like 'Général Jacqueminot'." [JR10/24] "In 1884, Bennett exhibited these [*'pedigree'*] roses at several English rose shows, and frequently they took first place because of the perfection of their blossoms. But he never released them to commerce. One day, Mrs. Evans, a dealer in flowers, was visiting Bennett at Shepperton with her young son. They were so struck by the beauty of the new rose, particularly as a cutting variety, that she acquired from Bennett all rights to the variety, paying $5,000. Such a sum for one variety is unique in rose history!" [JR10/23] "Everyone remembers the fuss made about the sale of the rose 'William Francis Bennett' for $5,000…[I]t was a good rose." [JR19/55]

Appendix One

Rose Identification

For many involved with "old" roses, the greatest delight of all is to find a gnarled old bush in some out-of-the-way cemetery or abandoned dooryard garden, and then, all the meantime dreaming heady reveries of the fabled—and frequently fabulous—past, to make an attempt to identify the plant. The following will perhaps assist the ambitious rosarian in his or her brave endeavor.

Methodology of Identification

Identification of roses old or new is an intricate and demanding affair, and one should begin any attempt with the clear understanding that assured success is unlikely. Disenheartening words! But let us consider:

Even in their purest form, many of the most significant roses are already such a complex brew of species that Science despairs of sorting out *what crossed with what and when.* For instance, the Damask Perpetual may derive from *Rosa gallica*, *R. phœnicia*, and/or *R. moschata*—not to mention *R. damascena*—all bred,, interbred, and re-bred together as well as—who knows?—with other species or hybrids. The other groups are no less complex; and consequently every cultivar may be considered not so much a representative of a particular "family," but rather a citizen of the world. Combinations may bring characteristics which are misleading in appearance; atavism may produce "memories" of far-distant ancestors. Indeed, our understanding of the groups and reliance on how we have labeled them may give us tunnel vision at the very moment when peripheral vision is called for; for instance, should we find a climber with Noisette characteristics, we might sift and sift through the Noisette listings, not realizing that many if not all of the Sempervirens hybrids were the result of crossings with Noisettes—the identity of that rose may be found in the Sempervirens listing, not in the Noisette listings. Thus, perhaps it is best to regard divisions of cultivars as indicating not species derivations so much as horticultural concepts. The pragmatic French breeders would, as an example, regard as a "China" not something demonstrably free of non-*chinensis* characteristics—whatever *R. chinensis* might be; rather, if the entity bloomed repeatedly)ruling out the old European roses and their primary hybrids), was well-branched with branches which could bloom from every node (ruling out Damask Perpetuals), was restrained in growth (ruling out typical Hybrid Perpetuals and Noisettes), had fairly regular broad-based thorns rather than bristles and broad-based thorns all mixed together (ruling out typical Bourbons), and had a blossom which was less than impeccable in form and/or doubleness (ruling out Teas), they would probably—but not necessarily—have considered it a "*China,*" be its parentage China, Bourbon, "pure" Tea, Noisette × Tea, China × Tea, or whatever. We must therefore scrutinize every fact or attribute very closely indeed all the while doing just the opposite and guarding against setting too much store by any single fact or attribute!

Distribution

It is important that such foundlings not be allowed merely to languish in the study-gardens of specialists, awaiting rediscovery of their official names. The mystery of their past does not obscure their beauty—to some it enhances it!—and there is thus no reason to "punish" them for the fact that insouciant horticulturists have let their names fade along with their flowers. And things happen. A "hundred year" storm could wipe out both parent plant and newly-rooted cuttings; or the caring rosarian him- or herself could expire or lose interest, the end result being perhaps to extinguish the remaining earthly stock of some most desirable cultivar. The plants must be made available and *distributed* for the delight of the horticulturist and the richness of Horticulture. But—how to do this without having the same cultivar being shipped around the world by 16 different nurseries under 16 different names? One can only make suggestions. *First,* the discoverer assigns a provisional name composed of the word "Unknown" followed by an appropriate word or two such as the name of the town, street, or person involved in the discovery (for example, "Avalon"), completing the provisional name with an honest guess as to what the classification *might* be ("Tea," perhaps).Those wishing to vend this discovery would thus do so under the name 'Unknown Avalon Tea', which would accomplish making it available under a comprehensible name (names of the 'WX8j1' sort being *in*comprehensible) while equally making it patently obvious even to blockheads that it is an *unknown.* Provisional names not including "Unknown" run the risk of having their names taken as the "real thing," leading to unnecessary confusion and frustration on all sides. *Second,* let us hope that at some point a wise rosarian—a *wise* one, not an *ambitious* one—will stand up and venture to opine that the 'Unknown Avalon Tea' is very possibly 'Egine', Vibert's 1852 Tea, stating and one hopes publishing a detailed rationale for this suggestion. As likely as the identification might be, prudence would seem to dictate that we not immediately shout "Hurrah! Yes, this is it!", carve this opinion in stone, and start celebrating a solemn but joy-filled *Te Deum*. That wise rosarian, wise as he is, could be wrong. Rather, let these and any other sincere and earnest attempts at identification be gathered under a name which—as "Unknown" did in the first instance—allows us to offer the cultivar while being perfectly straightforward with the enterprising customers who venture to buy the offering (and rosarians who buy and love "unknowns" are thrice-blessed by our patron goddess Flora). It thus would be appropriate to offer this example not as 'Egine', but rather as '*Possible* Egine', with the name of the person suggesting the identification attached, for a set period of 5 years or 10 to give *other* wise rosarians, as well as cranky rosarians and the like, to state their objections or suggest other likely identifications. After that period is over, shall we indeed just call it 'Egine'? If no substantive objections can be stated in the space of 5 or 10 years, not one, is there any reason to be held hostage by mute paralysis?

Documentation

When a subject for identification is first chosen, it would be wise to complete and keep on file a form with the following information: Provisional Name; Seemingly in which Group; Main Color of the Flower; Other Colors or Tintings, specifying locations; Degree of Doubleness; Form of Blossom; Stamens and Pistils Hidden or Evident; Size of Average Blossom; Size of Exceptional Blossom; Strength and Type of Fragrance; Any Further Remarks on the Blossom; Form of Bud; Form and Characteristics of Ovary; Flower-Stem Stiff or Bending; Flower-Stem Smooth or Prickly; Description of the Thorniness, Color, and Tendency to Branch of the Canes; Description of the Growth; Description of the Thorns; Description of the Leaves; Description of the Stipules; Plant Thick with Leaves or Scant of Leaves?; Characteristics of the Roots; What

Cultivar Does This Remind You Of, and Why?; Why Do You Think It Is *Not* the Variety It Reminds you Of?; Geographical Location Specimen Found; Estimated Age of Property or Garden or Community Where Found; Identifiable Roses and/or Other Significant Plants in the Same Garden; with any other observations or remarks.

Classification

The first question to ask in attempting identification is "What does this entity *look* like?", and the second, "How does it behave?". If the identifier's experience with "old" roses is well-rounded, and the plant looks or acts like a Bourbon—a rather schizophrenic group, by the way—very likely the breeder who originally classed it and named it felt the same way. Here is a rough attempt at a key to identification, in the use of which one must remember that other characteristics may take precedence in certain cases over those mentioned, and that the characteristics specified may in some cases be suppressed in the particular cultivar without prejudicing that cultivar's placement in a particular group—*and* that personal quirks or market conditions may have induced a breeder to place a cultivar in what we would now consider to be an inappropriate class!

I. Once-blooming, or feeble remontancy.
- A. Growth more compact; foliage rough, dull; spination bristly or needle-like; flowers open radially. Old European Roses.
- B. Growth more diffuse; foliage smooth, glossy; spination unequal, both bristly and with heavy, often hooked, thorns; flowers open spirally.
    - 1. Inflorescence a large cluster of flowers; individual blossoms smallish. Hybrid Noisette.
    - 2. Inflorescence few or uni-flowered; individual blossoms largish.
        - a. Foliage slender, leaflets more acuminate; petals of heavier substance, usually opaque. Hybrid China.

b. Foliage broad, stout, leaflets more obtuse; petals of a more delicate substance, often quasi-translucent. Hybrid Bourbon.

II. Markedly remontant.

A. Leaves, blossoms medium to tiny in size; secondary growths twiggy, though bush may grow to 1 m (ca. 3 ft) or more.

1. Flowers in large terminal panicles on primary canes; fragrance faint or lacking; *R. multiflora* characters frequently present. Polyanthas.

2. Flowers not in large clusters on primary canes; fragrance moderate to strong; *R. multiflora* characters lacking.

a. Plant, leaves, and flowers markedly reduced in size. Lawrencianas (see *The Old Rose Adventurer*).

b. Plant of average size, though in many cases scandent; flowers usually 5-7 cm in diameter, frequently nodding. Teas, old type.

B. Leaves, growths of average or large size; flowers usually in smaller clusters or solitary; fragrance generally strong.

1. Leaves soft, slender, downy; not stiff or rugose in age; spination bristly, often unequal, but all spines tendentially needle-like, narrow or only slightly enlarged at the base; spines straight or in a shallow arc; inflorescence multi-flowered, terminal or quasi-terminal on the cane; calyx narrow to narrowly funnel-shaped, grading into the stem; sepals tendentially foliaceous; flower buds round or squat; flowers open radially, not spirally. Damask Perpetuals.

2. Leaves more leathery, more stiff; spination occasional, sometimes remote, usually including at least some large, laterally flattened thorns, enlarged at the base, often strongly hooked; inflorescence often few- or uni-flowered, though in large clusters in certain climbers or on the strongest-growing canes; ovary more oval to spherical, often much enlarged, usually abruptly widening where it joins the stem; sepals tendentially entire; flower buds more conical; flowers open spirally, not radially.

a. Canes of plant much elongated, arching or quasi-climbing in maturity.

i. Inflorescence composed of many-flowered clusters; leaves more or less narrowly oval-acuminate, tendentially matte-green, not undulate; flower medium-sized or small.

AA. Leaves, stems reduced in size; scent generally faint; *R. multiflora* characters present. Climbing Polyanthas.

BB. Leaves, stems of average size; scent generally strong. Noisettes, old type.

ii. Inflorescence few-flowered, or flowers solitary; leaves moderately or broadly oval, tendentially glossy green, often undulate; flower average to large in size. Tea-type Noisettes and miscellaneous HT Climbers and climbing sports.

b. Canes of plant moderately or not much elongated; plant bushy or quasi-bushy.

i. Plant stocky, well ramified.

AA. Plant glabrous, often glaucous, green; flowers large, well-formed, often nodding; ovary usually large, spherical. Teas.

BB. Plant at least minutely hirsutulous; ovary medium-sized, oval to elongate.

aa. Petals of heavy substance; flowers shallow, convex; petals often quilled in age. Chinas.

bb. Petals delicate; flowers deeper, concave, rounded when fully open; petals not quilled in age. China-type Bourbons.

ii. Plant open, moderately or poorly ramified.

AA. Plants usually more restrained on growth; flowers usually in few-flowered clusters or solitary; bud urn-shaped in early stages of expansion; spination tendentially equal, not mixed; thorns usually broad-based, laterally flattened. Hybrid Teas.

BB. Plants usually more robust in growth; flowers frequently in few- or many-flowered clusters on strongest canes; opening bud often not urn-shaped; spination tendentially mixed, both bristly and broad-based.

aa. Petals of heavy substance; flowers usually large, more or less erect at the tips of the canes; growth usually robust, stout. Hybrid Perpetuals.

bb. Petals delicate; flower usually nodding, medium-sized; growth more slender, long. Bourbons.

Having come this far, some groups may be whittled down further—remembering meantime that each group has a large, unspecified, miscellaneous contingent of entries which do not fit neatly into any of the various types and clans: Hybrid-Tea-like Teas; Pernetiana Hybrid Perpetuals; undecided entities hovering between China, Tea, and Bourbon; Polyanthas that are actually dwarf Sempervirenses or dwarf Wichuraianas; cluster-flowered Hybrid Teas; recessive Hybrid Perpetuals more like Damask Perpetuals or Bourbons; progressive Bourbons more like Hybrid Teas; and so on! But let us try:

Teas

I. Thorns sparse, strong; flower with fairly faint scent; petals large and rounded; pedicel upright and strong. Tea/China hybrids.

II. Thorns abundant; flowers tendentially with medium to strong scent; petals, particularly inner ones, tendentially narrow and acuminate; pedicel weak, often bending under weight of flower.

  A. Color of flower predominantly light pink to white; ovary globular, much inflated at maturity; flower bud rounded, slightly pointed; leaves leathery. 'Adam' clan.

  B. Color of flower predominantly intense pink, coppery pink, coppery rose-red, to ivory,, yellow, or buff.

    1. Growth bushy, spreading; leaflets ovalish, light green; tendency towards blooming in clusters; bud short; pedicel short and weak; ovary small, widening towards the top. 'Caroline' clan.

      a. Secondary branches tendentially upright.

        i. Foliage ample, flowers large, fragrant, salmon-pink. 'Mme. Damaizin' group.

        ii. Foliage scant to moderate; flowers medium-sized or smallish, not or only lightly fragrant, bright pink, coppery at the nub. Comtesse de Labarthe' group.

      b. Secondary branches tendentially pendant; flower bright red to deep crimson to wine-lee. 'Souvenir de David d'Angers' group.

2. Growth upright; leaflets elongate, dentate, purplish at first, then dark green; tendentially uni- to few-flowered inflorescence; bud long, pointed; pedicel relatively long, moderately strong; ovary large, spherical or often pyriform, much enlarged at maturity.
   a. Flowers ivory, primrose, yellow, buff, or apricot in color. 'Safrano' clan.
   b. Flowers intense pink to coppery red shades, with yellow reflections and nub. 'Red Safrano' clan.

Hybrid Perpetuals

Leaflets small, crowded on rachis; leaves somewhat sparse on bush; flowers relatively small, flat or cupped, red. 'Géant des Batailles' type.

Leaflets large, not markedly crowded on rachis; leaves fairly to very ample on bush; flowers medium to large.

Canes spreading, long, and slender.

Flower flat, very large. 'Baronne Prévost' type.

Flower cupped to globular-imbricated.

Canes brownish; thorns large. 'Charles Lefebvre' type.

Canes greenish; thorns medium to small.

Flowers white to blush. 'Mme. Récamier' type.

Flowers pink, red, or maroon.

Thorns numerous, hooked; canes rough. 'Général Jacqueminot' type.

Thorns rare; canes smooth. 'Mme. Victor Verdier' type.

Canes upright, strong, medium to thick.

Canes rigid, stiff.

Internodes short; thorns large. 'Souvenir de la Reine d'Angleterre' type.

Internodes average length; thorns small. 'La Reine' type.

Canes not markedly rigid.

Canes short, stocky, smooth; leaves glossy. 'Victor Verdier' type.

Canes more slender, elongate to climbing; leaves not markedly glossy.

Internodes long; flowers medium to dark red, flat; ovary round. 'Triomphe de l'Exposition' type.

Internodes not markedly long; flowers light pink to light red, imbricated; ovary elongate. 'Jules Margottin' type.

Polyanthas

I Bush dwarf; primary inflorescence on main canes a tendentially leafless, much ramified cluster of many small, usually semi-double, cupped Ranunculus-form flowers; petals short, rarely or never reflexing; petal-nubs usually white; pedicel strong, upright; little or no scent in flower. Multiflora-type Polyanthas.

II Bush medium to tall; primary inflorescence on main canes a few- to moderately-branched cluster comprised of a number of medium-sized double or full, pointed or often quilled or "cactus-form" flowers of tendentially Tea- or China-rose form; petals long, outer ones usually reflexing in age; petal nubs usually yellowish; pedicel tendentially weak; flower often nodding; flower with moderate scent. Tea-type Polyanthas.

To leap from "Safrano clan" or "Général Jacqueminot type" and land—correctly—on a specific cultivar name takes more than a little intuition combined with just less than infinite luck. If one is very lucky indeed, one, having noticed "deep, irregular serrations in the leaf, purple at the edge," or "scent of plums in marmalade," will recall from one's studies references to such, and a name will perhaps come to mind. Otherwise—woe!—more whittling, more tedious sifting—often to no end at all, many if not most cultivars being very hazily defined even in the best old sources, and *wrongly* defined in many modern sources. One may very easily be left with half a dozen or more candidates jostling for precedence, all undifferentiated and perhaps undifferentiatable! Still, there are other factors to consider:

Certain flower forms are more typical of some decades than of others. For instance, the "flat" form of 'Souvenir de la Malmaison' or 'Baronne Prévost' was not much favored after perhaps 1860. A truly "full" flower—showing no stamens or pistils—is a rarity among cultivars introduced after about 1910 or 1915, but is to be expected, particularly in "exhibition-class" cultivars, prior to 1895 or 1900. An often unexpected variable would be just what is meant in the literature by the citing of certain color names. A "white" from the pre-'Frau Karl Druschki' era can look rather primrose or pinkish to us; "red" usually means what we would call "deep rose." Depending upon the climate in which the blossom as described was seen, equally veracious authors could describe the same rose as being anything from white or blush with yellow or salmon to being "deep pink." Worse, one must consider what stage of the flower the era was interested in, was describing—a "red" Tea might be one that is only "deep rose" when the bud is first expanding, then quite pink when fully open; the definitive "yellow" Tea, 'Safrano', was nevertheless known as early as 1844 for turning *whitish* by the end of its first day open. We have seen insular commentators pronounce as "daft" descriptions which vary from their own, obviously limited, experience with particular cultivars; we have meantime seen with our own eyes how extremely a cultivar's blossoms may vary with differing conditions. Should three people, for instance, march up to describe their own 'Gloire de Dijon', one saying that it is "white," one saying that it is "pink," and one saying that it is "yellow," they will all have been telling the truth. In this indeed we see the very *raison d'être* of this book—to show how diverse truth is with these roses! Objectivity, or at least varied subjectivity, must rule the day. To continue, then—study of the development of the cultivars, knowledge of the stated or inferential goals of the breeders of each era, and familiarity with the "manners and customs" of the breeding-stock to which breeders had recourse can give important hints.

Some cultivars had very wide distribution and thus by sheer force of numbers would be more likely to have survived here and there than would an introduction which never "caught on." Particularly in those areas most remote from France, England, and Germany, the survivors are often cultivars which were "old favorites" even when originally planted. Even when novelty-minded outlanders would manage to get rare, new introductions, they would be precisely the ones most likely to *discard* last year's novelties to make way for *this* year's novelties, thus constantly renewing their collections, and indeed tending to retain only those which performed the best—which would usually turn out to be, at length, the same "old favorites" we should have considered to begin with. They were "old favorites" for a reason! Thus, "likelihood" is something to be remembered and figured into calculations. Every factor is worthy of careful consideration. The very fact that a cultivar is rather ambiguous may be significant; look in the literature for cultivars that are listed under different groups by different "authorities"—ambiguity is not erased by the passage of time!

But if, after these extended and profound lucubrations, one is still left with an unidentified red Hybrid Perpetual, light yellow Tea, or pink China, so be it! That is the stage at which we may finally enjoy the plant not because it was introduced in such-and-such a year by so-and-so, and not because one celebrity or another lavished perfumed praises on it—no; we may finally cast aside these spurs towards faddish attraction and genuinely enjoy the rose for what it really it: Nature's simple gift of quiet and most pure beauty.

Appendix Two

Distinguished Seed Bearers

"Distinguished seed-bearers which have exercised, and still exercise, such a predominant influence upon Rose advancement." [WD] Origins and a short description are included for each cultivar not otherwise mentioned in this book.

1848

Compiled from *The Rose Garden*, by William Paul.

Damask Perpetuals
'Louis-Philippe I', '[Perpétuelle] D'Esquermes' [*Miellez, -1835, vivid rose, large and full*], 'St. Fiacre' [*Mauget, 1844, violet and crimson*]

Bourbons

'Amarantine' [*probably intending 'Amaranthine', Thibault,-1842, rosy pink*], 'Augustine Lelieur' [*Breeder unknown, -1835, rose-colored, large and double*], 'Bouquet de Flore', 'Célimène' [*Breeder unknown, -1835, silvery blush*], 'Cérès' [*Breeder unknown, -1841, pale glossy rose*], 'Comice de Seine-et-Marne', 'Comte de Rambuteau' [*Rolland, 1843, dark rose tinted with lilac*], 'Duc de Chartres' [*Breeder unknown, -1844, rosy crimson*], 'Émile Courtier', 'Gloire des Rosomanes', 'Mme. Nérard', 'Malvina' [*Vibert, 1829, rosy pink*], 'Marianne' [*Laffay, 1845, rosy pink*], 'Pierre de St.-Cyr', 'Proserpine', 'Thérèse Margat' [*Breeder unknown, -1842, rose-pink, edges lighter*]

Hybrid Bourbons

'Athalin', 'Capitaine Sissolet', 'Céline', 'Charles Duval', 'Coupe d'Hébé', 'Daphné' [*V. Verdier, 1835, light carmine*], 'Dombrowski', 'Great Western', 'Henri Barbet' [*Breeder unknown, -1835, light carmine, large and double*], 'Legouvé' [*Vibert, 1828, bright carmine*], 'Lord John Russell' [*Laffay, 1835, brilliant rose, fading; very abundant*], 'Majestueuse' [*Breeder unknown, -1836, bright rose, large and full*], 'Paul Perras

Hybrid Chinas

'Aurore' [*Laffay, -1835, light crimson, sometimes with a white line at the center of the petal*], 'Chénédolé', 'Duc de Devonshire' [*Laffay, -1835, rosy lilac striped with white*], 'Fulgens' [*i.e., 'Malton'*], 'Général Allard', 'Jenny', 'Magna Rosea' [*Breeder unknown, -1848, light rose, very large and very double*], 'Maréchal Soult' [*Laffay, 1838, light vermilion; introduced as a Hybrid Perpetual; poss. there was another 'Maréchal Soult' Hybrid China raised by Hooker*], 'Petit-Pierre' [*Breeder unknown, -1841, purplish red, very large and very double*], 'Riégo' [*Vibert, 1831, Rubiginosa/China hybrid; see* The Old Rose Adventurer]

Hybrid Perpetuals
'Comtesse Duchâtel', 'Duc d'Alençon' [*Breeder unknown, -1845, crimson, pale in Summer*], 'Duc d'Isly' [*Lacharme, 1845, "an autumnal Tuscany"*], 'Duchesse de Sutherland', 'Édouard Jesse' [*which we list as a Hybrid Bourbon*], 'La Bouquetière' [*Laffay, 1843, pale rose*], 'Lady Elphinstone' [*Laffay, 1842, rosy crimson*], 'Mme. Laffay', 'William Jesse' [*which we list as a Hybrid Bourbon*]

1877

According to Cranston's *Cultural Directions for the Rose* (our reference JC), the following may be taken as good seed-bearers.

Damask Perpetuals
'[Rose] du Roi'

Chinas
'Fabvier', 'Mrs. Bosanquet', 'Old White' [*? 'Alba' of Wm. Paul? Or the China 'Mme. Desprez'*]

Bourbons
'Bouquet de Flore', 'Louise Odier', 'Pierre de St.-Cyr', 'Sir Joseph Paxton'

Hybrid Bourbons
'Charles Lawson', 'Coupe d'Hébé', 'Paul Ricault', 'Paul Perras'

Hybrid Chinas
'Blairii No. 2', 'Brennus', 'Chénédolé', 'Fulgens' [*i.e., 'Malton'*], 'Général Allard', 'Magna Rosea' [*see above under "1848"*]

Hybrid Perpetuals
'Baronne Prévost', 'Black Prince', 'Centifolia Rosea', 'Charles Lefebvre', 'Dr. Andry', 'Duchesse de Sutherland', 'Duc de Cazes', 'Duc de Rohan'

[*Lévêque, 1861, red*], 'François Lacharme' [*V. Verdier, 1861, carmine*], 'Géant des Batailles', 'Général Jacqueminot', 'Gloire de Santenay' [*Ducher, 1859, purple*], 'John Hopper', 'Jules Margottin', 'King's Acre' [*Cranston, 1864, rose*], 'La Reine', 'Le Rhône' [*Guillot fils, 1862, vermilion*], 'Lord Clyde' [*W. Paul, 1862, crimson*], 'Lord Raglan', '[Mlle.] Annie Wood', 'Mme. Charles Crapelet', 'Mme. Hector Jacquin', 'Pierre Notting', 'Peter Lawson', 'Prince Léon' [*? 'Prince Léon Kotschoubey', Marest, 1852, flesh*], 'Sénateur Vaïsse', 'Souvenir de Leveson-Gower', 'Thorin', 'William Jesse' [*which we list as a Hybrid Bourbon*]

1882

Cited in *The Rose*, by Henry B. Ellwanger.

Bourbons

'Louise Odier'

Teas

'Adam', 'Alba Rosea' [*i.e., 'Mme. Bravy'*], 'Catherine Mermet', 'Comtesse de Labarthe', 'Devoniensis', 'Duchesse d'Edinburgh', 'Mme. de St.-Joseph', 'Mme. de Tartas', 'Mme. Falcot', 'Safrano', 'Parks' Yellow Tea-Scented China'

Hybrid Perpetuals

'Anna de Diesbach', 'Antoine Ducher', 'Baron Chaurand', 'Baron de Bonstetten', 'Baronne Adolphe de Rothschild', 'Beauty of Waltham', 'Charles Lefebvre', 'Comtesse d'Oxford', 'Dr. de Chalus' [*HP, Touvais, 1871, scarlet*], 'Duchesse d'Edinburgh', 'Duchesse de Sutherland', 'Duke of Edinburgh', 'Géant des Batailles', 'Général Jacqueminot', 'Jean Cherpin', 'John Hopper', 'Jules Margottin', 'La Reine', 'Lion des Combats', 'Marguerite de St.-Amande' [*de Sansal, 1864, light pink*], '[Mlle.] Annie Wood', 'Mlle. Marie Rady', 'Mme. Boutin', 'Mme. Charles Wood', 'Mme. Julia Daran', 'Mme. Laffay', 'Mme. Récamier', 'Mme.

Victor Verdier', 'Mme. Vidot', 'Paul Neyron', 'Sénateur Vaïsse', 'Souvenir de la Reine d'Angleterre', 'Souvenir de la Reine des Belges' [*de Fauw, 1850, carmine*], 'Thomas Mills', 'Triomphe des Beaux-Artes', 'Triomphe de l'Exposition', 'Victor Verdier'

Noisettes
'Chromatella', 'Gloire de Dijon', 'Lamarque', 'Ophirie', 'Solfatare'

1910

"A few good seed-bearing kinds...," as listed in *The Rose Annual* [NRS10/55-56]; we list them as published there, as it appears that this is the order in which they came to mind for the writer, a prioritizing which may be of interest.

'Antoine Rivoire', 'Mme. Abel Chatenay', 'Pharisäer', 'Joseph Hill' [*HT, Pernet-Ducher, 1903, salmon-pink*], 'Frau Karl Druschki', 'Mme. Edmée Metz' [*? 'Edmée Metz', HT, Soupert & Notting, 1900, rose-colored*], 'Mme. Ravary', '[Monsieur] Paul Lédé', 'Le Progrès' [*HT, Pernet-Ducher, 1903, yellow*], 'Gustav Grünerwald', 'Laurent Carle', 'Killarney', 'Earl of Warwick' [*HT, W. Paul, 1904, salmon-pink*], '[Mme.] Caroline Testout', 'White Lady' [*HT, W. Paul, 1889, white*], 'Kaiserin Auguste Viktoria', 'Mme. Lambard', 'Souvenir de William Robinson', 'Richmond', 'Mme. Mélanie Soupert', 'Warrior' [*HT, W. Paul, 1906, scarlet*], 'Mme. Gamon', 'Captain Hayward', 'Mrs. John Laing', 'Mme. Jean Dupuy', 'Betty', 'General MacArthur', 'G. Nabonnand', 'Farbenkönigin' [*HT, Hinner, 1902, rose-red*], 'Lady Battersea' [*HT, G. Paul, 1901, pink*], 'Étoile de France' [*HT, Pernet-Ducher, 1905, red*], 'Mme. Hoste', 'Corallina', 'White Lady' [*again*], 'Lady Roberts', 'Lady Mary Fitzwilliam', 'Prince de Bulgarie', 'Instituteur Sirdey' [*HT, Pernet-Ducher, 1905, yellow*], 'Marie Van Houtte', 'Countess of Caledon', 'Mme. Segond-Weber', 'Dr. Grill',

'Marquise Litta de Breteuil', 'Mme. Berkeley', 'President', 'Souvenir d'un Ami', 'Beryl', 'Souvenir de Pierre Notting'

Appendix Three

Single and Nearly Single Roses

Damask Perpetuals
'Marbrée', 'Portlandica'

Chinas
'Beauty of Glenhurst', 'Miss Lowe's Variety', 'Mutabilis', 'Pourpre', 'Rose de Bengale'

Teas
None.

Bourbons

'Bardou Job'

Hybrid Bourbons, Hybrid Chinas, and Hybrid Noisettes
'L'Admiration', 'Paul's Carmine Pillar'

Hybrid Perpetuals
'Maharajah'

Noisettes and Climbers
'Cooper's Burmese Rose', 'Climbing Dainty Bess', 'Climbing irish Fireflame', 'Crimson Conquest', 'Cupid', 'Dawn', 'Flying Colours', 'Gigantea Blanc', 'Irish Beauty', 'Lady Waterlow', 'Manettii', 'Milkmaid', 'Mrs. Rosalie Wrinch', 'Nancy Hayward', 'Noëlla Nabonnand', 'Paul's Single White Perpetual', 'Sénateur Amic', 'Sunday Best'

Polyanthas
'Cineraria', 'Cyclope', 'Fireglow', 'Jessie', 'Papa Hémeray'

Hybrid Teas
'Cecil', 'Dainty Bess', 'Ellen Wilmott', 'Frances Ashton', 'Innocence', 'Irish Brightness', 'Irish Elegance', 'Irish Fireflame', 'Irish Glory', 'Irish Modesty', 'Isobel', 'Kathleen', 'Kathleen Mills', 'K. of K.', 'Lulu', 'Old Gold', 'Sheila', 'Vesuvius', 'White Wings'

Appendix Four

***R. multiflora* 'Polyantha'**

A note on the parent of the Polyantha roses:

"This species originated in Japan, whence it was introduced into France for the first time, as far as we know, around 1862. It was the *Fleuriste de Paris* which received the first slip, which still exists, and which, planted in the nursery of Longchamps, grew into a strong shrub which, each year, is covered with thousands of blossoms of a very beautiful white. Here are the characteristics of the Type: Shrub extremely bushy, very vigorous; non-blooming branches nearly climbing, growing to nearly two meters [ca. 6 feet], in the case of young plants on their own roots; strong thorns, enlarged at the base, slightly hooked; 5-7 leaflets, sometimes even nine pairs of oval-elliptical leaflets, which are soft, gentle to the touch, villose, and thoroughly but shallowly dentate; rachis rust-colored, with short prickles similarly colored, enlarged at the base and sharply barbed on each side; blooming branches comparatively slender, with smaller leaflets which are more rounded and more obviously dentate than those of the sterile branches; inflorescence in long, pyramidal, subconical panicles, quite upright, much branched; buds very small, solitary, or most often clustered, on a shortly-villose flower stalk; blossoms lightly and pleasantly fragrant, the scent somewhat resembling that of Tea roses, pure white, or slightly sulphurous; 5 wedge-shaped petals, very large at the summit, which, in the middle, exhibits a large notch, giving it the appearance of the 5-armed Maltese Cross…; hips…very small, with deciduous sepals, beautiful glossy red, as if varnished, at maturity, with many long and narrow seeds. It blooms around the end of May, and is very ornamental. If perhaps this species originated in Japan, it is also, we are told, found in China…It is from this latter country that Monsieur A. Leroy's firm has received it with no other name than that of 'new rose.'

"It is evidently quite variable, and the small number of seedlings it has given us have sometimes differed from the Type so much that none of the characteristics of the original are preserved. Along the same lines, Monsieur Jean Sisley tells us, in a letter written September 8, 1873, 'This single 'Polyantha'…produced, *without artificial pollination*, very distinct and notable varieties. Guillot fils has obtained double blossoms, yellow as those of the Banksia, and double reds, as well as one he calls remontant, and one with foliage like that of *R. microphylla*; but *none* of these varieties has that characteristic which distinguishes the Type: blooming in a panicle, which, to my way of thinking, makes it distinct from all other roses—as well as more meritorious.'

"June 30 of that same year, Monsieur Sisley wrote to us, ' 'Polyantha' is very hardy…It seeds easily, producing many varieties, which however are not out yet—single pinks, double pinks, single and double yellows, and a very double white. This last is going to be released to commerce. [A footnote adds: *This very double white-blossomed plant looks like a miniature*

Noisette; it seems to be the equivalent of the Pompon Chinas, and could be used, like them, in borders...It was to be seen at the last exposition at the Palais de l'Industrie, in the booth of Messrs. Lévêque and son...under the name 'Pâquerette', in allusion to the small size of all its parts, and the elegance of its flower."]...Ph. Rambaux has shown some seedlings which he calls Noisettes because they have that look—but they are from 'Polyantha'.'

"We have had a chance to see and study the growth and bloom of Monsieur Rambaux's plants, and cannot hesitate to say that they have the appearance of Teas and Noisettes, and that their flowers have, in color, fragrance, and general character, the look of these two groups. All the plants are freely remontant, blooming until frost stops them. The hips are nearly all subspherical, smooth, and glossy, varying from 7 to 10 millimeters [ca. .25-.45 inch], and in color varying from orange red to brownish violet; one exceptional variety has longly oval-acuminate sepals which are persistent, while all the others are deciduous.

"In a letter of October 25, 1875, on the same subject, Monsieur Sisley adds, 'I forgot to tell you that the seeds of my children of 'Polyantha' are three or four times larger than those of their mother." [R-H76]

Appendix Five

The Rose in California

The Rose has played a role as garden *conquistador* or colonialist throughout history accompanying mankind as it has forged into and beyond the frontiers of traditional civilization. Historians have rarely picked up their chisels, styluses, quills, or fountain pens to record the traveling companionship of what is surely Man's best *horticultural* friend as societies migrated and matured. Perhaps the following words on the Rose in California can stand as a representative of the role the Rose has played in all such treks through the millennia, and will also be of interest as showing the speed with which new introductions were embraced by gardeners thousands of miles away from the place of origin of most of the cultivars.

"It is fit to tell the children how those cuttings crossed the plains, cherished and kept moist all the weary way that the pioneer women might have a reminder of home in a new, strange land. And how those pioneer roses reveled in the warm, red soil of the foothills, and cheered many lives which were full of loneliness and longing and often of deep disappointment! With what affection the roses spread a mantle of beauty and fragrance over the forsaken ruins of solitary camps, and how they grow to this day in such solitary places until their stems looks like the trunks of old grape vines, but are still full of sap to push out new wood and new bloom aloft…There are few, if any, places in the world where the rose enters more fully into daily life than it does in California…It is…as an arbor plant that the rose comes most fully into California life. To live under the rose is literally a possibility in California. Under the shade of the rose the hammock can be drawn and the table spread for *al fresco* refreshment. Many a rural table is spread for months on a rose fringed veranda or in a simple arbor made of poles to support the masses of rose bloom and foliage in which the birds build their nests and from which their songs break forth to greet the dawn or dismiss the evening twilight. California open air life is delightful and the rose is its charming priestess." [EJW]

Roses preferred in Southern California,May 1886 *(from JR10/66)*: 'William Allen Richardson' (N), 'Marie Van Houtte' (T), 'Alfred Colomb' (HP), 'Comtesse d'Oxford' (HP), 'Elisa Boëlle' (HP), 'La France' (B), 'Paul Neyron' (HP), 'Rosy Morn' (HP), 'Julius Finger' (HT), 'William Francis Bennett' (HT), 'American Beauty' (HP)

Recommended for Southern California, 1904 *(from L):*
White: 'Mabel Morrison' (HP), 'Niphetos' (T), 'Lamarque' (N), 'Aimée Vibert' (N), 'The Bride' (T), 'Devoniensis' (T), 'Kaiserin Auguste Viktoria' (HT)

Flesh-Color to Blush: 'Mme. Laurette Messimy' (Ch), '[Mlle.] Augustine Guinoisseau' (HT), 'Duchesse de Brabant' [alias 'Comtesse de Labarthe']

(T), 'Viscountess Folkestone' (HT), 'Captain Christy' (HT), 'Souvenir de la Malmaison' (B)

Pink to Rose: 'Hermosa' (B), 'Mme. Caroline Testout' (HT), 'Paul Neyron' (HP), 'Maman Cochet' (T), 'Comtesse Riza du Parc' (T), 'Triomphe du Luxembourg' (T), 'Catherine Mermet' (T), 'Mrs. John Laing' (HP), 'Magna Charta' (HP)

Rose to Red and Carmine: 'Papa Gontier' (T), 'Duchess of Albany' (HT), 'Reine Marie Henriette' (Cl. HT), 'Mme. Lambard' (T), 'Bon Silène' (T)

Scarlet to Deep Red: 'Gloire des Rosomanes' (B), 'Cramoisi Supérieur' (Ch), 'Général Washington' (HP), 'Ulrich Brunner fils' (HP), 'Général Jacqueminot' (HP)

Dark Crimson: 'Black Prince' (HP), 'Prince Camille de Rohan' (HP), 'Empereur du Maroc' (HP), 'Xavier Olibo' (HP)

Sulphur to Light Yellow: 'Céline Forestier' (N), 'Chromatella' (N), 'Isabella Sprunt' (T)

Deep Yellow to Apricot: 'Safrano' (T), 'Perle des Jardins' (T), 'Rêve d'Or' (N), 'Maréchal Niel' (N), 'Mlle. Franziska Krüger' (T), 'Mme. Falcot' (T), 'William Allen Richardson' (N)

Various: 'Marie Van Houtte' (T), 'Rainbow' (T), 'Archiduc Charles' (Ch), 'Homère' (T), 'Mme. de Watteville' (T), 'Fortune's Double Yellow' (HGig), 'Gloire de Dijon' (N), 'Dr. Grill' (T), 'Grace Darling' (HT), '[Mlle.] Cécile Brunner' (Pol)

Southern California, the Rosarian's Carbonek

(or veritable site of the Holy Grail)

"California is 'different' and eastern experience is oftentimes deceiving." [ARA19/133] "In this favored section not only is it possible and easy to produce outdoor roses the year round, but it is also practicable to grow all the different classes and types." [ARA21/58] "Only after an exhaustive search from Canada to Mexico did he [*Capt. George C. Thomas Jr.*] conclude his prospecting for a spot in America best suited for rose-perfection. Later I called at this sport, near Beverly Hills, Calif., where his dreams for finer roses began to be realized." [ARA33/111]

Appendix Six

Cultivars by Year

The indicated dates are inclusive of "circa" and "pre-" dates; that is, "circa 1835" and "-1835" would be included under "1835" for the purposes of this Appendix. This listing of course only includes cultivars mentioned in this book. It is fascinating to compare and contrast the introductions year by year!—in their nature and names.

Damask Perpetuals
1633: 'Monthly Rose'
1775: 'Portlandica'
1807: 'Bifera'

1811: 'Henriette'
1812: 'Quatre Saisons d'Italie'
1814: 'Venusta'
1815: 'Jeune Henry'
1817: 'Palmyre'
1819: 'Rose du Roi'
1820: 'La Moderne'
1821: 'Buffon', 'Préval'
1826: 'Belle de Trianon', 'Belle Fabert', 'Le Prince de Galles'
1830: 'Portland Pourpre', 'Rose de Trianon'
1831: 'Félicité Hardy'
1832: 'Louis-Philippe I'
1835: 'La Volumineuse', 'Quatre Saisons Blanc Mousseux'
1836: 'Bernard', 'Césonie', 'Jeanne Hachette', 'Portland Blanc'
1839: 'Henriette Boulogne'
1840: 'Marquise Boccella'
1841: 'Desdémona'
1843: 'Capitaine Rénard', 'Yolande d'Aragon'
1844: 'Duchesse de Montmorency', 'Ebène', 'Jacques Amyot', 'Mogador'
1845: 'Amanda Patenotte', 'Indigo'
1846: 'Amandine', 'Joasine Hanet'
1847: 'Adèle Mauzé', 'Blanche-Vibert', 'Duchesse de Rohan', 'Julie de Krudner', 'Mathilde Jesse', 'Sapho', 'Sydonie'
1848: 'Casimir Delavigne'
1849: 'Celina Dubos'
1850: 'Marie Robert'
1852: 'Céline Bourdier'
1853: 'Lesueur'
1854: 'Christophe Colombe'
1856: 'Robert Perpétuel'
1859: 'Comte de Chambord', 'Laurent Heister'
1860: 'Pergolèse'

1863: 'Delambre', 'Jules Lesourd'
1868: 'Jacques Cartier'
1869: 'Marie de St. Jean', 'Miranda'
1874: 'Mme Souveton'
1883: 'Rembrandt'
1888: 'Président Dutailly'
1895: 'Panachée de Lyon'
2001: 'Papa Vibert'

Chinas
1790: 'Slater's Crimson China'
1793: 'Parsons' Pink China'
1804: 'Bengale Centfeuilles', 'De Cels'
1806: 'Pumila'
1809: 'Bichonne'
1810: 'Beau Carmin', 'Blue Rose', 'Cruenta'
1815: 'Rouletii'
1817: 'Animating'
1819: 'La Spécieuse'
1820: 'Bengale Pompon'
1825: 'Archiduc Charles', 'Belle de Monza', 'Bengale d'Automne', 'Laffay', 'Le Vésuve'
1826: 'Papillon'
1827: 'Darius'
1831: 'Fimbriata à Pétales Frangés'
1832: 'Cramoisi Supérieur', 'Fabvier'
1834: 'Belle Hébé', 'Louis-Philippe'
1835: 'Duchesse de Kent', 'Mme. Desprez', 'Napoléon', 'Reine de la Lombardie'
1837: 'Eugène de Beauharnais'
1838: 'Bengale Sanguinaire', 'Némésis', 'St. Priest de Breuze'
1839: 'Pompon de Paris'

1844: 'Rose de Bengale'
1848: 'Douglas'
1852: 'Elise Flory'
1854: 'Lucullus'
1855: 'Viridiflora'
1869: 'Ducher'
1872: 'Marquisette'
1873: 'Sanglant'
1886: 'Bengale Nabonnand'
1887: 'Miss Lowe's Variety', 'Mme. Laurette Messimy', 'Princesse de Sagan'
1888: 'Red Pet'
1893: 'Institutrice Moulins'
1894: 'Duke of York', 'Mme. Eugène Résal', 'Mutabilis'
1895: 'Irène Watts', 'Souvenir de Catherine Guillot'
1896: 'Queen Mab'
1897: 'Alice Hoffman', 'Antoinette Cuillerat', 'Aurore', 'Souvenir d'Aimée Terrel des Chênes', 'Souvenir de J.-B. Guillot'
1898: 'Jean Bach Sisley'
1901: 'L'Ouche', 'Maddalena Scalarandis'
1902: 'Comtesse du Caÿla'
1903: 'Alice Hamilton', 'Arethusa'
1904: 'Beauty of Rosemawr', 'Unermüdliche'
1905: 'Charlotte Klemm'
1906: 'Bébé Fleuri'
1910: 'Laure de Broglie'
1913: 'Bengali'
1922: 'Primrose Queen'
1930: 'Purpurea'
1948: 'Granate'
1950: 'Rosada'
1985: 'Beauty of Glenhurst'

Teas

1810: 'Hume's Blush Tea-Scented China'
1824: 'Parks' Yellow Tea-Scented China'
1825: 'Roi de Siam'
1827: 'Catherine II'
1829: 'Hyménée'
1832: 'Bougère'
1834: 'Smith's Yellow China'
1835: 'Bon Silène', 'Caroline', 'Gigantesque', 'Triomphe du Luxembourg'
1836: 'Cels Multiflore'
1838: 'Adam', 'Devoniensis', 'Elise Sauvage'
1839: 'Goubault', 'Safrano'
1840: 'Le Pactole'
1841: 'Niphetos', 'Rival de Pæstum'
1842: 'La Sylphide'
1843: 'Abricotée', 'Fortune's Five-Colored Rose', 'Maréchal Bugeaud'
1844: 'Mme. Bravy'
1845: 'Mme. Mélanie Willermoz'
1846: 'Mme. de St.-Joseph', 'Souvenir d'un Ami'
1851: 'David Pradel', 'Mlle. de Sombreuil'
1852: 'Canari', 'Mme. Pauline Labonté'
1853: 'Laurette'
1854: 'Louise de Savoie', 'Souvenir d'Elisa Vardon'
1855: 'Archimède', 'Cornelia Cook', 'Mme. de Vatry'
1856: 'Général Tartas', 'Souvenir de David d'Angers'
1857: 'Comtesse de Labarthe'
1858: 'Enfant de Lyon', 'Homère', 'Mme. Damaizin', 'Mme. Falcot', 'Socrate'
1859: 'Duc de Magenta', 'Mme. de Tartas', 'Narcisse', 'Rubens'
1860: 'Esther Pradel', 'Regulus'
1864: 'Mme. Charles'
1865: 'Isabella Sprunt'

1866: 'Mme. Margottin'
1867: 'Jean Pernet', 'Safrano à Fleurs Rouges'
1868: 'La Tulipe', 'Marie Sisley', 'Mme. Céline Noirey'
1869: 'Catherine Mermet', 'Chamoïs', 'Grossherzogin Mathilde von Hessen'
1870: 'Hortensia', 'Mme. Azélie Imbert', 'Victor Pulliat'
1871: 'Comtesse de Nadaillac', 'Coquette de Lyon', 'La Nankeen', 'Ma Capucine', 'Marie Van Houtte', 'Mme. Camille', 'Perfection de Monplaisir', 'Souvenir de Paul Neyron'
1872: 'Amazone', 'Anna Olivier', 'Henry Bennett', 'Mme. Caroline Küster', 'Mme. Dr. Jutté', 'Perle de Lyon', 'Vallée de Chamonix'
1873: 'A. Bouquet', 'Aureus', 'Helvetia', 'Isabella Nabonnand', 'Mont Rosa'
1874: 'Aline Sisley', 'Duchess of Edinburgh', 'Jean Ducher', 'Lutea Flora', 'Marie Guillot', 'Mme. Devoucoux', 'Perle des Jardins', 'Shirley Hibberd'
1875: 'Maréchal Robert'
1876: 'Charles Rovelli', 'Comtesse Riza du Parc', 'Letty Coles', 'Mlle. Lazarine Poizeau', 'Mme. Welche', 'Souvenir de George Sand'
1877: 'American Banner', 'La Princesse Vera', 'Louis Richard', 'Mme. la Comtesse de Caserta', 'Mme. Maurice Kuppenheim', 'Mme. Nabonnand', 'Mystère', 'Paul Nabonnand', 'Souvenir de Marie Detry', 'Triomphe de Milan'
1878: 'Alphonse Karr', 'Général Schablikine', 'Innocente Pirola', 'Mlle. Blanche Durrschmidt', 'Mlle. la Comtesse de Leusse', 'Mme. Lambard'
1879: 'Jules Finger', 'Mlle. Franziska Krüger', 'Mlle. Marie Moreau', 'Mme. Angèle Jacquier', 'Mme. Barthélemy Levet', 'Mme. la Duchesse de Vallombrosa', 'Mme. P. Perny', 'Reine Emma des Pays-Bas'
1880: 'Mme. Caro', 'Mme. Chédane-Guinoisseau', 'Mme. Joseph Schwartz'

1881: 'Comtesse Alban de Villeneuve', 'Étoile de Lyon', 'Mme. Cusin'

1882: 'André Schwartz', 'Baron de St.-Triviers', 'Blanche Nabonnand', 'Hermance Louis de la Rive', 'Jeanne Abel', 'Honourable Edith Gifford', 'Mme. Crombez', 'Mme. Dubroca', 'Mme. Eugène Verdier', 'Mme. Léon Février', 'Mme. Remond', 'Papa Gontier', 'Princess of Wales', 'Rose Nabonnand', 'Souvenir de Germaine de St.-Pierre', 'Souvenir de Thérèse Levet'

1883: 'Édouard Gautier', 'Impératrice Maria Féodorowna de Russie', 'Marie d'Orléans', 'Mme. de Watteville', 'Mme. F. Brassac', 'Souvenir du Rosiériste Rambaux', 'Sunset', 'Vicomtesse de Bernis'

1884: 'Charles de Legrady', 'Mme. Fanny Pauwels', 'Rosalie', 'Souvenir de Gabrielle Drevet', 'White Bon Silène'

1885: 'Camille Roux', 'Comtesse de Frigneuse', 'Edmond de Biauzat', 'Exadelphé', 'Flavien Budillon', 'Marquise de Vivens', 'Mlle. Suzanne Blanchet', 'Mme. David', 'Reine Olga', 'Souvenir de l'Amiral Courbet', 'Souvenir de Victor Hugo', 'The Bride'

1886: 'Archiduchesse Marie Immaculata', 'Château des Bergeries', 'Claudius Levet', 'Dr. Grill', 'Duchesse de Bragance', 'Lady Stanley', 'Lady Zoë Brougham', 'Luciole', 'Marie Lambert', 'Mlle. Claudine Perreau', 'Mme. A. Étienne', 'Mme. Agathe Nabonnand', 'Mme. Honoré Defresne', 'Mme. la Princesse de Radziwill', 'Mme. Scipion Cochet', 'Namenlose Schöne', 'S.A.R. Mme. la Princesse de Hohenzollern, Infante de Portugal', 'Vicomtesse de Wauthier'

1887: 'Comtesse Anna Thun', 'Miss Ethel Brownlow', 'Mme. Claire Jaubert', 'Mme. Hoste', 'Mme. Joseph Godier', 'Mme. Philémon Cochet', 'Princesse Beatrix', 'Souvenir du Général Charreton', 'Thérèse Levet', 'V. Viviand Morel', 'White Catherine Mermet'

1888: 'Adèle de Bellabre', 'Annie Cook', 'Baronne Henriette de Loew', 'Capitaine Lefort', 'Comtesse Julie Hunyady', 'Edmond Sablayrolles', Ernest Metz', 'Francisca Pries', G. Nabonnand', 'Joseph Métral', 'Lady Castlereagh', 'Mme. Jules Cambon', 'Mme.

Pierre Guillot', 'Mme. Thérèse Deschamps', 'Monsieur Charles de Thézillat', 'Souvenir d'Espagne'

1889: 'Duchesse Marie Salviati', 'Georges Farber', 'J.-B. Varonne', 'Marion Dingee', 'Mlle. Jeanne Guillaumez', 'Mme. Marthe du Bourg', 'Mme. Olga', 'Mme. Philippe Kuntz', 'Mrs. James Wilson', 'Sappho', 'Souvenir d'Auguste Legros', 'Souvenir de François Gaulain', 'Souvenir du Dr. Passot', 'The Queen', 'White Pearl'

1890: 'Antoinette Durieu', 'Bella', 'Charles de Franciosi', 'Comtesse de Vitzthum', 'Comtesse Eva Starhemberg', 'Elisa Fugier', 'Général D. Mertschansky', 'Maurice Rouvier', 'Medea', 'Miss Marston', 'Miss Wenn', 'Mlle. Christine de Noué', 'Mme. Elie Lambert', 'Mme. la Princesse de Bessaraba de Brancovan', 'Pearl Rivers', Professeur Ganiviat', 'Souvenir de Clairvaux', 'Souvenir de Lady Ashburton', 'Souvenir de Mme. Lambard', 'Souvenir de Mme. Sablayrolles'

1891: 'Dr. Grandvilliers', 'Elise Heymann', 'Henry M. Stanley', 'Maud Little', 'Mme. Pélisson', 'Mme. Victor Caillet', 'Monsieur Édouard Littaye', 'Monsieur Tillier', 'Mrs. Jessie Fremont', 'Rainbow', 'Sénateur Loubet', 'Souvenir de Mme. Levet', 'Waban'

1892: 'Archiduc Joseph', 'Comtesse Festetics Hamilton', 'Golden Gate', 'Henri Plantagenet Comte d'Anjou', 'Léon XIII', 'Léonie Osterrieth', 'Madeleine Guillaumez', 'Maman Cochet', 'Mme. la Baronne Berge', 'Mme. Ocker Ferencz', 'Winnie Davis'

1893: 'Bridesmaid', 'Colonel Juffé', 'Comtesse Dusy', 'Corinna', 'Erzherzog Franz Ferdinand', 'Graziella', 'Improved Rainbow', 'Mme. Édouard Helfenbein', 'Perle de Feu', 'Princesse Alice de Monaco', 'Souvenir de Geneviève Godard'

1894: 'Comte Chandon', 'Fiametta Nabonnand', 'Francis Dubreuil', 'Jean André', 'Mme. Charles Franchet', 'Mme. Laurent Simons', 'Monsieur le Chevalier Angelo Ferrario', 'Rose d'Evian', 'Souvenir de Laurent Guillot'

1895: 'Auguste Comte', 'Comtesse Bardi', 'Comtesse Lily Kinsky', 'Grand-Duc Pierre de Russie', 'Isaac Demole', 'Léon de Bruyn',

'Marie Soleau', 'Mlle. Marie-Louise Oger', 'Mme. Émilie Charrin', 'Mme. Henry Graire', 'Mme. von Siemens', 'Mrs. J. Pierpont Morgan', 'Princesse de Venosa', 'Senator McNaughton', 'Souvenir du père Lalanne', 'Sylph', 'Zephyr'

1896: 'Baronne M. de Tornaco', 'Émilie Gonin', 'Enchantress', 'Général Billot', 'General Robert E. Lee', 'Gloire de Deventer', 'Mlle. Anna Charron', 'Mlle. Marie-Thérèse Molinier', 'Princess Bonnie', 'Raoul Chauvry', 'Souvenir de Jeanne Cabaud', 'White Maman Cochet'

1897: 'Baronne Ada', 'Baronne Henriette Snoy', 'Dr. Pouleur', 'Empress Alexandra of Russia', 'Frau Geheimrat von Boch', 'Marguerite Ketten', 'Mme. C.P. Strassheim', 'Mme. Derepas-Matrat', 'Mme. Jacques Charreton', 'The Sweet Little Queen of Holland'

1898: 'Albert Stopford', 'Beryl', 'F.L. Segers', 'Fürstin Infantin de Hohenzollern', 'Lucie Faure', 'Lucy Carnegie', 'Margherita di Simone', 'Meta', 'Mlle. Jeanne Philippe', 'Mme. Ada Carmody', 'Mme. Berkeley', 'Mme. Joseph Laperrière', 'Mme. Lucien Duranthon', 'Mrs. Oliver Ames', 'Muriel Grahame', 'Palo Alto', 'Peach Blossom', 'Princesse Étienne de Croy', 'Reichsgraf E. von Kesselstatt', 'Rosa Mundi', 'Winter Gem'

1899: 'Alliance Franco-Russe', 'Antoine Weber', 'Captain Philip Green', 'Frances E. Willard', 'Général Galliéni', 'Georges Schwartz', 'Hovyn de Tronchère', 'Maid of Honour', 'Mme. Clémence Marchix', 'Mme. C. Liger', 'Mme. Errera', 'Mme. Gustave Henry', 'Mrs. Edward Mawley', 'Santa Rosa', 'Souvenir de William Robinson', 'Sunrise'

1900: 'Burbank', 'Comte Amédé de Foras', 'Corallina', 'Garden Robinson', 'Lady Mary Corry', 'Mme. Adolphe Dohair', 'Mme. Antoine Rébé', 'Mme. Erenst Perrin', 'Mrs. Reynolds Hole', 'Sulphurea', 'The Alexandra'

1901: 'Boadicea', 'Capitaine Millet', 'Dr. Félix Guyon', 'Ivory', 'Marquise de Querhoënt', 'Miss Agnes C. Sherman', 'Mlle. Emma Vercellone',

'Mme. Antoine Mari', 'Mme. Jean Dupuy', 'Mme. Vermorel', 'Mrs. B.R. Cant'

1902: 'Abbé Garroute', 'Belle Panachée', 'Comtesse de Noghera', 'Comtesse Sophie Torby', 'Fortuna', 'Julius Fabianics de Misefa', 'Lady Roberts', 'Marguerite Gigandet', 'Marie Segond', 'Morning Glow', 'Peace', 'Professeur d'André', 'Souvenir de Pierre Notting'

1903: 'Anna Jung', 'Betty Berkeley', 'Comtesse Emmeline de Guigné', 'Empereur Nicolas II', 'Freiherr von Marschall', 'Konigin Wilhelmina', 'Mlle. Blanche Martignat', 'Mme. Achille Fould', 'Perle des Jaunes'

1904: 'Albert Hoffman', 'Mme. Albert Bernardin', 'Uncle John'

1905: 'Blumenschmidt', 'Golden Oriole', 'Joseph Paquet', 'Minnie Francis', 'Mme. Constant Soupert', 'Mme. Gamon', 'True Friend'

1906: 'Helen Good', 'Lena', 'Mme. Paul Varin-Bernier', 'Mme. Therese Roswell', 'Mrs. Myles Kennedy', 'Nelly Johnstone', 'Penelope'

1907: 'Canadian Belle', 'Harry Kirk', 'Hugo Roller', 'Mrs. Dudley Cross', 'Souvenir of Stella Gray'

1908: 'Alix Roussel', 'Molly Sharman-Crawford', 'Nita Weldon', 'Primrose', 'Rhodologue Jules Gravereaux', 'Rosomane Narcisse Thomas', 'William R. Smith'

1910: 'Lady Hillingdon', 'Miss Alice de Rothschild', 'Mrs. Alice Broomhill', 'Mrs. Foley-Hobbs', 'Mrs. Hubert Taylor', 'Recuerdo di Antonio Peluffo'

1911: 'Alexander Hill Gray'

1912: 'American Perfection', 'Madison', 'Mme. Barriglione', 'Mme. E. Vicaro', 'Mrs. Herbert Hawksworth', 'Number 27'

1913: 'Clementina Carbonieri', 'Maria Star'

1914: 'Lady Plymouth', 'Mrs. Campbell Hall', 'Mrs. S.T. Wright'

1916: 'Mme. Charles Singer'

1918: 'Mevrouw Boreel van Hogelander'

1920: 'Souvenir de Gilbert Nabonnand'

1922: 'Rosette Delizy'

1924: 'Lorraine Lee'
1927: 'Simone Thomas'
1929: 'Susan Louise'
1936: 'Baxter Beauty'
Unintroduced, bred in the 1990s: 'Sweet Passion'

Bourbons
1820: 'Rose Édouard'
1821: 'Burboniana'
1825: 'Gloire des Rosomanes'
1828: 'Pompon de Wasemmes'
1831: 'Charles Desprez', 'Mme. Desprez'
1832: 'Mrs. Bosanquet'
1834: 'Hermosa', 'Reine des Île-Bourbons'
1837: 'Émile Courtier'
1838: 'Acidalie', 'Mme. Nérard', 'Pierre de St.-Cyr'
1839: 'Bouquet de Flore'
1841: 'Proserpine'
1842: 'Comice de Seine-et-Marne', 'Georges Cuvier', 'Souchet'
1843: 'Souvenir de la Malmaison'
1844: 'Deuil de Duc d'Orléans', 'Reine des Vierges'
1845: 'Vicomte Fritz de Cussy'
1846: 'Leveson-Gower', 'Maréchal du Palais', 'Triomphe de la Duchère'
1847: 'Duchesse de Thuringe', 'Eupémie'
1848: 'Apolline', 'Delille'
1849: 'Toussaint-Louverture'
1850: 'Scipion Cochet', 'Souvenir d'un Frère'
1851: 'Louise Odier', 'Mlle. Blanche Laffitte', 'Souvenir de l'Exposition de Londres'
1852: 'Comice de Tarn-et-Garonne', 'Dr. Leprestre', 'Prince Albert', 'Réveil', 'Sir Joseph Paxton', 'Velouté d'Orléans'
1854: 'Omer-Pacha'

1855: 'Impératrice Eugénie', 'Marquis de Balbiano'
1856: 'Impératrice Eugénie', 'Mme. Massot'
1858: 'Comtesse de Barbantane', 'Edith de Murat'
1859: 'Amarante', 'Baron G.-B. Gonella', 'Monsieur Gourdault'
1860: 'Catherine Guillot', 'Dr. Brière', 'Duc de Crillon', 'Garibaldi'
1861: 'Baronne de Noirmont', 'Louise d'Arzens', 'Mme. Adélaïde Ristori'
1862: 'Deuil du Dr. Reyaud', 'Emotion', 'Lady Emily Peel', 'Mme. Alfred de Rougemont', 'Président Gausen', 'Reynolds Hole'
1863: 'Héroïne de Vaucluse', 'Mlle. Joséphine Guyet', 'Mme. Doré', 'Reverend H. D'Ombrain'
1864: 'Adrienne de Cardoville', 'Monsieur Dubost', 'Prince Napoléon', 'Souvenir de Louis Gaudin'
1865: 'Baronne de Maynard', 'Béatrix', 'Coquette des Blanches', 'Mme. Charles Baltet', 'Mme. Cornélissen', 'Souvenir de Président Lincoln'
1866: 'Souvenir de Mme. August Charles'
1867: 'Boule de Neige', 'Coquette des Alpes', 'La France', 'Mme. Gabriel Luizet'
1868: 'Le Roitelet', 'Zéphirine Drouhin'
1869: 'Mlle. Favart'
1872: 'Amédée de Langlois', 'Belle Nanon', 'Perle des Blanches', 'Reine Victoria', 'Souvenir d'Adèle Launay'
1873: 'Olga Marix'
1874: 'Comtesse de Rocquigny', 'Mme. de Sévigné', 'Mme. Thiers'
1876: 'Queen of Bedders'
1877: 'Mme. François Pittet', 'Robusta'
1878: 'Mme. Pierre Oger'
1879: 'Alexandre Pelletier', 'Perle d'Angers'
1880: 'Mme. Isaac Pereire'
1881: 'Mlle. Madeleine de Vauzelles'
1882: 'Malmaison Rouge', 'Mme. Fanny de Forest', 'Mme. Olympe Térestchenko', 'Victoire Fontaine'
1884: 'Mlle. Berger'

1886: 'Gloire d'Olivet', 'Mme. Chevalier'
1887: 'Bardou Job', 'Mlle. Claire Truffaut', 'Mlle. Marie Drivon', 'Mme. Létuvée de Colnet'
1888: 'Kronprinzessin Viktoria von Preussen', 'Mme. Ernest Calvat'
1889: 'Marie Dermar', 'Monsieur A. Maillé', 'Souvenir de Monsieur Bruel', 'Zigenerblut'
1890: 'Mlle. Andrée Worth', 'Mme. Dubost', 'Souvenir de Victor Landeau'
1891: 'Bijou de Royat-les-Bains', 'Mlle. Alice Marchand', 'Mlle. Berthe Clavel', 'Mrs. Paul', 'Président de la Rocheterie', 'Souvenir du Lieutenant Bujon'
1892: 'Monsieur Cordeau'
1893: 'Mme. Edmond Laporte', 'Mme. Nobécourt'
1894: 'Champion of the World', 'Lorna Doone'
1895: 'Mlle. Marie-Thérèse Devansaye', 'Philémon Cochet'
1897: 'Gruss an Teplitz'
1899: 'Dunkelrote Hermosa', 'Mme. Arthur Oger'
1900: 'J.B.M. Camm', 'Mme. Eugène E. Marlitt'
1904: 'Mme. d'Enfert'
1905: 'Capitaine Dyel, de Graville'
1909: 'Frau O. Plegg', 'Leuchtfeuer', 'Variegata di Bologna'
1912: 'Martha'
1913: 'Hofgärtner Kalb'
1918: 'Jean Rameau'
1919: 'Kathleen Harrop'
1920: 'Adam Messerich'
1927: 'Frau Dr. Schricker'
1950: 'Souvenir de St. Anne's'
2001: 'Charles XII'

Hybrid Bourbons, Hybrid Chinas, and Hybrid Noisettes

1814: 'Vibert'
1816: 'Cerise Éclatante', 'La Philippine'
1820: 'George IV'
1824: 'De Vergnies'
1825: 'Chévrier', 'La Nubienne', 'Roxelane'
1826: 'Duchesse de Montebello', 'La Pudeur'
1827: 'Belle de Vernier', 'La Dauphine'
1828: 'Las-Cases'
1829: 'Athalin', 'Belle de Crécy', 'Comtesse de Coutard', 'Malton'
1830: 'Belle Violette', 'Brennus'
1831: 'Riégo', 'Triomphe de Laffay'
1833: 'Lady Stuart'
1834: 'Le Vingt-Neuf Juillet'
1835: 'Bijou des Amateurs', 'Céline', 'Général Allard', 'Louis-Philippe', 'Mme. Plantier', 'Ohl'
1836: 'Gloriette'
1838: 'Great Western', 'William Jesse'
1840: 'Cardinal de Richelieu', 'Charles Duval', 'Charles Louis No. 1', 'Charles Louis No. 2', 'Chénédolé', 'Coupe d'Hébé', 'Comtesse de Lacépède'
1841: 'Captaine Sissolet', 'Deuil du Maréchal Mortier', 'Duc de Sussex'
1842: 'Dombrowski', 'Edward Jesse', 'Prince Charles'
1845: 'Comtesse Molé', 'Paul Ricault', 'Richelieu'
1846: 'Belmont', 'Jenny', 'Le Météore'
1847: 'Frédéric II de Prusse'
1851: 'Joseph Gourdon'
1853: 'Charles Lawson', 'Vivid'
1855: 'Impératrice Eugénie'
1856: 'L'Admiration'
1859: 'Souvenir de Némours'
1863: 'Arthur Young'

1866: 'Paul Verdier'
1868: 'Mme. Lauriol de Barney'
1870: 'Paul Perras'
1873: 'Catherine Bonnard'
1874: 'Souvenir de mère Fontaine'
1876: 'Mme. Galli-Marie', 'Souvenir de Paul Dupuy'
1877: 'La Saumonée', 'Mme. Jeannine Joubert'
1879: 'Jules Jürgensen'
1885: 'Catherine Ghislaine', 'Mrs. Degraw'
1892: 'Frances Bloxam', 'Francis B. Hayes'
1895: 'Paul's Carmine Pillar'
1897: 'Mme. Auguste Rodrigues'
1898: 'Purity'
1909: 'Parkzierde', 'Zigeunerknabe'
1927: 'Ekta'

Hybrid Perpetuals
1833: 'Gloire de Guérin'
1834: 'Perpétuelle de Neuilly'
1835: 'Sisley'
1837: 'Prince Albert', 'Princesse Hélène'
1838: 'Miss House'
1839: 'Comte de Paris', 'Duchesse de Sutherland', 'Mme. Laffay'
1840: 'Ornement du Luxembourg', 'Princesse de Joinville'
1841: 'Mrs. Elliot'
1842: 'Baronne Prévost', 'Comtesse Duchâtel', 'Dr. Marx'
1844: 'La Reine', 'Louise Peyronny'
1845: 'Cornet', 'Jacques Laffitte', 'Mrs. Cripps', 'Ponctué'
1846: 'Géant des Batailles'
1847: 'Duchesse de Galliera', 'Gerbe de Roses'
1848: 'Pie IX'

1849: 'Caroline de Sansal', 'Colonel Foissy', 'Comte Bobrinsky', 'Général Cavaignac', 'Mme. Campbell d'Islay', 'Triomphe de Valenciennes'

1850: 'Comte Odart', 'Desgaches', 'Lion des Combats', 'William Griffith'

1851: 'Auguste Mie', 'Dr. Jamain', 'Duchesse d'Orléans', 'Général Bedeau', 'Mère de St. Louis'

1852: 'Comte de Nanteuil', 'Génie de Châteaubriand', 'Lady Stuart', 'Reine de Castille', 'Rubens', 'Souvenir de Leveson-Gower', 'Vicomtesse Laure de Gironde'

1853: 'Alphonse de Lamartine', 'Général Jacqueminot', 'Jules Margottin', 'Marguerite Lecureaux', 'Mme. Domage', 'Mme. Récamier', 'Ville de St.-Denis'

1854: 'Duchesse de Cambacérès', 'Lord Raglan', 'Mme. de Trotter', 'Mme. Désirée Giraud', 'Mme. Masson', 'Mme. Schmitt', 'Mme. Vidot', 'Panachée d'Orléans', 'Prince Noir'

1855: 'Arthur de Sansal', 'Mme. Knorr', 'Monsieur de Montigny', 'Pæonia', 'Pauline Lansezeur', 'Souvenir de la Reine d'Angleterre', 'Triomphe de l'Exposition'

1856: 'Belle Angevine', 'Bouquet Blanc'

1857: 'Cardinal Patrizzi', 'Duc de Constantine', 'Louise d'Autriche', 'Mme. Marie Van Houtte', 'Reine de Danemark', 'Souvenir de Béranger'

1858: 'Anna Alexieff', 'Anna de Diesbach', 'Ardoisée de Lyon', 'Bouquet de Marie', 'Comtesse C'ecile de Chabrillant', 'Dr. Bretonneau', 'Empereur du Maroc', 'François I', 'François Arago', 'Giuletta', 'Orderic Vital', 'Oriflamme de St.-Louis', 'Virginale'

1859: 'Boccace', 'Eugène Appert', 'Louis XIV', 'Louis Gulino', 'Mlle. Bonnaire', 'Mlle. Eugénie Verdier', 'Mlle. Marie Dauvesse', 'Mme. Boll', 'Mme. Céline Touvais', 'Mme. Charles Crapelet', 'Montebello', 'Sénateur Vaïsse', 'Triomphe d'Alençon', 'Victor-Emmanuel', 'Victor Verdier'

1860: 'Amiral Gravina', 'Enfant de France', 'Général Washington', 'Léonie Lartay', 'Reine des Violettes', 'Robert de Brie'

1861: 'Alexandre Dumas', 'Bicolor Incomparable', 'Charles Lefebvre', 'Clémence Joigneaux', 'Duc de Cazes', 'La Brillante', 'Maurice Bernardin', 'Mlle. Léonie Persin', 'Mme. Auguste van Geert', 'Mme. Boutin', 'Mme. Charles Wood', 'Mme. Clémence Joigneaux', 'Mme. Julia Daran', 'Olivier Belhomme', 'Prince Camille de Rohan', 'Reine d'Espagne', 'Simon de St.-Jean', 'Souvenir de Monsieur Rousseau', 'Souvenir de Comte de Cavour', 'Triomphe de Caen', 'Turenne', 'Vulcain'

1862: 'Beauty of Waltham', 'Comtesse de Polignac', 'Duc d'Anjou', 'Henri IV', 'Jean Goujon', 'John Hopper', 'Mme. Crespin', 'Peter Lawson', 'Président Lincoln', 'Souvenir de Charles Montault', 'Vainqueur de Goliath'

1863: 'Alpaïde de Rotalier', 'Centifolia Rosea', 'Charles Margottin', 'Claude Million', 'Comte de Falloux', 'Duc d'Harcourt', 'Eugène Verdier', 'George Paul', 'La Duchesse de Morny', 'Léopold I, Roi des Belges', 'Lord Macaulay', 'Marie Baumann', 'Michel-Ange', 'Mlle. Gabrielle de Peyronny', 'Mme. Charles Verdier', 'Mme. Victor Verdier', 'Paul de la Meilleraye', 'Pierre Notting'

1864: 'Abbé Berlèze', 'Achille Gonod', 'Baronne Prévost Marbré', 'Belle Normande', 'Charles Wood', 'Comtesse de Paris', 'Dr. Andry', 'Duc de Wellington', 'Duchesse de Caylus', 'Jean Rosenkrantz', 'John Gould Veitch', 'John Keynes', 'La Tendresse', 'Marie Boisée', 'Mlle. Marie de la Villeboisnet', 'Monsieur Bonçenne', 'Prince Eugène de Beauharnais', 'Princess of Wales', 'Rushton-Radclyffe', 'Souvenir de William Wood', 'Triomphe de la Terre des Roses'

1865: 'Abel Grand', 'Alba Mutabilis', 'Alfred Colomb', 'Aurore Boréale', 'Camille Bernardin', 'Denis Hélye', 'Elisabeth Vigneron', 'Fisher-Holmes', 'Gloire de Ducher', 'Jean Cherpin', 'Joséphine de Beauharnais', 'Louis Noisette', 'Mlle. Berthe Lévêque', 'Mlle. Marie Rady', 'Mme. Fillion', 'Nardy Frères', 'Prince de Portia', 'Prudence Besson', 'Souvenir du Dr. Jamain', 'Xavier Olibo'

1866: 'André Leroy d'Angers', 'Antoine Ducher', 'Baronne Maurice de Graviers', 'Black Prince', 'Horace Vernet', 'Mlle. Annie Wood', 'Mlle. Madeleine Nonin', 'Mlle. Thérèse Levet', 'Monsieur Lauriol de Barney', 'Napoléon III', 'Paul Verdier', 'Souvenir de Monsieur Boll', 'Thorin', 'Velours Pourpre', 'Ville de Lyon'

1867: 'Alba Carnea', 'Aristide Dupuy', 'Aurore du Matin', 'Baron Haussmann', 'Comte Raimbaud', 'Comtesse de Falloux', 'Comtesse de Turenne', 'Dr. Hurta', 'Duchesse d'Aoste', 'Général Barral', 'Général Désaix', 'Lisette de Banger', 'Meyerbeer', 'Mlle. Elise Chabrier', 'Mme. Alice Dureau', 'Mme. Chirard', 'Mme. Noman', 'Président Willermoz', 'Prince de Joinville', 'Souvenir de Caillat', 'Souvenir de Mme. de Corval', 'Vicomtesse de Vezins'

1868: 'Baronne Adolphe de Rothschild', 'Berthe Baron', 'Devienne-Lamy', 'Duke of Edinburgh', 'Dupuy-Jamain', 'Jeanne Sury', 'Marquise de Gibot', 'Marquise de Mortemart', 'Marquise de Verdun', 'Maurice Lepelletier', 'Mme. Clert', 'Mme. Hersilie Ortgies', 'Mme. Lierval', 'Monsieur Journaux', 'Notaire Bonnefond', 'Thyra Hammerich', 'Vicomte Maison', 'Victor le Bihan'

1869: 'Abbé Giraudier', 'Anny Laxton', 'Baron Chaurand', 'Blanche de Méru', 'Charles Turner', 'Clémence Raoux', 'Comtesse d'Oxford', 'Elisa Boëlle', 'Ferdinand de Lesseps', 'Général de la Martinière', 'Hippolyte Jamain', 'Jules Seurre', 'La Motte Sanguin', 'Lena Turner', 'Louis Van Houtte', 'Marquise de Castellane', 'Mme. la Générale Decaen', 'Paul Neyron', 'Princesse Louise', 'Souvenir de Mme. Hennecart', 'Suzanne Wood'

1871: 'Abbé Bramerel', 'Baron de Bonstetten', 'Baronne de Prailly', 'François Michelon', 'L'Espérance', 'Le Havre', 'Lyonnais', 'Maxime de la Rocheterie', 'Mme. Bellon', 'Mme. de Ridder', 'Mme. Georges Schwartz', 'Mme. Hippolyte Jamain', 'Mme. Renard', 'Monsieur Jean Cordier', 'Prince Stirbey'

1872: 'Bessie Johnson', 'Duhamel-Dumonceau', 'Étienne Levet', 'Félicien David', 'Golfe-Juan', 'John Laing', 'Mme. Scipion Cochet', 'Mme. Soubeyran', 'Mrs. Laing', 'Souvenir de John Gould Veitch', 'Souvenir de Spa'

1873: 'Albert Payé', 'Comtesse de Bresson', 'Deuil de Dunois', 'Étienne Dubois', 'Marguerite Jamain', 'Miller-Hayes', 'Mme. Bernutz', 'Mme. Louis Lévêque', 'Monsieur Étienne Dupuy', 'Panachée Langroise', 'Souvenir de la Princesse Amélie des Pays-Bas', 'Thomas Mills', 'Triomphe de Toulouse'

1874: 'Antoine Mouton', 'Bernard Verlot', 'Comtesse de Serenyi', 'Crimson Bedder', 'Duchess of Edinburgh', 'Firebrand', 'Gaspard Monge', 'Gonsoli Gaëtano', 'Hippolyte Jamain', 'Ingénieur Madèlé', 'John Stuart Mill', 'La Rosière', 'La Syrène', 'Marguerite Brassac', 'Miss Hassard', 'Monsieur E.Y. Teas', 'Peach Blossom', 'Philippe Bardet', 'Souvenir du Baron de Semur'

1875: 'Abel Carrière', 'Alexandre Chomer', 'Alexis Lepère', 'Arthur Oger', 'Avocat Duvivier', 'Colonel de Sansal', 'Duc de Montpensier', 'Eugène Fürst', 'Général Duc d'Aumale', 'Henry Bennett', 'Jean Liabaud', 'Jean Soupert', 'Mme. Ferdinand Jamin', 'Mme. Grandin-Monville', 'Prince Arthur', 'Sir Garnet Wolseley', 'Souvenir d'Arthur de Sansal', 'Star of Waltham', 'Triomphe de France'

1876: 'Angèle Fontaine', 'Baronne de Medem', 'Berthe du Mesnil de Mont Chauveau', 'Charles Martel', 'Comtesse Hélène Mier', 'Duc de Chartres', 'Duchesse d'Ossuna', 'Emily Laxton', 'Empress of India', 'Magna Charta', 'Marchioness of Exeter', 'Marie Louise Pernet', 'Mlle. Léonie Giessen', 'Mme. Maurice Rivoire', 'Mme. Sophie Tropot', 'Mme. Théobald Sernin', 'Mme. Verlot', 'Monseigneur Fournier', 'Monsieur Fillion', 'Mrs. Baker', 'Princesse Charles d'Aremberg', 'Sultan of Zanzibar', 'Tancrède'

1877: 'Alfred K. Williams', 'Bathélemy-Joubert', 'Bicolore', 'Boïldieu', 'Comtesse de Flandres', 'Dames Patronesses d'Orléans', 'Dr. Auguste Krell', 'Fontenelle', 'Mme. Gabriel Luizet', 'Mme. Roger', 'Mme.

Thévenot', 'Président Schachter', 'Princesse Lise Troubetzkoï', 'Souvenir d'Adolphe Thiers', 'Souvenir d'Auguste Rivière'

1878: 'A Geoffey de St.-Hilaire', 'Alexandre Dutitre', 'Benjamin Drouet', 'Deuil de Colonel Denfert', 'Dr. Baillon', 'Édouard Fontaine', 'François Gaulain', 'John Bright', 'Jules Chrétien', 'Kaiser Wilhelm I', 'Léon Renault', 'Lord Beaconsfield', 'Mabel Morrison', 'Mme. Amélie Baltet', 'Mme. Charles Meurice', 'Mme. Charles Truffaut', 'Mme. Eugène Verdier', 'Mme. Loeben de Sels', 'Monsieur le Préfet Limbourg', 'Pierre Caro', 'Princesse Marie Dolgorouky', 'Rosy Morn', 'Souvenir de Laffay', 'Souvenir de Mme. Robert', 'Souvenir de Victor Verdier', 'William Warden'

1879: 'Abraham Zimmermann', 'Alsace-Lorraine', 'Ambrogio Maggi', 'Amédée Philibert', 'Baron Taylor', 'Catherine Soupert', 'Charles Darwin', 'Comte de Mortemart', 'Comte Florimund de Bergeyck', 'Comte Horace de Choiseul', 'Countess of Rosebery', 'Duchess of Bedford', 'Édouard André le Botaniste', 'Ferdinand Chaffolte', 'Gloire de Bourg-la-Reine', 'Henriette Petit', 'Jean Lelièvre', 'Mlle. Jules Grévy', 'Mme. Elisa Tasson', 'Mme. Georges Vibert', 'Monsieur Eugène Delaire', 'Panachée d'Angers', 'Rosiériste Harms', 'Souvenir d'Aline Fontaine', 'Souvenir de Monsieur Faivre', 'Vincent-Hippolyte Duval'

1880: 'Comte Frédéric de Thun de Hohenstein', 'Crown Prince', 'Dr. Hogg', 'Duke of Teck', 'François Levet', 'Georges Moreau', 'Guillaume Gillemot', 'Mme. Montel', 'Monsieur Alfred Leveau', 'Souvenir de Mme. Alfred Vy', 'Souvenir de Président Porcher'

1881: 'A.-M. Ampère', 'Archiduchesse Elizabeth d'Autriche', 'Comte Adrien de Germiny', 'Comte de Flandres', 'Comtesse Henriette Combes', 'Ernest Prince', 'François Olin', 'Friedrich von Schiller', 'Gustave Thierry', 'Mary Pochin', 'Mlle. Elisabeth de la Rocheterie', 'Mlle. Marie Chauvet', 'Mme. Crozy', 'Mme. Fortuné Besson', 'Mme. Marie Lavalley', 'Mme. Marthe d'Halloy', 'Mme. Pierre Margery', 'Mme. Rambaux', 'Mme. Yorke', 'Monsieur Albert la

Blotais', 'Monsieur Jules Monges', 'Pride of Waltham', 'Souvenir de Mme. Berthier', 'Souvenir de Monsieur Droche', 'Ulrich Brunner fils', 'Violette Bouyer'

1882: 'Adélaïde de Meynot', 'Alexandre Dupont', 'Baron de Wolseley', 'Baron Nathaniel de Rothschild', 'Beauty of Beeston', 'Duchesse of Connaught', 'Earl of Pembroke', 'Heinrich Schultheis', 'Joachim du Bellay', 'Lecoq-Dumesnil', 'Léon Say', 'Marguerite de Roman', 'Merveille de Lyon', 'Michel Strogoff', 'Mlle. Hélène Croissandeau', 'Mlle. Marie Closon', 'Mme. Alexandre Jullien', 'Mme. Apolline Foulon', 'Mme. François Bruel', 'Mme. Louise Vigneron', 'Mme. Marie Lagrange', 'Mme. Veuve Alexandre Pommery', 'Monsieur Joseph Chappaz', 'Monsieur Jules Maquinant'

1883: 'Alphonse Soupert', 'Boileau', 'Charles Lamb', 'Colonel Félix Breton', 'Directeur Alphand', 'Directeur N. Jensen', 'Éclair', 'Emperor', 'Grandeur of Cheshunt', 'Lord Bacon', 'Mlle. Hélène Michel', 'Mlle. Suzanne-Marie Rodocanachi', 'Mme. Bertha Mackart', 'Monsieur Francisque Rive', 'Monsieur le Capitaine Louis Frère', 'Président Sénélar', 'Princesse Radziwill', 'Prosper Laugier', 'Réveil du Printemps', 'Secrétaire J. Nicolas', 'Souvenir de Léon Gambetta', 'White Baroness'

1884: 'Aline Rozey', 'Amiral Courbet', 'Baronne Nathaniel de Rothschild', 'Charles Bonnet', 'Comtesse Cahen d'Anvers', 'Desirée Fontaine', 'Duc de Marlborough', 'Édouard Hervé', 'Félix Mousset', 'Général Appert', 'Hans Mackart', 'Laurent de Rillé', 'Lord Frederic Cavendish', 'Louis Philippe Albert d'Orléans', 'Mme. Edmond Fabre', 'Mme. Eugénie Frémy', 'Mme. Francis Buchner', 'Mme. Lucien Chauré', 'Monsieur Hoste', 'Mrs. George Dickson', 'Olivier Métra', 'Pride of Reigate', 'Queen of Queens', 'Souvenir d'Alphonse Lavallée', 'Souvenir de l'Ami Labruyère', 'Victor Hugo'

1885: 'Clara Cochet', 'Comtesse de Fressinet de Bellanger', 'Elise Lemaire', 'Frédéric Schneider II', 'Gloire Lyonnaise', 'Her Majesty', 'La Nantaise', 'Le Triomphe de Saintes', 'Léon Delaville', 'Louis

Calla', 'Marshall P. Wilder', 'Mme. A. Labbley', 'Mme. Baulot', 'Mme. Lefebvre', 'Mme. Rosa Monnet', 'Prince Waldemar', 'Princesse Amédée de Broglie', 'Princesse de Béarn', 'Princesse Marie d'Orléans', 'Professeur Maxime Cornu', 'Souvenir de Victor Hugo'

1886: 'A. Drawiel', 'Aly Pacha Chérif', 'American Beauty', 'Baronne de St.-Didier', 'Bijou de Couasnon', 'Charles Dickens', 'Comte de Paris', 'Dr. Antonin Joly', 'Duc de Bragance', 'Duchesse de Bragance', 'Erinnerung an Brod', 'Florence Paul', 'Inigo Jones', 'Jean-Baptiste Casati', 'Jules Barigny', 'Louis Rolet', 'Mme. de Selve', 'Mme. Édouard Michel', 'Mme. Henri Pereire', 'Mme. Léon Halkin', 'Mme. Lureau Escalaïs', 'Mme. Marcel Fauneau', 'Monsieur Jules Deroudilhe', 'Monsieur Mathieu Baron', 'Orgeuil de Lyon', 'Prince Henri d'Orléans', 'Princesse Hélène d'Orléans', 'Théodore Liberton'

1887: 'Cæcilie Scharsach', 'Duc d'Audiffret-Pasquier', 'Earl of Dufferin', 'James Bougault', 'Katkoff', 'Lady Helen Stuart', 'Louis Donadine', 'Louis Lille', 'Mme. Alphonse Seux', 'Mme. César Brunier', 'Mme. Sophie Stern', 'Mrs. John Laing', 'Silver Queen', 'Sir Rowland Hill', 'Tartarus'

1888: 'Caroline d'Arden', 'Comtesse Bertrand de Blacas', 'Comtesse Branicka', 'Comtesse de Roquette-Buisson', 'Comtesse O'Gorman', 'Ferdinand Jamin', 'Victor Lemoine'

1889: 'Adrien Schmitt', 'Benoît Pernin', 'Buffalo-Bill', 'Duchesse de Dino', 'Émile Bardiaux', 'Gloire de l'Exposition de Bruxelles', 'Gustave Piganeau', 'Lady Arthur Hill', 'Marchioness of Lorne', 'Mlle. Marie Magat', 'Mme. la Comtesse de St.-Andréol', 'Mme. Renahy', 'Mme. Thibaud', 'Oscar II, Roi de Suède', 'Souvenir de Grégoire Bordillon', 'Souvenir de Rosiériste Gonod', 'Vick's Caprice', 'Vicomte de Lauzières'

1890: 'Anna Scharsach', 'Antonie Schurz', 'Belle de Normandy', 'Belle Yvrienne', 'Crimson Queen', 'Jeannie Dickson', 'L'Ami Maubray', 'Margaret Haywood', 'Mme. Cécile Morand', 'Mme. Lemesle',

'Monsieur Jules Lemaître', 'Professeur Chargueraud', 'Roger Lambelin'

1891: 'Frère Marie Pierre', 'Général Baron Berge', 'Jeanne Masson', 'L'Étincelante', 'Margaret Dickson', 'Mme. Théodore Vernes', 'Monsieur de Morand', 'Président Carnot', 'Salamander'

1892: 'Claude Jacquet', 'Duchess of Fife', 'Duke of Fife', 'Grand-Duc Alexis', 'Impératrice Maria Feodorowna', 'Mme. Anatole Leroy', 'Mme. Henri Perrin', 'Mme. Louis Ricard', 'Spencer', 'Violet Queen'

1893: 'American Belle', 'Baron Elisi de St.-Albert', 'Capitaine Peillon', 'Captain Hayward', 'Charles Gater', 'Georges Rousset', 'La Vierzonnaise', 'Lucien Duranthon', 'Marchioness of Londonderry', 'Monsieur Édouard Detaille', 'Oakmont', 'Paul's Early Blush', 'Rose de France'

1894: 'Achille Cesbron', 'Baronne Gustave de St. Paul', 'Mme. Marguerite Marsault', 'Mrs. Harkness', 'Mrs. R.G. Sharman-Crawford'

1895: 'Éclaireur', 'François Coppée', 'Graf Fritz Metternich', 'Haileybury', 'Helen Keller', 'Mme. Verrier Cachet', 'Souvenir de Bertrand Guinoisseau', 'Venus'

1896: 'Comte Raoul Chandon', 'Comtesse Renée de Béarn', 'Coquette Bordelaise', 'Mlle. Marie Achard', 'Tom Wood'

1897: 'Baron Girod de l'Ain', 'Baron T'Kint de Roodenbeke', 'Comte Charles d'Harcourt', 'Jubilee', 'Merrie England', 'Miss Ethel Richardson', 'Oskar Cordel', 'Principessa di Napoli', 'Reverend Alan Cheales', 'Robert Duncan', 'Waltham Standard'

1898: 'Ernest Morel', 'Mme. Rose Caron', 'Mrs. F.W. Sanford', 'Souvenir d'Alexandre Hardy', 'Souvenir de Mme. Sadi Carnot'

1899: 'General von Bothnia-Andreæ', 'Gloire d'un Enfant d'Hiram', 'Mrs. Cocker', 'Mrs. Rumsey', 'Souvenir d'André Raffy', 'Souvenir de Henri Lévêque de Vilmorin', 'Souvenir de Maman Corbœuf', 'Souvenir de Mme. Jeanne Balandreau'

1900: 'Ami Charmet', 'Gruss an Pallien', 'Mme. Charles Montigny', 'Mme. Ernest Levavasseur', 'Mme. Petit', 'Rosslyn', 'Souvenir de Mme. Chédane-Guinoisseau', 'Ulster'
1901: 'Ben Cant', 'Capitaine Jouen', 'Frau Karl Druschki', 'Léon Robichon', 'Mary Corelly', 'Monsieur Louis Ricard', 'Queen of Edgely', 'Royat-Mondain', 'Victory Rose'
1902: 'Souvenir de McKinley', 'Vincente Peluffo'
1903: 'L'Ami E. Daumont', 'Mme. Cordier', 'Mme. Louise Piron', 'Mme. Roudillon'
1904: 'Maharajah', 'Monsieur Ernest Dupré'
1905: 'California', 'Dr. William Gordon', 'Hugh Dickson', 'Hugh Watson', 'J.B. Clark', 'M.H. Walsh', 'Mrs. John McLaren', 'Rosa Verschuren'
1906: 'Ami Martin', 'Barbarossa', 'Mlle. Renée Denis', 'Piron-Medard', 'Souvenir de Pierre Sionville'
1907: 'Adiantifolia', 'Charles Wagner', 'Dr. Georges Martin', 'Gloire de Chédane-Guinoisseau', 'Lady Overtoun', 'Mme. Jean Everaerts', 'Philipp Paulig', 'Rouge Angevin'
1908: 'Commandeur Jules Gravereaux', 'La Brunoyenne', 'Souvenir de Léon Roudillon'
1909: 'George Sand', 'Mme. Constant David'
1910: 'Georg Arends', 'Janine Viaud-Bruant', 'Juliet', 'Symmetry'
1911: 'Générale Marie Raiewesky', 'Heinrich Münch'
1912: 'George Dickson', 'Paula Clegg'
1913: 'Berti Gimpel', 'Camdeur Lyonnaise', 'Coronation', 'Leonie Lambert'
1914: 'Pæonia', 'Rembrandt'
1915: 'Emden', 'Louise Cretté', 'Marguerite Guillard', 'Miss Annie Crawford'
1916: 'Anne Laferrère', 'Henri Coupé'
1918: 'Fürst Leopold IV zu Schaumburg-Lippe'
1919: 'Dr. Ingomar H. Blohm', 'Gruss an Weimar'

1920: 'Dr. Müllers Rote', 'Ruhm von Steinfurth'

1921: 'Auguste Chaplain', 'Bischof Dr. Korum', 'Ferdinand Pichard', 'Schön Ingeborg'

1922: 'Sa Majesté Gustave V', 'Souvenir de Mme. H. Thuret'

1924: 'Henry Nevard', 'Suzanne Carrol of Carrolton'

1925: 'Edelweiss', 'Felbergs Rosa Druschki', 'Mme. Albert Barbier', 'Riccordo di Fernando Scarlatti'

1926: 'Mme. André Saint', 'St. Ingebert'

1927: 'Everest', 'Marie Menudel', 'Turnvater Jahn'

1928: 'Lyonfarbige Druschki'

1929: 'Arrillaga', 'Druschki Rubra', 'Isabel Llorach', 'Pfaffstädt', 'Président Briand', 'Prinzessin Elsa zu Schaumburg-Lippe'

1930: 'Martin Liebau'

1932: 'Arthur Weidling', 'Chot Pestitele', 'Druschka', 'Eliska Krásnohorská'

1933: 'General Stefanik', 'Harmony', 'Nuria de Recolons', 'Stämmler', 'Tatik Brada', 'Urdh'

1934: 'Dr. Bradas Rosa Druschki', 'Jan Böhm', 'Polar Bear', 'Prinz Max zu Schaumburg-Lippe'

1935: 'Symphony', 'Vyslanec Kalina'

1937: 'Bradova Lososova Druschki'

1938: '(Frau Karl Druschki × Cristata)'

1940: 'Magnolija'

1956: 'Hold Slunci'

1960: 'Waldfee'

Noisettes and Climbers

1802: 'Champneys' Pink Cluster'

1810: 'Fraser's Pink Musk'

1811: 'Fun Jwan Lo'

1812: 'Autumnalis'

1814: 'Blush Noisette', 'Noisette de l'Inde'

1824: 'Bougainville'
1825: 'Duchesse de Grammont'
1827: 'Blanc Pur'
1828: 'Aimée Vibert'
1830: 'Camélia Rose', 'Desprez à Fleur Jaune', 'Lamarque'
1832: 'La Biche'
1834: 'Bouquet Tout Fait', 'Fellemberg'
1835: 'Manettii'
1841: 'Climbing Aimée Vibert'
1842: 'Céline Forestier'
1843: 'Chromatella', 'Solfatare'
1844: 'Ophirie', 'Philomèle'
1845: 'Blairii No. 1', 'Blairii No. 2', 'Blairii No. 3', 'Fortune's Double Yellow'
1847: 'Pumila Alba'
1848: 'Caroline Marniesse', 'Vicomtesse d'Avesnes'
1853: 'Gloire de Dijon', 'Isis'
1856: 'Claudia Augusta', 'Dr. Kane', 'Mme. Schultz'
1857: 'Isabella Gray'
1858: 'Climbing Devoniensis', 'Cornélie', 'James Sprunt'
1859: 'Cinderella', 'L'Arioste'
1861: 'Gloire de Bordeaux'
1862: 'Mlle. Adèle Jougant'
1863: 'Pavillon de Pregny'
1864: 'Maréchal Niel'
1865: 'Glory of Waltham'
1868: 'Adrienne Christophle'
1869: 'Mme. Trifle', 'Rêve d'Or'
1870: 'Belle Lyonnaise', 'Mme. Bérard', 'Mme. Emilie Dupuy'
1871: 'Annie Vibert'
1872: 'Bouquet d'Or', 'Cheshunt Hybrid', 'Earl of Eldon', 'Marie Accary'
1873: 'Mme. Claire Carnot', 'Noisette Moschata'

1874: 'Climbing Jules Margottin'
1875: 'Anne-Marie Côte', 'Mme. Marie Berton', 'Multiflore de Vaumarcus'
1877: 'Deschamps', 'Lily Metschersky'
1878: 'Emilia Plantier', 'Mme. Auguste Perrin', 'Papillon', 'Reine Marie Henriette', 'William Allen Richardson'
1879: 'Duarte de Oliveira', 'Mlle. Mathilde Lenaerts', 'Mme. Alfred Carrière', 'Mme. Louis Henry', 'Setina'
1880: 'Les Fiançailles de la Princesse Stéphanie et de l'Archiduc Rodolphe', 'Reine Maria Pia'
1881: 'Beauté de l'Europe', 'Caroline Schmitt', 'Climbing Captain Christy', 'Mélanie Soupert', 'Mme. Julie Lassen', 'Reine Olga de Wurtemberg'
1882: 'Étendard de Jeanne d'Arc', 'Mme. Eugène Verdier'
1883: 'Paul's Single White Perpetual'
1884: 'Gaston Chandon'
1885: 'Comtesse Georges de Roquette-Buisson', 'Mme. Couturier-Mention', 'Waltham Climber I', 'Waltham Climber II', 'Waltham Climber III'
1886: 'Mme. Chauvry'
1887: 'Albert la Blotais', 'Elie Beauvilain', 'Fürst Bismarck', 'Fürstin Bismarck', 'Kaiser Wilhelm de Siegreiche', 'L'Abondance', 'L'Idéal', 'Meteor', 'Mlle. Claire Jacquier', 'Mlle. Jeanne Ferron', 'Mme. Jules Franke', 'Mme. la Duchesse d'Auerstädt', 'Monsieur Rosier', 'Souvenir de Mme. Joseph Métral' 'Triomphe des Noisettes'
1888: 'Marie Thérèse Dubourg', 'Mme. Rose Romarin', 'Monsieur Désir', 'Nardy'
1889: 'Climbing Niphetos', 'Climbing Perle des Jardins', 'Gigantea Blanc', 'Kaiserin Friedrich', 'La France de 89', 'Mlle. Geneviève Godard'
1890: 'Gribaldo Nicola', 'Mlle. Madeleine Delaroche', 'Mme. Brunner', 'Mme. Creux', 'Pink Rover'

1891: 'Mme. Pierre Cochet'
1892: 'Beauté Inconstante', 'Mlle. Marie Gaze', 'Climbing Queen of Queens'
1893: 'Alister Stella Gray', 'Baronne Charles de Gargan', 'Climbing La France', 'Climbing Souvenir de la Malmaison', 'Comtesse de Galard-Béarn', 'Dr. Rouges', 'Marie Robert', 'Princess May', 'Souvenir de Lucie'
1894: 'Climbing Cécile Brunner', 'Climbing White Pet', 'E. Veyrat Hermanos', 'Mme. Louis Blanchet'
1895: 'Belle Vichysoise'
1896: 'Empress of China', 'Mme. Chabanne', 'Weisser Maréchal Niel'
1897: 'Climbing Bridesmaid', 'Climbing Kaiserin Auguste Viktoria', 'Climbing Wootton', 'Lilliput', 'Mme. E. Souffrain'
1898: 'Ards Rover', 'Billard et Marré', 'Climbing Marie Guillot', 'Climbing Papa Gontier', 'Dawn', 'Eugene Jardine', 'Souvenir de Mme. Léonie Viennot'
1899: 'Climbing Mrs. W.J. Grant', 'Mme. Gaston Annouilh', 'Souvenir de Mme. Ladvocat'
1900: 'François Crousse', 'Irish Beauty', 'Mme. Jules Gravereaux', 'Noëlla Nabonnand', 'Oscar Chauvry', 'Rosabelle'
1901: 'Climbing Mme. Caroline Testout', 'Dr. Lande', 'Jeanne Corbœuf', 'Mme. Auguste Choutet', 'Mme. la Général Paul de Benoist', 'Purple East'
1902: 'Belle d'Orléans', 'Climbing Coltilde Soupert', 'Député Debussy', 'Gruss an Friedberg', 'Lady Waterlow', 'Mme. Driout'
1903: 'Gainesborough', 'Lady Clonbrock', 'Marie Bülow', 'Mme. Edmée Cocteau', 'Mme. Hector Leuilliot', 'Mme. Martignier', 'Tea Rambler'
1904: 'Climbing Le Vésuve', 'Climbing Mme. Louis Ricard', 'Crépuscule', 'Monsieur Georges de Cadoudal'
1905: 'Belle Portugaise', 'Comte de Torres'

1906: 'Climbing Captain Hayward', 'Climbing Frau Karl Druschki', 'Marguerite Desrayaux', 'Sarah Bernhardt', 'Tausendschön'
1907: 'Climbing White Maman Cochet', 'Henry Irving', 'Indiana', 'Mme. Léon Constantin', 'Souvenir d'Émile Zola'
1908: 'Ards Rambler', 'Climbing Liberty', 'Climbing Miniature', 'Frau Geheimrat Dr. Staub'
1909: 'Climbing American Beauty', 'Climbing Maman Cochet', 'Climbing Mosella', 'Étoile de Portugal'
1910: 'Dr. W. Van Fleet', 'Lafollette', 'Miss G. Mesman', 'Neervelt', 'Nymphe'
1911: 'Adele Frey', 'Climbing Gruss an Teplitz', 'Climbing Mrs. W.H. Cutbush', 'Florence Haswell Veitch'
1912: 'Climbing Richmond', 'Lemon Queen'
1913: 'Climbing Monsieur Paul Lédé', 'Effective', 'Mikado', 'Miss Marion Manifold', 'Mme. Foureau'
1915: 'Cupid', 'Mrs. Rosalie Wrinch', 'Paul's Lemon Pillar'
1916: 'Climbing Irish Fireflame', 'Colcestria', 'Geschwinds Gorgeous'
1917: 'Catalunya', 'Climbing Lady Hillingdon', 'Climbing Mme. Abel Chatenay', 'Purity'
1919: 'Black Boy'
1920: 'Climbing Château de Clos-Vougeot', 'Climbing Ophelia', 'Climbing Rosemary', 'Irène Bonnet', 'Souvenir de Claudius Denoyel'
1921: 'Vicomtesse Pierre de Fou'
1922: 'Climbing Mrs. Aaron Ward', 'Climbing Mrs. Herbert Stevens', 'Emmanuella de Mouchy', 'Flying Colours', 'Kitty Kininmonth', 'Marguerite Carels', 'Scorcher'
1923: 'Cherubim', 'Climbing General MacArthur', 'Climbing Jonkheer J.L. Mock', 'Phyllis Bide'
1924: 'Lucy Thomas', 'Sénateur Amic', 'Sunday Best'
1925: 'Dr. Domingos Pereira', 'Milkmaid'

1926: 'Apeles Mestres', 'Climbing Eva Teschendorff', 'Climbing Mme. Butterfly', 'Climbing Radiance', 'Queen of Hearts'
1927: 'Climbing Cracker', 'Climbing Hadley', 'Cooper's Burmese Rose'
1929: 'Climbing Columbia', 'Climbing Mme. Segond-Weber', 'Climbing Mrs. Henry Morse'
1930: 'Climbing Dame Edith Helen', 'Montarioso', 'Montecito', 'New Dawn'
1931: 'Climbing Étoile de Hollande', 'Climbing General-Superior Arnold Janssen', 'Crimson Conquest'
1932: 'Climbing Lorraine Lee', 'Doris Downes'
1933: 'Climbing Lady Sylvia', 'Princes van Oranje'
1935: 'Climbing Dainty Bess', 'Climbing Distinction', 'Glory of California', 'Mock's Rosa Druschki'
1936: 'Climbing Summer Snow'
1937: 'Climbing Gruss an Aachen', 'Nancy Hayward'
1938: 'Climbing Capitaine Soupa', 'Climbing Mme. Jules Bouché'
1940: 'Climbing König Friedrich II von Danemark', 'Climbing Marie Van Houtte', 'Climbing Wenzel Geschwind'
1941: 'Climbing Apotheker Georg Höfer', 'Climbing Pride of Reigate', 'Pennant'
1948: 'Climbing Orange Triumph'
1949: 'Climbing George Dickson', 'Climbing Snowbird'
1952: 'Climbing Pinkie'
1960: 'Climbing Mrs. B.R. Cant'
1962: 'Climbing Margo Koster'
1975: 'Archduchess Charlotte'
1977: 'Climbing China Doll'

Polyanthas
1875: 'Pâquerette'
1879: 'Anne-Marie de Montravel', 'Little White Pet'
1880: 'Mlle. Cécile Brunner'

1881: 'Mignonette'
1883: 'Jeanne Drivon', 'Perle d'Or'
1884: 'Miniature'
1885: 'Floribunda', 'Princesse Wilhelmina des Pays-Bas'
1886: 'Mlle. Joséphine Burland'
1887: 'Georges Pernet', 'Gloire des Polyantha', 'Miss Kate Schultheis', 'Rotkäppchen'
1888: 'Clara Pfitzer', 'Dr. Reymont', 'Flora', 'Hermine Madèlé', 'Marie Pavic', 'Minutifolia Alba', 'Mlle. Blanche Rebatel', 'Mme. Alégatière', 'Princesse Henriette de Flandres', 'Princesse Joséphine de Flandres'
1889: 'Bellina Guillot', 'Clotilde Soupert', 'Golden Fairy', 'Herzblättchen', 'Joséphine Morel', 'Little Dot', 'Mlle. Camille de Rochetaillée'
1890: 'Picotte', 'Schneeball', 'Souvenir de Mlle. Élise Châtelard'
1891: 'Mlle. Bertha Ludi'
1892: 'Étoile de Mai', 'Mme. E.A. Nolte', 'Petite Léonie', 'Princesse Elisabeth Lancellotti'
1893: 'Multiflore Nain Remontant'
1895: 'Kleiner Liebling', 'Mosella', 'Princesse Marie Adélaïde de Luxembourg'
1896: 'Perle des Rouges', 'Pink Soupert'
1897: 'Flocon de Neige', 'Gloire de Charpennes', 'La Proserpine', 'Ma Fillette'
1898: 'Amélie-Suzanne Morin', 'Archiduchesse Elisabeth Marie', 'Colibri', 'Little Gem', 'Ma Petite Andrée'
1899: 'Bouquet de Neige', 'Comtesse Antoinette d'Oultremont', 'Eugénie Lamesch', 'Leonie Lamesch', 'Mlle. Fernande Dupuy', 'Petit Constant'
1900: 'CharlesMetroz', 'Primula', 'Sisi Ketten'
1901: 'Katharine Zeimet', 'Mlle. Marthe Cahuzac', 'Schneewittchen', 'Snowball'

1903: 'Kleiner Alfred', 'Mlle. Alice Rousseau', 'Mme. Norbert Levavasseur', 'Schneekopf'
1904: 'Frau Cecilie Walter', 'Jacques Proust', 'Marguerite Rose', 'Mignon'
1905: 'Martha'
1906: 'Ännchen Müller', 'Princess Ena', 'Rösel Dach'
1907: 'Apfelblüte', 'Dr. Ricaud', 'Mrs. W.H. Cutbush'
1908: 'Diamant', 'Phyllis'
1909: 'Baptiste Lafaye', 'Cineraria', 'Cyclope', 'Frau Alexander Weiss', 'Frau Anna Pasquay', 'Frau Oberhofgärtner Schultze', 'Gustel Mayer', 'Jeanne d'Arc', 'Jessie', 'Louise Walter', 'Merveille des Polyanthas', 'Mme. Taft', 'Orléans-Rose', 'Tip-Top', 'White Cécile Brunner'
1910: 'Eileen Loow', 'Mlle. Marcelle Gaugin', 'Petite Marcelle', 'Yvonne Rabier'
1911: 'Bordure', 'Ellen Poulsen', 'Erna Teschendorff', 'Maman Turbat', 'Merveille des Rouges'
1912: 'Coronet', 'George Elger', 'Gloire d'Orléans', 'Ivan Misson', 'Jeanny Soupert', 'Madeleine Orosdy', 'Martha Keller', 'Mme. Arthur Robichon', 'Mme. Jules Gouchault', 'Papa Hémeray', 'Perle Orléanaise', 'Triomphe Orléanais'
1913: 'Excellens', 'Frau Elise Kreis', 'Loreley', 'Marie Brissonet', 'Marie-Jeanne', 'Mlle. Suzanne Bidard', 'Perle', 'Radium', 'Renoncule'
1914: 'Abondant', 'Betsy van Nes', 'Bouquet Blanc', 'Echo', 'Mary Bruni', 'Melle Fischer', 'Susanna'
1915: 'La Marne', 'Mauve', 'Petite Françoise', 'Siegesperle'
1916: 'Greta Kluis', 'Grete Schreiber', 'Magenta'
1917: 'Miss Edith Cavell', 'Mrs. William G. Koning'
1918: 'Éblouissant', 'Etoile Luisante', 'Maréchal Foch', 'Pink Cécile Brunner', 'Verdun'
1919: 'Evelyn Thornton', 'Frau Rudolf Schmidt', 'Indéfectible', 'Mevrouw Nathalie Nypels', 'Mimi Pinson', 'Schöne von Holstein', 'Stadtrat Meyn'

1920: 'Bloomfield Abundance', 'Coral Cluster', 'Evaline', 'Ideal', 'La Rosée', 'Le Loiret', 'Perle Angevine'
1921: 'Lady Reading'
1922: 'Denise Cassegrain'
1923: 'Chatillon Rose', 'Corrie Koster', 'Eva Teschendorff', 'Mrs. R.M. Finch'
1924: 'Baby Faurax'
1925: 'Rita Sammons'
1926: 'Golden Salmon'
1927: 'Kersbergen', 'Lindbergh', 'Marytje Cazant', 'Sunshine'
1928: 'Pink Pet'
1929: 'Dick Koster', 'Fireglow', 'Gloria Mundi', 'Paris', 'Sparkler'
1930: 'Little Dorrit', 'Nypels Perfection', 'Paul Crampel', 'The Allies'
1931: 'Flamboyant', 'Gabrielle Privat', 'Margo Koster'
1932: 'Baby Alberic', 'Cameo', 'Gloire du Midi', 'The Fairy'
1937: 'Jean Mermoz', 'Orange Triumph', 'Topaz'
1941: 'Spray Cécile Brunner'
1946: 'China Doll', 'Sneprinsesse'
1947: 'Pinkie'
1949: 'Muttertag', 'Pacific Triumph'
1950: 'Summer Dawn'
1951: 'Waverly Triumph'
1952: 'Border King'
1953: 'Lullaby'
1954: 'Alberich', 'Degenhard', 'Eberwein', 'Margo's Sister'
1955: 'Balduin', 'Bertram', 'Giesebrecht'
1956: 'Burkhard', 'Orange Morsdag', 'Red Triumph'
1958: 'Lillan'
1959: 'Vatertag'
1965: 'Milrose'
1971: 'Caid'
1978: 'Prevue'

1979: 'Casque d'Or', 'Fairy Changeling', 'Fairy Maid', 'Fairy Prince', 'Fairyland'
1980: 'Fairy Ring'
1982: 'Fairy Damsel'
1983: 'Pink Posy'
1984: 'Neiges d'Été'

Hybrid Teas

1849: 'Élise Masson', 'Gigantesque', 'Léonore d'Este'
1852: 'Adèle Bougère'
1864: 'Mme. Elisa de Vilmorin'
1872: 'Antonine Verdier', 'Mme. Lacharme'
1873: 'Captain Christy'
1878: 'Mlle. Brigitte Viollet', 'Mme. Étienne Levet'
1879: 'Beauty of Stapleford', 'Duchess of Connaught', 'Duchess of Westminster', 'Duke of Connaught', 'Jean Lorthois', 'Jean Sisley', 'Julius Finger', 'Michael Saunders', 'Mme. de Loeben-Sels', 'Pearl', 'Pierre Guillot'
1880: 'Honourable George Bancroft'
1881: 'Camoëns', 'Mme. Jules Grévy', 'Mme. Julie Weidmann'
1882: 'Distinction', 'Lady Mary Fitzwilliam'
1884: 'Bedford Belle', 'Grace Darling'
1886: 'Attraction', 'Directeur Constant Bernard', 'Mme. A. Schwaller', 'Mme. Joseph Desbois', 'The Puritan', 'Viscountess Folkestone', 'William Francis Bennett'
1887: 'Dr. Pasteur', 'Mlle. Germaine Caillot', 'Mme. André Duron', 'Mme. Ernest Piard', 'The Meteor'
1888: 'Comte Henri Rignon', 'Duchess of Albany', 'Mme. Angèle Favre', 'Souvenir of Wootton'
1889: 'Bona Weilschott', 'Mlle. Augustine Guinoisseau', 'Mme. Moser'

1890: 'Astra', 'Chloris', 'Danmark', 'Gustave Regis', 'Henri Brichard', 'Marquise de Salisbury', 'Mme. Angélique Veysset', 'Mme. Caroline Testout', 'Triomphe de Pernet père'

1891: 'Augustine Halem', 'Baronne G. de Noirmont', 'Carmen Sylva', 'Grand-Duc Adolphe de Luxembourg', 'Kaiserin Auguste Viktoria', 'Mme. Joseph Bonnaire', 'Mme. Pernet-Ducher', 'Mme. Veuve Ménier'

1892: 'Erinnerung an Schloss Scharfenstein', 'Erzherzogin Marie Dorothea', 'Lady Henry Grosvenor', 'Mme. Charles Boutmy'

1893: 'Marquise Litta de Breteuil', 'Mme. Joseph Combet', 'Mme. Jules Finger'

1894: 'Clara Watson', 'Charlotte Gillemot', 'Emin Pascha', 'Joséphine Marot', 'Mrs. W.C. Whitney', 'Mme. Abel Chatenay', 'Souvenir de Mme. Eugène Verdier', 'Souvenir du Président Carnot'

1895: 'Antoine Rivoire', 'Kathleen', 'Marjorie', 'Mavourneen', 'Mlle. Alice Furon', 'Mlle. Hélène Cambier', 'Mme. Charles Détraux', 'Mme. Tony Baboud', 'Mme. Wagram, Comtesse de Turenne', 'Mrs. W.J. Grant', 'Rosette de la Légion d'Honneur', 'Sheila', 'Souvenir d'Auguste Métral'

1896: 'Captain Christy Panaché', 'Ferdinand Batel', 'Ferdinand Jamin', 'Mme. Jules Grolez'

1897: 'Coronet', 'Countess of Caledon', 'Grossherzogin Viktoria Melitta von Hessen', 'L'Innocence', 'Marie Zahn', 'Mme. Adolphe Loiseau', 'Mme. Augustine Hamont', 'Mme. Eugénie Boullet', 'Mme. Paul Lacoutière', 'Violiniste Émile Lévêque'

1898: 'Aurore', 'Balduin', 'Clara Barton', 'Gardenia', 'Grossherzog Ernst Ludwig von Hesse', 'Marie Girard', 'Mme. Bessemer', 'Mrs. Robert Garrett', 'Papa Lambert', 'Souvenir de Mme. Ernest Cauvin'

1899: 'Abbé Millot', 'Admiral Dewey', 'Béatrix, Comtesse de Buisseret', 'Dr. Cazeneuve', 'Exquisite', 'Hofgärtendirektor Graebener', 'Johannes Wesselhöft', 'Jules Girodit', 'Jules Toussaint', 'Killarney', 'La Favorite', 'Ma Tulipe', 'Mme. Blondel', 'Mme. Cunisset-Carnot', 'Mme.

Georges Bénard', 'Mme. Ravary', 'Monsieur Bunel', 'Rosomane Gravereaux', 'Shandon'

1900: 'Bessie Brown', 'Irish Glory', 'Irish Modesty', 'La Tosca', 'Lady Clanmorris', 'Liberty', 'Magnafrano', 'Mme. Dailleux', 'Mme. Jean Favre'

1901: 'Abbé André Reitter', 'Gladys Harkness', 'Mildred Grant', 'Mme. Marie Croibier', 'Mme. Viger', 'Pharisäer', 'Pierre Wattinne', 'Prince de Bulgarie'

1902: 'Edmée et Roger', 'Mamie', 'Monsieur Paul Lédé', 'Paul Meunier', 'Reine Carola de Saxe'

1903: 'Amateur André Fourcaud', 'Becker's Ideal', 'Commandant Letourneux', 'Gertrude', 'Gustav Grünerwald'

1904: 'Cardinal', 'Frau J. Reiter', 'Irish Brightness', 'Lady Ashtown', 'Mme. Alfred Sabatier', 'Mme. Léon Pain', 'Reine Marguerite d'Italie'

1905: 'Adam Rackles', 'Andenken an Moritz von Frölich', 'Betty', 'General MacArthur', 'Irish Elegance', 'Lina Schmidt-Michel', 'Mme. Emilie Lafon', 'Mme. Gustav Metz', 'Richmond', 'Ruhm der Gartenwelt', 'The Dandy'

1906: 'Charles J. Graham', 'Souvenir de Monsieur Frédéric Vercellone'

1907: 'Australie', 'Avoca', 'Comtesse Icy Hardegg', 'Mme. Maurice de Luze', 'Mme. P. Euler', 'Mme. Segond-Weber', 'W.E. Lippiatt'

1908: 'Château de Clos-Vougeot', 'Madeline Gaillard', 'Radiance'

1909: 'Gruss an Aachen', 'His Majesty', 'Jonkheer J.L. Mock', 'Kaiserin Goldifolia', 'Lady Alice Stanley', 'Monsieur Charles de Lapisse', 'Mrs. Wakefield Christy-Miller'

1910: 'Mme. Jules Bouché', 'Mrs. Cynthia Forde', 'Mrs. Herbert Stevens'

1911: 'Mme. C. Chambard', 'Monsieur Fraissenon'

1912: 'Aviateur Michel Mahieu', 'British Queen', 'General-Superior Arnold Janssen', 'Killarney Queen', 'Ophelia'

1913: 'Double White Killarney', 'Irish Fireflame', 'Old Gold', 'Sachsengruss'

1914: 'Augustus Hartmann', 'Hadley', 'Killarney Brilliant'
1915: 'Mlle. Argentine Cramon', 'Red Radiance'
1916: 'Columbia', 'Isobel', 'Mme. Méha Sabatier'
1917: 'K. of K.', 'Kootenay', 'Mrs. Charles J. Bell'
1918: 'Golden Ophelia', 'Mme. Butterfly', 'Sunny South'
1919: 'Australia Felix', 'Étoile de Hollande', 'Lulu', 'Mrs. Henry Morse'
1920: 'Westfield Star'
1921: 'Innocence', 'Mrs. Oakley Fisher'
1923: 'Vesuvius'
1925: 'Dainty Bess'
1926: 'Cecil', 'Dame Edith Helen', 'Lady Sylvia'
1930: 'Minna', 'Rosa Gruss an Aachen'
1934: 'Kathleen Mills'
1935: 'Jean Muraour'
1936: 'Ellen Wilmott', 'Snowbird'
1937: 'Christobel', 'Frances Ashton'
1942: 'Gruss an Aachen Superior'
1947: 'White Wings'

Appendix Seven

Cultivars by Breeder or Introducer

Only breeders or family groups with two or more introductions included in this book are listed. When breeder and introducer are different, the variety is listed under the breeder's name only. Family groups (Cochet, Ducher, Guillot, etc.) are listed with the elder generation preceding the younger. Arrangement under each heading is chronological. In a number of cases, the breeder's company or family continued to release new offerings under his name after his decease. Close study of the listings for those breeders who undertook their crossings in a "scientific" manner will provide many insights. The indicated dates are inclusive of "circa" and "pre-" dates; that is, "ca. 1829" and "-1829" are, for the purposes of this appendix, listed indiscriminately as "1829." These listings do not give *all* of the breeder's respective releases, but only the ones in this book; complete listings of the entire œuvre of each breeder/introducer, with "circa" dates and "pre-" dates differentiated, will be found in our companion book *Roll-Call: The Old Rose Breeder*.

Alégatière, Alphonse
Lyon, France
1884: 'Miniature (Pol)
1888: 'Dr. Reymont' (Pol), 'Marie Pavic' (Pol)
1891: 'Joséphine Morel' (Pol)

Altmüller, Johann
Schwerin, Mecklenbourg, Germany
1913: 'Berti Gimpel' (HP)
1916: 'Grete Schreiber' (Pol)

Archer, W.E.B.
Sellindge, England
1925: 'Dainty Bess' (HT)
1936: 'Ellen Wilmott' (HT)

Avoux & Crozy
La Guillotière, Lyon, France
1856: 'Impératrice Eugénie' (B)
1858: 'Enfant de Lyon' (T)
1859: 'Narcisse' (T)

Barbier Brothers & Company
Orléans, France
1911: 'Bordure' (Pol)
1913: 'Renoncule' (Pol)

1915: 'La Marne' (Pol)
1916: 'Henri Coupé' (HP), 'Magenta' (Pol)
1918: 'Verdun' (Pol)
1919: 'Mimi Pinson' (Pol)
1925: 'Mme. Albert Barbier' (HP)
1926: 'Mme. André Saint' (HP)
1927: 'Marie Menudel' (HP)

Beluze, Jean
Lyon, France
1841: 'Rival de Pæstum' (T)
1843: 'Souvenir de la Malmaison' (B)
1844: 'Reine des Vierges' (B)
1846: 'Leveson-Gower' (B), 'Maréchal du Palais' (B), 'Triomphe de la Duchère' (B)
1855: 'Impératrice Eugénie' (HB)
1856: 'Mme. Schultz' (N)

Bénard, G.
Orléans, France
1899: 'Abbé Millot' (HT), 'Mme. Georges Bénard' (HT), 'Souvenir de Maman Corbœuf' (HP)

Bennett, Henry
Manor Farm Nursery, Shepperton, Stapleford, England
1874: 'Duchess of Edinburgh' (HP)
1879: 'Beauty of Stapleford' (HT), 'Duchess of Connaught' (HT), 'Duchess of Westminster' (HT), 'Duke of Connaught' (HT), 'Jean Sisley' (HT), 'Michael Saunders' (HT), 'Pearl' (HT), 'Viscountess Falmouth' (HT)
1880: 'Honourable George Bancroft' (HT)

1882: 'Distinction' (HT), 'Earl of Pembroke' (HP), 'Heinrich Schultheis' (HP), 'Lady Mary Fitzwilliam' (HT), 'Princess of Wales' (T)
1884: 'Grace Darling' (HT), 'Mrs. George Dickson' (HP)
1885: 'Her Majesty' (HP)
1886: 'The Puritan' (HT), 'Viscountess Folkestone' (HT), 'William Francis Bennett' (HT)
1887: 'Mrs. John Laing' (HP), 'Princess Beatrix' (T)
1888: 'Minutifolia Alba' (Pol)
1889: 'Golden Fairy' (Pol), 'Little Dot' (Pol)
1892: 'Lady Henry Grosvenor' (HT)
1893: 'Captain Hayward' (HP), 'Climbing Souvenir de la Malmaison' (Cl. B)

Berland
Bordeaux (?), France
1899: 'Mme. C. Liger' (T)
1901: 'Mme. la Général Paul de Benoist' (Cl. T)

Bernaix, Alexandre
Villeurbanne-Lyon, France
1886: 'Mlle. Joséphine Burland' (Pol), 'Mme. A Schwaller' (HT), 'Mme. A. Étienne' (T), 'Mme. Scipion Cochet' (T), 'Vicomtesse de Wauthier' (T)
1887: 'Mlle. Claire Jacquier' (Cl. Pol), 'Mme. César Brunier' (HP), 'Mme. la Duchesse d'Auerstädt' (N), 'Souvenir de Mme. Joseph Métral' (Cl. HT), 'V. Viviand-Morel' (T)
1888: 'Mlle. Blanche Rebatel' (Pol), 'Mme. Jules Cambon' (T)
1889: 'Georges Farber' (T), 'Mlle. Camille de Rochetaillée' (Pol), 'Mme. Marthe du Bourg' (T), 'Mme. Philippe Kuntz' (T)
1890: 'Mme. la Princesse de Bessaraba de Brancovan' (T), 'Souvenir de Mlle. Élise Châtelard' (Pol)

1891: 'Frère Marie Pierre' (HP), 'Mme. Victor Caillet' (T), 'Monsieur Édouard Littaye' (T), 'Monsieur Tillier' (T)
1892: 'Mme. E.A. Nolte' (Pol), 'Mme. Ocker Ferenca' (T)
1893: 'Comtesse de Galard-Béarn' (N)
1894: 'E. Veyrat Hermanos' (N), 'Monsieur le Chevalier Angelo Ferrario' (T), 'V. Vivo é Hijos' (T)
1895: 'Mme. Wagram, Comtesse de Turenne' (HT)
1897: 'Baronne Henriette Snoy' (T)

Bernaix fils (Pierre)
Villeurbanne-Lyon, France
1898: 'Mme. Berkeley' (T), 'Souvenir de Mme. Léonie Viennot' (Cl. T)
1899: 'Mme. Clémence Marchix' (T), 'Souvenir de William Robinson' (T)
1903: 'Betty Berkeley' (T)
1904: 'Mme. Alfred Sabatier' (HT)
1908: 'Madeleine Gaillard' (HT), 'Rosomane Narcisse Thomas' (T)

Bernède, H.B.
Bordeaux, France
1856: 'Général Tartas' (T)
1857: 'Comtesse de Labarthe' (T)
1859: 'Mme. de Tartas' (T)
1886: 'Mme. de Selve' (HP)

Besson, Antoine
Monplaisir, Lyon, France
1881: 'Mlle. Marie Chauvet' (HP)
1886: 'Dr. Antonin Joly' (HP), 'Orgeuil de Lyon' (HP)

Bizard
Angers, France
1838: 'Némésis' (Ch)
1839: 'Bouquet de Flore' (B)

Blair
Stamford Hill, England
1845: 'Blairii No. 1' (HCh), 'Blairii No. 2' (HCh), 'Blairii No. 3' (HCh)

Böhm, Jan
Blatná-Cechy, Czechoslovakia
1931: 'Climbing General-Superior Arnold Janssen' (HT)
1932: 'Chot Pestitele' (HP), 'Eliska Krásnohorská' (HP)
1933: 'General Stefanik' (HP)
1935: 'Vyslanec Kalina' (HP)

Bonfiglioli (A.) & Son
Bologna, Italy
1897: 'Principessa di Napoli' (T)
1913: 'Clementina Carbonieri' (T)

Bonnaire, Joseph
Lyon, France
1885: 'Souvenir de Victor Hugo' (T)
1886: 'Dr. Grill' (T), 'Mme. Chauvry' (Cl. T)
1887: 'Mme. André Duron' (HT), 'Mme. Ernest Piard' (HT)
1888: 'Capitaine Lefort' (T), 'Edmond Sablayrolles' (T)
1889: 'Mlle. Jeanne Guillaumez' (T), 'Souvenir d'Auguste Legros' (T)
1890: 'Elisa Fugier' (T), 'Henri Brichard' (HT), 'Souvenir de Mme. Sablayrolles' (T)
1891: 'Mme. Joseph Bonnaire' (HT)
1892: 'Madeleine Guillaumez' (T)

1893: 'Lucien Duranthon' (HP), 'Mme. Joseph Combet' (HT)
1894: 'Joséphine Marot' (HT), 'Souvenir de Laurent Guillot' (T)
1895: 'Rosette de la Légion d'Honneur' (HT)
1897: 'Mme. Jacques Charreton' (T)
1898: 'Mme. Lucien Duranthon' (T)
1899: 'Jules Toussaint' (HT), 'Ma Tulipe' (HT)
1902: 'Abbé Garroute' (T)
1907: 'Mme. Léon Constantin' (Cl. T)

Bougère** (or **Bougère-Breton)
Angers, France
1832: 'Bougère' (T)
1841: 'Niphetos' (T)

Boutigny, Jules-Philbert
Rouen, France
1901: 'Captaine Jouen' (HP), Monsieur Louis Ricard (HP)
1904: 'Climbing Mme. Louis Ricard' (HP), 'Monsieur Ernest Dupré' (HP)
1905: 'Capitaine Dyel, de Graville' (B)
1906: 'Souvenir de Pierre Sionville' (HP)
1909: 'Mme. Constant David' (HP)

Boyau, Joseph
Angers, France
1842: 'La Sylphide' (T)
1843: 'Solfatare' (N)
1844: 'Ebène' (DP)
1854: 'Prince Noir' (HP)
1862: 'Duc d'Anjou' (HP)
1866: 'Souvenir de Monsieur Boll' (HP)

Brada, Dr. Gustav
Czechoslovakia
1933: 'Tatik Brada' (HP)
1934: 'Dr. Bradas Rosa Druschki' (HP)
1937: 'Bradova Lososova Druschki' (HP)

Brassac, François
Toulouse, France
1873: 'Triomphe de Toulouse' (HP)
1874: 'Marguerite Brassac' (HP)
1876: 'Mme. Théobald Sernin' (HP)
1879: 'Duarte de Oliveira' (N)

Bruant, Georges *(see also Viaud-Bruant)*
Poitiers, France
1857: 'Souvenir de Béranger' (HP)

Buatois, Emmanuel
Dijon, France
1897: 'Antoinette Cuillerat' (Ch), 'Mme. Adolphe Loiseau' (HT), 'Mme. Derepas-Matrat' (T), 'Mme. Paul Lacoutière' (HT)
1898: 'Marie Girard' (HT)
1899: 'Jules Girodit' (HT), 'Mme. Cunisset-Carnot' (HT), 'Mme. Gustave Henry' (T)
1900: 'Mme. Dailleux' (HT)
1901: 'L'Ouche' (Ch)
1902: 'Député Debussy' (Cl. HT), 'Paul Meunier' (HT)

Budlong & Son Co.
Auburn, Rhode Island, U.S.A.
1912: 'Killarney Queen' (HT)
1913: 'Double White Killarney' (HT)

Burbank, Luther
Santa Rosa, California, U.S.A.
1893: 'Improved Rainbow' (T)
1899: 'Santa Rosa' (T)
1900: 'Burbank' (T)

California Nursery Company
Niles, California, U.S.A.
1890: 'Bella' (T), 'Belle de Normandy' (HP), 'Souvenir de Mme. Lambard' (T)
1895: 'Senator McNaughton' (T)
1905: 'California' (HP), 'Mrs. John McLaren' (HP), 'True Friend' (T)
1906: 'Mme. Therese Roswell' (T)
1911: 'Niles Cochet' (T)

Cant, Benjamin R.
Colchester, England
1875: 'Prince Arthur' (HP)
1901: 'Ben Cant' (HP), 'Mrs. B.R. Cant' (T)
1904: 'Maharajah' (HP)
1914: 'Augustus Hartmann' (HT)
1915: 'Cupid' (Cl. HT)
1916: 'Colcestria' (Cl. HT)
1918: 'Golden Ophelia' (HT)
1921: 'Mrs. Oakley Fisher' (HT)
1926: 'Cecil' (HT)

Cant, Frank
Colchester, England
1902: 'Lady Roberts' (T)
1924: 'Henry Nevard' (HP)

Cayeux, Henri
Lisbon, Portugal
1905: 'Belle Portugaise' (HGig)
1909: 'Étoile de Portugal' (HGig)

Chambard, C.
Lyon, France
1911: 'Mme. C. Chambard' (HT)
1915: 'Louise Cretté' (HP), 'Marguerite Guillard' (HP), 'Mlle. Argentine Cramon' (HT)
1920: 'Souvenir de Claudius Denoyel' (Cl. HT)

Chaplin Bros.
Waltham Cross, England
1921: 'Innocence' (HT)
1929: 'Climbing Mrs. Henry Morse' (HT)
1931: 'Crimson Conquest' (Cl. HT)
1932: 'Baby Alberic' (Pol)

Chauvry, J.-B.
Bordeaux, France
1891: 'Mlle. Berthe Clavel' (B)
1896: 'Raoul Chauvry' (T)
1897: 'Mme. Auguste Rodrigues' (HB), 'Mme. E. Souffrain' (N)
1898: 'Ma Petite Andrée' (Pol)
1899: 'Mme. Gaston Annouilh' (N)
1900: 'Oscar Chauvry' (N)
1901: 'Climbing Mme. Caroline Testout' (HT)

Chédane-Guinoisseau
Angers, France

1875: 'Duc de Montpensier' (HP)
1880: 'Mme. Chédane-Guinoisseau' (T)
1895: 'Mlle. Marie-Thérèse Devansaye' (B), 'Mme. Verrier-Cachet' (HP), 'Souvenir de Bertrand Guinoisseau' (HP)
1900: 'Souvenir de Mme. Chédane-Guinoisseau' (HP)
1906: 'Ami Martin' (HP), 'Mlle. Renée Denis' (HP)
1907: 'Gloire de Chédane-Guinoisseau' (HP), 'Rouge Angevin' (HP)

Chenault, R.
Orléans, France

1930: 'Purpurea' (Ch)
1937: 'Jean Mermoz' (Pol)

Cherpin, Jean
Lyon, France

1853: 'Marguerite Lecureaux' (HP)
1865: 'Béatrix' (B)
1873: 'Sanglant' (Ch)

Clark, Alister
Bulla, Australia

1918: 'Sunny South' (HT)
1919: 'Australia Felix' (HT), 'Black Boy' (Cl. HT), 'Queen of Hearts' (Cl. HT)
1922: 'Flying Colours' (HGig), 'Kitty Kininmonth' (HGig), 'Scorcher' (Cl. HT)
1923: 'Cherubim' (N)
1924: 'Lorraine Lee' (HGig), 'Sunday Best' (Cl. HP)
1925: 'Milkmaid' (N)
1927: 'Climbing Cracker' (HGig)

1932: 'Doris Downes' (HGig)
1935: 'Glory of California' (HGig)
1936: 'Baxter Beauty' (T)
1937: 'Nancy Hayward' (HGig)
1941: 'Pennant' (HGig)

Cochet père (Pierre)
Grisy-Suisnes, France
1824: 'Bougainville' (N)
1850: 'Scipion Cochet' (B)
1855: 'Arthur de Sansal' (HP)

Cochet Bros. (Scipion & Pierre fils)
Grisy-Suisnes, France
1855: 'Souvenir de la Reine d'Angleterre'

Cochet-Aubin
Grisy-Suisnes, France
1866: 'Mlle. Berthe Lévêque' (HP)

Cochet, Scipion
Grisy-Suisnes, France
1869: 'Souvenir de Mme. Hennecart' (HP)
1887: 'Mme. Philémon Cochet' (T)
1891: 'Baronne G. de Noirmont' (HT), 'Mme. Pierre Cochet' (N)
1892: 'Maman Cochet' (T)
1893: 'Marie Robert' (N)

Cochet, Pierre (fils)
Grisy-Suisnes, France
1895: 'Philémon Cochet' (B)
1898: 'Ernest Morel' (HP)

Cocker (James) and Sons
Aberdeen, Scotland
1892: 'Duchess of Fife' (HP)
1899: 'Mrs. Cocker' (HP)

Conard & Jones Co.
West Grove, Pennsylvania, U.S.A.
1898: 'Eugene Jardine' (N), 'Little Gem' (Pol), 'Mme. Bessemer' (HT), 'Palo Alto' (T), 'Peach Blossom' (T), 'Rosa Mundi' (T)
1902: 'Belle d'Orléans' (N)
1903: 'Henry Irving' (HP)
1907: 'Canadian Belle' (T)
1909: 'Climbing Mosella' (Pol), 'Kaiserin Goldifolia' (HT)

Cook, Anthony
Baltimore, Maryland, U.S.A.
1855: 'Cornelia Cook' (T)

Cook (John) & Son
Baltimore, Maryland, U.S.A.
1886: 'American Beauty' (HP)
1888: 'Annie Cook' (T), 'Souvenir of Wootton' (HT)
1889: 'Marion Dingee' (T)
1896: 'White Maman Cochet' (T)
1898: 'Mrs. Robert Garrett' (HT)
1904: 'Cardinal' (HT)
1908: 'Radiance' (HT)

Coquereau
Maître-École, Angers, France
1832: 'Cramoisi Supérieur' (Ch)

1843: 'Chromatella' (N)

Corbœuf-Marsault
Orléans, France
1890: 'Mlle. Madeleine Delaroche' (N)
1894: 'Mme. Marguerite Marsault' (HP), 'Climbing White Pet' (Pol)
1900: 'Mme. Charles Montigny' (HP), 'Mme. Petit' (HP)
1901: 'Jeanne Corbœuf' (Cl. HT)
1907: 'Dr. Ricaud' (Pol)
1910: 'Mlle. Marcelle Gaugin' (Pol)

Couturier fils/Couturier-Mention
Paris?, France
1854: 'Mme. Vidot' (HP)
1885: 'Mme. Couturier-Mention' (Cl. Ch)

Cranston, John
King's Acre, England
1874: 'Climbing Jules Margottin' (HP), 'Crimson Bedder' (HP)
1875: 'Sir Garnet Wolseley' (HP)

Croibier (Jean) & Son
Lyon, France
1901: 'Mme. Marie Croibier' (HT)
1908: 'Commandeur Jules Gravereaux' (HP)
1910: 'Mme. Jules Bouché' (HT)
1913: 'Candeur Lyonnaise' (HP)
1927: 'Lindbergh' (Pol)
1937: 'Christobel' (HT)

Curtis, Sanford, & Co.
Torquay, England
1841: 'Climbing Aimée Vibert' (N)
1872: 'Bessie Johnson' (HP)
1898: 'Mrs. F.W. Sanford' (HP)

Damaizin, Frédéric
Lyon, France
1856: 'Claudia Augusta' (N)
1858: 'Bouquet de Marie' (HP), 'Mme. Damaizin' (T)
1862: 'Mme. Crespin' (HP)
1864: 'Mme. Charles' (T)
1865: 'Abel Grand' (HP)
1867: 'Général Barral' (HP)
1869: 'Marie de St.-Jean' (HP)
1873: 'Étienne Dubois' (HP)
1874: 'La Rosière' (HP)

Dauvesse, D.
Orléans, France
1852: 'Velouté d'Orléans' (B)
1854: 'Panachée d'Orléans' (HP)

De Ruiter, G.
Hazerswoude, The Netherlands
1929: 'Gloria Mundi' (Pol), 'Paris' (Pol), 'Sparkler' (Pol)
1932: 'Cameo' (Pol), 'Gloire du Midi' (Pol)
1954: 'Alberich' (Pol), 'Degenhard' (Pol), 'Eberwein' (Pol)
1955: 'Balduin' (Pol), 'Bertram' (Pol)
1956: 'Burkhard' (Pol)

de Sansal, Arthur
Farcy-les-Lys, France
1868: 'Marquise de Gibot' (HP)
1869: 'Général de la Martinière' (HP), 'Miranda' (DP)

de Vergnies
France
1824: 'De Vergnies' (HCh)
1830: 'Belle Violette' (HCh)

Delbard-Chabert
Paris, France
1965: 'Milrose' (Pol)
1979: 'Casque d'Or' (Pol)

Descemet, Jean
St.-Denis, France
1810: 'Beau Carmin' (Ch)
1814: 'Venusta' (DP)
1815: 'Jeune Henry' (DP)

Desprez
Yèbles, France
1830: 'Desprez à Fleur Jaune' (N)
1831: 'Charles Desprez' (B), 'Mme. Desprez' (B)
1835: 'Mme. Desprez' (Ch)
1838: 'Bengale Sanguinaire' (Ch), 'St. Priest de Breuze' (Ch)
1840: 'Marquise Boccella' (DP)
1842: 'Baronne Prévost' (HP), 'Comice de Seine-et-Marne' (B)
1849: 'Caroline de Sansal' (HP)

Dickerson, Brent C.
Los Alamitos, California, U.S.A.
2001: 'Charles XII' (B), 'Papa Vibert' (DP)

Dickson, Alexander
Hawlmark, Newtownards, Ireland
1887: 'Earl of Dufferin' (HP), 'Lady Helen Stewart' (HP), 'Miss Ethel Brownlow' (T)
1888: 'Caroline d'Arden' (HP), 'Lady Castlereagh' (T)
1889: 'Lady Arthur Hill' (HP), 'Mrs. James Wilson' (T)
1890: 'Jeannie Dickson' (HP)
1891: 'Margaret Dickson' (HP)
1893: 'Marchioness of Londonderry' (HP)
1894: 'Mrs. R.G. Sharman-Crawford' (HP)
1895: 'Helen Keller' (HP), 'Kathleen' (HT), 'Marjorie' (HT), 'Mavourneen' (HT), 'Mrs. W.J. Grant' (HT), 'Sheila' (HT)
1896: 'Tom Wood' (HP)
1897: 'Climbing Kaiserin Auguste Viktoria' (HT), 'Countess of Caledon' (HT), 'Miss Ethel Richardson' (HP), 'Robert Duncan' (HP)
1898: 'Ards Rover' (Cl. HP), 'Beryl' (T), 'Meta' (T), 'Muriel Grahame' (T)
1899: 'Killarney' (HT), 'Mrs. Edward Mawley' (T), 'Shandon' (HT)
1900: 'Bessie Brown' (HT), 'Irish Beauty' (Cl. HT), 'Irish Glory' (HT), 'Irish Modesty' (HT), 'Lady Clanmorris' (HT), 'Lady Mary Corry' (T), 'Liberty' (HT), 'Rosslyn' (HP), 'Ulster' (HP)
1901: 'Gladys Harkness' (HT), 'Mildred Grant' (HT)
1902: 'Mamie' (HT)
1903: 'Gertrude' (HT)
1904: 'Dean Hole' (HT), 'Irish Brightness' (HT), 'Lady Ashtown' (HT)
1905: 'Betty' (HT), 'Hugh Watson' (HP), 'Irish Elegance' (HT), 'M.H. Walsh' (HP)
1906: 'Charles J. Graham' (HT), 'Lena' (T), 'Mrs. Myles Kennedy' (T)

1907: 'Avoca' (HT), 'Harry Kirk' (T), 'Souvenir of Stella Gray' (T), 'W.E. Lippiatt' (HT)
1908: 'Ards Rambler' (Cl. HT), 'Molly Sharman-Crawford' (T), 'Nita Weldon' (T)
1910: 'Miss Alice de Rothschild' (T), 'Mrs. Cynthia Forde' (HT), 'Mrs. Foley-Hobbs' (T), 'Mrs. Hubert Taylor' (T)
1911: 'Alexander Hill Gray' (T)
1912: 'Climbing Richmond' (HT), 'George Dickson' (HP), 'Mrs. Herbert Hawksworth' (T)
1913: 'Irish Fireflame' (HT)
1914: 'Killarney Brilliant' (HT), 'Lady Plymouth' (T), 'Mrs. S.T. Wright' (T)
1916: 'Climbing Irish Fireflame' (HT)
1917: 'K. of K.' (HT), 'Kootenay' (HT)
1919: 'Kathleen Harrop' (B)
1920: 'Climbing Ophelia' (HT)
1922: 'Climbing Mrs. Aaron Ward' (HT)
1926: 'Dame Edith Helen' (HT)

Dickson, Hugh
Belfast, Ireland
1905: 'Hugh Dickson' (HP), 'J.B. Clark' (HP)
1907: 'Lady Overtoun' (HP)
1913: 'Coronation' (HP)
1923: 'Climbing General MacArthur' (HT)

Dingee-Conard
West Grove, Pennsylvania, U.S.A.
1889: 'The Queen' (T)
1890: 'Pearl Rivers' (T)
1891: 'Henry M. Stanley' (T), 'Maud Little', 'Mrs. Jessie Fremont' (T)
1894: 'Virginia' (T)

1896: 'Pink Soupert' (Pol), 'Princess Bonnie' (T)
1897: 'Climbing Bridesmaid' (T), 'Coronet' (HT)
1898: 'Climbing Marie Guillot' (T)
1901: 'Victory Rose' (HP)
1902: 'Climbing Clotilde Soupert' (Pol)
1908: 'Primrose' (T)
1912: 'Number 27' (T)
1920: 'Climbing Rosemary' (HT)

Dot, Pedro
Barcelona, Spain
1926: 'Apeles Mestres' (Cl. HP)
1929: 'Isabel Llorach' (HP)
1933: 'Nuria de Recolons' (HP)
1948: 'Granate' (Ch)
1950: 'Rosada' (Ch)

Drögemüller, Heinrich
Neuhauss, Hanover, Germany
1887: 'Fürst Bismarck' (N), 'Fürstin Bismarck' (Cl. HT), 'Kaiser Wilhelm der Siegreiche' (Cl. T)
1889: 'Kaiserin Friedrich' (Cl. T)
1894: 'Emin Pascha' (HT)

Duboc fils
Rouen, France
1892: 'Mme. Louis Ricard' (HP)
1894: 'Mlle. Honorine Duboc' (HP)

Dubreuil, Francis
Lyon, France
1884: 'Amiral Courbet' (HP)

1885: 'Floribunda' (Pol), 'Marquise de Vivens' (T)
1886: 'Attraction' (HT), 'Duchesse de Bragance' (T)
1887: 'Louis Lille' (HP), 'Princesse de Sagan' (Ch)
1888: 'Président Dutailly' (DP)
1893: 'Graziella' (T), 'Perle de Feu' (T)
1894: 'Francis Dubreuil' (T)
1895: 'Panachée de Lyon' (HP), 'Princesse de Venosa' (T)
1896: 'Général Billot' (T), 'Perle des Rouges' (Pol)
1898: 'Jean Bach Sisley' (Ch)
1899: 'Dr. Cazeneuve' (HT)
1900: 'Ami Charmet' (HP)
1903: 'Mme. Martignier' (Cl. T)
1904: 'Crépuscule' (N)
1906: 'Bébé Fleuri' (Ch), 'Sarah Bernhardt' (Cl. HT)
1909: 'Cyclope' (Pol)
1910: 'Laure de Broglie' (Ch), 'Petite Marcelle' (Pol)
1911: 'Merveille des Rouges' (Pol)

Ducher, Jean-Claude
Lyon, France
1853: 'Alphonse de Lamartine' (HP)
1854: 'Louise de Savoie' (T)
1858: 'Edith de Murat' (B)
1865: 'Gloire de Ducher' (HP), 'Louis Noisette' (HP), 'Nardy Frères' (HP)
1866: 'Mlle. Madeleine Nonin' (HP), 'Ville de Lyon' (HP)
1867: 'Président Willermoz' (HP)
1868: 'La Tulipe' (T)
1869: 'Chamoïs' (T), 'Ducher' (Ch), 'Rêve d'Or' (N)
1870: 'Coquette de Lyon' (T), 'Hortensia' (T), 'Victor Pulliat' (T)
1871: 'La Nankeen' (T), 'Marie Van Houtte' (T)

1872: 'Amazone' (T), 'Anna Olivier' (T), 'Bouquet d'Or' (N), 'Marquisette' (Ch), 'Perle de Lyon' (T), 'Vallée de Chamonix' (T)
1873: 'Aureus' (T), 'Helvetia' (T), 'Mont Rosa' (T)

Widow Ducher
Lyon, France
1874: 'Jean Ducher' (T), 'Mme. Devoucoux' (T)
1875: 'Maréchal Robert' (T)
1876: 'Mme. Welche' (T), 'Souvenir de George Sand' (T)
1877: 'Louis Richard' (T), 'Mme. Maurice Kuppenheim (T), 'Souvenir de Marie Detrey' (T), 'Triomphe de Milan' (T)
1878: 'Innocente Pirola' (T), 'William Allen Richardson' (N)
1879: 'Jean Lorthois' (HT), 'Jules Finger' (T), 'Mme. Louis Henry' (N)
1880: 'Mlle. Cécile Brunner' (Pol)

Ducher "Children and Successors"
Lyon, France
1881: 'Climbing Captain Christy' (HT), 'Ernest Prince' (HP), 'François Olin' (HP)

Ducher fils (Antoine)
Lyon, France
1888: 'Adèle de Bellabre' (T)
1889: 'Souvenir du Rosiériste Gonod' (HP)

Dupuy-Jamain
Paris, France
1850: 'Comte Odart' (HP)
1868: 'Dupuy-Jamain' (HP)

Duval, Charles
Montmorency, France
1832: 'Louis-Philippe I' (DP)
1840: 'Comtesse de Lacépède' (HCh)
1841: 'Charles Duval' (HB)
1846: 'Jenny' (HCh)

Duval, Hippolyte
Montmorency, France
1879: 'Alsace-Lorraine' (HP), 'Monsieur Alexandre Pelletier' (B), 'Vincent-Hippolyte Duval' (HP)

Easlea, Walter
Leigh-on-Sea, England
1910: 'Juliet' (HP)
1919: 'Lulu' (HT)
1927: 'Everest' (HP)

Ellwanger (Henry B.) & Barry
Rochester, New York, U.S.A.
1884: 'Rosalie' (T)
1885: 'Marshall P. Wilder' (HP)

Elsa von Württemberg, Herzogin
Württemberg, Germany
1929: 'Pfaffstädt' (HP), 'Prinzessin Elsa zu Schaumburg-Lippe' (HP)
1934: 'Prinz Max zu Schaumburg-Lippe' (HP)

Faudon
St.-Didier-au-Mont-d'Or, France
1868: 'Jeanne Sury' (HP)
1869: 'Hippolyte Jamain' (HP)

Felberg-Leclerc, Walter
Trier, Germany
1913: 'Hofgärtner Kalb' (B)
1925: 'Felbergs Rosa Druschki' (HP)
1927: 'Frau Dr. Schricker' (B)

Fontaine, François
Clamart, France
1852: 'Prince Albert' (B)
1854: 'Duchesse de Cambacérès' (HP)
1857: 'Louise d'Autriche' (HP)
1859: 'Mme. Charles Crapelet' (HP), 'Montebello' (HP)
1861: 'Mlle. Léonie Persin' (HP), 'Reine d'Espagne' (HP)
1863: 'Mme. Doré' (B)
1865: 'Mlle. Marie Rady' (HP)
1868: 'Mme. Lierval' (HP), 'Vicomte Maison' (HP)
1874: 'Souvenir de Mère Fontaine' (N)
1877: 'Angèle Fontaine' (HP)
1878: 'Édouard Fontaine' (HP)
1879: 'Souvenir d'Aline Fontaine' (HP)
1882: 'Victoire Fontaine' (B)
1884: 'Desirée Fontaine' (HP)

Franceschi-Fenzi, Dr.
Santa Barbara, California, U.S.A.
1930: 'Montarioso' (HGig), 'Montecito' (HGig)
uncertain date: 'Madeleine Lemoine' (HGig)

Frettingham
Beeston?, England
1882: 'Beauty of Beeston' (HP)
1884: 'Lord Frederic Cavendish' (HP)

Gamon, André
Lyon, France
1892: 'Étoile de Mai' (Pol)
1900: 'Comte Adédé de Foras' (T)
1902: 'Belle Panachée' (T), 'Reine Carola de Saxe' (HT)
1903: 'Mlle. Blanche Martignat' (T)
1905: 'Mme. Gamon' (T)
1908: 'Alix Roussel' (T)
1911: 'Monsieur Fraissenon' (HT)

Garçon
Rouen, France
1871: 'Mme. Hippolyte Jamain' (HP)
1875: 'Triomphe de France' (HP)
1877: 'Boïldieu' (HP)
1878: 'Monsieur le Préfet Limbourg' (HP)
1880: 'Mme. Isaac Pereire' (B)
1882: 'Étendard de Jeanne d'Arc' (N)
1893: 'Mme. Edmond Laporte' (B)

Gautreau, Victor
Brie-Comte-Robert, France
1865: 'Camille Bernardin' (HP), 'Denis Hélye' (HP)
1867: 'Mlle. Élise Chabrier' (HP), 'Vicomtesse de Vezins' (HP)
1869: 'Mme. la Générale Decaen' (HP)
1873: 'Souvenir de Spa' (HP)
1879: 'Mlle. Jules Grévy' (HP)

Geduldig, Philipp
Aachen, Germany
1907: 'Mme. Jean Everaerts' (HP)

1909: 'Gruss an Aachen' (HT)
1914: 'Pæonia' (HP)

Geschwind, Rudolf
Karpona, Hungary
1867: 'Dr. Hurta' (HP)
1886: 'Erinnerung an Brod' (HP)
1887: 'Cæcilie Scharsach' (HP), 'Meteor' (N), 'Rotkäppchen' (Pol), 'Tartarus' (HP)
1889: 'Herzblättchen' (Pol), 'Marie Dermar' (B), 'Zigeunerblut' (B)
1890: 'Anna Scharsach' (HP), 'Antonie Schurz' (HP), 'Astra' (HT), 'Chloris' (HT), 'Picotte' (Pol)
1892: 'Erinnerung an Schloss Scharfenstein' (HT)
1897: 'Gruss an Teplitz' (B)
1900: 'Mme. Eugène E. Marlitt' (B)
1902: 'Julius Fabianics de Misefa' (T)
1909: 'Parkzierde' (B), 'Zigeunerknabe' (HB)
1916: 'Geschwind's Gorgeous' (Cl. HT)

Godard, Antoine
Lyon, France
1888: 'Marie-Thèse Dubourg' (N)
1889: 'Mlle. Geneviève Godard' (Cl. T), 'Souvenir du Dr. Passot' (T)
1890: 'Antoinette Durieu' (T), 'Mme. Creux' (N)
1892: 'Mlle. Marie Gaze' (N)
1893: 'Souvenir de Geneviève Godard' (T)
1894: 'Mme. Louis Blanchet' (N)
1895: 'Mme. Tony Baboud' (HT)
1898: 'Mlle. Jeanne Philippe' (T)
1900: 'Mme. Jean Favre' (HT)
1901: 'Marquise de Querhoënt' (T), 'Mme. Auguste Choutet' (Cl. HT)
1902: 'Souvenir de McKinley'

Gonod, J.-M.
Lyon, France
1864: 'Achille Gonod' (HP)
1865: 'Mme. Fillion' (HP)
1867: 'Souvenir de Mme. de Corval' (HP)
1868: 'Mme. Clert' (HP)
1871: 'Monsieur Jean Cordier' (HP)
1876: 'Mme. Maurice Rivoire' (HP), 'Monsieur Fillion' (HP)
1878: 'Princesse Marie Dolgorouky' (HP)
1881: 'Beauté de l'Europe' (N)
1882: 'Adélaïde de Maynot' (HP), 'Malmaison Rouge' (B)
1883: 'Souvenir de Léon Gambetta' (HP)
1884: 'Souvenir de l'Ami Labruyère' (HP)
1886: 'Louis Rollet' (HP)
1887: 'Louis Donadine' (HP)

Good & Reese Co.
Springfield, Ohio, U.S.A.
1896: 'General Robert E. Lee' (T)
1899: 'Frances E. Willard' (T)
1903: 'Gainesborough' (Cl. HT)
1906: 'Helen Good' (T)

Goubault, Maurice
Angers, France
1839: 'Goubault' (T)
1841: 'Ophirie' (N)

Grandes Roseraies du Val de la Loire
Orléans, France
1913: 'Radium' (Pol)
1922: 'Denise Cassegrain' (Pol)

Granger, Louis-Xavier
Grisy-Suisnes, France
1854: 'Mme. de Trotter' (HP)
1857: 'Reine de Danemark' (HP)
1860: 'Général Washington' (HP), 'Robert de Brie' (HP)
1861: 'Baronne de Noirmont' (B), 'Maurice Bernardin' (HP)
1862: 'Comtesse de Polignac' (HP), 'Président Lincoln' (HP)
1864: 'Duc de Wellington' (HP)
1869: 'Clémence Raoux' (HP)

Granger, Théophile
Grisy-Suisnes, France
1880: 'Souvenir du Président Porcher' (HP)

Gravereaux, Jules
Roseraie de l'Haÿ, l'Haÿ, France
1912: 'Madeleine Orosdy' (Pol)
1913: 'Maria Star' (T)
1915: 'Petite Françoise' (Pol)

Grootendorst (F.J.) & Sons
Boskoop, The Netherlands
1846: 'Sneprincesse' (Pol)
1949: 'Muttertag' (Pol)
1956: 'Orange Morsdag' (Pol)

Guérin, Modeste
Angers, France
1829: 'Caroline' (T), 'Malton' (HCh)
1833: 'Gloire de Guérin' (HP)
1834: 'Louis-Philippe' (Ch)
1855: 'Mme. de Vatry' (T)

Guillot père (Laurent)
Lyon, France
1844: 'Mme. Bravy' (T)
1847: 'Duchesse de Thuringe' (B)
1851: 'Souvenir de l'Exposition de Londres' (B)
1852: 'Canari' (T), 'Elise Flory' (Ch), 'Réveil' (B), 'Souvenir de Leveson-Gower' (HP)
1854: 'Lord Raglan' (HP)
1858: 'Comtesse de Barbantane' (B)
1859: 'Baron G.-B. Gonella' (B), 'Louis Gulino' (HP), 'Monsieur Gourdault' (B), 'Sénateur Vaïsse' (HP), 'Victor-Emmanuel' (HP)
1862: 'Emotion' (B)
1863: 'Pavillon de Pregny' (N)
1864: 'Triomphe de la Terre des Roses' (HP)
1867: 'Mme. Noman' (HP)
1868: 'Victor le Bihan' (HP)
1869: 'Comtesse d'Oxford' (HP), 'Élisa Boëlle' (HP)

Guillot fils (Jean-Baptiste)
Lyon, France
1858: 'Mme. Falcot' (T)
1859: 'Louis XIV' (HP), 'Mlle. Eugénie Verdier' (HP)
1860: 'Catherine Guillot' (B)
1863: 'Eugène Verdier' (HP), 'Paul de la Meilleraye' (HP)
1864: 'Abbé Berlèze' (HP)
1865: 'Joséphine de Beauharnais' (HP)
1866: 'Horace Vernet' (HP), 'Mme. Margottin' (T)
1867: 'La France' (B)
1868: 'Adrienne Christophle' (Cl. T), 'Marie Sisley' (T), 'Mme. Céline Noirey' (T)
1869: 'Catherine Mermet' (T)

1871: 'Abbé Bramerel' (HP), 'Catherine Bonnard' (HCh), 'Comtesse de Nadaillac' (T), 'Mme. Camille' (T)
1872: 'Marie Accary' (N)
1873: 'Mme. Claire Carnot' (N)
1874: 'Aline Sisley' (T), 'Marie Guillot' (T)
1875: 'Anne-Marie Côte' (N), 'Pâquerette' (Pol)
1878: 'Mlle. Blanche Durrschmidt' (T)
1879: 'Mme. Angèle Jacquier' (T), 'Pierre Guillot' (HT)
1881: 'Étoile de Lyon' (T), 'Mignonette' (Pol), 'Mme. Cusin' (T), 'Monsieur Jules Monges' (HP)
1882: 'Honourable Edith Gofford' (T), 'Jeanne Abel' (T)
1883: 'Mme. de Watteville' (T)
1884: 'Gloire Lyonnaise' (HP)

Guillot & fils
Lyon, France
1884: 'Souvenir de Gabrielle Drevet' (T)
1885: 'Comtesse de Frigneuse' (T)
1886: 'Luciole' (T), 'Mme. Joseph Desbois' (HT)
1887: 'Gloire des Polyantha' (Pol), 'Mme. Hoste' (T), 'Mme. Laurette Messimy' (Ch)
1888: 'Ernest Metz' (T), 'Mme. Pierre Guillot' (T)
1889: 'J.-B. Varonne' (T), 'Mme. Renahy' (HP), 'Souvenir de François Gaulain' (T)
1890: 'Miss Wenn' (T), 'Mlle. Christine de Noué' (T)
1891: 'Augustine Halem' (HT)

Guillot, Pierre
Lyon, France
1893: 'Mme. Édouard Helfenbein' (T), 'Mme. Jules Finger' (HT)
1894: 'Charlotte Gillemot' (HT), 'Mme. Eugène Résal' (Ch)

1895: 'Irène Watts' (Ch), 'Souvenir d'Auguste Métral' (HT), 'Souvenir de Catherine Guillot' (Ch)
1896: 'Émilie Gonin' (T), 'Mme. Jules Grolez' (HT), 'Souvenir de Jeanne Cabaud' (T)
1897: 'Souvenir de J.-B. Guillot' (Ch)
1898: 'Margherita di Simone' (T)
1900: 'François Crousse' (Cl. T)
1902: 'Comtesse du Caÿla' (Ch)
1904: 'Climbing Le Vésuve' (Ch), 'Mme. Léon Pain' (HT)
1907: 'Mme. P. Euler' (HT)

Guillot, Marc
St.-Priest, Isère, France
1929: 'Président Briand' (HP)

Guinoisseau (Bertrand)-Flon
Angers, France
1854: 'Lucullus' (Ch)
1858: 'Empereur du Maroc' (HP)
1873: 'Comtesse de Bresson' (HP)

Guinoisseau fils
Angers, France
1889: 'Mlle. Augustine Guinoisseau' (HT)

Hall, Dr. J. Campbell
Rowantree House, Monaghan, Ireland
1914: 'Mrs. Campbell Hall' (T)
1915: 'Miss Annie Crawford' (HP)

Hardy, Alexandre
Paris, France

1829: 'Hyménée' (T)
1831: 'Félicité Hardy' (DP)
1835: 'Bon Silène' (T), 'Gigantesque' (T), 'Ohl' (HCh), 'Triomphe du Luxembourg' (T)
1836: 'Cels Multiflore' (T)
1837: 'Eugène de Beauharnais' (Ch)
1840: 'Ornement du Luxembourg' (HP)
1842: 'Prince Charles' (HB)
1847: 'Pumila Alba' (N)

Harkness & Company
Hitchin, England

1894: 'Mrs. Harkness' (HP)
1897: 'Merrie England' (HP)
1979: 'Fairy Changeling' (Pol), 'Fairy Maid' (Pol), 'Fairy Prince' (Pol), 'Fairyland' (Pol)
1980: 'Fairy Ring' (Pol)
1982: 'Fairy Damsel' (Pol)

Heers, C.W.
Manly, Australia

1930: 'The Allies' (Pol)
1949: 'Pacific Triumph' (Pol)

Henderson, Peter
New York City, New York, U.S.A.

1879: 'Little White Pet' (Pol), 'Setina' (Cl. B)
1883: 'Sunset' (T)
1893: 'Climbing La France' (B)

Hill, E.G.
Richmond, Indiana, U.S.A.
1899: 'Climbing Mrs. W.J. Grant' (HT)
1905: 'General MacArthur' (HT), 'Richmond' (HT)
1907: 'Indiana' (Cl. HT)
1916: 'Columbia' (HT)
1918: 'Mme. Butterfly' (HT)

Hinner, Wilhelm
Trier, Germany
1901: 'Pharisäer' (HT)
1905: 'Andenken an Moritz von Frölich' (HT)
1910: 'Georg Arends' (HP)
1911: 'Heinrich Münch' (HP)

Hjort, Samuel
Thomasville, Georgia, U.S.A.
1940: 'Climbing Marie Van Houtte' (T)
1960: 'Climbing Mrs. B.R. Cant' (T)

Hobbies Ltd.
Dereham, England
1912: 'Lemon Queen' (Cl. HT)
1913: 'Effective' (Cl. HT)

Hoopes, Bro. & Thomas Co.
West Chester, Pennsylvania, U.S.A.
1909: 'Climbing American Beauty' (Cl.)
1917: 'Purity' (Cl.)

Hosp, F.P.
Riverside, California, U.S.A.
1894: 'Climbing Mlle. Cécile Brunner' (Pol)
1898: 'Climbing Papa Gontier' (T)

Jacques, Antoine A.
Neuilly, France
1821: 'Burboniana' (B)
1829: 'Athalin' (HB)
1831: 'Fimbriata à Pétales Frangés' (Ch)

Jamain, Hippolyte
Paris, France
1851: 'Dr. Jamain' (HP)
1861: 'Mme. Boutin' (HP)
1872: 'Antonine Verdier' (HT)
1873: 'Marguerite Jamain' (HP), 'Mme. Bernutz' (HP)
1875: 'Colonel de Sansal' (HP)
1876: 'Berthe du Mesnil de Mont Chauveau' (HP)
1877: 'Duchesse d'Ossuna' (HP), 'Mme. Thévenot' (HP)
1880: 'Souvenir de Mme. Alfred Vy' (HP)

Jantet
France
1816: 'Cerise Éclatante' (HCh), 'La Philippine' (HCh)

Kersbergen
Boskoop, The Netherlands
1927: 'Kersbergen' (Pol)
1930: 'Paul Crampel' (Pol)

Ketten Bros.
Luxembourg
1897: 'Dr. Pouleur' (T), 'La Proserpine' (Pol), 'Marguerite Ketten (T)
1898: 'F.L. Segers' (T), 'Princesse Étienne de Croy' (T)
1900: 'Sisi Ketten' (Pol)
1901: 'Capitaine Millet' (T), 'Mlle. Marthe Cahuzac' (Pol)
1902: 'Edmée et Roger' (HT)
1905: 'Joseph Paquet' (T)
1911: 'Générale Marie Raiewsky' (HP)

Kiese (Hermann) & Company
Wieselbach-Erfurt, Germany
1895: 'Venus' (HP)
1912: 'Paula Clegg' (HP)
1913: 'Loreley' (Pol), 'Mikado' (Cl. HT), 'Perle' (Pol)
1915: 'Siegesperle' (Pol)
1918: 'Fürst Leopold zu Schaumburg-Lippe' (HP)
1919: 'Gruss an Weimar' (HP)
1921: 'Schön Ingeborg' (HP)
1930: 'Martin Liebau' (HP)

Kluis & Koning
Boskoop, The Netherlands
1916: 'Greta Kluis' (Pol)
1917: 'Mrs. William G. Koning' (Pol)

Kordes, Wilhelm
Sparrieshoop, Germany
1930: 'Minna' (HT)
1932: 'Druschka' (HP)
1937: 'Climbing Gruss an Aachen' (HT), 'Orange Triumph' (Pol)
1960: 'Waldfee' (HP)

Koster & Sons
Boskoop, The Netherlands
1929: 'Dick Koster' (Pol)
1931: 'Margo Koster' (Pol)

Labruyère, Eugène
Lyon, France
1872: 'Reine Victoria' (B)
1874: 'Firebrand' (HP)

Lacharme, François
Lyon, France
1844: 'Deuil de Duc d'Orléans' (B), 'Louise Peyronny' (HP)
1845: 'Cornet' (HP), 'Mme. Mélanie Willermoz' (T)
1850: 'Desgaches' (HP)
1851: 'Mère de St. Louis' (HP)
1853: 'Mme. Récamier' (HP)
1855: 'Marquis de Balbiano' (B), 'Pæonia' (HP)
1856: 'Mme. Massot' (B)
1858: 'Anna de Diesbach' (HP), 'Virginale' (HP)
1859: 'Victor Verdier' (HP)
1861: 'Charles Lefebvre' (HP), 'Louise d'Arzens' (B)
1862: 'Lady Emily Peel' (B), 'Mme. Alfred de Rougemont' (B)
1863: 'Mlle. Gabrielle de Pyeronny' (HP), 'Mme. Charles Verdier' (HP)
1865: 'Alfred Colomb' (HP), 'Baronne de Maynard' (B), 'Coquette des Blanches' (B), 'Prudence Besson' (HP), 'Souvenir du Dr. Jamain' (HP), 'Xavier Olibo' (HP)
1866: 'Thorin' (HP)
1867: 'Boule de Neige' (B), 'Coquette des Alpes' (B)
1869: 'Louis Van Houtte' (HP)
1871: 'Lyonnais' (HP)
1872: 'Mme. Lacharme' (HT), 'Perle des Blanches' (B)

1873: 'Captain Christy' (HT)
1874: 'Comtesse de Serenyi' (HP), 'Hippolyte Jamain' (HP), 'Souvenir du Baron de Semur' (HP)
1875: 'Henry Bennett' (HP), 'Jean Soupert' (HP)
1876: 'Mlle. Léonie Giessen' (HP)
1877: 'Mme. François Pittet' (B)
1878: 'Mme. Lambard' (T)
1879: 'Catherine Soupert' (HP), 'Julius Finger' (HT)
1881: 'Violette Bouyer' (HP)
1883: 'Alphonse Soupert' (HP), 'Éclair' (HP)
1885: 'Clara Cochet' (HP)

Laffay, Jean
Bellevue-Meudon, France
1825: 'Archiduc Charles' (Ch), 'Bengale d'Automne' (Ch), 'Chévrier' (HCh), 'Laffay' (Ch), 'Le Vésuve' (Ch), 'La Nubienne' (HCh), 'Roi de Siam' (T)
1826: 'Duchesse de Montebello' (HN), 'La Pudeur' (HB)
1827: 'Catherine II' (T), 'Darius' (Ch)
1830: 'Brennus' (HB)
1831: 'Triomphe de Laffay' (HN)
1832: 'Fabvier' (Ch), 'Mrs. Bosanquet' (B)
1834: 'Belle Hébé' (Ch), 'Bouquet Tout Fait' (N)
1835: 'Céline' (HB), 'Duchesse de Kent' (Ch), 'Général Allard' (HCh), 'Napoléon' (Ch), 'Quatre Saisons Blanc Mousseux' (DP)
1837: 'Prince Albert' (HP), 'Princesse Hélène' (HP)
1838: 'Great Western' (HB), 'William Jesse' (HB)
1839: 'Comte de Paris' (HP), 'Duchesse de Sutherland' (HP), 'Mme. Laffay' (HP)
1840: 'Coupe d'Hébé' (HB)
1841: 'Duc de Sussex' (HCh), 'Mrs. Elliot' (HP)
1842: 'Comtesse Dûchatel' (HP), 'Dr. Marx' (HP), 'Edward Jesse' (HB)

1844: 'La Reine' (HP)
1845: 'Comtesse Molé' (HP), 'Indigo' (DP), 'Mrs. Cripps' (HP), 'Ponctué' (HP)
1847: 'Julie de Krudner' (DP), 'Mathilde Jesse' (DP)
1851: 'Auguste Mie' (HP)
1852: 'Rubens' (HP), 'Sir Joseph Paxton' (B)

Lambert, Elie
Lyon, France
1882: 'Marie Remond' (T)
1886: 'Marie Lambert' (T), 'Mlle. Claudine Perreau' (T)
1890: 'Mme. Elie Lambert' (T)

Lambert & Reiter
Trier, Germany
1891: 'Kaiserin Auguste Viktoria' (HT)

Lambert, Peter
Trier, Germany
1895: 'Mosella' (Pol)
1897: 'Frau Geheimrat von Boch' (T), 'Grossherzogin Viktoria Melitta von Hessen' (HT), 'Oskar Cordel' (HP)
1898: 'Balduin' (HT), 'Papa Lambert' (HT), 'Reichsgraf E. von Kesselstatt' (T)
1899: 'Eugénie Lamesch' (Pol), 'Hofgärtendirektor Graebener' (HT), 'Leonie Lamesch' (Pol)
1901: 'Frau Karl Druschki' (HP), 'Katharina Zeimet' (Pol), 'Mme. Jean Dupuy' (T), 'Schneewittchen' (Pol)
1903: 'Freiherr von Marschall' (T), 'Gustav Grünerwald' (HT), 'Kleiner Alfred' (Pol), 'Schneekopf' (Pol)
1904: 'Frau Cecilie Walter' (Pol), 'Unermüdliche' (Ch)
1905: 'Lina Schmidt-Michel' (HT), 'Martha' (Pol)

1908: 'Frau Geheimrat Dr. Staub' (Cl. HT), 'Climbing Miniature' (Pol), 'Philipp Paulig' (HP)
1909: 'Cineraria' (Pol), 'Frau Alexander Weiss' (Pol), 'Frau Oberhofgärtner Schultze' (Pol), 'Gustel Mayer' (Pol), 'Tip-Top' (Pol)
1913: 'Leonie Lambert' (HP)
1914: 'Echo' (Pol)
1919: 'Dr. Ingomar H. Blohm' (HP)
1920: 'Adam Messerich' (B)
1921: 'Bischof Dr. Korum' (HP)
1926: 'St. Ingebert' (HP)
1929: 'Druschki Rubra' (HP)

Laperrière, Joseph
Champagne-au-Mont-d'Or, France
1898: 'Mme. Joseph Laperriére' (T)
1900: 'Mme. Antoine Rébé' (T)

Lartay, Clém.
Bordeaux, France
1850: 'Lion des Combats' (HP)
1852: 'Reine de Castille' (HP)
1860: 'Enfant de France' (HP), 'Léonie Lartay' (HP)
1861: 'Gloire de Bordeaux' (N)
1871: 'L'Ésperance' (HP)
1872: 'Belle Nanon' (B)

Laxton Bros. (Philip & Thomas)
Bedford, England
1869: 'Anny Laxton' (HP), 'Princess Louise' (HP)
1876: 'Emily Laxton' (HP), 'Empress of India' (HP), 'Marchioness of Exeter' (HP)

1879: 'Charles Darwin' (HP)
1880: 'Dr. Hogg' (HP)
1884: 'Bedford Belle' (HT)

Lédéchaux, Henri
Villecresne, France
1862: 'Mlle. Adèle Jougant' (Cl. T)
1875: 'Mme. Ferdinand Jamin' (HP)

Widow Lédéchaux
Villecresne, France
1878: 'Léon Renault' (HP)
1884: 'Comtesse Cahen d'Anvers' (HP)
1886: 'Château des Bergeries' (T)
1895: 'François Coppée' (HP)

Leenders Bros.
Tegelen, The Netherlands
1909: 'Jonkheer J.L. Mock' (HT)
1912: 'General-Superior Arnold Janssen' (HT)
1918: 'Mevrouw Boreel van Hogelander' (T)
1919: 'Mevrouw Nathalie Nypels' (Pol)
1930: 'Nypels Perfection' (Pol)
1931: 'Climbing Étoile de Hollande' (HT)
1942: 'Gruss an Aachen Superior' (HT)

Lens, Louis
Wavre-Notre-Dame, Belgium
1929: 'Climbing Columbia' (HT)
1935: 'Climbing Distinction' (Pol)

Leroy, Anatole
Angers, France
1892: 'Mme. Anatole Leroy' (HP)
1903: 'Mme. Cordier' (HP)

Levavasseur & Sons
Orléans, France
1903: 'Mme. Norbert Levavasseur' (Pol)
1907: 'Mrs. W.H. Cutbush' (Pol)
1909: 'Jeanne d'Arc' (Pol), 'Mme. Taft' (Pol), 'Orléans-Rose' (Pol)
1910: 'Eileen Loow' (Pol)
1912: 'Gloire d'Orléans' (Pol)
1913: 'Excellens' (Pol)
1918: 'Maréchal Foch' (Pol)

Lévêque, René
Ivry-sur-Seine, France
1844: 'Duchesse de Montmorency' (DP)
1847: 'Duchesse de Rohan' (DP)

Levêque, Louis
Ivry-sur-Seine, France
1864: 'John Gould Veitch' (HP), 'Mme. Elisa de Vilmorin' (HT)
1867: 'Baron Haussmann' (HP)
1868: 'Devienne-Lamy' (HP)
1869: 'Mlle. Favart' (B)
1873: 'Deuil de Dunois' (HP), 'Mme. Louis Lévêque' (HP)
1875: 'Avocat Duvivier' (HP)
1877: 'Princesse Lise Troubetzkoï' (HP)
1878: 'Alexandre Dutitre' (HP)
1879: 'Abraham Zimmermann' (HP), 'Amédée Philibert' (HP), 'Comte Horace de Choiseul' (HP), 'Mme. Élisa Tasson' (HP)

1880: 'Comte Frédéric de Thun de Hohenstein' (HP)
1881: 'Comte Adrien de Germiny' (HP), 'Comte de Flandres' (HP), 'Mme. Marthe d'Halloy' (HP)
1882: 'Baron Nathaniel de Rothschild' (HP), 'Léon Say' (HP), 'Mme. Olympe Terestchenko' (B), 'Mme. Veuve Alexandre Pommery' (HP)
1883: 'Directeur Alphand' (HP), 'Mlle. Suzanne-Marie Rodocanachi' (HP), 'Princesse Radziwill' (HP)
1884: 'Duc de Marlborough' (HP), 'Laurent de Rillé' (HP), 'Mme. Francis Buchner' (HP)
1885: 'Comtesse de Fressinet de Bellanger' (HP), 'Mme. Baulot' (HP), 'Princesse Amédée de Broglie' (HP), 'Professeur Maxime Cornu' (HP)
1886: 'A. Drawiel' (HP), 'Aly Pacha Chérif' (HP), 'Baronne de Dt.-Didier' (HP), 'Comte de Paris' (HP), 'Mme. Léon Halkin' (HP)
1887: 'Mme. Sophie Stern' (HP)
1888: 'Comtesse Branicka' (HP), 'Comtesse de Roquette-Buisson' (HP), 'Comtesse O'Gorman' (HP), 'Ferdinand Jamin' (HP), 'Victor Lemoine' (HP)
1889: 'Duchesse de Dino' (HP), 'Émile Bardiaux' (HP), 'Laforcade' (HP), 'Mme. Olga' (T), 'Mme. Thibaut' (HP)
1890: 'Belle Yvrienne' (HP), 'Mlle. Andrée Worth' (B), 'Professeur Charguereaud' (HP)
1891: 'Mme. Théodore Vernes' (HP)
1892: 'Grand-Duc Alexis' (HP), 'Impératrice Maria Feodorowna' (HP)
1894: 'Mme. Laurent Simons' (T)
1895: 'Belle Vichysoise' (N), 'Mlle. Marie-Louise Oger' (T), 'Mme. Henry Graire' (T)
1896: 'Comte Raoul Chandon' (HP), 'Comtesse Renée de Béarn' (HP)
1897: 'Baron T'Kint de Roodenbeke' (HP), 'Comte Charles d'Harcourt' (HP)
1898: 'Mme. Rose Caron' (HP), 'Souvenir d'Alexandre Hardy' (HP), 'Souvenir de Mme. Sadi Carnot' (HP)

1899: 'Souvenir de Henri Lévêque de Vilmorin' (HP)
1902: 'Vincente Peluffo' (HP)
1903: 'Empereur Nicolas II', 'Mme. Achille Fould' (T)

Levet, Antoine
Lyon, France
1866: 'Mlle. Thérèse Levet' (HP)
1869: 'Abbé Giraudier' (HP), 'Mme. Trifle' (N), 'Paul Neyron' (HP)
1870: 'Belle Lyonnaise' (N), 'Mme. Azélie Imbert' (T), 'Mme. Bérard' (N), 'Mme. Émilie Dupuy' (Cl. T), 'Paul Perras' (HB)
1871: 'François Michelon' (HP), 'Ma Capucine' (T), 'Perfection de Monplaisir' (T), 'Souvenir de Paul Neyron' (T)
1872: 'Étienne Levet' (HP), 'Henry Bennett' (T), 'Mme. Dr. Jutté' (T)
1873: 'Monsieur Étienne Dupuy' (HP)
1874: 'Antoine Mouton' (HP), 'Perle des Jardins' (T), 'Shirley Hibberd' (T)
1875: 'Mme. Marie Berton' (N)
1876: 'Mlle. Lazarine Poizeau' (T), 'Mme. Sophie Tropot' (HP), 'Souvenir de Paul Dupuy' (HCh)
1878: 'Mlle. Brigitte Viollet' (HT), 'Mme. Étienne Levet' (HT), 'Pierre Carot' (HP), 'Reine Marie Henriette' (Cl. HT)
1879: 'Mlle. Mathilde Lenaerts' (N), 'Mme. Barthélemy Levet' (T), 'Souvenir de Monsieur Faivre' (HP)
1880: 'François Levet' (HP), 'Les Fiançailles de la Princesse Stéphanie et de l'Archiduc Rodolphe' (N), 'Mme. Caro' (T)
1881: 'Mme. Crozy' (HP), 'Ulrich Brunner fils' (HP)
1882: 'Mme. Eugène Verdier' (Cl. T), 'Mme. François Bruel' (HP), 'Souvenir de Thérèse Levet' (T)
1885: 'Edmond de Biauzat' (T)
1886: 'Claudius Levet' (T), 'Mme. Honoré Defresne' (T)
1889: 'Souvenir de Monsieur Bruel' (B)

Levet, Étienne
Lyon, France
1891: 'Souvenir de Mme. Levet' (T)

Liabaud, Jean
Lyon, France
1861: 'Clémence Joigneaux' (HP), 'Mme. Clémence Joigneaux' (HP), 'Simon de St.-Jean' (HP)
1864: 'Monsieur Bonçenne' (HP)
1865: 'Jean Cherpin' (HP)
1867: 'Mme. Gabriel Luizet' (B)
1868: 'Marquise de Mortemart' (HP), 'Notaire Bonnefond' (HP)
1869: 'Baron Chaurand' (HP), 'Jules Seurre' (HP)
1871: 'Baron de Bonstetten' (HP), 'Baronne de Prailly' (HP)
1873: 'A. Bouquet' (T), 'Souvenir de la Princesse Amélie des Pays-Bas' (HP)
1875: 'Alexandre Chomer' (HP), 'Jean Liabaud' (HP)
1877: 'Mme. Gabriel Luizet' (HP)
1880: 'Mme. Montel' (HP)
1881: 'A.-M. Ampère' (HP), 'Mme. Pierre Margery' (HP)
1882: 'Alexandre Dupont' (HP), 'Mme. Marie Legrange'(HP)
1884: 'Monsieur Hoste' (HP)
1886: 'Monsieur Jules Deroudilhe' (HP)
1887: 'Mme. Alphonse Seux' (HP)
1889: 'Mlle. Marie Magat' (HP), 'Vicomte de Lauzières' (HP)
1891: 'Jeanne Masson' (HP)
1892: 'Claude Jacquet' (HP)
1893: 'Capitaine Peillon' (HP), 'Colonel Juffé' (T)
1894: 'Mme. Antoine Rivoire' (HP), 'Mme. Charles Franchet' (T)
1896: 'Mlle. Marie Achard' (HP), 'Mme. Chabanne' (HP)

Lille, Léon
Lyon-Villeurbanne, France
1893: 'Multiflora Nain Remontant' (Pol)
1897: 'Flocon de Neige' (Pol), 'Gloire de Charpennes' (Pol)
1898: 'Colibri' (Pol)
1924: 'Baby Faurax' (Pol)

Marest
Paris, France
1849: 'Comte Bobrinsky' (HP)
1855: 'Souvenir d'Elisa Vardon' (T)
1858: 'Comtesse Cécile de Chabrillant' (HP)
1868: 'Monsieur Journaux' (HP)

Margottin père (Jacques-Julien)
Bourg-la-Reine, France
1845: 'Vicomte Fritz de Cussy' (B)
1849: 'Colonel Foissy' (HP), 'Général Cavaignac' (HP)
1851: 'Général Bedeau' (HP), 'Louise Odier' (B)
1853: 'Jules Margottin' (HP), 'Mme. Domage' (HP)
1855: 'Triomphe de l'Exposition' (HP)
1857: 'Mme. Marie Van Houtte' (HP)
1858: 'Anna Alexieff' (HP)
1859: 'Duc de Magenta' (T)
1861: 'Alexandre Dumas' (HP), 'Souvenir de Comte de Cavour' (HP)
1862: 'Jean Goujon' (HP)
1863: 'Charles Margottin' (HP), 'Révérend H. D'Ombrain' (B)
1867: 'Duchesse d'Aoste' (HP)
1869: 'Charles Turner' (HP)
1871: 'Mme.de Ridder' (HP)
1878: 'Deuil du Colonel Denfert' (HP), 'Dr. Baillon' (HP)

1879: 'Comte de Mortemart' (HP), 'Gloire de Bourg-la-Reine' (HP), 'Henriette Pettit' (HP)

Margottin fils (Jules)
Pierrefitte, France
1877: 'La Saumonée' (HCh), 'Mme. Jeannine Joubert' (HB)
1903: 'Mme. Edmée Cocteau' (Cl. HT)

Mari, Antoine
Nice, France
1901: 'Dr. Félix Guyon' (T), 'Mme. Antoine Mari' (T), 'Mme. Vermorel' (T)
1904: 'Mme. Albert Bernardin' (T)

Mauget
Orléans, France
1827: 'Blanc Pur' (N), 'La Dauphine' (HB)
1834: 'Reine des Île-Bourbons' (B)

May, John M.
Summit, New Jersey, U.S.A.
1885: 'The Bride' (T)
1892: 'Francis B. Hayes' (HB)
1893: 'Oakmont' (HP)
1894: 'Mrs. W.C. Whitney' (HT)
1895: 'Mrs. J. Pierpont Morgan' (T)

May, H.B.
Summit, New Jersey, U.S.A.
1906: 'Princess Ena' (Pol)
1908: 'Climbing Liberty' (HT)

McGredy (Samuel) & Son
Portadown, Ireland

1909: 'His Majesty' (HT), 'Lady Alice Stanley' (HT), 'Mrs. Wakefield Christie-Miller' (HT)
1910: 'Mrs. Herbert Stevens' (HT)
1912: 'British Queen' (HT)
1913: 'Old Gold' (HT)
1916: 'Isobel' (HT)
1919: 'Mrs. Henry Morse' (HT)
1923: 'Vesuvius' (HT)

Merryweather (H.) & Sons
Southwell, Nottinghamshire, England

1908: 'Phyllis' (Pol)
1909: 'Jessie' (Pol)

Miellez
Esquermes, France

1835: 'Louis-Philippe' (HB)
1838: 'Elise Sauvage' (T)
1841: 'Le Pactole' (T)
1849: 'Toussaint-Louverture' (B)

Moreau, F. *(called "Louis")*
Fontenay-aux-Roses, France

1862: 'Vainqueur de Goliath' (HP)
1867: 'Lisette de Béranger' (HP)

Moreau-Robert
Angers, France

1864: 'Prince Eugène de Beauharnais' (HP)
1865: 'Souvenir du Président Lincoln' (B)
1866: 'Souvenir de Mme. Auguste Charles' (B)

1867: 'Général Désaix' (HP)
1868: 'Jacques Cartier' (DP), 'Maurice Lepelletier' (HP)
1871: 'Mme. Renard' (HP)
1872: 'Souvenir d'Adèle Launay' (B)
1874: 'Gaspard Monge' (HP), 'Ingénieur Madèlé' (HP), 'Mme. de Sévigné' (B), 'Philippe Bardet' (HP)
1877: 'Bathélemy-Joubert' (HP), 'Fontenelle' (HP), 'Mme. Roger' (HP), 'Souvenir d'Adolphe Thiers' (HP)
1878: 'Souvenir de Mme. Robert' (HP)
1879: 'Mme. Georges Vibert' (HP), 'Panachée d'Angers' (HP), 'Perle d'Angers' (B)
1880: 'Georges Moreau' (HP)
1881: 'Archiduchesse Elisabeth d'Autriche' (HP), 'Mme. Yorke' (HP), 'Monsieur Albert la Blotais' (HP)
1882: 'Joachim du Bellay' (HP)
1883: 'Boileau' (HP), 'Rembrandt' (DP)
1885: 'Mme. Lefebvre' (HP)
1887: 'Dr. Pasteur' (HT), 'Katkoff' (HP), 'L'Abondance' (N)
1889: 'La France de 89' (Cl. HT), 'Monsieur A. Maillé' (B), 'Souvenir de Grégoire Bordillon' (HP)
1890: 'Mme. Lemesle' (HP), 'Souvenir de Victor Landeau' (B)
1891: 'Souvenir du Lieutenant Bujon' (B)
1892: 'Monsieur Cordeau' (B)
1893: 'Mme. Nobécourt' (B)

Morse, Henry
Norwich, England
1920: 'Climbing Château de Clos-Vougeot' (HT), 'Westfield Star' (HT)

Müller, Dr. F.
Weingarten, Bavaria, Germany
1897: 'Marie Zahn' (HT)

1898: 'Grossherzog Ernst Ludwig von Hesse' (HT)
1920: 'Dr. Müllers Rote' (HP)
1927: 'Turnvater Jahn' (HP)

Nabonnand, Gilbert
Golfe-Juan, France

1872: 'Golfe-Juan' (HP)
1873: 'Isabelle Nabonnand' (T)
1874: 'Duchess of Edinburgh' (T)
1877: 'La Princesse Vera' (T), 'Lily Metschersky' (N), 'Mme. la Comtesse de Caserta' (T), 'Mme. Nabonnand' (T), 'Mystère' (T), 'Paul Nabonnand' (T)
1878: 'Alphonse Karr' (T), 'Général Schablikine' (T), 'Papillon' (Cl. T)
1879: 'Mlle. Franziska Krüger' (T), 'Mlle. Marie Moreau' (T), 'Mme. la Duchesse de Vallombrosa' (T), 'Mme. P. Perny' (T), 'Reine Emma des Pays-Bas' (T)
1881: 'Comtesse Alban de Villeneuve' (T), 'Mélanie Soupert' (N), 'Mme. Julie Lassen' (N), 'Mme. Marie Lavalley' (N), 'Reine Olga de Wurtemberg' (N)
1882: 'Baronne de St.-Triviers' (T), 'Blanche Nabvonnand' (T), 'Hermance Louisa de la Rive' (T), 'Mme. Crombez' (T), 'Mme. Dubroca' (T), 'Mme. Léon Février' (T), 'Papa Gontier' (T), 'Rose Nabonnand' (T), 'Souvenir de Germain de St.-Pierre' (T)
1883: 'Impératrice Marie Féodorowna de Russie' (T), 'Marie d'Orléans' (T), 'Mme. F. Brassac' (T), 'Vicomtesse de Bernis' (T)
1885: 'Camille Raoux' (T), 'Comtesse Georges de Roquette-Buisson' (N), 'Exadelphé' (T), 'Flavien Budillon' (T), 'Mlle. Suzanne Blanchet' (T), 'Reine Olga' (T)
1886: 'Bengale Nabonnand' (Ch), 'Lady Zoë Brougham' (T), 'Lordy Stanley' (T), 'Mme. Agathe Nabonnand' (T), 'Mme. la Princesse de Radziwill' (T), 'S.A.R. Mme. la Princesse de Hohenzollern, Infante de Protugal' (T)

1887: 'Bardou Job' (B), 'L'Idéal' (N), 'Mme. Claire Jaubert' (T), 'Mme. Jules Franke' (N), 'Monsieur Rosier' Cl. T)
1888: 'Baronne Henriette de Loew' (T), 'G. Nabonnand' (T), 'Mme. Rose Romarin' (Cl. T), 'Mme. Thérèse Deschamps' (T), 'Monsieur Charles de Thézillat' (T), 'Nardy' (N)
1890: 'Général D. Mertchanky' (T), 'Maurice Rouvier' (T)
1892: 'Archiduc Joseph' (T), 'Comtesse Festetics Hamilton' (T)
1894: 'Fiametta Nabonnand' (T)
1895: 'Isaac Demole' (T), 'Marie Souleau' (T), 'Mme. von Siemens' (T), 'Souvenir du Père Lalanne' (T)
1898: 'Albert Stopford' (T), 'Lucie Faure' (T), 'Lucy Carnegie' (T)
1899: 'Captain Philip Green' (T), 'Général Galliéni' (T)
1900: 'Garden Robinson' (T), 'Mrs. Reynolds Hole' (T), 'Noëlla Nabonnand' (Cl. T)
1901: 'Miss Agnes C. Sherman' (T)
1902: 'Comtesse de Noghera' (T), 'Comtesse Sophie Torby' (T), 'Lady Waterlow' (Cl. HT), 'Marguerite Gigandet' (T), 'Marie Segond' (T), 'Professeur d'André' (T)
1903: 'Alice Hamilton' (Ch), 'Anna Jung' (T), 'Comtesse Emmeline de Guigné' (T)

Nabonnand, Clément & Paul
Golfe-Juan, France
1906: 'Marguerite Desrayaux' (N)

Nabonnand, Paul
Golfe-Juan, France
1909: 'Frau O. Plegg' (B)
1916: 'Anne Laferrère' (HP), 'Mme Charles Singer' (T)
1920: 'Irène Bonnet' (Cl. HT), 'Souvenir de Gilbert Nabonnand' (T)
1922: 'Emmanuella de Mouchy' (HGig), 'Marguerite Carels' (Cl. HT), 'Rosette Delizy' T), 'Sa Majesté Gustave V' (HP)

1924: 'Lucy Thomas' (Cl. HP), 'Sénateur Amic' (HGig), 'Suzanne Carrol of Carrolton' (HP)

Nérard
Vaise, France
1838: 'Mme. Nérard' (B)
1846: 'Géant des Batailles' (HP)

Nicolas, J.H.
Newark, New York, U.S.A.
1933: 'Harmony' (HP)
1934: 'Polar Bear' (HP)

Noisette (Louis, Philippe, and Étienne)
Paris, France and Charleston, South Carolina, U.S.A.
1814: 'Blush Noisette' (N), 'Noisette de l'Inde' (N)
1829: 'Comtesse de Coutard' (HCh)
1905: 'Minnie Francis' (T)

Nonin, Auguste
Chatillon, France
1913: 'Bengali' (Ch)
1917: 'Catalunya' (B)
1923: 'Chatillon Rose' (Pol)

Oger, Pierre
Caen, France
1850: 'Souvenir d'un Frère' (B)
1852: 'Dr. Leprestre' (B)
1858: 'Orderic Vital' (HP)
1861: 'Triomphe de Caen' (HP)
1863: 'Michel-Ange' (HP)

1864: 'Belle Normande' (HP), 'La Tendresse' (HP), 'Marie Boisée' (HP)
1867: 'Safrano à Fleurs Rouges' (T)
1868: 'Marquise de Verdun' (HP)
1875: 'Arthur Oger' (HP)
1876: 'Charles Martel' (HP), 'Tancrède' (HP)
1877: 'Bicolore' (HP)
1878: 'Mme. Pierre Oger' (B)
1879: 'Jean Lelièvre' (HP)
1881: 'Gustave Thierry' (HP)
1883: 'Réveil du Printemps' (HP)

Page, C.G.
Washington, D.C., U.S.A.
1859: 'Amarante' (B), 'Cinderella' (N)

Paul, A.
Cheshunt, England
1853: 'Vivid' (HB)

Paul, George
Cheshunt, England
1872: 'Cheshunt Hybrid' (Cl. HT)
1876: 'Sultan of Zanzibar' (HP)
1878: 'John Bright' (HP)
1880: 'Duke of Teck' (HP)
1883: 'Grandeur of Cheshunt' (HP), 'Paul's Single White Perpetual' (Cl. HP), 'White Baroness' (HP)
1891: 'Mrs. Paul' (B)
1892: 'Frances Bloxam' (HCh), 'Violet Queen' (HP)
1893: 'Charles Gater' (HP), 'Paul's Early Blush' (HP)
1895: 'Haileybury' (HP), 'Paul's Carmine Pillar' (HCh)
1897: 'Lilliput' (Cl. Pol), 'Reverend Alan Cheales' (HP)

1898: 'Dawn' (Cl. HT)
1900: 'J.B.M. Camm' (B)
1901: 'Purple East' (Cl.)
1903: 'Tea Rambler' (Cl.)
1905: 'The Dandy' (HT)
1906: 'Nelly Johnstone' (T)
1910: 'Symmetry' (HP)

Paul, William
Waltham Cross, England
1862: 'Beauty of Waltham' (HP)
1863: 'Lord Macaulay' (HP)
1864: 'Princess of Wales' (HP)
1866: 'Black Prince' (HP)
1867: 'Prince de Joinville' (HP)
1868: 'Duke of Edinburgh' (HP)
1874: 'Peach Blossom' (HP)
1875: 'Star of Waltham' (HP)
1876: 'Magna Charta' (HP)
1878: 'Rosy Morn' (HP)
1880: 'Crown Prince' (HP)
1881: 'Pride of Waltham' (HP)
1882: 'Queen of Queens' (HP)
1883: 'Charles Lamb' (HP), 'Emperor' (HP), 'Lord Bacon' (HP)
1885: 'Waltham Climber I' (Cl. HT), 'Waltham Climber II' (Cl. HT), 'Waltham Climber III' (Cl. HT)
1886: 'Charles Dickens' (HP), 'Florence Paul' (HP), 'Inigo Jones' (HP)
1887: 'Silver Queen' (HP)
1888: 'Duchess of Albany' (HT)
1889: 'Marchioness of Lorne' (HP), 'Sappho' (T)
1890: 'Crimson Queen' (HP), 'Medea' (T), 'Pink Rover' (Cl. HT)
1891: 'Salamander' (HP)

1892: 'Climbing Queen of Queens' (HP), 'Spencer' (HP)
1893: 'Corinna' (T), 'Princess May' (N)
1894: 'Clio' (HP), 'Duke of York' (Ch), 'Lorna Doone' (B)
1895: 'Sylph' (T), 'Zephyr' (T)
1896: 'Enchantress' (T), 'Queen Mab' (Ch)
1897: 'Empress Alexandra of Russia' (T), 'Waltham Standard' (HP)
1898: 'Aurora' (HT), 'Mme. Ada Carmody' (T)
1899: 'Exquisite' (HT)
1900: 'Corallina' (T), 'Sulphurea' (T), 'The Alexandra' (T)
1901: 'Boadicea' (T)
1902: 'Fortuna' (T), 'Morning Glow' (T)
1903: 'Arethusa' (Ch)
1905: 'Dr. William Gordon' (HP)
1906: 'Climbing Captain Hayward' (HP)
1907: 'Hugo Roller' (T), 'Mrs. Dudley Cross' (T)
1910: 'Florence Haswell Veitch' (Cl. HT)
1912: 'Coronet' (Pol), 'Ophelia' (HT)
1915: 'Paul's Lemon Pillar' (Cl. HT)
1923: 'Corrie Koster' (Pol)

Pernet père (Jean)
Lyon, France
1859: 'Mlle. Bonnaire' (HP)
1864: 'Prince Napoléon' (B)
1867: 'Jean Pernet' (T), 'Mme. Chirard' (HP)
1868: 'Baronne Adolphe de Rothschild' (HP)
1869: 'Marquise de Castellane' (HP)
1871: 'Mme. Bellon' (HP)
1872: 'Mme. Caroline Küster' (N)
1874: 'Gonsoli Gaëtano' (HP)
1876: 'Charles Rovelli' (T), 'Marie Louise Pernet' (HP)
1881: 'Souvenir de Monsieur Droche' (HP)

1882: 'Merveille de Lyon' (HP)
1884: 'Baronne Nathaniel de Rothschild' (HP), 'Mlle. Berger' (B)
1885: 'Mme. David' (T), 'Souvenir de l'Amiral Courbet' (T), 'Souvenir de Victor Hugo' (T)
1886: 'Mme. Chevalier' (B)
1887: 'Albert la Blotais' (Cl. HP), 'Triomphe des Noisettes' (N)
1888: 'Monsieur Désir' (Cl. T)
1890: 'Marquise de Salisbury' (HT), 'Mme. Dubost' (B), 'Triomphe de Pernet père' (HT)
1891: 'Général Baron Berge' (HP)
1892: 'Mme. la Baronne Berge' (T)

Pernet fils (Joseph)/Pernet-Ducher
Lyon, France
1879: 'Ambrogio Maggi' (HP), 'Ferdinand Chaffolte' (HP)
1883: 'Édouard Gauthier' (T)
1884: 'Charles de Legrady' (T)
1887: 'Georges Pernet' (Pol), 'Mlle. Germaine Caillot' (HT), 'Mme. Joseph Godier' (T)
1888: 'Comte Henri Rignon' (HT)
1889: 'Gustave Piganeau' (HP)
1890: 'Gustav Regis' (HT)
1891: 'Mlle. Bertha Ludi' (Pol), 'Mme. Pernet-Ducher' (HT)
1892: 'Beauté Inconstante' (Cl. T)
1893: 'Marquise Litta de Breteuil' (HT)
1894: 'Mme. Abel Chatenay' (HT), 'Souvenir de Mme. Eugène Verdier' (HT), 'Souvenir du Président Carnot' (HT)
1895: 'Antoine Rivoire' HT), 'Mlle. Alice Furon' (HT), 'Mlle. Hélène Cambier' (HT)
1896: 'Ferdinand Batel' (HT), 'Ferdinand Jamin' (HT)
1897: 'L'Innocence' (HT), 'Mme. Eugénie Boullet' (HT), 'Violiniste Émile Lévêque' (HT)

1899: 'Mme. Ravary' (HT), 'Monsieur Bunel' (HT)
1901: 'Prince de Bulgarie' (HT)
1902: 'Monsieur Paul Lédé' (HT)
1903: 'Mme. Hector Leuilliot' (Cl. HT)
1907: 'Mme. Maurice de Luze' (HT)
1908: 'Château de Clos-Vougeot' (HT)
1916: 'Mme. Méha Sabatier' (HT)
1922: 'Climbing Mrs. Herbert Stevens' (HT)

Perny, Pierre
Nice, France
1888: 'Mme. Angèle Favre' (HT)
1891: 'Dr. Grandvilliers' (T)
1894: 'Mme. Erenestine Verdier' (T)
1895: 'Grand-Duc Pierre de Russie' (T)

Perrier, Jean
Rivières, France
1890: 'Professeur Ganiviat' (T)
1895: 'Mme. Émilie Charrin' (T)

Piper, George Wren
Uckfield, England
1899: 'Sunrise' (T)
1902: 'Peace' (T)

Plantier
La Guillotière, France
1825: 'Gloire des Rosomanes' (B)
1835: 'Mme. Plantier' (HN)
1855: 'Inpératrice Eugénie' (B)
1858: 'Ardoisée de Lyon' (HP)

Portemer père
Gentilly, France
1837: 'Émile Courtier' (B)
1845: 'Paul Ricault' (HCh)
1847: 'Duchesse de Galliera' (HP)
1849: 'Léonore d'Este' (HT)
1850: 'William Griffith' (HP)
1852: 'Lady Stuart' (HP)
1863: 'Arthur Young' (HCh), 'Pierre Notting' (HP)
1864: 'Charles Wood' (HP), 'Jean Rosenkrantz' (HP)

Postans, R.B.
England
1879: 'Countess of Rosebery' (HP), 'Duchess of Bedford' (HP)

Pradel, Henri
Montauban, France
1851: 'David Pradel' (T), 'Mlle. Blanche Laffitte' (B)
1852: 'Comice de Tarn-et-Garonne' (B), 'Vicomtesse Laure de Gironde' (HP), 'Mme. Pauline Labonté' (T)
1854: 'Omer-Pacha' (B)
1860: 'Esther Pradel' (T), 'Garibaldi' (B)
1861: 'Mme. Adélaïde Ristori' (B)
1862: 'Deuil du Dr. Raynaud' (B), 'Président Gausen' (B)
1864: 'Maréchal Niel' (N)
1874: 'Mme. Thiers' (B)

Prévost fils
Rouen, France
1825: 'Roxelane' (HCh)
1826: 'Belle de Trianon' (DP)

1830: 'Camélia Rose' (N), 'Portland Pourpre' (DP)

Pries
Malaga, Spain
1888: 'Francisca Pries' (T), 'Souvenir d'Espagne' (T)
1890: 'Miss Marston' (T)

Prince, George
Oxford, England
1894: 'Clara Watson' (HT)
1901: 'Mary Corelly' (HP)

Puyravaud, Jouannem
Roseraie de Goubière, Ste.-Foy-la-Grande, France
1899: 'Hovyn de Tronchère' (T)
1900: 'Mme. Adolphe Dohair' (T)
1903: 'Amateur André Fourcaud' (HT)
1909: 'Baptiste Lafaye' (Pol)

Quétier
Meaux, France
1851: 'Duchesse d'Orléans' (HP)
1852: 'Comte de Nanteuil' (HP)

Widow Rambaux
Lyon, France
1879: 'Anne Marie de Montravel' (Pol)
1881: 'Mme. Rambaux' (HP)
1883: 'Souvenir du Rosiériste Rambaux' (T)
1884: 'Perle d'Or' (Pol)

Renaud-Guépet
Châlon-sur-Saône, France
1887: 'James Bougault' (HP)
1889: 'Mme. la Comtesse de St.-Andréol' (HP)

Robert
Angers, France
1850: 'Marie Robert' (DP)
1851: 'Joseph Gourdon' (HB), 'Mlle. de Sombreuil' (T)
1852: 'Adèle Bougère' (HT), 'Céline Bourdier' (DP)
1853: 'Isis' (N), 'Laurette' (T), 'Lesueur' (DP)
1854: 'Christophe Colombe' (DP)
1855: 'Archimède' (T)
1856: 'Belle Angevine' (HP), 'Bouquet Blanc' (HP), 'L'Admiration' (HCh), 'Robert Perpétuel' (DP), 'Souvenir de David d'Angers' (T)

Robert & Moreau
Angers, France
1858: 'Cornélie' (N), 'Homère' (T), 'Marbrée' (DP), 'Socrate' (T)
1859: 'Boccace' (HP), 'L'Arioste' (N), 'Laurent Heister' (DP), 'Rubens' (T)
1860: 'Amiral Gravina' (HP), 'Comte de Chambord' (DP), 'Duc de Crillon' (B), 'Pergolèse' (DP), 'Regulus' (T)
1862: 'Souvenir de Charles Montault' (HP)
1863: 'Delambre' (DP), 'Duc d'Harcourt' (HP), 'Héroïne de Vaucluse' (B), 'Jules Lesourd' (DP)

Robichon, Altin
Orléans, France
1901: 'Léon Robichon' (HP)
1904: 'Jacques Proust' (Pol), 'Marguerite Rose' (Pol)
1908: 'Diamant' (Pol)

1912: 'Mme. Arthur Robichon' (Pol)
1927: 'Sunshine' (Pol)

Roeser
Crécy-en-Brie, France
1829: 'Belle de Crécy' (HCh)
1848: 'Caroline Marniesse' (N), 'Vicomtesse d'Avesnes' (N)

Rousset, Georges
France
1893: 'Georges Rousset' (HP)
1894: 'Achille Cesbron' (HP)

Schmidt, J.-C.
Erfurt, Germany
1895: 'Kleiner Liebling' (Pol)
1905: 'Blumenschmidt' (T)
1906: 'Ännchen Müller' (Pol), 'Tausendschön' (Mult)
1915: 'Emden' (HP)
1919: 'Frau Rudolf Schmidt' (Pol)

Schmitt
Lyon, France
1854: 'Mme. Schmitt' (HP)
1881: 'Caroline Schmitt' (N)
1882: 'Monsieur Joseph Chappaz' (HP)
1889: 'Adrien Schmitt' (HP)

Schwartz, Joseph
Lyon, France
1871: 'Mme. Joseph Schwartz' (HP), 'Prince Stirbey' (HP)
1873: 'Noisette Moschata' (N), 'Olga Marix' (B)

1876: 'Comtesse Riza du Parc' (T)
1877: 'Alfred K. Williams' (HP)
1878: 'Emilia Plantier' (B), 'François Gaulain' (HP), 'Jules Chrétien' (HP), 'Lord Beaconsfield' (HP), 'Mme. Auguste Perrin' (N)
1879: 'Jules Jürgensen' (HB), 'Mme. Alfred Carrière' (N)
1880: 'Guillaume Gillemot' (HP), 'Mme. Joseph Schwartz' (T), 'Reine Maria Pia' (Cl. T)
1881: 'Camoëns' (HT), 'Comtesse Henriette Combes' (HP), 'Mme. Jules Grévy' (HT)
1882: 'André Schwartz' (T), 'Mme. Fanny de Forest' (N)\\B)
1883: 'Colonel Félix Breton' (HP), 'Jeanne Drivon' (Pol), 'Monsieur Francisque Rive' (HP), 'Président Sénélar' (HP), 'Secrétaire J. Nicolas' (HP)
1884: 'Aline Rozey' (HP), 'Gaston Chandon' (Cl. HT), 'Général Appert' (HP), 'Victor Hugo' (HP)

Widow Schwartz
Lyon, France
1886: 'Jean-Baptiste Casati' (HP), 'Monsieur Mathieu Baron' (HP)
1887: 'Mlle. Jeanne Ferron' (Cl. Pol), 'Mlle. Marie Drivon' (B)
1888: 'Flora' (Pol), 'Mme. Ernest Calvat' (B)
1889: 'Bellina Guillot' (Pol)
1890: 'Roger Lambelin' (HP)
1891: 'Mme. Veuve Ménier' (HT), 'Monsieur de Morand' (HP)
1892: 'Mme. Henri Perrin' (HP)
1893: 'Baron Elisi de St.-Albert' (HP), 'Dr. Rouges' (Cl. T), 'Souvenir de Lucie' (Cl)
1896: 'Mlle. Anna Charron', 'Mlle. Marie-Thérèse Molinier' (T)
1897: 'Aurore' (Ch), 'Souvenir d'Aimée Terrel des Chênes' (Ch)
1899: 'Georges Schwartz' (T), 'La Favorite' (HT)
1900: 'Charles Metroz' (Pol), 'La Tosca' (HT), 'Mme. Ernest Perrin' (T)

Schwartz, André
Lyon, France
1901: 'Mlle. Emma Vercellone' (T)
1904: 'Monsieur Georges de Cadoudal' (Cl. T)
1905: 'Comte de Torres' (Cl. HT)
1906: 'Souvenir de Monsieur Frédéric Vercellone' (HT)
1910: 'Mrs. Alice Broomhall' (T)

Souchet, Charles
Bagnolet, France
1842: 'Georges Cuvier' (B), 'Souchet' (B)

Soupert (Jean) & Notting (Pierre)
Luxembourg
1857: 'Duc de Constantine' (HP)
1868: 'Le Roitelet' (B), 'Mme. Hersilie Ortgies' (HP)
1875: 'Eugène Fürst' (HP)
1876: 'Comtesse Hélène Mier' (HP), 'Princesse Charles d'Aremberg' (HP)
1877: 'Robusta' (B)
1878: 'Mme. Loeben de Sels' (HP)
1879: 'Comte Florimund de Bergeyck' (HP), 'Mme. de Loeben-Sels' (HT)
1881: 'Mme. Julie Weidmann' (HT)
1884: 'Mme. Fanny Pauwels' (T)
1885: 'Princesse Wilhelmina des Pays-Bas' (Pol)
1886: 'Archiduchesse Marie Immaculata' (T), 'Directeur Constant Bernard' (HT), 'Théodore Liberton' (HP)
1887: 'Comtesse Anna Thun' (T), 'Miss Kate Schultheis' (Pol), 'Thérèse Lambert' (T)

1888: 'Clara Pfitzer' (Pol), 'Comtesse Julie Hunyadi' (T), 'Hermine Madèlé' (Pol), 'Princesse Henriette de Flandres' (Pol), 'Princesse Joséphine de Flandres' (Pol)
1889: 'Bona Weillschott' (HT), 'Clotilde Soupert' (Pol), 'Duchesse Marie Salviati' (T), 'Gloire de l'Exposition de Bruxelles' (HP), 'Oscar II, Roi de Suède' (HP)
1890: 'Charles de Franciosi' (T), 'Comtesse de Vitzthum' (T), 'Comtesse Eva Starhemberg' (T), 'Gribaldo Nicola' (N)
1891: 'Grand-Duc Adolphe de Luxembourg' (HT)
1892: 'Erzherzog Franz Ferdinand' (T), 'Léon XIII' (T), 'Léonie Osterrieth' (T), 'Petite Léonie' (Pol), 'Princesse Elisabeth Lancellotti' (Pol)
1893: 'Baronne Charles de Gargan' (Cl. T), 'Comtesse Dusy' (T)
1894: 'Comte Chandon' (T)
1895: 'Auguste Comte' (T), 'Comtesse Bardi' (T), 'Comtesse Lily Kinsky' (T), 'Graf Fritz Metternich' (HP), 'Léon de Bruyn' (T), 'Princesse Marie Adélaïde de Luxembourg' (Pol)
1896: 'Baronne M. de Tornaco' (T), 'Gloire de Deventer' (T)
1897: 'Baronne Ada' (T), 'Ma Fillette' (Pol), 'Mme. C.P. Strassheim' (T), 'The Sweet Little Queen of Holland' (T)
1898: 'Amélie-Suzanne Morin' (Pol), 'Archiduchesse Elisabeth-Marie' (Pol), 'Gardenia' (HT)
1899: 'Comtesse Antoinette d'Oultremont' (Pol), 'Mme. Errera' (T), 'Petit Constant (Pol), 'Rosomane Gravereaux' (HT)
1900: 'Mme. Jules Gravereaux' (Cl. T), 'Primula' (Pol)
1901: 'Pierre Wattinne' (HT)
1902: 'Souvenir de Pierre Notting' (T)
1904: 'Reine Marguerite d'Italie' (HT)
1905: 'Mme. Constant Soupert' (T)
1906: 'Mme. Paul Varin-Bernier' (T)
1907: 'Comtesse Icy Hardegg' (HT), 'Mme. Segond-Weber' (HT)
1910: 'Recuerdo di Antonio Peluffo' (T)

1912: 'Aviateur Michel Mahieu' (HT), 'Ivan Misson' (Pol), 'Jeanny Soupert' (Pol)

Spek, Jan
Boskoop, The Netherlands
1920: 'Ideal' (Pol)
1930: 'Rosa Gruss an Aachen' (HT)

Sprunt, Rev. James
Kenansville, North Carolina, U.S.A.
1855: 'Isabella Sprunt' (T)
1868: 'James Sprunt' (Cl. Ch)

Standish & Noble
Bagshot, England
1862: 'Reynolds Hole (B)
1877: 'Queen of Bedders' (B)
1882: 'Duchess of Connaught' (HP)

Stevens, Walter
Hoddesdon, England
1926: 'Lady Sylvia' (HT)
1833: 'Climbing Lady Sylvia' (HT)

Tanne, Remi
Rouen, France
1921: 'Auguste Chaplain' (HP), 'Ferdinand Pichard' (HP)

Tantau, M.
Ütersen, Germany
1919: 'Schöne von Holstein' (Pol), 'Stadtrat Meyn' (Pol)
1933: 'Stämmler' (HP), 'Urdh' (HP)

1937: 'Topaz' (Pol)
1959: 'Vatertag' (Pol)

Thierry, Gustave
Caen, Normandy, France
1840: 'Chénédolé' (HCh)
1846: 'Le Météore' (HCh)

Thomas, Desiré
St.-Denis, France
1853: 'Ville de St.-Denis' (HP)
1862: 'Peter Lawson' (HP)

Touvais, Jean
Petit-Montrouge, France
1859: 'Mme. Céline Touvais' (HP)
1861: 'Bicolore Incomparable' (HP), 'Duc de Cazes' (HP), 'Mme. Julia Daran' (HP)
1863: 'Centifolia Rosea' (HP), 'Mlle. Joséphine Guyet' (B)
1867: 'Alba Carnea' (HP)
1873: 'Albert Payé' (HP)
1874: 'La Syrène' (HP), 'Lutea Flora' (T)

Trouillard, Victor
Angers, France
1842: 'Céline Forestier' (N)
1857: 'Cardinal Patrizzi' (HP)
1858: 'Dr. Bretonneau' (HP), 'François I' (HP), 'François Arago' (HP)
1859: 'Eugène Appert' (HP)
1863: 'Comte de Falloux' (HP)
1864: 'Mlle. Marie de la Villeboisnet' (HP), 'Souvenir de Louis Gaudin' (HP)

1866: 'André Leroy d'Angers' (HP), 'Monsieur Lauriol de Barney' (HP)
1867: 'Aristide Dupuy' (HP), 'Comtesse de Falloux' (HP)
1868: 'Mme. Lauriol de Barney' (B)

Turbat (Eugène) & Co.
Orléans, France
1910: 'Yvonne Rabier' (Pol)
1911: 'Maman Turbat' (Pol)
1912: 'George Elger' (Pol), 'Mme. Jules Gouchault' (Pol)
1913: 'Marie Brissonet' (Pol), 'Marie-Jeanne' (Pol)
1914: 'Abondant' (Pol)
1915: 'Mauve' (Pol)
1918: 'Éblouissante' (Pol), 'Étoile Luisante' (Pol)
1919: 'Indéfectible' (Pol)
1920: 'La Rosée' (Pol), 'Le Loiret' (Pol)
1931: 'Flamboyant' (Pol)

Türke, Robert
Meissen, Germany
1890: 'Schneeball' (Pol)
1905: 'Charlotte Klemm' (Ch)
1909: 'Leuchtfeuer' (B)
1910: 'Nymphe' (Cl.)

Turner, Charles
Slough, England
1874: 'John Stuart Mill' (HP), 'Miss Hassard' (HP)
1876: 'Mrs. Baker' (HP)

Van Fleet, Walter
Glenn Dale, Maryland, U.S.A.
1898: 'Clara Barton' (HT)

1900: 'Magnafrano' (HT)
1904: 'Beauty of Rosemawr' (Ch)
1907: 'Charles Wagner' (HP)
1910: 'Dr. W. Van Fleet' (Cl.)

Varangot, Victor
Melun, France
1844: 'Jacques Amyot' (DP), 'Mogador' (DP)

Verdier, Victor
Paris, France
1834: 'Perpétuelle de Neuilly' (HP)
1842: 'Dombrowski' (HB)
1845: 'Richelieu' (HCh)
1847: 'Frédéric II de Prusse' (HB)
1848: 'Apolline' (B), 'Douglas' (Ch)

Verdier, Victor & Charles
Paris, France
1855: 'Mme. Knorr' (HP)
1861: 'La Brillante' (HP), 'Olivier Belhomme' (HP), 'Turenne' (HP), 'Vulcain' (HP)
1862: 'Henri IV' (HP)

Verdier, Charles
Paris, France
1864: 'Duchesse de Caylus' (HP)
1866: 'Paul Verdier' (HP)
1869: 'Blanche de Méru' (HP)
1884: 'Souvenir d'Alphonse Lavallée' (HP)
1890: 'Souvenir de Lady Ashburton' (T)

Verdier, Eugène
Paris, France

1861: 'Mme. Charles Wood' (HP), 'Prince Camille de Rohan' (HP)
1863: 'Claude Million' (HP), 'George Paul' (HP), 'La Duchesse de Morny' (HP), 'Mme. Victor Verdier' (HP)
1864: 'Comtesse de Paris' (HP), 'Dr. Andry' (HP), 'Rushton-Radclyffe' (HP), 'Souvenir de William Wood' (HP)
1865: 'Alba Mutabilis' (HP), 'Fisher-Holmes' (HP), 'Mme. Charles Baltet' (B), 'Prince de Portia' (HP)
1866: 'Baronne Maurice de Graviers' (HP), 'Mlle. Annie Wood' (HP), 'Napoléon III' (HP), 'Velours Pourpre' (HP)
1867: 'Comtesse de Turenne' (HP), 'Meyerbeer' (HP), 'Souvenir de Caillat' (HP)
1869: 'Lena Turner' (HP), 'Suzanne Wood' (HP)
1872: 'Félicien David' (HP), 'John Laing' (HP), 'Mrs. Laing' (HP), 'Souvenir de John Gould Veitch' (HP)
1873: 'Miller-Hayes' (HP), 'Thomas Mills' (HP)
1874: 'Bernard Verlot' (HP), 'Monsieur E.Y. Teas' (HP)
1875: 'Abel Carrière' (HP), 'Général Duc d'Aumale' (HP), 'Mme. Grandin-Monville' (HP), 'Mme. Prosper Laugier' (HP)
1876: 'Baronne de Medem' (HP), 'Duc de Chartres' (HP), 'Mme. Galli-Marie' (HCh), 'Mme. Verlot' (HP)
1877: 'Comtesse de Flandres' (HP), 'Dr. Auguste Krell' (HP), 'Président Schlachter' (HP), 'Souvenir d'Auguste Rivière' (HP)
1878: 'A. Geoffrey de St.-Hilaire' (HP), 'Benjamin Drouet' (HP), 'Mme. Amélie Baltet' (HP), 'Mme. Charles Truffaut' (HP), 'Mme. Eugène Verdier' (HP), 'Souvenir de Laffay' (HP), 'Souvenir de Victor Verdier' (HP)
1879: 'Édouard André le Botaniste' (HP), 'Rosiériste Harms' (HP)
1882: 'Baron de Wolseley' (HP), 'Lecoq-Dumesnil' (HP), 'Mlle. Marie Closon' (HP)

1883: 'Directeur N. Jensen' (HP), 'Mme. Bertha Mackart' (HP), 'Prosper Laugier' (HP)
1884: 'Édouard Hervé' (HP), 'Félix Mousset' (HP), 'Hans Mackart' (HP), 'Louis-Philippe d'Orléans' (HP), 'Mme. Edmond Fabre' (HP), 'Mme. Eugénie Frémy' (HP), 'Olivier Métra' (HP)
1885: 'Léon Delaville' (HP), 'Louis Calla' (HP), 'Prince Waldemar' (HP), 'Princesse Marie d'Orléans' (HP)
1886: 'Duc de Bragance' (HP), 'Duchesse de Bragance' (HP), 'Jules Barigny' (HP), 'Mme. Édouard Michel' (HP), 'Prince Henri d'Orléans' (HP), 'Princesse Hélène d'Orléans' (HP)
1887: 'Duc d'Audiffret-Pasquier' (HP), 'Mlle. Claire Truffaut' (B)
1888: 'Comtesse Bertrand de Blacas' (HP)
1889: 'Buffalo-Bill' (HP)
1890: 'Souvenir de Clairvaux' (T)
1893: 'Rose de France' (HP)

Verschuren (H.A.) & Sons
Haps, The Netherlands
1899: 'General von Bothnia-Andreæ' (HP)
1903: 'Koningin Wilhelmina' (T)
1905: 'Rosa Verschuren' (HP)
1910: 'Neervelt' (Cl. HT)
1919: 'Étoile de Hollande' (HT)

Veysset
Royat-les-Bains, France
1890: 'Mme. Angélique Veysset' (HT)
1891: 'Bijou de Royat-les-Bains' (B)
1899: 'Mme. Blondel' (HT), 'Souvenir de Mme. Ladvocat' (N)
1901: 'Royat Mondain' (HP)

Viaud-Bruant
Poitiers, France
1910: 'Janine Viaud-Bruant' (HP)
1913: 'Mme. Foureau' (N)

Vibert, Jean-Pierre
Chennevières-sur-Marne/Longjumeaux/Angers, France
1817: 'Palmyre' (DP)
1820: 'Bengale Pompon' (Ch), 'Thisbé' (HN)
1828: 'Aimée Vibert' (N), 'Las-Cases' (HB)
1831: 'Riégo' (HCh)
1836: 'Césonie' (DP), 'Gloriette' (HN), 'Portland Blanc' (DP)
1841: 'Desdémona' (DP)
1843: 'Yolande d'Aragon' (DP)
1844: 'Jeanne Hachette' (DP), 'Philomèle' (N)
1845: 'Amanda Patenotte' (DP)
1846: 'Amandine' (DP), 'Belmont' (HCh), 'Jacques Laffitte' (HP)
1847: 'Adèle Mauzé' (DP), 'Blanche-Vibert' (DP), 'Euphémie' (B), 'Gerbe de Roses' (HP), 'Joasine Hanet' (DP), 'Sapho' (DP), 'Sydonie' (DP)
1848: 'Casimir Delavigne' (DP), 'Pie IX' (HP)
1849: 'Élise Masson' (HT)

Vigneron, Jacques
Olivet, France
1859: 'Mlle. Marie Dauvesse' (HP)
1860: 'Dr. Brière' (B)
1864: 'Monsieur Dubost' (B)
1865: 'Elisabeth Vigneron' (HP), 'Glory of Waltham' (Cl. HP)
1867: 'Mme. Alice Dureau' (HP)
1869: 'La Motte Sanguin' (HP)
1871: 'Maxime de la Rocheterie' (HP)
1872: 'Amédée de Langlois' (B)

1875: 'Alexis Lepère' (HP)
1877: 'Dames Patronesses d'Orléans' (HP)
1879: 'Monsieur Eugène Delaire' (HP)
1880: 'Monsieur Alfred Leveau' (HP)
1881: 'Mlle. Elisabeth de la Rocheterie' (HP), 'Mlle. Madeleine de Vauzelles' (B)
1882: 'Mlle. Hélène Croissandeau' (HP), 'Mme. Alexandre Jullien' (HP), 'Mme. Apolline Foulon' (HP), 'Mme. Louise Vigneron' (HP), 'Monsieur Jules Maquinant' (HP)
1883: 'Mlle. Hélène Michel' (HP), 'Monsieur le Capitaine Louis Frère' (HP)
1884: 'Mme. Lucien Chauré' (HP)
1886: 'Bijou de Couasnon' (HP), 'Gloire d'Olivet' (B), 'Mme. Marcel Fauneau' (HP)
1887: 'Mme. Létuvée de Colnet' (B)
1889: 'Mme. Moser' (HT)
1890: 'Monsieur Jules Lemaître' (HP)
1891: 'L'Étincelante' (HP), 'Mlle. Alice Marchand' (B), 'Président de la Rocheterie' (B)
1892: 'Mme. Charles Boutmy' (HT)
1895: 'Éclaireur' (HP), 'Mme. Charles Détraux' (HT)
1897: 'Mme. Augustine Hamont' (HT)
1899: 'Mlle. Fernande Dupuy' (Pol), 'Souvenir d'André Raffy' (HP)
1900: 'Mme. Ernest Levavasseur' (HP)
1903: 'Mme. Roudillon' (HP)
1908: 'Souvenir de Léon Roudillon' (HP)
1913: 'Mlle. Suzanne Bidard' (Pol)

Vilin, Rose
Grisy-Suisnes, France
1868: 'Thyra Hammerich' (HP)
1872: 'Duhamel-Dumonceau' (HP)

1886: 'Mme. Henri Pereire' (HP)
1899: 'Bouquet de Neige' (Pol), 'Gloire d'un Enffant de Hiram' (HP), 'Souvenir de Mme. Jeanne Balandreau' (HP)
1901: 'L'Ami E. Daumont' (HP)
1903: 'Mlle. Alice Rousseau' (Pol)

Widow Vilin & Son
Grisy-Suisnes, France
1904: 'Mme. d'Enfert' (B)
1907 'Dr. Georges Martin' (HP)

Vogel, Max
Sangerhausen, Germany
1932: 'Arthur Weidling' (HP)
1935: 'Jean Muraour' (HT)
1938: 'Climbing Capitaine Soupa' (HT)
1940: 'Climbing König Friedrich II von Dänemark' (HP), 'Climbing Wenzel Geschwind' (HT)
1941: 'Climbing Apotheker Georg Höfer' (HT), 'Climbing Pride of Reigate' (HP)

Walsh, M.H.
Woods Hole, Massachusetts, U.S.A.
1897: 'Jubilee' (HP)
1901: 'Snowball' (Pol)

Walter, Louis
Saverne, France
1906: 'Rösel Dach' (Pol)
1909: 'Frau Anna Pasaquay' (Pol), 'Louise Walter' (Pol)
1911: 'Adèle Frey' (Cl. HT)
1912: 'Martha Keller' (Pol)

Weber, Antoine
Dijon, France
1893: 'Princesse Alice de Monaco' (T)
1899: 'Antoine Weber' (T)

Weeks (O.L.) Wholesale Rose Grower
Chino/Ontario, California, U.S.A.
1949: 'Climbing Snowbird' (HT)
1977: 'Climbing China Doll' (Pol)

Weigand, Christoph
Bad Sonen a Taunus, Germany
1914: 'Susanna' (Pol)
1920: 'Ruhm von Steinfurth' (HP)
1935: 'Symphony' (HP)

Welter, Nicola
Trier, Germany
1899: 'Johannes Wesselhöft' (HT)
1900: 'Gruss an Pallien' (HP)
1901: 'Abbé André Reitter' (HT)
1903: 'Marie Bülow' (N)
1904: 'Albert Hoffmann' (T), 'Frau J. Reiter' (HT)
1906: 'Barbarossa' (HP)

Of Unknown Provenence: 'American Perfection' (T), 'Anaïse' (HB), 'Annie Vibert' (N), 'Belle Blanca' (HGig), 'Belle de Vernier' (HCh), 'Bijou des Amateurs' (HCh), 'Buffon' (DP), 'Capitaine Rénard' (DP), 'Capitaine Sissolet' (HB), 'Climbing Anna Olivier' (T), 'Climbing Louis-Philippe' (Ch), 'Climbing Old Blush' (Ch), 'Climbing Pale Pink China' (Ch), 'Climbing Perle d'Or' (Pol), 'Climbing Pink Pet' (Pol), 'Climbing Pompon de Paris' (Ch), 'Climbing Rouletii' (Ch), 'Delille' (B), 'Deuil du

Maréchal Mortier' (HCh), 'Élise Lemaire' (HP), 'Fun Jwan Lo' (Cl. T), 'Henriette' (DP), 'Henriette Boulogne' (DP), 'Honorine de Brabant' (B), 'König Friedrich II von Dänemark' (HP), 'La Moderne' (DP), 'La Volumineuse' (DP), 'Lady Stuart' (HCh), 'Le Prince de Galles' (DP), 'Le Vingt-Neuf Juillet' (HCh), 'Maréchal Bugeaud' (T), 'Mme. A. Labbley' (HP), 'Mme. Barriglione' (T), '(Mme. Caroline Testout × *R. gallica* Splendens)' (HCh), 'Mme. E. Vicaro' (T), 'Mme. Jules Thibaud' (Pol), 'Monthly Rose' (DP), 'Mrs. J.F. Redly' (HP), 'Orange Koster' (Pol), 'Pale Pink China' (Ch), 'Pompon de Paris' (Ch), 'Quatre Saisons d'Italie' (DP), 'Reine de la Lombardie' (Ch), 'Riccordo di Fernando Scarlatti' (HP), 'Rouge Marbrée' (B), 'Simone Thomas' (T), 'Sophie's Perpetual' (B), 'Souvenir d'Anselme' (HB), 'Verdun Superior' (Pol), 'Weeping China Doll' (Pol), 'White Koster' (Pol)

Appendix Eight

Cultivars Listed by Color

Rose colors varying as they characteristically do, these listings must necessarily strike an average between the extremes of recorded experience, while meantime readers must also bear in mind the vagaries of linguistic usage of color-terms over geography and the passage of time. The "yellow" of the 1800s can look quite pale to us; the "blush" of a rose described as such by a writer gardening in a cool climate may well be an unequivocal "pink" to those in warmer climates; the "*pourpre*" (translated as "purple") assigned by a Frenchman is redder than the blue-imbibing "purple" which comes to mind to Anglophones using the term; the "white" can be absolute ('Frau

Karl Druschki'), relative ('White Maman Cochet'), greenish ('Marie Guillot'), predominant ('Virginale'), or eventual ('Clotilde Soupert').

White to Near-White

Damask Perpetuals: 'Blanche-Vibert', 'Celina Dubos', 'Félicité Hardy', 'Marie de St.-Jean', 'Portland Blanc', 'Quatre Saisons Blanc Mousseux', 'Sapho'

Chinas: 'Duchesse de Kent', 'Mme. Desprez', 'Pumila'

Teas: 'Bella', 'Baronne M. de Tornaco', 'Blanche Nabonnand', 'Comtesse Dusy', 'Cornelia Cook', 'Elisa Fugier', 'Enchantress', 'Fiametta Nabonnand', 'Frances E. Willard', 'Grossherzogin Mathilde von Hessen', 'Innocente Pirola', 'Ivory', 'Lady Plymouth', 'Léon XIII', 'Léonie Osterrieth', 'Madison', 'Marie Guillot', 'Marie Lambert', 'Mlle. de Sombreuil', 'Mlle. Marie-Louise Oger', 'Mme. Adolphe Dohair', 'Mme. Joseph Schwartz', 'Molly Sharman-Crawford', 'Mrs. Herbert Hawksworth', 'Niphetos', 'Rival de Pæstum', 'Senator McNaughton', 'The Bride', 'The Queen', 'White Bon Silène', 'White Catherine Mermet', 'White Maman Cochet' 'White Pearl', 'William R. Smith'

Bourbons: 'Acidalie', 'Baronne de Maynard', 'Boule de Neige', 'Comtesse de Rocquigny', 'Coquette des Alpes', 'Coquette des Blanches', 'Duchesse de Thuringe', 'Lady Emily Peel', 'Louise d'Arzens', 'Mlle. Marie-Thérese Devansaye', 'Mme. Fanny de Forest', 'Mme. François Pittet', 'Mme. Massot', 'Perle des Blanches'

Hybrid Bourbons, Hybrid Chinas, and Hybrid Noisettes: 'Purity', 'Mme. Plantier', 'Triomphe de Laffay'

Hybrid Perpetuals: 'Belle Normande', 'Blanche de Méru', 'Bouquet Blanc', 'Bouquet de Marie', 'Candeur Lyonnaise', 'Edelweiss', 'Everest', 'Frau Karl Druschki', '(Frau Karl Druschki × Cristata)', 'Gloire Lyonnaise', 'James Bougault', 'Léon Robichon', 'Louise

Cretté', 'Mabel Morrison', 'Magnolija', 'Margaret Dickson', 'Marguerite Guillard', 'Miss House', 'Mlle. Bonnaire', 'Mme. André Saint', 'Mme. Noman', 'Nuria de Recolons', 'Polar Bear', 'Princess Louise', 'Virginale', 'White Baroness'

Noisettes and Climbers: 'Aimée Vibert', 'Aimée Vibert, Climbing', 'Autumnalis', 'Belle d'Orléans', 'Blanc Pur', 'Claudia Augusta', 'Clotilde Soupert, Climbing', 'Devoniensis, Climbing', 'Étendard de Jeanne d'Arc', 'Eugene Jardine', 'Eva Teschendorff, Climbing', 'Frau Karl Druschki, Climbing', 'Gigantea Blanc', 'Irish Beauty', 'Isis', 'Kaiserin Auguste Viktoria, Climbing', 'Marie Guillot, Climbing', 'Marie Accary', 'Mélanie Soupert', 'Milkmaid', 'Mme. Alfred Carrière', 'Mme. Jules Bouché, Climbing', 'Mme. Jules Franke', 'Montarioso', 'Montecito', 'Mrs. Herbert Stevens, Climbing', 'Niphetos, Climbing', 'Nymphe', 'Paul's Single White Perpetual', 'Pumila Alba', 'Purity', 'Snowbird, Climbing', 'Summer Snow, Climbing', 'Weisser Maréchal Niel', 'White Maman Cochet, Climbing', 'White Pet, Climbing'

Polyanthas: 'Amélie-Suzanne Morin', 'Anne-Marie de Montravel', 'Baby Alberic', 'Bellina Guillot', 'Bouquet Blanc', 'Bouquet de Neige', 'Clotilde Soupert', 'Colibri', 'Comtesse Antoinette d'Oultremont', 'Denise Cassegrain', 'Eva Teschendorff', 'Flocon de Neige', 'Flora', 'Hermine Madèlé', 'Jeanne d'Arc', 'Katharine Zeimet', 'Little Gem', 'Little White Pet', 'Lullaby', 'Minutifolia Alba', 'Mrs. William G. Koning', 'Multiflore Nain Remontant', 'Neiges d'Été', 'Pâquerette', 'Petite Marcelle', 'Prevue', 'Princesse Wilhelmina des Pays-Bas', 'Schneeball', 'Sneprinsesse', 'Snowball', 'White Cécile Brunner', 'White Koster', 'Yvonne Rabier'

Hybrid Teas: 'British Queen', 'Charlotte Gillemot', 'Double White Killarney', 'Gardenia', 'Innocence', 'Jean Muraour', 'Joséphine Marot', 'Kaiserin Auguste Viktoria', 'Kaiserin Goldifolia', 'L'Innocence', 'Mlle. Argentine Cramon', 'Mlle. Augustine

Guinoisseau', 'Mme. Jules Finger', 'Mrs. Herbert Stevens', 'Snowbird', 'The Puritan', 'White Wings'

Cream to Flesh and Blush

Damask Perpetuals: 'Julie de Krudner', 'La Moderne', 'La Volumineuse', 'Mme. Souveton', 'Palmyre'

Chinas: 'Ducher', 'Pompon de Paris'

Teas: 'A. Bouquet', 'Annie Cook', 'Baron de St.-Triviers', 'Baronne Ada', 'Baronne Henriette de Loew', 'Catherine II', 'Catherine Mermet', 'Cels Multiflore', 'Comtesse Lily Kinsky', 'Comtesse Emmeline de Guigné', 'Devoniensis', 'Francisca Pries', 'Frau Geheimrat von Boch', 'G. Nabonnand', 'Gigantesque', 'Gloire de Deventer, 'Graziella', 'Hermance Louisa de la Rive', 'Homère', 'Honourable Edith Gifford', 'Hume's Blush Tea-Scented China', 'Hyménée', 'Isabelle Nabonnand', 'La Princesse Vera', 'La Sylphide', 'La Tulipe', 'Laurette', 'Lucie Faure', 'Marie Sisley', 'Mlle. Blanche Durrschmidt', 'Mlle. Suzanne Blanchet', 'Mme. Ada Carmody', 'Mme. Antoine Mari', 'Mme. Bravy', 'Mme. Damaizin', 'Mme. Elie Lambert', 'Mme. Hoste', 'Mme. Léon Février', 'Mme. Lucien Duranthon', 'Mme. Mélanie Willermoz', 'Mme. Nabonnand', 'Mme. Olga', 'Mrs. Foley-Hobbs', 'Mrs. Hubert Taylor', 'Mrs. Myles Kennedy', 'Nita Weldon', 'Pearl Rivers', 'Princesse Alice de Monaco', 'Princesse de Venosa', 'Rubens', 'Souvenir d'Elisa Vardon', 'Winnie Davis'

Bourbons: 'Delille', 'Edith de Murat', 'Emotion', 'Gloire d'Olivet', 'Impératrice Eugénie', 'Maréchal du Palais', 'Marie Dermar', 'Mlle. Berger', 'Mlle. Blanche Laffitte', 'Mme. Alfred de Rougemont', 'Mme. Cornélissen', 'Mme. d'Enfert', 'Mme. Nérard', 'Mme. Olympe Terestchenko', 'Mrs. Paul', 'Olga Marix', 'Perle d'Angers', 'Reine des Vierges', 'Souvenir de la Malmaison', 'Souvenir de St. Anne's', 'Triomphe de la Duchère'

Hybrid Bourbons, Hybrid Chinas, and Hybrid Noisettes: 'Belmont', 'Comtesse de Lacépède', 'Comtesse Molé', 'Duc de Sussex', 'Gloriette', 'La Dauphine', 'La Pudeur', 'Lady Stuart', 'Thisbé'

Hybrid Perpetuals: 'Alba Carnea', 'Aline Rozey', 'Antonie Schurz', 'Bessie Johnson', 'Bicolore', 'Cæcilie Scharsach', 'Comtesse de Turenne', 'Élisa Boëlle', 'George Sand', Giuletta', 'Générale Marie Raiewesky', 'Gloire de Guérin', 'Gonsoli Gaëtano', 'Jeanne Masson', 'Lady Overtoun', 'Lady Stuart', 'Lisette de Béranger', 'Marguerite de Roman', 'Marguerite Jamain', 'Marie Boisée', 'Marquise de Mortemart', 'Mère de St. Louis', 'Merveille de Lyon', 'Miss Ethel Richardson', 'Mlle. Eugénie Verdier', 'Mme. Fortuné Besson', 'Mme. Hippolyte Jamain', 'Mme. Louis Lévêque', 'Mme. Maurice Rivoire', 'Mme. Récamier', 'Mme. Vidot', 'Mrs. F.W. Sanford', 'Paul's Early Blush', 'Prince Stirbey', 'Réveil du Printemps', 'Thyra Hammerich', 'Violette Bouyer'

Noisettes and Climbers: 'Anne-Marie Cote', 'Annie Vibert', 'Belle Blanca', 'Blush Noisette', 'Bouquet Tout Fait', 'Caroline Marniesse', 'Comtesse de Galard-Béarn', 'Cooper's Burmese Rose', 'Cupid', 'Député Debussy', 'Dr. W. Van Fleet', 'Emmanuella de Mouchy', 'Fraser's Pink Musk', 'Fun Jwan Lo', 'Gribaldo Nicola', 'Gruss an Aachen, Climbing', 'L'Arioste', 'La Biche', 'Madeleine Lemoine', 'Mlle. Madeleine Delaroche', 'New Dawn', 'Noisette de l'Inde', 'Noisette Moschata', 'Ophelia, Climbing', 'Philomèle', 'Pale Pink China, Climbing', 'Pompon de Paris, Climbing', 'Souvenir de la Malmaison, Climbing'

Polyanthas: 'Ivan Misson', 'Jeanny Soupert', 'Little Dot', 'Louise Walter', 'Marie Brissonet', 'Marie-Jeanne', 'Marie Pavic', 'Merveille des Polyanthas', 'Mignon', 'Mignonette', 'Mlle. Alice Rousseau', 'Mlle. Bertha Ludi', 'Mlle. Joséphine Burland', 'Perle', 'Perle Angevine', 'Princesse Joséphine de Flandres', 'Princesse Marie Adélaïde de Luxembourg'

Hybrid Teas: 'Abbé André Reitter', 'Adam Rackles', 'Admiral Dewey', 'Antoine Rivoire', 'Baronne G. de Noirmont', 'Bessie Brown', 'Carmen Sylva', 'Clara Watson', 'Edmée et Roger', 'Frau J. Reiter', 'Gertrude', 'Grace Darling', 'Grossherzogin Viktoria Melitta von Hessen', 'Gruss an Aachen', 'Gruss an Aachen Superior', 'Killarney', 'La Favorite', 'La Tosca', 'Lady Clanmorris', 'Lady Henry Grosvenor', 'Léonore d'Este', 'Marie Girard', 'Marjorie', 'Mavourneen', 'Mildred Grant', 'Mme. Adolphe Loiseau', 'Mme. Augustine Hamont', 'Mme. C. Chambard', 'Mme. de Loeben-Sels', 'Mme. Gustave Metz', 'Mme. Joseph Combet', 'Mme. Joseph Desbois', 'Mme. Jules Bouché', 'Mme. Lacharme', 'Mme. Léon Pain', 'Mme. Moser', 'Mme. Veuve Ménier', 'Monsieur Charles de Lapisse', 'Ophelia', 'Pearl', 'Prince de Bulgarie', 'Rosomane Gravereaux', 'Sachsengruss', 'Souvenir de Mme. Ernest Cauvin', 'Souvenir du Président Carnot', 'Violiniste Émile Lévêque', 'Westfield Star'

Shades of Pink

Damask Perpetuals: 'Adèle Mauzé', 'Amandine', 'Belle de Trianon', 'Bifera', 'Buffon', 'Comte de Chambord', 'Duchesse de Rohan', 'Henriette', 'Henriette Boulogne', 'Jacques Cartier', 'Marie Robert', 'Marquise Boccella', 'Miranda', 'Quatre Saisons d'Italie', 'Robert Perpétuel', 'Sydonie', 'Venusta'

Chinas: 'Alice Hoffmann', 'Beauty of Glenhurst', 'Belle Hébé', 'Elise Flory', 'Irène Watts', 'Jean Bach Sisley', 'L'Ouche', 'Marquisette', 'Napoléon', 'Parsons' Pink China', 'Rosada', 'Rouletii'

Teas: 'American Perfection', 'Anna Jung', 'Baronne Henriette Snoy', 'Boadicea', 'Bridesmaid', 'Burbank', 'Caroline', 'Charles Rovelli', 'Comte Amédé de Foras', 'Comtesse de Labarthe', 'Comtesse de Noghera', 'Corinna', 'David Pradel', 'Flavien Budillon', 'Grand-Duc Pierre de Russie', 'Helvetia', 'Henry Bennett', 'Hortensia', 'J.B. Varonne', 'Jeanne Abel', 'Lady Castlereagh', 'Lady Stanley', 'Letty

Coles', 'Maid of Honour', 'Maman Cochet', 'Marie d'Orléans', 'Marie Souleau', 'Maud Little', 'Maurice Rouvier', 'Miss Wenn', Mlle. Claudine Perreau', 'Mlle. la Comtesse de Leuss', 'Mlle. Marie Moreau', 'Mlle. Marie-Thérèse Molinier', 'Mme. Angèle Jacquier', 'Mme. Berkeley', 'Mme. C. Liger', 'Mme. Camille', 'Mme. Charles Franchet', 'Mme. David', 'Mme. de Tartas', 'Mme. de Vatry', 'Mme. Dubroca', 'Mme. Émilie Charrin', 'Mme. Joseph Laperrière', 'Mme. Pauline Labonté', 'Mme. Philémon Cochet', 'Mme. Scipion Cochet', 'Mme. von Siemens', 'Mont Rosa', 'Mrs. Campbell Hall', 'Mrs. Edward Mawley', 'Mrs. Jessie Fremont', 'Mrs. Oliver Ames', 'Number 27', 'Principessa di Napoli', 'Roi de Siam', 'Rosabelle', 'Rosalie', 'Rose d'Evian', 'Rose Nabonnand', 'Santa Rosa', 'Socrate', 'Souvenir de Gabrielle Drevet', 'Souvenir de Geneviève Godard', 'Souvenir de George Sand', 'Souvenir d'un Ami', 'Souvenir de Marie Detrey', 'Susan Louise', 'Sylph', 'Vicomtesse de Bernis', 'Vicomtesse de Wauthier', 'Winter Gem'

Bourbons: 'Adrienne de Cardoville', 'Apolline', 'Baron G.-B. Gonella', 'Baronne de Noirmont', 'Burboniana', 'Capitaine Dyel, de Graville', 'Champion of the World', 'Charles XII', 'Charles Desprez', 'Comtesse de Barbantane', 'Hermosa', 'Hofgärtner Kalb', 'J.B.M. Camm', 'Kathleen Harrop', 'La France', 'Le Roitelet', 'Louise Odier', 'Mrs. Bosanquet', 'Mlle. Alice Marchand', 'Mlle. Andrée Worth', 'Mlle. Claire Truffaut', 'Mlle. Favart', 'Mlle. Marie Drivon', 'Mlle. Madeleine de Vauzelles', 'Mme. Charles Baltet', 'Mme. Chevalier', 'Mme. de Sévigné', 'Mme. Doré', 'Mme. Dubost', 'Mme. Ernest Calvat', 'Mme. Létuvée de Colnet', 'Mme. Nobécourt', 'Mme. Thiers', 'Monsieur Alexandre Pelletier', 'Monsieur Dubost', 'Philémon Cochet', 'Pierre de St.-Cyr', 'Pompon de Wasammes', 'Reine des Île-Bourbons', 'Révérend H. D'Ombrain', 'Reynolds Hole', 'Scipion Cochet', 'Sophie's Perpetual', 'Souvenir de Mme. Auguste Charles'

Hybrid Bourbons, Hybrid Chinas, and Hybrid Noisettes: 'Anaïse', 'Blairii No. 1', 'Blairii No. 2', 'Blairii No. 3', 'Céline', 'Charles Louis No. 1', 'Comtesse de Coutard', 'Coupe d'Hébé', 'Duchesse de Montebello', 'Ekta', 'Frances Bloxam', 'Impératrice Eugénie', 'Jenny', 'L'Admiration', 'La Saumonée', 'Mme. Auguste Rodrigues', '(Mme. Caroline Testout × *R. gallica* Splendens)', 'Mme. Galli-Marie', 'Mme. Lauriol de Barney', 'Mrs. Degraw', 'Paul Perras', 'Roxelane', 'Souvenir de Némours'

Hybrid Perpetuals: 'Abel Grand', 'Adiantifolia', 'Alba Mutabilis', 'Albert Payé', 'Alexandre Dutitre', 'Angèle Fontaine', 'Anna Scharsach', 'Archiduchesse Elizabeth d'Autriche', 'Arrillaga', 'Arthur Weidling', 'Auguste Mie', 'Aurore du Matin', 'Baron Taylor', 'Baronne Adolphe de Rothschild', 'Baronne Nathaniel de Rothschild', 'Baronne de Prailly', 'Baronne Gustave de St.-Paul', 'Berthe Baron', 'Berthe du Mesnil de Mont Chauveau', 'Berti Gimpel', 'Boileau', 'Buffalo-Bill', 'California', 'Caroline d'Arden', 'Caroline de Sansal', 'Charles Bonnet', 'Chot Pestitele', 'Clara Cochet', 'Clémence Raoux', 'Clio', 'Colonel de Sansal', 'Comte Adrien de Germiny', 'Comte de Mortemart', 'Comtesse Branicka', 'Comtesse Cécile de Chabrillant', 'Comtesse de Bresson', 'Comtesse de Flandres', 'Comtesse de Fressinet de Bellanger', 'Comtesse de Roquette-Buisson', 'Comtesse de Serenyi', 'Comtesse Hélène Mier', 'Comtesse Henriette Combes', 'Coronation', 'Dr. Antonin Joly', 'Dr. Bradas Rosa Druschki', 'Dr. Georges Martin', 'Dr. William Gordon', 'Druschka', 'Duc de Constantine', 'Duchess of Edinburgh', 'Duchess of Fife', 'Duchesse d'Orléans', 'Duchesse de Bragance', 'Duchesse de Galliera', 'Duchesse de Sutherland', 'Édouard Fontaine', 'Élise Lemaire', 'Emden', 'Emily Laxton', 'Enfant de France', 'François Levet', 'Général Bedeau', 'Georg Arends', 'Gustave Thierry', 'Harmony', 'Heinrich Münch', 'Heinrich Schultheis', 'Henri Coupé', 'Her Majesty', 'Impératrice Maria Feodorowna', 'Jean-Baptiste Casati', 'Joséphine de Beauharnais', 'La Reine', 'La Tendresse', 'La Vierzonnaise', 'Lady

Arthur Hill', 'Leonie Lambert', 'Marchioness of Exeter', 'Marchioness of Londonderry', 'Margaret Haywood', 'Marquise de Gibot', 'Martin Liebau', 'Mary Corelly', 'Miss Annie Crawford', 'Miss Hassard', 'Mlle. Berthe Lévêque', 'Mlle. Elisabeth de la Rocheterie', 'Mlle. Élise Chabrier', 'Mlle. Honorine Duboc', 'Mlle. Léonie Giessen', 'Mlle. Léonie Persin', 'Mlle. Madeleine Nonin', 'Mlle. Marie Achard', 'Mlle. Marie Chauvet', 'Mlle. Marie de la Villeboisnet', 'Mlle. Marie Closon', 'Mlle. Marie Rady', 'Mlle. Renée Davis', 'Mlle. Suzanne-Marie Rodocanachi', 'Mme. A. Labbley', 'Mme. Alexandre Jullien', 'Mme. Alice Dureau', 'Mme. Alphonse Seux', 'Mme. Amélie Baltet', 'Mme. Anatole Leroy', 'Mme. Antoine Rivoire', 'Mme. Apolline Foulon', 'Mme. Bernutz', 'Mme. Boll', 'Mme. Céline Touvais', 'Mme. César Brunier', 'Mme. Charles Truffaut', 'Mme. Clert', 'Mme. Crozy', 'Mme. Edmond Fabre', 'Mme. Édouard Michel', 'Mme. Eugène Verdier', 'Mme. Eugénie Frémy', 'Mme. Francis Buchner', 'Mme. Gabriel Luizet', 'Mme. Georges Schwartz', 'Mme. Georges Vibert', 'Mme. Hersilie Ortgies', 'Mme. Knorr', 'Mme. la Générale Decaen', 'Mme. Lefebvre', 'Mme. Louis Ricard', 'Mme. Louise Piron', 'Mme. Louise Vigneron', 'Mme. Lureau-Escalaïs', 'Mme. Marcel Fauneau', 'Mme. Marie Van Houtte', 'Mme. Montel', 'Mme. Pierre Margery', 'Mme. Renard', 'Mme. Rose Caron', 'Mme. Scipion Cochet', 'Mme. Soubeyran', 'Mme. Théodore Vernes', 'Mme. Verlot', 'Mme. Verrier Cachet', 'Mme. Veuve Alexandre Pommery', 'Monsieur Étienne Dupuy', 'Monsieur Joseph Chappaz', 'Mrs. Cocker', 'Mrs. Cripps', 'Mrs. George Dickson', 'Mrs. J.F. Redly', 'Mrs. John Laing', 'Mrs. John McLaren', 'Mrs. R.G. Sharman-Crawford', 'Oakmont', 'Orderic Vital', 'Pæonia', 'Peach Blossom', 'Perpétuelle de Neuilly', 'Piron-Medard', 'Président Briand', 'Prince Henri d'Orléans', 'Princesse Amédée de Broglie', 'Princesse de Joinville', 'Princesse Hélène d'Orléans', 'Princesse Lise Troubetzkoï', 'Princesse Radziwill', 'Principessa di Napoli', 'Queen of Edgely', 'Queen of Queens', 'Reine de Danemark', 'Rembrandt',

'Rosa Verschuren', 'Rosslyn', 'Rosy Morn', 'Sa Majesté Gustave V', 'Schön Ingeborg', 'Silver Queen', 'Souvenir d'Arthur de Sansal', 'Souvenir de la Reine d'Angleterre', 'Souvenir de McKinley', 'Souvenir de Mme. Corbœuf', 'Souvenir de Mme. de Corval', 'Souvenir de Mme. H. Thuret', 'Souvenir de Mme. Hennecart', 'Souvenir de Mme. Robert', 'Souvenir de Victor Hugo', 'Spencer', 'Stämmler', 'Suzanne Carrol Of Carrolton', 'Suzanne Wood', 'Symphony', 'Ulster', 'Urdh', 'Vicomtesse Laure de Gironde', 'Victory Rose', 'William Griffith', 'William Warden'

Noisettes and Climbers: 'Adele Frey', 'Belle Portugaise', 'Belle Vichysoise', 'Bougainville', 'Bridesmaid, Climbing', 'Camélia Rose', 'Captain Christy, Climbing', 'Cécile Brunner, Climbing', 'Champneys' Pink Cluster', 'China Doll, Climbing', 'Cinderella', 'Colcestria', 'Columbia, Climbing', 'Dainty Bess, Climbing', 'Dawn', 'Doris Downes', 'Dr. Domingos Pereira', 'Dr. Rouges', 'Distinction, Climbing', 'Duchesse de Grammont', 'Gainesborough', 'Gaston Chandon', 'Glory of California', 'Indiana', 'Irène Bonnet', 'Jeanne Corbœuf', 'Jonkheer J.L. Mock, Climbing', 'Kitty Kininmonth', 'L'Abondance', 'La Follette', 'La France, Climbing', 'Lady Clonbrock', 'Lady Sylvia, Climbing', 'Lucy Thomas', 'Maman Cochet, Climbing', 'Manettii', 'Marguerite Carels', 'Marguerite Desrayaux', 'Marie Robert', 'Miniature, Climbing', 'Mlle. Mathilde Lenaerts', 'Mme. Abel Chatenay, Climbing', 'Mme. Auguste Perrin', 'Mme. Butterfly, Climbing', 'Mme. Caroline Testout, Climbing', 'Mme. Edmée Cocteau', 'Mme. la Général Paul de Benoist', 'Mme. Léon Constantin', 'Mme. Marie Lavalley', 'Mme. Segond-Weber, Climbing', 'Mrs. Henry Morse, Climbing', 'Mrs. W.H. Cutbush, Climbing', 'Multiflore de Vaumarcus', 'Old Blush, Climbing', 'Papillon', 'Pennant', 'Pink Pet, Climbing', 'Pink Rover', 'Pinkie, Climbing', 'Pompon de Paris, Climbing', 'Princess May', 'Queen of Queens, Climbing', 'Radiance, Climbing', 'Rosemary, Climbing',

'Rouletii, Climbing', 'Setina', 'Souvenir de Mme. Ladvocat', 'Tausendschön', 'Tea Rambler', 'Triomphe des Noisettes'

Polyanthas: 'Abondant', 'Apfelblüte', 'Balduin', 'Bertram', 'Bloomfield Abundance', 'Burkhard', 'Charles Metroz', 'China Doll', 'Degenhard', 'Echo', 'Eileen Loow', 'Ellen Poulsen', 'Evaline', 'Evelyn Thornton', 'Fairy Changeling', 'Fairy Maid', 'Fairyland', 'Georges Pernet', 'Giesebrecht', 'Gloire des Polyantha', 'Grete Schreiber', 'Herzblättchen', 'Joséphine Morel', 'La Marne', 'Le Loiret', 'Little Dorrit', 'Loreley', 'Madeleine Orosdy', 'Maman Turbat', 'Margo's Sister', 'Marguerite Rose', 'Mary Bruni', 'Melle Fischer', 'Mevrouw Nathalie Nypels', 'Milrose', 'Miniature', 'Mlle. Cécile Brunner', 'Mlle. Fernande Dupuy', 'Mlle. Marcelle Gaugin', 'Mme. Alégatière', 'Mme. Jules Gouchault', 'Mrs. R.M. Finch', 'Mrs. W.H. Cutbush', 'Nypels Perfection', 'Petite François', 'Phyllis', 'Pink Cécile Brunner', 'Pink Pet', 'Pink Posy', 'Pink Soupert', 'Pinkie', 'Princess Ena', 'Radium', 'Renoncule', 'Rita Sammons', 'Schöne von Holstein', 'Sisi Ketten', 'Spray Cécile Brunner', 'Summer Dawn', 'Susanna', 'The Allies', 'The Fairy', 'Waverly Triumph', 'Weeping China Doll'

Hybrid Teas: 'Abbé Millot', 'Amateur André Fourcaud', 'Astra', 'Aurora', 'Australia Felix', 'Béatrix, Comtesse de Buisseret', 'Beauty of Stapleford', 'Becker's Ideal', 'Camoëns', 'Captain Christy', 'Charles Dickens', 'Clara Barton', 'Columbia', 'Commandant Letourneux', 'Coronet', 'Dainty Bess', 'Dame Edith Helen', 'Distinction', 'Duchess of Connaught', 'Emin Pascha', 'Gladys Harkenss', 'Irish Glory', 'Isobel', 'Jean Sisley', 'Jonkheer J.L. Mock', 'Kathleen', 'Kathleen Mills', 'Killarney Queen', 'Lady Alice Stanley', 'Lady Ashtown', 'Lady Mary Fitzwilliam', 'Lady Sylvia', 'Lina Schmidt-Michel', 'Madeleine Gaillard', 'Marie Zahn', 'Minna', 'Mlle. Germaine Caillot', 'Mme. A. Schwaller', 'Mme. Abel Chatenay', 'Mme. Angèle Favre', 'Mme. Bessemer', 'Mme. Blondel', 'Mme. Butterfly', 'Mme. Caroline Testout', 'Mme. Charles Boutmy', 'Mme. Cunisset-Carnot', 'Mme. Dailleux', 'Mme. Ernest Piard', 'Mme. Eugénie Boullet', 'Mme.

Georges Bénard', 'Mme. Joseph Bonnaire', 'Mme. Marie Croibier', 'Mme. Maurice de Luze', 'Mme. Segond-Weber', 'Mme. Viger', 'Monsieur Fraissenon', 'Mrs. Charles J. Bell', 'Mrs. Henry Morse', 'Mrs. Robert Garrett', 'Mrs. Wakefield Christy-Miller', 'Mrs. W.C. Whitney', 'Papa Lambert', 'Pharisäer', 'Reine Carola de Saxe', 'Rosa Gruss an Aachen', 'Sheila', 'Sunny South', 'Viscountess Folkestone'

Deep Pink to Rose and Rose-Red

Damask Perpetuals: 'Amanda Patenotte', 'Belle Fabert', 'Bernard', 'Casimir Delavigne', 'Céline Bourdier', 'Césonie', 'Delambre', 'Duchesse de Montmorency', 'Jeanne Hachette', 'Joasine Hanet', 'Le Prince de Galles', 'Mathilde Jesse', 'Monthly Rose', 'Portlandica', 'Quatre Saisons d'Italie', 'Rose de Trianon', 'Yolande d'Aragon'

Chinas: 'Beauty of Rosemawr', 'Bébé Fleuri', 'Bengale Centfeuilles', 'Bengali', 'Douglas', 'Fimbriata à Pétales Frangés', 'Général Labutère', 'Institutrice Moulins', 'Le Vésuve', 'Rose de l'Inde'

Teas: 'Adam', 'Albert Stopford', 'Archiduc Joseph', 'Auguste Comte', 'Bon Silène', 'Bougère', 'Camille Roux', 'Captain Philip Green', 'Charles de Legrady', 'Claudius Levet', 'Ernest Metz', 'F.L. Segers', 'Freiherr von Marschall', 'Général D. Mertchansky', 'Henri Plantagenet, Comte d'Anjou', 'Joseph Paquet', 'Maréchal Bugeaud', 'Marquise de Vivens', 'Mevrouw Boreel van Hogelander', 'Minnie Francis', 'Miss Agnes C. Sherman', 'Miss Ethel Brownlow', 'Mme. A. Étienne', 'Mme. Céline Noirey', 'Mme. Ernestine Verdier', 'Mme. P. Kuntz', 'Mme. Victor Caillet', 'Monsieur Tillier', 'Morning Glow', 'Mrs. B.R. Cant', 'Mrs. J. Pierpont Morgan', 'Mrs. Reynolds Hole', 'Nelly Johnstone', 'Niles Cochet', 'Papa Gontier', 'Paul Nabonnand', 'Regulus', 'Reichsgraf E. von Kesselstatt', 'Reine Olga', 'Safrano à Fleurs Rouges', 'Sénateur Loubet', 'Souvenir de Clairvaux', 'Souvenir de David d'Angers', 'Sweet Passion', 'Triomphe du Luxembourg', 'V. Vivo é Hijos', 'Waban'

Bourbons: 'Adam Messerich', 'Béatrix', 'Catherine Guillot', 'Émile Courtier', 'Georges Cuvier', 'Héroïne de Vaucluse', 'Impératrice Eugénie', 'Jean Rameau', 'Leveson-Gower', 'Martha', 'Mme. Arthur Oger', 'Mme. Desprez', 'Mme. Isaac Pereire', 'Monsieur Cordeau', 'Prince Napoléon', 'Reine Victoria', 'Réveil', 'Rose Édouard', 'Sir Joseph Paxton', 'Souvenir d'Adèle Launay', 'Victoire Fontaine', 'Zéphirine Drouhin'

Hybrid Bourbons, Hybrid Chinas, and Hybrid Noisettes: 'Athalin', 'Capitaine Sissolet', 'Charles Duval', 'Charles Lawson', 'Général Allard', 'Las-Cases', 'Marguerite Lartay', 'Paul Ricault', 'Paul Verdier', 'Richelieu', 'Riégo', 'Vivid'

Hybrid Perpetuals: 'Abbé Giraudier', 'Adélaïde de Meynot', 'Alfred Colomb', 'Alpaïde de Rotalier', 'Alphonse Soupert', 'Ambrogio Maggi', 'American Beauty', 'American Belle', 'Ami Charmet', 'Anna Alexieff', 'Anna de Diesbach', 'Anny Laxton', 'Antoine Mouton', 'Aristide Dupuy', 'Baronne Prévost', 'Belle de Normandy', 'Benoist Pernin', 'Captain Hayward', 'Centifolia Rosea', 'Colonel Foissy', 'Comte de Falloux', 'Comte de Paris', 'Comte Florimund de Bergeyck', 'Comtesse Bertrand de Blacas', 'Comtesse Cahen d'Anvers', 'Comtesse de Falloux', 'Comtesse Duchâtel', 'Cornet', 'Countess of Rosebery', 'Dr. Hurta', 'Dr. Marx', 'Duchesse d'Aoste', 'Duchesse de Canbacérès', 'Duchesse de Caylus', 'Duchesse de Vallombrosa', 'Eliska Krásnohorská', 'Étienne Levet', 'Felbergs Rosa Druschki', 'Félicien David', 'François Michelon', 'Général Cavaignac', 'Général de la Martinière', 'George Paul', 'Gerbe de Roses', 'Grandeur de Cheshunt', 'Guillaume Gillemot', 'Helen Keller', 'Hippolyte Jamain' (both), 'Inigo Jones', 'Jacques Laffitte', 'Jean Goujon', 'Jean Rosenkrantz', 'Jeannie Dickson', 'John Hopper', 'Jules Margottin', 'L'Ami E. Daumont', 'L'Espérance', 'La Duchesse de Morny', 'Lena Turner', 'Louis Noisette', 'Louise Peyronny', 'Lyonnais', 'Magna Charta', 'Marchioness of Lorne', 'Marie Louise Pernet', 'Marie Menudel', 'Marquise de Castellane', 'Marquise de

Verdun', 'Maurice Lepelletier', 'Mlle. Hélène Croissandeau', 'Mlle. Thérèse Levet', 'Mme. Baulot', 'Mme. Bellon', 'Mme. Bertha Mackart', 'Mme. Charles Verdier', 'Mme. Chirard', 'Mme. Clémence Joigneaux', 'Mme. Cordier', 'Mme. Crespin', 'Mme. Ferdinand Jamin', 'Mme. Fillion', 'Mme. Henri Perrin', 'Mme. Laffay', 'Mme. Lierval', 'Mme. Rambaux', 'Mme. Renahy', 'Mme. Roger', 'Mme. Schmitt', 'Mme. Scipion Cochet', 'Mme. Sophie Stern', 'Mme. Sophie Tropot', 'Mme. Thibaut', 'Monsieur Alfred Leveau', 'Monsieur de Montigny', 'Monsieur Fillion', 'Monsieur Jules Monges', 'Mrs. Laing', 'Mrs. Rumsey', 'Nardy Frères', 'Olivier Belhomme', 'Paul Neyron', 'Paul Verdier', 'Pride of Waltham', 'Princesse Hélène', 'Princesse Marie d'Orléans', 'Princesse Marie Dolgorouky', 'Prudence Besson', 'Reine de Castille', 'Reverend Alan Cheales', 'Robert Duncan', 'Rose de France', 'Sisley', 'Souvenir de Béranger', 'Souvenir de l'Ami Labruyère', 'Souvenir de Leveson-Gower', 'Souvenir de Mme. Jeanne Balandreau', 'Souvenir de Monsieur Droche', 'Souvenir du Président Porcher', 'Théodore Liberton', 'Thomas Mills', 'Thorin', 'Triomphe de France', 'Triomphe de la Terre des Roses', 'Ulrich Brunner fils', 'Vicomtesse de Vezins', 'Ville de Lyon', 'Ville de St.-Denis', 'Vincent-Hippolyte Duval', 'Vincente Peluffo', 'Victor le Bihan', 'Victor Verdier'

Noisettes and Climbers: 'American Beauty, Climbing', 'Archduchess Charlotte', 'Capitaine Soupa, Climbing', 'Captain Hayward, Climbing', 'Dame Edith Helen, Climbing', 'Étoile de Portugal', 'Flying Colours', 'General-Superior Arnold Janssen, Climbing', 'Gloire de Bordeaux', 'La France de 89', 'Le Vésuve, Climbing', 'Marie Bülow', 'Mme. Julie Lassen', 'Monsieur Rosier', 'Mrs. B.R. Cant, Climbing', 'Mrs. Rosalie Wrinch', 'Mrs. W.J. Grant, Climbing', 'Papa Gontier, Climbing', 'Queen of Hearts', 'Reine Maria Pia', 'Scorcher', 'Souvenir de Lucie', 'Vicomtesse d'Avesnes', 'Vicomtesse Pierre de Fou', 'Wootton, Climbing'

Polyanthas: 'Ännchen Müller', 'Baptiste Lafaye', 'Dr. Reymont', 'Fairy Ring', 'Frau Anna Pasquay', 'Frau Oberhofgärtner Singer', 'Gabrielle Privat', 'Greta Kluis', 'Jean Mermoz', 'Kleiner Liebling', 'Mauve', 'Mimi Pinson', 'Mme. Arthur Robichon', 'Primula' 'Rösel Dach'

Hybrid Teas: 'Australie', 'Bona Weillschott', 'Countess of Caledon', 'Danmark', 'Dean Hole', 'Directeur Constant Bernard', 'Dr. Pasteur', 'Duchess of Albany', 'Duchess of Westminster', 'Élise Masson', 'Ferdinand Jamin', 'General-Superior Arnold Janssen', 'Gigantesque', 'Grand-Duch Adolphe de Luxembourg', 'Grossherzog Ernst Ludwig von Hesse', 'Gustav Grünerwald', 'Jean Lorthois', 'Killarney Brilliant', 'Magnafrano', 'Mamie', 'Marquise Litta de Breteuil', 'Mlle. Brigitte Viollet', 'Mme. Jules Grolez', 'Mme. Julie Weidmann', 'Mme. P. Euler', 'Mme. Wagram, Comtesse de Turenne', 'Mrs. W.J. Grant', 'Pierre Wattinne', 'Radiance', 'Red Radiance', 'Souvenir de Monsieur Frédéric Vercellone', 'Souvenir of Wootton'

Medium Red

Damask Perpetuals: 'Desdémona', 'Jeune Henry', 'Jules Lesourd', 'Laurent Heister', 'Rembrandt', 'Rose du Roi'

Chinas: 'Animating', 'Bengale d'Automne', 'Charlotte Klemm', 'Cramoisi Supérieur', 'Fabvier', 'Granate', 'La Spécieuse', 'Laffay', 'Miss Lowe's Variety', 'Red Pet', 'Reine de la Lombardie', 'Rose de Bengale', 'Sanglant', 'Slater's Crimson China', 'St. Priest de Breuze'

Teas: 'Betty Berkeley', 'Corallina', 'Duchess of Edinburgh', 'Empereur Nicolas II', 'Général Tartas', 'Georges Farber', 'Goubault', 'Jules Finger', 'Julius Fabianics de Misefa', 'Margherita di Simone', 'Marion Dingee', 'Marquise de Querhoënt', 'Meta', 'Mme. Antoine Rébé', 'Mme. Clémence Marchix', 'Mme. E. Vicaro', 'Mme. F. Brassac', 'Mme. Jules Cambon', 'Mme. la Princesse de Radziwill', 'Mme. Thérèse Deschamps', 'Monsieur Édouard Littaye', 'Princess Bonnie', 'Professeur Ganiviat', 'Rosa Mundi', 'S.A.R. Mme. la Princesse de

Hohenzollern, Infante de Portugal', 'Simone Thomas', 'Souvenir d'Auguste Legros', 'Souvenir de l'Amiral Courbet', 'Souvenir de Lady Ashburton', 'Souvenir du Dr. Passot', 'V. Viviand-Morel'

Bourbons: 'Belle Nanon', 'Bouquet de Flore', 'Comice de Seine-et-Marne', 'Comice de Tarn-et-Garonne', 'Dr. Brière', 'Duc de Crillon', 'Dunkelrote Hermosa', 'Fellemberg', 'Frau Dr. Schricker', 'Garibaldi', 'Gloire des Rosomanes', 'Gruss an Teplitz', 'Marquis de Balbiano', 'Mme. Adélaïde Ristori', 'Mme. Eugène E. Marlitt', 'Mme. Gabriel Luizet', 'Monsieur A. Maillé', 'Omer-Pacha', 'Président de la Rocheterie', 'Président Gausen', 'Queen of Bedders', 'Souvenir de l'Exposition de Londres', 'Souvenir de Monsieur Bruel', 'Souvenir de Victor Landeau', 'Souvenir de Lieutenant Bujon', 'Vicomte Fritz de Cussy'

Hybrid Bourbons, Hybrid Chinas, and Hybrid Noisettes: 'Bijou des Amateurs', 'Brennus', 'Catherine Bonnard', 'Cerise Éclatante', 'Chénédolé', 'Francis B. Hayes', 'Joseph Gourdon', 'Le Météore', 'Le Vingt-Neuf Juillet', 'Malton', 'Mme. Jeannine Joubert', 'Paul's Carmine Pillar', 'Souvenir d'Anselme', 'Souvenir de Paul Dupuy', 'William Jesse'

Hybrid Perpetuals: 'A. Geoffrey de St.-Hilaire', 'Abbé Berlèze', 'Abraham Zimmermann', 'Achille Cesbron', 'Achille Gonod', 'Adrien Schmitt', 'Alexandre Dupont', 'Alexis Lepère', 'Alfred K. Williams', 'Ami Martin', 'Amiral Courbet', 'Auguste Chaplain', 'Aurore Boréale', 'Baron Chaurand', 'Baron de Wolseley', 'Baron Nathaniel de Rothschild', 'Baronne de Medem', 'Bathélemy-Joubert', 'Beauty of Beeston', 'Beauty of Waltham', 'Belle Yvrienne', 'Ben Cant', 'Bijou de Couasnon', 'Boccace', 'Boïldieu', 'Camille Bernardin', 'Capitaine Jouen', 'Charles Lamb', 'Charles Margottin', 'Charles Turner', 'Charles Wagner', 'Clémence Joigneaux', 'Commandeur Jules Gravereaux', 'Comte Charles d'Harcourt', 'Comte de Paris', 'Comte Horace de Choiseul', 'Comte Odart', 'Comte Raimbaud', 'Comte Raoul Chandon', 'Comtesse d'Oxford', 'Comtesse Renée de Béarn',

'Crimson Bedder', 'Crimson Queen', 'Denis Hélye', 'Desgaches', 'Desirée Fontaine', 'Dr. Andry', 'Dr. Auguste Krell', 'Druschki Rubra', 'Duc d'Anjou', 'Duc d'Audiffret-Pasquier', 'Duc d'Harcourt', 'Duc de Bragance', 'Duc de Marlborough', 'Duc de Montpensier', 'Duchess of Bedford', 'Duchesse d'Ossuna', 'Duhamel-Dumonceau', 'Dike of Fife', 'Duke of Teck', 'Dupuy-Jamain', 'Earl of Pembroke', 'Éclaireur', 'Édouard André le Botaniste', 'Édouard Hervé', 'Elisabeth Vigneron', 'Émile Bardiaux', 'Ernest Morel', 'Ernest Prince', 'Étienne Dubois', 'Ferdinand Chaffolte', 'Ferdinand Jamin', 'Firebrand', 'Florence Paul', 'François I', 'François Coppée', 'Gaspard Monge', 'Général Baron Berge', 'Général Désaix', 'Général Duc d'Aumale', 'General von Bothnia-Andreæ', 'George Dickson', 'Georges Moreau', 'Georges Rousset', 'Gloire d'un Enfant d'Hiram', 'Gloire de Bourg-la-Reine', 'Gloire de Chédane-Guinoisseau', 'Golfe-Juan', 'Gustave Piganeau', 'Haileybury', 'Hans Mackart', 'Henry Bennett', 'High Dickson', 'Ingénieur Madèlé' 'Jan Böhm', 'Jean Lelièvre', 'Jeanne Sury', 'Joachim du Bellay', 'John Bright', 'John Gould Veitch', 'John Stuart Mill', 'Jules Barigny', 'Jules Seurre', 'Katkoff', 'L'Ami Maubry', 'L'Étincelante', 'La Brillante', 'La Motte Sanguin', 'La Nantaise', 'La Syrène', 'Lady Helen Stewart', 'Laforcade', 'Laurent de Rillé', 'Le Havre', 'Le Triomphe de Saintes', 'Léon Renault', 'Léon Say', 'Léonie Lartay', 'Léopold I, Roi des Belges', 'Lord Frédéric Cavendish', 'Lord Raglan', 'Lord Macaulay', 'Louis Lille', 'Louis Philippe Albert d'Orléans', 'Lucien Duranthon', 'Marie Baumann', 'Mary Pochin', 'Maurice Bernardin', 'Michel-Ange', 'Miller-Hayes', 'Mlle. Annie Wood', 'Mlle. Gabrille de Peyronny', 'Mlle. Hélène Michel', 'Mlle. Marie Magat', 'Mme. Boutin', 'Mme. Cécile Morand', 'Mme. Charles Crapelet', 'Mme. Charles Wood', 'Mme. Constant David', 'Mme. de Selve', 'Mme. de Trotter', 'Mme. Domage', 'Mme. Elisa Tasson', 'Mme. Ernest Levavasseur', 'Mme. François Bruel', 'Mme. Grandin-Monville', 'Mme. Henri Pereire', 'Mme. Jean Everaerts', 'Mme. Lucien Chauré', 'Mme. Marie Grange', 'Mme. Marthe d'Halloy', 'Mme. Prosper Laugier', 'Mme. Roudillon', 'Mme. Théobald Sernin', 'Mme. Thévenot', 'Mme. Victor Verdier', 'Monsieur de Morand', 'Monsieur E.Y. Teas', 'Monsieur Francisque Rive', 'Monsieur Hoste', 'Monsieur Jean Cordier', 'Monsieur Journaux', 'Monsieur Jules Lemaître', 'Monsieur le Capitaine Louis Frère', 'Monseigneur Fournier', 'Montebello', 'Mrs. Baker', 'Mrs. Elliot', 'Oliver Métra', 'Orgeuil de Lyon', 'Oriflamme de St. Louis', 'Oscar II, Roi de Suède', 'Oskar Cordel', 'Pæonia', 'Paul de la Meilleraye', 'Paula Clegg', 'Peter Lawson', 'Philipp Paulig', 'Philippe Bardet', 'Pierre Carot', 'Président Carnot', 'Président Sénélar', 'Président Willermoz', 'Prince de Joinville', 'Prince de Portia', 'Prince Waldemar', 'Princess of Wales', 'Princesse Charles d'Aremberg', 'Princesse de Béarn', 'Professeur Maxime Cornu', 'Prosper Laugier', 'Reine d'Espagne', 'Rouge Angevine', 'Rubens', 'Ruhm von Steinfurth', 'Rushton-Radclyffe', 'Sir Garnet Wolseley', 'Souvenir d'Adolphe Thiers', 'Souvenir d'André Raffy', 'Souvenir de Grégoire Bordillon', 'Souvenir de Laffay', 'Souvenir de Léon Gambetta', 'Souvenir de Léon Roudillon', 'Souvenir de Mme. Alfred Vy', 'Souvenir de Mme. Berthier', 'Souvenir de Mme. Chédane-Guinoisseau', 'Souvenir de Monsieur Boll', 'Souvenir de Monsieur Faivre', 'Souvenir de Monsieur Rousseau d'Angers', 'Souvenir de Pierre Sionville', 'Souvenir de Victor Verdier', 'Souvenir du Rosiériste Gonod', 'Star of Waltham', 'Tancrède', 'Tom Wood', 'Triomphe d'Alençon', 'Triomphe de l'Exposition', 'Turenne', 'Vainqueur de Goliath', 'Vicomte Maison', 'Vyslanec Kalina', 'Waldfee'

Noisettes and Climbers: 'Albert la Blotais', 'Apotheker Georg Höfer, Climbing', 'Ards Rambler', 'Cracker, Climbing', 'Crimson Conquest', 'Deschamps', 'Effective', 'Empress of China', 'François Crousse', 'Fürstin Bismarck', 'General MacArthur, Climbing', 'George Dickson, Climbing', 'Geschwinds Gorgeous', 'Glory of Waltham', 'Gruss an Teplitz, Climbing', 'Henry Irving', 'James Sprunt', 'Jules Margottin, Climbing', 'Lilliput', 'Meteor', 'Mikado',

'Miss Marion Manifold', 'Mlle. Geneviève Godard', 'Mme. Couturier-Mention', 'Mme. Rose Romarin', 'Nanc Hayward', 'Neervelt', 'Noëlla Nabonnand', 'Reine Marie Henriette', 'Reine Olga de Wutemberg', 'Richmond, Climbing', 'Sénateur Amic', 'Souvenir de Mère Fontaine', 'Souvenir de Mme. Joseph Métral', 'Sunday Best', 'Waltham Climber I', 'Waltham Climber II', 'Waltham Climber III'

Polyanthas: 'Alberich', 'Betsy van Nes', 'Border King', 'Bordure', 'Chatillon Rose', 'Cineraria', 'Fairy Damsel', 'Fairy Prince', 'Flamboyant', 'Frau Elise Kreis', 'Gloire de Charpennes', 'Gustel Mayer', 'Indéfectible', 'Jessie', 'Kersbergen', 'Lady Reading', 'Lillan', 'Lindbergh', 'Ma Petite Andrée', 'Maréchal Foch', 'Merveille des Rouges', 'Mlle. Blanche Rebatel', 'Mme. Norbert Levavasseur', 'Mme. Taft', 'Orléans-Rose', 'Papa Hémeray', 'Paris', 'Perle des Rouges', 'Rodhätte', 'Rotkäppchen', 'Souvenir de Mlle. Élise Châtelard', 'Sparkler', 'Stadtrat Meyn', 'Triomphe Orléanais', 'Verdun Superior'

Hybrid Teas: 'Admiral Dewey', 'Antonine Verdier', 'Attraction', 'Augustus Hartmann', 'Aviateur Michel Mahieu', 'Avoca', 'Balduin', 'Bedford Belle', 'Cardinal', 'Comtesse Icy Hardegg', 'Exquisite', 'Frances Ashton', 'General MacArthur', 'Henri Brichard', 'K. of K.', 'Mme. André Duron', 'Mme. Alfred Sabatier', 'Mme. Charles Détraux', 'Mme. Emilie Lafon', 'Mme. Étienne Levet', 'Mrs. Cynthia Forde', 'Pierre Guillot', 'Reine Marguerite d'Italie', 'Richmond', 'Rosette de la Légion d'Honneur', 'Ruhm der Gartenwelt', 'Triomphe de Pernet Père', 'Vesuvius'

Deep Red, Maroon, Purple, Violet, "Blue," and "Black"

Damask Perpetuals: 'Christophe Colombe', 'Ebène', 'Indigo', 'Jacques Amyot', 'Leseuer', 'Louis-Philippe I', 'Mogador', 'Pergolèse', 'Portland Pourpre', 'Président Dutailly', 'Rose de Rescht'

Chinas: 'Alice Hamilton' 'Beau Carmin', 'Belle de Monza', 'Bengale Nabonnand', 'Bengale Sanguinaire', 'Blue Rose', 'Cruenta', 'Darius', 'Eugène de Beauharnais', 'Louis-Philippe', 'Lucullus', 'Maréchal de Villars', 'Némésis', 'Papillon', 'Princesse de Sagan', 'Purpurea', 'Unermüdliche'

Teas: 'Aline Sisley', 'Alphonse Karr', 'André Schwartz', 'Capitaine Lefort', 'Colonel Juffé', 'Empress Alexandra of Russia', 'Francis Dubreuil', 'Garden Robinson', 'Général Billot', 'Isaac Demole', 'Joseph Métral', 'Mlle. Christine de Noué', 'Mme. Agathe Nabonnand', 'Mme. Cusin', 'Monsieur le Chevalier Angelo Ferrario', 'Penelope', 'Souvenir de François Gaulain', 'Souvenir de Germain de St.-Pierre', 'Souvenir de Thérèse Levet', 'Souvenir du Père Lalanne'

Bourbons: 'Amarante', 'Amédée de Langlois', 'Bardou Job', 'Catalunya', 'Deuil du Dr. Raynaud', 'Deuil du Duc d'Orléans', 'Dr. Leprestre', 'Frau O. Plegg', 'Lorna Doone', 'Malmaison Rouge', 'Mlle. Joséphine Guyet', 'Monsieur Gourdault', 'Prince Albert', 'Proserpine', 'Robusta', 'Souchet', 'Souvenir d'un Frère', 'Souvenir de Louis Gaudin', 'Souvenir du Président Lincoln', 'Toussaint-Louverture', 'Velouté d'Orléans', 'Zigeunerblut'

Hybrid Bourbons, Hybrid Chinas, and Hybrid Noisettes: 'Arthur Young', 'Belle de Crécy', 'Belle Violette', 'Cardinal de Richelieu', 'Chévrier', 'De Vergnies', 'Deuil du Maréchal Mortier', 'Dombrowski', 'Edward Jesse', 'George IV', 'Great Western', 'Jules Jürgensen', 'La Nubienne', 'La Philippine', 'Louis-Philippe', 'Ohl', 'Parkzierde', 'Prince Charles', 'Souvenir de Paul Dupuy', 'Vibert', 'Zigeunerknabe'

Hybrid Perpetuals: 'A. Drawiel', 'A.-M. Ampère', 'Abbé Bramerel', 'Abel Carrière', 'Alexandre Chomer', 'Alexandre Dumas', 'Aly Pacha Chérif', 'Alphonse de Lamartine', 'Alsace-Lorraine', 'Amédée Philibert', 'Amiral Gravina', 'André Leroy d'Angers', 'Anne Laferrère', 'Antoine Ducher', 'Ardoisée de Lyon', 'Arthur de Sansal', 'Arthur Oger', 'Avocat Duvivier', 'Barbarossa', 'Baron de Bonstetten', 'Baron Elisi de St.-Albert', 'Baron Haussmann', 'Baron T'Kint de Roodenbeke', 'Baronne de St.-Didier', 'Baronne Maurice de Graviers', 'Benjamin Drouet', 'Bernard Verlot', 'Black Prince', 'Capitaine Peillon', 'Cardinal Patrizzi', 'Charles Darwin', 'Charles Gater', 'Charles Lefebvre', 'Charles Martel', 'Charles Wood', 'Claude Jacquet', 'Claude Million', 'Colonel Félix Breton', 'Comte de Bobrinsky', 'Comte de Flandres', 'Comte Frédéric de Thun de Hohenstein', 'Comtesse de Polignac', 'Comtesse O'Gorman', 'Crown Prince', 'Dames Patronesses d'Orléans', 'Deuil de Dunois', 'Deuil du Colonel Denfert', 'Devienne-Lamy', 'Directeur Alphand', 'Directeur N. Jensen', 'Dr. Baillon', 'Dr. Bretonneau', 'Dr. Hogg', 'Dr. Ingomar H. Blohm', 'Dr. Jamain', 'Dr. Müllers Rote', 'Duc de Cazes', 'Duc de Chartres', 'Duc de Wellington', 'Duchess of Connaught', 'Duchesse de Dino', 'Duke of Edinburgh', 'Earl of Dufferin', 'Éclair', 'Empereur du Maroc', 'Emperor', 'Empress of India', 'Erinnerung an Brod', 'Eugène Appert', 'Eugène Fürst', 'Eugène Verdier', 'Félix Mousset', 'Fisher-Holmes', 'François Arago', François Gaulain', 'Fréderic II de Prusse', 'Friedrich von Schiller', 'Fürst Leopold zu Schaumburg-Lippe', 'Géant des Batailles', 'Général Appert', 'Général Barral', 'Général Jacqueminot', 'General Stefanik', Général Washington', 'Génie de Châteaubriand', 'Gloire de Ducher', 'Gloire de l'Exposition de Bruxelles', 'Graf Fritz Metternich', 'Grand-Duc Alexis', 'Gruss aus Pallien', 'Henri IV', 'Henriette Petit', 'Henry Nevard', 'Horace Vernet', 'J.B. Clark', 'Janine Viaud-Bruant', 'Jean Cherpin', 'Jean Liabaud', 'Jean Soupert', 'John Keynes', 'John Laing', 'Jubilee', 'Jules Chrétien', 'Kaiser Wilhelm I', 'König Friedrich II von

Dänemark', 'La Brunoyenne', 'La Rosière', 'Lecoq-Dumesnil', 'Léon Delaville', 'Lion des Combats', 'Lord Bacon', 'Lord Beaconsfield', 'Louis XIV', 'Louis Donadine', 'Louis Gulino', 'Louis Rollet', 'Louis Van Houtte', 'Louise d'Autriche', 'M.H. Walsh', 'Maharajah', 'Marguerite Brassac', 'Marshall P. Wilder', 'Maxime de la Rocheterie', 'Meyerbeer', 'Michel Strogoff', 'Mlle. Jules Grévy', 'Mlle. Marie Dauvesse', 'Mme. Charles Meurice', 'Mme. Charles Montigny', 'Mme. de Ridder', 'Mme. Julia Daran', 'Mme. Lemesle', 'Mme. Léon Halkin', 'Mme. Loeben de Sels', 'Mme. Marguerite Marsault', 'Mme. Masson', 'Mme. Rosa Monnet', 'Mme. Yorke', 'Monsieur Albert la Blotais', 'Monsieur Bonçenne', 'Monsieur Édouard Détaille', 'Monsieur Ernest Dupré', 'Monsieur Eugène Delaire', 'Monsieur Jules Deroudilhe', 'Monsieur Lauriol de Barney', 'Monsieur le Préfet Limbourg', 'Monsieur Louis Ricard', 'Monsieur Mathieur Baron', 'Napoléon III', 'Notaire Bonnefond', 'Ornement du Luxembourg', 'Pauline Lansezeur', 'Pie IX', 'Pierre Notting', 'Président Lincoln', 'Présudent Schlachter', 'Prince Albert', 'Prince Arthur', 'Prince Camille de Rohan', 'Prince Eugène de Beauharnais', 'Prnce Noir', 'Professeur Charguereaud', 'Reine des Violettes', 'Riccordo di Fernando Scarlatti', 'Rosiériste Harms', 'Salamander', 'Secrétaire J. Nicolas', 'Sénateur Vaïsse', 'Simon de St.-Jean', 'Sir Rowland Hill', 'Souvenir d'Alexandre Hardy', 'Souvenir d'Aline Fontaine', 'Souvenir d'Alphonse Lavallée', 'Souvenir d'Auguste Rivière', 'Souvenir de Bertrand Guinoisseau', 'Souvenir de Caillat', 'Souvenir de Charles Montault', 'Souvenir de Henri L'evêque de Vilmorin', 'Souvenir de John Gould Veitch', 'Souvenir de la Princesse Amélie des Pays-Bas', 'Souvenir de Mme. Sadie Carnot', 'Souvenir de William Wood', 'Souvenir de Baron de Semur', 'Souvenir du Comte de Cavour', 'Souvenir du Dr. Jamain', 'Sultan of Zanzibar', 'Symmetry', 'Tartarus', 'Triomphe de Caen', 'Triomphe de Toulouse', 'Velours Pourpre', 'Venus', 'Vicomte de Lauzières', 'Victor-Emmanuel',

'Victor Hugo', 'Victor Lemoine', 'Violet Queen', 'Vulcain', 'Waltham Standard', 'Xavier Olibo'

Noisettes and Climbers: 'Ards Rover', 'Black Boy', 'Château de Clos-Vougeot, Climbing', 'Cheshunt Hybrid', 'Étoile de Hollande, Climbing', 'Florence Haswell Veitch', 'Frau Geheimrat Dr. Staub', 'Hadley, Climbing', 'König Friedrich II von Dänemark, Climbing', 'Liberty, Climbing', 'Lily Metschersky', 'Louis-Philippe, Climbing', 'Miss G. Mesman', 'Mme. Louis Ricard, Climbing', 'Mme. Martignier', 'Monsieur Désir', 'Purple East', 'Sarah Bernhardt', 'Souvenir de Claudius Denoyel', 'Wenzel Geschwind, Climbing'

Polyanthas: 'Baby Faurax', 'Eberwein', 'Éblouissant', 'Erna Teschendorff', 'Frau Rudolf Schmidt', 'Gloire d'Orléans', 'Ideal', Jacques Proust', 'Magenta', 'Miss Edith Cavell', 'Muttertag', 'Red Triumph', 'Verdun'

Hybrid Teas: 'Adèle Bougère', 'Andenken an Moritz von Frölich', 'Château de Clos-Vougeot', 'Chloris', 'Dr. Cazeneuve', 'Duke of Connaught', 'Erinnerung an Scholss Scharfenstein', 'Étoile de Hollande', 'Hadley', 'His Majesty', 'Honourable George Bancroft', 'Jules Toussaint', 'Liberty', 'Ma Tulipe', 'Marquise de Salisbury', 'Mme. Élisa de Vilmorin', 'Mme. Jules Grévy', 'Mme. Méha Sabatier', 'Shandon', 'Souvenir d'Auguste Métral', 'The Dandy', 'The Meteor', 'W.E. Lippiatt', 'William Francis Bennett'

Sulphur to Light Yellow and Paler Buff

Damask Perpetuals: —None—

Chinas: 'Primrose Queen'

Teas: 'Alexander Hill Gray', 'Alix Roussel', 'Anna Olivier', 'Canari', 'Château des Bergeries', 'Comtesse de Frigneuse', 'Comtesse de Vitzthum', 'Comtesse Eva Starhemberg', 'Coquette de Lyon', 'Duchesse de Bragance', 'Élise Sauvage', 'Enfant de Lyon', 'Étoile de

Lyon', 'Exadelphé', 'Golden Gate', 'Harry Kirk', 'Isabella Sprunt', 'Jean Pernet', 'Le Pactole', 'Léon de Bruyn', 'Louise de Savoie', 'Lutea Flora', 'Maréchal Robert', 'Medea', 'Miss Alice de Rothschild', 'Mme. Azélie Imbert', 'Mme. Albert Bernardin', 'Mme. Barthélemy Levet', 'Mme. C.P. Strassheim', 'Mme. Chédane-Guinoisseau', 'Mme. Derepas-Matrat', 'Mme. Devoucoux', 'Mme. Fanny Pauwels', 'Mme. Marthe du Bourg', 'Mme. Paul Varin-Bernier', 'Mme. Pelisson', 'Mme. P. Perny', 'Monsieur Charles de Thézillat', 'Mrs. Dudley Cross', 'Muriel Grahame', 'Namenlose Schöne', 'Narcisse', 'Parks' Yellow Tea-Scented China', 'Peace', 'Perfection de Monplaisir', 'Perle des Jardins', 'Primrose', 'Princess Beatrix', 'Safrano', 'Shirley Hibberd', 'Smith's Yellow China', 'Sulphurea', 'Triomphe de Milan', 'True Friend', 'Uncle John', 'Victor Pulliat', 'Zephyr'

Bourbons: 'Kronprinzessin Viktoria von Preussen'

Hybrid Bourbons, Hybrid Chinas, and Hybrid Noisettes: None, though some of the "whites" will have yellow or buff tintings in the blossom.

Hybrid Perpetuals: 'Hold Slunci', 'Pfaffstädt', 'Prinzessin Elsa zu Schaumburg-Lippe', 'St. Ingebert'

Noisettes and Climbers: 'Alister Stella Gray', 'Baronne Charles de Gargan', 'Belle Lyonnaise', 'Céline Forestier', 'Chromatella', 'Mosella, Climbing', 'Comtesse Georges de Roquette-Buisson', 'Desprez à Fleur Jaune', 'Emilia Plantier', 'Gruss an Friedberg', 'Isabella Gray', 'Lamarque', 'Lemon Queen', 'Maréchal Niel', 'Mlle. Adèle Jougant', 'Mlle. Marie Gaze', 'Mme. Chabanne', 'Mme. Gaston Annouilh', 'Mme. Jules Gravereaux', 'Mme. Louis Henry', 'Mme. Schultz', 'Paul's Lemon Pillar', 'Perle des Jardins, Climbing', 'Rêve d'Or', 'Solfatare'

Polyanthas: 'Archiduchesse Elisabeth-Marie', 'Coronet', 'Diamant', 'Étoile de Mai', 'Frau Cecilie Walter', 'George Elger', 'Golden Fairy', 'La Rosée', 'Martha Keller', 'Mlle. Marthe Cahuzac', 'Mme. E.A.

Nolte', 'Princesse Elisabeth Lancellotti', 'Schneewittchen', 'Siegesperle', 'Topaz'

Hybrid Teas: 'Golden Ophelia', 'Gustav Regis', 'Johannes Wesselhöft', 'Kootenay', 'Mlle. Alice Furon', 'Mme. Pernet-Ducher', 'Mme. Tony Baboud', 'Paul Meunier', 'Souvenir de Mme. Eugène Verdier'

Deep Yellow to Deeper Buff and Fawn, Bronze, Apricot, Copper, Coral, Coral-Pink, Salmon, Orange, Nasturtium, Coppery-Red, and Orange-Red

Damask Perpetuals: —None—

Chinas: 'Arethusa', 'Comtesse du Caÿla', 'Mme. Eugène Résal', 'Queen Mab'

Teas: 'Abricotée', 'Alliance Franco-Russe', 'Antoine Weber', 'Antoinette Durieu', 'Archimède', 'Aureus', "Baxter Beauty', 'Beryl', 'Canadian Belle', 'Chamoïs', 'Charles de Franciosi', 'Comte Chandon', 'Comtesse Anna Thun', 'Comtesse de Nadaillac', 'Comtesse Festetics Hamilton', 'Comtesse Sophie Torby', 'Dr. Félix Guyon', 'Dr. Grandvilliers', 'Edmond de Biauzat', 'Élise Heymann', 'Esther Pradel', 'Fortuna', 'Fürstin Infantin von Hohenzollern', 'Général Galliéni', 'General Robert E. Lee', 'Général Schablikine', 'Georges Schwartz', 'Golden Oriole', 'Henry M. Stanley', 'Jean André', 'Jean Ducher', 'Koningen Wilhelmina', 'La Nankeen', 'Lady Hillingdon', 'Lady Mary Corry', 'Lady Roberts', 'Lady Zoë Brougham', 'Lena', 'Lorraine Lee', 'Louis Richard', 'Luciole', 'Lucy Carnegie', 'Ma Capucine', 'Medeleine Guillaumez', 'Marguerite Gigandet', 'Marguerite Ketten', 'Maria Star', 'Marie Segond', 'Mlle. Blanche Martignat', 'Mlle. Franziska Krüger', 'Mlle. Lazarine Poizeau', 'Mme. Achille Fould', 'Mme. Barriglione', 'Mme. Carot', 'Mme. Charles', 'Mme. Constant Soupert', 'Mme. Crombez', 'Mme. Dr. Jutté', 'Mme. Édouard Helfenbein', 'Mme. Ernest Perrin', 'Mme. Errera',

'Mme. Eugène Verdier', 'Mme. Falcot', 'Mme. Gamon', 'Mme. Gustave Henry', 'Mme. Henry Graire', 'Mme. Honoré Dufresne', 'Mme. Jean Dupuy', 'Mme. la Comtesse de Caserta', 'Mme. la Duchesse de Vallombrosa', 'Mme. Laurent Simons', 'Mme. Margottin', 'Mme. Maurice Kuppenheim', 'Mme. Pierre Guillot', 'Mme. Remond', 'Mme. Vermorel', 'Mme. Welche', 'Mrs. Alice Broomhall', 'Mrs. S.T. Wright', 'Palo Alto', 'Peach Blossom', 'Perle de Feu', 'Perle de Lyon', 'Perle des Jaunes', 'Raoul Chauvry', 'Reine Emma des Pays-Bas', 'Rhodologue Jules Gravereaux', 'Sappho', 'Souvenir d'Espagne', 'Souvenir de Jeanne Cabaud', 'Souvenir de Laurent Guillot', 'Souvenir de Mme. Levet', 'Souvenir de Mme. Sablayrolles', 'Souvenir de Pierre Notting', 'Souvenir of Stella Gray', 'Sunrise', 'Sunset', 'The Sweet Little Queen of Holland', 'Vallée de Chamonix', 'Virginia'

Bourbons: —None—

Hybrid Bourbons, Hybrid Chinas, and Hybrid Noisettes: —None—

Hybrid Perpetuals: 'Bischof Dr. Korum', 'Bradova Lososova Druschki', 'Gruss an Weimar', 'Isabel Llorach', 'Juliet', 'Lyonfarbige Druschki', 'Mme. Albert Barbier', 'Prinz Max zu Scaumburg-Lippe', 'Tatik Brada'

Noisettes and Climbers: 'Adrienne Christophle', 'Anna Olivier, Climbing', 'Apeles Mestres', 'Beauté de l'Europe', 'Billard et Barré', 'Bouquet d'Or', 'Cherubim', 'Crépuscule', 'Duarte de Oliveira', 'E. Veyrat Hermanos', 'Earl of Eldon', 'Fürst Bismarck', 'Irish Fireflame, Climbing', 'Kaiser Wilhelm der Siegreiche', 'Kaiserin Friedrich', 'Les Fiançailles de la Princesse Stéphanie et de l'Archiduc Rodolphe', 'Lorraine Lee, Climbing', 'Margo Koster, Climbing', 'Marie Thérèse Dubourg', 'Mlle. Claire Jacquier', 'Mme. Auguste Choutet', 'Mme. Bérard', 'Mme. Brunner', 'Mme. Caroline Küster', 'Mme. Chauvry', 'Mme. Creux', 'Mme. E. Souffrain', 'Mme. Emilie Dupuy', 'Mme. Eugénie Verdier', 'Mme. Foureau', 'Mme. la Duchesse d'Auerstädt', 'Mme. Pierre Cochet', 'Mme. Trifle', 'Monsier Paul Lédé, Climbing',

'Mrs. Aaron Ward', Climbing', 'Nardy', 'Ophirie', 'Orange Triumph, Climbing', 'Oscar Chauvry', 'Prinses van Oranje', 'William Allen Richardson'

Polyanthas: 'Caid', 'Cameo', 'Casque d'Or', 'Coral Cluster', 'Corrie Koster', 'Dick Koster', 'Dr. Ricaud', 'Étoile Luisante', 'Eugénie Lamesch', 'Frau Alexander Weiss', 'Gloire du Midi', 'Gloria Mundi', 'Golden Salmon', 'Kleiner Alfred', 'Leonie Lamesch', 'Margo Koster', 'Martha', 'Marytje Cazant', 'Mlle. Suzanne Bidard', 'Mme. Jules Thibaud', 'Mosella', 'Orange Koster', 'Orange Morsdag', 'Orange Triumph', 'Pacific Triumph', 'Paul Crampel', 'Princesse Henriette de Flandres', 'Sunshine', 'Vatertag'

Hybrid Teas: 'Augustine Halem', 'Betty', 'Cecil', 'Charles J. Graham', 'Christobel', 'Erzherzogin Marie Dorothea', 'Hofgärtendirektor Graebener', 'Irish Brightness', 'Irigh Elegance', 'Irish Fireflame', 'Irish Modesty', 'Jules Girodit', 'Lulu', 'Mlle. Hélène Cambier', 'Mme. Paul Lacoutière', 'Mme. Ravary', 'Monsieur Paul Lédé', 'Mrs. Oakley Fisher', 'Old Gold'

Mixed Coloration

(see also "Striped or Mottled," below)

Damask Perpetuals: —None—

Chinas: 'Antoinette Cuillerat', 'Aurore', 'Bichonne', 'De Cels', 'Duke of York', 'Laure de Broglie', 'Maddalena Scalarandis', 'Mme. Laurette Messimy', 'Mutabilis', 'Viridiflora'

Teas: 'Abbé Garroute', 'Adèle de Bellabre', 'Albert Hoffmann', 'Amazone', 'Archiduchesse Marie Immaculata', 'Blumenschmidt', 'Capitaine Millet', 'Clementina Carbonieri', 'Comtesse Alban de Villeneuve', 'Comtesse Bardi', 'Comtesse Julie Hunyady', 'Comtesse Riza du Parc', 'Dr. Grill', 'Dr. Pouleur', 'Duc de Magenta', 'Duchesse Marie Salviati', 'Edmond Sablayrolles', 'Édouard Gautier', 'Émilie Gonin',

'Erzherzog Franz Ferdinand', 'Fortune's Five-Colored Rose', 'Helen Good', 'Hovyn de Tronchère', 'Hugo Roller', 'Impératrice Maria Féodorowna de Russie', 'Marie Van Houtte', 'Miss Marston', 'Mlle. Anna Charron', 'Mlle. Emma Vercellone', 'Mlle. Jeanne Guillaumez', 'Mlle. Jeanne Philippe', 'Mme. Claire Jaubert', 'Mme. de St.-Joseph', 'Mme. de Watteville', 'Mme. Jacques Charreton', 'Mme. Joseph Godier', 'Mme. la Baronne Berge', 'Mme. la Princesse de Bessaraba de Brancovan', 'Mme. Lambard', 'Mme. Ocker Ferencz', 'Mrs. James Wilson', 'Princess of Wales', 'Princesse Étienne de Croy', 'Professeur d'André', 'Rosette Delizy', 'Rosomane Narcisse Thomas', 'Souvenir de Gilbert Nabonnand', 'Souvenir de Mme. Lambard', 'Souvenir de Paul Neyron', 'Souvenir de Victor Hugo', 'Souvenir de William Robinson', 'Souvenir du Général Charreton', 'Souvenir du Rosiériste Rambaux', 'The Alexandra', 'Thérèse Lambert'

Bourbons: 'Mme. Edmonde Laporte', 'Mme. Pierre Oger'

Hybrid Bourbons, Hybrid Chinas, and Hybrid Noisettes: 'Belle de Vernier'

Hybrid Perpetuals: 'Catherine Soupert', 'Comte de Nanteuil', 'Frédéric Schneider II', 'Frère Marie Pierre', 'Turnvater Jahn'

Noisettes and Climbers: 'Beauté Inconstante', 'Caroline Schmitt', 'Comte de Torres', 'Dr. Lande', 'Elie Beauvilain', 'Fortune's Double Yellow', 'Gloire de Dijon', 'L'Idéal', 'Lady Waterlow', 'Marie Van Houtte, Climbing', 'Mme. Claire Carnot', 'Mme. Hector Leuilliot', 'Monsieur Georges de Cadoudal', 'Pavillon de Pregny', 'Perle d'Or, Climbing', 'Phyllis Bide', 'Souvenir d'Émile Zola', 'Souvenir de Mme. Léonie Viennot'

Polyanthas: 'Clara Pfitzer', 'Excellens', 'Fireglow', 'Jeanne Drivon', 'La Proserpine', 'Ma Fillette', 'Miss Kate Schultheis', 'Perle d'Or', 'Perle Orléanaise', 'Petite Constant', 'Petite Léonie', 'Scheekopf', 'Tip-Top'

Hybrid Teas: 'Comte Henri Rignon', 'Ellen Wilmott', 'Ferdinand Batel', 'Julius Finger', 'Mme. Jean Favre', 'Monsieur Bunel'

Striped or Mottled

Damask Perpetuals: 'Capitaine Rénard', 'Marbrée', 'Panachée de Lyon', 'Papa Vibert'

Chinas: 'Archiduc Charles'

Teas: 'American Banner', 'Belle Panachée', 'Improved Rainbow', 'Mystère', 'Rainbow'

Bourbons: 'Bijou des Royat-les-Bains', 'Honorine de Brabant', 'Mlle. Berthe Clavel', 'Rouge Marbree', 'Variegata di Bologna'

Hybrid Bourbons, Hybrid Chinas, and Hybrid Noisettes: 'Catherine Ghislaine'

Hybrid Perpetuals: 'Baron Girod l'Ain', 'Baronne Prévost Marbré', 'Belle Angevine', 'Coquette Bordelaise', 'Ferdinand Pichard', 'Fontenelle', 'François Olin', 'Louis Calla', 'Marguerite Lecureaux', 'Merrie England', 'Mme. Auguste van Geert', 'Mme. Campbell d'Islay', 'Mme. Desirée Giraud', 'Mme. Petit', 'Mrs. Harkness', 'Panachée d'Angers', 'Panachée d'Orléans', 'Panachée Langroise', 'Ponctué', 'Pride of Reigate', 'Robert de Brie', 'Roger Lambelin', 'Royat Mondain', 'Souvenir de Mme. Jeanne Balandreau', 'Thomas Mills', 'Triomphe de Valenciennes', 'Vick's Caprice'

Noisettes and Climbers: 'Mme. Driout', 'Mme. Louis Blanchet', 'Pride of Reigate, Climbing'

Polyanthas: 'Cyclope', 'Floribunda', 'Mlle. Camille de Rochetaillée', 'Picotte'

Hybrid Teas: 'Captain Christy Panaché', 'Mme. Angélique Veysset'

Leaves Striped or Mottled

Only: ***Noisettes and Climbers:*** 'Souvenir de Mme. Ladvocate'

Appendix Nine

Gigantea Hybrids

The following group, though often seen listed indiscriminately as "Teas" or "Climbers," without further clarification, are derived at least partially from *Rosa gigantea*. As such, they may be of particular interest to collectors who wish to specialize.

In the Chapter on Teas: 'Baxter Beauty', 'Lorraine Lee', 'Susan Louise'

In the Chapter on Noisettes and Climbers: 'Belle Blanca', 'Belle Portugaise', 'Climbing Cracker', 'Climbing Lorraine Lee', 'Cooper's Burmese Rose', 'Doris Downes', 'Emmanuella de Mouchy', 'Étoile de Portugal', 'Flying Colours', 'Fortune's Double Yellow', 'Gigantea

Blanc', 'Glory of California', 'Kitty Kinonmonth', 'Lafollette', 'Madeleine Lemoine', 'Montecito', 'Montarioso', 'Nancy Hayward', 'Pennant', 'Sénateur Amic'

Appendix Ten

Miscellany

Addenda and Corrigenda to
The Old Rose Adventurer
and
Roll-Call: The Old Rose Breeder
plus
A Statement, A Letter, A Salutation

The kindness of interested and knowledgeable readers, the proceeds of continuing research, and sheer luck, have all provided us with some updates:

The Old Rose Adventurer.

Chapter One: Preliminary.

The Poetess Sappho, Achilleus Tatios, and the Pseudo-Anacreon

One of the stanchions of rose lore has always been that Sappho was the first to call the Rose the Queen of Flowers; Rivers indeed quotes the following as from her: "If Jupiter wished to give to the flowers a Queen, the rose would be their Queen" [R9]. Peter Harkness quite properly probed this, and it seems found on consultation with a university don that nothing of the sort could be found in Sappho. On hearing of his finding, I immediately took an interest in finding out who indeed *was* the first to use this phrase. On December 15, 1999, I posted the following on the newsgroup rec.gardens.roses: "Turn we then to the question 'Who *did* first call the rose the Queen of Flowers'? I owe to Dr. Axel Bergmann the information that a Greek rhetorician by the name of Achilleus Tatios called the rose the Queen of Flowers around the end of the 2nd century AD; and so did, more mysteriously, a pseudo-Anacreon 'in the times of the Western Roman Empire' in his poem *In Myrillam*: 'Rose, thou art the Queen of Flowers, [in the same way as] thou, Myrilla [art] the rose among virgins.' This information is relayed by Dr. Bergmann from the book *Die Rose. Geschichte und Symbolik in enthnographischer und kulturhistorischer Beziehung* [by M.J. Schleiden], Leipzig: Engelmann, 1873 (reprinted 1973)...". The question coming up again on a private discussion group the following July, I looked further into the question, and wrote the following: "Tatios...has not yet found a place on my bookshelves—am on Hesiod right now; but may be combing the bookstores for him soon, as here's what I read in the copy of the *Encyclopædia Americana* which I have at hand: 'Greek rhetorician: flourished 5th century AD. He wrote *Leucippe and Cleitophon*, an erotic story in eight books, of pleasing but florid style, and without much regard to unity or consistency of plot.' ... His 'florid' style of course played right into our rosarians' hands... Dr. Bergmann, and, separately, Harkness, mention him as existing around 180 alias the end of the 2nd century AD; our quote above puts him in the 5th century alias the 400s, which would also thus put him into a chronological horse-race with the pseudo-Anacreon mentioned earlier, 'the times of the Western Roman Empire' ending in 476, whose line concerning the Queen of Flowers I quoted previously. It would be nice to have the actual line from Tatios as well! Anyone up for reading an erotic story in eight books?"

Chapter Two: Gallicas.

Belle Sultane
Fleeting correspondence with a resident of Damascus revealed that there is a traditional rose grown there which bears the name 'Sultana'. Unfortunately, description and a promised photograph never ensued. Rosarians going to Damascus, however, might do well to ask for the rose 'Sultana'. Is our 'Belle Sultane' simply at length Beautiful 'Sultana' originating in the Levant?

Camayeux
Twice, late in his career, Vibert, the introducer of this well-known cultivar, specifies that 'Camayeux' was a sport, not a seedling, once indeed in the context of roses that were first released as seedlings but later found out to be sports. See our book *The Old Rose Informant* for details.

Dona Sol
We can put on record that at least the cataloguer at Weilburg considered this rose to be a Hybrid China rather than a Gallica or Centifolia; and Weilburg was very interested in Hybrid Chinas.

Insigne Destekles (Vibert, -1835)
Another still-existing Gallica may be added to our treasury. "Marbled lilac pink." [TCN] "Full double, rosy marbled." [WRP] "Marbled pink, large,

full, beautiful." [LF] "Medium-sized, full, marbled pink." [V8] "Flowers lilac, marbled with white and rose, of medium size, full; form, reflexed. Habit, branching; growth, moderate." [P] The meaning of the interesting name has yet to be determined.

Moïse

The date and attribution were omitted in the main text. This Gallica is "Parmentier, 1828."

Ohl

As we have seen in this present book, 'Ohl' turns out to be not a Gallica, but rather a Hybrid China.

Chapter Three: Damasks.

Common Damask (Breeder unknown, -1629)

We must separate what was known as the 'Common Damask' from the theoretical species *R. damascena.* It may have been *common* at one time, but remains to be rediscovered today. Are the 'Red Damask' (listed in *The Old Rose Adventurer*) and the 'Common Damask' synonymous? The question is one to be probed; as we will see below, the Damask is the "Red Rose" in Bulgaria at least. Here are some descriptions of the 'Common Damask': 'The Damaske Rose bush is more usually noursed up to a competent height to stand alone, (which we call Standards,) then any other Rose: the barke both of the stocke and branches is not fully so greene as the red [*Gallica*] or white [*Alba*] Rose: the leaves are greene with an eye of white upon them, so like unto the red Rose, that there is no great difference between them, but that the leaves of the red Rose seeme to bee of a darker greene. The flowers are of a fine deepe blush colour, as all know, with some pale threds in the middle, and are not so thicke and double as the white, nor being blowne, with so large and great leaves as the red, but of the most excellent sweet pleasant s[c]ent, far surpassing all other Roses or Flowers, being neyther heady nor too strong, nor stuffing or unpleasant sweet, as many other flowers." [PaSo] "*York and Lancaster*, differeth only from the ordinary *Damask Rose*, in that the flowers are parted and marked, with a pale blush almost white upon the *Damask Rose* colour, from which in no other thing it differeth." [Rea] Thus we see that the 'Common Damask' flower was the color of the darker shade of the 'York and Lancaster' blossom. "The common Damaske Rose in stature, prickley branches, and in other respects is like the white Rose [*Alba*]; the especiall difference consists in the colour and smell of the flours: for these are of a pale red colour, of a more pleasant smell, and fitter for meat and medicine." [Gerard in Johnson, 1636] "The industrial rose grown in Bulgaria is the red rose (Rosa Damascena, Miller. [*thus, in this particular author's work, the term "red rose" refers not to the Gallica, but to the Damask*]) and the white rose (Rosa Alba, L.). The red rose is a bush which grows from 1½-2 m in height [ca. 4.5-6 feet], growing with canes fairly interlaced, and blooming from May to the middle of June. Its young shoots are reddish and overspread with very close-set dark-colored prickles. It has large slender green stipules in which the mid-vein is pilose and bears stipitate glands intermixed with bristles. The bush's leaves are elliptical in form, and crenelate, but without a pedicel, and pilose on the upper surface. The flowers are grouped in twos, threes, and up to sevens on each branch; indeed, on some bushes can be found clusters of 30 on a branch. At anthesis, the blossom is 4-5 cm across [to ca. two inches]; the cane, calyx, and little conical receptacle are covered with viscose glands. The petals are rounded and pink in color. The blossom has a very likeable scent. It is supposed that the oil-giving red rose derives from a cross between Rosa gallica and Rosa canina." [Zla (illustrating but not describing three further varieties of Damasks: 'De Brazigovo', 'De Pavel-Bania', and 'De Bachmanlaré')] "The *common Damask Rose*, although it be not so ancient an inhabitant of England as the common *red Rose*, yet it is so well known, and all the parts thereof, so that it needeth no further description." [Rea]

Chapter Five: Centifolias.

Alain Blanchard
We are informed by several sources that the person after whom this rose was named was a defender of Rouen against the English, choosing death instead of payment of ransom after the fall of the city.

Tour de Malakoff
Some have noted the home city of the releasers of this Centifolia, point to that city's own Malakoff Tower, and feel that the name commemorates that tower. Others, including the author, note the release-date of the rose in question, the fact that, far away, in Angers, France, Monsieur Robert had named a Gallica 'Tour Malakoff' the previous year, and connect the name with the then-current Crimean War with *its* Malakoff's Tower in the temporary defenses of Sebastopol. No doubt Soupert & Notting were proud to be able to give a name which had a timely meaning to many throughout Europe, and an extra meaning to locals.

Chapter Nine: Albas.

Princesse de Lamballe
Several warm partisans of the Princess have become exercised over the fact that that the book spells her name as 'Princesse de Lamballé'; the correct spelling is 'Princesse de Lamballe', without the *accent aigue* over the terminal "e."

Chapter Twenty-Three: Sempervirenses.

We are happy to be able to supply further notes on the names of some, and correct one name:

Adélaïde d'Orléans
Named for the Duc d'Orléans' sister.

Félicité-Perpétue
The correct name of this rose is *not* 'Félicité et Perpétue', but rather 'Félicité-Perpétue'.

Princesse Louise
This name commemorates Louis-Philippe's eldest daughter, soon to become the Queen of Belgium on her marriage to Léopold I; the Sempervirens 'Reine des Belges' is named after her in this later incarnation.

Princesse Marie
This name refers to the second daughter of the Duc d'Orléans, Louis-Philippe. She was a gifted sculptress.

Chapter Twenty-Four: Boursaults.

Drummond's Thornless
We can throw this rose back another decade or so, and make its date - 1834.

Chapter Twenty-Six: Wichuraianas.

We add one more variety, significant in being used in breeding-work.

[Sylvia] (W. Paul, 1911)
"Flower pale lemon-yellow passing to cream and pure white, small double flowers in large loose sprays. Growth very vigorous." [GeH] "Bud pale lemon yellow, becoming white upon opening; flowers double, like big

white grapes, very fragrant. Climbing bush, reblooms very well in Fall." [JR35/102]

Chapter Twenty-Seven: Multifloras.

We add one more to clear up the classification of this rose, which was often classed as a Polyantha because it was descended from *R. multiflora* 'Polyantha'; but it was a climbing Multiflora.

[**Ornement des Jardins**] (Widow Rambaux & Dubreuil, 1881) trans., "Garden-Ornament"
"Non-remontant hybrid rose. This variety, coming from the Polyantha [*i.e., R. multiflora* 'Polyantha'], only preserves certain of its characteristics. It's a very vigorous bush of luxuriant growth, giving at first bloom innumerable quantities of flowers of a flesh-pink color, very well formed, nuanced to a greater or lesser degree depending upon the vigor of the canes, and coming in corymbs of varying size. It is easily trained on close-set pillars and can grow to 3 or 4 meters in height [ca. 9-12 feet]." [JR5/186]

Appendix Ten: Loose Ends.

We add an interesting letter from Fred Lautzenheiser about Iranian roses, bringing us full circle after our studies and travels, back to the quote on page 11 in Chapter One of the *Adventurer*: "However, it will do to believe that the rose originated in Persia…" [l'H51]:

"I lived in Tehran for almost 5 years, and being a lover of roses, I did keep my eyes out for them when I was there, although I never mounted a full rose expedition. There would have been certain difficulties, one of the principal ones being that society is structured differently there, and people's gardens are private and behind high walls; you would have to go through the whole introduction thing and get to know each family individually to find out what roses were growing in a particular neighborhood, whereas here [*the U.S.A.*] one just drives down the street and looks, or goes rummaging freely through the cemetery of choice. Public gardens in Iran (except for some historic sites) had gone over almost 100% to modern Western roses so they weren't much good for rose-hunting.

"Some roses could be found in outer courtyards of mosques and emamzadehs (small shrines, not really full public mosques), and in smaller towns one could see roses growing in the occasional odd place—of course, due to lack of water, they couldn't grow in most waste spaces.

"In the course of my various jaunts in Iran, I came across mostly fœtidas and damasks. Although there were gallicas, I did not find them as often. I don't know about the Levant [*this letter came pursuant to a request made for information on roses growing in the Levant*], but in Iran, there is not the cultural background of quoting Latin names for things or even of pinning them down very exactly at all. If you mentioned 'rose' ('*gol*,' which by the way is also the generic word for 'flower'—how's that for ambiguity??), people would respond with inexact words that to us would mean a class rather than a specific variety—*gol-e-chai* (tea rose—they meant HT, maybe occasionally actual tea roses); '*nastaran*' (any single garden rose—not just the variety we see named that in the catalogues), *gol-e-Mohammadi* (far and away the favorite of the traditional roses there—the double pink damask used for rosewater—and quite frankly, probably any other damask as well!), and *gol-e-zard* ('yellow rose'—most often the fœtidas but also hemisphærica, which is much less common). I never got to meet a TRADITIONAL gardener who would have known individual varieties much more specifically. They were a dying breed (already dead in most places). In the cities one saw gardeners for the municipality or private plant fanciers, all of whom planted the latest imports from Europe or Japan. They were not in the least interested in native plants.

"I did take a close look at any wild roses I was able to find—they were much more available than garden roses, since one could always just take a hike up the mountain. The taxonomy of Iranian roses is rather confusing—the *Flora Iranica*, published by the University of Graz over a considerable span of time, does include a volume on *Rosa*; but since the Revolution intervened and I never received the rest of the series, I was missing that particular volume, and besides all the volumes I did receive are in Tehran in a friend's house, if he kept them. (Univ. Graz never answered the letters I wrote after returning re: obtaining the rest of the series.) There was a common rose that looked like *Rosa acicularis*, but wasn't. The wild *Rosa fœtida* grew up in the mountains, as I know by photos Iranian friends of mine gave me, though I never ran across a bush of it. Friends who went to Afghanistan reported *R. fœtida* 'Bicolor' growing wild there. The commonest rose was *Rosa canina*. The one wild rose that was everywhere in the desert (as opposed to populated places near mountains, where the Dog Rose abounded) was *Hulthemia persica*. It was more often than not just *nastaran* to the Iranians, although it is so strikingly different from any other rose and has the peculiarity of having only one leaflet. I tried transplanting it to a courtyard in Tehran, but it is really impossible—the roots go down so far that you can't possibly avoid wounding it mortally if you try to dig it up. I tried planting seeds and hips, but they didn't work either. In general, my 'gardening' there was eminently unsuccessful; one simply has to be at home to water these things several times a day, especially when the temperature is above 100 and the poor things are in pots. (Families where the mother and other women stay at home have wonderful plants.) I eventually gave it up almost completely, having an erratic schedule and not wishing to sacrifice other aspects of life there.

"Some rose moments stand out in my memory—the Emamzadeh *Gol-e-Zard* in south Tehran, with its Redbuds and 'Persian Yellow' growing all around the sides of the courtyard, although I never managed to catch it at the peak of its glory; the beautiful (though trampled) specimen of *Rosa hemisphærica* I found in the dust at a bus stop in Darband (a search of the area turned up nothing, as it was simply not possible to disturb the entire neighborhood so I could take a peek inside each courtyard—I would have ended up being arrested as a suspicious character); many a spring day spent in Garmsar, above Kashan, with everyone distilling rosewater and the smell of roses permeating the air; a night spent in an unoccupied, centuries-old pleasure dome above a valley near there, and being awakened at 4:30 a.m. by the rose pickers and their donkeys going out to pick before the sun ruined the flowers; and a particularly lovely yellow rose blooming next to a waterway in Garmsar, made even more poignant by the fact that I had just used up the last frame of my color film brought from Tehran!!!

"I wonder if there is anyone who has had the leisure and funds to do a more thorough investigation of Iranian roses and garden plants. I think the key would be settling into a fairly traditional locale and becoming known as a plant person, and getting to know everyone in the community. Then people would come to one and the secrets would begin to come out. I can't see any other way to do the project justice. —Maybe when I retire...

"None of this answers your question at all—I never saw anything looking like 'La Belle Sultane' in Iran—but since you were asking about the Middle East in general, I thought I would add my two cents."

• Addenda and Corrigenda to *Roll-Call: The Old Rose Breeder.*
References to the city "Nanci" should be spelled "Nancy." Rouen's rose 'Sophie de Bavière' is probably a synonym of Cottin's 'Célanire'. Breeder Debeaumont was located in Rouen, France. The Dubreuil of Rouen indeed had the first name "Alphonse"; he was a professor at Rouen and subsequently at Paris; his father was chief gardener at the *Jardin des Plantes* in Rouen. The horticulturist Lecomte of Nancy, France, appears to have

been a different person from the Lecomte of Rouen. The rose 'Mme. Edmond Laporte' should be allotted to Garçon, not to Boutigny. Prévost fils' rose 'Quesné' should be dated 1826. Pernet père's 'Souvenir de l'Amiral Courbet' of 1885 is—as we have seen in *The Old Rose Advisor*—a Tea, not an HP (his 'Souvenir de Victor Hugo' of the same year is not the well-known Tea, but rather an HP, as listed). Assignment of C.S. Sargent to "Hartford" probably ultimately derives from someone mishearing "Harvard"; he should be located at Harvard's Arnold Arboretum.

• A Statement.

"A Statement I saw some time ago in a gardening paper made me a little sad. It was a letter from a head gardener, who said—I cannot remember the exact words—that the improvement of late years in Tea and Hybrid Tea Roses had been so great that he was planting nothing else, and was doing away entirely with all Hybrid Perpetuals. Now, this is one of those wholesale and wanton follows of fashion that, I confess, exasperate me not a little. Why discard one beautiful thing because another is as, or even more, beautiful? Why turn our backs on the old and faithful friend, because forsooth the new acquaintance pleases us? Are our hearts so small and mean that we have not room in them for more than one liking at a time? Moreover in all things the slavish following of a fashion because it is a fashion, whatever its intrinsic merits, is odious and unworthy, reducing sentient human beings to the level of a flock of sheep hurrying blindly and foolishly through a gap…I am sick of that word 'fashion'; and now, that is should be imported into our gardens, into the culture of God's loveliest gifts to poor man, into the purest, sweetest, most san and wholesome of recreations, is indeed too much. But so it is, alas! And we hear on all sides, from morning till night, not that Hybrid Teas are beautiful, but that they 'are all the fashion'…I would as soon drown one of my homely tabby cats because it was not a pale lavender Persian, as destroy my Hybrid Perpetuals because they were not Tea Roses; and though I should be charmed to possess a lavender Persian as well as the humble tabby, I can thoroughly appreciate the delights and merits of the very newest Tea Rose without abating one jot of my love for 'Ulrich Brunner [fils], 'Duke of Edinburgh', 'Mrs. John Laing'...the dear old 'Général Jacqueminot', or the new and superb 'Frau Karl Druschki'. For without blindly following the fashion of the moment, it is singularly foolish to despise what is new, if at the same time it is worthy of admiration." [K1]

• A Letter.

From Revue-Horticole, 1843:

Bellevue, November 20, 1843.

In our discussion concerning roses yesterday at my nursery, you told me that you did not believe that I could develop any rose more beautiful than 'La Reine'. I told you that, in my opinion, roses still haven't reached their apogee. Indeed, the more a person advances with his seedlings, the more he merely advances in a botanical labyrinth. The more I sow, the more I see the immensity of what lies before me!...You see, Monsieur, all a person needs is faith...

—Laffay

• A Salutation.

From HmC:

Goodbye, summer. Good-bye, good-bye!

As the leaves fall, our hearts are heavy. We feel the cold of winter as the roses feel it, be we cannot slumber in the earth till spring wakens us...at least not yet.

But away with sentiment! Let us think only of next year's roses, and of the sun which is shining behind the clouds.

The End.

Bibliography

Key to Citations

A: *Roses, or A Monograph...*, by Henry Andrews, 1805 and 1828.
AbR: *Cours Complet d'Agriculture...*, by Abbé Rozier, 1793.
AC: *La Rose*, by A. de Chesnel, 1838.
ADE: Departmental Archives of Essonne at Corbeil, France.
Adk: *Catalogue*, by Alexander Dickson, year as indicated.
ADVDM: Departmental Archives of Val-de-Marne at Creteil, France.
ADY: Departmental Archives of Yvelines at Versailles, France.
AHB: *The Tree Rose*, by A[rthur] H[enry] B[osanquet], 1845.
An: *Annales de Flore et de Pomone*, 1832-1848.
AnM-L: *Annales du Comice Horticole de Maine-et-Loire*, 1859.
ARA: *American Rose Annual*, year as indicated. Quoted by kind permission of the American Rose Society.
Au: *The Australasian Rose Book*, by R.G. Elliott, ca. 1925.
AxD: *Rose Catalogue*, Alex. Dickson & Sons, Ltd., Newtownards, Ireland, year as indicated.
BBF: *The Flower-Garden, or Breck's Book of Flowers*, by Joseph Breck, 1851.
BBF66: *New Book of Flowers*, by Joseph Breck, 1866.
BCD: Interpolated material by Brent C. Dickerson.
BJ: *Le Bon Jardinier*, 1865 edition.
BJ06: *Le Bon Jardinier*, 1806 edition.
BJ09: *Le Bon Jardinier*, 1809 edition.
BJ09s: *Supplément à...Bon Jardinier*, 1809.
BJ17: *Le Bon Jardinier*, 1817 edition.

BJ24: *Le Bon Jardinier*, 1824 edition.
BJ30: *Le Bon Jardinier*, 1830 edition.
BJ40: *Le Bon Jardinier*, 1840 edition.
BJ53: *Le Bon Jardinier*, 1853 edition.
BJ58: *Le Bon Jardinier*, 1858 edition.
BJ63: *Le Bon Jardinier*, 1863 edition.
BJ70: *Le Bon Jardinier*, 1870 edition.
BJ77: *Le Bon Jardinier*, 1877 edition.
Bk: *Roses and How to Grow Them*, by Edwin Beckett, 1918.
Br: *A Year in a Lancashire Garden*, by Henry Bright, 1879.
BSA: *The Garden Book of California*, by Belle Sumner Angier, 1906.
Bu: *The Rose Manual*, by Robert Buist, 1844.
B&V: *List of Roses Now in Cultivation at Château Eléonore, Cannes…*, by Henry Charles Brougham, 3rd Baron Brougham & Vaux, 1898.
C: *Beauties of the Rose*, by Henry Curtis, 1850-1853. Facsimile reprint, 1980, by Sweetbriar Press; additional material by Leonie Bell.
CA: *Descriptive Catalogue*, California Nursery Company, 1888 *et sequitur*, year as indicated.
Cal: *Catalogue* of Calvert & Company, 1820.
Capt27: Article "Tea Roses for Southern Clmates," by Capt. Goerge C. Thomas, in ARA27.
Capt28: Article "Climbing Roses for Southern Climates," by Capt. George C. Thomas, in ARA28.
CaRoI (*et seq.*): *The California Rosarian*, published by the California Rose Society, 1930-1932.
Cat12: *Official Catalogue of Roses*, by the [British] National Rose Society, 1912 edition.
CC: *Catalogue* for the Wasamequia Nurseries, New Bedford, MA, by Henry H. Crapo, 1848. In ARA26.
CdF: *La Culture des Fleurs*, anonymous, 1712.
C'H: *Dictionnaire Universel des Plantes…*, by Pierre-Joseph Buc'hoz, 1770.

C&Jf: *Fall Catalog*, The Conard & Jones Co., yearly 1897-1924, as specified. Quoted by kind permission of the Conard-Pyle Co.

C&Js: *Spring Catalog*, The Conard & Jones Co., yearly 1897-1924, as specified. Quoted by kind permission of the Conard-Pyle Co.

Ck: *Catalogue, Marie Henriette Chotek Rosenschulen*, by Marie Henriette Chotek, 1926.

CM: *Histoire des Roses*, by Charles Malo, 1821.

C-Pf: *Fall Catalog*, The Conard-Pyle Co., yearly 1925-1934, as specified. Quoted by kind permission of the Conard-Pyle Co.

C-Ps: *Spring Catalog*, The Conard-Pyle Co., yearly 1925-1934, as specified. Quoted by kind permission of the Conard-Pyle Co.

Cr: *Catalogue* of Cranston's Nurseries, various years as noted.

C-T: *Almanach des Roses*, by Claude-Thomas Guerrapain, 1811.

Cw: *La Rose Historique*, by Edm. Van Cauwenberghe, 1927.

Cx: *Les Plus Belles Roses au Début de Iième Siècle*, by the Société Nationale d'Horticulture de France, 1912.

Cy: *The French Revolution. A History*, by Thomas Carlyle, 1837.

Cy2: *Oliver Cromwell's Letters and Speeches*, 3rd edition, by Thomas Carlyle, 1849.

Cy3: *The History of Friedrich II of Prussia, Called Frederick the Great*, by Thomas Carlyle, 1865.

D: *A General History and Collection of Voyages and Travels*, by Robert Kerr, 1824.

D&C12: *Catalog*, Dingee & Conard Co., 1912.

DH: *Journal d'Horticulture Pratique et de Jardinage*, 1844-1847, edited by Martin-Victor Paquet.

DO: *Roses for Amateurs*, by Rev. H. Honywood D'Ombrain.

DP: *Sommaire d'une Monographie du Genre Rosier...*, by de Pronville, 1822.

DP: Article "My Favorites...," by D. Bruce Phillips, in *Pacific Horticulture*, vol. 43, no. 3, 1982. Quoted by kind permission of *Pacific Horticulture.*

Dr: *Everblooming Roses*, by Georgia Torrey Drennan, 1912.

DuC: *The Flowers and Gardens of Madeira*, by Florence duCane, 1909.

E: *Gardens of England*, by E.T. Cook, 1911.

ECS: City Archives of Soisy-sous-Etioles, France.

Ed: *The Amateur's Rosarium*, by R. Wodrow Thomson, 1862.

EER: Article "A Short History of theTea Rose," by E.E. Robinson, in *The Rose*, vol. 17, no. 3, 1969.

EER2: Article "The Early Hybrid Perpetuals," by E.E. Robinson, in *The Rose*, vol. 13, no. 3, 1965.

EJW: *California Garden-Flowers*, by E.J. Wickson, 1915.

EL: *The Rose*, by Henry B. Ellwanger, 1882.

ElC: Article "Old Roses and New Roses," by Henry B. Ellwanger, in *Century Magazine*, vo. 4, 1883.

ET: Article "Help Wanted in Texas?", by Edward Teas, from ARA28.

ExRé: *Guide pour servir à la visite de notre Exposition Rétrospective de la Rose*, from Roseraie de l'Haÿ, 1910.

F: *Les Roses*, by Louis Fumierre, 1910.

Fa: *In a Yorkshire Garden*, by Reginald Farrer, 1909.

FeR: *La France en Russie*, by Eugène Delaire, 1900.

Fl: *The Florist*, vol. 1, 1848.

FlCa: *Floricultural Cabinet*, date as specified.

F-M: *The Book of the Rose*, 4th edition, by Andrew Foster-Melliar, 1910.

F-M2: *The Bookd of the Rose*, 2nd edition, by Andrew Foster-Melliar, 1902.

F-M3: *The Book of the Rose*, 1st edition, by Andrew Foster-Melliar, 1894.

F-M4: *The Book of the Rose*, 3rd edition, by Andrew Foster-Melliar, 1905.

FP: *The Book of Roses*, by Francis Parkman, 1871.

Fr: *Dictionnaire du Jardinier Français*, by Monsieur Fillassier, 1791.

FRB: *Tea Roses*, by F.R. Burnside, 1893.

GAS: *Climbing Roses*, by G.A. Stevens, 1933. Quoted by kind permission of the copyright holder, the McFarland Co.

G&B: *Roses*, by Gemen & Bourg, ca. 1908.

GeH: *The Rose Encyclopædia*, be Geoffrey W. Henslowe, 1934.

Gf: *Catalogue*, J.-B. Guillot fils, 1856.
GG: *In a Gloucestershire Garden*, by Henry N. Ellacombe, 1896.
GJB: *Vägledning genom Linnés park 1836*, manuscript by G.J. Billberg, 1836.
Gl: *The Culture of Flowers and Plants*, by George Glenny, 1861.
Go: *The Rose Fancier's Manual*, by Mrs. Gore, 1838.
God: *Catalogue des Rosiers*, by Godefroy, 1831.
Gp: *Catalogue*, by J.-B. Guillot père, 1844/1845.
Gp&f: *Catalogue*, J.-B. Guillot père & fils, 1852.
Gx: *"La Malmaison" Les Roses de l'Impératrice Joséphine*, by Jules Gravereaux, 1912.
H: *A Book About Roses*, by S. Reynolds Hole, 1906 printing.
Hd: *The Amateur's Rose Book*, by Shirley Hibberd, 1874.
HDk: *Catalogue*, year as indicated, by High Dickson.
Hj: Unpublished correspondence with Thomasville Nurseries, Inc. Quoted by kind permission of Thomasville Nurseries, Inc.
HmC: *My Roses and How I Grew Them*, by Helen (Crofton) Milman, 1899.
Hn: *The Amateur Gardener's Rose Book*, by Julius Hoffmann, English language edition, 1905.
HoBoIV: *The Horticultural Review and Botanical Magazine*, 1854.
HRH: *A Gardener's Year*, by H. Rider Haggard, 1905.
HstI (*et sequitur*): *The Horticulturist*, 1846-1875.
Ht: *Le Livre d'Or des Roses*, by Paul Hariot, 1904.
HuD: *Catalogue* from the Royal Nurseries of Hugh Dickson, Belfast, Ireland, year as indicated.
Hÿ: *Les Roses Cultivées à l'Haÿ en 1902,* from Roseraie de l'Haÿ, 1902.
J: *Roses for English Gardens*, by Gertrude Jekyll, 1902.
J-A: *Le Jardinier-Amateur*, edited by Eugène Pirolle, 1826.
J-As: *Premier Supplément, le Jardinier-Amateur*, edited by Eugène Pirolle, 1827.
JC: *Cultural Directions for the Rose*, 6th edition, by John Cranston, 1877.

JDR: *Journal des Roses*, year as indicated, edited by Jean Cherpin, published 1854-1859 in Lyon.

JF: *Les Roses*, by Hippolyte Jamain & Eugène Forney, 1873.

Jg: *Rosenlexikon*, by Auguste Jäger, pub. 1970, data collected in the 1920s and 1930s.

JHP: *Journal d'Horticulture Pratique*, 1850.

JP: *Roses: Their History, Development, and Cultivation*, by Rev. Joseph H. Pemberton, 1920.

JPV: *Réponse à … Pirolle*, by Jean-Pierre Vibert, 1827.

JR: *Journal des Roses*, year as indicated, edited by Cochet & Bernardin, published 1877-1914 in Melun.

Jwa: *Warren's Descriptive Catalogue*, by J.L.L.F. Warren, 1844.

K: *The Rose Manual*, by J.H. Nicolas, 1938. Quoted by kind permission of the publishers, Doubleday & Co., Inc.

K1: *Eversley Gardens and Others*, by Rose G. Kingley, 1907.

K2: *Roses and Rose-Growing*, by Rose G. Kingley, 1908.

Kr: *The Complete Book of Roses*, by Gerd Krüssman, 1981. Quoted by kind permission of the publisher, Timber Press.

L: *Gardening in California*, 3rd revised edition, by William S. Lyon, 1904.

LADR: *Les Amis des Roses*, issues 1946-1962, as indicated.

Lam: *Encyclopédie Méthodique…*, section on roses by Lamarck, 1804.

Lam/Poir: *Encyclopédie Méthodique. Botanique. Supplément*, by J.L.M. Poiret, 1816.

LaQ: *Instruction pour les Jardins Fruitiers et Potagiers…*, by Jean de la Quintinye, 1695.

Lc: *Les Rosiers*, by Jean Lachaume, revised by Georges Bellair, ca. 1921.

L-D: *La Rose…*, by Jean Louis Augustin Loiseleur-Deslongchamps, 1844.

LeB: *Traité des Jardins…*, by Abbé le Berriays, 1789.

LeR: *Histoire Généalogique des Rosiers*, by Antoine LeRouge, unpublished manuscript dated 1819, with additional material from 1820.

LF: *Prix Courant des Espèces et Variétés de Roses*, by Jean Laffay, 1841.

LF1: Death Certificate of Jean Laffay, town records of the Municipality of Cannes, France, 1878.

L'H: *l'Horticulteur Français*, 1851-1872, year as indicated.

LR: *La Rose*, by J. Bel, 1892.

LS: *Nomenclature de Tous les Noms de Roses*, 2nd edition, by Léon Simon, 1906.

Lu: *Luther Burbank. His Methods and Discoveries*, vol. 9, by Luther Burbank, 1914.

M: *Gardening in California*, by Sidney B. Mitchell, 1923. Quoted by kind permission of the publishers, Doubleday & Co., Inc.

MaCo: *Manuel Complet de l'Amateur des Roses*, by Boitard, 1836.

MaRu: *La Nouvelle Maison Rustique...*, by J.-F. Bastien, 1798.

MCN: *Minutier Central des Notaires* at the French National Archives in Paris.

Mdv: *The Virgin Unmask'd*, by Bernard Mandeville, 1709.

MH: *The Magazine of Horticulture*, edited by C.M. Hovey, Boston & New York, various years as indicated.

M'I: *The Book of the Garden*, by Charles M'Intosh, 1855.

M-L: *Travaux du Comice Horticole de Maine-et-Loire*, various years as indicated.

MLS: Article "Roses in Kansas City," by Minnie Long Sloan, in ARA28.

MonL/deP: *Monographie de Genre Rosier*, translation of Lindley by de Pronville, with an added appendix by de Pronville, 1824.

M-P: *The Culture of Perennials*, by Dorothy M.-P. Cloud, 1925. Quoted by kind permission of the publishers, Dodd, Mead & Co., Inc.

M-R: *Catalogue*, by Moreau-Robert, year as indicated.

MR8: *Modern Roses 8*, published by The McFarland Company, 1980. Quoted by kind permission of The American Rose Society and The McFarland Company.

M-V: *l'Instructeur-Jardinier*, 1848-1851, edited by Martin-Victor Paquet.

Mz: *Catalogue*, by Miellez of Esquermes, various years as indicated.

N: *Die Rose*, by Thomas Nietner, 1880.

No: *Manuel Complet du Jardinier*, by Louis Noisette, 1825.

No26: *Manuel Complet du Jardinier*, by Louis Noisette, 1826 edition.

No28: *Manuel Complet du Jardinier, Supplément No. I*, by Louis Noisette, 1828.

No35: *Manuel Complet du Jardinier, Supplément No. II*, by Louis Noisette, 1835.

NRS: *Rose Annual*, year as indicated, issued by the [British] National Rose Society. Quoted by kind permission of the Royal National Rose Society.

OB: *Oekonomisch-Botanische Beschreibung*, by Rössig, 1799.

OM: *The Rose Boo*, by H.H. Thomas, 1916.

P: *The Rose Garden*, 1st edition, by William Paul, 1848.

P1: *The Rose Garden*, 10th edition, by William Paul, 1903.

P2: *Contributions to Horticultural Literature, 1843-1892*, by William Paul, 1892.

PaSo: *Paradisi in Sole: Paradisus Terrestris*, by John Parkinson, 1629.

Pd: *Le Bilan d'un Siècle*, by Alfred Picard, tome 3, 1906.

Pf: *Catalogue Descriptif...du Genre Rosa*, by Prévost fils, 1829.

Pfs: *Supplément au Catalogue des Roses...*, by Prévost fils, 1830.

PH: *Henderson's Handbook of Plants and General Horticulture*, "New Edition" (*i.e.*, 2nd), by Peter Henderson, 1889.

PlB: *Choix des Plus Belles Roses*, by Martin-Victor Paquet *et al.*, 1845-1854.

PP28: Article "Proof of the Pudding" in ARA28.

Pq: *Le Jardinier Pratique*, by Jacquin & Rousselon, 1852.

PS: Article "Roses in Brazil," by Mrs. Paul C. Schilling, in ARA28.

R1(through 7): *The Garden*, vols. 1-7, "founded and conducted by William Robinson," 1872-1875.

R8: *The Rose-Amateur's Guide*, 8th edition, by Thomas Rivers, 1863.

R9: *The Rose-Amateur's Guide*, 4th edition, by Thomas Rivers, 1846.

RATS: Article "Roses Across the Sea" in ARA28.

Rea: *Flora: seu De Florum Cultura*, 1665.

RG: *Rosetum Gallicum*, by Desportes, 1828.

R-H: *Revue-Horticole*, year as indicated, issues 1829-1877. Quoted by kind permission of the publishers.

R-HC: *Revue-Horticole*, centenary number, 1929. Quoted by kind permission of the publishers.

Riv: *Roses et Rosiers*, by Rivoire père & fils, with Marcel Ebel, 1933.

RJC: *Revue des Jardins et des Champs*, year as indicated, 1860-1871, edited by Jean Cherpin.

R&M: *Catalogue*, by Robert & Moreau, year as indicated.

Ro: *The English Flower-Garden*, 8th edition, by William Robinson, 1903.

RP: Article "Roses—The Ophelia Strain and Kindred Spirits," by Reginald Parker, in *The Rose*, vol. 13, no. 3, 1965.

RR: Article "Check List of Red Tea Roses," by R. Robinson, in *The Rose*, vol. 13, no. 1, 1964.

Rsg: *Die Rosen/Les Roses*. Rössig's *Die Rosen*, with parallel French version by de Lahitte, 1802-1820.

RZ: *Rosen-Zeitung*, vol. 1, 1886.

S: *Dictionnaire des Roses*, by Max Singer, 1885.

SAP: *Journal de la Société d'Agronomie Pratique*, 1829.

SBP: *Parsons on the Rose*, by Samuel B. Parsons, 1888.

SDH: *Newry Roses*, catalogs by T. Smith of Daisy Hill Nursery, 1903-1929.

SHj: Article "Old Roses for the South," 1949, and address "Tea Roses for Florida," 1951, by Samuel J. Hjort. Quoted by kind permission of Sarah L. Hjort of Thomasville Nurseries, Inc.

SHP: *Annales de la Société d'Horticulture de Paris*, year as indicated.

Sn: *Rosenverzeichnis*, 3rd edition, Rosarium Sangerhausen, 1976.

SNH: *Journal de la Société Nationale d'Horticulture*, year as indicated.

SRh: *Société d'Horticulture Pratique du Rhône*, year as indicated.

S-V: *Catalogue des Plantes…*, by J. Sisley-Vandael, 1835-1836.

S-Vs: *Supplément…*, by J. Sisley-Vandael, 1839.

Sx: *The American Rose Culturist*, by C.M. Saxton, 1860.

T1: *The Old Shrub Roses*, by Graham S. Thomas, 1956. Quoted by kind permission of the author and of the publishers J.M. Dent & Sons, Ltd.

T1H: Writings of Dr. Hurst in *The Old Shrub Roses* by Graham S. Thomas.

T2: *Climbing Roses Old and New*, by Graham S. Thomas, 1983. Quoted by kind permission of the author and of the publishers J.M. Dent & Sons, Ltd.

T3: *Shrub Roses of Today*, by Graham S. Thomas, 1980. Quoted by kind permission of the author and of the publishers J.M. Dent & Sons, Ltd.

T4: *The Graham Stuart Thomas Rose Book*, by Graham Stuart Thomas, 1994. Quoted by kind permission of the publishers, Sagapress and Timber Press.

Th: *The Practical Book of Outdoor Rose Growing*, by Capt. George C. Thomas, 1920. Quoted by very kind permission of the Thomas family.

Th2: *Roses for All American Climates*, by Capt. George C. Thomas, 1924. Quoted by very kind permission of the Thomas family.

ThGl: *The Gladiolus*, by Matthew Crawford, 1911.

T&R: *Les Roses*, by Claude-Antoine Thory and Pierre-Joseph Redouté, 1817-1824.

TS: Article "Roses of Australia," by T.A. Stewart, in ARA28.

TW: *Cultivated Roses*, by T.W. Sanders, 1899.

URZ: *Ungarische Rosenzeitung*, edited by Ernst Kaufmann, date as indicated. Basic translation kindly supplied by Mr. Erich Unmuth.

V1: *Observations sur la Nomenclature et le Classement des Roses*, by Jean-Pierre Vibert, 1820.

V2: *Essai sur les Roses*, by Jean-Pierre Vibert, 1824-1830.

V3: *Catalogue*, by Jean-Pierre Vibert, 1826.

V4: *Catalogue*, by Jean-Pierre Vibert, 1836.

V5: Page from town records of Montfort-l'Amaury containing *l'Acte de décès* concerning the death of Jean-Pierre Vibert, 1866.

V6: *Le Mouvement Horticole*, 1866.

V7: Minutes of the February 8, 1866, meeting of the *conseil d'administration de la Société Nationale d'Horticulture.*

V8: *Catalogue*, by Jean-Pierre Vibert, 1844.

V9: *Catalogue*, by Jean-Pierre Vibert, 1831.

VD: Article "Roses on the Mexican Coast," by V.E. Dillon, in ARA28.

V-H: *Flore des Serres et des Jardins de l'Europe*, by Louis Van Houtte, 1845-1880.

VPt: *Almanach Horticole*, 1844-1848, year as indicated, edited by Martin-Victor Paquet.

Vrp: *Réponse à...Pirolle*, by Jean-Pierre Vibert, 1827.

W: *Climbing Roses*, by Helen Van Pelt Wilson, 1955. Quoted by kind permission of Helen Van Pelt Wilson.

War: *Warren's Descriptive Catalogue*, by J.L.L.F. Warren, 1844.

Way45: *Catalog*, by Wayside Gardens, 1945.

WD: *Roses and Their Culture*, 3rd edition, by W.D. Prior, 1892.

W/Hn: Interpolations by translator John Weathers in *The AmateurGardener's Rose Book*, by Julius Hoffmann, 1905.

Who: *The Western Horticultural Review*, vols. As indicated, 1850-1853.

Wr: *Roses and Rose Gardens*, by Walter P. Wright, 1911.

WRP: *Manual of Roses*, by William R. Prince, 1846.

Ÿ: *Inventaire de la Collection*, from Roseraie de l'Haÿ, 1984. Quoted by kind permission of the *Service des Espaces Verts du Conseil Général du Val de Marne.*

Zla: *La Rose et l'Industrie de l'Essence de Roses en Bulgarie*, by Dr. As. Zlataroff, 1926.

Works Consulted

Almanach Horticole. 1844-1848. Edited by Martin-Victor Paquet. Paris: Cousin.

American Rose Annual. 1916-1940. American Rose Society.

Les Amis des Roses. 1946-1961. Société Français des Rosiéristes.

Anderson, Frank J. 1979. *An Illustrated Treasury of Redouté Roses.* New York: Abbeville Press.

Andrews, H. C. 1805 & 1828. *Roses or A Monograph of the Genus Rosa.* Knightsbridge: Andrews.

Annales de Flore et de Pomone. 1832-1848. Paris: Rousselon.

Annales du Comice Horticole de Maine-et-Loire. 1859. Angers.

Angier, Belle Sumner. 1906. *The Garden Book of California.* San Francisco: P. Elder & Co.

Anonymous. 1712. *La Culture des Fleurs.* Lyon: Besson.

Anonymous. 1764. *L'École du Jardinier Fleuriste.* Paris: Panckoucke.

Barron, Leonard. 1905. *Roses and How to Grow Them.* New York: Doubleday.

Bastien, J.-F. 1798. *La Nouvelle Maison Rustique...* Paris.

Beales, Peter. 1979. *Edwardian Roses.* Norwich: Jarrold.

Beales, Peter. 1979. *Late Victorian Roses.* Norwich: Jarrold.

Beales, Peter. 1985. *Classic Roses.* London: Collins Harvill.

Bean, W. J. 1970- . *Trees and Shrubs Hardy in the British Isles,* 8th edition. London: Murray.

Beckett, Edwin. 1918. *Roses and How to Grow Them.* London: C. A. Pearson.

Bel, J. 1892. *La Rose.* Paris: Baillière.

Billberg, Gustaf Johan. 1836. *Vägledning genom Linnés Park.* Manuscript unpublished until 1996, until it appeared with an article "Rosenlabyrinten Mme. Humlegården" by Maria Flinck in *Rosenbladet* 2: 18-21. Stockholm.

Boitard, Pierre. 1836. *Manuel Complet de l'Amateur de Roses, leur Monographie, leur Histoire et leur Culture.* Paris: Roret.

Le Bon Jardinier, Almanach pour l'Année 1806. 1806. Paris: Onfroy.

Le Bon Jardinier, Supplément... to the 1806 edition. Paris: Onfroy.

Le Bon Jardinier... 1809. Paris: Onfroy.

Le Bon Jardinier... 1817. Paris: Audot.

Le Bon Jardinier... 1824. Paris: Audot.

Le Bon Jardinier... 1830. Paris: Audot.

Le Bon Jardinier... 1840. (Title page missing).

Le Bon Jardinier... 1853. Paris: Dusacq.

Le Bon Jardinier... 1858. Paris: Maison Rustique.

Le Bon Jardinier... 1863. Paris: Maison Rustique.

Le Bon Jardinier... 1865. Paris: Maison Rustique.

Le Bon Jardinier... 1869. Paris: Maison Rustique.

Le Bon Jardinier... 1870. Paris: Maison Rustique.

Le Bon Jardinier... 1877. Paris: Maison Rustique.

Bosanquet, Arthur Henry (as "A.H.B."). 1845. *The Tree Rose.* London: Gardener's Chronicle.

Breck, Joseph. 1851. *The Flower Garden; or, Breck's Book of Flowers.* Boston: Jewett.

Breck, Joseph. 1866. *New Book of Flowers.* New York: Orange Judd.

Breon, Nicolas. 1825. *Catalogue des Plantes Cultivées aux Jardins Botanique et de Naturalisation de l'Île Bourbon.* St.-Denis, Île-Bourbon: Impr. du Gouv.

Bright, Henry. 1879. *A Year in a Lancashire Garden.* London: Macmillan.

Brontë, Charlotte. 1850. *Biographical Notice of Ellis and Acton Bell.* Republished in Penguin Classics edition of Anne Brontë's *Agnes Gray,* 1988.

Brougham, Henry Charles, 3rd Baron Brougham & Vaux. 1898. *List of Roses Now in Cultivation at Château Éléonore, Cannes...* London: Bumpus.

Buc'hoz, Pierre-Joseph. 1770. *Dictionnaire Universel des Plantes...*Paris: Lacombe.

Buist, Robert. 1844. *The Rose Manual.* Philadelphia: Buist.

Bunyard, Edward A. 1936. *Old Garden Roses.* London: Country Life.

Burbank, Luther. 1914. *Luther Burbank. His Methods and Discoveries.* New York & London: Luther Burbank Press.

Burnside, F. R. 1893. *Tea Roses.* Hereford: Jakeman & Carver.

California Nursery Company. 1888 *et sequitur. Catalogue.* Niles, CA: California Nursery Company.

The California Rosarian. 1930-1932. Point Loma, CA: California Rose Society.

Calvert & Company. 1821. *Catalogue of Roses.* Calvert: Rouen.

Cannes, France. Town records.

Carlyle, Thomas. 1837. *The French Revolution. A History.* Reprint (no date). New York: Modern Library.

Carlyle, Thomas. 1849. *Oliver Cromwell's Letters and Speeches,* 3rd edition. Chicago: Belford, Clark & Co.

Carlyle, Thomas. 1858-1865. *The History of Friedrich II of Prussia, Called Frederick the Great.* Republication (no date). New York: Merrill & Baker.

Cauwenberghe, Edm. Van. 1927. *La Rose Historique...*Brussels: Féd. Des Soc. Hort.

Chotek, Marie Henriette. 1926. *Catalogue, Marie Henriette Chotek Rosenschulen.* Trnava: Chotek.

Cloud, Dorothy M.-P. 1925. *The Culture of Perennials.* New York: Dodd, Mead & Company.

Comice Horticole de Maine-et-Loire. Various dates, 1830s-1850s. *Travaux du Comice Horticole de Maine-et-Loire.*

The Conard & Jones Company. 1897-1924. *Catalog.* West Grove, PA.: Conard & Jones.

The Conard-Pyle Company. 1925-1934. *Catalog.* West Grove, PA.: Conard-Pyle.

Cook, E. T. 1911. *Gardens of England.* London: Black.

Cours Complet d'Agriculture. 1793. Abbé Rozier, ed. Paris.

Cranston, John. 1877. *Cultural Directions for the Rose,* 6th edition. Liverpool: Blake & Mackenzie.

Cranston and Mayo's. Various dates. *A Descriptive Catalogue*...King's Acre: Cranston and Mayo's.

Crapo, Henry H. 1848. *Catalogue for the Wasamequia Nurseries, New Bedford, Mass.* Reprint ARA26.

Crawford, Matthew. 1911. *The Gladiolus.* Appendix by Dr. Walter Van Fleet. Chicago & New York: Vaughan's.

Curtis, Henry. 1850-1853. *Beauties of the Rose.* Bristol: Lavars.

De Chesnel, A. 1838. *La Rose,* 2nd edition. Paris: Soc. Repr. Des Bons Livres.

De Pronville, Aug. 1818. *Nomenclature Raisonnée...du Genre Rosier.* Paris: Huzard.

De Pronville, Aug. 1822. *Sommaire d'une Monographie du Genre Rosier.* Paris: Huzard.

De Pronville, Aug. 1824. Appendix to *Monographie du Genre Rosier, Traduite de l'Anglais de M. J. Lindley.* Paris: Audot.

Descemet, Jean. 1741. *Catalogue des Plantes du Jardin de M[essieu]rs les Apoticaires de Paris.* Paris: no imprint.

Desportes, Narcisse Henri François. 1828. *Rosetum Gallicum*...Le Mans: Pesche & Paris: Huzard.

Dickerson, Brent C. 1982-1983. "Education of a Gardener." *Pacific Horticulture* 43(4): 8-10.

Dickerson, Brent C. 1989. "The Portland Rose." *The Garden, Journal of the Royal Horticultural Society* (January): 9-14.

Dickerson, Brent C. 1990. "Notes Towards an Understanding of 19th Century Rose-Breeding. *The Yellow Rose* (March): 2-6.

Dickerson, Brent C. 1992. *The Old Rose Advisor,* first edition. Portland, OR: Timber Press.

Dickerson, Brent C. 1997. *Handbook of Old Roses.* In manuscript.

Dickerson, Brent C. 1997-1998. "Åter till Rosenlabyrinten." *Rosenbladet* 1997(4), 1998(1). Stockholm.

Dickerson, Brent C. 1999. *The Old Rose Adventurer.* Portland, OR: Timber Press.

Dickerson, Brent C. 2000. *Roll-Call: The Old Rose Breeder.* Lincoln, NE: Authors Choice.

Dickerson, Brent C. 2001. *The Old Rose Informant.* Lincoln, NE: Authors Choice.

Dickson, Alexander. Various dates. *Catalogue,* Royal Irish Nurseries. Newtownards: Dickson.

Dickson, Hugh. Various dates. *Catalogue,* Royal Nurseries. Belfast: Dickson.

Dingee & Conard Co. 1912. *Catalog.* West Grove, Pennsylvania.

Dobson, Beverly. 1985. *Combined Rose List 1985.* Irvington, NY: Dobson.

Dobson, Beverly. 1987. *Combined Rose List 1987.* Irvington, NY: Dobson.

D'Ombrain, Rev. H. Honywood. 1908. *Roses for Amateurs.* London: L. Upcott Gill.

Drennan, Georgia Torrey. 1912. *Everblooming Roses.* New York: Duffield.

DuCane, Florence. 1909. *The Flowers and Gardens of Madeira.* London: Black.

Ellacombe, Henry N. 1896. *In a Gloucestershire Garden.* London: Arnold.

Elliott, R. G. No date (ca. 1925). *The Australasian Rose Book.* Melbourne: Whitcombe & Tombs.

Ellwanger, Henry B. 1883. "Old and New Roses." *Century Magazine* 26: 350-358.

Ellwanger, Henry B. 1896. *The Rose.* New York: Dodd, Mead & Company.

Encyclopédie Méthodique. 1804. Botanical contributions by Lamarck. Paris.

Encyclopédie Méthodique. Botanique...Supplément. 1816. Continuation by J. L. M. Poiret. Paris.

Farrer, Reginald. 1909. *In a Yorkshire Garden.* London: Arnold.

Festing, Sally. 1986. "The Second Duchess of Portland and Her Rose." *Garden History* 14: 194-200.

Ferrari. 1633. *Flora, seu, De Florum Cultura.* Rome.

Fillassier, Monsieur. 1791. *Dictionnaire du Jardinier Français.* Paris: Desoer.

Fillery, J. W. 1960. *Old Fashioned Roses in New Zealand.* Ilfracombe: Stockwell.

The Floricultural Cabinet 4: 224-231; 1838. London.

The Floricultural Cabinet 9: 30-31; 1841. London.

The Florist & Horticultural Journal. 1852. Philadelphia.

The Florist & Pomologist. 1848. London.

Foster-Melliar, Andrew. 1894. *The Book of the Rose,* 1st edition. London: Macmillan.

Foster-Melliar, Andrew. 1902. *The Book of the Rose,* 2nd edition. London: Macmillan.

Foster-Melliar, Andrew. 1905. *The Book of the Rose,* 3rd edition. London: Macmillan.

Fumierre, Louis. 1910. *Les Roses.* Rouen: Cagniard.

Furber, Robert. 1730. *Twelve Months of Flowers.* London.

The Garden. 1872-1875. London.

The Garden. 1987. London.

Gautreau, Philippe. Unpublished correspondence with the present author.

Gemen & Bourg. No date (ca. 1908). *Roses.* Luxembourg: Buck.

Glenny, George. 1861. *The Culture of Flowers and Plants.* London: Houlston.

Godefroy. 1831. *Catalogue des Rosiers cultivées Chez M. Godefroy...* Paris: Huzard & Audot.

Gore, Mrs. Catherine Grace Francis. 1838. *The Rose Fancier's Manual.* London: Colburn.

Gravereaux, Jules. 1912. *"La Malmaison" Les Roses de l'Impératrice Joséphine.* Paris: Ed. d'Art.

Griffiths, Trevor. 1984. *The Book of Old Roses.* London: Michael Joseph.

Griffiths, Trevor. 1987. *The Book of Classic Old Roses.* London: Michael Joseph.

Griffiths, Trevor. 1990. *A Celebration of Old Roses.* London: Michael Joseph.

Grimm, Hedi, & Wernt Grimm. Unpublished correspondence with the present author.

Guerrapain, Claude-Thomas. 1811. *Almanach des Roses.* Troyes: Gobelet.

Guillot, Jean-Baptiste (père). 1844. *Catalogue...* Lyon: Guillot.

Guillot, Jean-Baptiste (père et fils). 1852. *Catalogue...* Lyon: Guillot.

Guillot, Jean-Baptiste (fils). 1856. *Catalogue...* Lyon: Guillot.

Haggard, H. Rider. 1905. *A Gardener's Year.* London: Longmans Green.

Harkness, Jack. 1978. *Roses.* London: Dent.

Hariot, Paul. 1904. *Le Livre d'Or des Roses.* Paris: Laveur.

Henderson, Peter. 1889. *Henderson's Handbook of Plants and General Horticulture.* New York: Henderson.

Henslow, T. Geoffrey W. 1934. *The Rose Encyclopaedia.* London: Pearson.

Hibberd, Shirley. 1874. *The Amateur's Rose Book.* London: Groomsbridge.

Hoffmann, Julius. 1905. *The Anateur's Rose Book.* John Weathers, trans. London: Longmans Green.

Hole, S. Reynolds. 1906. *A Book About Roses.* London: E. Arnold.

L'Horticulteur Français. 1851-1872. Paris: Hérincq.

The Horticultural Review and Botanical Magazine. 1854. Cincinnati.

The Horticulturist. 1846-1875. Edited by A. J. Downing *et alia.* New York.

How to Grow Roses. 1980. Editors of Sunset Books. Menlo Park: Lane.

L'Instructeur Jardinier. 1848-1851. Paris: Paquet.

Jacquin, P.-J., & H. Rousselon. 1852. *Le Jardinier Pratique.* Paris: Lefèvre & Guérin.

Jäger, August. 1970. *Rosenlexikon.* Leipzig: Zentralantiquariat.

Jamain, Hippolyte, & Eugène Forney. 1873. *Les Roses.* Paris: Rothschild.

Le Jardinier-Amateur. 1826. Eugène Pirolle, ed. Paris: Renard.

Le Jardinier-Amateur, Premier Supplément. 1826-1827. Eugène Pirolle, ed. Paris: Renard.

Le Jardinier Prévoyant, Almanach pour...MDCCLXXII. 1772. Paris: Didot.

Jekyll, Gertrude. 1902. *Roses for English Gardens.* London: Country Life.

Journal de la Société d'Agronomie Pratique. 1829. Paris.

Journal de la Société d'Horticulture Pratique du Rhône. Issues 1859-1863. Lyon.

Journal de la Société Nationale d'Horticulture. 1863, 1865, 1869. Paris: Société Nationale d'Horticulture.

Journal des Roses. 1854-1859. J. Cherpin, ed. Lyon: Cherpin.

Journal des Roses. 1877-1914. Cochet & Bernardin, eds. Melun: Cochet.

Journal d'Horticulture Pratique. 1850.

Journal d'Horticulture Pratique et de Jardinage. 1844-1847. Paris: Cousin.

Keays, Ethelyn Emery. 1936. *Old Roses.* New York: Macmillan.

Kerr, Robert. 1824. *A General History and Collection of Voyages and Travels.* Edinburgh: Blackwood.

Kingsley, Rose G. 1907. *Eversley Gardens and Others.* London: Allen.

Kingsley, Rose G. 1908. *Roses and Rose-Growing.* New York: Macmillan.

Krüssmann, Gerd. 1981. *The Complete Book of Roses.* Portland, OR: Timber Press.

Lachaume, Jean. No date (ca. 1921). *Les Rosiers.* Revised by Georges Bellair. Paris: Maison Rustique.

Laffay, Jean. 1841. *Prix Courant des Espèces et Variétés de Roses...* Bellevue-Meudon: Laffay.

La Quintinye, Jean de. 1693. *The Complete Gard'ner.* John Evelyn, trans. London: Gillyflower.

La Quintinye, Jean de. 1695. *Instructions pour les Jardins Fruitiers et Potagers...* Geneva: Ritter.

Le Berriays. 1789. *Traité des Jardins, ou Le Nouveau De La Quintinye,* 3rd edition. Paris.

Lemonnier, Daniel. Unpublished correspondence with the present author.

Leproux, Dominique. 1986. "Les Roses Anciennes, un marché en expansion." *Revue-Horticole,* pp. 40-41.

LeRouge, Antoine. 1819-1820. *Histoire Généalogique des Rosiers en deux volumes contenans 560 Espèces et variétés / Dediée à mon Amie.* Unpublished manuscript, partially based on Guerrapain. From the Cochet collection.

Liger, Louis. 1706. *The Compleat Florist,* 2nd edition. Trans. Francis Gentil. London.

Loiseleur-Deslongchamps, Jean Louis Augustin. 1844. *La Rose...*Paris: Audot.

Louette, Yvan. Unpublished correspondence with the present author.

Lyon, William S. 1904. *Gardening in California.* 3rd revised edition. Los Angeles: G. Rice.

McFarland, J. Horace. 1928. *Roses and How to Grow Them.* Garden City: Doubleday.

M'Intosh, Charles. 1855. *The Book of the Garden.* Edinburgh: Blackwood.

The Magazine of Horticulture. Examined were issues from 1840 through 1852. Boston & New York: Hovey & Company.

Malo, Charles. 1821. *Histoire des Roses.* Paris: Janet.

Mandeville, Bernard. 1709. *The Virgin Unmask'd...* London: Morphew/Woodward.

Massiot, Georges. Unpublished correspondence with the present author.

Miellez. 1853. *Plantes de Serres et de Pleine Terre / Prix-Courant.* Lille: Miellez.

Miellez. 1853. *Supplément.* Lille: Miellez.

Miellez. 1854. *Plantes de Serres et de Pleine Terre / Prix-Courant.* Lille: Miellez.

Miellez. 1856. *Plantes de Serres et de Pleine Terre / Prix-Courant.* Lille: Miellez.

Miller, Philip. 1724. *The Gardener's and Florist's Dictionary.* London.

Miller, Philip. 1731. *The Gardener's and Florist's Dictionary.* London.

Miller, Philip. 1754. *The Gardener's Dictionary.* London.

Miller, Philip. 1768. *The Gardener's Dictionary.* London.

Milman, Helen (Crofton). 1899. *My Roses and How I Grew Them.* London: Lane.

Mitchell, Sydney B. 1923. *Gardening in California.* New York: Doubleday.

Modern Roses 8. 1980. Harrisburg, PA: McFarland Company.

Montaigne, Michel Eyquem de. 1962. *Oeuvres Complètes.* Stanford, CA: Stanford University Press.

Montfort l'Amaury, France. Town records.

Moreau-Robert. 1865. *Catalogue Générale.* Angers: Moreau-Robert.

Le Mouvement Horticole. 1866.

National [British] Rose Society. 1912. *Official Catalogue of Roses.* Croyden: National Rose Society.

Nelson, E. Charles. Unpublished correspondence with the present author.

Nicolas, J. H. 1938. *The Rose Manual.* New York: Doubleday.

Nietner, Thomas. 1880. *Die Rose.* Berlin: Hempel & Parey.

Noisette, Louis. 1825. *Manuel Complet du Jardinier.* Paris: Rousselon.

Noisette, Louis. 1826. *Manuel Complet du Jardinier...tome quatrième.* Paris: Rousselon.

Noisette, Louis. 1828. *Manuel Complet du Jardinier...Supplément No 1.* Paris: Rousselon.

Noisette, Louis. 1829. *Manuel Complet du Jardinier...*Brussels edition. Brussels: Wahlen & Tarlier.

Noisette, Louis. 1835. *Manuel Complet du Jardinier...*Paris: Rousselon.

Nottle, Trevor. 1983. *Growing Old-Fashioned Roses.* Australia: Kangaroo Press.

Nottle, Trevor. Unpublished correspondence with the present author.

Paquet, Martin-Victor (*inter alia*). 1845-1854. *Choix des Plus Belles Roses.* M.-V. Paquet, ed. Paris: Dusacq.

Parker, Reginald. 1965. "Roses, the Ophelia Strain and Kindred Spirits," *The Rose* 13: 173-180.

Parkinson, John. 1629. *Paradisi in Sole Paradisus Terrestris*; facsimile reprint (1976) by Dover Books. Originally published London.

Parkman, Francis. 1871. *The Book of Roses.* Boston: Tilton.

Parsons, Samuel B. 1888. *Parsons on the Rose.* New York: Orange Judd.

Paul, William. 1848. *The Rose Garden,* 1st edition. London: Sherwood, Gilbert & Piper.

Paul, William. 1892. *Contributions to Horticultural Literature, 1843-1892.* Waltham Cross: Paul.

Paul, William. 1903. *The Rose Garden,* 10th edition. London: Simpkin.

Pemberton, Rev. Joseph J. 1920. *Roses: Their History, Development, and Cultivation.* London: Longmans Green.

Phillips, Roger, & Martyn Rix. 1988. *Roses.* New York: Random House.

Phillips, Roger, & Martyn Rix. 1993. *The Quest for the Rose.* New York: Random House.

Picard, Alfred. 1906. *Le Bilan d'un Siècle.* Paris: Impr. Nationale.

Prévost fils. 1829. *Catalogue Descriptif, Méthodique et Raisonné, des Espèces, Variétés et Sous-Variétés du Genre Rosier, Cultivées chez Prévost fils...* Rouen: Prévost.

Prévost fils. 1830. *Supplément au Catalogue des Roses...* Rouen: Prévost.

Prince, William R. 1846. *Prince's Manual of Roses.* New York: Clark & Austin.

Prior, W. D. 1892. *Roses and Their Culture.* 3rd edition. London: Routledge.

Rea, John. 1665. *Flora: seu De Florum Cultura.* London.

Redouté, Pierre-Joseph. 1828. *Les Roses,* 3rd edition. Text by Claude-Antoine Thory. Paris: Dufart.

Redouté, Pierre-Joseph. 1833. *Choix des Plus Belles Fleurs.* Paris: Roret.

Redouté, Pierre-Joseph. 1978. *P. J. Redouté Roses.* Locality unknown: Miller Graphics.

Redouté, Pierre-Joseph. 1990 (reprint). *Redouté's Roses.* Secaucus, NJ: Wellfleet.

Revue des Jardins et des Champs. 1860-1862. Paris: Cherpin.

Revue-Horticole. 1829-1877. Paris: Librarie Agricole.

Revue-Horticole. 1929. Special centenary number. Paris: Maison Rustique.

Rivers, Thomas. 1846. *The Rose-Amateur's Guide*, 4th edition. Facsimile edition, published 1979 by Coleman; original edition London: Longman *et al.*

Rivers, Thomas. 1863. *The Rose-Amateur's Guide,* 8th edition. London: Longmans Green.

Rivoire père & fils, & Marcel Ebel. 1933. *Roses et Rosiers.* Paris: Baillière.

Robert & Moreau. 1862. *Extrait du Catalogue des Rosiers, Vignes, et Diverses Plantes...*Angers: Robert & Moreau.

Robinson, William. 1903. *The English Flower-Garden,* 8th edition. London: Murray.

Rockwell [F. F.] and Grayson [Esther C.]. 1966. *The Rockwells' Complete Book of Roses.* New York: Doubleday.

Rosarium Sangerhausen. 1976. *Rosenverzeichnis,* 3rd edition. Sangerhausen: Rosarium Sangerhausen.

Rosarium Sangerhausen. No date (ca. 1980). *Der Welt Bedeutendster Rosengarten.* Sangerhausen: Rosarium Sangerhausen.

Rose Annual. 1910-1930. Croyden: National Rose Society.

Rosen-Zeitung. 1886. Frankfurt: Fey.

Roseraie de l'Haÿ. 1902. *Les Roses Cultivées à l'Haÿ en 1902.* Grisy-Suisnes: Cochet.

Roseraie de l'Haÿ. 1910. *Guide pour servir à la visite de notre Exposition Rétrospective de la Rose.* Paris: Exp. Int. d'Hort. De Paris.

Roseraie de l'Haÿ. 1984. *Inventaire de la Collection.* L'Haÿ: Cons. Gén. Du Val-de-Marne.

Rössig, D. 1799. *Oekonomisch-Botanische Beschreibung...der Rosen.* Leipzig.

Rössig, D. 1802-1820. *Die Rosen / Les Roses.* German / French edition, French translation by M. de Lahitte. Leipzig.

Sanders, Thomas William. 1899. *Cultivated Roses.* London: Collingridge.

Simon, Léon. 1906. *Nomenclature de Tous les Noms de Roses,* 2nd edition. Paris: Libr. Hort.

Singer, Max. 1885. *Dictionnaire des Roses.* Tournai: Singer.

Sisley-Vandael, J. 1835-1836. *Catalogue de Plantes...* Paris: Sisley-Vandael.

Sisley-Vandael, J. 1839. *Supplément...* Paris: Sisley-Vandael.

Smith, Thomas. Various dates. Catalogs for *Newry Roses.* Ireland.

Société Nationale d'Horticulture de France. 1912. *Les Plus Belles Roses au Debut du Xxème Siècle.* Paris: Société Nationale d'Horticulture.

Soulange-Bodin. 1835. *Coup-d'Oeil Historique sur les Progrès de l'Horticulture Française depuis 1789.* Paris: Soc. Roy. D'Hort.

The Southern Horticulturalist. 1869. Tangipahoa, LA.

Stevens, G. A. 1933. *Climbing Roses.* New York: Macmillan.

Testu, Charlotte. 1984. *Les Roses Anciennes.* Paris: Flammarion.

Thierry, Gustave. 1835. *Culture de Rosier/Établissement Horticole de G. Thierry, Horticulteur, rue Bagatelle, à Caen (Calvados) 1835-1836.* Caen: Thierry.

Thomas, Capt. George C. 1920. *The Practical Book of Outdoor Rose Growing.* Philadelphia: J. B. Lippincott & Co.

Thomas, Capt. George C. 1924. *Roses for All American Climates.* New York: Macmillan.

Thomas, Graham S. 1956. *The Old Shrub Roses.* London: Dent.

Thomas, Graham S. 1980. *Shrub Roses of Today.* London: Dent.

Thomas, Graham S. 1983. *Climbing Roses Old and New.* London: Dent.

Thomas, Graham S. 1994. *The Graham Stuart Thomas Rose Book.* Portland, OR: Sagapress & Timber Press.

Thomas, Harry H. 1916. *The Rose Book.* London: Cassell.

Thomson, R. Wodrow. 1862. *The Amateur's Rosarium.* Edinburgh: Paton & Ritchie.

Thomson, Richard. 1959. *Old Roses for Modern Gardens.* Princeton: Van Nostrand.

Thory, Claude Antoine. 1820. *Prodrome de la Monographie des Espèces et Variétés Connues du Genre Rosier...* Paris: Dufart.

Ungarische Rosenzeitung, edited by Ernst Kaufmann. Selections with basic translation kindly supplied by Mr. Erich Unmuth.

Unmuth, Erich. Unpublished correspondence with the present author.

Van Houtte, Louis. 1845-1880. *Flore des Serres et des Jardins de l'Europe.* Ghent: Van Houtte.

Van Mons, J. B. 1835. *Arbres Fruitiers...* Louvain.

Verrier, Suzanne. 1991. *Rosa Rugosa.* Deer Park, WI: Capability's.

Verrier, Suzanne. 1995. *Rosa Gallica.* Deer Park, WI: Capability's.

Vibert, Jean-Pierre. 1820. *Observations sur la Nomenclature et le Classement des Roses.* Paris: Huzard.

Vibert, Jean-Pierre. 1824-1830. *Essai sur les Roses.* Paris: Huzard.

Vibert, Jean-Pierre. 1826. *Catalogue.* Paris: Huzard.

Vibert, Jean-Pierre. 1827. *Réponse de M. Vibert...aux Assertions de M. Pirolle...* Paris: Huzard.

Vibert, Jean-Pierre. 1831. *Catalogue.* Paris: Huzard.

Vibert, Jean-Pierre. 1836. *Catalogue.* Paris: Huzard.

Vibert, Jean-Pierre. 1844. *Catalogue.* Angers: Vibert.

Warren, J. L. L. F. 1844. *Annual Descriptive Catalogue of Fruit and Ornamental Trees, Grape-Vines, Shrubs and Herbaceous Plants, Roses, Dahlias, Green-House Plants, etc., etc.* Boston: Warren.

Wayside Gardens. 1945. *Catalog.*

The Western Horticultural Review. 1850-1853. Cincinnati.

Weston, Richard. 1770. *The Universal Botanist and Nurseryman...* London: Bell.

Weston, Richard. 1775. *The English Flora...* London: Weston.

Wickson, E. J. 1915. *California Garden-Flowers.* San Francisco: Pacific Rural.

Wilson, Helen Van Pelt. 1955. *Climbing Roses.* New York: Barrows.

Wright, Walter P. 1911. *Roses and Rose Gardens.* London: Headley.

Young, Norman. 1971. *The Complete Rosarian.* New York: St. Martin's.

Zlataroff, Dr. As. *La Rose, et l'Industrie de l'Essence de Roses en Bulgarie.* Sofia: Imprimerie de la Cour.

Selected Works Not Consulted

—*Not* consulted due, in most cases to unavailability, and, in a few cases, to prospects of very lean pickings. Occasionally, a particular work listed below was subsumed by another to which we were able to devote the requisite attention. To *point the way* is no less a valuable favor in fields of enquiry than to *conclude*; indeed, to toss a weight tome down onto the desk of Public View meanwhile giving the world to understand that *this is it—there's nothing more to find out* is unfair to both subject and reader. In the present case, not only is there still much much more to find out, there is also much much more to review. The horizon recedes as we approach it! Information from and about the *Orient* is sorely missed: "When we count over the numerous varieties of splendid flowering plants already received from China and Japan, it seems almost incredible to what an extent we are already indebted to those two countries, which have been hitherto so completely closed to us, that we have been kept in utter ignorance as to the extent of their Floral productions, except as regards those that have been obtained almost by stealth from their prolific shores." [WRP] The *German* side of matters has never been adequately treated. *Italian, Portuguese,* and *Spanish* rosarians, writers, and editors have doubtless made many important contributions which have not been disseminated properly, not to mention whole continents'-worth of experience existing in—but not emanating from—*Africa*, *South America*, and *Australia*. *Periodicals*, in their thirst for copy, publish many facts which never appear in books, facts which are particularly pertinent because they often reflect local conditions which would be of interest to horticulturists gardening under similar conditions; the *Bulletins*, *Minutes*, *Proceedings*, *Annals*, and other such effusions of horticultural societies, associations, circles, committees, and the like—especially those of rose-breeding areas—were written by specialists for specialists, and consequently contain obscure or minute facts of great interest to the specialists of the *present* day, though completely forgotten in the intervening "dark ages." Nurserymen's

Catalogs have much value, and in some cases contain interesting short essays by or about roses and/or breeders. In short, in this case it seems that to "point the way" is merely to point in all directions while sternly admonishing those who make it this far *not to stop here!* Some suggestions:

Annales de la Société d'Horticulture de Paris. Paris: Mme. Huzard.

Les Amis des Roses. 1897-ca. 1942, 1962-present. Lyon, France: Les Amis des Roses.

Belmont, Abel. 1896. *Dictionnaire Historique et Artistique de la Rose.* Melun: no impr.

Bessa, Pancrace. 1836. *Flore des Jardiniers.* Paris: Audot.

Biedenfeld, Freiherr Ferdinand L.C. von. 1847. *Das Buch der Rosen.* Weimar: no impr.

Brassac, François. *Annuaire Méridionale,* various years ca. 1880.

Buc'hoz, Pierre-Joseph. 1786. *Dissertation sur les Roses.* Paris: no impr.

Buc'Hoz, Pierre-Joseph. 1804 and 1807. *Monographie de la Rose et de la Violette.* Paris: no impr.

Buist, Robert. 1855. *R. Buist's Catalogue...* Philadelphia: T.K. & P.G. Collins.

Le Censeur de Lyon. Ca. 1848.

Claxton, Écroyde. 1879. *Tea Roses and How to Grow Them.* Liverpool: William Potter.

Desportes, Narcisse Henri François. 1829. *Roses Cultivées en France...* Paris: no impr.

Drapiez, Pierre A.J. 1828-1835. *Herbier de l'Amateur de Fleurs.* Brussels: de Mat.

Dupuis, Aristide, & Hérincq, François. 1871. *Horticulture...* Paris: Guérin.

The Florist & Pomologist. Issues of 1849 and later. London.

Forney, Eugène. 1875. *La Taille du Rosier.* Paris: Goin.

The Garden. Founded and conducted by William Robinson. Issues of 1876 and later. London.

Hérincq, François, & Jacques, Antoine. 1845-1857. *Flore des Jardins de l'Europe.* Paris: Libr. Agr.
L'Horticulteur Belge. 1833. Brussels.
L'Horticulteur Chalonnais. Ca. 1840? Chalon-sur-Saône.
L'Horticulteur Provençal., Ca. 1850?
L'Horticulteur Universel. 1839-1847. Paris: Cousin.
Hy, Abbé F. 1904. *Sur les Roses Hybrides de l'Anjou.* Angers: no impr.
Jacques, Antoine A. & Hérincq, François. 1847. *Manuel des Plantes.* Paris: Libr. Agr.
Jullien, Th. P. 1863. *La Rose; étude Historique...* Rheims: no impr.
Kannegiesser, Friedrich-August. 1804. *Die Gattung der Rosen.* Freiburg, Germany: no impr.
Komlosy, Franz. 1868-1872. *Rosenalbum.* Vienna: Sommer.
Lachaume, Jean. 1874. *Le Rosier...* Paris: Bibl. Du Jardinier.
Lelieur, M. J.-B. 1811. *De la Culture du Rosier.* Paris: Didot.
Lyon-Horticole. Lyon, France.
Maxwell (T.C.) & Bros. 1860. *Descriptive Catalogue...*
McIntosh, Charles. 1829-1832. *Flora & Pomona.* London: Kelly.
Nestel, H. 1866-1879. *Nestels Rosengarten.* Stuttgart: no impr.
Nouveau Jardinier Illustré. No date. Paris: Libr. Cent. D'Agr.
Paul, William. Various dates. *The Rose Garden*, editions 2-9. London.
Perrault, Pierre. 1894. *La Rose-Thé.* Paris: Charpentier & Fasquelle.
Pirolle. 1824-1825. *L'Horticulteur Français.* Paris: Roret.
Prince, William. 1822. *Catalogue...* New York: T&J Swords.
Proceedings of the IX All India Rose Convention. 1988. Lucknow, India.
Revue-Horticole. Issues 1878-present. Paris, etc.
Rivers, Thomas. 1837. *A Descriptive Catalogue of Roses...* London: Rivers.
Rivers, Thomas. Various dates. *The Rose-Amateur's Guide*, editions other than no. 4 and no. 8. London.
Rosen-Zeitung. 1886-1933.

Les Roses, Étrennes aux Dames. 1814. No author. 143 pages. Little-known illustrated book of plates, descriptions, calendar, and poem excerpts. Paris: Hocquart.

Shaw, Henry. 1879-1882. *The Rose*... St. Louis: Studley.

Sulzberger, Robert. 1888. *La Rose*... Namur: no impr.

Theunen, Auguste. 1893. *Guide à Usage des Amateurs de Roses*. Antwerp: no impr.

Travaux du Comice Horticole de Maine-et-Loire, fl. 1840s.

Vallot, Antoine. 1862. *Journal de la Santé du Roi Louis XIV.* Paris: Durand.

Ventenat, Étienne Pierre. 1803. *Choix des Plantes*... Paris: Crapelet.

Welcome, Mrs. M.D. 1881. *An Essay*... Yarmouth, Maine: no impr.

—*—

☞ Note ☜

The intelligence of my Readers, and the alphabetical arrangement of each chapter in this book, renders an Index largely redundant here. But fear not, oh ye seekers of indexes! A comprehensive Index, encompassing not only both volumes of *The Old Rose Advisor* but also *The Old Rose Adventurer* and *The Old Rose Informant* is in preparation for separate publication as this present book goes to press, and will fully satisfy even the most alarmed Reader.

—*—

— Some Numbers —

Of *Damask Perpetuals* in this book, there are entries for 67.
Of *Chinas*, 75.
Of *Teas*, 474.
Of *Bourbons*, 156.
Of *Hybrid Bourbons, Hybrid Chinas,* and *Hybrid Noisettes*, 85.
Of *Hybrid Perpetuals*, 858.
Of *Noisettes* and *Climbers*, 308.
Of *Polyanthas*, 238.
Of *Hybrid Teas*, 253.

Making a total of 2,514 entries in this second edition of
The Old Rose Advisor,
an increase of 182 over the first edition.
With the total of 2,510 entries in *The Old Rose Adventurer*,
including the 4 added to it in our present Appendix 10,
these two companion books cover
5,024 different roses.

"Vive l'Horticulture! Vive la Rose!"

— * —

About the Author

Brent C. Dickerson is the internationally-known author of the most influential modern works on old roses. This is the enlarged second edition of his acclaimed first book *The Old Rose Advisor*; also in print are his definitive works *The Old Rose Adventurer*, *Roll Call: The Old Rose Breeder*, and *The Old Rose Informant*, the latter two books also being available from iuniverse.

Made in the USA
Coppell, TX
09 January 2021